TESI GREGO~~RIANA~~

Serie Teologia

98

AIDAN O' BOYLE

TOWARDS A CONTEMPORARY WISDOM CHRISTOLOGY

Some Catholic Christologies in German,
English and French 1965-1995

EDITRICE PONTIFICIA UNIVERSITÀ GREGORIANA
Roma 2003

Vidimus et approbamus ad normam Statutorum Universitatis

Romae, ex Pontificia Universitate Gregoriana
die 03 mensis martii anni 2001

R.P. Prof. GERARD O'COLLINS, S.J.
Prof.ssa NURIA CALDUCH-BENAGES, M.S.F.N.

ISBN 88-7652-963-2
© Iura editionis et versionis reservantur
PRINTED IN ITALY

GREGORIAN UNIVERSITY PRESS
Piazza della Pilotta, 35 - 00187 Rome, Italy

ACKNOWLEDGMENTS

With the publication of this dissertation I would like especially to acknowledge and thank the following:

Most Rev. Thomas A. Finnegan, Bishop Emeritus of Killala, for assigning me to the Pontifical Gregorian University in September 1995 for studies in theology and for his encouragement during the time of my studies;

Most Rev. John Fleming, Bishop of Killala and formerly Rector of the Pontifical Irish College, Rome for his support during my years at the College;

My director, Rev. Gerald O' Collins, sj, for his unfailing commitment, encouragement, and guidance in directing this work;

Sr. Nuria Calduch-Benages, mn, the second reader of the dissertation, for her helpful observations and recommendations on this study;

Those who read various chapters during the development of the thesis;

My family and friends who have supported me with their prayers and encouragement.

INTRODUCTION

The Wisdom tradition of ancient Israel has exerted a major influence upon the interpretation of Jesus of Nazareth both in the New Testament and the later Christian tradition. This dissertation examines to what extent the Wisdom elements present in the Scriptures have been incorporated into some recent Catholic Christology and explores the contribution that the Wisdom tradition can make to a contemporary interpretation of Jesus Christ. Our basic claim is that an understanding of Jesus Christ as the incarnation of Wisdom offers a rich basis for expressing his significance for Christians today.

1. Scope and Originality

While, in recent years, many biblical scholars have come to recognize ever more fully the importance of the Wisdom theme in New Testament Christology[1], the relationship between the biblical theme of Wisdom Christology and contemporary Catholic Christology has not been appraised. This thesis examines to what extent the Wisdom elements present in the Scriptures have been incorporated into some contemporary Catholic Christology in three language areas (English, French and German). From each area *some representative* theologians have been chosen: German (W. Kasper, K. Rahner, we also include in this group, from the Low Countries, E. Schillebeeckx); English (J. Dupuis, D. Edwards, E. Schüssler Fiorenza); French (L. Bouyer, C. Duquoc, J. Moingt). Furthermore, we also show how the language of Wisdom can be retrieved as a *root metaphor* which can generate new perspectives on five

---

[1] Among the works we could note, for example, are: F. CHRIST, *Jesus Sophia*; F.W. BURNETT, *The Testament of Jesus–Sophia*; ASSOCIATION CATHOLIQUE FRANÇAISE POUR L'ÉTUDE DE LA BIBLE, *La Sagesse biblique*.

issues which face contemporary Christology: the call to justice, outlining the significance of Wisdom for feminist concerns in Christology, the dialogue with other religions, grounding ecological and environmental thinking, and presenting a face of God for the modern world.

2. Structure and Methodology

The dissertation unfolds over ten chapters. Chapters one to five, following a historical-biblical methodology, appraise the degree of indebtedness of portions of the New Testament to sapiential material and ways of thinking. Chapter six similarly elaborates the reception of the Wisdom theme in the Church and how it influenced the development of Christology in patristic and medieval theology. The purpose of these chapters is not to undertake original historical or exegetical research, but rather, in light of contemporary scholarship, to explore the sapiential themes that have particular relevance for the concerns of contemporary Christology.

Chapters seven, eight and nine, adopting an analytic–expository methodology and drawing on the insights gleaned in the previous six chapters, consider in turn the relevant writings of some representative Catholic Christologies in the language areas of German, English and French, and examine to what extent the Wisdom elements present in the Scriptures have been incorporated into this material. Chapter ten, by way of evaluation, identifies five cogent theological issues which can benefit from being considered from a Wisdom Christology perspective.

3. Overview of Contents

The objective of the opening chapter is to provide a context for understanding the New Testament's use of Wisdom speculation in the process of christological reflection. To this end the development in the relationship between personified Wisdom, Sophia, and the one God, Yahweh, as seen in the Wisdom writings of the Second Temple Period is our chief concern. The relationship between Sophia and Yahweh in the writings of Philo and the Wisdom texts from Qumran are also discussed. This chapter also inquires into the origin and theological significance of Sophia and brings together in the form of a composite profile the threads of what has been said about the personification of Wisdom. In addressing the theological significance of Sophia, the chapter recognizes that it is the interpretation of Sophia as a personification of God's own self in creative and saving involvement with the world which best describes Sophia as divine and thus provides a female image for God without distorting the structure of Israel's faith and falling into the error of ditheism. In tracing the development of the personification of Wisdom in the writings of the Second Temple Period, this chapter highlights a certain particularization: Wisdom is linked to the Torah in Sirach and to God's Spirit in Wisdom. This trend of particularization takes a further and dramatic step in the New Testament.

Moving to the New Testament, the objective of chapter two is to set out and evaluate the conclusions contemporary biblical scholarship has drawn regarding the Wisdom influences on the formation of some of the christological hymns of the New Testament. It is the thesis of this chapter that some of these hymn fragments found in the Pauline corpus, the Fourth Gospel, and Hebrews are fundamentally expressions of Wisdom Christology that go back to early Jewish Christianity and reflect the fact that some of the earliest christological thinking about Jesus amounted to what today would be called a very high Christology indeed. We note the fact that nowhere in these hymns is Christ ever directly called Wisdom. Rather Wisdom's actions, status or attributes are predicated of Christ. The interest of the hymn writers was simply in transferring adequately exalted language to the one they worshipped. The early Christians were searching for a way to predicate divinity of Christ while at the same time not relinquishing a belief in only one God. Wisdom material made possible the adequate expression of this monotheistic faith.

Chapter three's objective is to gain as clear a perspective as possible on Paul's intention and understanding when he identified Christ as Wisdom. We also highlight the influence of the Wisdom theme on the Letter of James. Paul found the widespread Wisdom terminology an important tool for asserting the centrality and finality of Christ's role in God's purpose for humanity and creation. We affirm that, when Paul is set against the background of pre–Christian Jewish reflection on divine Wisdom, what he is saying is that the same divine Wisdom who was active in creation has now been active in Jesus. Hence, not only was the creator God acting in and through Jesus Christ but that divine Wisdom is now to be recognized as wholly identified with him. Consequently, for Paul, the distinctive character of divine Wisdom is to be established not from creation or speculative knowledge, but from the cross (I Cor 1:18–25). What we see in Christ's life, death, and resurrection is the very power by which God created and sustains the world (I Cor 8:6). In the

Letter of James the author returns to traditional topics: guarding one's speech and passions, enduring suffering and temptations, seeking Wisdom. It is the conventional Wisdom of a practical sort that is to be sought to cope with the trials and tribulations of life.

Chapter four deals with the teaching of the Synoptic Gospels in their final, edited form. It considers what place these individual evangelists gave to the concept of Jesus as teacher of Wisdom and also if they incorporate the notion of Jesus as divine Wisdom in person into their overall christologies. Secondly, we ask whether there are hints in any of the Synoptics that Jesus, during his earthly career, had intimated that his own story was the story of Wisdom in person. We conclude that Matthew stands alone within the Synoptic tradition in maintaining a full Wisdom Christology, identifying Jesus as the personification of Wisdom. Matthew follows the general lines of the Wisdom thought in Sirach and Baruch where Wisdom retains a strong practical and moral sense. Matthew identifies Jesus implicitly with Wisdom and shows how he fulfils the principal moral functions attributed to Wisdom in the Old Testament and Jewish tradition.

The purpose of chapter five is to appraise the conclusions contemporary scholarship has drawn regarding the influence of Wisdom on the formation of the Fourth Gospel. It is the thesis of this chapter that Wisdom's influence on the Christology of the Fourth Evangelist is not merely significant, but fundamental, even though no word of the *sophia/sophos* family appears in the text. John sees in Jesus the supreme example of divine Wisdom active in history and indeed divine Wisdom herself.

The survey of the biblical Wisdom tradition in these five chapters present two complementary processes at work in Wisdom Christology. First, the sages of Israel, and Jesus as presented in the Gospels, offer proverbs and Wisdom sayings which articulate the religious dimension of human experience. The second process relates the universal presence of Lady Wisdom to specific historical events of revelation thus highlighting a particularization of the tradition. The Wisdom Christology of the New Testament, continuing the correlation between Lady Wisdom and the events of salvation history, particularizes the tradition in a dramatic way and interprets Jesus as the Wisdom of God.

Chapter six focuses on how the Wisdom theme was received in the church and influenced the development of Christology in patristic and medieval theology. The chapter considers the writings of several authors who were influenced by the Wisdom theme including Justin Martyr, Origen, Athanasius, Pope Leo I, Augustine, and Hildegard of Bingen. While Wisdom Christology in itself was not a major theme in post–biblical development, the early Christian centuries saw continuing use of Wisdom categories in christological reflection both alone and in combination with thought about the Logos. In the East, from mid–second century onwards, the Apologists and others exegeted Proverbs, Sirach, and Wisdom christologically, identifying Wisdom with Jesus Christ in order to ground their argument for his eternal origin and divinity. While not as predominant in the West, traces of Wisdom Christology are highlighted in the writings of Jerome and Augustine. Eight hundred years later the theme featured in the work of Thomas Aquinas. In later centuries in the West, while largely replaced by considerations of Logos Christology (in itself partially shaped by Wisdom texts), the Wisdom tradition continued to make sporadic appearances in christological reflection, while the major application of Wisdom texts turned in the direction of mariology. This led to a more profound and comprehensive vision of Mary's participation in the plan of salvation as well as providing a rich basis for the church to articulate our devotion to her as more elevated than the angels and the saints.

In these six chapters we examine the major influences exerted by the Wisdom tradition of ancient Israel upon the interpretation of Jesus of Nazareth both in the New Testament and the Christian tradition. In chapter seven we examine to what extent these Wisdom elements present in the Scriptures and the tradition of the church have been incorporated into some representative Catholic Christologies of the German (and Dutch)–speaking world. The three theologians whose Christology we examine are Walter Kasper, Karl Rahner and Edward Schillebeeckx.

The objective of chapter eight is to examine to what extent the Wisdom elements present in the Scriptures and the tradition of the church have been incorporated into some representative Catholic Christologies of the English–speaking world. Jacques Dupuis, Denis Edwards, and Elizabeth Schüssler Fiorenza are the three theologians whose Christology we review in this chapter.

Chapter nine examines to what extent the Wisdom elements present in the Scriptures and the tradition of the church have been incorporated into some representative Catholic Christologies of the French–speaking world. The three theologians whose Christology we survey are Louis Bouyer, Christian Duquoc and Joseph Moingt.

The final chapter of this dissertation opens up new avenues for Wisdom Christology. In the light of what has been presented, chapter ten aims to show that the language of Wisdom can be retrieved as a *root metaphor* which can generate new perspectives on issues facing contemporary theology. In the contemporary life of the church, at least five important areas are amenable to being led along the path of Wisdom: the call to justice, outlining the significance of Wisdom for feminist concerns in Christology, the dialogue with other religions, grounding ecological and environmental thinking, and presenting a face of God for the modern world.

The chapter highlights some issues raised by these new perspectives and not dealt with in this dissertation. As one of the most evocative images of the Bible, we propose to show that the figure of Wisdom was of decisive importance for the early church's interpretation of Jesus Christ, that it continues to have an impact upon the endeavors of theological reflection, and that it offers an immense resource for the future development of Christology.

PART ONE

WISDOM IN THE BIBLE AND TRADITION

CHAPTER I

The Figure of Wisdom
in the Writings of the Second Temple Period

Our objective here is to provide a context for understanding the New Testament's use of Wisdom speculation in the process of christological reflection. To this end the development in the relationship between personified Wisdom, Sophia, and the one God, Yahweh, as seen in the writings of the Second Temple Period is our chief concern. The relationship between Sophia and Yahweh in the writings of Philo and the Wisdom texts from Qumran will also be discussed. As often in advocacy exegesis, particular Wisdom texts and commentators have been selected to highlight this relationship.

1. Israel's Wisdom Tradition

The Hebrew term for Wisdom (*hokmah*) occurs in one form or another (verb, noun or adjective) three hundred and eighteen times in the Old Testament and approximately three-fourths of these occurrences appear in the five books which have come to represent Israel's «Wisdom literature».[1] J.L. Crenshaw offers the following helpful definition of Wisdom literature:

> Formally, wisdom consists of proverbial sentence or instruction, debate, intellectual reflection; thematically, wisdom comprises self-evident intuitions

---

[1] The figure of three hundred and eighteen is given by R.E. MURPHY, «Wisdom in the Old Testament», 920. The five books usually classified as Wisdom literature are; Job, Proverbs, Ecclesiastes, Sirach and Wisdom. In addition the counsels in Tobit 4:3-21, 12:6-13 and the poem in Baruch 3:9-4:4 should be mentioned. Sirach and Wisdom are not considered canonical within Judaism or the Protestant tradition where they are understood as apocryphal books.

about mastering life for human betterment, groping after life's secrets with regard to innocent suffering, grappling with finitude, and quest for truth concealed in the created order and manifested in Dame Wisdom. When a marriage between form and content exists, there is wisdom literature. Lacking such oneness, a given text participates in biblical wisdom to a greater or lesser extent.[2]

The Wisdom literature of Israel has always posed problems for biblical scholars because of its consistent defiance of attempts at schematization or simple categorization. In contrast to the Old Testament's general preoccupation with divine purpose and order in Israel's life and history, the Wisdom writers, at least until we reach parts of Sirach, endeavoured to communicate insights that transcend space and time. They deal with experiences that are common to humanity, not with particular and distinct historical events that are unrepeated and unrepeatable.[3] Their teachings aimed to elicit assent from any intelligent individual, Israelite or non-Israelite. Accordingly, the wise usually remained silent about the specifics of national history, choosing rather to dwell on things accessible to every human being.

In recent times biblical scholars have come to a new evaluation of the centrality of Wisdom in the ancient tradition and scriptures of the Hebrew people.[4] They have come, as well, to a new appreciation of the importance of the figure of personified Wisdom, Sophia, who is increasingly related to divine creating, guiding and saving in this world. Within the Old Testament she remains an elusive and allusive figure, despite the considerable attention given to the figure of Wisdom. Since she is found in works which span centuries and diverse geographic areas, it is impossible to harmonize all descriptions of her essence and role. Concepts

---

[2] Cf. J.L. CRENSHAW, *Old Testament Wisdom*, 19. This definition suggests that, for example, while some Psalms or the Joseph story may reflect Wisdom ideas and concepts about the nature of life, they are not Wisdom literature *per se*; they merely reflect a Wisdom view of the world.

[3] Sirach seems to have been the first to deliberately link the traditional faith story about Israel's salvation history with Wisdom's generalizations (Sir 24). Later Wisdom 10 reinterprets Israel's history, attributing to Sophia the saving deeds normally attributed to Yahweh. As we shall see there is a gradual particularizing of Sophia in the wisdom tradition.

[4] Cf. J.L. CRENSHAW, *Old Testament Wisdom*; M. GILBERT, ed., *La Sagesse*; B. LANG, *Frau Weisheit*; B.L. MACK, *Logos und Sophia*; D.F. MORGAN, *Wisdom in the Old Testament*; G. VON RAD, *Wisdom in Israel*; R.B.Y. SCOTT, *The Way of Wisdom*.

were fluid and developing and her status increased in dignity and power with the passage of time.[5]

However, even for the most superficial reader of the Wisdom literature it is striking to note the way in which Sophia functions within that tradition. First, in the midst of an overwhelmingly patriarchal religion we are suddenly presented with a strongly positive feminine dimension. Second, at the heart of a faith and tradition deeply committed to monotheism we are presented with a figure who appears to take on the functions and attributes of the one God, Yahweh, in a way which we might otherwise have associated with the common exchange of attributes between gods and goddesses within the context of polytheistic religions.[6] It is important, therefore, to come to some kind of understanding of the relationship which is portrayed as existing between Sophia and Yahweh, always keeping at the forefront of our minds the context of Jewish monotheism. At the same time we note the wider context of polytheism in the ancient Near East, and so the question of the influence of ancient Near Eastern goddess figures on Sophia is one which cannot be ignored and we shall return to this matter later in the chapter. First we shall ask, in the context of the Wisdom literature, who is Sophia and how was the relationship between Sophia and Yahweh understood? These questions will also be addressed in the context of the writings of Philo and the Wisdom texts from Qumran. In so doing we are providing a context for understanding this relationship as it impinged upon the first-century Christian authors' presentation of the Jesus-God the Father relationship. A profile of personified Wisdom will emerge and consideration will be given to the questions of Sophia's origin and theological significance. We begin with an overview of the five major Wisdom books of the Old Testament so that Israel's journey in the experience and understanding of Sophia is clearly presented.

---

[5] Personification is no stranger to the Old Testament. Justice leads Israel out of Babylon (Is 58:4); in Psalm 85:10 Kindness and Truth meet, Justice and Peace kiss. Wine is arrogant (Prov 20:1). But the personification of Wisdom is simply unique in the Old Testament, both for its quantity and quality. E.A. Johnson argues that the figure of Sophia became the most developed personification in the Jewish tradition. Cf. E.A. JOHNSON, «Jesus, the Wisdom of God».

[6] J. Ochshorn remarks on the fact that «what is striking in much of the extant literature is the representation of divinities and mortals of both sexes in a wide variety of roles» (p. 90). Thus we find that Isis teaches Osiris the art of agriculture and Baal does the same for his sister/lover Anath. Cf. J. OCHSHORN, The Female Experience, 75-90.

1.1 *Job the Steadfast*

The structure of the book of Job is essential for understanding it. Job was known in Hebrew tradition as a holy man (1:1-5), and the story of his trial and restoration is found in the prologue (chapters 1-2) and epilogue (42:7-17) that form the framework. The poetic dialogue (chapters 3-31) deals with the profound theological problem of the meaning of suffering in the life of a just man. It is a literary creation, not a report of a literal debate. In a series of disputation speeches Job defends his integrity against the charges of the thee friends who think they are defending God. In chapters 29-31 he closes the debate with a formal protestation of his innocence and issues a challenge to God. At this point Elihu intervenes to speak against Job (chapters 32-37). Finally, the Lord appears in a theophany to deliver two speeches (chapters 38-41), and Job gives his final reaction (42:1-6).[7]

The date of Job is unknown, despite a general tendency to regard it as post-exilic.[8] The question is complicated by the claims of some scholars that portions of the work are later additions (the poem on the search for Wisdom in Job 28 and the Elihu speeches in Job 32:1-37:24). Specific indicators for dating the book are exceedingly rare, as there are no historical allusions within the book and all literary and theological arguments to answer the question of date are quite frail. As M. Pope (who regards the seventh century B.C. as the «best guess») remarks, the date remains an «open question».[9]

Some commentators have argued that the figure of Wisdom makes her initial appearance in the Wisdom poem of Job 28.[10] However, this assessment has not gone unchallenged.[11] Regardless, this ode to the search for Wisdom is hard to situate in the dialogue or, indeed, in the book as a

---

[7] Cf. R. MacKenzie – R.E. Murphy, «Job», 466. The subheads of the five Wisdom books under review in this chapter are taken from R.E. Murphy, *The Tree of Life*.

[8] Cf. L. Alonso Schökel – J.L. Sicre Díaz, *Job*; D. Cox, *Man's Anger*; C. Duquoc, ed., *Job and the Silence of God*; J. Lévèque, *Job et son Dieu*; J. Vermeylen, *Job*.

[9] Cf. M.H. Pope, *Job*, xxxvii.

[10] Cf. E.A. Johnson, «Jesus, the Wisdom of God», 264.

[11] J.D.G. Dunn believes that in Job 28 we cannot really speak of Wisdom in terms of a divine attribute, or of a personification. M. Scott argues that the Wisdom reference in Job 28 may represent an early level of reflection and would be better characterized as a «hymn to Wisdom» than as a formal attempt at personification. Cf. J.D.G. Dunn, *Christology in the Making*, 168; M. Scott, *Sophia and the Johannine Jesus*, 50.

whole. Many scholars are of the opinion that it is a later insertion in the book. The point of chapter 28 is simple: God alone knows where Wisdom is. The position in the chapter of this poem on Wisdom could make it appear as a continuation of Job's words in chapter 27. But the whole tenor of the poem is tangential to the points Job is making.[12] Rather, chapter 28 represents another perspective that Job brings to bear on the mystery of the suffering of its main character: humans do not have the Wisdom to solve the mystery; they can only «fear God». Scholars have described the Wisdom poem of Job 28 in different ways: as an interlude (MacKenzie – Murphy)[13], a bridge (Lévêque)[14], or simply as a later insertion (Dhorme).[15]

Wisdom is presented as something inestimably precious, something which is sought as humans seek precious stones, something whose location only God knows, something which is found by the one who fears the Lord.

> Whence then comes Wisdom?
> And where is the place of understanding?
> It is hid from the eyes of all living,
> and concealed from the birds of the air [...]
> God understands the way to it,
> and he knows its place.
> For he looks to the ends of the earth,
> and sees everything under the heavens.
> When he gave to the wind its weight,
> and meted out the waters by measure;
> when he made a decree for the rain,
> and a way for the lightning of the thunder;
> then he saw it and declared it;
> he established it, and searched it out.
> And he said to man,
> «Behold, the fear of the Lord, that is Wisdom;
> and to depart from evil is understanding»   (Job 28:20-21, 23-28)

It is clear we do not find a personal description of Sophia in these verses and her female character is not stressed. However, Wisdom does appear to be understood as related to the works of creation, yet distinct from

---

[12] Cf. R.E. MURPHY, *The Tree of Life*, 41.

[13] Cf. R.A.F. MACKENZIE – R.E. MURPHY, «Job», 481. In their analysis of Job 28 the authors refer to J. LÉVÊQUE, *Job et son Dieu*, and P. DHORME, *Le Livre de Job*.

[14] Cf. J. LÉVÊQUE, *Job et son Dieu*, 56.

[15] Cf. P. DHORME, *Le Livre de Job*, 110.

them. The poem stresses the transcendence of divine Wisdom and its inaccessibility. Humans can explore and find treasure, but Wisdom, most precious of all, is beyond their reach. Wisdom is located with God and in his creation. The final verse associates Wisdom with fear of the Lord.

1.2 *Proverbs: The Wisdom of Words*

The Book of Proverbs is an anthology of short, two-line sayings (chapters 10–29), prefaced by long poetic instructions (chapters 1–9) and concluded by a section of longer sayings and short poems (chapters 30–31). It is too facile, although quite traditional, to characterize Proverbs as a compendium of ethics, of Israelite morality. This view is strengthened by the optimistic note that sounds frequently in the work: Wisdom (Justice) prospers, while folly (wickedness) self-destructs. However, while a moral code undergirds the book, the real intent is to train a person, to form character, to show what life is really like and how best to cope with it.[16]

While a date for Proverbs is hard to determine two stages can be inferred. First was the family or clan collections of proverbs. Then, under Solomon and other kings (Prov 25:1), the collecting and editing of the traditional Wisdom was fostered. Proverbs itself represents a special redaction of some of these earlier materials. A probable date for the book is the late sixth or early fifth century B.C.[17]

In chapters 1–9 of Proverbs we find a series of carefully constructed long poems and a vision of the pursuit of Wisdom. These chapters stand out from the rest of the book in regard to both form (long poems) and content (exhortatory tone, strong emphasis on moral right and wrong). It appears that Proverbs 1–9 serves as an introduction or prologue to and hermeneutical key for all that follows. While there is uncertainty, the most common opinion is that these chapters are post-exilic.[18]

---

[16] Cf. L. ALONSO SCHÖKEL – J. VÍLCHEZ LÍNDEZ, *Sapienciales. I. Proverbios*; A. BARUCQ, *Le Livre des Proverbes*; D. COX, *Proverbs*; B. GEMSER, *Sprüche Salomos*; T.P. MCCREESH, «Proverbs», 454; W. MCKANE, *Proverbs*; R.B.Y. SCOTT, *Proverbs*.

[17] On the dating of Proverbs cf. T.P. MCCREESH, «Proverbs», 453.

[18] Cf. J. CRENSHAW, «Wisdom», 954. Cf. R.E. MURPHY, *The Tree of Life*, 19. However, a date in the monarchical period has been put forward in B. WITHERINGTON, *Jesus the Sage*, 36. B. Lang has argued that there is no hard evidence of specifically post-exilic vocabulary in Proverbs 1–9: Cf. B. LANG, *Frau Weisheit*, 46-48.

Whatever about the dating of Proverbs 1–9, the figure of Wisdom looms large in these chapters. She makes her appearance in Proverbs 1:20-33; 3:13-24; 4:5-9, and 8:1-9:6. In Proverbs 1:20-33 Sophia is portrayed in the style of an Old Testament prophet threatening her audience with ridicule and doom in the public streets, the town squares and the city gates. In the ancient world the main gate of a town was the hub of life. It served as a market place where produce and products were sold and traded, as the place of justice where civil and criminal cases were tried, as the civic centre where gatherings of all sorts were possible, and as the social and intellectual centre of the community where the elders and the leisured could sit, socialize and converse.[19] In such a public place Sophia preaches her message, challenging her hearers to heed her warnings and setting before them the choice between folly and disaster on the one hand, and the fear of God and life on the other. Only at the end of her public speech does she offer peace and security to those who obey her. She does not merely call to the sage or educated but to the untutored youth, the mockers, even the fools. The audience she seeks is everyone, for her concern is with the business of daily living, not with some esoteric scholarly pursuit of wisdom.[20]

Proverbs 3:13-24 can be divided into two parts: vv.13-18 are a hymn in praise of Wisdom and vv. 21-24 are an admonition to follow the ways of Wisdom. Wisdom is first celebrated in vivid images. We are told that she is more precious than jewels (Prov 3:15) and that she is a tree of life to those who hold on to her (Prov 3:18). Then the great theme of her role with God in creation is announced: «The Lord by Wisdom founded the earth; by understanding he established the heavens» (Prov 3:19). J.L. Crenshaw suggests that the view of Wisdom as a revealer comes not through belief in the scrutiny of human nature, but in direct encounter with God, and thus with the mind of God.[21] This in turn leads to an understanding of at least some aspects of Wisdom as hidden unless she is revealed in such an encounter. This helps to explain the stress placed here on the preciousness of Wisdom, worth a great deal more than riches. Yet among her benefits are length of days, riches, honour and contentment.

Once more, and with great flourish, Sophia appears in Proverbs 8:3-36. Again she addresses the «simple» in public places (8:5). Her proclamation

---

[19] Cf. J. HAYES, *An Introduction*, 328-332.

[20] Cf. D.A. KIDNER, *Proverbs*, 39; R.E. MURPHY, «Wisdom's Song», 456-460.

[21] Cf. J.L. CRENSHAW, «The Acquisition of Knowledge», 251.

is encouraging: truth, more precious than silver or gold (8:10-11,19); love, for those who love her (8:17). Her first claim is the honesty and integrity of her message which is in contrast to the foolish woman of Proverbs 2:16; 5:3; 7:21. Furthermore, Wisdom propounds truth and justice (8:7-8). This claim connotes more than simple honesty; these words are associated with the Lord, who is truthful and just. It is not surprising that her instruction is beyond price (8:10-11); a claim many times repeated in Wisdom literature (Job 28:15-29; Prov 2:4; 3:14-16; Wis 7:8; 8:5).

In Proverbs 8:12-16 she continues the description of the high qualities that she communicates (the Hebrew text emphasizes the *I* or *ego* throughout the next several verses): prudence, knowledge, and aversion to anything evil. Indeed, the qualities of counsel, strength, and understanding enable Wisdom to be the basis for royal rule (these qualities are divine, according to Job 12:13, and in Isaiah 11:2 they are gifts of the Lord's spirit to the messianic figure). Not only royalty, but anyone who will love her (8:17-21) has the opportunity for riches.

Then the figure of Wisdom begins the famous description of her relationship to God and to creation:

> The Lord created me at the beginning of his work,
> the first of his acts of old.
> Ages ago I was set up,
> at the first, before the beginning of the earth.
> When there were no depths I was brought forth,
> when there were no springs abounding with water.
> Before the mountains had been shaped,
> before the hills, I was brought forth;
> before he had made the earth with its fields,
> or the first of the dust of the world.
> When he established the heavens I was there,
> when he drew a circle on the face of the deep,
> when he made firm the skies above,
> when he established the fountains of the deep,
> when he assigned to the sea its limit,
> so that the waters might not transgress his command,
> when he marked out the foundations of the earth,
> then I was beside him, like a master workman;
> and I was daily his delight,
> rejoicing before him always,
> rejoicing in his inhabited world
> and delighting in the sons of men.   (Prov 8:22-31)

This remarkable speech of Sophia has a very deliberate purpose within the book; if Proverbs 1–9 is the introduction to the collection of individual sayings that follow, this powerful motivating figure sweeps all the practical Wisdom of Israel into the orbit of her activity. Yet this cannot exhaust the meaning of one who originates from God before creation, is a cause for joy, plays on the earth, and is involved with human beings. The functions of Sophia are manifold; they are as broad as life itself, in keeping with her eternal origins from the source of all life.

Sophia asserts several important things about herself in this poem. One is that God begot or «created» her as the first-born. She was created «at the beginning of his work» (8:22). Sophia existed before all natural things, before springs of water, mountains, seas and the sky above. The second important theological insight concerns Sophia's presence with God and her co-operation with God in the creation of all creatures. Sophia is God's companion and co-worker in creation. Third, Sophia is God's delightful companion and she delights in the inhabited world and in the human community. Sophia is revealed as profoundly relational, interrelated with God, with all creatures, and with human creatures in a particular way. M. Gilbert makes clear the structure of this entire passage and the logic of its development. The passage moves from the procreation of Wisdom (8:22), to the forming of her parts in the womb (8:23), to her infancy existing before the creation of the world (8:24-26), to her assisting in the creation of the world (8:27-30a), and then finally she is seen as the link or bond between Yahweh and human beings (8:30b-31).[22]

In Proverbs 9:1-6 Sophia is presented as the hostess inviting the «simple» to the banquet of bread and wine. She does not invite the well-to-do to her banquet, however, though she is presented as a wealthy householder who has built a perfect house. This description is in deliberate contrast to that of the foolish woman in Proverbs 9:13-18, who issues another invitation to the «simple» to partake of bread and water (stolen, v. 17!), an invitation that the author characterizes as a trip to Sheol.[23] These

---

[22] Cf. M. GILBERT, «Le Discours de la Sagesse», 214-215.

[23] R.J. Clifford has noted numerous parallels between the personification in Proverbs 9 and an important Ugaritic text from the fourteenth century B.C. The Canaanite goddess Anat is involved and she cries out: «Eat of food, ho! Drink of the liquor of wine, ho! [...] She raises her voice and cries "Hear, O Aqht the hero, Ask silver and I will give it to you, Gold and I will bestow it on you. Only give your bow to Anat [...] Ask for life, O Aqht the hero. Ask for life and I will give it to you, Not-dying and I will grant it to you

images of Sophia building her house and inviting her hearers to a great banquet will influence the whole Wisdom tradition.

Proverbs includes some notable paradoxes. On the one hand, we learn in the prologue that the purpose of this book is that human beings may know Wisdom and receive instruction in wise dealings. On the other hand Wisdom, in the persona of Lady Wisdom, is said to be seeking human beings. Wisdom seems to involve the investigation of natural and human phenomena and deducing practical lessons from them, but also Wisdom is something that God must reveal if anyone is to know it. Wisdom is both a challenge to the listener, and in other contexts the required response of that same listener.[24]

Later we will address the question of Wisdom's identity in Proverbs. At this stage it is sufficient to note that, while it can be said that she reflects female deities of Israel's neighbours, it is clear nonetheless that Sophia of Proverbs is thoroughly integrated within Israel's monotheistic faith in Yahweh. B. Witherington notes that Sophia does not seem to be presented or used *primarily* as a polemic against other forms of international Wisdom or polytheistic faith, but rather as an aesthetic device meant to stress the moral beauty and personal character of God's Wisdom as opposed to other kinds of worldly wisdom which might allure or attract our attention as a way of life or living.[25] We do not have to choose between Yahweh and Sophia. Ultimately the revelation of Wisdom is the revelation of God.

[...] For Baal, when he gives life, gives a feast. For the one brought to life he gives a feast and makes him drink"». The similarity in language and content is striking. Clifford also notes how Anat laughs in scorn of human folly, like what we find in Proverbs. Cf. R.J. CLIFFORD, «Proverbs IX», 300-303. B. Witherington uses this in support of his view of a monarchical rather than a post-exilic point of origin for this personification of Wisdom. Cf. B. WITHERINGTON, *Jesus the Sage*, 48-49.

[24] These two perspectives are brought together by two considerations: (1) G. von Rad has shown that at least *part* of the discussion about Lady Wisdom implies that Wisdom is inherent in creation, as a sort of ordering principle or pattern (*Wisdom in Israel*, 144-146); (2) this being so, the human scrutiny of the human and natural world amounts to an encounter with what may be called the voice of God in both nature and ordinary human affairs. In any case the final editor makes quite clear in Proverbs 1:7 that the beginning of being wise entails proper respect for, trust in, and commitment to Yahweh.

[25] Cf. B. WITHERINGTON, *Jesus the Sage*, 50-51.

1.3 *Qoheleth the Sceptic*

The Book of Ecclesiastes is the clearest example of counter-order Wisdom in the Hebrew Scriptures. The view espoused here challenges the adequacy of most basic Wisdom assumptions about everyday life. Yet even if it was recognized in early Judaism that Ecclesiastes was a serious challenge to such an approach to life, the epilogue of the book, written after his time, perhaps by a disciple, makes clear that Qoheleth was still seen as a sage who stood within the Wisdom tradition even if he offered a fundamental rethinking of various Wisdom generalizations about life. Qoheleth represents the sceptical side of Israelite Wisdom. He does not reject the Wisdom movement, but he does challenge some of its cherished beliefs. That he shares many ideas with the more conventional sages is clear. Qoheleth believes in God and in the fear of God (3:14; 5:6) and in an ethical code and in God's judgment on human behaviour (11:9). Although he points out that Wisdom has its limitations, he never recommends folly.

Qoheleth's quarrel is with any theology that ignores experience and thereby tends to become unreal. Thus he attacks the simplistic statements of the traditional theology of retribution (3:16-18; 7:15; 8:12-14; 9:1-3) because they do not square with experience; God judges, but how that works is very much a mystery. He attacks the glib statements about the advantages of Wisdom, because experience shows that the one fate comes to the wise and the foolish (2:13-16; 9:1-3,11). Above all he rejects the Wisdom tradition's emphasis on industriousness if it means total absorption in work, because such feverish labour robs one of enjoyment (2:22-23; 4:7-8; 5:11-16). Tremendously impressed by the transitory nature (vanity) of all things, he believes that enjoyment is the thing to be focused on in life, not a pursuit of luxury because it is not worth the labour involved (2:1-11), but an acceptance of the ordinary joys which God sees fit to give us (2:24; 3:12, 22; 5:17; 11:9-10).[26]

Of the five books which have come to represent Israel's Wisdom literature, Ecclesiastes is of least significance for our project. It is striking that we do not find here any personification of Wisdom and so Ecclesiastes cannot hope to help us significantly in providing a context for

---

[26] Cf. J.L. CRENSHAW, «Qoheleth in Current Research»; M.V. FOX, *Qoheleth and his Contradictions*; D. MICHEL, *Qohelet*; R.N. WHYBRAY, «Qoheleth, Preacher of Joy». On the history of the book's interpretation, cf. R.E. MURPHY, «Qoheleth Interpreted».

understanding the New Testament's use of Sophia speculation in the process of christological reflection.

1.4 *Sirach: Wisdom's Traditionalist*

Among the earliest of the deutero-canonical Old Testament books, the Book of Sirach is one of the rare biblical works that was actually composed by the author to whom it is ascribed. One of the longest books of the Bible, Sirach contains the most extensive portion of Israelite Wisdom literature to come down to us.[27] Originally written in Hebrew[28], the work comes from the pen of a Jewish writer who lived and worked as a scribe in Jerusalem, although there is considerable evidence of Hellenistic influence.[29] The evidence suggests that the entire book was composed by one author, Ben Sira, who lived during the third and early second centuries B.C. Ben Sira's grandson states in the foreword to his Greek translation that he reached Egypt in the thirty-eighth year of the reign of King Euergetes, 132 B.C. Going back two generations (forty to fifty years) from 132 B.C., we come to a date around 180 B.C. for the composition of the book.[30]

Ben Sira wrote in a time of cultural upheaval. Israel was occupied by the Seleucid dynasty, and the pressure to conform to Greek ways created

---

[27] Cf. H.V. KIEWELER, *Ben Sira*; R.A.F. MACKENZIE, *Sirach*; T. MIDDENDORP, *Die Stellung*; G.L. PRATO, *Il problema*; L. SCHRADER, *Leiden und Gerechtigkeit*; P.W. SKEHAN – A.A. DI LELLA, *The Wisdom of Ben Sira*; O. WISCHMEYER, *Die Kultur*.

[28] Fragments of early Hebrew manuscripts have been recovered at Qumran and Masada but the Greek text remains our only complete source. Nevertheless, quite a lot of Sirach has survived in Hebrew. A. Di Lella estimates that about 68% is now extant in Hebrew. The earliest fragments recovered were the so-called Cairo Geniza fragments, identified in 1896 by Solomon Schechter and published in the early 20th century; the Qumran and Masada material came later. Cf. P.W. SKEHAN – A.A. DI LELLA, *The Wisdom of Ben Sira*; G.W.E. NICKELSBURG, *Jewish Literature*, 64-65. On comparing the original Hebrew to the grandson's Greek translation, cf. H.J. Cadbury's analysis in «The Grandson of Ben Sira», 219-225.

[29] The influence of Hellenistic thought and the possible polemic against it in Sirach is discussed at length in M. HENGEL, *Judaism and Hellenism*, 131-153.

[30] The fact that Sirach does not reflect the problems that arose in Palestine with the advent of Antiochus IV Epiphanes to power in 175 B.C., and the ensuing Maccabean revolt triggered by the desecration of the Temple in 167 B.C., supports the 180 B.C. date for the composition of Sirach. Cf. J.L. CRENSHAW, *Old Testament Wisdom*, 149-151; A.A. DI LELLA, «Sirach», 497; R.E. MURPHY, *The Tree of Life*, 65; P.W. SKEHAN – A.A. DI LELLA, *The Wisdom of Ben Sira*, 15.

diverse reactions within Judaism, as some accommodated to Greek culture and others rejected all Hellenistic influences. Ben Sira's response is that of a traditionalist. Although he is not against accepting what is good in Greek culture, his fundamental argument is that it is only in relationship with the God of Israel that one can find true Wisdom. One of the major purposes of the Wisdom of Sirach is to stress the need for both a Torah-centred and Temple-centred orientation among Jews, especially in view of the ever growing influence of Hellenism in Jewish culture. He is not willing to appropriate Hellenistic or international Wisdom thought in any way that he sees as compromising or significantly altering what he takes to be the true and traditional Jewish faith.

The personification of Wisdom in Sirach is found in a variety of texts including1:4-20; 4:11-19; 6:19-31; 15:1-8; 24:1-29. D. Edwards has singled out Wisdom's personification in three places in Sirach: the beginning (1:1-30), the middle (24:1-33) and the end (51:1-27).[31] Kathleen O'Connor speaks of Sophia holding up the structure of the book through these three sections. She notes that the figure of Sophia provides the basis and structure of Sirach's theology.[32] In Sirach 1:1-10 we read of Sophia's close connection with God and that Sophia can be attained only through «fear of the Lord» (1:11-20).

In Sirach 24 Sophia's great central speech is set in the assembly of the Most High, in the heavenly Court, and there she proclaims her divine origins and her search for rest and inheritance:

> I came forth from the mouth of the Most High,
> and covered the earth like a mist.
> I dwelt in high places,
> and my throne was in a pillar of cloud.
> Alone I have made the circuit of the vault of heaven
> and have walked in the depths of the abyss.
> In the waves of the sea, in the whole earth,
> and in every people and nation I have gotten a possession.
> Among all these I sought a resting place;
> I sought in whose territory I might lodge.   (Sir 24:3-7)

Sophia proclaims that she has come forth from God. She is born from God's mouth, as a Word of God.[33] She speaks of her role in creation, of

---

[31] Cf. D. EDWARDS, *Jesus the Wisdom of God*, 25.

[32] Cf. K.M. O'CONNOR, *The Wisdom Literature*, 137.

[33] P.W. Skehan has shown that Sirach 24, both in terms of content and structure, is not simply Ben Sira's version of the similar material in Proverbs 8. As an example of the similarities and differences between Sirach 24 and Proverbs 8, in both poems we read

her exploration of the universe and of her sway over all nations in terms usually reserved for God alone. She covers the earth like mist, as the breath of God covers the waters (Gen 1:2). Like God she journeys through the vault of heaven and has dominion over all things. This transcendent Wisdom seeks a permanent home, a resting place, and the Creator chooses a place for her to dwell:

> Then the Creator of all things gave me a commandment,
> and the one who created me assigned a place for my tent.
> And he said, «Make your dwelling in Jacob,
> and in Israel receive your inheritance»
> From eternity, in the beginning,
> he created me,
> and for eternity I shall not cease to exist.
> In the holy tabernacle I ministered before him,
> and so I was established in Zion.
> In the beloved city likewise he gave me a resting place,
> and in Jerusalem was my dominion.
> So I took root in an honoured people,
> in the portion of the Lord, who is their inheritance.   (Sir 24:8-12)

Sophia, who was with God in the beginning and shall not cease to be, has made her home in Israel. It is in the holy city that she has set up her tent and come to rest. Sophia is clearly seen as a created being, for not only do we hear that she comes forth «from the mouth of the Most High» (24:3), but she is said to have also been created, though created «from eternity» (24:8-9). She comes forth from God and is of God, and divine

---

that Wisdom opens her mouth to speak but only in Sirach 24 do we also read that Wisdom came forth from the mouth of the Most High. Cf. P.W. SKEHAN, «Structures». While Skehan is right in pointing out the differences between the two, nevertheless, a recent turn in criticism of the Hebrew bible has been to approach the question of the similarities and differences between Sirach and Proverbs from an «inter-textual perspective». In such a perspective, Sirach's dependence on Proverbs becomes a little clearer. Sirach never cites his sources exactly as they are written, but usually makes some change in words, form, etc. In this he is like the Book of Revelation which alludes to the Old Testament more than any New Testament book, yet intriguingly never once quotes it directly. The «inter-textual» relationship between Sirach and Proverbs is complex. It may reflect a learned scribal convention which prided itself in making knowing allusions to existing texts while showing its virtuosity by doing so obliquely rather than directly. Consequently, a sophisticated readership would recognize the allusion while applauding the author's dexterity in not simply quoting. For a pithy summary of the relationship of Sirach to Proverbs from an inter-textual perspective cf. R. BAUCKHAM, *James*, 74-83.

qualities may be attributed to her, but her subordination to the Most High is clear. From her home in Jerusalem she grows tall «like a cedar in Lebanon» and «like choice myrrh» spreads her fragrance, and like a vine her «blossoms become glorious and abundant fruit» (24:13-17). Settled in the holy city, Sophia, as in Proverbs 9, sends out a warm invitation to her great banquet:

> Come to me, you who desire me,
> and eat your fill of my produce.
> For the remembrance of me is sweeter than honey,
> and my inheritance sweeter than the honeycomb.
> Those who eat me will hunger for more
> and those who drink me will thirst for more. (Sir 24:19-21)

Here it is Sophia herself who is the food and drink. She is the source of nourishment and life.

What is most innovative in Sirach's portrayal of Sophia's role is the dialectical relationship developed between Sophia and Torah.[34] B. Witherington has noted that the three major theological ideas in Sirach are Wisdom, Torah and Fear of the Lord.[35] The key term *sophia/hokmah* is found more frequently than the other two, but all three come together in Sirach 19:20 where we read: «All Wisdom is the fear of the Lord, and in all Wisdom there is the fulfilment of the Law». At the very heart of Wisdom is the fear of the Lord, and this is also at the heart of the

---

[34] E.P. Sanders has argued that it is too simple to say that in Sirach the Wisdom tradition is subsumed by or fully identified with the Torah. Cf. E.P. SANDERS, *Paul and Palestinian Judaism*, 332-334. Cf. G.T. SHEPPARD, *Wisdom as a Hermeneutical Construct*, 46, n. 69; B. WITHERINGTON, *Jesus the Sage*, 85-86, 96-98. These scholars argue that what is being described is the increasing particularization of Wisdom. What begins as an attribute of God becomes an attribute of creation and thus available to all creatures everywhere, and then finally becomes an attribute of Torah. This means that God's Wisdom may be found not merely by examining creation or the behaviour of creatures, but by consulting his written revelation to his chosen people. But none of this negates that Wisdom may be found beyond Torah as well, for Ben Sira has not given up the creation theology of the sage, as is clear from the hymn of thanksgiving in Sirach 39:12-35. Wisdom then endures forever and may be found everywhere, though it has established its *legal* and indeed permanent residence in Jacob, in Jerusalem, in Torah. Sirach 24 may well have been the spark that fueled later rabbinic speculation about the eternity of Torah, but Ben Sira is not arguing for that in this poem. Cf. B. WITHERINGTON, *Jesus the Sage*, 96-97. For a view identifying Wisdom and Torah in Sirach, cf. G. VON RAD, *Wisdom in Israel*, 245

[35] Cf. B. WITHERINGTON, *Jesus the Sage*, 78.

Deuteronomistic approach to Torah. We could say then that Torah is «the manifestation of Wisdom in history».[36] Following Wisdom teaching leads to the same goal and is based on the same principle of reverence for the biblical God that we find in Torah. Sirach takes matters further by saying that all Wisdom entails fulfilling what the Law requires (19:20). Further-more, keeping the Law leads to Wisdom (15:1). Sophia hears the command from the Most High: «Make your dwelling in Jacob, and in Israel your inheritance» (24:8). So she does (24:10-12) and Sirach identifies her with «the Law which Moses commanded us» (24:23). Or, phrased differently, the benefits Wisdom has and gives are the benefits the Law provides because the Law is a written manifestation of Wisdom.

Hence, not only does divine Wisdom reappear in the guise we have known from Proverbs, but she also comes to represent that most lasting symbol of Yahweh's will and influence among the people, the Book of the Law. Sirach 24:23 is an echo of Exodus 24:7 («the book of the covenant») and Deuteronomy 33:4 («Moses commanded us a law»).[37] This dialectical relationship had already been prepared for by Psalm 19, which links creation with Law, and by Deuteronomy 4:6-9 which describes observance of the Law as giving evidence of Wisdom to the nations. M. Scott argues that this development may turn out to be double-edged as far as Sophia is concerned: on the one hand, it can be viewed as a positive expansion of the influence of Sophia in the realm of that most sacred part of Israel's relationship with God. On the other hand, it may be seen as a negative move in respect of Sophia's development, confining her, as it surely does, to the manageable limits of a book.[38]

Why should this be so? M. Scott suggests that, as we saw in Proverbs, Sophia was able to appear in a symbolic role as the presence and all-pervading power of God at work in creation, while remaining within the confines of Yahweh's control. This presentation may have been governed to an extent by the situation in which the book was compiled. Ben Sira

---

[36] Cf. G. BOCCACCINI, *Middle Judaism*, 94.

[37] G.T. Sheppard talks about the sapientializing of other sacred Hebrew traditions in Sirach. This is particularly evident in Sirach 24. Ben Sira approaches the Law, the Prophets, and the other books from a Wisdom perspective and draws freely from all of them to make the points he wishes to make about Wisdom. It is true that this leads to a more Torah-centred approach to life, but this is achieved by Ben Sira's using Wisdom, and a Wisdom hermeneutic, to achieve that end. In Sirach 24 we hear Wisdom endorse Torah, by claiming that Torah embodies all the traits and positive attributes of Wisdom. Cf. G.T. SHEPPARD, *Wisdom as a Hermeneutical Construct*, 19-71.

[38] Cf. M. SCOTT, *Sophia and the Johannine Jesus*, 54.

was not just trying to reassert the old values of Wisdom thinking.[39] He was also attempting to establish a new sort of conservatism among Jews, with Wisdom and Torah in tandem, that could withstand the challenges presented by Hellenism without giving up some benefits from and dialogue with Hellenism.[40] To this end he felt it necessary to ground Wisdom not just in creation but also in the history of Israel, and in particular to connect it with Torah. When we consider Sirach's very strong attempts to delineate the sphere of woman's influence and to keep her under male control[41], we can hardly be surprised at his attempt also to bring Sophia very closely under control, in the most obvious way available: through confining her to the well-defined parameters of the Torah. The personalized symbol is thus prevented from developing individual personality by confinement to the impersonal concept of the Torah.[42]

Sirach continues with a series of images which show that the Torah, Wisdom's presence and expression in Israel, is more abundant than the seas and great rivers of the world overflowing with abundance and life (24:24-29). In the final poem in Sirach 51:13-27 Ben Sira speaks as an old man, at times almost identifying himself with his beloved Wisdom:

---

[39] J.T. Sanders has demonstrated at length the extensive parallels between Proverbs and Sirach. Nevertheless, Sanders notes that Ben Sira does not simply recycle material from Proverbs but develops it in some new ways as well as reaffirming older ideas and values, including linking Wisdom with Torah. The linking of Torah with Wisdom does not amount to a subsuming of the latter under the heading of the former. «Ben Sira has not given up the traditional sage orientation of Judaic Wisdom, for Torah is to be followed because it is a sage, not sage advice because it comports with Torah». Cf. J.T. SANDERS, *Ben Sira*, 3-26, 16; B. WITHERINGTON, *Jesus the Sage*, 84-85.

[40] J. Marböck criticizes the idea that Ben Sira is simply a reactionary. He offers both old and new things in his book and does not settle for reiterating what he had learned about the fear of the Lord from Proverbs and elsewhere. It is true, however, that the basic trajectory of his thought is in a more conservative direction as is shown both by his attempt to tie Wisdom to Torah and to tie the present Jewish community to its priestly and prophetic past in Sirach 44-50. Cf. J MARBÖCK, *Weisheit im Wandel*, 175-176.

[41] Cf. H. MCKEATING, «Jesus Ben Sira's Attitude». B. Witherington argues that Ben Sira was trying to inculcate a highly patriarchal honour-shame type of culture where women were often stereotyped as either saints or sinners, and were thought to be mainly responsible for the sexual purity or impurity of the society. Proper blame for male sexual aggression when it took place was usually not placed where it ought to have been placed in an honour-shame culture. Ben Sira does not escape from stereotyping women, often seeing them chiefly as temptresses. Cf. B. WITHERINGTON, *Jesus the Sage*, 91-92.

[42] This manifestation of Sophia in Torah is further developed by Baruch 3:37-4:2, which sees her as gifted to humanity in the form of the book of the Law.

[...] Draw near to me, you who are untaught,
and lodge in my school.
Why do you say you are lacking in these things,
and why are your souls very thirsty?
I opened my mouth and said,
Get these things for yourselves without money.
Put your neck under the yoke,
and let your souls receive instruction;
it is to be found close by.
See with your own eyes that I have laboured little
and found for myself much rest.   (Sir 51:23-27)

Sirach's theology would enable Judaism to understand true Wisdom in terms of the Torah and Torah piety, the joyful and enthusiastic pursuit of God's will. Sirach provided an unique development to the figure of Wisdom and also gave an explicit definition. This narrowed down, in a sense, the broad view of Wisdom as presented in Proverbs 8. Both perspectives are valid. The figure of Wisdom is adapted to the circumstances of the time (with Sirach, the Torah), but she also retains the mysterious identity of Proverbs 8.

1.5 *The Wisdom of Solomon: A View from the Diaspora*

The Book of Wisdom is not in the Hebrew Bible and is known to us only in the Greek. Although it has been argued that some or all of the book was originally written in Hebrew, it is generally held today, because of various linguistic features, that Greek was the original language.[43] Clearly, then, despite the claim for Solomonic authorship, Wisdom was written many centuries after the time of Solomon. It was probably written around the beginning of the Christian era[44] and, while the direction of the influence can be debated, the well documented degree of affinity between Wisdom and the writings of Philo also suggest a date around this time.[45] If we assign to Wisdom a date in the last half of the first century B.C., we

---

[43] Cf. J. GEYER, *Wisdom of Solomon*; C. LARCHER, *Le Livre de la Sagesse* I; A. SISTI, *Il libro della Sapienza*; A.G. WRIGHT, «Wisdom»; J. ZIEGLER, ed., *Sapientia Salomonis*.

[44] Cf. A.G. WRIGHT, «Wisdom», 510.

[45] The view that Wisdom is, or can be identified with, the divine spirit of God is an idea we find in Wisdom literature for the first time in the Book of Wisdom, but this idea is also found in Philo. Cf. J. BLENKINSOPP, *Wisdom and Law*, 149. Philo's dates are from c. 20 B.C. to c. 50 A.D. If the affinities between his writings and the Book of Wisdom are any clue, it is likely it also came from this period and locale. Cf. J. LAPORTE, «Philo».

shall not be far wrong. Wisdom, then, is the last of the Old Testament books.

The place of composition is apparently Egypt, probably Alexandria, the great intellectual and scientific centre of the Mediterranean world and one of the largest centres of the Jewish Diaspora. The author of the book claims to be Solomon. The claim was questioned by Origen, Eusebius, Augustine and Jerome[46], and it is clear from the preceding data that the claim is simply a literary device, conventional in Old Testament Wisdom literature. The author of Wisdom remains anonymous and the most we can say is that he was a learned Greek-speaking Jew and probably a teacher and that he was familiar with Hellenistic philosophy, rhetoric and culture. In Wisdom we see the results of a substantive interaction between Judaism and Hellenism.[47]

The first half of Wisdom (1:1-11:1) is divided into two sections. The first section, sometimes called the Book of Eschatology, deals with the problem of retribution for good and evil and with the immortality that Sophia offers (1:1-6:21). The second section describes Sophia and her operations in the world and explains how she is to be found (6:22-11:1). Here Sophia is closely identified with God and shares remarkably in divine transcendence.[48]

Yet, we are told in beautiful images that Sophia is readily accessible to those who seek her: «He who rises early to seek her will have no difficulty, for he will find her sitting at his gates» (Wis 6:14). She goes seeking those worthy of her, appears to them in their paths, and «meets them in every thought» (6:16). The author claims to have been led by Sophia to the knowledge of various sciences. It is natural that all this knowledge would come from Sophia, since she is understood as the divine

---

[46] Cf. A.G. WRIGHT, «Wisdom», 510.

[47] B. Witherington argues that the author of Wisdom is attempting to forge a new marriage of mainly Jewish ideas with some Greek ones in order to show his audience that whatever is really of worth that they might be seeking in Hellenistic religion or culture can in fact be found in Judaism. This strategy suggests that the author is not arguing for his audience to give up entirely social interaction with the dominant culture. The point is rather that at the substantive level: whatever Hellenistic philosophy and culture in general may offer, this can also be found with Sophia. Cf. J. KLOPPENBORG, «Isis and Sophia», 84; B. WITHERINGTON, *Jesus the Sage*, 103.

[48] On the structure of Wisdom cf. J.M. REESE, «Plan and Structure»; D. WINSTON, *The Wisdom of Solomon*.

Creator: «For Wisdom, the fashioner of all things, taught me» (7:22). Sophia is the divine artisan at work in creation (7:22; 8:6). The author offers an extraordinary celebration of the praises of Sophia:

> For in her there is a spirit that is intelligent, holy,
> unique, manifold, subtle,
> mobile, clear, unpolluted,
> distinct, invulnerable, loving the good, keen,
> irresistible, beneficent, humane,
> steadfast, sure, free from anxiety,
> all-powerful, overseeing all,
> and penetrating through all spirits
> that are intelligent and pure and most subtle.
> For Wisdom is more mobile than any motion;
> because of her pureness she pervades and
> penetrates all things.   (Wis 7:22-24)

These twenty-one attributes (the perfect number seven multiplied by three) explain how it is that Sophia can teach all these things. Sophia is identified with spirit, a spirit which is utterly pure, pervades all things, and is thus also utterly immanent. Yet this immanence is balanced by transcendence and Sophia is portrayed as «holy, unique, [...] all-powerful [...] and overseeing all».[49] Wisdom goes on to describe Sophia's relationship to God:

> For she is a breath of the power of God,
> and a pure emanation of the glory of the Almighty;
> therefore nothing defiled gains entrance into her.
> For she is a reflection of eternal light,
> a spotless mirror of the working of God,
> and an image of his goodness.
> Though she is but one, she can do all things,
> and while remaining in herself, she renews all things;
> in every generation she passes into holy souls
> and makes them friends of God and prophets;
> for God loves nothing so much as the man
> who lives with Wisdom.
> For she is more beautiful than the sun,
> and excels every constellation of the stars.
> Compared with the light she is found to be superior,
> for it is succeeded by the night,

---

[49] Cf. R.E. MURPHY, *The Tree of Life*, 88.

but against Wisdom evil does not prevail,
She reaches mightily from one end of the earth to the other,
and she orders all things well.   (Wis 7:25 - 8:1)

Sophia is radically related to God. Now her divine character is expressed in a manner that goes beyond: «The Lord created me at the beginning of his work» (Prov 8:22) or «I came forth from the mouth of the Most High» (Sir 24:3). As R.E. Murphy says: «The general image is a sort of radiation from the divinity: vapour, effusion, reflection, mirror image».[50]

Sophia is God's presence to the universe in continuous creation. The author goes beyond other biblical writers in this treatment of continuous creation and in attributing this ongoing work to Sophia.[51] Hence we find the author saying of Sophia that «while remaining in herself, she renews all things» (Wis 7:27), and «she reaches mightily from one end of the earth to the other and she orders all things well» (8:1). She is the «mother of all good things» (7:12), the «fashioner of all things» (7:22) and «renews all things» (7:27).

After celebrating the unity between Sophia and God in continuous creation, Wisdom goes on to describe her as «living with God» (8:3) and associated with all God's works (8:4). The book celebrates the author's love for Sophia. The relationship is described in personal and intimate terms. She is understood as a friend (6:12-16), and friendship with her means friendship with God (7:14). She is very often seen as the beloved whom Solomon seeks as spouse (7:28; 8:2,9,16).

The theme of the unity between Sophia and God comes to a significant climax in Wisdom 10 in which she is presented as Saviour. We are told explicitly that human beings are «saved» by Sophia (9:18), and in a remarkable way Wisdom 10 reinterprets Israel's history, attributing to

---

[50] Cf. R.E. MURPHY, *The Tree of Life*, 144.

[51] Cf. C. LARCHER, *Études*, 391. B. Witherington argues that here we see the beginnings of a groping beyond mere personification of an attribute of God to a hypostasis. On the one hand Wisdom can be distinguished from creation, for creation is something she helped fashion, but on the other hand the sage can say that she penetrates both all spirits (7:23) and all things (7:24). That is, she comes from the very being of the Creator as spirit, light, glory and penetrates the very being of creation and creature. It is because of her purity that she is able to relate to both Creator and creature in this way. Cf. B. WITHERINGTON, *Jesus the Sage*, 109. Also in favour of this view are J.L. Crenshaw and B. Mack. Cf. J.L. CRENSHAW, *Old Testament Wisdom*, 176; B.L. MACK, *Logos und Sophia*, 67-70. However, all the scholars are clear that the author of Wisdom did not want to say anything that would compromise his belief in monotheism.

Sophia the saving deeds normally attributed to Yahweh. Sophia is accredited with God's work of salvation. It was Sophia who was at work in the «deliverance» and «preservation» of Adam, Noah, Abraham, Lot, Jacob and Joseph (10:1, 8). It was Sophia who delivered the Hebrew people in the Exodus:

> A holy people and blameless race
> Wisdom delivered from a nation of oppressors.
> She entered the soul of a servant of the Lord,
> and withstood dread kings with wonders and signs.
> She gave to holy men the reward of their labours;
> she guided them along a marvellous way,
> and became a shelter to them by day,
> and a starry flame through the night.
> She brought them over the Red Sea,
> and led them through deep waters.   (Wis 10:15-18)

Clearly in Wisdom we have moved beyond even the close linking of Sophia and Yahweh given by Proverbs and Sirach. Yet Sophia is never identified with God. In Wisdom 9:17-18 we hear that God sends Wisdom from on high. Here and elsewhere she is seen as subordinate to the biblical God. In a new development she is identified as «a holy and disciplined spirit» (1:5), and we read that «Wisdom is a kindly spirit» (1:6). The two parallel phrases in 9:17 also suggest that Wisdom is being identified with God's holy Spirit: «Who has learned thy counsel, unless thou has given Wisdom and sent thy holy Spirit from on high?» Thus while she is sent from heaven, and even from or from beside God's glorious throne (9:4, 10), she is not simply identical with the Almighty who still dwells in heaven once Sophia has been sent. Sophia had been traditionally associated with creation (Prov 8:22-31), and she even roamed the created world (Sir 24:5). Now she penetrates all things (Wis 1:7; 7:24; 8:1). While the Jews of the Diaspora recognized that she dwelt in the Temple in Jerusalem (Sir 24:8-12), they recognised her in their Greek world as well (Wis 7:16-28). Wisdom's end result is an intriguing marriage of Jewish and Hellenistic ideas, though clearly the former predominate, and the latter are used in the service of those Jewish ideas.

2. Wisdom in Other Writings

2.1 Wisdom in the Writings of Philo

Philo's significance for us lies not so much in the possibility of direct influence on the New Testament writers themselves, as in his witness to a particular trend of Jewish philosophical reflection and speculation at the time of the formation of the New Testament. Consequently, we need not be over concerned with any possible direct influence from Philo's conception of the Wisdom relationship to God on New Testament Christology, but we should see his significance rather as a pointer to a certain trend in Sophia speculation at the time in which New Testament thinking was developing.

Philo's writings display a «unique blend of Jewish monotheism with middle-Platonic and Stoic philosophy».[52] The resulting synthesis of ideas makes it extremely difficult to make any definitive statement of «Philo's view» on a particular subject. The relationship of God and Sophia, or of Logos and Sophia, is no exception to this observation. In general, however, Philo sees Sophia as belonging to the upper realm of the divine, while the Logos replaces her traditional role as God active in the world of sensory perception. M. Scott believes that this switch may very well have come about as a result of Sophia's gender, a possibility which is reinforced by Philo's willingness to assert that she is in actual fact «male»![53] He almost invariably sees the female realm as something negative or evil.[54]

All the universal qualities which Philo considers most admirable are subsumed under the category of «male»: the rational, the noetic-ideal and incorporeal, the heavenly, indivisible and unchanging, the active principle. Their opposites are categorized as «female»: the irrational, the sense-perceptible and material, the earthly, divisible and changing, the passive principle. The superiority of that which is «male» over that which is «female» is one of the most consistently applied principles in Philo's thought. Thus he is often found to compare the relative value of the various components of his conceptual universe according to their «maleness» and «femaleness». We can conceive, therefore, of a kind of *gender gradient* underlying much of Philo's thought, whose positive («male») and negative («female») poles are consistently defined, and whose predominant feature is hierarchy.

---

[52] Cf. J.D.G. DUNN, *Christology in the Making*, 15; E.A. JOHNSON, «Jesus, the Wisdom of God», 287. For much more detailed analysis, see the traditional reference books: E.R. GOODENOUGH, *By Light, Light*; H.A. WOLFSON, *Philo*. An English translation of the works of Philo may be found in F.H. COLSON – G.H. WHITAKER, *Philo*, ten volumes and two supplementary volumes.

[53] Cf. M. SCOTT, *Sophia and the Johannine Jesus,* 58. Here Scott quotes a text from Philo's *De Fuga et Inventione*, 51-52.

[54] Cf. R.A. BAER, *Philo's Use of the Categories Male and Female.*

What we may be seeing in Philo's version of the relationship between God and divine Wisdom is a reaction against the increasing freedom, typified by Wisdom, of expressing God's activity in the world in feminine terms through the use of the figure Sophia. To an extent Philo would only be continuing a trend already hinted at in Sirach 24:23 and Baruch 3:37-4:2, namely the limitation of Sophia to the Torah. However, Philo appears to take this trend much more radically forward in two ways. First, he effectively removes Sophia from the world and confines her to the realm of the divine. We find this, for example, in his description of the giving of the tabernacle as a «copy» of Sophia:

> When God willed to send down the image of divine excellence from heaven to earth in pity for our race, that it should not lose its share in the better lot, he constructs as a symbol of the truth the holy tabernacle and its contents to be a representation and copy of Wisdom (*Quis Rerum Divinarum Heres Sit*, 112).[55]

Thus it is not Sophia that is sent into the world, but only a mere representation of her in the form of the tabernacle. We also find that, instead of Sophia descending into the world to impart her gifts, it is the Logos who comes on her behalf:

> The Divine Word descends from the fountain of Wisdom like a river to lave and water the heaven-sent celestial shoots and plants of virtue-loving souls which are as a garden (*De Somniis* 2.242).[56]

This process of keeping Sophia in the upper realm of the divine leads B.L. Mack to comment:

> Sophia thus represents the otherworldly sphere of salvation. That is, she is no longer immanent Wisdom, but appears rather, together with her gifts, in the realm of the beyond and is in fact understood as hidden Wisdom [...] From now on Wisdom embodies the divine.[57]

Second, Philo attempts to remove Sophia's gender significance by calling her «male»[58], denigrating all that is female by associating it with the created, evil, material world. We find this, for example, in his reflections on the creation and fall accounts:

---

[55] This text is quoted by M. SCOTT, *Sophia and the Johannine Jesus*, 60-61.

[56] Cf. M. SCOTT, *Sophia and the Johannine* Jesus, 61.

[57] Cf. B.L. MACK, *Logos und Sophia*, 121.

[58] See the text quoted from Philo in M. SCOTT, *Sophia and the Johannine Jesus*, 59.

Pleasure does not venture to bring her wiles and deceptions to bear on the man, but on the woman, and by her means on him. This is a telling and well-made point: for in us mind corresponds to man, the senses to woman; and pleasure encounters and holds parley with the senses first, and through them cheats with her quackeries the sovereign mind itself (*De Opificio Mundi*, 165).[59]

Only in relation to God does Philo depict Wisdom as «female»; she is his daughter, his wife, and the mother of his creation.[60] Wisdom is decidedly «male» in relation to humanity. Philo is explicit about the exchange of genders that takes place, depending on whether Wisdom's relationship is with God or with humanity:

[...] while Wisdom's name is feminine, her nature is masculine [...] For that which comes after God, even though it were chiefest of all other things, occupies a second place, and therefore was termed feminine to express its contrast with the Maker of the Universe who is masculine, and its affinity to everything else [...] Let us, then, pay no heed to the discrepancy in the gender of the words, and say that the daughter of God, even Wisdom, is not only masculine but father, sowing and begetting in souls aptness to learn, discipline, knowledge, sound sense, good and laudable actions (*De Fuga et Inventione*, 51-52).[61]

Far removed from the irrational, sense-perceptible, «female» world, Wisdom enjoys a supra-cosmological status, affirmed above all by her close affiliation and frequent virtual identity with the figure of the Logos.[62] The whole universe was framed through the Logos[63]; equally, it is through divine Wisdom that the cosmos was wrought.[64] Both divine Wisdom and the Logos are allegorized as the indivisible turtledove, identifying them

---

[59] Cf. M. SCOTT, *Sophia and the Johannine Jesus*, 61.

[60] Cf. PHILO, *De Cherubim*, 49; *Quod Deterius Potiori Insidiari Soleat*, 54; *De Ebrietate*, 30-31.

[61] Cf. S. LEA MATTILA, «Wisdom, Sense Perception, Nature».

[62] E.R. GOODENOUGH, *By Light, Light*, 23 declares that «Philo flatly identifies the Logos with Sophia». H.A. WOLFSON, *Philo*. I. 258 says Philo calls one «only another word» for the other. B.L. MACK, *Logos und Sophia*, 110, n.10 observes that most scholars have commented on the identity of the figures of Wisdom and Logos in Philo.

[63] PHILO, *De Specialibus Legibus*, 1.18.

[64] PHILO, *Quis Rerum Divinarum Heres Sit*, 199; *De Fuga et Inventione*, 109.

with the «monad».[65] They are both called the «eldest» or «chiefest»[66], and
are both said to have many names, including «the beginning», «the image
of God», and «the one who sees God».[67] Wisdom is «God's archetypal
luminary»[68]; the Logos too, is the model or pattern of light.[69] Both are
compared to the heavenly food or manna which God rained down upon
Israel.[70] Like the Logos, Wisdom is involved in the activity of the creative
and kingly powers of God. Philo thus makes every effort to strip Sophia
of her feminine influence, largely, it seems, because of his antipathy
toward that gender group and his inherent sense of the supremacy of all
that is male, including God. We may, therefore, conclude with J.C.
Engelsmann that the «growing tension between Yahweh and Sophia [...]
appears to have been resolved by repression [...] (in) the writings of
Philo».[71]

2.2 *Wisdom Texts from Qumran*

While the subject of Wisdom at Qumran is a relatively new topic on the
agenda of Dead Sea Scrolls research[72], it has long been recognised that the

---

[65] PHILO, *Quis Rerum Divinarum Heres Sit*, 127, 234.

[66] PHILO, *De Fuga et Inventione*, 101; *Quis Rerum Divinarum Heres*, 205; *De
Virtutibus*, 62.

[67] PHILO, *De Confusione Linguarum*, 146; *Legum Allegoriarum*, 1.43; *De Fuga et
Inventione*, 101.

[68] PHILO, *De Migratione Abrahami*, 40.

[69] PHILO, *De Somniis*, 1.75.

[70] PHILO, *De Fuga et Inventione*, 137-138; *Quis Rerum Divinarum Heres*, 79, 191.

[71] Cf. J.C. ENGELSMANN, *The Feminine Dimension of the Divine*, 75.

[72] The term «Dead Sea Scrolls», used in its widest sense, covers manuscripts and
fragments discovered independently from 1947 to 1965 at a half-dozen sites in the cliffs
west of the Dead Sea. In its narrow sense it refers to what was discovered near Qumran,
the original and most important site. The discovery of the Dead Sea Scrolls was an
epoch-making event for the study of the Bible, early post-biblical Judaism and the
beginnings of Christianity. Written in Hebrew, Aramaic, and Greek, and dating roughly
from 200 BC to the mid first century AD, they afford an unparalleled insight into some
aspects of Palestinian Jewish life and ideology at a very crucial period in the
development of Jewish and Christian religious thought. There are eleven more or less
complete Dead Sea Scrolls and thousands of fragments belonging originally to almost
six hundred manuscripts which amounts to a substantial body of literature covering the
Hebrew Bible. Cf. R.E. BROWN, «Dead Sea Scrolls», 1069; F.M. CROSS, *The Ancient*

foundational documents of the Qumran library, works such as the Community Rule, Damascus Document and Thanksgiving Hymns, contain Wisdom elements.[73] Furthermore, small fragments of the biblical Wisdom books have been discovered at Qumran.[74] These Qumran Wisdom texts did not arise in an intellectual and religious vacuum. Rather, they arose in a society and culture in which the ideas and literary forms of Wisdom writings were well known. We have already noted that Israel's Wisdom was part of an international movement that also found literary expressions in ancient Egypt and Mesopotamia. We have also noted that the Jewish Wisdom books are generally acknowledged to have been organised in their present form in post-exilic times (after 587 BC). The Qumran Wisdom writings are also part of larger post-exilic Jewish movements toward collecting and codifying Israel's Wisdom during the so-called Second Temple period.

At the outset we must acknowledge that the subject of Wisdom texts from Qumran is much more comprehensive than what is presented in these pages. The objective here, as with the Wisdom literature of the Old Testament, is solely to examine Wisdom texts from Qumran to the degree that they help us in providing a context for the understanding of the New Testament's use of Sophia speculation in the process of christological reflection. Generally, we can say that the most important contributions of the Qumran Wisdom texts to New Testament studies lie in their extending what we know about Wisdom teaching and Wisdom teachers in Jesus' time.[75] The Qumran Wisdom scrolls tell us about the language and theological concepts of a Palestinian Jewish group active from the second century BC to the first century AD. But can we be more specific?

The most extensive Wisdom writing in the Qumran library is a Wisdom instruction designated as Sapiential Work A.[76] There are substantial parts of this work in 4Q416, 417 and 418 while other parts are preserved in 1Q26, 4Q415 and 4Q423.[77] Since there are textual overlaps among the

---

Library; J.T. MILIK, *Ten Years of Discovery*; G. VERMES, *The Dead Sea Scrolls.*

[73] Cf. F.M. CROSS, *The Ancient Library*; J.A. FITZMYER, *Responses*; W.L. LIPSCOMB – J.A. SANDERS, «Wisdom at Qumran»; C. ROMANIUK, «Le Thème de la Sagesse», J.C. VANDERKAM, *The Dead Sea Scrolls Today.*

[74] Cf. G.W. NEBE, «Qumranica. I.».

[75] Cf. D.J. HARRINGTON, *Wisdom Texts from Qumran.*

[76] Cf. D.J. HARRINGTON, *Wisdom Texts from Qumran*, 40-59.

[77] The references to the Qumran texts follow the usual conventions. Thus, 4Q416 2 iii 4 refers to Text 416 from Qumran Cave 4, fragment 2, column iii, line 4. On the presence of large parts of Sapiential Work A in texts from caves 1 and 4 see R.H.

various manuscripts, we can be sure that they belong to the same work. The fact that parts of six copies exist indicates the popularity and importance of the work at Qumran.[78]

This Qumran sapiential work is a Wisdom instruction expressed in small units and put together without much apparent concern for logical or thematic progression. In form and content it is similar to Sirach, parts of Proverbs (especially 22:17-24:22), late Egyptian Wisdom writings, Jesus' instruction in the Synoptic Gospels, and the letter of James. In the instructional setting the senior sage gives advice to a novice sage. In some places the senior sage's appeal is to pragmatism or to reward and punishment at the judgment, while in other places there are deductions from and symbolic uses of Scripture.

Fragment 1 of 4Q416 is badly damaged, so much so, that there is not a single complete line of text left. Nevertheless, this fragment may be very important. Before the writing starts there is an extensive margin on the right-hand side. Such a margin would seem to designate the beginning of the work. What can be deciphered here indicates that it started, theologically, with a cosmic and eschatological framework.

The cosmic aspect is suggested by phrases such as «season by season [...] and the host of the Heavens he has established [...] and luminaries for their portents, and signs of their festivals».[79] The eschatological aspect is indicated by the best preserved parts of the fragment: «In heaven he shall pronounce judgment upon the work of wickedness, but all his faithful children will be accepted with favour by Him [...] and every spirit of flesh will be laid utterly bare but the sons of Heaven shall rejoice in the day when it is judged».[80] It would appear that the Wisdom instructions that follow in the main part were intended to help the one who is being

---

EISENMAN– M.O. WISE, *The Dead Sea Scrolls Uncovered*, 241-254; D.J. HARRINGTON – J. STRUGNELL, «Qumran Cave 4 Texts»; J.T. MILIK – D. BARTHÉLEMY, *Qumran Cave, I*, 100-102; B. Z. WACHOLDER–M.G. ABEGG, *A Preliminary Edition*, 54-154, 166-171.

[78] Cf. T. ELGVIN, «Admonition Texts» 137-152; T. ELGVIN, «The Reconstruction of Sapiential work A», 559-580; F. GARCÍA MARTÍNEZ, *The Dead Sea Scrolls*, 383-393; D.J. HARRINGTON, «Wisdom at Qumran», 137-152; L.H. SCHIFFMAN, *Reclaiming the Dead Sea Scrolls*, 203-206.

[79] The translations of the Wisdom texts used come from D.J. HARRINGTON, *Wisdom Texts from Qumran*. Harrington's translations have been helped greatly by the translations of F. GARCÍA MARTÍNEZ, *The Dead Sea Scrolls*; J.A. SANDERS, *The Psalms Scrolls*; G. VERMES, *The Dead Sea Scrolls*.

[80] Cf. D.J. HARRINGTON, *Wisdom Texts from Qumran*, 27.

instructed both to align himself with the correct order of the cosmos and to prepare for the divine judgment when the righteous will be vindicated and wickedness will be destroyed forever. If fragment 1 of 4Q416 is indeed the beginning of the great sapiential instruction, then it must have provided the theological perspective in which the sage's advice on various issues was to be interpreted. That perspective seems to have been cosmic and eschatological.

Furthermore, the hymn to the Creator in 11Q5 xxvi 9-15 celebrates God's Wisdom and understanding made manifest in creation. In talking about creation it introduces the theme of God's Wisdom: «He establishes the dawn by the knowledge of his heart». The reason why God is blessed is because of the Wisdom he showed in creation: «who establishes the world by His Wisdom. By His understanding he stretched out the heavens [...] ». The Wisdom language in the Thanksgiving hymns (1QH) is also prominent in the context of creation.[81] The speaker reflects on God's Wisdom in creating heaven and earth, and in forming «the spirit of Man»: «In the Wisdom of your knowledge You did establish their destiny before they were» (i 19-20). The very structure of the universe has been shaped by the Wisdom of God: «Without it nothing is or shall be, for the God of knowledge has established it» (xii 10-11). While all these expressions are based on the Hebrew Bible and are not especially innovative, they do, nevertheless, demonstrate something of the Qumran community's awareness of the Wisdom theme and its strong links with creation.

A further theme to be found at Qumran, which concerns us here, is the personification of Wisdom in some of the Wisdom texts. In this context, while no one of the other Qumran Wisdom texts is nearly so extensive as Sapiential Work A, some are quite substantial and help us see how personified Wisdom was presented in the Qumran Wisdom texts. The manuscripts from Qumran Cave 4 include an important, though fragmentary, Wisdom text. 4Q184 is a somewhat lurid description of Lady Folly, well known from the early chapters of Proverbs. The text is clearly intended to warn those seeking righteousness against the seductions of folly and sin. Fragment 1 of 4Q184 contains a poem variously known as «the Wiles of the Wicked Woman»[82] and «the seductress».[83] It is a very

---

[81] Cf. D.J. HARRINGTON, *Wisdom Texts from* Qumran, 78-80; S. HOLM–NIELSEN, *Hodayot*; B. KITTEL, *The Hymns of Qumran.*

[82] Cf. J.M. ALLEGRO, «The Wiles»; S. WHITE CRAWFORD, «Lady Wisdom».

[83] Cf. VERMES, *The Dead Sea Scrolls*, 273.

negative description of Lady Folly in the tradition of and in dependence on Proverbs 2,5,7, and 9. By re-using the language of Proverbs 1–9 and concentrating only on Lady Folly, the poem has created a harshly negative portrait that is intended to warn the readers against her enticements:

> *1* [...] she utters folly [...] for perversities she is always searching. She sharpens the words of her mouth, *2* and she imparts mockery so as to lead people astray with evil nonsense. Her heart is set up as a snare, and her kidneys as nets; her eyes are defiled *3* with iniquity; her hands descend to the pit; her feet go down to work wickedness and to talk in the guilt of transgression [...] She is the beginning of all the ways of iniquity. Alas, there shall be ruin to all who possess her, and destruction to all *9* who take hold of her. For her ways are ways of death, and her paths are roads to sin; her tracks lead astray *10* to iniquity and her paths to the guilt of transgression.[84] (4Q184 1 i 1-3, 8-10)

The great Psalms Scroll from Qumran Cave 11, designated 11Q5, contains all or part of over forty canonical psalms (from Psalms 101 to 150) as well as Sirach 51:13-19,30.[85] Other small fragments of Sirach had been found at 2Q18. What is important here is that, with the finding of Sirach 51:13-30, we have evidence at Qumran for the vivid personification of Wisdom as a female figure for whom those who wish to be wise should search. Only part of the first half of the autobiographical poem (Sir 51:13-19) is preserved in column xxi of the Cave 11 Psalms Scroll. The presence of the second half (Sir 51:23-30) is indicated by the last words of *v 30* in the beginning of column xxii.[86]

The connection between Wisdom and Torah is also found in the Qumran Wisdom texts. Fragment 1 and 2 of 4Q185 constitute two columns of a Wisdom instruction.[87] Though the text is very fragmentary, it appears that the «words of the Lord» provide the appropriate guidance for those who wish to pursue the way of Wisdom and righteousness. All are told to walk «in the way He laid down for Jacob, and in the path He appointed for Isaac».[88] In the background is the connection between Wisdom and Torah. This link emerges as a common theme in these Qumran texts. 4Q525 is a sapiential instruction in which the speaker uses the first person singular

---

[84] Cf. D.J. HARRINGTON, *Wisdom Texts from Qumran*, 31-32.

[85] Cf. M.R. LEHMANN, «11Q5 and Ben Sira».

[86] Cf. D.J. HARRINGTON, *Wisdom Texts from Qumran*, 28.

[87] Cf. J.M. ALLEGRO, *Qumran Cave 4*; J. STRUGNELL, «Notes on Volume V».

[88] Cf. D.J. HARRINGTON, *Wisdom Texts from Qumran*, 37.

(«listen to me») to address a second person plural audience («sons»). Its most prominent feature also is the series of five beatitudes in fragment 2, column ii, where Wisdom is manifested in the Torah:

> *2 ii* Happy are they who cling to her statutes and do not cling *2* to the ways of iniquity. Happy are they who rejoice in her and do not babble in the ways of iniquity. Happy are they who seek her with pure hands and do not search for her *3* with a deceitful heart. Happy is the man who has attained Wisdom, and walks by *4* the Law of the Most High, and fixes his heart on her ways, and gives heed to her admonitions, and in her chastisements delights always, *5* and does not forsake her in the stress of his troubles.[89] (4Q525 2 ii 1-5)

This link between Wisdom and the Torah is carried on in fragment 4. The text describes those who fear God and love God as keeping "her ways" and walking in «her statutes».[90] Again the feminine singular suffixes could refer to Wisdom personified or to Torah, and indeed are probably intended to refer to both.

The Community Rule (1QS), though not a Wisdom book in itself, does include so many sapiential elements that we can at least talk about Wisdom influences or elements in it. In the appendix to the Community Rule, also called the Messianic Rule (1QSa), there is the description of the «messianic banquet» (1QSa 1 ii 11-12) in which the community's meal in the present prepares for and reflects the heavenly banquet at which the Messiah of Aaron (the priest) and the Messiah of Israel (a David figure) play prominent roles.[91] According to Psalm 154, the appropriate topics of conversation for the community of the righteous as they eat and drink together are Wisdom and the Torah: «When they eat in fullness, she is mentioned; and when they drink in community together, their meditation is on the Law of the Most High» (11Q5 xviii 11-12).

We have focussed on the most substantial and important manuscripts in our examination of Wisdom texts from Qumran. The evidence has given us some ideas and motifs about Wisdom that were present at Qumran: the cosmic and eschatological context of the Wisdom instructions, Wisdom as God's agent in creation, the close connection between Wisdom and Torah, the personification of Wisdom as a female figure for whom those who wish to be wise should search, the description of the «messianic

---

[89] Cf. D.J. HARRINGTON, *Wisdom Texts from Qumran*, 66.

[90] Cf. D.J. HARRINGTON, *Wisdom Texts from Qumran*, 67.

[91] Cf. D.J. HARRINGTON, *Wisdom Texts from Qumran*, 78.

banquet» where Wisdom and the Torah are the topics of conversation. These are familiar to us from our study of the biblical Wisdom literature. They emphasize the influence of the Wisdom literature on the community at Qumran, notwithstanding the distinctive and particular character of these Qumran Wisdom texts.

3. Lady Wisdom, Sophia: Origin and Theological Significance

We have seen that a presentation of the meaning of Wisdom from the Second Temple Period, which is foundational for understanding early Christianity's language about Jesus as the Wisdom of God, involves the personification of Wisdom in female form. Consistent with this personification, *Wisdom* is a feminine noun in both Hebrew (*hokmah*) and Greek (*sophia*). It has become common to name this personification Sophia even when the reference is to the Hebrew text. The obvious reason for doing so (besides the fact that Greek texts use *sophia*) is that Sophia is a woman's name, thereby reminding us of the female personification in a way that the neuter-sounding word *Wisdom* does not. Sophia is the most striking personification in the Bible.[92] While it is practically impossible to articulate a synthesis of personified Wisdom as presented in the Old Testament a certain profile seems desirable to clarify the foregoing discussion.

3.1 *Sophia: A Profile*

1. Sophia has a divine origin and dwelt with God: Proverbs 8:22-31; Sirach 24:3-4; Wisdom 7:25-26; 9:9-10.

2. Being the exclusive property of God Sophia is as such inaccessible to human beings: Job 28:12-13, 20-21, 23-27.

3. Sophia existed before creation and had a role in creation: Proverbs 8:22-31; Sirach 1:4, 9-10; Wisdom 7:22; 8:4-6; 9:2,9.

4. Sophia is identified with the divine spirit: Sirach 24:3-4; Wisdom 1:7; 9:17; 12:1; and she is also immanent in the world: Wisdom 7:24; 8:1.

---

[92] We have noted that personification as a literary device is not unknown in biblical literature. The justice or vindication (*ṣedeq*) of Israel will go before the Israelites when they leave from Babylon (Is 58:8). In Psalm 85:11 kindness and truth meet; justice and peace kiss. In Proverbs 20:1 wine and strong drink are personified as proud and riotous figures; they impersonate the effects they produce. However, the personification of Wisdom is simply unique in the Old Testament, both for its quantity and quality.

5. Sophia accounts for the coherence and permanence of the cosmos: Wisdom 1:7; 7:24-27; 8:1; 11:25.

6. Sophia has a particular mission to human beings: Proverbs 1:20-33; 8:1-9:6; Sirach 24:7,12,19-22; Wisdom 7:27-28; 8:2-3.

(a) She speaks to them in the world (Prov 1, 8, 9; Sir 24:19-22; Wis 6:12-16; 7:22a; 8:7-9; 9:10-16).

(b) She promises her followers life, prosperity and blessing (Prov 1:32; 3:13-18; 8:1-5,35; 9:1-6; Sir 1:14-20; 6:18-31; 15:1-8; 24:19-33; Wis 7:7-14).

(c) She invites to her feast those who are not yet wise: (Prov 9:1-6).

7. Sophia is particularly associated with Israel:

(a) She dwells in Israel, by divine command (Sir 24:8-12)

(b) She can be identified with the Torah (Sir 24:23; Bar 4:1)

(c) She was at work in Israel's history (Wis 10:1-21)

(d) It was God who «found» Sophia and gave her to Israel (Bar 3:29-37)

8. Sophia is a gift from God: Proverbs 2:6; Sirach 1:9-10,26; 6:37; Wisdom 7:7; 9:4. But at the same time she is associated with effort and discipline: Proverbs 4:10-27; 6:6; Sirach 4:17; 6:18-36; Wisdom 1:5; 7:14.

9. A list of the passages where Sophia is found to be personified: Proverbs 1, 8, 9; Sirach 1:9-10; 4:11-19; 6:18-31; 14:20-15:8; 51:13-21; Baruch 3:9-4:4; Wisdom 6:12-11:1.[93]

3.2 Origin of Sophia

The question of Sophia's identity has been a challenge to biblical scholars and the issue remains unsettled. Various attempts have been made to capture the elusive origins of this figure.[94] However hard it may be to

---

[93] I am indebted in this profile to R.E. MURPHY, *The Tree of Life*, 145-146 and B. WITHERINGTON, *Jesus the Sage*, 114-115. Murphy also draws our attention to the profile of Sophia by B.L. MACK, *Logos und Sophia*. Mack prefers to use a different terminology for Sophia: *verborgen*, or «hidden», for the remoteness of Sophia in Job 28 and Baruch 3:9 - 4:4; *nahe*, or «near» for the intimate presence of Proverbs 8:22-31. There is also the terminology used by J. MARBÖCK, *Weisheit im Wandel*, 127-133, who speaks of Sophia «from above» and «from below» (categories seemingly derived from current christological discussion). Thus Sirach 24 is «from above» and Sirach 31:12-32:13 is «from below». Cf. C. LARCHER, *Études sur le livre de la Sagesse*, 398-414.

[94] For bibliography on this question of the origins of Sophia see J.D.G. DUNN, *Christology in the Making*, 326, n. 26; M. HENGEL, *Judaism and Hellenism*, II, 101-102, n. 331; J.S. KLOPPENBORG, «Isis and Sophia», 58, n. 7-9; R.E. MURPHY, *The Tree of Life*, 147-148, n. 5.

determine Sophia's origins and whatever problems there may be in specifying her exact relationship to the one God, Yahweh, one thing may be said with certainty: Sophia emerged in the context of an ancient Near Eastern world widely accustomed to the cult of a variety of goddesses. The biblical tradition itself reflects this in the warnings given against the dangers of ensnarement in their grasp, particularly with reference to the destruction of the cult of Asherah (Judg 3:7, 6:26-30; 1 Kgs 14:23, 15:13; 2 Kgs 21:7, 23:4,7, 2 Chr 15:16).[95]

Of all the various ancient Near Eastern goddesses mooted as a possible background for the understanding of the development of Sophia, the most widely acknowledged and advanced has been the Egyptian Isis.[96] Varying degrees of influence have been proposed, but only rarely has an attempt been made to deny altogether an influence of some kind.[97] Perhaps the greatest difficulty has been encountered by those seeking a direct influence at an *early* stage in Israel's Sophia speculation. M. Hengel is able to show early traces of an Isis-Astarte relationship in Palestine,[98] but has to admit that a connection with Proverbs «is still uncertain».[99] However, more convincing material has been brought to light concerning the influence of the figure of Isis on Sirach and more especially Wisdom.[100]

---

[95] Cf. W.L. REED, «Asherah».

[96] Cf. B.L. MACK, *Logos und Sophia;* J. REESE, *Hellenistic Influence*; J.S. Kloppenborg, building on the studies of Mack and Reese, has made a strong case for Isis being behind the figure of Sophia in Wisdom 7–9. Cf. J.C. Kloppenborg, «Isis and Sophia», 57-84. This view has been questioned somewhat by J.J. COLLINS, *Jewish Wisdom in the Hellenistic Age*.

[97] Cf. G. PFEIFER, *Ursprung und Wesen*. He is the only recent advocate of such an extreme position, which is described by J.C. KLOPPENBORG, «Isis and Sophia», 59 as «exaggerated and ill-considered».

[98] Cf. M. HENGEL, *Judaism and Hellenism*, I, 158.

[99] Cf. M. HENGEL, *Judaism and Hellenism*, II, 102, n.331. For a similar viewpoint see B. Witherington, *Jesus the Sage*, 40-41. However, a different view is presented by H. CONZELMANN, «The Mother of Wisdom».

[100] H. Conzelmann, among others, has suggested that in Sirach 24 we see a clear dependence on an Isis aretology. Cf. H. CONZELMANN, «The Mother of Wisdom», 228; M. HENGEL, *Judaism and Hellenism*, I, 158-159. Even if it does prove to be the case that some ideas have been borrowed from an Isis liturgy, it is done to supplant any such pagan deity and redirect the listener to the worship of the Jewish God, cf. M. HENGEL, *Judaism and Hellenism*, I, 162.

As early as 1937, W.L. Knox proposed an Isis influence on the figure of Sophia in Sirach.[101] He saw in Sirach 24 «the answer of orthodox Judaism» to those finding it «hard to resist the attractions of Isis».[102] His study pointed out the flexibility and adaptability of Isis, in particular in relation to her influence on the Syrian Astarte, which in turn he believed to have influenced the picture of Sophia. The wandering quest of Isis has been altered to present a Sophia who comes down to earth and searches out her disciples, while indulging in self-praise «modelled on Isis of the aretalogy».[103]

The Book of Wisdom shows the greatest affinity to Isis traditions. Both B.L. Mack[104] and J.M. Reese[105] have dealt with this in some detail, but it has again been thoroughly rehearsed in recent times by J.S. Kloppenborg.[106] While acknowledging the value of Reese's work, Kloppenborg asserts that «what is required is not a lot of parallel terms and titles but a demonstration that complete configurations of specifically Isiac-mythologumena are mirrored in Wisdom».[107] He does not doubt that Wisdom owes a great deal to older biblical traditions, but at the same time stresses that it «goes far beyond the traditional *topoi* of Wisdom in Proverbs, Job and Sirach».[108] In his analysis, both Isis and Sophia create, sustain and regulate the universe. Of particular importance is the parallelism between Sophia and Isis in their role as saviour[109], a role not specifically attributed to Sophia in other earlier Wisdom writings. Kloppenborg shows how the saving acts of Sophia in Wisdom 9-10 have been chosen not so much for their place in the traditional religious piety of Israel, but rather because they are «incidents which are precisely of the sort over which Isis also had control».[110] Two examples of such incidents are the reference to the guiding of Noah's ark (Wis 10:4), which «corre-

---

[101] Cf. W.L. KNOX, «The Divine Wisdom»; ID., *St Paul*, 53-89.

[102] Cf. W.L. KNOX, «The Divine Wisdom», 236.

[103] Cf. W.L. KNOX, «The Divine Wisdom», 237.

[104] Cf. B.L. MACK, *Logos und Sophia*, 63-107.

[105] Cf. J.M. REESE, *Hellenistic Influence on the Book of Wisdom*.

[106] Cf. J.S. KLOPPENBORG, «Isis and Sophia», 57-84.

[107] Cf. J.S. KLOPPENBORG, «Isis and Sophia», 61.

[108] Cf. J.S. KLOPPENBORG, «Isis and Sophia», 78.

[109] Cf. C.T. BLEEKER, «Isis as Saviour Goddess», 1-16; J.J. COLLINS, *Jewish Wisdom in the Hellenistic Age*, 204.

[110] Cf. J.S. KLOPPENBORG, «Isis and Sophia», 70.

sponds closely to one of Isis' major competences, the protection and guiding of sailors»,[111] and her support of the righteous man in prison (Wis 10:14), which is «closely parallelled by Isis' promise to save prisoners when they pray for her presence».[112]

Kloppenborg goes on to show strong links between Sophia's relationship with the king in Wisdom 6:1-9:17 and the similar functions of Isis.[113] Both represent the divine power by which the king comes to power and rules, and by which he sustains the prosperity and longevity that one associates with a good king. Both Sophia and Isis are intimates of God and the king. Kloppenborg sums up: «The mythic power which informed Egyptian ideology is captivated and transformed for Judaism, enabling Jews to maintain themselves in an atmosphere of intense religious and political propaganda».[114] His final section reflects on the reason for this transformation, outlining the social setting to which the work was addressed.[115] In the end, the figure of Sophia functions as both a stimulus to Jews suffering under pagan attack, and as an apologetic designed to allow for «communication with the dominant group to whose privileges and position Alexandrian Jews aspired».[116]

M. Scott argues that by attempting to outline areas of *function* which correspond, rather than concentrating on mere verbal or linguistic overlaps, Kloppenborg has achieved a significant methodological breakthrough in dealing with the relationship between the ancient Near Eastern goddess and Sophia.[117] He has also rooted this in a plausible sociological analysis. What is important for us is not whether he is correct in every detail of his analysis, but that he has conclusively shown the need for a Jewish writer to counter the claims of a widely known goddess by using a corresponding symbol from *within* his own tradition: that is, by using the overtly feminine figure of Sophia. But if biblical Sophia, while fashioned in many ways along the lines of the goddess, is nevertheless not intended as a second deity within the religious context of Jewish monotheism, what is to be made of her significance?

---

[111] Cf. J.S. KLOPPENBORG, «Isis and Sophia», 70.

[112] Cf. J.S. KLOPPENBORG, «Isis and Sophia», 71.

[113] Cf. J.S. KLOPPENBORG, «Isis and Sophia», 73-78.

[114] Cf. J.S. KLOPPENBORG, «Isis and Sophia», 78.

[115] Cf. J.S. KLOPPENBORG, «Isis and Sophia», 79-84.

[116] Cf. J.S. KLOPPENBORG, «Isis and Sophia», 84.

[117] Cf. M. SCOTT, *Sophia and the Johannine Jesus*, 72.

3.3 *Theological Significance of Sophia*

Debate on the theological meaning and interpretation of Sophia has remained unresolved, not least because the differences apparent in the various scriptural books written in diverse contexts make it impossible to apply any one interpretation to every text where Sophia appears. The principal options held out to us are as follows: (1) Wisdom is the personification of cosmic order[118]; (2) Wisdom is a hypostasis[119]; (3) Wisdom is a personification of a divine attribute[120]; (4) Wisdom is a personification of God's own self in creative and saving involvement with the world.[121] If we hope to establish what the first Christians meant in identifying Christ as Wisdom, we must attempt to reach some sort of decision as to which of these options is the best interpretation of these Old Testament passages, that is to say, which of these options represents the meaning that the first Christians would assign to these passages.[122]

---

[118] This view sees Sophia as the personification of the meaning which God has implanted in creation. Cf. G. VON RAD, *Wisdom in Israel*, 144-176. For a critique of von Rad's position see O. PLÖGER, *Sprüche Salomos (Proverbia)*, 93; B. WITHERINGTON, *Jesus the Sage*, 41-42.

[119] This view of Sophia has the meaning of a quasi-personification of certain attributes proper to God occupying an intermediate position between personalities and abstract beings. With this understanding, monotheism gave rise to such quasi-personifications of divine qualities in order to allow for more concrete experience of the transcendent God's actions. In time these hypostases broke off to acquire their own independent existence, leading to polytheism. Sophia appears mid-way in this process, not yet an independent personality in her own right but certainly more than an unimaginable, abstract being. Cf. O.S. RANKIN, *Israel's Wisdom Literature*, 224; H. RINGGREN, *Word and Wisdom*, 147.

[120] In this interpretation the attribute of Wisdom is understood in the anthropological sense of insightful knowledge and discerning intelligence; its personification is compared with similar personalizations of qualities in the scriptures, such as «steadfast love and faithfulness will meet, righteousness and peace will kiss each other» (Ps 85:10). Cf. F.W. DILLISTONE, «Wisdom, Word and Spirit»; C. LARCHER, *Études sur le livre de la Sagesse*, 402-410; R. N. WHYBRAY, *Wisdom in Proverbs*, 92-104.

[121] In this interpretation the attribute of Wisdom is used as a way of asserting the transcendent God's nearness to the world in such a way that transcendence was not compromised.

[122] A various combination of possible solutions have been listed by different scholars in their treatment of this question. For example, E.A. Johnson treats of five proposed solutions: (1) Wisdom is the personification of cosmic order; (2) Wisdom is the personification of the Wisdom sought and learned in Israel's Wisdom schools; (3) Wisdom is the poetic personification of a divine attribute; (4) Wisdom is a hypostasis;

In this regard, J.D.G. Dunn has highlighted a number of key points which are worth affirming here by way of summary of our discussion thus far.[123] First, a *development* in the talk about Wisdom can be observed by setting out the passages in the most likely chronological order. We saw that in Job 28 we cannot really speak of a divine attribute, or of a personification. Wisdom may be simply the order given to the world by God. Proverbs affirms a significant development where Wisdom speaks in the first person. We saw the arguments for the influence of figures from wider religious thought and worship. Many scholars support the view that Proverbs, and more clearly Sirach, have been greatly influenced by the cult of Isis from Egypt. The central issue of comparison is that Isis proclaims herself as the divine agent who created and sustains the universe, as the teacher who has revealed to humanity the principles and the laws of morality and civilization. The divine status of Sophia and her role in creation comes to clearest expression in the Book of Wisdom where we see her as the fashioner of all things who pervades all creation. With Dunn we may conclude that, «however deeply rooted in Palestinian soil and Jewish faith was the late Israelite talk of Wisdom, many of the images and words used to describe her were drawn from wider religious thought and worship, the aim being to present the worshippers of Yahweh with as attractive as possible an alternative to the cults and speculations more widely prevalent in their time».[124]

Second, we should bear in mind that language which denoted a hypostasis or independent deity in polytheism would certainly have a different connotation within a monotheistic religion. A monotheistic faith could not countenance another god within the heavenly realm. There is no evidence that the Wisdom tradition we have been examining was willing to diffuse its monotheism under the impact of Hellenistic culture.[125]

---

(5) Wisdom is a personification of God's own self in creative and saving involvement with the world. J.D.G. Dunn treats of four proposed solutions which overlap with Johnson's. Cf. J.D.G. DUNN, *Christology in the Making*, 168-176; E.A. JOHNSON, «Jesus, the Wisdom of God», 271-276. Those in support of this final proposition include P.E. BONNARD, «De la Sagesse personnifiée»; J.D.G. DUNN, *Christology in the Making,* 176; J.S. KLOPPENBORG, «Isis and Sophia».

[123] Cf. J.D.G. DUNN, *Christology in the Making*, 168-176.

[124] Cf. J.D.G. DUNN, *Christology in the Making*, 169-170.

[125] Thus when H. Ringgren examined the hypostatization of divine qualities and functions in the Near East he concludes that words like *Maat* (truth, righteousness, order and regularity in the cosmos) and *Mesaru* (righteousness) came to denote independent

Hence, in order to understand what meaning words and statements from an Isis hymn, on the one hand, and Sirach on the other, had for those who used them, we must interpret them within the context in which they were used. We have seen that, within the Wisdom tradition, no worship is offered to Wisdom. In the context of faith in Yahweh there is no clear indication that the Wisdom language of these writings has gone beyond vivid personification. While taking up some of the more widespread language of near Eastern religious speculation, the Jewish Wisdom tradition does so in conscious awareness of its use elsewhere. It does *not* draw the same conclusions for worship and practice as the polytheistic religions do. On the contrary, as Dunn concludes, the Jewish Wisdom writers «*adapt* this wider speculation to their own faith and make it serve to commend their own faith; to Wisdom understood and worshipped as a divine being (one of Isis' names), they pose the alternative of Wisdom manifested by the law given to Israel by the one God».[126]

Third, the Wisdom spoken of is the *Wisdom of God* and signifies God's wise ordering of creation. The Jewish Wisdom writers do not give Wisdom the status of an independent entity or a divine personality side by side with Yahweh. We have little or no grounds for believing that the Wisdom writers thought of Wisdom as a hypostasis or intermediary being.[127] Wisdom was a way of asserting God's nearness, his involvement

---

deities. *Maat*, originally a function of the high god in Egyptian religion becomes a self-existent being. Since the word *maat* is female, it was natural that this being should become a goddess, the daughter of the god. Similarly with *Mesaru* in the Babylonian realm. But what makes it clear to Ringgren that these are more than merely poetic personifications or abstractions, is that we know of many priests of *Maat*, and that *Mesaru* had its own image in the temple and was worshiped there. This is precisely what is lacking in the Wisdom tradition. Cf. H. RINGGREN, *Word and Wisdom*, 45-59.

[126] Cf. J.D.G. DUNN, *Christology in the Making*, 171.

[127] J.D.G. Dunn makes the point that this view of Wisdom as a divine hypostasis involves the importation of a concept whose appropriateness here is a consequence of the technical meaning it acquired in the much later Trinitarian controversies of the early Church. Dunn argues that it has not been demonstrated that Hebrew thought was already contemplating such distinctions within its talk of God. On the contrary, for a Jew to say that Wisdom «effects all things», that Wisdom «delivered Israel from a nation of oppressors», that love of Wisdom «is the keeping of her laws»" (Wis 8:5; 10:15; 6:18*)*, was simply to say in a more picturesque way that God created all things wisely, that God's wise purpose is clearly evident in the exodus from Egypt and most fully expressed in the law he gave through Moses. Cf. J.D.G. DUNN, *Christology in the Making*, 174. Dunn cites G.F. MOORE, «Intermediaries in Jewish Theology» in support of his position. Those in agreement with Dunn, against the view of Sophia as a hypostasis, include R.E.

with the world, his concern for his people. Wisdom provided an understanding of God's *immanence*, his active concern in creation, revelation and redemption, while at the same time protecting his transcendence and wholly otherness.[128] Dunn affirms that «we can say with confidence that it is very unlikely that pre-Christian Judaism ever understood Wisdom as a divine being in any sense independent of Yahweh. The language may be the language of the wider speculation of the time, but within Jewish monotheism and Hebraic literary idiom Wisdom never becomes more than a *personification*, a personification not of a divine attribute but a personification rather of a *function* of Yahweh, a way of speaking about God himself, of expressing God's active involvement with his world and his people without compromising his transcendence».[129] Maintaining as it does that Sophia is God's active and gracious presence in the world, this interpretation of Wisdom will be most useful to us when we begin to inquire after the significance of some of the earliest Christian reflections on Jesus of Nazareth which interpreted him in terms of the Wisdom tradition.

4. Summary and Conclusions

We have traced the remarkable and significant development of the personification of Wisdom in the Jewish sapiential tradition, a development that involved the evolution and creation of a variety of forms as well as the development and genesis of new ideas. Throughout we have noted a development in the relationship between Sophia and Yahweh: from the time of her earliest appearances in Proverbs to that in Wisdom at the

---

Murphy, G. von Rad, R.B.Y. Scott and B. Witherington (though he does suggest a possible hypostasis presentation of Sophia in Wisdom, see *Jesus the Sage*, 109). Cf. M. HENGEL, *Judaism and Hellenism*. II. 98, n. 294.

[128] J.D.G. Dunn has called attention to the judgment of rabbinic specialists, who use the hermeneutical key of *transcendence/immanence* to interpret Sophia's appearance. They argue that Wisdom, Word, God's Name and so forth were not introduced into Judaism to offset the utter transcendence of God. Rather, these were ways of asserting the transcendent God's nearness to the world in such a way that transcendence was not compromised. Thus to say that Sophia is the fashioner of all things, that she delivered Israel from a nation of oppressors, or that her gifts are justice and life is to speak of the transcendent God's relation to the world, of *Yahweh's* nearness and activity. Dunn concludes that the Wisdom of God in Jewish thought is simply God revealing and known. Cf. J.D.G. DUNN, «Was Christianity a Monotheistic Faith?», 319, n. 51.

[129] Cf. J.D.G. DUNN, *Christology in the Making*, 176.

beginning of the Christian era. In doing so we have had to keep in mind the nature of Israel's religion as being *monotheistic:* Sophia was seen as a symbolic figure in female guise, who took on some of the roles traditionally associated with Yahweh, while remaining within his control.

In Proverbs Sophia asserting several important theological features about herself: she was created as God's first-born; she was God's co-worker in creation; she reveals herself as profoundly relational, interrelated with God, with all creatures, and with humans in a particular way. Furthermore, we noted the paradox at the heart of Wisdom in Proverbs: on the one hand, Wisdom involves the investigation of natural and human phenomena and deducing practical lessons from them, but equally, Wisdom is something that God must reveal if anyone is to know it.

Moving to Sirach, we saw two things: first, the development of Sophia's role as creator, giver of life and sustainer of those who accepted her after her settling on earth, which went beyond the initial steps of the first speeches in Proverbs 1 and 8. Second, in the dialectical relationship developed between Sophia and Torah, we recognized the beginnings of what might be an attempt to suppress the gender-significance of Sophia and to define her parameters. The personalized symbol is thus prevented from developing individual personality by confinement to the impersonal concept of the Torah. While it was not possible fully to substantiate the consciousness of such suppression in the mind of the author of Sirach, the possibility was heightened by the observation of the negative, almost chauvinistic attitude towards women presented in the book as a whole. Such an attitude was noted in an even more explicit form in the works of Philo. Again, with Sirach 24, the probable influence of goddess features in the presentation of Sophia was noted, in particular those of the goddess Isis who by that period was influential throughout the Graeco-Roman world.

The Book of Wisdom provided us with both an unrestricted picture of Sophia as God at work in the life and salvation history of Israel, and with a clear view of the manner in which pagan goddess influence may actually have worked in Sophia's development. She was seen to be almost indistinguishable from God (Wis 7:25-26), and at one and the same time quite distinct in her function (Wis 9:4). Clearly here we have moved beyond the relationship between Sophia and Yahweh given by Proverbs and Sirach. As the Saviour of Israel, both collectively and of the individual, and in her relationship with the king, she clearly took on some configurations from Isis, but in doing so did not succumb to the danger of being swallowed up by Isis into a form of independent goddess worship. Rather, the assimilation of traits of Isis was used to serve Jewish monotheistic faith.

With regard to the Alexandrian philosopher Philo, his significance for the study of New Testament background lies in his witness to a particular trend of Jewish philosophical reflection and speculation at the time of the formation of the New Testament. Philo also sought to use the figure of Sophia within the context of Jewish monotheism. However, this usage was also heavily influenced both by his Platonic base and his understanding of the nature of human sexuality. This led him to withdraw Sophia largely to the upper realm of the divine, replacing her function in the divine by the work of the Logos. Philo's Sophia is influenced by the goddess Isis. However, Philo is at great pains to obliterate any cultic influence by removing or transmuting her sexuality, on at least one occasion even making her male. This is effectively done in terms of her role in the divine by the substitution of the male Logos.

The objective in examining some Wisdom texts from Qumran was to provide a context for the understanding of the New Testament's use of Sophia speculation in the process of christological reflection. Generally, the most important contributions of the Qumran Wisdom texts to New Testament studies lie in their extending what we know about Wisdom teaching and Wisdom teachers during the time of Jesus. The cosmic and eschatological aspects of Qumran provided the theological perspectives in which the sage's advice on various issues was interpreted. The personification of Wisdom as a female figure in the Qumran Wisdom texts, together with the connection between Wisdom and Torah as found in these texts, were noted.

Regarding Sophia's origin and theological significance, Sophia emerged in the context of an ancient Near Eastern world widely accustomed to the cult of a variety of goddesses, the most widely acknowledged as a possible background for the understanding of the development of Sophia being the Egyptian Isis. The use of material from contemporary religious circles, however, in no way implied that there was an attempt to *copy* the goddess religions in terms of setting up a Sophia cult in Israel. Rather, it served somewhat as a *counter* to them, which may be reflected in the contrast between Sophia and Dame Folly in Proverbs 1–9. While monotheism was in no way threatened by Sophia's appearance in Proverbs, in her appearance lay the possibility of the beginnings of a feminine expression of God within Israel's tradition.

We brought together in the form of a composite profile the threads of what has been said about the personification of Wisdom. This led us to address the question of the theological significance of Sophia. A number of solutions to this question have been proposed. The Wisdom literature reflects so many shades of meaning that each of the interpretations can be supported by appeal to certain texts. It was the interpretation of Sophia as a personification of God's own self in creative and saving involvement with the world which best describes Sophia as divine and thus provides a female image for God without distorting the structure of Israel's monotheistic faith.

A certain particularization of the tradition was detected as the personification developed so that Wisdom obtains names. She is linked to the Torah in Sirach and to God's Spirit in Wisdom. It is striking that what happens to Sophia is what happens in general in Sirach and Wisdom, for in both these books we saw a drawing on the particular traditions of Israel's history and a focus on God's chosen people and their future direction. This trend of particularization takes a further and dramatic step in the New Testament Wisdom material.

CHAPTER II

Wisdom in the Christological Hymns

We have established a context for understanding the New Testament's use of Wisdom speculation in the process of christological reflection. To this end the development in the relationship between personified Wisdom, Sophia, and the one God, Yahweh, as seen in the writings of the Second Temple Period, together with the writings of Philo and the Wisdom texts from Qumran, was our chief concern. Our objective now is to set out and evaluate the conclusions contemporary biblical scholarship has drawn regarding the Wisdom influences on the formation of some of the christological hymns of the New Testament. We will specifically consider Philippians 2:6-11, Colossians 1:15-20, Hebrews 1:2-4 and John 1:1-16.

1. Singing Wisdom's Praises

Many influences were brought to bear on early Jewish Christianity in establishing and determining the structure and system of belief statements and creedal confessions about Jesus Christ: the experience of the Spirit, the preaching by the apostles of the life, death and resurrection of Jesus, reflection on the apostles' preaching and the structure and system of prayer and worship. This prayer and worship, was largely expressed in various liturgical forms and prayers: hymns, testimonia and doxologies.[1] We will

---

[1] So far as we can tell the earliest Christians in Palestine maintained the traditions of Jewish worship virtually unchanged. They attended the Temple daily (Acts 2:46, 3:1, 5:12, 21, 42). They seem also to have observed the traditional hours of prayer (Acts 3:1, 5:21) at Temple and/or Synagogue (Acts 6:9, Jn 9). They continued to observe the Law and the «tradition of the elders», including the Sabbath, with faithfulness (Mt 23:3, 23, 24:20, Acts 21:20, Gal 2:3, 12). However, at the same time new forms of worship seem to have been developing. These centred on gathering in private houses (Acts 2:46, 5:42).

be concerned here with one particular expression of earliest Christian worship, its hymnody.[2]

Although there are references to Christians singing «psalms and hymns and spiritual songs»[3] the New Testament does not contain a collected book of hymns similar to the Old Testament Book of Psalms. Rather first-century Christian canticles and hymns are incorporated into larger writings of another genre. Sometimes the New Testament hymn or song is clearly

---

We hear of different elements entering into these meetings: worship and prayer (Acts 1:14, 2:42, 4:23-31, 12:12), teaching, that is both the Scriptures (Old Testament) and the Jesus-tradition, both passing them on and interpreting them (Acts 2:42, 5:42), and common meals (Acts 2:42, 46). There is nothing to indicate that these fell into a regular pattern or formed a unified service of worship. It is more likely that there were at least two different kinds of gathering: one, possibly more formal, for prayer and teaching, following somewhat the pattern of the Synagogue service, and the other for fellowship meals, which may also have included other elements, such as singing, introduced, as appropriate, in more spontaneous manner. The new patterns of worship which began to emerge in these meetings were not wholly different from what had gone before: reading of the Scriptures (Old Testament). But there were also distinctively Christian elements: the Lord's Prayer, the use of *abba* in prayers, the recollection of the words and mighty acts of Jesus, all of which must have been transmitted through the earliest communities, not least the centrality of Jesus in his presence (Mt 18:20), and expected imminent return (I Cor 16:22), and those elements in the common meal which recalled the table-fellowship of Jesus' ministry, the last supper in particular, and which were to develop into what we now know as the Lord's Supper. For consideration of the patterns of worship which characterized the church of the New Testament period see J.D.G. DUNN, *Unity and Diversity,* 124-149.

[2] There is a precedent and also parallels in early Judaism and elsewhere for the earliest Christians composing hymns. In the pagan world there was already a close connection between hymn writing and singing in temples coupled with significant theological content: see R. MCMULLEN, *Paganism in the Roman Empire,* 150. Philo speaks about the singing of hymns among the Jewish *therapeutae,* men and women who had abandoned the world for the sake of solitude and contemplation in the first century A.D. Cf. PHILO, *De Vita,* 28-29, 68-80, in C.D. YONGE, *The Works of Philo,* 706. Composing hymns seems to have been a regular practice in the Qumran community: see G. VERMES, *The Dead Sea Scrolls,* 165-208.

[3] Cf. Colossians 3:16, Ephesians 5:19, also Acts 16:25, Hebrews 2:12, I Corinthians 14:15,26; James 5:13. «Psalm» is a Christian composition, evidently thought comparable to Old Testament hymns. The letter of Pliny to Trajan (10.96-97) says that Christians met before dawn on a stated day and sang in alternation (antiphonally?) «a hymn to Christ as a God». The earliest preserved Christian hymn collection may be the *Odes of Solomon,* a Jewish Christian collection in Syriac of the 2nd century. The earliest preserved musically annotated Christian hymn seems to be Oxyrhynchus Papyrus 1786 of the early 3rd century. Cf. R.E. BROWN, *An Introduction,* 489-491.

designated, as in the heavenly singing of Revelation 4:8, 10-11; 5:9. The canticles of the Lucan infancy narratives, while not designated as songs, are set off from the surrounding text as oracles of praise.[4] The Johannine prologue by its very situation at the beginning of the Gospel stands apart.

A greater problem is presented by the proposal that there are hymns woven into the heart of letters and detectable only by scholarly investigation. Most often nothing in the context states that a hymn is being introduced and quoted although occasionally the transition to the incorporated hymn is awkward. Criteria for detecting a hymn are not easy to apply, and as a result the detection of hymns is an «inexact science».[5] Various backgrounds have been suggested for the formation of such hymns. Among the suggested Pagan parallels are the Orphic Hymns (5th-4th centuries B.C.), the Isis Hymn of Cyme (2nd century B.C.), and the Mithras Liturgy. As we shall see, a Jewish background for many of these hymns is supplied by the personified Wisdom poems of the Old Testament.

When first-century Christians began expressing their experience of the saving significance of Jesus and his ultimate origin in God's gracious goodness, they combed the Jewish religious traditions and Hellenistic

---

[4] The Church has long been familiar with the four psalms of Luke 1-2 as part of its own worship: the *Magnificat* (Lk 1:46-55), the *Benedictus* (Lk 1:68-79), the *Gloria in excelsis* (Lk 2:14) and the *Nunc dimittis* (Lk 2:29-32).

[5] This will be illustrated in debates to be reported about some individual hymns - debates as to where they end or how they are to be divided or which lines are original. Moreover, the line of demarcation between hymns and confessional formulae (eg., I Cor 15:3-8) or doxologies (eg., I Tim 6:15-16) is not clear. The following is a list of hymns often detected by scholars in New Testament letters (scholarly estimates run from five to thirty); it does not claim to be complete, and those marked with an asterisk are the most agreed upon: Philippians 2:6-11*, I Corinthians 13, Romans 3:24-26, Romans 6:1-11, Romans 8:31-39, Romans 11:33-36, Colossians 1:15-20*, Ephesians 1:3-14, Ephesians 1:20-23, Ephesians 2:14-18, Ephesians 5:14*, Titus 3:4-7, I Timothy 3:16*, II Timothy 2:11-13*, Hebrews 1:3, I Peter 1:3-5, I Peter 1:18-21, I Peter 2:21-25, I Peter 3:18-22. Although M. Barth gives eleven criteria and E. Stauffer twelve for detecting the presence of hymnic material in the New Testament, the common consensus points to two general criteria. P.T. O'Brien describes these as follows: (a) *stylistic*: a certain rhythmical lilt when the passages are read aloud, the presence of *parallelismus membrorum* (an arrangement into couplets), the semblance of some metre, and the presence of rhetorical devices such as alliteration, *chiasmus*, and antithesis; and (b) *linguistic*: an unusual vocabulary, particularly the presence of theological terms, which is different from the surrounding context». Cf. P.T. O'BRIEN, *The Epistle to the Philippians*, 188-189. Cf. also M. BARTH, *Ephesians 1–3*, 7–8; E. STAUFFER, *New Testament Theology*, 337-338.

interpretative elements.[6] This attempt, firstly in the christological hymns, to express adequately the theological significance of the origin and saving work of Jesus Christ led early Jewish Christians to draw on the exalted language of Jewish Wisdom speculation.[7] In other words early Christianity, influenced by the Jewish Wisdom tradition, appropriated the hymn-like praise of personified Wisdom in order to express its experience of and devotion to Jesus Christ.[8] While there is no one single dominant interpretative background for these hymns, we will contend that the Wisdom tradition is a very important source for many of the New Testament christological hymns, though the word «wise/wisdom» is not actually used in any of them.

2. The Christological Hymns

It will be seen from what follows that the christological hymns have a characteristic V pattern that chronicles the pre-existence, earthly existence, and post-existence of the Son. In short, they are exercises in narrative Christology tracing the full life of the Son, not just his earthly ministry. This fuller presentation of Christ involves discussing his role in creation as well as redemption. The creators of these various hymns were

---

[6] The monograph of L.W. Hurtado has been singularly helpful in showing that in addition to «Wisdom», Jewish thinkers also theologized about two other divine agents as they grappled with God's dealings with the world. They reflected upon the «exalted patriarchs» like Enoch and Moses and the «principal angels» like Daniel, Michael, and Raphael. According to Hurtado the Jewish category of «divine agency» provided the earliest Christians with the conceptual framework needed to explain Jesus' exaltation to God's «right hand». That is, the earliest Jewish Christians could more readily proclaim that God had exalted Jesus to the position of glory at God's right hand because they were used to placing other exalted figures in this supreme position, namely, Wisdom and Enoch and Michael. Cf. L.W. HURTADO, *One God, One Lord*.

[7] The use of Jewish Wisdom speculation was coupled to some degree with the use of other sources including the christological interpretation of the Psalms, especially Psalms 2, 8, 22, 110, 118. Cf. M. HENGEL, «Psalm 110», 43-73. Cf. also M. HENGEL, «Hymns and Christology», 78-96, 188-190; R.P. MARTIN, «Some Reflections on New Testament Hymns», 37-49. Though this section intends to focus on the degree of indebtedness to Jewish Wisdom speculation, the importance of other sources is not being minimized.

[8] Both E. Schüssler Fiorenza and R.P. Martin speak of the astonishing exalted language of the christological hymns and argue that they do not belong to a later stage of christological development but are among the earliest christological statements found in the New Testament. Cf. E. SCHÜSSLER FIORENZA, «Wisdom Mythology», 17-41. Cf. also R.P. MARTIN, *Carmen Christi*, xi.

concerned to make clear that the subject being discussed was a person, not merely a divine attribute or power of God. In each of these hymns, in one way or another whether through reference to death on a cross, making purification for sins, or being in the flesh, the author makes clear that he is talking about a real human figure who acted on the stage of history. We have already noted that the criteria for detecting a hymn woven into the heart of a letter of the New Testament are not easy to apply and as a result the task is an «inexact science». We will confine our analysis to Philippians 2:6-11, Colossians 1:15-20, Hebrews 1:2b-4, and John 1:1-18.

2.1 *Philippians 2:6-11: The Servant Song*

Although the unity of many of the Pauline letters has been questioned in the endless ingenuity of scholarship, only two have remained subjects of major debate: II Corinthians and Philippians.[9] There is today a widespread, though far from unanimous, view that Philippians represents a conflation of two or three originally separate letters.[10] However, defenders of the unity of Philippians point out the considerable links in language, ideas and formal construction across the supposed parts and also the difficulty of accounting for the process of compilation.[11] Despite the arguments in favour of unity, the sharp breaks at 3:1 and 4:9 remain a

---

[9] For commentaries on Philippians see: F.W. BEARE, *A Commentary*; P. BONNARD, *L'épître de Saint Paul*; J. GNILKA, *Der Philipperbrief*; G.F. HAWTHORNE, *The Letter to the Philippians*. The subheads of the four christological hymns under review in this chapter are taken from B. WITHERINGTON, *Jesus the Sage*.

[10] The following division into two or three letters is proposed: (1) following what seems to be a typical conclusion to a Pauline letter, a sharp change of tone and content occurs in 3:2 where Paul begins a polemical passage warning against a set of adversaries as yet unmentioned; (2) after a similar conclusion in 4:2-9 Paul seems to make a fresh start at 4:10 acknowledging at length the Philippians' gift; (3) the injunction to «rejoice» in 4:4 flows very naturally from the similar theme in 3:1. Hence a division may be set out as follows: Letter A: 4:10-20 (a letter acknowledging a gift); Letter B: 1:1 -3: 1a; 4:4– 7:23 (a letter urging unity and joy); Letter C: 3:1b– 4:3, 8-9 (the body of a polemical letter). On this schema letters A and B date from the closing period of Paul's stay in Ephesus (54-57 A.D.) with letter C following some months later. G. Bornkamm, J. Gnilka, E.J. Goodspeed and L.E. Keck have argued in favour of two original letters while F.W. Beare, J.A. Fitzmyer, R.H. Fuller, H. Koester, E. Lohse, W. Marxsen and W. Schmithals have argued in favour of three. For a summary of the debate and the works of the scholars involved see R.E. BROWN, *An Introduction*, 496-498.

[11] Cf. D.E. GARLAND, «The Composition and Unity», 141-173 (extensive bibliography); B. MENGEL, *Studien zum Philipperbrief*, 58-60.

grave obstacle.[12] Those who argue for several letters date letters A and B from the closing period of Paul's stay in Ephesus (54-57 A.D.) with letter C following some months later.

At least two of the letters contained in Philippians (A and B) presuppose that Paul is in prison. Traditionally, this imprisonment has been identified with the «house arrest» in Rome (Acts 28:16-30). Though the Roman origin of Philippians has had its defenders in recent years[13], this view is largely rejected today.[14] As alternatives to Rome as the place of imprisonment, Caesarea and Corinth have been proposed. However, most modern scholars assign the imprisonment to Paul's lengthy stay in Ephesus in the course of his third missionary journey (Acts 19:1–20:1).[15]

Philippians 2:6-11 is perhaps the most illustrious example of the New Testament christological hymns. It contains one of the best-known and loved New Testament descriptions of the gallantry of Christ: one who emptied himself and took on the form of a servant, even unto death on a cross. The literature on the hymn alone is immense, and controversy over its interpretation shows no signs of diminishing.[16] The distinctive qualities of this Christ-hymn passage, rhythmic character, use of parallelism, occurrence of rare and uncharacteristic language, have led to the widespread view that Paul is here quoting a hymn composed independently of Philippians.[17]

---

[12] Cf. B.D. RAHTJEN, «The Three Letters of Paul to the Phillipians», 167-173.

[13] Cf. F.W. BEARE, *A Commentary*; G.B. CAIRD, *Paul's Letters from Prison*.

[14] Cf. B. BYRNE, «The Letter to the Philippians»,792.

[15] Cf. R.E. BROWN, *An Introduction*, 495-496.

[16] There is an enormous literature devoted to the hymn and a detailed consideration lies beyond the possibilities of this dissertation. For a summary of the literature on Philippians 2:6-11 see R.P. MARTIN, *Carmen Christi*, 63-95. This book presents a scholarly treatment of various interpretations of Philippians' christological hymn and must be taken into account if the complexities of this passage are to be appreciated. Cf. also N. CAPIZZI, *L'uso di Fil 2:6-11*, 23-94.

[17] R.P. Martin argues that the main lines of evidence for this conclusion, which is largely accepted now as proven, are given as (i) stylistic, which shows that we are dealing with the language of liturgy rather than epistolary prose; (ii) linguistic, which reveals many exceptional terms, phrases and words in the section; and (iii) contextual, supporting the view that Philippians 2:6-11 is detachable from the epistolary context of the Pauline letter of which it forms a part. Cf. R.P. MARTIN, *Carmen Christi*, 42. Cf. also D. GEORGI, «Der vorpaulinische Hymnus», 263-294; O. HOFIUS, *Der Christushymnus*; E. KÄSEMANN, «A Critical Analysis», 45-88; J. MURPHY-O'CONNOR, «Christological

The discussion has therefore centred on questions concerning the hymn's original literary form, authorship, background, setting and meaning as well as its use and redaction by Paul. In its theological flow, the hymn is bipartite, with the theme of lowliness / abasement in 2:6-8 and that of exaltation in 2:9-11. Beyond this fundamental division scholars offer a great variety of more detailed analyses. Of the various proposals those of E. Lohmeyer and J. Jeremias deserve mention.[18] The former divides the hymn into six strophes (A-F) of three lines each (A: v.6; B: v.7a-c; C: vv.7d-8; D: v.9; E: v.10; F: v.11). The latter divides the hymn into three strophes (A-C) of four lines each (A: vv.6-7b; B: vv.7c-8b; C: vv.9-11) with vv. 8c, 10c, and 11c viewed as Pauline additions.[19]

Also debated is whether the hymn was originally composed in Greek, probably with its origin in the mission that evangelized Greek-speaking Jews, or in Aramaic with its origin in the Palestinian missionary enterprise.[20] A plausible case has been made for the latter and for the possibility that Paul learned the hymn in the late 30s in the first years after his conversion.[21] Dispute about the precise focus of the Christology is centred on 2:6-7: Is *being in the form of God* the same as being equal to God and thus being uncreated (as in the Johannine prologue: *The Word*

Anthropology», 25-50; N.T. WRIGHT, «*Harpagmos*», 321-352.

[18] Cf. E. LOHMEYER, *Kyrios Jesus*; J. JEREMIAS, «Zur Gedankenführung», 146-154.

[19] It is important to take seriously the caution of M.D. Hooker and other scholars, that the structure which scholars perceive in the hymn must not determine the meaning of the hymn's content or determine what additions Paul might have made to correct the theology of the original hymn. Cf. M.D. HOOKER, «Philippians 2:6-11», 151-164.

[20] The term *Hellenization* means a variety of things generally pertaining to Greek culture and its impact on the non-Greek world after the conquests of Alexander the Great and his successors from the fourth century B.C. onwards. The term refers to the effects of Greek language, lifestyle, education, philosophy, religion, technology and other factors on a culture, in this case a Jewish culture, that was not indigenously Greek prior to its being «hellenized». The issue of the degree of hellenization in first-century Palestine is a complex one and calls for a cautious assessment of all the data for and against significant hellenization of Palestine and, in particular, of Galilee. While the issue is beyond the scope of this thesis, the following references on the topic are helpful: H.D. BETZ, «Hellenism», 127-135; M. HENGEL, *Judaism and Hellenism*, I-II; ID., *The Hellenization of Judea*; F.E. PETERS, *The Harvest of Hellenism*. Regarding the debate as to whether Philippians 2:6-11 was originally composed in Greek, B. Witherington and N.T. Wright argue that the hymn was likely composed in Greek. Cf. B. WITHERINGTON, *Jesus the Sage*, 253, n.18; N.T. WRIGHT, *The Climax of the Covenant*, 98.

[21] Cf. J.A. FITZMYER, «The Aramaic Background», 470-483.

was God), or does it mean being in the image / likeness of God (as in Gen 1:27: *God created Adam in his image*) and thus not being equal to God? Does the hymn posit an incarnation of a divine figure as does the Johannine prologue, or is there a play on two Adam-figures?[22]

Turning to our specific question concerning the source(s) of the hymn, exclusive or in combination, a wide range of christological speculation and theory is invoked.[23] These proposed sources include the gnostic scheme of the primal Man myth,[24] the Genesis story of Adam as well as later Jewish speculation about a second Adam,[25] the Suffering Servant imagery in Deutero-Isaiah,[26] as well as the figure of divine Wisdom in post-exilic Judaism.[27] Sometimes only one source is recognized in the hymn, but more often the confluence of motifs from several sources, both Hellenistic and Jewish, is detected.[28]

J.D.G. Dunn has maintained that Philippians 2:6-11 is best understood as an expression of Adam Christology.[29] Dunn argues that it is a fundamental conviction of Paul that in his life and death Jesus was one with humanity and that his resurrection inaugurated a new humanity. This comes to expression in this Christ-hymn. For Dunn, Philippians 2:6-11 presents an implicit contrast between Adam and Christ. It was the Christ of Philippians 2:6-11 who undid Adam's wrong. He rejected Adam's sin

---

[22] If the hymn is incarnational and was phrased in Aramaic in the 30s, the highest form of New Testament Christology was articulated early indeed. For incarnational interpretations see L.D. HURST, «Re-enter the Pre-existent Christ», 449-457; C.A. WANAMAKER, «Philippians 2:6-11», 179-193. For non-incarnational interpretations see G.E. HOWARD, «Philippians 2:6-11», 368-387; J. MURPHY-O'CONNOR, «Christological Anthropology», 25-50.

[23] R.P. Martin has observed that «[...] scholars have been able to detect a bewildering array of categories so that the verses of this hymn appear like a christological miscellany with many contributions». Cf. R.P. MARTIN, *Carmen Christi*, 297.

[24] Cf. E. KÄSEMANN, «A Critical Analysis», 45-88.

[25] Cf. J.D.G. DUNN, *Christology in the Making*, 114-121; J. HERING, «Kyrios Anthropos», 196-209.

[26] Cf. L. CERFAUX, «L'hymne au Christ-Serviteur de Dieu», 117-130; J. JEREMIAS, *The Servant of God*, 182-188; D. STANLEY, «The Theme of the Servant of Yahweh», 385-425.

[27] Cf. D. GEORGI, «Der vorpaulinische Hymnus», 263-294; J.T. SANDERS, *The New Testament*, 9-11; B. WITHERINGTON, *Jesus the Sage*, 257-266.

[28] Cf. J.T. SANDERS, *The New Testament*, 58-74.

[29] Cf. J.D.G. DUNN, *Christology in the Making*, 114-121, here 119.

while freely following Adam's course to the bitter end of death and God bestowed on him the status which Adam himself was intended to inherit.

Against Dunn, N.T. Wright has convincingly shown that finding elements of an Adam Christology in the hymn in no way means squeezing everything into a purely Adamic pattern and ruling out a Christology of pre-existence and incarnation.[30] The Philippians hymn neither mentions Adam by name, nor does it refer clearly to his being created (out of the earth), his sin, and that sinful disobedience as being more than countered by Christ's obedience. In 1992 Dunn himself acknowledged that «the majority of scholars» would hardly agree with him in finding an expression of Adam Christology in Philippians 2:6-11.[31]

Both J.T. Sanders and B. Witherington critique the thesis that the source of this hymn is to be found in the Deutero-Isaianic figure of the Suffering Servant (as presented by L. Cerfaux, D. Stanley).[32] Both Sanders and Witherington argue that this position fails to notice that the servant language in Philippians 2:6-11 came to the author through reflection on such language in Sirach and especially in Wisdom. Furthermore, for Witherington, such language as *in the form of God* and *being found in human form* is extremely odd if the author is simply applying the Suffering Servant language to Jesus here. He argues that in the Isaianic material the Suffering Servant gave up no divine prerogatives or heavenly existence to become a servant. It is much more convincing, contends Witherington, to suggest that various sorts of Wisdom ideas are here being predicated of Christ while acknowledging that the Wisdom material in Sirach and Wisdom to some degree draws on the Isaianic presentation.

In his attempt to explain the historical religious background of Philippians 2:6-11, D. Georgi postulates a redeemer myth not as a single myth that existed in a single religion, Gnosticism, but as a «developing myth»[33] and he finds the particular form of «developing myth» that lies behind Philippians 2:6-11 almost exclusively in the *Sapientia Salomonis*.[34]

---

[30] Cf. N.T. WRIGHT, *The Climax of the Covenant*, 90-97. Those who agree with Wright, against Dunn, include B. Witherington, C.F.D. Moule, C.A. Wanamaker and T.F. Glasson.

[31] Cf. J.D.G. DUNN, «Christology (N.T.)», 979-991, here 983.

[32] Cf. J.T. SANDERS, *The New Testament*, 73-74; B. WITHERINGTON, *Jesus the Sage*, 260-261. Maintaining the Isaianic origin of Philippians 2:6-11 see L. CERFAUX, «L'hymne», 117-130; D. STANLEY, «The Theme of the Servant of Yahweh», 385-425.

[33] Cf. D. GEORGI, «Der vorpaulinische Hymnus», 263-294.

[34] Cf. D. GEORGI, «Der vorpaulinische Hymnus», 268-270.

J.T. Sanders, B. Witherington and D. Georgi all argue that the servant language of Philippians 2:6-11 came to the author through reflection on such language in Sirach and especially in Wisdom. For Witherington, the material in Wisdom 5–7 can illuminate the question of the origin of Philippians 2:6-11. He argues that, for example, in Wisdom 5:15-16 we read of the righteous (called servants of God's Kingdom in 6:4) who will receive a glorious crown; or again in 6:3: «your dominion was given you from the Lord» for being obedient servants while on earth. Seen in this light, Philippians 2:6-11 becomes on the one hand a hymn about a royal figure who, like Solomon, humbles himself by becoming God's servant, obeys God, and is rewarded in the end in royal fashion, and on the other hand, it is a story about a king who *is* the very image of Wisdom, both before, during, and after his earthly career, and is shown to be thus by his behaviour during all three stages of his career.

Therefore, we can say that scholars have discovered various backgrounds for the key concepts and images of this hymn, finding these backgrounds mainly in the Old Testament. The main argument put forward in favour of a Wisdom background concerns the juxtaposition of servant, humility and exaltation language found in both the Christ hymn of Philippians 2 and parts of the Wisdom literature of the Old Testament. No specific connections between Philippians 2:6-11 and the Wisdom literature are identified. The connections made, or the lack thereof, lead us to suspect that, with Philippians 2:6-11, we are not on as solid a Wisdom foundation as we shall see to be the case with some of the other hymns to be appraised.

2.2 *Colossians 1:15-20: Ode to the Cosmic Christ*

In its vision of Christ, of his body the church, and of the mystery of God hidden for ages, the Letter to the Colossians is truly majestic, and certainly a worthy representative of the Pauline heritage. That evaluation should not be forgotten amidst the major scholarly debate about whether or not the letter was written by Paul himself, a problem that has cast a long shadow on discussions about Colossians. The differences from the undisputed Pauline epistles has persuaded most modern scholars that Paul did not write Colossians and that the letter is Deutero-Pauline, composed after Paul's lifetime, between 70-80 A.D., by someone who knew the Pauline tradition.[35] Some describe the letter as Pauline but say that it was heavily interpolated or edited.[36]

It seems clear from the letter that the «philosophers» at Colossae pursued their Wisdom in multiple ways. First, they relied on the powers of the universe whose harmony and proportion reflected a divine ordering. Since Jesus Christ had established peace among all things (all elements) once and for all (Col 1:20b), they were assured that order and balance among the elements were secured. Second, through ascetical practices of fasting, abstinence, and observance of special days they tried to liberate their minds from distractions and prepare themselves to receive and comprehend revelatory insight from above. Third, like thousands of their compatriots they reverenced demons and angels, who acted as messengers between heaven and earth.[37]

In Colossians 2:8, 16-23, the author vigorously argues that the three avenues just described do not lead to divine knowledge. Repeating in different ways his foundational point that only in Christ is there Wisdom (2:3), the author maintains that dying with Christ in baptism liberated the Colossians from the control of the «elemental spirits of the universe» (2:20). No divine knowledge will come from study of what we today would call first principles, natural law, and the elements by which all reality is held together. Further, fasting and such may well have an effect contrary to the ecstatic experience anticipated, for they may set into motion drives to gratify the flesh (2:23). Moreover, seeking revelation from angels and engaging in profound investigations of visionary experiences will not lead to humility, but to pride and community-

---

[35] At the present moment about sixty percent of critical scholarship holds that Paul did not write the letter to the Colossians. R.F. COLLINS, *Letters that Paul did not Write*, surveys the various scholars and the nuances of their views. Cf. also R.E. BROWN, *An Introduction*, 610-617; J. GNILKA, *Der Kolosserbrief*; A. LINDEMANN, *Der Kolosserbrief*; E. LOHSE, *A Commentary on the Epistles*.

[36] E. Schweizer suggests that Colossians was jointly written by Paul and Timothy. The position taken by M.P. Horgan is that Colossians is Deutero-Pauline, composed after Paul's lifetime, between 70-80 A.D. by someone who knew the Pauline tradition, for a church which was perceived as needing further instruction in faith because of the threats posed by some opponents. E. Lohse regards Colossians as the product of a Pauline school tradition, probably located in Ephesus. Cf. M.P. HORGAN, «The Letter to the Colossians», 877-882; E. LOHSE, *A Commentary on the Epistles*; E. SCHWEIZER, *The Letter to the Colossians*. On the cultural context within which Colossians was written see R.E. DEMARIS, *The Colossian Controversy*, 94-96.

[37] Cf. R.E. DEMARIS, *The Colossian Controversy*, 131-132, 142.

destroying elitism (2:18). In brief, the author insists that the Colossians stay close to Christ, the Head (2:19). They must adhere to the Wisdom of the hymn and not wander down avenues which might be heralded as passages to divine Wisdom, but which in reality are dead ends. It seems that the goal of the author's polemic against the errors is to prompt his readers to hasten back to the Wisdom of Colossians 1:15-20 and abandon any inkling they might have had to find divine knowledge in any other place than in Christ.

Turning to the christological hymn itself, it has long been recognized that Colossians 1:15-20 is an independent unit that has the character of a primitive Christian hymn.[38] By means of special vocabulary, parallelisms within and between the stanzas, artistic repetition of prepositions, and the refrain *all things*, the composer of Colossians 1:15-20 has created a wondrous hymn to draw attention to the one who is absolute in every way, Jesus Christ. The hymn sings of the universal lordship and absolute primacy of Jesus Christ over all. No creature is excluded from his power.[39] Differences in language, style, and thought, from the rest of the letter and from the undisputed Pauline letters suggest that this hymnic section was not composed by the author of the letter but rather that it was, for the most part, traditional material adapted by the author of Colossians to serve the instructional purposes of the letter.[40]

Although it is agreed that a hymn is present here, there are many different suggestions concerning its structure and the elements in the hymn

---

[38] The hymn has been the subject of an extensive bibliography, much of it in German. For treatments in English see J.F. BALCHIN, «Colossians 1:15-20», 65-93; P. BEASLEY-MURRAY, «Colossians 1:15-20», 169-183; J. FOSSUM, «Colossians 1:15-18a», 183-201; E. LOHSE, *Colossians*, 41-61; J. MURPHY-O'CONNOR, «Tradition and Redaction», 231-241; T.E. POLLARD, «Colossians 1:12-20», 572-575; J.M. ROBINSON, «A Formal Analysis», 270-287; B. VAWTER, «The Colossians Hymn», 62-81; N.T. WRIGHT, «Poetry and Theology», 444-468.

[39] J.N. Aletti has detailed six ways in which Colossians 1:15-20 expresses the primacy of Christ: eminence, universality, uniqueness, totality, priority and definitive accomplishment. Cf. J.-N. ALETTI, *Colossiens 1:15-20*, 93-94.

[40] Two differences frequently proposed are (the italicized) phrases in 1:18a: «He is the head of the body, *the church*»; and 1:20b: «Making peace *through the blood of his cross*». Cf. J.N. ALETTI, *Colossiens 1:15-20*; P. BENOIT, «L'hymne christologique», 226-263; R. DEICHGRÄBER, *Gotteshymnus und Christushymnus*; B. VAWTER, «The Colossians Hymn», 62-81; N.T. WRIGHT, «Poetry and Theology», 444-468. Both Aletti and Wright argue for the integral, non-redacted nature of Colossians 1:15-20.

that are redactional.[41] This latter question, however, does not affect the hymn as it stands in Colossians, but is of importance for those who attempt to recover the original hymn or to determine the theology of the redactor.[42] Most would agree that the original hymn was constructed in two strophes: (i) vv.15-18a and (ii) vv.18b-20.[43] J.D.G. Dunn traces the basic movement of thought here from Christ's (pre-existent) role in creation (first strophe) to his role in redemption (second strophe), from his relationship with the old creation (protology) to his relationship with the new (eschatology).[44] Dunn argues that «the claim is not simply that salvation and creation are continuous, one and the same divine energy working in each, but also that the divine energy put forth in creation reaches its completion and goal in Christ, that the divine manifestation in and to creation reaches a wholeness and a fullness of expression in Christ».[45]

Turning to our central question, the many attempts to identify the background of the hymn include the following accounts of the material: a Stoic hymn mediated by Hellenism,[46] a Jewish midrash on Genesis 1:1 in the light of Proverbs 8:22,[47] Jewish material related to the Day of Expiation[48], a Christianized hymn to a gnostic redeemer figure[49], Jewish Wisdom speculation[50], Jewish and Christian missionary theology growing out of Old Testament thought.[51]

---

[41] The structure of the hymn is debated. Proposed divisions of the existing lines include: (i) three strophes (vv. 15-16: creation; 17-18a: preservation; 18b-20 redemption); (ii) two strophes of unequal length (15-18a: creation; 18b-20: reconciliation); or (iii) two strophes of approximately the same length (15-16 and 18b-20), separated by a refrain (17-18a, which is sometimes thought to match the preface to the hymn in 13-14). Cf. R.E. BROWN, *An Introduction*, 603.

[42] For a summary of the views of modern commentators concerning redactional elements, see the chart in P. BENOIT, «L'hymne christologique», 238.

[43] This thesis is well defended by E. LOHSE, *Colossians*, 44-45.

[44] Cf. J.D.G. DUNN, *Christology in the Making*, 188.

[45] Cf. J.D.G. DUNN, *Christology in the Making*, 194.

[46] Cf. E. NORDEN, *Agnostos Theos*.

[47] Cf. C.F. BURNEY, «Christ as the ἀρχή of Creation», 160-177; W.D. DAVIES, *Paul and Rabbinic Judaism*.

[48] Cf. E. LOHMEYER, *Die Briefe an die Philipper*.

[49] Cf. E. KÄSEMANN, «A Primitive Christian Baptismal Liturgy», 149-168.

[50] Cf. J.T. SANDERS, *The New Testament*; B. WITHERINGTON, *Jesus the Sage*, 266-272.

[51] Cf. N. KEHL, *Der Christushymnu*.

While many elements from diverse settings may be interwoven in the hymn, most commentators would agree that Jewish Wisdom motifs are prominent.[52] Indeed numerous parallels between this hymn and the Book of Wisdom, and also some parallels with Sirach, have been identified:[53]

«For she is a reflection of eternal light, a spotless mirror of the working of God, and an image of his goodness» (Wis 7:26)
«He is the image of the invisible God» (Col 1:15a)

«I will tell you what Wisdom is [...] I will trace her course from the beginning of creation [...]» (Wis 6:22)
«[...] the first-born of all creation [...]» (Col 1:15b)

«For He created all things that they might exist [...]» (Wis 1:14)
«for in him all things were created, in heaven and on earth, [...] all things were created through him and for him» (Col 1:16)

«[...] the thrones of rulers [...], [...] if you delight in thrones and scepters [...], [...] I preferred her to scepters and thrones [...]» (Wis 5:23, 6:21, 7:8)
«[...] whether thrones or dominions or rulers or powers [...]» (Col 1:16)
«[...] because of her pureness she pervades and penetrates all things» (Wis 7:24)
«Because of him his messenger finds the way, and by his word all things hold together» (Sir 43:26)
«He himself is before all things, and in him all things hold together, [...] for in him all the fullness of God was pleased to dwell» (Col 1:17,19).

«[...] and that which holds all things together knows what is said [...] she orders all things well» (Wis 1:7, 8:1)
«[...] and by his word all things hold together» (Sir 43:26)
«[...] in him all things hold together» (Col 1:17)

«[...] compared with the light she is found to be superior» (Wis 7:29)
«He is before all things, [...] that in everything he might be pre-eminent» (Col 1:17, 18)[54]

In Colossians 1:15 Christ is called «the image (*eikôn*) of the invisible God, the first-born of all creation». While in isolation this verse could be

---

[52] Cf. M.R. D'ANGELO, «Colossians», 313-324.

[53] E. Schweizer argues that we can quote the parallels to the first stanza (vv. 15-18a) word for word in the Wisdom literature. B. Witherington also lists some of the parallels. Cf. E. SCHWEIZER, «The Church», 1-11, esp. 7; B. WITHERINGTON, *Jesus the Sage*, 267.

[54] For links between Colossians 1:15-20 and Sirach 24: Cf. J. JERVELL, *Imago Dei*, 200-213.

taken merely in an Adamic sense as referring to Christ as the first created being, the archetypal human being who visibly reflects God, the invisible Creator, the context suggests finding the background in personified Wisdom, the perfect image of God (Wis 7:26) and the agent of creation (Prov 8:22-31). The verses which follow speak of «all things» being «created through him and for him», of his being «before all things», of «all things holding together» in him, and of the plenitude of deity dwelling in him (Col 1:16-17,19). Wisdom 7:22b– 8:1 describes the nature and works of Wisdom, naming among her attributes the following: «she is a reflection of eternal light, a spotless mirror of the working of God, and an image of his goodness» (Wis 7:26; see Prov 8:22-31). It is the category of Wisdom as the *eikôn* of God which opens up the possibility of recognizing full «re-presentation» on the divine side. The context of Colossians 1:15, therefore, prompts us to interpret «the image of the invisible God» as pointing to Christ's divinity and his being the perfect revealer of God. Christ is the «first born» in the sense of being prior to and supreme over all creation, just as by virtue of his resurrection from the dead he is supreme vis-à-vis the Church (Col 1:18). The emphatic and repeated «*kai autos*» (and he) of Colossians 1:17,18 underlines the absolute «pre-eminence» of Christ in the orders of creation and salvation history, both cosmologically and soteriologically.[55] It seems that, while there is an element of uniqueness involved in talking about the pre-existence and incarnation of a personal being who took on flesh and became Jesus the Messiah, the sapiential material with its exalted praise of Wisdom helped prepare the way for such an idea.

2.3 *Hebrews 1:2b-4: The Radiance Reprise*

By all standards the letter to the Hebrews is one of the most impressive works of the New Testament. Consciously rhetorical, carefully constructed, ably written in quality Greek, and passionately appreciative of Christ, Hebrews offers an exceptional number of unforgettable insights that have shaped subsequent Christianity.[56]

Yet in other ways the letter is a conundrum. Hebrews tells us virtually nothing specific about the author, locale, circumstances, and addressees.

---

[55] Cf. I.H. MARSHALL, «Incarnational Christology», 9; G. O'COLLINS, *Christology*, 33-35.

[56] For commentaries on Hebrews see: H.W. ATTRIDGE, *Hebrews*; J. HÉRING, *L'Epître aux Hébreux*; O. KUSS, *Der Brief an die Hebräer*; O. MICHEL, *Der Brief an die Hebräer*; C. SPICQ, *L'Épître aux Hébreux*, I-II.

Almost all information pertinent to background must come from an analysis of the argumentation advanced by the author. Although Hebrews is included in the Pauline corpus and was part of that corpus in its earliest attested form, it is certainly not a work of the apostle. This fact was recognized, largely on stylistic grounds, even in antiquity. Numerous alternative candidates for authorship have been proposed. Arguments for none are decisive.[57]

Only a general date range can be established with any certainty for the composition of Hebrews. The development of the traditions evident in the text, the author's reference to his dependence on the original hearers of the word of salvation (2:3), and his remark that the addressees had been believers for some time (5:12) would seem to suggest that at least several decades have elapsed since the beginning of the Christian movement. Very few commentators would want to date the work much before 60 A.D., a date that can serve as a rough *terminus a quo*. The upper end of the date range is apparently anchored by the use of Hebrews in I Clement, which is conventionally dated to 96 A.D., but both the dependence and the date have been challenged.[58]

In the eschatological context of the last days[59], Hebrews 1:1-3 immediately affirms the superiority of Christ over all that has gone before in Israel. The main contrast is between two divine revelations: one by the prophets and the other by a pre-existent Son through whom God created

---

[57] We have to be satisfied with the irony that one of the most sophisticated rhetoricians and elegant theologians of the New Testament is an unknown. The quality of his Greek and his control of the Scriptures in Greek suggest that he was a Jewish Christian with a good Hellenistic education and some knowledge of Greek philosophical categories. Cf. H.W. ATTRIDGE, *Hebrews*; J. HÉRING, *L'Épître aux Hébreux*; P.E. HUGHES, *Hebrews*; O. KUSS, *Der Brief an die Hebräer*; C. SPICQ, *L'Épître aux Hébreux*, I-II.

[58] Nowhere does I Clement cite Hebrews explicitly, as it does Pauline epistles. Similarities to Hebrews in theme and vocabulary, however, appear frequently throughout. It is clear that, at the very least, Hebrews and I Clement stand within the same stream of ecclesiastical tradition. Some scholars have claimed that the connection between the two works is no more than that, a shared common tradition. It seems only this general time frame, from 60-90 A.D. can, with any degree of certainty, be determined as the date for Hebrews. Cf. K. BEYSCHLAG, *Clemens Romanus*, 351; R.E. BROWN, *An Introduction*, 696; G. THEISSEN, *Untersuchungen*, 35-37.

[59] Eschatology is a key theme in Hebrews: see W.D. DAVIS – D. DAUBE, ed., *The Background of the New Testament*, 363-393; C.E. CARLSTON, «Eschatology and Repentance», 296-302.

the world and who has now spoken to us. The description, in language that suggests it was drawn from a hymn[60], suggests that the writer is interpreting Christ against the background of the Old Testament portrayal of divine Wisdom. Just as Wisdom is the effusion of God's glory, the spotless mirror of God's power who can do all things (Wis 7:25-27), God's Son is the reflection of God's glory and the imprint of God's being, upholding the universe by his word of power (Heb 1:3). The evidence for the influence of Wisdom material is clear:

«[...] when he established the heavens I was there [...] then I was beside him like a master worker [...]» (Prov 8:22-36)
«[...] for Wisdom, the fashioner of all things, taught me» (Wis 7:22)
«[...] and an associate in his works [...] the fashioner of what exists [...]» (Wis 8:4-6)
«[...] He has spoken to us by a Son, whom He appointed heir of all things, through whom also He created the world» (Heb 1:2)

«For she is a breath of the power of God, and a pure emanation of the glory of the Almighty [...]» (Wis 7:25)
«He reflects the glory of God and bears the very stamp of his nature» (Heb 1:3)

«[...] that which holds all things together knows what is said» (Wis 1:7)
«[...] and in every people and nation I have gotten a possession» (Sir 24:6)
«[...] He upholds the universe by his word of power» (Heb 1:3b)

«Give me the Wisdom that sits by your throne [...]» (Wis 9:4)
«[...] from the throne of thy glory send her [...]» (Wis 9:10)
«[...] He sat down at the right hand of the Majesty on high» (Heb 1:3d)

Both the form (participial style, balanced clauses) and the content (the pattern of pre-existence, incarnation, and exaltation) of these verses also suggest that the author drew on an early Christian hymn, the vehicle, as we have noted, through which such a high Christology based on the Wisdom tradition first emerged. The precise limits of the hymnic material are disputed. Some scholars include the relative clauses at the end of v. 2.[61] Others begin the hymn with v. 3a.[62] Some critics have been sceptical of the

---

[60] Cf. J. FRANKOWSKI, «Early Christian Hymns», 183-194.

[61] Cf. G. SCHILLE, *Frühchristliche Hymnen*, 42; R. DEICHGRÄBER, *Gotteshymnus und Christushymnus*, 138.

[62] Cf. J. GRASSER, *Hebräer 1:1-4*, 63.

whole line of analysis.[63] The parallels in form and content to other possible hymnic materials in the New Testament do suggest that a traditional fragment of hymnology at least has served as the inspiration for these verses. It is also clear that the author has modified whatever source material he may have utilized.

H.W. Attridge suggests that it is possible that the christological hymn the author may have used had a confessional character and that this, at least in part, is what the author has in mind when he reminds his addressees of their «confession» (Heb 3:1; 4:14; 10:23).[64] The hymn probably had a liturgical setting, and the presumed connection with the confession has led to more precise suggestions about that setting, either in a baptismal context[65] on the basis of the allusion to baptism and confession at 10:22, or in a eucharistic context[66] on the basis of the connection at 13:15 between «sacrifices of praise» and «confessing the name» of Jesus. On the presumption of a connection between hymn and confession either setting would be possible. The presumption, however, is hardly secure. While the festive affirmation of these verses certainly give expression to some of what the community confessed, it is not necessarily the precise formula to which the «confession» alludes. Whatever the relationship of possible hymn and confession, there is no definite indication of what the hymn's original setting may have been.[67]

B. Witherington reflects on the way that the Redeemer, after making purification, sat down at the right hand of God.[68] He makes two points. First, in Wisdom 9:4 the same is said of Wisdom; she sits by the throne of God as God's consort. The implication is that the redeemer is in some

---

[63] Cf. D.W.B. ROBINSON, «The Literary Source», 178-186; J. FRANKOWSKI, «Early Christian Hymns», 183-194; J.P. MEIER, «Symmetry and Theology», 504-533.

[64] Cf. H.W. ATTRIDGE, *Hebrews*, 42.

[65] A baptismal setting, for this and other New Testament hymns, is conjectured by G. FRIEDRICH, «Das Lied vom Hohenpriester», 95-115. Cf. also E. BRANDENBURGER, «Text und Vorlagen», 222.

[66] Cf. G. BORNKAMM, «Das Bekenntnis», 196; S. NOMOTO, «Herkunft und Struktur», 11; E. KÄSEMANN, *The Wandering People of God*, 167-174. For doubts about a eucharistic setting, see R. DEICHGRÄBER, *Gotteshymnus und Christushymnus*, 117; K. WENGST, *Christologische Formeln*, 187.

[67] Many recent critics are cautious about identifying a specific *Sitz im Leben* for the hymn. Cf. J. GRASSER, *Hebräer 1:1-4*, 69; W.R.G. LOADER, *Sohn und Hohepriester*, 71. F. LAUB, *Bekenntnis und Auslegung*, 43-44.

[68] Cf. B. WITHERINGTON, *Jesus the Sage*, 280.

sense divine and divinely favoured by God. Second, the point may be that the Son made one definitive purification, once for all time, and so thereafter he sat down, in contrast to the levitical priests, who could only stand and offer sacrifices in God's presence which had to be offered over and over as sinning went on. It will be seen that here we have some precedent for two of the major tenets of the high priestly Christology of Hebrews, that Christ was a holy priest and that his priesthood is forever because he is an eternal being. Thus, even in the apparently least sapiential portions in this christological hymn, a sapiential explanation seems possible and helpful.[69]

J.P.Meier is very likely right in saying that «what the author of Hebrews 1:2b-4 is doing is bringing together in one periodic sentence a Christology of pre-existent Wisdom and a Christology of Jesus who is enthroned as Son or Lord at the time of his resurrection and ascension».[70] Furthermore, J.D.G. Dunn concludes his study saying that «in Hebrews we have a concept of pre-existent sonship, a sonship which Philo ascribed to the Logos and which the Wisdom tradition in equivalent measure ascribed to Wisdom».[71]

A notable point also is the similarity between the hymn in Hebrews and Colossians 1:15-17, even though the clauses are somewhat rearranged. The Wisdom parallels are important in this regard. When he refers to the Son, the author of the Hebrews hymn is not merely talking about a personification or a hypostasization but about a person. This Wisdom figure he identifies as Jesus Christ. He chooses the Wisdom language because he wants to indicate that Jesus is not merely a good likeness of God, or a copy of him, or a reflection of him, but in fact God in God's final self-expression, beaming forth to humankind. The point is that the Son is the exact likeness of God and therefore in a true sense may be called God, or God's Son, or divine. What other term is left, if he is above the angels (Heb 1:4) and the exact representation of God? The author views the Son as not merely an act or power or an attribute of God but as a person who exactly represents or bears the impress of God.

2.4 John 1:1-16: The Logos Hymn

The Gospel of John has been dated as early as 40 A.D. and as late as 110 A.D. But the latest possible date has been fixed by the discovery in

---

[69] Cf. H. GESE, *Essays on Biblical Theology*, 200-202.

[70] Cf. J.P. MEIER, «Symmetry and Theology», 185.

[71] Cf. J.D.G. DUNN, *Christology in the Making*, 209.

Egypt of the John Rylands Papyrus 457 which contains John 18:31-33,37-38.[72] This fragment is usually dated between 125 and 150 A.D. No one, therefore, is now inclined to propose a date later than 100-110 A.D. for the composition of the Gospel. The earliest date for its composition hinges upon the question of whether or not it presupposes the destruction of the Temple in 70 A.D. Most agree that it does, although there have been persistent attempts to argue otherwise. The reasons for positing a post-70 A.D. date include the view of the Temple implicit in John 2:13-22. Most would argue that the passage attempts to present Christ as the replacement of the Temple that has been destroyed. Given all the different consider-ations, most often the Gospel is assigned a date of 90-95 A.D., a date in line with previous decades of scholarship that had concluded that John is the last of the four gospels to be written. There are some, however, who argue that the date might well have been as early as 80-85 A.D.[73]

Serving as a preface to the Gospel, the prologue is a hymn that encapsulates John's view of Christ: a divine being who is God's Word (1:1,14), who is also the light (1:5,9) and God's only Son (1:14,18), and who comes into the world and becomes flesh. Although rejected by his own, he empowers all who do accept him to become God's children, so that they share in God's fullness, a gift reflecting God's enduring love that surpasses the loving gift of the Law through Moses.[74]

Without question John 1:1-18 has had more impact on Christian thinking about the Son of God as a pre-existent, divine being than any other New Testament passage. Here is where the early church derived its Logos Christology and its basic understanding of the incarnation.[75] The conviction has prevailed in recent research that the prologue is based on a poem or hymn which was taken up by the evangelist and used for the beginning of his Gospel.[76] Discussion is confined to asking what verses

---

[72] Cf. R. KYSAR, «The Gospel of John», 918.

[73] For commentaries on the Gospel of John see J. ASHTON, ed., John; ID, The Fourth Gospel; C.K. BARRETT, John; R.E. BROWN, The Gospel According to John; R. BULTMANN, John; C.H. DODD, The Fourth Gospel; J. GNILKA, Johannesevangelium; R. SCHNACKENBURG, St. John, I-III.

[74] Beyond the commentaries there is an abundant literature on the prologue: C.K. BARRETT, The Prologue; C.H. GIBLIN, «Two Complementary Literary Structures», 87-103; J.L. STANLEY, «The Structure of John's Prologue», 241-264; C.A. EVANS, Word and Glory; E. HARRIS, Prologue and Gospel.

[75] Cf. C.H. DODD, The Fourth Gospel, 292-296.

[76] Against the view that the tradition came as a hymn see E.L. MILLER, «The Logic of the Logos Hymn», 552-561.

belong to this hymn, what was its original form, where it originated and what occasioned it.

The main reasons for thinking that the prologue makes use of a Logos hymn are as follows: (i) Literary criticism can point to poetical and rhythmical sentences, verses and perhaps strophes, and distinguish them from prose elements or additions, as in vv. 6-8 and, perhaps, also vv. 12, 13, 15. While the «rhythm» of the hymn is debatable, the fact itself can hardly be doubted. (ii) The structure and the movement of thought also reveal breaks and sudden switches. These are again particularly clear in the two interpolations about John the Baptist (vv. 6-8,15) as well as the unexpected nature of vv. 17-18. The impression they give of being attached loosely or merely by external association reinforces the idea that a well-constructed and finished hymn has been worked over and added to. (iii) Analysis of the style is also important. It is possible to detect in several verses or portions of verses the absence of typical criteria of Johannine style, and their frequent presence elsewhere. These observations agree with the analysis of rhythm and content.[77] (iv) Analysis of the style is supported by observations on the terminology and concepts used in the re-discovered Logos hymn. It is remarkable that the title of Logos is used only here (1:1,14). Other theological concepts confined to the prologue are the «dwelling» of the Logos (in a tent) among men (v.14), his «fullness» and his communication of «grace» (v. 16), very important theological expressions which are, however, missing from the subsequent characteristic vocabulary of the fourth evangelist. J.D.G. Dunn argues that «the links with the Gospel, both verbal (particularly life, light and darkness, world, glory) and structural (particularly v. 11), are probably best explained as theological concepts and themes common to both authors or by the hypothesis that the Logos hymn itself actually influenced the composition of the Gospel in part at least. Whatever the precise facts of the matter, we most probably have here a Logos hymn which originally had an existence independent of the Gospel».[78]

In its pattern it is not unlike the hymns already reviewed. In Philippians 2:6-11 we have a sequence not unlike that of the prologue. The Philippians hymn begins with Christ Jesus being in the form of God, as the prologue begins by telling us that the Word was God. Philippians says that Jesus

---

[77] Cf. R. SCHNACKENBURG, «Logos-Hymnus», 69-109, here 77-82.

[78] Cf. J.D.G. DUNN, *Christology in the Making*, 239; R. SCHNACKENBURG, *St. John*. I, 224-249.

emptied himself and took on the form of a servant, becoming (or being born) in the likeness of man; the prologue says that the Word became flesh. Philippians says that God has exalted Jesus so that every tongue will proclaim that Jesus is the Lord, to the glory of the Father; the prologue ends on the theme of God the only Son being ever at the Father's side, and v. 14 speaks of the glory of an only Son coming from the Father. In both instances the exaltation or glory is witnessed by men.[79]

An analysis of Colossians 1:15-20 also shows similarities to the prologue. In Colossians we hear that the Son is the image of the invisible God; in the prologue he is the Word of God. In Colossians all things are created in, through, and unto the Son; in the prologue all things are created through, in and not apart from the Word. In Colossians the Son is the beginning; in the prologue «in the beginning was the Word». In Colossians all the fullness dwells in the Son and all things are reconciled through him; in the prologue we have all had a share in the fullness of the Word-became-flesh.[80]

Reconstructions of the pre-Johannine hymn differ.[81] However, some variant of the following outline would be common: v. 1, (v. 2), vv. 3-4, (v. 5), (vv. 9ab), (v. 10ab), v. 10c-11, v. 12ab, v. 14a(b)c, v. 16. The hymn celebrates the pre-existent Word and its activity in creation (vv. 1-5); the activity of the Word in guiding and illuminating humans, who often reject divine Wisdom (vv. 9ab, 10-12); and the incarnation of the Word, which has enabled humans to partake of divine fullness (vv. 14,16).

Much of what we have said would not be new to anyone familiar with the Wisdom tradition. The background of this poetic description of the descent of the Word into the world and the eventual return of the Son to the Father's side (1:18) lies in the Old Testament picture of personified Wisdom (especially Sirach 24 and Wisdom 9), who was in the beginning with God at the creation of the world and came to dwell with human beings when the law was revealed to Moses. In the early stages of the hymn the readers encounter the Wisdom and Logos figure of pre-Christian Judaism, the wise utterance of God personified. However, in v. 14 they move beyond the pre-Christian to something unprecedented.[82] While v. 14b echoes the idea of Wisdom pitching her tent in Israel (Sir 24:8), the

---

[79] Cf. R.E. BROWN, *The Gospel According to John*, 20.

[80] Cf. J.M. ROBINSON, «A Formal Analysis», 278-279; R.E. BROWN, *The Gospel According to John*, 20.

[81] Cf. G. ROCHAIS, «La Formation du Prologue Jn 1:1-18», 5-44.

[82] Cf. G. O'COLLINS, *Christology*, 42, n. 22.

most important affirmation in the hymn, namely *the Word became flesh*, is unparalleled in pre-Christian Jewish thought.[83]

Regarding the source of the hymn, J. Ashton argues that: «[...]the Jewish Wisdom tradition that has long been acknowledged to have influenced, directly or indirectly, the author of the hymn, is still the best place to start».[84] Proverbs 8:22-35 is the earliest passage in the Bible to show a real affinity with the Johannine prologue:

«The Lord created me at the beginning of his work [...] before the beginning of the earth [...]» (Prov 8:22-23)
«In the beginning was the Word, and the Word was with God, and the Word was God» (Jn 1:1)

«For he who finds me finds life and obtains favour from the Lord» (Prov 8:35)
«In him was life, and the life was the light of men» (Jn 1:4)

This sort of Wisdom speculation had gone a step further by the time of Ben Sirach to include speculation about God's written word, the Torah. As we have seen, Torah and Wisdom were interrelated, the former being the consummate expression of the latter:

«All this is the book of the covenant of the Most High God, the law that Moses commanded us as an inheritance for the congregations of Jacob» (Sir 24:23)

At the end of the prologue in John 1 it is said that the Son eclipses the Torah, for Torah which came from Moses gave the law, but through the Logos we receive grace and truth:

«For the law was given through Moses; grace and truth came through Jesus Christ» (Jn 1:17)

Ben Sirach opens his work with a phrase that, also, anticipates the prologue:

«All Wisdom comes from the Lord, and is with him forever» (Sir 1:1).
«In the beginning was the Word, and the Word was with God, and the Word was God» (Jn 1:1)

---

[83] Cf. J.D.G. DUNN, *Christology in the Making*, 242-243.

[84] Cf. J. ASHTON, «The Transformation of Wisdom», 161-186, 162. Cf. also G. ROCHAIS, «La Formation du Prologue», 5-44, here 5-9.

On the idea of Wisdom providing life and light we recall:

«For she is a breath of the power of God, and a pure emanation of the glory of the Almighty [...] for she is a reflection of eternal light [...]» (Wis 7:25-26)
«In him was life, and the life was the light of men» (Jn 1:4)

In Wisdom 10, Wisdom is shown to have watched over the great men of Genesis, from Adam to Joseph, and to have planned and executed the crossing of the Red Sea. With this portrayal of Wisdom as the active agent in salvation history the stage was set for her transformation into the Johannine Logos.

This Wisdom character and background of the Logos hymn has long been recognized. R. Bultmann, before he favoured the Gnostic redeemer myth theory, argued at length for its sapiential character.[85] In view of the general demise of the Gnostic redeemer myth theory to explain these hymns, Bultmann's earlier suggestion should be heeded.[86] C.H. Dodd also has shown the extensive indebtedness of this hymn to Wisdom material.[87] H. Gese has taken the argument a step further providing even more evidence of indebtedness to Wisdom than Dodd.[88]

We should note that Solomon's prayer for Wisdom takes Word and Wisdom as synonymous agents of divine creation: «God of my fathers and Lord of mercy, you made all things by your Word, and by your Wisdom fashioned man» (Wis 9:1-2). Despite the fact that, in the literature of pre-Christian Judaism, Wisdom, Word, and for that matter Spirit, were «near alternatives as ways of describing the active, immanent power of God»[89], why did John choose Word and not Wisdom? Several considerations may have told against Wisdom and for the choice of Word.[90] First, it would have been difficult for John to speak of Wisdom becoming flesh given that, in the Old Testament, Wisdom is personified as Lady Wisdom and Jesus was male. Second, in Sirach 24:23 Wisdom was identified with the Torah. Hence, had John said that Wisdom was made flesh, it could have implied that the Torah was God and had been made flesh. No New

---

[85] Cf. R. BULTMANN, «Der religionsgeschichtliche Hintergrund», 3-26.

[86] Cf. M. HENGEL, *The Son of God*, 33-35; L.W. HURTADO, «Jesus as Lordly Example», 117; J.T. SANDERS, *The New Testament*, 58-62.

[87] Cf. C.H. DODD, *The Fourth Gospel*, 274-278.

[88] Cf. H. GESE, *Essays on Biblical Theology*, 190-198.

[89] Cf. J.D.G. DUNN, *Christology in the Making*, 196; T.E. FRETHEIM, «Word of God», 961-968; T.H. TOBIN, «Logos», 348-356.

[90] Cf. G. O'COLLINS, *Christology*, 41-44.

Testament writer, including John, identified Jesus with Torah.[91] Third, Paul (I Thess 2:13, Rom 9:6, I Cor 14:36, II Cor 2:17, Phil 1:14) and Luke (especially in Acts) prepared the way for John's prologue by their use of *logos* for God's revelation through Christ.[92] Moreover the *logos* is already personified in Wisdom 18:15 where it is said:

«Your all-powerful Word leaped from heaven, from the royal throne, into the midst of the land [...]».

Since it had already been said in Wisdom 9:10 that Wisdom was present and sent forth from the throne, it is clear how indistinguishable the terms were in the Book of Wisdom.[93]

Finally, in John 1:14 we find the tabernacling or tenting of the *logos* with God's people (Jn 1:14). This idea already appeared in Sirach 24:8 which speaks about the creator choosing a place for Wisdom to tent:

«Then the Creator of all things gave me a commandment, and the one who created me assigned a place for my tent [...] In the holy tabernacle I ministered before him, and so I was established in Zion [...] All this is the book of the covenant of the Most High God, the law which Moses commanded us [...]» (Sir 24: 8,10,23).

In the Johannine prologue we find the idea of Wisdom in the person of the divine Logos tabernacling in the midst of God's people.[94]

The intermingling of these Wisdom themes prepares the way for the climactic utterance of John 1:14: *And the Word became flesh and lived among us*. The author's central insight is summed up here, the identification of Jesus Christ, revered and worshipped by Christians, with the figure of Wisdom. This stems from the realisation, expressed throughout the hymn, that the history of Wisdom has been re-enacted by Christ: the divine plan seen at work throughout the history of Israel has actually taken flesh in him.

3. Summary and Conclusions

We have set out and evaluated the conclusions contemporary biblical scholarship has drawn regarding the Wisdom influences on the formation

---

[91] The closest approach to such identification is found in Galatians 6:2 («Bear one another's burdens, and so fulfill the law of Christ») and Romans 10:4 («For Christ is the end of the law [...]»).

[92] Cf. J.D.G. DUNN, *Christology in the Making*, 230-239.

[93] Cf. H. GESE, *Essays on Biblical Theology*, 198.

[94] Cf. J.D.G. DUNN, *Christology in the Making*, 239.

of some of the christological hymns of the New Testament. We specifically considered Philippians 2:6-11, Colossians 1:15-20, Hebrews 1:2-4 and John 1:1-16.

In these four hymns Christ is praised and exalted. He is the universal and saving Lord, his triumph secured through the humiliation of the cross (Phil 2:6-11 and Col 1:15-20). While the word «wise/wisdom» is not actually used in any of the hymns, language and categories borrowed from the Wisdom tradition are one of the major vehicles through which Christ's victory over death and the cosmic powers is proclaimed. Wisdom's actions, status and attributes are predicated of Christ. The reflection on and worship of Jesus by early Christians caused them to go back and look at the Scriptures in a new light and to use these texts to express their new faith. The application of this material to Christ led to the discussion of such subjects as the Son's incarnation and his role in creation. The Philippians' hymn already implicitly suggests the incarnation of the Son by the way it discusses his pre-existence. Philippians 2:6-11 also makes clear that there was no difficulty in using God's name of the Son or in discussing the universal worship of the Son.

The subsequent hymns expanded on these ideas, further developing the understanding of the Son's role in creation, his role in heaven, and the sacrificial character of his death. While stressing that Christ is both the creator and the redeemer of his creation, the hymns say only the bare minimum about his earthly life, referring to his incarnation, rejection, and death. Nevertheless, the latter was sufficient to make clear that the hymns were not simply exercises in myth making. Jesus was a recent historical figure, whom some people still remembered when the earliest of these hymns were created.

Philippians 2:6-11 is perhaps the most illustrious of the New Testament christological hymns. It stands out as an ode in praise of Christ and his achievement, and contains one of the best-known and loved New Testament descriptions of the graciousness of Christ: one who emptied himself and took on the form of a servant, even unto death on a cross. Considerable debate centres around whether the hymn posits an incarnation of a divine figure as does the Johannine prologue or plays on two Adam-figures. If the hymn is incarnational and was phrased in Aramaic in the 30s, the highest form of New Testament Christology was articulated early indeed.

Concerning the source(s) of the hymn, exclusive or in combination, a wide range of christological speculation and theory is invoked including the gnostic scheme of the primal Man myth, the genesis story of Adam as well as later Jewish speculation about a second Adam, the Suffering Servant imagery in Deutero-Isaiah, as well as the figure of divine Wisdom in post-exilic Judaism. Scholars have discovered various backgrounds for the key concepts and images of the Philippians hymn, finding these backgrounds especially in the Old Testament. The juxtaposition of servant, humility and exaltation language found in both the Christ hymn of Philippians 2 and parts of the Wisdom literature of the Old Testament is the basis upon which a claim is made for a Wisdom background here.

Turning to Colossians 1:15-20, the many attempts to identify the background of the hymn include the following accounts of the material: a Stoic hymn mediated by Hellenism, a Jewish midrash on Genesis 1:1 in the light of Proverbs 8:22, Jewish material related to the Day of Expiation, a Christianized hymn to a gnostic redeemer figure, Jewish Wisdom speculation, Jewish and Christian missionary theology growing out of Old Testament thought. While acknowledging that parts of these backgrounds may form part of the hymn, most commentators agree that Jewish Wisdom motifs are preeminent. Parallels between Colossians 1:15-20 and the Book of Wisdom, and also some parallels with Sirach, were identified.

In Colossians 1:15 Christ is called «the image (*eikôn*) of the invisible God, the first-born of all creation». While in isolation the verse could be taken merely in an Adamic sense as referring to Christ as the first created being, the archetypal human being who visibly reflects God, the invisible Creator, the context suggests finding the background in personified Wisdom, the perfect image of God (Wis 7:26) and the agent of creation (Prov 8:22-31). The verses which follow speak of «all things» being «created through him and for him», of his being «before all things», of «all things holding together» in him, and of the plenitude of deity dwelling in him (Col 1:16-17,19). Wisdom 7:22b–8:1 describes the nature and works of Wisdom, naming among other attributes the following: «she is a reflection of eternal light, a spotless mirror of the working of God, and an image of his goodness» (Wis 7:26; see Prov 8:22-31). It is the category of Wisdom as the *eikôn* (image) of God which opens up the possibility of recognizing full «re-presentation» of the divine reality.

In the eschatological context of the last days, Hebrews 1:1-3 immediately affirms the superiority of Christ over all that has gone before in Israel. The main contrast is between two divine revelations: one by the prophets and the other by a pre-existent Son through whom God created the world and who has now spoken to us. The description suggests that the writer is interpreting Christ against the background of the Old Testament portrayal of divine Wisdom. Just as Wisdom is the outpouring of God's glory (Wis 7:25-27), God's Son is the image of God's glory and the mark of God's being (Heb 1:3). Evidence of the influence of Wisdom material on the hymn was cited. In order to indicate that Jesus is not merely a good likeness of God but in fact God in God's final self-expression, this hymn's author make use of the Wisdom language.

Turning to the Johannine prologue, these verses have had more impact on Christian thinking about the Son of God as pre-existent and a divine being than any other New Testament passage. Here is where the early church derived its Logos Christology and its basic understanding of the incarnation. Regarding the source of the hymn, the Jewish Wisdom tradition has long been acknowledged to have influenced, directly or indirectly, the author. The background of the poetic description of the descent of the Word into the world and the eventual return of the Son to the Father's side lies in the Old Testament picture of personified Wisdom (especially Sirach 24 and Wisdom 9) who was, in the beginning, with God at the creation of the world and came to dwell with human beings when the law was revealed to Moses. In vv. 4-5 the thought of the Logos as *light* is equally familiar to the Wisdom tradition (particularly Wisdom 7:26). In vv. 10-12b the origins are again mainly to be found in the Wisdom tradition, particularly the idea of Wisdom as hidden from or rejected by men, but revealed to Israel in the Torah (Sir 24; Bar 3:9–4:4).

There were considerations which may have told against Wisdom and for John's choice of Word. While the terms were interchangeable in the Book of Wisdom (Wis 9:10 and Wis 18:15), it may be that the evangelist simply used the term *logos* to better prepare for the replacement motif, Jesus superseding Torah as God's *logos*.

Finally, we observed the tabernacling or tenting of the *logos* with God's people (Jn 1:14). The idea already appeared in Sirach 24:8 which speaks about the creator choosing a place for Wisdom to tent. The place chosen was the earthly tabernacle in Zion and in particular in the book of the covenant in that tabernacle, the Torah. The interacting of these Wisdom themes prepares the way for the definitive utterance of John 1:14: *And the Word became flesh and lived among us*. The author's central insight speaks of the identification of Jesus Christ, revered and worshipped by Christians, with the figure of Wisdom. The basis of this statement is that the history of Wisdom has been re-enacted by Christ. The divine plan seen at work throughout the history of Israel has actually taken flesh in him.

In understanding and interpreting Christ, these New Testament christological hymns use various strands from the accounts of Wisdom. First, like Wisdom, Christ pre-existed all things and dwelt with God (Jn 1:1-2). Second, the lyric language about Wisdom being the breath of the divine power, reflecting the divine *glory*, mirroring *light*, and being an *image* of God appears to be echoed by Hebrews 1:3 (*he is the radiance of God's glory*), John 1:9 (*the true light that enlightens every man*) and Colossians 1:15 (*the image of the invisible God*). Third, these hymns apply to Christ the language about Wisdom's cosmic significance as God's agent in the creation of the world: *all things were made through him, and without him was not anything made that was made* (Jn 1:3, also Col 1:16, Heb 1:2).

The composers of the christological hymns were concerned to make clear that the subject being discussed was a person, not merely a divine attribute or power of God. In each case whether through reference to flesh (Jn 1:1-16), or death on the cross (Phil 2:6-11), or making purification for sin (Heb 1:1-3), they were trying to ensure that these hymns would not be treated as mere myths or discussions about abstract concepts or attributes of God or the world. In short, there was a need always to say more of an historical nature than had been said in previous Wisdom hymns, while still appropriating an amount of the form and content of those hymns. The earliest Christians were searching for a way to adequately praise the divine Christ and at the same time not relinquish a belief in the one true God. The early Jewish discussion on the relationship between God and God's Wisdom facilitated this sort of christological development. The language about personified or hypostasised Wisdom found in Job 28, Proverbs 8, Sirach 24, Wisdom 7,9 and elsewhere were well suited for the task of adequately expressing the theological significance of the origin and saving work of Jesus Christ and expressing the early Christians' experience of and devotion to him. With the exception of Philippians 2:6-11, where the testimony is more circumspect, evidence has been presented or cited that the influence of the earlier praise of personified Wisdom was both extensive and intensive on the christological hymns under review. Some commentators propose that it was the latest Wisdom thought, in the Book of Wisdom, that had the greatest impact on the christological hymns. In other words, Jewish Wisdom speculation, probably outside Palestine and certainly Hellenized, to some degree provides a background for some of the New Testament christological hymns. The hymns of Colossians, Hebrews and John reflect a sophisticated form of Hellenistic Jewish

Christianity, influenced by philosophical and religious speculation about the cosmos, linking Hellenistic Jewish speculation about the relation between God and the world with Jesus.

Wisdom Christology, as it is expressed in these hymns, is a very high Christology indeed. When the sapiential hymn material was applied to the historical Jesus, this led to the predicating of pre-existence, incarnation, and even divinity to this same historical person. The existence of these hymns in so many different sources, Pauline, Johannine, in Hebrews, strongly suggests that a Wisdom Christology was both widespread and popular with a variety of Christian writers and their audiences.

CHAPTER III

Wisdom in the Writings of Paul and the Letter of James

Our primary objective here is to gain as clear a perspective as possible on what Paul's intention and understanding was when he identified Christ as Wisdom. We will also highlight the influence of the Wisdom literature on the Letter of James.

1. The Life of Paul

Next to Jesus, Paul[1] has been the most influential figure in the history of Christianity.[2] Although all the New Testament writers are working out the implications of the life, death, and resurrection of Jesus for particular communities of believers, Paul, in his numerous letters, does this on the widest scale of all.[3] That range, plus the depth of his thought and the

---

[1] In his letters the apostle calls himself *Paulos*, the name also used in 2 Peter 3:15 and from Acts 13:9 on. Prior to that in Acts he is called *Saulos* (7:58; 8:1,3; 9:1). It is likely the apostle was called *Paulos* from birth, and *Saoul* was the *signum* (added name) used in Jewish circles. Many Jews of the period had two names, one Semitic (Saul) and the other Greek or Roman (Paul); cf. Acts 1:23; 10:18; 13:1. The names were often chosen for their similarity of sound. There is no evidence that «Saul» was changed to «Paul» at the time of his conversion; indeed *Saulos* is used in Acts even after this event. Cf. *NJBC*, 1329-1330.

[2] Cf. C.K. BARRETT, *Paul*; J.C. BEKER, *Paul the Apostle*; J.D.G. DUNN, *The Theology of Paul*; E.E. ELLIS, *Paul and His Recent Interpreters*; J.A. FITZMYER, *Paul and His Theology*; W. MILLS, *Periodical Literature on the Apostle Paul*; A.J.M. WEDDERBURN, «Some Recent Pauline Chronologies», 103-108.

[3] Competing chronologies have been offered by scholars regarding dates for Paul's career as a believer in Jesus. R.E. Brown presents two types: the «traditional» one (still followed by the majority and favoured by Brown himself) and the «revisionist» one (supported by a smaller group of adherents). Brown notes that differences about the date

passion of his involvement, have meant that, since his letters became part of the New Testament, no Christian has been unaffected by what he has written.[4]

There are two sources for his life: biographical details in his own letters and accounts of his career in Acts (beginning with 7:58).[5] Paul never tells us where he was born; but the information in Acts that he was a citizen of Tarsus, the prosperous capital of Cilicia (21:39; 22:3), is perfectly plausible.[6] Tarsus had a considerable Jewish colony; and by his own testimony, in his early years as a Christian, Paul hastened to go to Cilicia

---

of Jesus' crucifixion and the reliability of the data in Acts are responsible for many of the assigned datings. Only rarely does a chronological difference have theological import in reading Paul's letters. Cf. R.E. BROWN, *An Introduction*, 428.

[4] It would appear that there were only a few early Christian writers or proclaimers equal in brilliance to Paul. Perhaps we might mention the authors of the Fourth Gospel and Hebrews, but on the whole most early Christians, rather than being in danger of surpassing Paul's acumen, were struggling to come to grips with the profundity of Paul's writings (cf. 2 Pet 3:15-16).

[5] There are three views of how to assess these sources: (a) virtually complete trust in Acts. The traditional lives of Paul are guided strongly by Acts, fitting and adapting information from the letters into the Acts framework. (b) Distrust of Acts. By way of reaction and as part of a scepticism about the historical value of Acts, what that book reports about Paul has been questioned (eg., Becker, Jewett, Knox, Lüdemann). (c) A mediate stance uses Paul's letters as a primary source and cautiously supplements matters from Acts, not hastening to declare apparent differences contradictory. The author of Acts has often been criticized for not fully understanding Paul's theology, for highlighting themes that were not Pauline, for simplifying Paul's career, and for avoiding many of the controversies in Paul's life. We should not overlook, however, the extraordinary tribute he paid by devoting to Paul half the book's lengthy description of the spread of Christianity. Whether or not Paul was that important in the estimation of non-Pauline Christians, Acts has forever placed Paul alongside Peter in the Christian «pantheon» as the two most important figures in the following of Jesus. Cf. R. Brown, *An Introduction*, 422-437; *NJBC*, 1331.

[6] While Paul never tells us where he was born, his name, Paulos, would connect him with some Roman town. He boasted of his Jewish background and traced his lineage to the tribe of Benjamin (Rom 11:1; Phil 3:5; 2 Cor 11:22). He was an «Israelite» (Rom 11:1; Phil 3:5; 2 Cor 11:22), «a Hebrew, born of Hebrews [...], as to the law a Pharisee» (Phil 3:6), one «extremely zealous for the traditions of my fathers» and one who excelled his peers «in Judaism» (Gal 1:14). In calling himself a «Hebrew», he may have meant that he was a Greek-speaking Jew who could also speak Aramaic and could read the Old Testament in the original. Paul's letters, however, reveal that he knew Greek well and could write it and that in addressing Gentile churches he usually quoted the Greek version of the Old Testament (LXX). Cf. *NJBC*, 1332.

(Gal 1:21).[7] The majority of scholars maintains that Paul was reared and educated at Tarsus. He wrote good Greek, had basic Hellenistic rhetorical skills, quoted from the Scriptures in Greek, and knew Deutero canonical books composed or preserved in Greek.[8]

To what extent did upbringing in the diaspora influence Paul, besides obvious language and rhetorical abilities? Acculturation by Jews in language and education led to varied degrees of accommodation and even assimilation, so that no universal judgments can be made.[9] He would have known something about the religion of the Gentiles among whom he lived, having had some awareness, probably prejudiced and unsympathetic, of pagan myths and Greco-Roman civic religious festivals. Paul's education would probably have included a summary acquaintanceship with the moral or ethical stances of the Stoics, the Cynics, and the Epicureans. On a simpler level Paul would have known how ordinary Gentiles lived and worked, so that later in life he would not have come among them as a stranger.

After a period of persecuting Christians, according to both Galatians 1:13-17 and Acts 9:1-9, Paul received a divine revelation in which he encountered Jesus and after which he stayed at Damascus. That report leaves many issues unresolved.[10] In I Corinthians 9:1 Paul says he *saw*

---

[7] Acts 16:37-38 and 22:25-29 identify Paul as a Roman citizen by birth. Some have suggested that Tarsus' inhabitants received that privilege, but citizenship may have come to Paul through his family rather than through the status of Jews in Tarsus. If Luke's information about Paul's origins is correct, it helps explain both the Hellenistic and the Jewish background of Paul. Tarsus was heavily hellenized by Antiochus IV Epiphanes (175-164 B.C.), who also established a colony of Jews there to foster commerce and industry. Cf. *NJBC*, 1332-1333.

[8] Tarsus had a reputation for culture and excellent schools and although those structures would have been Gentile, an essential training in writing, rhetoric, and dialectic may have been made available to Jewish boys in order to allow them to function competitively. Cf. *NJBC*, 1384-1385.

[9] Cf. J.M.G. BARCLAY, «Paul among Diaspora Jews», 89-120.

[10] Paul clearly regarded the experience near Damascus as the turning point in his life and in that sense a «conversion». It was for him an encounter with the risen Lord that he never forgot. When his apostolate was subsequently challenged, he was wont to expostulate, «Am I not an apostle? Have I not seen Jesus our Lord?» (I Cor 9:1; cf. 15:8). As a result of that «revelation of Jesus Christ» (Gal 1:12), he became «a servant of Christ» (Gal 1:10), someone with a compulsion to preach the Gospel of Christ. Luke recounts the Damascus experience three times in Acts: once in a narrative that depicts Paul eventually sojourning for several days in Damascus (9:3-19); and twice in speeches,

Jesus (also 15:8); but in none of the three accounts of the experience in Acts does that happen, even though he does see light. Paul's theology was influenced most of all by this experience near Damascus and by his faith in the risen Christ as the Son of God that developed from that experience. Paul himself speaks of that experience as a revelation of the Son accorded him by the Father (Gal 1:16); in it he «saw Jesus the Lord» (I Cor 9:1). He spoke of it as an event in which he had been «seized» by Christ Jesus (Phil 3:12) and in which a «necessity» had been laid upon him to preach the Gospel to the Gentiles (I Cor 9:16). Theologically the encounter with the risen Lord revealed to Paul that the scandal of the cross was not the end of the story of Jesus. Acts 26:17 has Jesus say that he is sending Paul to the Gentiles, and in Galatians 1:16 Paul says that God was pleased «to reveal His Son to/in me that I might preach him among the Gentiles».

2. The Theology of Paul

No other follower of Jesus in New Testament times left behind a written testimony comparable to that of Paul. Of the twenty-seven books of the New Testament, half have Paul's name attached, all of them in letter form.[11] The seven undisputed Pauline letters (I Thess, Gal, Phil, Phlm, I

---

before a crowd in Jerusalem (22:6-16) and before Festus and King Agrippa (26:12-18). Each of these accounts stresses the overwhelming and unexpected character of the experience which occurred during Paul's persecution of Christians. Puzzling, however, are the variant details in the accounts: whether Paul's companions stand by speechless or fall to the ground; whether or not they hear the heavenly voice; though Jesus addresses Paul «in the Hebrew language», he quotes a Greek proverb (26:14). The failure to harmonize such details reflects Luke's lack of concern for consistency. Yet in each account the essential message is conveyed to Paul: «Saul, Saul, why do you persecute me?» – «Who are you, Sir?» – «I am Jesus (of Nazareth) whom you are persecuting.» Cf. *NJBC*, 1333.

[11] It is no accident that letters were the first Christian literature of which we know: since they can be designed to answer immediate, pressing problems, they were consistent with an urgent eschatology. The first Christian generations were strongly eschatological: for them the *last things* were at hand, and undoubtedly Jesus would return soon. That these letters were written by Paul clarifies another factor in the appearance of Christian literature. Paul was a travelling apostle who proclaimed Jesus in one town and then moved on to another. Letters became his means of communication with converts who lived at a distance from him. Thus in the 50s of the first century Paul produced the earliest surviving Christian documents: I Thessalonians, Galatians, Philippians, Philemon, I-II Corinthians, and Romans. There is a somewhat different tone and emphasis to each, corresponding to what Paul perceived as the needs of the respective community at a particular time. Cf. W.G. DOTY, *Letters in Primitive Christianity*.

and II Cor, Rom) were probably the first New Testament books to be composed. That is explicable, in part, because the early Christians thought that Christ would return soon, and so only «immediate literature» that dealt with existing problems was of import.[12]

Pauline theology is a very large subject to which many books have been devoted.[13] Although they widely agree that we should not impose on Paul the organizational principles of later theology, scholars are far from agreement on the key issue in Paul's thought.[14] In place of a central

---

[12] Yet letters continued to be written even when more permanent literature (Gospels, Acts) had begun to be produced. In the canonical order accepted in modern Bibles, all the New Testament letters, which by name or history are associated with apostles, come after the Acts of the Apostles. The thirteen letters/epistles that bear Paul's name come first. They are divided into two smaller collections: nine addressed to communities at geographical places (Romans, I-II Corinthians, Galatians, Ephesians, Philippians, Colossians, I-II Thessalonians) and four addressed to individuals (I-II Timothy, Titus, Philemon). Each collection is arranged in descending order of length (the one exception is that Galatians comes before Ephesians, even though Ephesians is about 200 words longer than Galatians). Hebrews, long associated with Paul, follows; and then come the Epistles associated with James, Peter, John and Jude. The first three are in the order of their names in Galatians 2:9, followed by Jude who is not mentioned by Paul. Cf. R.E. BROWN, *An Introduction*, 409-421.

[13] Even a sketch is beyond the scope of this thesis. A presentation of any aspect of Pauline theology must take into account the character of Paul's writings, which do not offer a systematic presentation of his thought. Most of what Paul wrote was composed *ad hoc*, to handle concrete problems by letters. In them he developed certain topics and exhorted his churches to the practice of a more intense Christian life. Almost every extant letter exemplifies this twofold purpose. This also explains how he could mingle elements of revelation, fragments of the primitive kerygma, teachings of Christ, interpretations of the Old Testament, a personal understanding of the Christ-event, and even his own private opinions. Any attempt, therefore, to sketch «pauline theology» must try to reckon with the varied nuances of the apostle's thought and expression. For bibliography cf. R.E. BROWN, *An Introduction*, 442-445.

[14] The Reformation emphasis on justification by faith still has followers. F.C. Baur stressed the antithesis between human flesh and the divine Spirit. Bultmann gives the main thrust to anthropology because the Pauline affirmations concerning God relate the deity to human beings. A concept of salvation-history is seen as central to many who do not drive a sharp wedge between Paul and Judaism (cf. W.D. DAVIES, *Paul and Rabbinic Judaism*). Beker stresses a Jewish apocalyptic context: the Christ-event as the consummation and end of history. Fitzmyer prefers the language of *eschatology* over *apocalyptic* and speaks of christocentric soteriology: Christ crucified and raised for our sanctification. All these have their elements of truth, provided we realize that they are analytical judgments and that probably Paul never thought out «the centre of his theology». He did express himself, however, about his «gospel», and christocentrism is

theological theme some scholars have thought of a narrative.[15] Just as Judaism had a basic story of how God chose and called Israel, so also, some would logically suppose, Christians had a basic story that retold God's choice of Israel by recalling how God had renewed the call through the ministry, crucifixion, and resurrection of Jesus. Surely Paul had preached the story about Jesus when he first came to a place. In many ways this «commonsense approach» to Paul is more convincing than any presentation wherein he was abstractly systematic in his thought. In the revelation Paul, who already knew the love shown by the God of his Israelite ancestors, discovered a love that went beyond his previous imagination. He felt «taken over» by Christ Jesus (Phil 3:12). With awe Paul exclaims: «The Son of God loved me and gave himself for me» (Gal 2:20). What he avows in Romans 8:35-37 must have been uttered many times in his many travails: «Who will separate us from the love of Christ? Will anguish or persecution or famine or nakedness or peril or the sword? [...] in all these things we are conquerors because of him who loved us». This love became the driving factor of Paul's life when he came to understand how encompassing it was: «the love of Christ impels us once we come to the conviction that one died for all» (II Cor 5:14).

How can people know the love of Christ unless they hear about it? «And how are they to hear without a preacher? And how can men preach unless they are sent?» (Rom 10:14-15). Thus the mission to the Gentiles, who would otherwise not hear, is not for Paul an abstract conclusion but an inevitable translation into action of the overflowing love that he had experienced. Although Paul offers arguments for his position that Gentiles were not bound to accept the observance of the Law of circumcision, his

---

closest to that (Rom 1:3-4; 4:24-25). For a summary of the debate and the works of the scholars, cf. R.E. BROWN, *An Introduction*, 437-442.

[15] B. Witherington speaks of «a fourfold narrative that gives Paul's Christology its essential shape and contours»: (i) first, there is the story of Christ himself, the one who was in the form of God (Phil 2:6) but set aside his divine prerogatives and status in order to take the status of a human, indeed even a slave among humans, who died a slave's death on a cross and because of this was highly exalted by God; (ii) a second, larger story, the story of Israel, also informs Paul's discussions of the Christ; (iii) a further and larger story into which the story of Christ and Israel fits is the story of a world gone wrong; (iv) transcending yet involved in all of the stories just mentioned of Christ, of Israel, of the world, is the story of God. This is the story of the interrelationship of Father, Son, and Holy Spirit, and this story also informs Paul's Christology in important ways. Cf. B. WITHERINGTON, *The Many Faces of the Christ*, 104-107.

most basic argument would have been existential: They had to become aware of the love manifested by God in Christ, and nothing must be allowed to stand in the way.

The key to Pauline theology should be formulated in terms of what the apostle stated over and over again in various ways: «For since, in the Wisdom of God, the world did not know God through Wisdom, it pleased God through the folly of what we preach to save those who believe. For Jews demand signs and Greeks seek Wisdom, but we preach Christ crucified, a stumbling block to Jews and folly to Gentiles, but to those who are called, both Jews or Greeks, Christ the Power of God and the Wisdom of God» (I Cor 1:21-24; cf. Rom 1:16; 2 Cor 4:4). This «word of the cross» (I Cor 1:18) thus puts Christ himself at the centre of soteriology and all else in Paul's teaching has to be oriented to this christocentric soteriology.

2.1 Pauline Christology: Shaping the Fundamental Structures

In an influential monograph, M. Hengel argued that more developments in Christology happened with the period of Paul's ministry than in the whole of the next seven centuries.[16] Paul says little about Jesus' life, apart from his final suffering and makes no attempt to focus his Christology on the pre-Good Friday Christ (Rom 1:3; Gal 4:4; I Cor 11:23-26; 2 Cor 10:1). Apart from I Corinthians 7:10-11; 9:14 and 11:23-25, he never refers to Jesus' teaching as such or cites Jesus as his authority for his own emphases.[17] However, it would be wrong to underestimate how central and dominant Paul's Christology is to the rest of his thinking. Indeed, his thought revolves around the Son, whom he calls with great regularity *Jesus Christ*.[18] Paul compares Christ to important figures in the story of God's people (Adam, Abraham), but he also speaks about Christ's

---

[16] Cf. M. HENGEL, *The Son of God*, 2 and 77. Hengel's claims may be exaggerated (cf. J.D.G. DUNN, *Christology in the Making*, 351, n. 1) but he is correct enough to underline the importance of Paul's treatment of Christology and the extent to which subsequent Christian understanding of Christ has been dependent on Paul's formulations.

[17] There is, however, the further question as to whether there are echoes of Jesus tradition in Paul's letters and if so whether Paul was aware that he was echoing utterances of Jesus. This involves a long-standing debate. Cf. J.D.G. DUNN, «Jesus Tradition in Paul», 169, n. 2.

[18] B. Witherington notes that some 270 of 531 uses of the term *Christ* in the New Testament occur in the Pauline corpus. Cf. B. WITHERINGTON, *The Many Faces of the Christ*, 123.

relationship to the Father and to the Holy Spirit, without fully articulating a description of the Trinity (2 Cor 1:3; Rom 15:6). A notable feature of Paul's treatment of Christ's death, resurrection, and exaltation is the extent to which he relies on what are generally agreed to be earlier formulations (Rom 1:3-4; 3:24-25; 4:25; 8:34; Gal 1:4; 2:20; Phil 2:9-11). We assume that the source material he adopted and adapted he also endorsed, and thus it tells us something about his own views.[19]

Paul sees an Adamic significance of Christ, a significance for the history and salvation of humankind analogous to that of Adam. Adam sums up humankind in its mortality and submissiveness to human appetite and selfish desire. In Adam, all die; death is the end for all who share human traits and family likenesses. Christ, in contrast, opens up the possibility of a new beginning, a humanity no longer enslaved by its animal nature, no longer subservient to selfish desire, and no longer fearful of death. In Christ all shall be made alive (I Cor 15:22).[20] It is precisely as last Adam that Christ has undone the damage wrought by Adam, that in a figure analogous in significance to Adam the remedy to the cancer of human sin is presented.[21]

---

[19] E. Schweizer argues that to a large extent Paul's importance lies in the way he brought together a wide variety of material (hymns, creeds, confessions, Old Testament formulae, doxologies) and focused them by his understanding of Christ's death and resurrection. While there is a large element of truth in this, Paul's letters are not just a repository of earlier Christian fragments that have now been focused. Paul's narrative approach to Christology provides him with a large framework in which many truths can be expressed and understood, and through it all Paul has made his source material his own so that we can rightly speak of Pauline Christology. Cf. E. SCHWEIZER, *Jesus Christ*, 27.

[20] This may seem a thin strand indeed out of which to build one of the principal factors of Pauline Christology. The Adam / Christ parallel comes to clear expression in only two passages in the Pauline letters (Rom 5:12-21 and I Cor 15:20-22, 44-49). However, it is argued that these passages are more significant than at first appears and make explicit what is more frequently implicit elsewhere. Cf. J.D.G. DUNN, «Jesus Tradition in Paul», 171.

[21] Morna Hooker has shown how far the Adam / Christ parallel extends in Paul in terms of what she calls «interchange in Christ». Adam exchanged his share in divine glory for slavery to sin and death. Christ changed places with this Adam, sharing Adam's subjection to sin and death in order that Adam might experience Christ's victory over sin and death. The pattern of interchange is most obvious in passages referring to Christ's death (Rom 8:3; 2 Cor 5:21; 8:9; Gal 3:13; 4:4; Phil 2:6-8). But it embraces the whole of Jesus' life: it was because his life had a representative character that his death could have the same character (Rom 8:3; Gal 4:4; Phil 2:6-8). Because of this Adamic

Adam Christology also embraces the thought of Christ's resurrection and exaltation. It also includes the affirmation of the lordship of Christ. In appointing Christ as Lord, God had put all things under his feet (I Cor 15:25-27; Phil 3:21; Eph 1:20-22; Heb 1:13–2:8; I Pet 3:22). The exaltation of Christ as Lord fulfills the divine purpose in creating humanity; the lordship of Christ completes the lordship of Adam. The Creator's plan, which broke down in Adam, has been made right again in Christ and achieved its original goal. Those «in Adam» share in the tensions of a fractured creation; those «in Christ» will share in the fulfilment and completion of God's purpose for creation as a whole. This links us into one of the most pervasive and characteristic motifs in Paul's writings, the understanding of believers as «in Christ». The «in Christ» language is a natural outworking of Adam Christology. Christ is the eldest of a new family of God, the firstborn of (the new) creation (Rom 8:29; Col 1:18). In his parallel to and contrast with Adam, he provides an alternative template for humanity.[22] However, Paul did not just call on the figure of Adam to illuminate the significance of Jesus and his work. He also made use of the figure of divine Wisdom.

3. Wisdom in the Writings of Paul

Perhaps one of the most enduring developments of Pauline Christology was the application of Wisdom categories to Jesus. Divine Wisdom, as we have seen, was serving as one of the most important bridge concepts for a Judaism seeking to present itself intelligibly and appealingly within the context of the wider religiophilosophic thought of the time. In Judaism itself, Wisdom (along with Spirit and Word) was one important way of speaking of God in his creative, revelatory, and redemptive immanence.[23] Judaism's distinctive claim was that this Wisdom was now identified with the Torah (Sir 24:23). In passages such as I Corinthians 8:6 and Colossians

---

character of Christ's entire ministry, Paul thinks of the process of salvation as a sharing in Christ's sufferings, a becoming like him in his death (as in Rom 8:17; 2 Cor 1:5; 4:10-12, 16-18; Phil 3:10-11). Cf. M.D. HOOKER, *From Adam to Christ*. Cf. also J.D.G. DUNN, *Christology in the Making*, 107-128.

[22] However, a number of scholars are more modest in their claims for the existence of an Adam Christology in the writings of Paul. Cf. C.K. BARRETT, *Paul*, 109-112; J.A. FITZMYER, *According to Paul*, 10, 15, 26; M. HENGEL, *The Cross of the Son of God*, 7, 8, 89-90.

[23] Cf. G. O' COLLINS, *Christology*, 41; J.D.G. DUNN, *Christology in the Making*, 196.

1:15-17, the first Christians in effect were doing something similar, yet identifying this divine Wisdom with Christ.[24]

Paul names Christ as «the Wisdom of God» (1 Cor 1:24) whom God «made our Wisdom» (1 Cor 1:30), while in Colossians 2:3 Paul speaks of Christ «in whom are hidden all the treasures of Wisdom and knowledge». The clearest link between divine Wisdom and Christ comes in I Corinthians 1:17-2:13. Yet even there Paul's impulse is to explain «God's hidden Wisdom» not so much as the person of Christ himself but rather as God's «secret purpose from the very beginning to bring us to our destined glory» (I Cor 2:7).[25] In other words, when Paul calls Christ «the Wisdom of God» God's eternal plan of salvation overshadows everything.

What then is Paul doing when he uses Wisdom language of Christ, when he says of Christ what was said of Wisdom in pre-Christian Judaism, when he seems even to identify Christ with Wisdom? The answer is best discovered by examining Paul's chief Wisdom passages. The most explicit linguistic identification of Jesus with divine Wisdom in the writings of Paul occurs in his first Letter to the Corinthians and also, less explicitly, in the Letter to the Romans.

3.1 *The First Letter to the Corinthians*

Paul's known contacts with Corinth[26] lasted nearly a decade, and there is more Pauline correspondence to that city than to any other place.[27] It seems that the disturbed state of the Christians at Corinth explains the

---

[24] Where Jewish Wisdom writers said to the wider world, «Here in the Torah is the divine Wisdom on which you depend and which you seek», Paul and the first Christians could express the significance of their gospel in similar terms: «Here in Christ is the sum and epitome of the divine Wisdom by which the world was created and is sustained».

[25] Cf. G. O' COLLINS, *Christology*, 39.

[26] Corinth was situated in between ports on the Aegean and Adriatic seas. Called «the light of all Greece» by Cicero, this spot had already been settled for more than four thousand years when the Greek city effectively came to an end through defeat by the Romans in 146 B.C. The replacement city to which Paul came in 50/51-52 A.D. had been founded a century before (44 B.C.) as a Roman colony by Julius Caesar. In one sense, Corinth was like Philippi; but its strategic placement attracted a more cosmopolitan population, for poor immigrants came from Italy to dwell there, including freed slaves of Greek, Syrian, Jewish, and Egyptian origin. Cf. *NJBC*, 798-799.

[27] Traces of as many as seven letters have been detected. Cf. R.E. BROWN, *An Introduction*, 548-549.

need for so much attention.[28] Paul himself tells us that I Corinthians was written in the Spring from Ephesus (16:8), but the year is a matter of some dispute. The suggested dates range from 52 to 57 A.D. with the majority opting for a date close to the middle of that span. When all of Paul's complex relations with the Corinthians are taken into account, the most probable date is the Spring of 54 A.D.[29]

I Corinthians is a complex reaction to two sets of data about the situation in Corinth. In a letter (7:1), probably carried by Stephanas and others (16:17), the Corinthians brought to Paul's attention a series of problems on which they wanted his advice. Such official information was supplemented by gossip and rumour. Chloe's people (1:11), on their return to Ephesus from a business trip to Corinth, recounted to Paul those aspects of the life of the Church there that surprised them, but which apparently were not problematic for the Corinthians. These observations revealed to Paul certain basic flaws in the Corinthians' understanding of Christian community. In consequence, he integrated his replies to their questions into an effort to bring them to a true appreciation of authentic life in Christ.

3.1.1 I Corinthians 1–4: The Background

What then is the problem? A careful reading of I Corinthians 1–4 indicates that at least four issues are involved:[30]

(1) There is «quarreling» and «divisiveness» among the Corinthians, with their various teachers as rallying points. This is indicated by explicit statements in 1:10-12, 3:3-4, and 3:21, plus indirect statements in 3:5-9 and 4:1-2 as to how they should regard these teachers. However, there is no hint that the teachers were themselves party to this quarrelling; indeed, Paul's affirmations of Apollos in 3:5-9 and 16:12 would seem to indicate they were not.

---

[28] R. Brown notes that, paradoxically, the range of their problems (rival «theologians», factions, problematic sexual practices, marital obligations, liturgy, church roles) makes the correspondence exceptionally instructive for troubled Christians and churches of our times. Attempts to live according to then the Gospel i multiethnic and cross-cultural society at Corinth raised issues still encountered in multiethnic, multiracial, and cross-cultural societies today. Cf. R.E. BROWN, An Introduction, 511.

[29] Cf. C.K. BARRETT, The First Epistle; G.D. FEE, The First Epistle.

[30] Cf. N.A. DAHL, «Paul and the Church at Corinth», 313-335; G.D. FEE, The First Epistle, 48-49; B. WITHERINGTON, Jesus the Sage, 300-301.

(2) This quarrelling is in some way being carried on in the name of «Wisdom». The Greek word-group «Sophia/Sophos» («Wisdom»/«Wise») dominates the discussion throughout chapters 1–3. The high incidence in these three chapters of this otherwise infrequent word group,[31] plus the fact that in most cases the word is used in a perjorative sense, is an indication that this is a Corinthian way of speaking, not Paul's.

(3) Related to these first two terms are the repeated references to the Corinthians' «boasting» (1:29-31; 3:21; 4:7) and being «puffed up» (4:6). Their quarrels took the form of boasting, apparently in the name of Wisdom (3:18-21; 4:6). The problem, however, probably goes much deeper than that.[32]

(4) Apart from 3:5-23 the whole response has a decidedly apologetic ring to it, in which Paul is defending not only his own past ministry among them (1:16-17; 2:1-3:4), but also his present relationship to them, since he is being «judged» by them (4:1-21).

3.1.2 *The Role of Wisdom in I Corinthians 1–4*

In recent scholarship on I Corinthians 1–4 the role of Wisdom has become a focal point.[33] The impetus behind Paul's use of Wisdom categories in christological reflection here has been variously explained. Some scholars led by U. Wilckens argue that in Corinth Sophia was a christological title used by an enthusiastic Christian group whom Paul opposed; in his response and critique he used the categories of his opponents.[34] Others make the case that Paul independently associated Christ with Sophia through first characterizing him as the new Torah, already identified with Sophia since the time of Sirach 24:23. Thus when

---

[31] The «wisdom/wise» word group appears 44 times in the first ten epistles (plus one in the Pastorals); 28 of these are in I Corinthians, 26 in chapters 1-3. Cf. G.D. FEE, *The First Epistle*, 48, n. 7.

[32] J. Munck observes that their view of Christian leaders as teachers of Wisdom really ministers to their own exaltation. It is true that they boast about these great names, but only to boast about themselves. Cf. J. MUNCK, *Paul and the Salvation of Mankind*, 59, 157.

[33] Cf. J.A. DAVIES, *Wisdom and Spirit*; A. FEUILLET, *Le Christ*. For a further representative sampling of the most helpful studies on the relevant data see the list of works in: B. WITHERINGTON, *Jesus the Sage*, 299, n. 12.

[34] Cf. U. WILCKENS, *Weisheit und Torheit*; U. WILCKENS, «Kreuz und Weisheit», 27-108. Substantial objections are raised by H. Koester in his review of Wilckens' book in *Gnomon* 33 (1961) 590-595.

Paul wrote that God has made Christ Jesus «our Wisdom, our righteous-ness and sanctification and redemption» (I Cor 1:30), he was giving to Jesus the salvific function which pious Jews ascribed to Sophia-Torah.[35] Again, scholars differ over whether in these verses Paul was explicitly identifying Jesus with personified Wisdom and thus using «Wisdom» as a christological title, or whether the Wisdom of God meant simply God's plan of salvation.[36] In the latter case Paul would be intending to say that, contrary to all human expectations, God's eternal plan of salvation was fulfilled through the crucifixion of Jesus and its proclamation. In either case, through evocative use of the Jewish Wisdom tradition, Paul was making the point that the same Divine Wisdom active in the creating and saving ordering of the world is present in a definitive way in Jesus. By so implicating Divine Sophia with Jesus Christ, he also implied that God's Wisdom is now to be read off not from nature or the Torah but from the history of Jesus culminating in the cross.

In I Corinthians 1:17–2:13 we have both the earliest clear link between Christ and Wisdom and also the most explicit:

> For Jews demand signs and Greeks seek Wisdom, but we preach Christ crucified, a stumbling-block to Jews, and folly to Gentiles, but to those who are called, both Jews and Greeks, Christ the Power and the Wisdom of God [...] Christ Jesus, whom God made our Wisdom, our righteousness and sanctification and redemption (1:22-24, 30).

It is clear from the context (I Cor 1:17–2:13) that Paul is confronting some opposition in Corinth and is responding to the assertions and language used by his opponents.[37] In terms of their understanding and concept of Wisdom, Paul's presentation of his message was unimpressive and its particular content, «the word of the cross» was foolishness (I Cor 1:18-25; 2:1-5). Presumably they had their own idea as to what constituted God's method of salvation and saw it as an expression or enactment of

---

[35] Cf. W.D. DAVIES, *Paul and Rabbinic Judaism*, 147-176; M. Hengel, *The Son of God*, 74.

[36] The former position is argued by A. Feuillet, *Le Christ*; the latter by J.D.G. Dunn, *Christology in the Making*, 177. For a review of recent studies and a typology of scholarly positions taken on the interpretation of Christ and Sophia in Paul, cf. V. BRANICK, «Source and Redaction Analysis», 251-269. Also J.A. DAVIES, *Wisdom and Spirit*.

[37] Cf. C.K. BARRETT, *The First Epistle*, 60; A. PEARSON, *The Pneumatikos-Psychikos Terminology*, 31.

divine Wisdom, though what precisely they understood by «Wisdom» remains obscure. It evidently gave rise to an elitist spirituality, no doubt based on their superior insight into and knowledge of divine Wisdom (I Cor 2:10–3:4,8).

3.1.3 I Corinthians 1:18–2:5: Paul's Polemic against False Wisdom

In I Corinthians 1–4 Paul reacts against two aspects of Sophia: he strongly insists that eloquent Wisdom is not an appropriate expression for the Gospel (1:17; 2:1-5; 4:20) and he derides the Corinthians' obsession with Wisdom as a means of salvation (2:6–3:4). Both of these aspects together must be considered the organizing principles of his polemical argument from 1:17 to 3:4.[38] In 2:1-5 the focus is on avoiding purely ornamental rhetoric in the preaching lest the audience be carried away by the form of the message rather than by the plain unvarnished truth that Paul wished to convey. Paul agrees here that he does speak Wisdom of a sort, a Wisdom not of this age but rather a Wisdom of God in a mystery, a Wisdom that involved a revelation from God through the Holy Spirit (2:10). For Paul, receiving the Spirit is primary and Wisdom and knowledge come through the Spirit.[39]

Moreover, the Corinthians' notion of Wisdom had cosmological ramifications: Wisdom for the Corinthians had something to do with the «rulers of this age» (2:6,8), and gave them a clearer understanding of the cosmic realities behind this world.[40] However, there is no indication that the Corinthians thought of this Wisdom as active in creation, as a personification of divine action, or as a personal being, an emanation from the unknowable God. Still less can we conclude that the Corinthians had evolved anything properly to be called a Wisdom Christology, in which Christ was identified with a (pre-existent) heavenly being (Wisdom).[41] Paul's polemic in terms of Wisdom is directed rather against worldly

---

[38] Cf. R.A. HORSLEY, «Wisdom of Word», 224-239.

[39] Cf. J.A. DAVIES, Wisdom and the Spirit, 108.

[40] In this regard R.A. Horsley has shown how much light can be shed on the Corinthian teaching confronted in I Corinthians by setting it against the background of Jewish Wisdom tradition, particularly in the Wisdom of Solomon and Philo. Cf. R.A. HORSLEY, «How can some of you say», 203-231.

[41] Cf. W. SCHMITHALS, Gnosticism in Corinth, 138-140; H. CONZELMANN, «Paulus und die Weisheit», 231-244, here 237; B.A. PEARSON, «Hellenistic-Jewish Wisdom», 43-66.

evaluation of the message of the cross and against over-evaluation of rhetorical skill (1:18-2:5). Insofar as Christology was involved, the fault probably lay in an unbalanced emphasis on the exalted glory of Christ («the Lord of glory»), resulting in a perfectionist soteriology which had no place for the eschatological «not yet».[42] But we cannot speak of a Christology of pre-existent Wisdom, or of «Wisdom» as a title used by the Corinthians for Christ.[43]

---

[42] Cf. J.M. ROBINSON, «Kerygma and History», 30-40; J.H. WILSON, «The Corinthians», 90-107.

[43] The Hellenistic Jewish tradition presented by Philo and the Book of Wisdom has been presented as the background to the particular religiosity which Paul is challenging in I Corinthians. This tradition elucidates the two aspects of Sophia to which Paul reacts against in I Corinthians, the «Wisdom of word» (2:4) as well as the more soteriologically substantive Sophia. In this regard R.A. Horsley and B. Witherington suggest that in the person of Apollos there is even a possible historical link between the Hellenistic Jewish tradition represented by the Book of Wisdom and Philo and the Corinthian situation, although such a direct link is hardly necessary for the analogy to be valid and helpful, given the general mobility of people, ideas and religious cults in the Hellenistic-Roman world. Both Horsley and Witherington argue that we should take more seriously the tradition about Apollos in Acts 18:24-28 that he, an Alexandrian Jew, was an «eloquent man», and well versed in the scriptures and that he was noted for speaking «boldly in the synagogue» (Acts 18:26). Paul insists that there is no conflict between himself and Apollos (I Cor 3:5-9), but Horsley and Witherington argue that Paul may be presenting a common front with Apollos in order to counter the Corinthian divisiveness which is clearly linked to Apollos (1:10-17; 3:5-15, with the warning in 3:10-15; 4:6). Indeed his reputation for eloquence is not the only element of the tradition which links Apollos with the conflicts behind I Corinthians. Although he «taught accurately the things concerning Jesus» (Acts 18:25), it was necessary for Priscilla and Aquila, two close associates of Paul from his Corinthian mission, to take him aside and «expound to him the Way of God more accurately» (Acts 18:26). Moreover, his major deficiency, according to the tradition (Acts 18:25) was his misunderstanding of baptism, which was one of the basic sources of the conflict in Corinth (I Cor 1:12-17). On this question G.D. Fee focuses on I Corinthians 3:5-9 where Paul acknowledges that Apollos' work was not in competition with his own, but rather that it «watered» what he had «sown». For Fee, it is not so much that Apollos himself advocated understanding the Gospel in terms of Wisdom, although he acknowledges that this cannot be ruled out given Apollos' origins in Alexandria, but that the Corinthians themselves had become enamoured with Wisdom and saw Apollos as best fitting their new understanding. This would be especially so if their love of Wisdom included a fascination for the values of the Greek philosophical, rhetorical tradition. B. Witherington has made a case for the essential historicity of the material in Acts 18:24-28 (B. WITHERINGTON, *Women in the Ministry of Jesus*, 153-154). However, such a view regarding the conflict between Paul and Apollos is far from being unanimously held. Cf. J.A. DAVIES, *Wisdom and Spirit*; M.D. GOULDER, «Sophia in I

The Corinthians' eloquence in religious language was an integral part
of a whole pattern of religious expression and helps to clarify, indirectly,
what Paul writes in I Corinthians.[44] The Corinthians made distinctions in
religious status or achievement expressed in terms such as *teleios* versus
nepios, the mature or perfect who enjoy the solid food (of Sophia) versus
those who could handle only milk-like nourishment (2:6–3:4). These
Corinthians also referred to the exalted status of perfection as being
«powerful», of «noble birth», «wealthy» and «reigning like kings»
according to Paul's rejection of such language in I Corinthians 1:26 and
4:8. This is all standard language for Philo, who used it to make the same
distinction in religious status: the perfect or wise as the highest status
versus those making progress as the intermediate state and the bad or
worthless persons who are obviously lost.[45] If the Corinthians were
thinking in similar terms, then it is evident how their eloquence is directly
related to what Paul viewed as a spiritual arrogance on their part and to the
divisiveness in the newly formed Corinthian community. Lacking Paul's
christocentrism and oriented toward individual possession of Sophia and
perfection, the Corinthian *teleioi* apparently had a divisive effect on the
community as a whole (I Cor 1:10-11; 3:4).

In 1:17 Paul describes his own task as that of «preaching the Gospel»,
which he here elaborates with a striking contrast: «not with words of
human Wisdom, lest the cross of Christ be emptied of its power». The
long elaboration of this comment in 1:18–2:16 suggests that «words of
human Wisdom» is a Corinthian value. Thus Paul's general intent with
these words seems clear: to set forth his own ministry, both its content and
form, in sharp contrast to the Corinthians' present stance.[46]

Corinthians», 516-534. Cf. also: G.D. FEE, *The First Epistle*, 56-57; R.A. HORSLEY,
«Wisdom of Word», 224-239; B. WITHERINGTON, *Jesus the Sage*, 99-114, 118-123, 299-
303.

[44] For a detailed analysis which sorts through Paul's argument concerning the
language and principles of the Corinthians: cf. H. CONZELMANN, *A Commentary on the
First Epistle*; J.C. HURD, *The Origins of I Corinthians*.

[45] «Since food for babes is milk, and for mature (perfect) men is cake, there must also
be as milk-like foods for the soul during its infancy the elementary education of school
studies, and as foods for mature (perfect) men instruction through Wisdom and
moderation and all virtue» (*De Agricultura, 8-9*) quoted in R.A. HORSLEY, «Wisdom of
Word», 233.

[46] The precise meaning of the negative phrase «words of human Wisdom» is not quite
clear: is the emphasis on the content (Wisdom) or form (Word), or perhaps both? The
emphasis appears, on initial reading, to be on content; Paul is about to set out the divine

Having set up the contrast in v. 17 between the «Wisdom of logos» and the cross, Paul now moves to a series of arguments that will have this contrast as its point of reference. In a series of three paragraphs (1:18-31) Paul tries to persuade the Corinthians to understand that their own existence as Christians, especially in regard to their Christian beginnings, stands in total contradiction to their present «boasting». Each of the paragraphs is predicated on the same reality, namely that the cross is not something to which one may add human Wisdom and thereby make it superior; rather, the cross stands in absolute, uncompromising contradiction to human Wisdom. The cross in fact is folly to Wisdom humanly conceived; but it is God's folly, folly that is at the same time his Wisdom and Power.[47]

What Paul offers as an alternative is described as the mystery of God (2:1) or, more vividly, as the Wisdom of God in a mystery.[48] The content of this particular mystery seems to be what Paul preached and is now explaining, Christ crucified as the Wisdom and Power of God (1:24). This is a Wisdom that shames the wise and powerful of the world because it is something they did not generate nor could have inherited. It is strictly from God and therefore when we obtain it we have no grounds whatsoever for human pride or boasting.

In every possible way Paul has tried to show the Corinthians the folly of their present fascination with Wisdom, which has inherent within it the

---

Wisdom of the cross in contrast to merely «human Wisdom». But it probably also includes a concern over form, since according to 2:1-5 the human Wisdom with which they are most enamoured is that characterized by the Greek philosophical, rhetorical tradition. Recent scholarship has been so enamoured with Wisdom as content that it has generally neglected Wisdom as speech and rhetoric. For a corrective, cf. R.A. HORSLEY, «Wisdom of Word», 233-236; R. SCROGGS, «Paul», 33-55.

[47] G.D. Fee argues that Paul's concern here is not so much to do with the Corinthians' being able to *perceive* the cross as Wisdom, but on the actual *effective work* of the cross in the world. Thus in saying that Christ is the «Wisdom of God», Paul is not using philosophical categories, nor is he personifying Wisdom in Christ. Rather, this is an evangelical statement, a statement about the effectual working of the Christian Gospel. Christ is the «Wisdom of God» precisely because he is «the Power of God for the salvation of everyone who believes» (1:18-25). Cf. G.D. FEE, *The First Epistle*, 77. Fee argues that 1:24 is not a christological statement but a soteriological one.

[48] R.E. Brown has pointed out that it is not necessary to look elsewhere than in Jewish sources, both prophetic-apocalyptic and late sapiential, to explain Paul's use of the term *mysterion*. He refers to Sirach 4:18 where Wisdom is the one who reveals the secrets of God, and in 14:10 she is said to have secrets herself. In Wisdom 6:22 the origin of Wisdom is called a *mysterion*, and in 7:21 Wisdom teaches «mysteries». Cf. R.E. BROWN, «The Semitic Background», 40-50.

folly of self-sufficiency and self-congratulation. Even the preacher whom God used to bring them to faith had to reject self-reliance. But Paul does not glory in his weaknesses for their own sake, nor simply to contrast himself to the sophists. Rather, he does so to remind the Corinthians that the real power does not lie in the person or presentation of the preacher but in the work of the Spirit, as is evidenced by their own existence (2:1-5). With 2:5 the argument that began in 1:18 now comes full circle. The message of the cross, which is folly to the «wise», is the saving power of God to those who believe. The goal of all the divine activity, both on the cross and in choosing the Corinthians, and now in Paul's preaching that brought the cross and the Corinthians together, has been to disarm the wise and powerful so that those who believe must trust God alone and completely.

3.1.4 *I Corinthians 2:6–3:17: Paul's Exposition of Authentic Wisdom*

Beginning at I Corinthians 2:6, Paul's argument undergoes a significant shift, in terms of content, expression and tone.[49] Up to this point Paul's comments concerning Wisdom have been predominantly, if not quite exclusively, negative. Yet now he seems to change direction completely. He not only admits the validity and the legitimacy of some sort of Wisdom but also asserts that he himself speaks such Wisdom (2:6).

The Wisdom of which Paul is now speaking is of a radically different kind from that which the Corinthians are currently pursuing. In 2:7 Paul qualifies what he means by the Wisdom of God in four ways. The first three describe the nature of God's Wisdom so as to distinguish it from the Wisdom of this age. First, it is Wisdom *in mystery*. As Paul will develop more fully in Colossians and Ephesians,[50] the term *mystery* ordinarily refers to something formerly hidden in God from all human eyes but now revealed in history through Christ and made understandable to his people through the Spirit.[51] Second, to clarify the phrase *in mystery*, God's Wisdom *has been hidden*. God's Wisdom, salvation through a crucified

---

[49] Cf. J.A. DAVIES, *Wisdom and Spirit*, 85. In a treatment of I Corinthians 2:6-3:17 (pp. 88-137), two questions raised by Davies can serve here to guide our study: how does Paul define the relationship between Wisdom and Spirit? What is his understanding of the purpose or function of Wisdom?

[50] Cf. Colossians 1:26-27; 2:2; 4:3; Ephesians 1:9; 3:3; 4:9; 6:19.

[51] For further discussion of «mystery» in this passage and in Paul, cf. S. KIM, *The Origin of Paul's Gospel*, 75-78.

Messiah, has been hidden in God from eternity until such time («now») as he was ready to reveal it.

Third, God's secret Wisdom, long hidden and still hidden to some, was *destined* by God himself *for our glory before time began.* What Paul has in mind is God's gracious activity in Christ, whereby through the crucifixion he determined eternal salvation for his people, including the Corinthian believers. Fourth, God's Wisdom is something that *none of the rulers of this age understood.* The reason for their failure is that it was *hidden in God* and could only be grasped by a revelation of the Spirit (2:10).[52]

In I Corinthians 2:10–3:4 Paul offers an answer to questions concerning how the Spirit functions in relation to the giving and receiving of divine Wisdom. The communication of Wisdom by the Spirit involves three aspects:[53] (a) a source for such communication: Paul identifies the source with God's Spirit (I Cor 2:10-11); (b) the act or process of communication itself: Paul describes the process in terms of receiving, understanding and speaking (I Cor 2:12-13); (c) a recipient for the communication: Paul restricts the reception of the Spirit's communication to the «spiritual» (*pneumatikos,* 1:13).

Paul's contention is that the Spirit functions as the source of christological Wisdom. In our reading of the Jewish Wisdom literature we noted that the locus of divine Wisdom had been made available to all in the Torah and those who wished to know God's Wisdom had to diligently search out Torah's truths. Paul's perspective, however, is markedly different. First, he stresses that God's Wisdom has found a new locus in Christ (1:24, 30 and 2:7). Though Christ as the new locus of divine Wisdom has been hidden in history (2:8), we can come to a knowledge of the hidden aspects of divine Wisdom which transcend the previously revealed Wisdom of the Torah through the Spirit leading us to knowledge of the meaning of the Christ-event and its implications.[54]

---

[52] As we have noted, the Corinthians, with a view to the external form of their language, had attempted to authenticate an inspired Wisdom surpassing the kerygma. But, as Paul makes plain in I Corinthians 2:4, the conclusive and definitive demonstration of Wisdom is not found in external manifestation such as eloquence. It can be observed rather in an internal conviction, in the power produced by the Spirit in conjunction with the preaching of the kerygma.

[53] I am indebted here to the work of J.A. DAVIES, *Wisdom and Spirit,* 100-131.

[54] The analogy of I Corinthians 2:11 adds to this argument: even a human being has within him secrets of his own that no other person can penetrate but which are known solely to his own spirit. How much more then is this true of God as the divine being. The

For Paul, the Spirit alone is a complete and reliable guide to all divine Wisdom while Torah, even if fully and completely interpreted, is not. Its incompleteness and inadequacy has been decisively shown up by the event of the crucifixion (cf. I Cor 2:8-9), but through the Spirit God has now revealed to us not only the significance of that event but also, in its light, of God's Wisdom now laid open to us.

From Paul's argument regarding the exclusivity of the Spirit as the source of christological Wisdom, we move to the process of communicating christological Wisdom itself. Paul notes that we have received God's Spirit that we might know and speak the Wisdom of God. Both the knowledge and the communication of Wisdom are made dependent upon receiving the Spirit. The *reception of the Spirit* forms the basis, the starting point, in *understanding* and *imparting* Christian Wisdom. Indeed, it is here that the Pauline idea distinctively begins. While we do not yet know all God's Wisdom, all of it is potentially knowable to us, for the christological key to its meaning has already been revealed to us by the Spirit.

The *reception of the Spirit* and the kerygma has opened up the possibility for us to come to know God's Wisdom completely. But, as Paul points out (3:1), all are not yet fully mature or spiritual in this sense. Since the Spirit's Wisdom does not come to all of us at once, or to all uniformly, then the «things» (2:10) of divine Wisdom must be spoken and shared. This process is a product of our initial receipt of the Spirit and of a maturing understanding of the whole divine purpose and its centre in Christ.

For Paul, our receipt of God's Spirit forms the basis for a growing understanding of divine Wisdom. However, a full comprehension of all the implications of the Christ-event does not take place at the time of our first experience of receiving spiritual Wisdom. The intended result of our possession of the Spirit is that we might come to know the whole Wisdom of God but such knowledge is only progressively realized by the one who is maturing in the Spirit and participating in the speaking and sharing of spiritual insights.

3.1.5 *I Corinthians 8:6*

In I Corinthians 8:6 Paul speaks of Jesus Christ «through whom are all things and through whom we exist». We have already noted that pre-

---

Spirit of God is the one source fully privy to God's innermost thoughts and plans, so the Spirit is competent to reveal to us the whole Wisdom of God.

Christian Judaism was well accustomed to speaking of Wisdom in just such terms.[55] I Corinthians 8:6 has been seen as an extension of the thought of I Corinthians 1-2. J.D.G. Dunn claims that «as there (I Cor 1–2) he claims that the crucified Christ is the one who fulfils God's plan of salvation as God's Wisdom, so here (I Cor 8:6) he extends the thought to assert in effect that God's plan of salvation is continuous with his power in creation. Here the «folly» to the Gentiles would be that he has united creation and salvation so closely together (breaking down the typical Hellenistic dualism between spirit and matter; cf. 6:12-20). The «stumbling block» to the Jews would be that the one Lordship of God (Deut 6:4) has to be divided with a crucified Christ. For Paul, Christ who, because he is now Lord, shares in God's rule over creation and believers, therefore his Lordship is the continuation and fullest expression of God's own creative power».[56] In I Corinthians 8:6 Christ is being identified with the creative power and action of God.[57]

3.2 *The Letter to the Romans*

The contribution that the Letter to the Romans has made to Christian thinking is inestimable. Longer than any other New Testament letter, Romans has been the most studied of the apostle's writings.[58] The Pauline authorship of Romans is universally acknowledged. The situation in Paul's life that served as the context of the letter is relatively easy to discern. Romans 15 suggests that Paul wrote the Letter shortly before he made his last trip to Jerusalem (15:25). He probably wrote it in Corinth or in

---

[55] "The Lord by Wisdom founded the earth, by understanding he established the heavens» (Prov 3:190); «For she (Wisdom) is an initiate in the knowledge of God, and an associate in his works. If riches are a desirable possession in life, what is richer than Wisdom who effects all things? And if understanding is effective, who more than she is fashioner of what exists?» (Wis 8:4-6). Cf. A. FEUILLET, *Le Christ*, 75; R.A. HORSLEY, «Confessional Formula in I Corinthians 8:6», 130-135.

[56] Cf. J.D.G. DUNN, *Christology in the Making*, 182.

[57] What seems to be a clear statement of Christ's pre-existence and an important landmark in the development of the doctrine of the incarnation may simply be Paul drawing out the implications of Christ's Lordship in response to the particular problems of the Corinthian church and using the language of the pre-Christian Jewish Wisdom tradition. When we remove I Corinthians 8:6 from this context it becomes a vehicle for a Christology of pre-existence. But whether Paul intended it to be thus understood is doubtful.

[58] For bibliography cf. J.A. FITZMYER, *The Letter to the Romans*.

Cenchreae, sometime in the winter of 57-58 A.D., after an evangelization of Illyricum (15:19) and of Macedonia and Achaia (15:26).[59] Paul spent the winter of 57/58 in Corinth, and afterward (Acts 20:2–21:15) went back through Macedonia, Asia and Caesarea to Jerusalem, where he was arrested.[60]

Paul wrote Romans, conscious that his apostolate in the eastern Mediterranean area was over. Having preached «all the way from Jerusalem to Illyricum» (15:19), he looked westward to Spain. He planned to visit the Roman church en route, to fulfill the desire of years (1:13; 15:22, 24, 28). Before heading west, he had to attend to one last matter: to carry personally to Jerusalem the collection taken up in Gentile churches that he had founded (15:25) in order to manifest to the Jewish Christian mother church the solidarity existing between the poor of that community and the Gentile Christians of Galatia, Macedonia, and Achaia. These Gentile Christians contributed to that collection, realizing that they had «shared in the spiritual blessings» of the mother church (15:27). So before he departed from Corinth for Jerusalem, Paul wrote to the Roman church to announce his coming visit. Writing as «the apostle of the Gentiles» (11:13), he wanted to introduce himself to this church that did not know him personally. Conscious too of his apostolic commission, he fashioned this letter of introduction as an extended exposé of his understanding of the Gospel (1:16-17), which he was also eager to preach at Rome (1:15), about which he had heard so much.

The Letter to the Romans is an essay-letter presenting Paul's missionary reflections on the historical possibility of salvation, rooted in God's uprightness and love, now offered to all human beings through faith in Christ Jesus. In view of his eastern apostolate, and especially of the Judaizing crisis (at this stage a past history), Paul came to realize that justification and salvation depended not on deeds prescribed by the law, but on faith in Christ Jesus, the Son whom the Father's love did not spare. Through faith and baptism human beings share in the effects of the Christ-event, in the plan of salvation conceived by the Father and brought to realization in the death and resurrection of Jesus Christ.[61]

---

[59] Cf. J.A. FITZMYER, «The Letter to the Romans», 830-831; C.D. MYERS, «Epistle to the Romans», 816-830.

[60] Thus there is virtual scholarly unanimity that Paul wrote to Rome from Corinth in 57/58 A.D.

[61] Cf. C.K. BARRETT, *A Commentary*; E. KÄSEMANN, *Commentary on Romans*; S. LYONNET, *Epistulam ad Romanos*.

3.2.1 *Sapiential Influences in Romans*

In Romans 9–11 the influence of sapiential material has been detected. The first occurs in Romans 9:20-23:

> But who indeed are you, a man, to answer back to God? Will what is moulded say to the moulder, «Why have you made me thus?» Has the potter no right over the clay, to make out of the same lump one vessel for beauty and another for menial use? What if God, desiring to show his wrath and to make known his power, has endured with much patience the vessels of wrath made for destruction; in order to make known the riches of his glory for the vessels of mercy, which he has prepared beforehand for glory. (Rom 9:20-23)

Here Paul uses Old Testament texts (Is 29:16 and Jer 18:1) but then combines them with material that clearly does not come from those sources.[62] Neither in Isaiah 29 nor Jeremiah 18 are there references to the two sorts of vessels created for two different purposes. Wisdom 15:7, however, says:

> For when a potter kneads the soft earth
> and labouriously moulds each vessel
> for our service,
> he fashions out of the same clay
> both the vessels that serve clean uses
> and those for contrary uses,
> making all in like manner;
> but which shall be the use of each of these
> the worker in clay decides. (Wis 15:7)

In the Book of Wisdom this discussion comes in the course of a polemic against the making of idols, but in Sirach 33:12-13 Ben Sira is discussing the creation of human beings and says that God distinguished them and appointing them to different ways. Some he blessed and exalted, others he cursed and brought down. «As clay in the hand of the potter, for all his ways are as he pleases, so men are in the hand of him who made them as he decides» (33:13). The conclusion arrived at is: Paul draws on the material from Isaiah and perhaps also from Jeremiah but the form of the tradition he uses depends on the later use of the material in Wisdom and Sirach.[63] In addition it appears that the question «Why have you made me

---

[62] Cf. E.E. JOHNSON, *The Function of Apocalyptic*, 132.

[63] Cf. C.E.B. CRANFIELD, *The Letter to the Romans*. II, 491-492; E. KÄSEMANN, *Commentary on Romans*, 272.

thus?» in Romans 9:20 seems indebted to the rhetorical questions in Wisdom 12:12.[64]

A presentation of Wisdom influences on Romans must also include reference to the praise of God's Wisdom in Romans 11:33-36:[65]

> O the depths of the riches and Wisdom and knowledge of God !
> how unsearchable are his judgments
> and how inscrutable are his ways.
> For who has known the mind of the Lord?
> Or who has been his counsellor?
> Or who has given a gift to him
> that he might be repaid?
> For from him and through him and to him are all things;
> To him be the glory for ever. Amen.

In view of the whole argument of Romans 9–11 it does not seem that Paul has Christ specifically in focus. Rather the emphasis is placed on the mysterious secret of God's eschatological plan.

3.3 Concluding Remarks

The most explicit linguistic identification of Jesus with divine Wisdom in the writings of Paul occurs in the First Letter to the Corinthians. Paul names Christ as «the Wisdom of God» (I Cor 1:24) whom God «made our Wisdom» (I Cor 1:30). The clearest link between divine Wisdom and Christ comes in I Corinthians 1:17–2:13. Paul explains «God's hidden Wisdom» not in terms of the person of Christ himself but rather as «a secret and hidden Wisdom of God, which God decreed before the ages for our glorification» (I Cor 2:7). In Colossians 2:3 Paul speaks of Christ «in whom are hid all the treasures of Wisdom and knowledge.»

In the context of pre-Christian Jewish talk of divine Wisdom, what Paul is saying is that the same divine Wisdom which was active in creation, Christians believe to have been active in Jesus. The creator God was himself acting in and through Christ. The distinctive character of divine Wisdom is to be read off not from creation or in terms of speculative knowledge but from the cross (I Cor 1:18-25). What we see in Christ's life, death, and resurrection is the very Wisdom and Power by which God

---

[64] Cf. B. WITHERINGTON, *Jesus the Sage*, 325.

[65] E. Norden has shown that this passage has a strophic arrangement involving a parallel construction of nine lines. Cf. E. NORDEN, *Agnostos theos*, 241.

created and sustains the world (I Cor 8:6). That divine Wisdom which shaped the world and established the covenant with Israel, and which had hitherto been seen as expressed most clearly in the Torah, is now to be recognized as most fully and finally manifested in Jesus the crucified and risen one.

4. The Letter of James

According to its opening verse, this epistle is written by «James, a servant of God and of the Lord Jesus Christ». Much has been written concerning the identity of the figure presented as the author.[66] In the New Testament there are several men named James. At least two of them, both members of the Twelve, may be dismissed as extremely unlikely candidates for authorship: the brother of John and son of Zebedee, James («the Great») who died in the early 40s; and James, son of Alphaeus, of whom we know nothing. The use of the title *servant*, which suggests a church official, and the unmistakable tone of authority throughout the letter all indicate someone of authority, well known in the church. This conclusion is confirmed by Jude 1:1, where the writer refers to himself as «brother of James». Such a person is identifiable in the New Testament as James, «brother of the Lord» (Gal 1:19; cf. Mt 13:55; Mk 6:3) and leader of the early church in Jerusalem (Acts 12:17; 15:13; I Cor 15:7; Gal 2:9, 12). This identification has been traditionally accepted in the church and is generally held by modern scholars.[67] Did this James write the epistle attributed to him? Contemporary scholarship is divided; the most widely held view is that a Christian versed in both Hellenism and Judaism wrote the letter under the name of James of Jerusalem in the latter part of the first century A.D.[68]

The epistle consists of a long series of exhortations, mostly brief and loosely connected, some developed at length. The one common trait, which gives the letter its distinctive quality, is a concern that the faith of the recipients be not merely theoretical or abstract, but implemented in action, in every aspect of their lives. It helps us understand how Jews, who had come to believe that Jesus was the Messiah, wrestled with the practical implications of their discipleship. In a situation where trials and temptations abound and where the poor suffer at the hands of the rich,

---

[66] Cf. L.T. JOHNSON, *The Letter of James*; S. LAWS, *The Letter of James*.

[67] Cf. R.E. BROWN, *An Introduction*, 725-727, 741; *NJBC*, 909.

[68] Cf. R.E. BROWN, *An Introduction*, 725-727, 741; *NJBC*, 909.

James exhorts them to joy, endurance, Wisdom, confident prayer, and faithful response to the liberating word of God in a hostile world, as they wait for the coming of the Lord.[69]

4.1 *Wisdom Influences on the Letter of James*

It is widely recognised that the author of James is indebted to the Wisdom material of the Old Testament.[70] His presentation is not a Wisdom of a counter order, as was true with Jesus and Qoheleth, but rather a more traditional and conventional form of Wisdom like that found in Proverbs and Sirach. The author of James returns to traditional topics, not only like guarding one's speech and passions but also enduring suffering (like Job) and temptations, seeking Wisdom (1:5) and the like.[71] Missing in James is any real sense of God's new eschatological activity or in-breaking reign in the present which changes the social order of things even now. Instead the audience is only exhorted to be patient until the Lord comes (5:7).[72]

From the outset of James, the author makes clear that it is Wisdom, conventional Wisdom of a practical sort, that is to be sought to cope with the trials and temptations of life (cf. James 1:2-6). We are not exhorted to seek first the Kingdom of God in the here and now, or to learn the teachings of Jesus, but rather to pray to God for Wisdom from above. The beginning of James resonates with the exhortation in Wisdom 7:7-8: «Therefore I prayed and understanding was given me; I called on God, and the spirit of Wisdom came to me».[73] In James the suggestion is that

---

[69] Five major themes have been identified in James: (i) living with trials; this theme is announced in 1:2-4 and discussed in 5:7-11; (ii) the need for Wisdom; the theme is announced in 1:5 and discussed in 3:13–4:10; (iii) the dangers of wealth; the theme is announced in 1:9-11 and discussed in 2:1-13 and 4:13-16; (iv) Christian speaking; the theme is announced in 1:19, 26 and discussed in 3:1-12; (v) faith in action; the theme is announced in 1:22-25 and discussed in 2:14-16.

[70] Cf. E. BAASLAND, «Der Jakobusbrief», 119-139; R. BAUCKHAM, *James*; É. COTHENET, «La Sagesse», 413-419; C.H. FELDER, *Wisdom, Law and Social Concern*; D.E. GOWAN, «Wisdom and Endurance», 145-153; P.J. HARTIN, *James and the Q Sayings*; R.P. MARTIN, *James*, xxxvii-xciii; R.W. WALL, *Community of the Wise*; B. WITHERINGTON, *Jesus the Sage*, 236-244.

[71] Cf. T.B. MASTON, «Ethical Dimensions of James», 23-39.

[72] This in itself may explain why, on the surface, James seems so foreign to much of the rest of the New Testament and has been neglected.

[73] On the association of Spirit and Wisdom in both James and earlier Jewish sapiential material, cf. J.A. KIRK, «The meaning of Wisdom in James», 24-38.

Wisdom should be sought from God since it comes from above. James does not exhort his audience to observe life or nature to gain Wisdom. It is something passed down from one's teachers or directly from God. James reflects a knowledge of the «hidden» quality of divine Wisdom but does not develop the idea of personified Wisdom.

Furthermore, there is no evidence of any movement amounting to a proclaiming of Good News to those outside the community (unless a passing hint in 1:18 suggests it). James is focused specifically on inculcating a certain kind of community ethic, concentrating almost exclusively on behaviour within the community (4:11; 5:9). It is to good works and the good life that James is exhorting his charges (2:14; 3:13-18), not to a proclaiming of Good News to the world. The works to which James is exhorting his audience are the following: (i) to care for widows and orphans in the community (1:27); (ii) to keep oneself unstained from the world (1:27b); (iii) to fulfill the royal law, according to Scripture (2:8-13); (iv) to bridle one's tongue and one's passions (3:1-12; 4:1-10); (v) to persevere in faith through suffering and trials (1:2-15; 5:10-11); (vi) to pray for the sick and suffering (5:13-15, 16b-17); (vii) to confess sins to one another in the community (5:16); and (viii) to retrieve the erring community member (5:19).

There is very little here that Ben Sira could not have said, except the unreserved condemnation of the rich in James (see Sir 31:1-8), and there are various places where the echoes are clear. For example, in Sirach 35:12-14 we read «for the Lord is the judge, and with him there is no partiality. He will not show partiality in the case of a poor man; and he will listen to the prayer of one who is wronged. He will not ignore the supplication of the fatherless, nor the widow when she pours out her story» (cf. James 1:27-29). The concern for carefully controlled speech is expressed in Sirach 23:7-15, 27:4-5 in ways similar to James 3:1-12, especially in regard to the avoiding of cursing and abusive speech. The connection of Wisdom and the Law is at least implied in James (1:5; 2:8) which may be another echo of Sirach (24:23).

Despite the pervasive sapiential content of the book there is no reflection in James whatsoever on the concept of Jesus as Wisdom. Also notable for its absence is any of the more radical teachings of Jesus about, for example, loving enemies or leaving the dead to bury the dead. James has chosen either to draw on the more conventional parts of the Jesus tradition, or to use the often unconventional teaching of Jesus for some very conventional and traditional purposes, or to remain silent about certain aspects of Jesus' teaching that inculcated a counter order of things.

Qoheleth offered aphorisms and meditations of a counter order because of the limits, and in some cases the bankruptcy, he saw in conventional Wisdom. Jesus offered aphorisms and parables of a counter-order not merely as a critique of the *status quo* but as a positive alternative made possible by the in-breaking of God's eschatological reign even in the present. James offers neither, returning in the main to the sort of things which by now are quite familiar to us from Proverbs and Sirach.[74]

5. Summary and Conclusions

Our main objective has been to gain as clear a perspective as possible on what Paul's intention and understanding was when he identified Christ as Wisdom as well as highlighting Wisdom influences on the Letter of James. One of the most enduring developments of Pauline Christology was the application of Wisdom categories to Jesus. Paul found the Wisdom language an important resource in articulating Christ's definitive role in God's plan for all of creation. Furthermore, these Pauline expressions of a Wisdom Christology are crucial in any attempt to trace back to the earliest understanding of the risen Christ as a cosmic power.

The most explicit linguistic identification of Jesus with divine Wisdom in the writings of Paul occurs in the First Letter to the Corinthians. Paul speaks of Christ as «the Wisdom of God» (I Cor 1:24) whom God «made our Wisdom» (I Cor 1:30). In Colossians 2:3 Paul talks of Christ «in whom are hidden all the treasures of Wisdom and knowledge». I Corinthians 1: 17–2:13 is the clearest link between divine Wisdom and Christ. Yet even there Paul's impulse is to explain «God's hidden Wisdom» not as the person of Christ himself but rather as God's «secret purpose from the very beginning to bring us to our destined glory» (I Cor 2:7). When Paul calls Christ «the Wisdom of God» God's eternal plan of salvation overshadows everything.

---

[74] B. Witherington argues that we can conclude from James that at least one form of early Jewish Christianity could be very traditional indeed, even though it drew on the Jesus tradition in numerous ways and places. James was capable of using aphorisms and aphoristic beatitudes of Jesus in a proverbial way, and Witherington suggests that because it is James' intention to do precisely this that he does not attribute any of his material to Jesus. Proverbial Wisdom was normally anonymous or the collective and accumulated Wisdom of many generations of sages. James is using the Jesus tradition as though it were proverbial Wisdom. Cf. B. WITHERINGTON, *Jesus the Sage*, 236-245.

The impetus behind Paul's use of Wisdom categories in christological reflection has been variously explained. U. Wilckens argues that in Corinth Wisdom was a christological title used by an enthusiastic Christian group whom Paul opposed; in his response and critique he used the categories of his opponents. W.D. Davies makes the case that Paul independently associated Christ with Wisdom through first characterizing him as the new Torah, already identified with Wisdom since the time of Sirach 24:23. A. Feuillet argues that Paul was explicitly identifying Jesus with personified Wisdom and thus using Wisdom as a christological title. J.D.G. Dunn presents Paul's understanding of the Wisdom of God as simply God's plan of salvation. In either case, through evocative use of the Jewish Wisdom tradition, Paul was making the point that the same divine Wisdom active in the creating and saving ordering of the world is present in a definitive way in Jesus. By so implicating divine Wisdom with Jesus Christ he also implied that God's Wisdom is now to be read off not from nature or the Torah but from the history of Jesus culminating in the cross (I Cor 1:18-25).

In I Corinthians 1-4 Paul reacts against two aspects of Wisdom: eloquent Wisdom is not an appropriate expression for the Gospel (1:17; 2:1-5; 4:20) and the Corinthians have an obsession with Wisdom as a means of salvation (2:6-3:4). Paul's polemic in terms of Wisdom is directed against worldly evaluation of the message of the cross and against over-evaluation of rhetorical skill (1:18-2:5). Furthermore, Paul reveals here that he does speak Wisdom, a Wisdom not of this age but rather a Wisdom of God in a mystery, a Wisdom that involved a revelation from God through the Holy Spirit (2:10). For Paul, receiving the Spirit is crucial and Wisdom comes through the Spirit.

In I Corinthians 1:17 Paul describes his own task as that of «preaching the Gospel», which he here elaborates with a striking contrast: «not with words of human Wisdom, lest the cross of Christ be emptied of its power». Having set up the contrast in v. 17 between «the Wisdom of logos» and the cross, Paul moves to a series of arguments that have this contrast as its point of reference. What Paul offers as an alternative is described as the mystery of God (2:1) or, more vividly, as the Wisdom of God in a mystery. The content of this mystery is what Paul preached and is here amplifying for the benefit of the Corinthians, Christ crucified as the Wisdom and Power of God (1:24). This is a Wisdom that shames the wise and powerful of the world because it is something they did not generate nor could have inherited. It is strictly from God and therefore when one obtains it there are no grounds whatsoever for human pride or boasting.

In 2:7 Paul qualifies what he means by the Wisdom of God in four ways. First, it is Wisdom in *mystery*. Paul is referring to something formerly hidden in God from all human eyes but now revealed in history through Christ and made understandable to his people through the Spirit. Second, to clarify the phrase *in mystery*, God's Wisdom *has been hidden*. God's Wisdom, salvation through a crucified Messiah, has been hidden in God from eternity until such time («now») as he was ready to reveal it.

Third, God's secret Wisdom, long hidden and still hidden to some, was *destined* by God himself *for our glory before time began*. Fourth, God's Wisdom is something that *none of the rulers of this age understood*. The reason for their failure is that it was *hidden in God* and could only be grasped by a revelation of the Spirit (v. 10).

In I Corinthians 2:10–3:4 Paul offers an answer to questions concerning how the Spirit functions in relation to the giving and receiving of divine Wisdom. The communication of Wisdom by the Spirit involves three aspects: (a) a source for such communication, Paul identifies the source with God's Spirit (I Cor 2:10-11); (b) the act or process of communication itself, Paul describes the process in terms of receiving, understanding and speaking (I Cor 2:12-13); (c) a recipient for the communication, Paul restricts the reception of the Spirit's communication to the «spiritual» (*pneumatikos*, 1:13).

I Corinthians 8:6 has been seen as an extension of the thought of I Corinthians 1–2. As there Paul claims that the crucified Christ is the one who fulfils God's plan of salvation as God's Wisdom, so in I Corinthians 8:6 Paul extends the thought to assert in effect that God's plan of salvation is continuous with his power in creation. What we actually see in Christ's life, death, and resurrection is the very Wisdom and Power by which God created and sustains the world.

Against the background of pre-Christian Jewish understanding of divine Wisdom, Paul argues that, given our understanding of the Wisdom of God active in creation, revelation, and salvation, we can speak of Jesus in terms of this Wisdom.[75] Applying the understanding of the Wisdom language within Jewish monotheism, Jesus is to be seen as the expression of God's Wisdom fully realized and hence superior to any previous manifestation of the Wisdom of God. It seems the first Christians were using the vocabulary available to them in order that they might express as fully as possible the significance of Jesus. What was understood by divine Wisdom is now seen and proclaimed to have been most fully expressed and finally realized in Jesus our Lord.

---

[75] Cf. J.D.G. DUNN, *Christology in the Making*, 196.

While there is not yet a fully developed Wisdom Christology in Paul, there are the elements of one present. We have seen how Paul draws on the late sapiential presentation of the Old Testament to articulate his understanding about Jesus Christ. He also seems happy to adopt or adapt some Wisdom hymns to his own ends (Col 1:15-20). For Paul the revealed Wisdom that he claims to be privy to is Wisdom about God's eschatological plan of salvation in Christ for all the world. Here Paul transfers what the Wisdom writers have said about Wisdom to Christ (1 Cor 10:4). Sometimes what the sages were prepared to say was offered by the Torah, Paul now claims is available from Christ (Rom 10:4), and sometimes what was said of God is now said of Christ (1 Cor 8:6).

We highlighted sapiential influences on parts of the Letter to the Romans, specifically Romans 9:20-23 (influenced by Wis 12:12; Wis 15:7; Sir 33:12-13) and Romans 11:33-36.

Turning to the Letter of James, the author's presentation here is not a Wisdom of a counter order, as was true with Jesus and Qoheleth, but rather a more traditional and conventional form of Wisdom like that found in Proverbs and Sirach. Missing in James is any real sense of God's new eschatological activity or in-breaking reign in the present which changes the social order of things even now. The author returns to traditional topics: guarding one's speech and passions, enduring suffering and temptations, seeking Wisdom. It is the conventional Wisdom of a practical sort that is to be sought to cope with the trials and tribulations of life. Despite the pervasive sapiential content of the letter there is no reflection on the concept of Jesus as Wisdom.

CHAPTER IV

Wisdom in the Synoptic Gospels

We address here primarily the Synoptic Gospels in their final edited
form. We consider what place these individual Evangelists may have
given to the concept of Jesus as teacher of Wisdom and also if they
incorporate the notion of Jesus as Divine Wisdom in person into their
respective Christologies. We also ask whether there are hints in any of the
Synoptics that Jesus, during his earthly career, had intimated that his own
story was the story of Wisdom in person.

1. The Gospel of Mark

1.1 *Authorship, Date, and Place of Composition*

Little is known about the origin, date, and authorship of the Gospel of
Mark. Intensive study of the materials of which Mark is composed has
convinced scholars that much of that material as it currently appears must
have had a period of oral circulation in the Greek language before it was
included in the Gospel. In addition it appears that some of the material in
Mark was written down, perhaps even in rudimentary collections, before
the writer incorporated it into his Gospel.[1]

Nothing in the Gospel identifies its author by name, though we can
determine some hints from the Gospel itself. His confusion about

---

[1] Cf. the following commentaries and theological works on the Gospel of Mark: E.
BEST, *Mark*; J. ERNST, *Das Evangelium*; R.A. GUELICH, *Mark*; J. GNILKA, *Das
Evangelium*; R.H. GUNDRY, *Mark*; W. HARRINGTON, *Mark*; M.D. HOOKER, *Mark*; S.P.
KEALY, *Mark's Gospel*; J.D. KINGSBURY, *Christology of Mark's Gospel*; Q. QUESNELL,
Mind of Mark; V. TAYLOR, *Gospel according to Mark*.

Palestinian geography[2] and his fluency in Greek make it likely he grew up in an area outside Palestine. The author's origin outside Aramaic-speaking Palestine is confirmed by the type of readers for whom he was writing. Mark, like all of the evangelists, wrote for the community of his concern. It seems to have been a mixed community with Christians of Gentile and of Jewish background. Sustained interest in the Gentile mission and a care to translate Jewish expressions and explain Jewish customs indicate the Gentile element (7:2-4), which would have been predominant. But a care to do justice to the privilege of Israel is a gesture to the feelings of Jewish Christians.

The time and place of the composition of the Gospel remain a matter of some speculation.[3] The evidence for Markan priority, for example the tendency of both Luke and Matthew to shorten and polish Mark's stories, remains convincing to most scholars.[4] The view that Mark wrote in Rome about the year 65 A.D. has become prevalent because of Mark's traditional association with Peter.[5] But this has not gone unchallenged because the traditional data which points to this provenance and date are of uncertain

---

[2] The Greek of 7:31 shows the author assumes Sidon is south of Tyre and that the Sea of Galilee is in the midst of the Decapolis, inaccurate in both cases.

[3] The first three Gospels in the canon (Synoptics) have much in common and are significantly different from John. Similarities and dissimilarities among the Synoptics give rise to the question of inter-relationship, the so-called Synoptic problem. The priority of Mark was first suggested at the end of the 18th century as an alternative to the traditional view of Matthean priority. Debate in the 1830s to 1860s resulted in the Marcan priority becoming the predominant scholarly opinion. Cf. F. NEIRYNCK, «Synoptic Problem», 587-595.

[4] Luke 5:29 eliminates the ambiguity from the story in Mark 2:15-17 concerning the owner of the house where the meal was held; Matthew 17:13 eliminates a potential confusion about the subject of Jesus' conversation in Mark 9:11-13; Matthew 8:28-34 and Luke 8:26-39 both condense and clarify Mark 5:1-20 but in different ways.

[5] The earliest record we have of such data is in material cited by the Church historian Eusebius. In that account Eusebius (Hist. Eccl. 3:39.14-17) quotes Papias, who in his turn was quoting someone he, Papias, identified as «the elder». In that third hand account, we learn that Mark had been Peter's «interpreter», and that he had written down «accurately all that he remembered» although «not in order». Furthermore, I Peter 5:13 describes Mark as Peter's co-worker. Nevertheless, as an interpretative principle, it is better not to lean too heavily on the assumption that Peter was Mark's sole or even primary conduit to Jesus' public ministry. For diverse views of this tradition cf. M. HENGEL, Studies, 47-50, 64-84; W.G. KÜMMEL, Introduction, 95-97. Cf. also R.E. BROWN, An Introduction, 158-161; NJBC, 596.

worth.[6] We are forced back to the text of the Gospel, to an anonymous writing of the first Christian century. Nothing in the Gospel points necessarily, or even at all, to Roman provenance. Latinisms are now seen to be no more than predictable traces of a Roman administrative and military presence.[7] Persecution was a fact of wide Christian experience, not a prerogative of Roman Christians. We may assume that Mark wrote for a determined community and in face of concrete circumstances.[8] We are left to tease out a plausible setting for, and a likely date of, his Gospel.

Among those who give credence to the Papias tradition, the usual understanding is that Mark wrote just before or after Peter's death and thus in the mid or late 60s.[9] Internally that dating is supposed to be supported by the failure of Mark to show any knowledge of the details of the First Jewish Revolt against Rome in 66-70 A.D. and to mention the fall of Jerusalem. Some who posit a post-70 A.D. date for Mark ask whether many people outside Palestine knew details of the revolt, and whether the fall of Jerusalem warranted symbolic mention in a Gospel before it was seen as God's judgment because of what happened to Jesus. Yet the attention that Josephus and the Jewish apocalypses give to that fall and to the destruction of the Temple leads others to object that Christians with Jewish roots could scarcely have ignored the symbolism of these events after they had occurred.[10]

Regarding a terminus after which Mark is not likely to have been written, inter-relationship between the Synoptics constitute an argument. If Mark was used independently by both Matthew and Luke, and they were written in the 80s or early 90s, as most scholars believe, a date beyond 75

---

[6] Cf. P.J. ACHTEMEIER, «The Gospel of Mark», 542; R.E. BROWN, An Introduction, 158-161.

[7] Cf. R.E. BROWN, An Introduction, 161-163; M. HENGEL, Studies, 29.

[8] The consensus that evangelists wrote for definite, well-defined communities has been challenged in a set of essays: R. BAUCKHAM, ed., The Gospels for all Christians.

[9] M. Hengel dates the atmosphere of Mark 13 to the period after the suicide of Nero, specifically to 69 A.D. when three emperors lost their lives. Cf. M. HENGEL, Studies, 21-28.

[10] Matthew 22:7 and Luke 21:20 are seen as more precise with respect to the destruction of Jerusalem than is Mark; and during Jesus' passion Matthew 27:25 and Luke 23:28 warn the Jerusalem populace of punishment for the «children»(next generation). Yet the references are still only by allusion. The failure of New Testament works to make specific and detailed mention of the destruction of Jerusalem and the Temple is difficult to explain. Cf. R.E. BROWN, An Introduction, 163-164.

seems unlikely. The other end of the spectrum is more problematic, for there is no way of knowing with certainty how early Mark was written. Most scholars surmise that the developed state of the Greek Jesus tradition in Mark implies that several decades have passed since the time of Jesus. Therefore, there is wide scholarly agreement that Mark was written in the late 60s or just after 70 A.D.[11]

1.2 *Wisdom Influences on the Gospel of Mark*

When we come to consider the possible influence of Wisdom themes on the Synoptic Gospels it is not the Gospel of Mark that comes to mind. In effect, in so far as Mark emphasises the teaching activity of Jesus, he gives us less actual teaching than the parallels in Matthew and Luke. The Jesus of Mark appears, above all, as the wonder-worker. The large amount of space devoted to healings and exorcisms proves that Mark revered Jesus as a man of deeds as well as words.[12]

However, some scholars have argued that a Wisdom dimension to the Gospel of Mark might be more significant than at first appears.[13] H. Humphrey argues that Mark 6:30–8:21 is a clearly unified part of the Gospel of Mark which was elaborated from traditional materials into a complex, concentrically organized, literary structure, in order to develop a portrayal of Jesus which identifies him with the figure of Wisdom in Jewish literature and thought.[14] The strongest evidence for this, according

---

[11] For an overview of the debate cf. R.E. BROWN, *An Introduction*, 163-164; *NJBC*, 596-597.

[12] Cf. D.J. HARRINGTON, «Gospel according to Mark», 597.

[13] Cf. H.M. HUMPHREY, «Jesus as Wisdom», 48-53. Humphrey has elaborated his position further in *He is Risen!*

[14] Cf. H.M. HUMPHREY, «Jesus as Wisdom», 48-53. Mark 6:30-8:21 begins with the first miracle of the loaves and ends with Jesus linking the miracles of feeding with his call to «understand». He argues that the overall unity of 6:30–8:21 is indicated in 8:19 by the explicit reference back to the story of the feeding of the 5,000 in Mark 6:34-44 with possibly an earlier suggestion of unity in 8:17: «Do you not yet perceive or understand?» The only time that the first part of that question had appeared before in Mark was again as a question to the disciples in 7:18, and the use of the verb *understand* occurs first as a narrative comment about the disciples' failure to understand in 6:52, then again as an appeal by Jesus to everybody to *listen to* Jesus and to *understand* and finally is repeated again in 8:21 by way of closing off not only 8:17-21 through an inclusion but also the entirety of 6:30–8:2's theme of the disciples' failure to *perceive or understand* some hidden quality about Jesus which Mark apparently thought ought to have been obvious from the events narrated. Humphrey puts forward further

to Humphrey, comes from the concentrated use of the *bread* motif as a metaphor for *teaching* in this section and the parallels with the figure of Wisdom in Proverbs and Sirach to be found in this block of material where other titles for Jesus are absent.[15] For Humphrey, what we find coming to expression in Mark 6:30–8:21 is a continuation of the sapiential emphasis already in the Jewish scriptures.[16]

Humphrey argues that in Mark 7:1-23 Jesus displays a knowledge of the function of the Law which has been misunderstood by the Pharisees and in his rejection of their «tradition» shows the authoritative knowledge of what is pleasing to God. This corresponds to a characteristic of Wisdom from the Jewish scriptures (in Sirach 24:23 Wisdom in Israel is principally found in the Law). In Mark 7:1-13 there is a strong indictment of the Pharisees. In rejecting them as hypocrites, Jesus uses a quotation from Isaiah 29:13-14 and employs a theme that is also found in Sirach 1:29-30 («Be not a hypocrite in men's sight, and keep watch over your lips [...]»). Jesus' illustration of this radical failure of the Pharisees is then given in terms of their failure to respect the Law of Moses to honour one's father and mother in Mark 7:9-12, a theme which recalls the concern also of Sirach 3:3-16. Like Wisdom, Jesus calls out to the people to «understand» his words (7:14) and again, when questioned by the disciples about the parable concerning cleanliness and uncleanliness (7:14-16), he asks them: «Do you not understand either» (7:18)? It seems plausible that at the heart of this episode Jesus is portrayed in a way similar to that of the figure of Wisdom in the Jewish scriptures. Wisdom holds the key to true knowledge.

---

arguments in favour of the unity of Mark 6:30-8:21 based on the frequent use of the *bread* (fifteen of the eighteen uses of the word here) and *boat* (the opening and closing images are the same: Jesus is alone with his disciples in a boat) motifs respectively in this section.

[15] The thematic unity of the *bread* motif suggested here is as follows: Jesus comes to Israel as its true teacher, as the one who can satisfy Israel's hunger for knowing God's will and can do so abundantly. The use of *bread* as a metaphor for what Jesus brings to Israel (7:27), for Jesus himself (8:14), and for his teaching (8:15-21) points in this direction. The parallels with personified Wisdom in Proverbs and Sirach will be elaborated above.

[16] It must be noted that the position taken here by H.M. Humphrey implicitly challenges other analyses of this material. Cf. N.A. BECK, «Reclaiming a Biblical Text», 49-56; R.M. FOWLER, *Loaves and Fishes*; Q. QUESNELL, *The Mind of Mark*.

In Mark 7:15-23 Jesus teaches the disciples not to be like the Pharisees, «without understanding» (7:18), but to understand Jesus' teaching. The list of «all these evil things» in 7:23 parallels concerns found in various parts of the Book of Sirach (5:14-6:4).

It is also possible that Mark could have expected his readers to have understood that the two feeding miracles (6:30-44 and 8:1-10) metaphorically illustrated in some way the comment in 6:34: Jesus «saw a great throng, and he had compassion on them, because they were like sheep without a shepherd; and he began to teach them many things.» Mark's readers could well have been expected to recognize the «feeding with bread» as motifs associated with Wisdom. In Mark 8:19-21 Jesus asks the disciples to recall the number of baskets of scraps collected on the two occasions of his feeding miracles and then asks them: «Do you not yet understand»? (8:21).[17]

Marie Sabin contends that Mark images God's Kingdom as a state of new consciousness. Here, women are followers and reflectors of Jesus as Wisdom, prophets entrusted with bearing witness to the resurrection.[18]

---

[17] Particularly helpful in this regard are the references in Sirach 15:3 («She will feed him with the bread of understanding») and Proverbs 9:5 («Come, eat of my bread»). Regarding Jesus' discussion with the disciples at the end of this section, H.M. Humphrey argues that the numbers of baskets of scraps collected must be significant in order to make sense of the narrative. He suggests that «twelve» could refer to the twelve minor prophets and «seven» to the seven major prophets and the seven writings with «five» referring to the five books of the Law. Taken together, then, the two feeding narratives associate the entire complex of the Jewish canon, attributed to Wisdom, with Jesus, whose teaching of the crowd satisfies their hunger abundantly because it is «the bread of understanding». Cf. H.M. HUMPHREY, «Jesus as Wisdom», 52.

[18] Cf. M. SABIN, «Women Transformed», 149-168. This essay is excerpted from the final chapter of a book-length manuscript *Reopening the Word*. Sabin's thesis is that, in the Jewish Wisdom writings, the life-sustaining activities of God are imaged through the personification of Wisdom as a female figure: the faithful, provident wife of Proverbs, the female Wisdom «poured out» in Sirach as a divine life-force upon creation, and the radiant feminine Wisdom who mirrors God in the Wisdom of Solomon. It is in keeping with these traditions that Mark dramatizes women as the immediate foils to the foolish disciples, as symbols of the wise. Mark works out this metaphorical antithesis in three distinct, although overlapping, ways: in the first part of the Gospel he shows Jesus' healing miracles to be acts in which women are «raised up» to a new status (chapters 1-7); in the second part, he shows women acting out the roles the male disciples have failed to perform (chapters 14-15); at the end, he uses language which suggests that women are so transformed by Jesus' resurrection that they become both bearers and symbols of God's renewed creation (16:1-8).

Reading Mark as midrashic homily and further placing the homiletic discourse in the context of the Wisdom tradition, Sabin presents the disciples' weaknesses functioning as metaphors for folly. As Proverbs' Wisdom invites the unwise to her banquet, so the Markan Jesus calls not the righteous but sinners. As a community of sinners, these disciples are also a community of fools, failing to grasp the basic instructions of their teacher, Wisdom/Jesus, the instructions to serve others, to become dispossessed of themselves, to be awake to God's presence. In Mark's symbolic narrative the foolish disciples seek to make themselves great, are dumb-founded at the idea of voluntary poverty, and fall asleep at the critical hour. For Sabin, Mark further follows the conventions of the Wisdom traditions in setting up antithesis to folly in two distinctive ways: first, hinting at some future change in the foolish disciples and, second, describing disciples who are wise.[19]

A more tentative position than that of Humphry and Sabin is put forward by J. Schlosser, who argues that the sapiential dimension of Mark may be «less insignificant» than at first appears.[20] His objective, which seems more limited than Humphrey's or Sabin's, is simply to enrich our understanding of the Gospel of Mark through the use of sapiential themes.[21] He focuses on Mark 6:1-6a and notes the Wisdom parallels. In this passage Jesus was teaching in the synagogue on the Sabbath. Though the people of Nazareth acknowledged his Wisdom, they rejected him. Schlosser also notes the Wisdom parallels with Mark 7:1-23 where Jesus displays a knowledge of the function of the Law misunderstood by the Pharisees. Jesus calls on the people to *understand* (7:14). Like the figure

---

[19] Sabin argues that Mark accomplishes the first through his patterns of scriptural allusion which in effect create dual time-frames and a double lens through which to view the disciples: while he shows the disciples of the present to be weak, vulnerable, and faithless, yet through biblical allusion he links them to rich traditions of the past (the twelve tribes of Israel) and to images of future metanoia (the friends of the Bridegroom). Called as sinners and fools, they are yet called to a transformed state, and the biblical allusions serve as a foil which point to this calling. But Mark also describes disciples who are wise; while he shows the foolish disciples to be men, he depicts the wise as women. Cf. M. SABIN, «Women Transformed», 155-159.

[20] Cf. J. SCHLOSSER, «Jésus le sage», 321-356: «Pourtant la dimension sapientielle pourrait bien être moins insignifiante qu'il n'y paraît au premier abord [...]» (p. 321).

[21] Cf. J. SCHLOSSER, «Jésus le sage», 323: «Mon objectif se limite à montrer comment la prise en compte de la sagesse nous aide à reconnaître que certains aspects de l'évangile de Marc prennent un relief assez surprenant. Il s'agit en somme d'enrichir notre lecture de l'évangile.»

of Wisdom in the Jewish scriptures, Jesus holds the key to true knowledge.[22]

1.3 Concluding Remarks

It has not been our purpose here to summarize Mark's structure for his Gospel or of his theology, but to suggest that our understanding of them may benefit by recalling some sapiential themes. We have noted Humphry's argument in favour of the integrity of Mark 6:30–8:21 and its possible emphasis on Jesus as Wisdom. Specifically at issue here is Jesus' authoritative knowledge of the Law presented by Mark in this section and his calling on the people to «understand» (7:14). Also the possible linking of *feeding* and *bread* motifs with Wisdom as *the bread of understanding,* presented in Sirach 15:3 and Proverbs 9:5, are seen as worth considering, though we have pointed out that this position implicitly challenges other analyses of this material. However, it is in light of these tentative parallels that Humphrey makes the case that this specific section of Mark's Gospel seems to elaborate a traditional sequence of materials which emphasized the portrayal of Jesus in terms of the figure of Wisdom. We have seen a somewhat comparable position adopted by Sabin who highlights that, just as Proverbs' Wisdom invites the unwise to her banquet, so the Markan Jesus calls not the righteous but sinners. Moreover, she believes that Mark further follows the conventions of the Wisdom traditions in setting up an antithesis to folly, hinting at some future change in the foolish disciples, and describing disciples (the women) who are wise. Schlosser's position is more general, simply attempting to enrich our understanding of Mark through the use of sapiential themes.

Having considered the arguments, we find no compelling reason for detecting in Mark's mind a connection with personified Wisdom. Mark would seem to relate the word *authority* with miracles. For him the questions asked by the people of Nazareth call the reader's attention to the authority of the teacher. The implied answers point back to the baptism of Jesus, his preaching and miracles. Therefore we are unable to say that Mark has a developed theology of Wisdom or that a discernible Wisdom theology permeates his Gospel.

---

[22] Schlosser also draws our attention to the less convincing parts of Humphrey's argument: «Les indices relevés par l'auteur ne sont pas tous convaincants, tant s'en faut, mais son essai mériterait d'être pris en compte dans une étude plus développée. Cf. J. SCHLOSSER, «Jésus le sage», 329, n. 2.

2. The Gospel of Luke

2.1 *Authorship, Date, and Place of Composition*

While nowhere in the Gospel of Luke does its author reveal his identity and it cannot be deduced from the text, by the latter half of the second century this work was being attributed to Luke, the companion of Paul.[23] From the Gospel itself it emerges that the author is not an eyewitness of the ministry of Jesus, but that he depends on those who were (1:2). He is rather a second, or third, generation Christian. Furthermore, he is scarcely a native Palestinian; his knowledge of its geography and customs seems inadequate and argues in favour of another origin (see 4:44 and 17:11). He is obviously a well-educated person, a writer of considerable merit, acquainted with both Old Testament literary traditions and Hellenistic literary techniques.[24] It seems wise to accept the tradition that Luke composed this Gospel, for there seems no reason why anyone in the ancient church would invent this datum and make a relatively obscure figure the author of a Gospel.[25] In Colossians 4:14 Luke is identified as «the beloved physician».[26] This detail is picked up and used in subsequent

---

[23] For comprehensive bibliographies on the Gospel of Luke cf. J.A. FITZMYER, *Gospel According to Luke*. For bibliography of material post-1980 cf. R.E. BROWN, *An Introduction*, 276-278.

[24] Of the four evangelists he had the best control of Greek and uses several different styles with ease: imitative introductory formulation in his prologue, septuagintal style in the infancy narrative, classical polish in Paul's Areopagus declamation in Athens (Acts 17:16-31), and a pattern in Stephen's preaching different from that of Peter and Paul. It has been claimed that Lucan style becomes less biblical and more Hellenistic as the narrative moves from the Gospel (centred in Palestine) to Acts (on the way to Rome). Cf. R.E. BROWN, *An Introduction*, 268.

[25] For commentaries on and studies of the Gospel of Luke cf. D.L. BOCK, *Luke*; H. CONZELMANN, *Theology of Luke*; J. ERNST, *Das Evangelium*; J.A. FITZMYER, *Gospel According to Luke*; J.A. FITZMYER, *Luke the Theologian*; J. JEREMIAS, *Die Sprache des Lukasevangeliums*; J. JERVELL, *Luke and the People of God*; E. KLOSTERMANN, *Das Lukasevangelium*; R.F. O'TOOLE, *The Unity of Luke's Theology*.

[26] There have been several attempts to establish that the evangelist was a physician by pointing to technical medical language and perceptions introduced into material taken over by Mark (for instance, Luke 4:38 adds «high» to the fever in Mark 1:30; Luke 8:43 softens the harsh criticism of physicians in Mark 5:26). However, contemporary scholarship is of the view that the Lucan expressions are no more technical than those used by other educated Greek writers who are not physicians. Cf. R.E. BROWN, *An Introduction*, 269.

church tradition about the author of the Third Gospel and Acts.[27] Paul's statements in Philemon 1:24 and Colossians 4:14 refer to Luke as a fellow worker or companion.[28] In 2 Timothy 4:11 he is named as Paul's «sole companion». This association finds some support in the «We» sections of Acts (a form of self-reference in certain passages of Acts where Paul is not travelling alone: 16:10-17; 20:5-15; 21:1-18; 27:1–28:16), at least if we are willing to explain them as diary material.

Differences do exist between Paul's theology and Luke's «paulinism» but they need not call into question the relationship between Luke and Paul. We can still admit that Luke was a companion or fellow worker of Paul for a time, without having been with him inseparably.[29] In other words, these differences may come from an insufficient and brief acquaintance. If we suppose that Luke did not collaborate with Paul during the crucial time of the latter's struggle with the Judaizers and if we accept that Luke never read Paul's letters, we would expect his view of Paul, idyllic as it is in many ways, to differ from what we read in Paul's own letters.[30]

The identification of the author of the Third Gospel and Acts as Luke, a Syrian of Antioch, a physician, and a sometime collaborator of Paul, in no way necessitates an early dating (ie. pre-70 A.D.) of the composition of these two New Testament books. In the prologue to the Gospel, Luke speaks of his dependence on the first generation of Christian disciples

---

[27] The unity of the two volumes is maintained by the overwhelming number of scholars, based on continuity of style, thought, and plan.

[28] The way that Colossians 4:11 is phrased, i.e., all the men listed before that verse are of the circumcision, suggests that Luke who is listed after that verse is not a Jew. The name *Loukas*, which is a shortened Greek form of a Latin name (Lucius?), does not tell us whether he was Gentile or Jew. Outside the New Testament a prologue from the end of the 2nd century adds that Luke was a Syrian from Antioch who died in Boeotia in Greece (Cf. J.A. FITZMYER, *Gospel According to Luke*. I, 38-39). Scholars are about evenly divided on whether this attribution to Luke should be accepted as historical. Fitzmyer and Franklin argue strongly in favour. Cf. J.A. FITZMYER, *Luke the Theologian*, 1-22; E. FRANKLIN, *Luke*.

[29] Cf. J.A. FITZMYER, *Gospel According to Luke*. I, 47-51.

[30] The main objection against authorship by a companion of Paul comes from Acts in terms of historical and theological differences / discrepancies from the Pauline Letters. It does not make a great deal of difference whether or not the author of the Gospel was a companion of Paul, for in either case there would be no reason to think of him as a companion of Jesus. Therefore, as a second, or third, generation Christian he would have had to depend on traditions supplied by others.

(«eyewitnesses»), possibly on some of the second generation («ministers of the word», if these are to be understood as distinct from the eyewitnesses), and on «many» others who undertook to write accounts of the Christ-event before him. Among the latter must be included Mark, whose Gospel, we concluded, was composed about 68-70 A.D. The Lucan Gospel should be dated, therefore, later than Mark's.

J.A. Fitzmyer argues that when we reflect on the Lucan passages that allude to Jerusalem and its fate (13:35a; 19:43-44; 21:20 and possibly 23:28-31) and sees how the emphasis falls not on the Temple, but on the city, it is difficult to comprehend how it can be said that there is no reference in the Lucan Gospel to the destruction of Jerusalem.[31] It seems, therefore, that the dating of Luke-Acts must be not only post-Mark but also after the destruction of Jerusalem in 70 A.D. How much later? J.A. Fitzmyer suggests that Luke-Acts should be dated prior to the formation or circulation of the Pauline Corpus.[32] There is no evidence that Luke was acquainted with Paul's letters, much less with the Corpus as such. Furthermore, the Gospel of Luke does not reflect knowledge of the bitter persecutions of Christians during the latter part of Domitian's rule (81-96 A.D.). Luke does not reflect the severe controversy that existed between church and synagogue after the Pharisaic reconstruction of Judaism at Jamnia (85-90 A.D.). Hence the best solution is to adopt a date for Luke-Acts that is used by many today, 80-85 A.D.

External tradition that Luke was from Antioch does not tell us where and for whom the Gospel was written. The tradition that Luke was a companion of Paul raises a likelihood that Luke-Acts was addressed to churches descended from the Pauline mission. More specifically a late-second century prologue reports that the Gospel was written in Greece (Achaia) and that Luke died there.[33] From the internal evidence of the two-volume Lucan work, the concentration in the last half of Acts on Paul's career (independently of the «we» identification) makes it likely that the addressees were somehow connected with that apostle's proclamation of the gospel message. Brown argues that the early tradition that it was written in and to an area of Greece matches the internal evidence and might find some confirmation in Acts 16:9-10, which portrays Paul's

---

[31] Cf. J.A. FITZMYER, *Gospel According to Luke*, I, 56.

[32] Cf. J.A. FITZMYER, *Gospel According to Luke*, 57.

[33] Cf. J.A. FITZMYER, *Gospel According to Luke*, 38-39.

movement from Asia Minor to Macedonia as dictated by divine revelation.[34]

2.2 *Wisdom Influences on the Gospel of Luke*

In Luke's Gospel the texts linking Jesus and Wisdom are found principally in four places.

(a) «Yet, Wisdom is justified by all her children» (Lk 7:35). Dunn argues that this text «[...] is the conclusion to a brief passage which Luke has drawn from Q (Lk 7:31-35), wherein it formed what is clearly the final element of a collection of sayings relating to John the Baptist (Lk 7:18-35)».[35] It is a saying of Jesus about his own generation of Palestinian contemporaries who have failed to understand either John or himself. It finds its counterpart in Matthew 11:16-19, which we will consider later. The episode consists of a parable (vv. 31-32), an explanation of the parable (vv. 33-34) and an added Wisdom saying (v. 35). Fitzmyer points out that, in v. 35, Luke has added «all», an echo of «all the people» of v. 29.[36] In the Q source, *Wisdom's children* would have referred to John the Baptist and Jesus.[37] But Luke, by introducing *all*, seems to be deliberately including the disciples in *Wisdom's children*. God's wise, salvific plan has become foolishness for some of Jesus' contemporaries; his Wisdom is manifested as a mother whose children include not only John the Baptist and Jesus, but also «all» the people who, like tax-collectors and sinners, are willing to listen to John the Baptist or Jesus.

Luke, then, emphasizes the *children* of Wisdom, the people who accept both the Baptist and Jesus adding, for this purpose, vv. 29-30. For the same reason, he has followed this passage with the parable of the sinner who washes and anoints Jesus' feet while he sits at table in the house of the Pharisee. The sinner accepts Jesus; the Pharisee, it is implied, rejects him. The parable of the sower, which follows almost immediately, develops a similar theme. It is those who accept and those who reject the Word of God. As for the relationship of Jesus and the Baptist to Wisdom,

---

[34] R.E. Brown speaks of an area or region rather than thinking of Luke's intended audience as a single house-church or even as living in one city. Cf. R.E. BROWN, *An Introduction*, 269-271.

[35] Cf. J.D.G. DUNN, *Christology in the Making*, 197.

[36] Cf. J.A. FITZMYER, *Gospel According to Luke*, I, 678.

[37] Cf. R.A. EDWARDS, *A Theology of Q*, 58-61.

Luke is close to Q. Both Jesus and John are agents of Wisdom, but neither is identified with her.[38]

(b) «[...] I thank thee, Father, Lord of heaven and earth, that thou hast hidden these things from the wise and understanding and revealed them to babes [...] All things have been delivered to me by my Father; and no one knows who the Son is except the Father, and who the Father is except the Son [...]» (Lk 10:21-22). It is now widely accepted that this can be called a Wisdom saying.[39] However, regarding the relationship here between Jesus and Wisdom, appraisals have been more divided. While the endeavour to highlight a clear Wisdom Christology, Christ as Wisdom, in the Q material has been rebutted by several scholars,[40] the case seems at its strongest in this saying. In particular the unique mutual knowledge of the Father and the Son in v. 22 has been stressed as something that elsewhere is said only of Wisdom – only God knows Wisdom (Job 28:1-27; Sir 1:6,8; Bar 3:15-32) and only Wisdom knows God (Prov 8:12; Wis 7:25; 8:3; 9:4,9,11).

However, Dunn claims to demonstrate that, upon close examination, the parallels are not quite so exact.[41] First, the opening line of v. 22 («all things have been delivered to me by my Father») may be as much influenced by apocalyptic thought (*all things*, particularly Dan 7:14) as by Wisdom. Second, in the clearest parallels to v. 22b («no one knows who the Son is except the Father»), found in Job 28, Sirach 1, and Baruch 3, what is hidden to men and known only to God is the source of Wisdom (Job 28:20, 23; Sir 1:6; Bar 3:27, 29-31, 36), which for Ben Sira and Baruch at least, is now found in the Torah (Sir 24:23; Bar 3:37–4.1). Third, the Father-Son allusions sits awkwardly with the identification of Jesus as Wisdom, since Wisdom is more naturally spoken of in feminine imagery.

Dunn concludes that, at all these points, Israel's claim to election by Yahweh provides a closer parallel than Wisdom. He affirms that the exclusivity of the mutual knowledge of Father and Son in Luke 10:22 is

---

[38] Cf. R.E. BROWN, *An Introduction*, 240-241; J.D.G. DUNN, *Christology in the Making*, 197-198; J.A. FITZMYER, *Gospel According to Luke*. I, 677-681; *NJBC*, 696.

[39] Cf. particularly the parallels cited by F. CHRIST, *Jesus Sophia*, 82-91.

[40] Cf. D. LÜHRMANN, *Die Redaktion der Logienquelle*, 99; M.J. SUGGS, *Wisdom, Christology*, 96. For a different view cf. U. WILCKENS, *Weisheit und Torheit*, 515-517, 519.

[41] Cf. J.D.G. DUNN, *Christology in the Making*, 198-9.

less likely to have been influenced by Wisdom parallels, and more likely to have been swayed by the belief in one who had been specially favoured with the knowledge of God and charged with the task of making God's purpose known and bringing that purpose to completion in the world. Hence, he contends, Jesus is presented here as Wisdom's eschatological envoy rather than as Wisdom.

(c) «Therefore also the Wisdom of God said, "I will send them prophets and apostles, some of whom they will kill and persecute"» (Lk 11:49). This verse is part of three woes addressed to the lawyers among the Pharisees, dealing with the Law, the prophets, and Wisdom. Jesus addresses the first woe against the lawyers castigating them for minute legalistic interpretations of the Mosaic Law (v. 46). The second woe (vv. 47-48), more appropriately addressed to the Pharisees than to the lawyers, criticizes them for building monumental tombs to the honour and memory of prophets killed by their forebears, and consequently witnessing and consenting to what was done to these mouthpieces of God («for they killed them and you build their tombs», Lk 11:48). But God's Wisdom will not be thwarted, and Jesus' words take on a critical edge: Unless this generation breaks with the past, it will answer for all the injustice done to God's chosen ones (v. 50-51). The third woe against the lawyers (v. 52) reveals the sad plight of those learned men. The key of knowledge was given to them, the key to unlock the knowledge of God and his will in the Torah and its traditions, the key to the house that Wisdom built (Prov 9:1). They have not entered that house themselves and have prevented others from entering it. Their neglect is thus castigated.[42]

What we have here is a Q saying.[43] Thus in Q Jesus quotes a Wisdom saying in which divine Wisdom promises to send prophets (and apostles) to Israel. Where Q derived the saying from is a matter of debate. Dunn argues that it is likely that its origin lies in Wisdom 10–11 where Israel's history is ascribed to personified Wisdom. Dunn contends that «[...] the Q saying could go back to Jesus himself, although we should not entirely dismiss the possibility that it comes from a very early stage of the Palestinian Christian community's self-understanding (when prophetic inspiration was, in some cases at least, attributed to divine Wisdom and not yet to the exalted Christ), or from a particular community which greatly valued the Jewish Wisdom tradition and saw Jesus as the climax

---

[42] Cf. J.A. FITZMYER, *Gospel According to Luke*, II, 945-6.
[43] Cf. R.A. EDWARDS, *A Theology of Q*, 58.

of Wisdom's «stretching out her hand» to Israel and rejection by Israel (Prov 1: 20-31)».[44]

It seems, therefore, that in this verse (Lk 11:49) the authors of Q, and then Luke, do not intend to identify Jesus with Wisdom. In the first passage under consideration (Lk 7:31-35) we saw that Luke kept Jesus and the Baptist more or less on the same level with respect to Wisdom, who sent them both. Thus Luke remains consistent in this passage by seeing Jesus as an ambassador of Wisdom, in the line of the prophets. In the Book of Wisdom we saw that Wisdom herself is understood as a personification of one of God's attributes and personified Wisdom is identified with the Spirit (Wis 9:17). In this respect it has been argued that Luke follows this Old Testament development represented by the Book of Wisdom and thinks in terms of a Wisdom practically identified with the Spirit of God, who sent the prophets and who sends also the Baptist and Jesus with their followers.[45]

(d) «O Jerusalem, Jerusalem, killing the prophets and stoning those who are sent to you! How often would I have gathered your children together as a hen gathers her brood under her wings, and you would not» (Lk 13:34). Luke has derived this short passage from Q.[46] He has apparently altered the text slightly to improve its Greek. From a form-critical viewpoint, we can understand the passage as a minatory saying, a word of salvific concern uttered by a prophetic figure and teacher of Wisdom who approaches the city of Jerusalem. The episode portrays Jesus referring to himself as a heaven-sent messenger and herald of God's Wisdom commenting on the sad condition of Jerusalem, the metropolis of God's people.[47]

In comparing himself to a mother-bird, Jesus uses a readily understood image for his own love and concern for his contemporaries, thereby manifesting in a new way the salvific interest of God himself, which he was sent to proclaim (4:43). But Jerusalem will not seek its security under

---

[44] Cf. J.D.G. DUNN, *Christology in the Making*, 201-202.

[45] D.W. Smith puts forward the thesis that Luke relates Wisdom primarily with the Spirit, in line with the development of the Old Testament Book of Wisdom, and therefore has a Wisdom Pneumatology rather than a Wisdom Christology. Thus, it is interesting to note that in Acts 7:51-53 Stephen attributes the sending of prophets to the Spirit. Cf. D.W. SMITH, *Wisdom Christology*, 102-113.

[46] Cf. J.A. FITZMYER, *Gospel According to Luke*, I, 78.

[47] Cf. J.A. FITZMYER, *Gospel According to Luke*, I, 1033-1038.

the protective wings of heaven-sent Wisdom. So it will be left like a helpless fledgling, its «house» will be left abandoned. Whether «house» is understood as the Jerusalem Temple or in a broader sense of God's people resident there, the message of judgment is ominously the same.

Dunn inquires whether the one who speaks of gathering the children of Jerusalem («I») (13:34) is the same as the one who sends the prophets?[48] Both statements are appropriate as applied to Wisdom: Wisdom sends prophets (Prov 9:3; Wis 6:16; Sir 24:7-12; I Enoch 42:1), and the imagery of the mother hen is appropriate to maternal Wisdom (Sir 1:15), suggesting an affirmative answer.[49] Yet, if the saying followed Luke 11:49-51 in Q (the third of our four passages)[50], then, according to Q, Jesus distinguished himself from Wisdom as one of those sent by Wisdom. Jesus speaks in Luke 11:49 as one who stands in the tradition of the prophets who must perish in Jerusalem. It is unlikely that Q would intend a meaning for this saying different from other sayings in the Q material so it is unlikely that Q understood Jesus as the one who sends prophets and the «I» who would gather the children of Jerusalem.

The alternative explanation is that the one who laments over Jerusalem is not the one who sends the prophets, but is the climax of the prophetic appeal sent to Israel.[51] The saying could be a heart-rending expression of Jesus' frustration and disappointment at his rejection by the religious authorities centred in Jerusalem. The picture of the protective mother hen is wholly familiar from the Old Testament and does not necessarily embody any specific allusion to Wisdom (Deut 32:11; Ruth 2:12; Ps 17:8; 36:7; 57:1; 61:4; 63:7; 91:4; Is 31:5). It could also be argued that, since the imagery usually described God's protectiveness, Jesus' use of the image for his own concern implicitly implied a claim to have been divinely commissioned and to embody the «steadfast love» of Yahweh for Israel. Consequently, Jesus could again be speaking as the messenger of Wisdom, the one who brings God's final appeal to his people. This latter alternative gives an interpretation of the Q saying similar to the other passages under review.[52]

---

[48] Cf. J.D.G. DUNN, *Christology in the Making*, 203-204.

[49] Cf. F. CHRIST, *Jesus Sophia*, 138-148; M.J. SUGGS, *Wisdom, Christology*, 66-70.

[50] Cf. M.J. SUGGS, *Wisdom, Christology*, 64-66. Cf. also J.A.T. ROBINSON, «Jesus as Sophos and Sophia», 13.

[51] Cf. J.A. FITZMYER, *Gospel According to Luke*. II, 1034.

[52] In this saying, Q combines Wisdom language with more apocalyptically coloured language. Cf. N. PERRIN, «Wisdom and Apocalyptic», 543-572.

2.3 *Concluding Remarks*

In Luke's Gospel the texts linking Jesus and Wisdom are found principally in four places: 7:35; 10:21-22; 11:49; 13:34. Of the four passages, the two which illustrate most clearly Luke's use of Wisdom are 7:31-35 (on Wisdom justified by her children) and 11:49-51 (on Wisdom sending prophets). As we have seen, they are quite close to each other in meaning. In the first, Wisdom sends John the Baptist and Jesus in particular; in the second, Wisdom sends «prophets and apostles» in general. There is no reason to make Jesus the subject who sends the prophets and apostles in 11:49-51. Luke presents Jesus not as Wisdom but as the messenger of Wisdom, as the eschatological envoy of (God in his) Wisdom. The implication is that Jesus thought of himself in these terms. Influenced by his interest in the Holy Spirit, Luke has adopted and developed a theology first clearly stated in the Book of Wisdom where Wisdom is practically identified with the Spirit of God.[53]

3. **The Gospel of Matthew**

3.1 *Authorship, Date, and Place of Composition*

Those who accept Marcan priority and the existence of Q work with those two written sources for Matthew.[54] Overall, Matthew is remarkably faithful to Mark, almost as a scribe copying his source. Nevertheless, in the changes to what is taken over from Mark, we can detect Matthean thought and proclivities.[55] By including Q material, Matthew gives a strong emphasis to Jesus as teacher. In terms of content, Matthew appears to be reasonably faithful to Q even as he was to Mark. Yet the way in

---

[53] Luke thought of Jesus as the *principal* bearer of the Spirit. The virginal conception of Jesus by the Spirit (Lk 1:35); his special reception of the Spirit at his baptism (Lk 3:21-22); the special Lucan passages that refer to his relationship with the Spirit (4:1,14) and, most of all, Jesus' application to himself of the passage from Isaiah on the anointing by the Spirit (Lk 4:18-19) all set him apart, at least in degree, from the other bearers of the Spirit. For D.W. Smith, this is the key passage relating Jesus to the Spirit. The relationship of Jesus to Wisdom, at least during his earthly life, seems to be through his relationship with the Spirit, the giver of Wisdom. Cf. D.W. SMITH, *Wisdom Christology*, 102-113.

[54] For bibliographies on aspects of the Gospel of Matthew, cf. W.D. DAVIES and D.C. ALLISON, *Matthew*, I-III.

[55] R.E. Brown lists the characteristic changes made by Matthew with some examples of each. Cf. R.E. BROWN, *An Introduction*, 204-205.

which Q is used is not consistently the same, and the order of Q is adapted to Matthew's sense of order.[56] When we discuss material in Matthew not found in Mark or Q we enter an area that is not homogeneous and about which scholars seriously disagree. How much represents the Matthean evangelist's own composition / creation and how much did he draw from a source or sources (M) known to him alone among the four evangelists? Certainly Matthew could create his own compositions modelled on what he found in Mark and Q, yet he does seem to have had other sources that he followed: a body of special material about Peter (14:28-31; 16:17-19; 17:24-27).[57]

This new synthesis of Mark, Q, and M was necessitated by a severe crisis in the author's church. Stringently Jewish in origins, it had experienced the trauma of separation from the synagogue and a great influx of Gentiles into its ranks. This shift in its Christian existence demanded a new interpretation of old traditions, a new way of looking at Christ and his church, at the Old Testament and salvation history, at discipleship and morality.[58]

To achieve this new synthesis, the author divided salvation history into three periods: «all the prophets and the Law» up to the Baptist (Mt 11:13); the public ministry of Jesus, restricted to the land and people of Israel (Mt 10:5-6, 15:24); and the mission to all nations, a mission made possible by the great turning point, the death and resurrection of Jesus (Mt 27:51-54; 28:2-3; 16-20). Narrow, exclusive, Jewish-Christian statements could thus be retained by being referred to the unique period of Jesus' public ministry, while the evangelist could view his own time as under the final, universal mandate of 28:16-20.[59]

---

[56] Matthew rearranges the Q material into sermons or discourses. To a group of four beatitudes (Lk 6:20-23) Matthew 5:3-11 adds others to enlarge the number to eight. Matthew 6:9-13 fleshes out the Lord's Prayer by bringing to it additional petitions lacking in Luke 11:2-4.

[57] For works on the Gospel of Matthew cf. F.W. BEARE, *Gospel According to Matthew*; P. BENOIT, *L'Évangile*; W.D. DAVIES – D.C. ALLISON, *Matthew*, I-III; P.F. ELLIS, *Matthew*; W. GRUNDMANN, *Evangelium nach Matthäus*; D.A. HAGNER, *Matthew*, I-II; U. LUZ, *Evangelium nach Matthäus*; J.P.MEIER, *Matthew*; E. Schweizer, *Good News According to Matthew*.

[58] Cf. W.D. DAVIES, *The Setting of the Sermon on the Mount*; D.R.A. HARE, *The Theme of Jewish Persecution*; J.P. MEIER, *The Vision of Matthew*.

[59] Cf. R.E. BROWN, *An Introduction*, 171-174.

We cannot say with any certainty who was the author of this Gospel. He is probably not the apostle Matthew. The author of the final Greek text seems to have copied, with modifications and a few omissions, the Gospel according to Mark. Hence, it is improbable that, in its present form, it is the work of an eyewitness apostle. Why would an eyewitness need to copy from someone who was not? Today a more divisive issue is whether the unknown canonical evangelist was a Jewish Christian or a Gentile Christian. Current scholarship is in favour of a Jewish Christian; but significant commentators argue for Gentile authorship.[60] In support of identifying the evangelist as a Jewish Christian, the Papias tradition suggests a Jewish background for Matthew. The evangelist's use of the Old Testament indicates that he knew Hebrew and perhaps even Aramaic, an unlikely accomplishment for a Gentile. Although not conclusive and possibly reflecting sources rather than the evangelist himself, there are many features of Jewish thought and theology in Matthew.[61]

A number of locales have been suggested for the place of composition of this Gospel: Antioch, the Phoenician cities of Tyre or Sidon, southern Syria, even Alexandria and Edessa. The majority view relates Matthew to Syria and specifically to Antioch. The dominant influence that Matthew would have in subsequent Christianity suggests that it served as the Gospel of a major Christian church in an important city, such as Antioch. The interplay of Jewish and Gentile interests in Matthew is complex. There are passages that strongly echo the interests of a law-abiding Jewish Christianity (5:17-20; 10:5-6; 23:1-3); yet other passages revise the Law or Jewish observances (5:17-48; 23:1-36). The most plausible

---

[60] For a discussion of this question cf. J.P. MEIER, *The Vision of Matthew*, 17-27. An frequently-made argument for Gentile authorship is that Matthew omits or substitutes Greek for some of Mark's Aramaisms; much of that, however, may be simply a matter of stylistic preference or communicability.

[61] What we have in mind here are: the infancy narratives with a genealogy, a Moses parallelism for Jesus, and a knowledge of Jewish legends; the Sermon on the Mount with modifications of the Law; debates with the Pharisees; images of Peter's authority (keys of the kingdom, binding and loosening); a command to obey those who sit in Moses' seat (23:2-3); worry about flight on a Sabbath (24:20); and the special material in the passion narrative that is almost a midrash on Old Testament passages. Overall likelihood, then, favours the Jewish Christian identity of the evangelist. Cf. W.D. DAVIES– D.C. ALLISON, *Matthew*. I, 26-27.

interpretation is that Matthew was addressed to a once strongly Jewish Christian church that had become increasingly Gentile in composition.[62]

The majority view considers 80-90 A.D. as the most plausible dating for Matthew but the arguments are not precise. Matthew betrays no awareness of the problem of Gnosticism; therefore, if Matthew was written in the Antioch area, it was probably written before the time of Ignatius (110 A.D.) for whom Gnosticism was a threat. The best argument for a post-70 A.D. date is the dependence of Matthew on Mark, a Gospel commonly dated, as we noted, to the 68-73 period.

3.2 Wisdom Influences on the Gospel of Matthew

It is clear that the author of Matthew wished to give Jesus' task of teaching pride of place.[63] For example, in 4:23, 9:35 and 11:1, the author cites teaching ahead of preaching and healing as the chief task of Jesus. This is especially significant when we note that, in his Markan source at Mark 1:39, there is no mention of teaching. In fact there is no parallel at all to Matthew 9:35. Regarding the content of this teaching, Wisdom material has an overwhelming predominance. Jesus offers beatitudes, aphorisms, parables, Wisdom discourses.[64]

The four passages highlighted from the Gospel of Luke all have Matthean parallels.

---

[62] J.P. MEIER has shown how the history of Christianity at Antioch fits that situation. Cf. R.E. BROWN – J.P. MEIER, *Antioch and Rome*, 45-72. Cf. also R.E. BROWN, *An Introduction*, 212-216.

[63] There was a great urgency in early Christianity to legitimate itself by offering the true interpretation of Jesus, Judaism, Torah and related matters. To this end early Jewish Christians set up schools or school-like settings where teachings of and about Jesus as well as the new interpretations of Torah were reflected on and transmitted to a generation of Christians who had not been in contact with the historical Jesus or involved with his earthly ministry. Witherington cites an extensive study of ancient schools by A. Culpepper who concludes that Matthew's Gospel was produced in and probably for a school setting, as is evidenced by the preoccupation with the sort of things that characterized schools. The veneration of the founder of the community, transmission of his teaching, admission or defining rituals (baptism, foot-washing), making boundaries evident by augmenting a clear sense of «we» versus «they» («their synagogues»), and conveying certain biographical details about the founder's life are notable in the Gospel of Matthew. Cf. A. CULPEPPER, *The Johannine School*, 253-255; B. WITHERINGTON, *Jesus the Sage*, 342-343.

[64] Cf. P.E. BONNARD, *La Sagesse en personne*, F.W. BURNETT, *Testament of Jesus Sophia*; F. CHRIST, *Jesus Sophia*; M.J. SUGGS, *Wisdom, Christology*.

(a) «Yet Wisdom is justified by her deeds» (Mt 11:19). This is Matthew's first Wisdom saying. As we have seen, Luke writes «Yet Wisdom is justified by all her children» (7:35). In both Matthew and Luke, the saying stands as the conclusion to a parable (Mt 11:16-17 / Lk 7:31-32) which has been applied to John and Jesus (Mt 11:18-19a / Lk 7:33-34); it follows a longer unit of material in Matthew which comprises 11:2-19. This unit is indicated by the reference to the *deeds of the Christ* (v. 2) and the *deeds* of Wisdom (v. 19).[65]

F.W. Burnett argues that the *Sitz im Leben* of this unit is earlier than Q.[66] He affirms that a strong case can be built for placing this pericope in the life-situation of Jesus. The tradition is strongly Semitic and the language readily translates back into Aramaic, which locates it at least as early as the Palestinian tradition. The children at play are a vivid description of a Palestinian street-scene. Vividness of detail has been found to be more characteristic of the earliest stage of the tradition than it has of its later development. Furthermore, the application of the parable (11:19) reflects a high estimate of the Baptist because it tends to put his ministry on a level with that of Jesus. This is more characteristic of Jesus than it is of the early Church.

It is generally agreed, however, that Luke's *children* (Lk 7:35) is more original than *deeds*, and that Matthew has introduced the thought of Wisdom's *deeds* (11:19) just as he prefaced the collection of sayings relating John and Jesus by referring to *the deeds of the Christ* (Mt 11:2). In creating a parallel between the *deeds* of Wisdom (v. 19b) and the *deeds of the Christ* (v. 2), Matthew identifies Jesus with Wisdom.[67] In light of the Lukan meaning, Matthew has gone beyond Q. Where Q presented Jesus at most as the envoy of Wisdom, Matthew has taken the step here of identifying Jesus with Wisdom.[68]

Matthew has certain concerns which explain the change. In his redactional activity with these materials (11:2-19), Matthew underscores John's honoured place and parallels him to Jesus. He changes the saying

---

[65] The fact that the materials exist in substantially the same order in Luke, indicates that they had already achieved that order and were handed on as a unit by the redactor of Q. Cf. R. BULTMANN, *Die Geschichte*, 164; M.J. SUGGS, *Wisdom, Christology*, 37-40.

[66] Cf. F.W. BURNETT, *Testament of Jesus-Sophia*, 81.

[67] Cf. J.D.G. DUNN, *Christology in the Making*, 198; M.J. SUGGS, *Wisdom, Christology*, 57.

[68] Cf. F. CHRIST, *Jesus Sophia*, 77.

in 11:11 to read «there has risen no one» rather than «none is» (Lk 7:28). And just as Jesus is «he who is to come» (11:3), so John is «Elijah who is to come» (11:14). Finally, Matthew calls attention to John's eschatological role with the words, «He who has ears to hear, let him hear» (11:15).

But Matthew also makes it clear that John's role is subordinate to that of Jesus.[69] Jesus is the Christ, the Coming One (11:2-3), while John is the messenger, the Elijah figure (11:10). Moreover, while John is greater than other people, Jesus, the «least», is yet greater (11:14). Through the changes in 11:19b, Matthew indicates that he does not consider Jesus to be the first among Wisdom's messengers, but rather to be identified with personified Wisdom herself.

The deeds of Wisdom (11:19b) refer back to Jesus' reply to John's question: «Are you he who is to come or shall we look for another?» (11:3). The woes against the Galilean cities (11:20-24), immediately followed by a three-fold reference to Jesus' «mighty works», confirms that in 11:19 Matthew identifies Wisdom with Jesus the Christ. Among the deeds described in 11:2-6 is the preaching of good news to the poor. In 11:20-24 Jesus speaks prophetically, castigating the Galilean cities which did not repent at his mighty works. Furthermore, in 12:38-42 Jesus is compared to the prophet Jonah. Finally, in the immediate context of 11:16-19, it is implied that Wisdom's preaching is successful in the case of the tax collectors and sinners with whom Jesus dines. In this way Matthew associates personified Wisdom with «works» and «mighty deeds».

In this context Matthew has altered the Q saying to identify Jesus with Wisdom in order to make clear the proper ranking of John with respect to Jesus. In so doing, he has associated and identified the deeds of Wisdom with the deeds of Christ. This is particularly true of the deed of prophetic preaching. This apparently liberal editorial activity is justified because, as we have seen, one of Wisdom's roles is that of prophet (Prov 1:20-33), a prophet moreover who is rejected and who pronounces judgment on those who do so. Such is the case in Matthew 11:16-19, 20-24.[70]

(b) «[...] no one knows the Son except the Father, and no one knows the Father except the Son and anyone to whom the Son chooses to reveal him»

---

[69] Cf. M.J. SUGGS, *Wisdom, Christology,* 56-58.

[70] On the motif of Sophia's rejected envoys in Q cf. D.A. HAGNER, *Matthew.* I, 224-228; A.D. JACOBSEN, «The Literary Unit of Q», 365-389; R.J. MILLER, «The Rejection of the Prophets», 225-240.

(Mt 11:27). There are several differences between the Matthean and Lucan versions of Matthew 11:25-27.[71] However, the most significant Matthean redactional change is the addition of vv. 28-30 to vv. 25-27, and the literary context in which he has placed the whole.[72] We can speak of an implicit personification of Wisdom in 11:25-27. The material pertaining to Jesus bears certain similarities to the various descriptions of Lady Wisdom. Wisdom is hidden, transcendent, known only to God. So too, Jesus is known only to the Father and to those chosen to become privy to that knowledge.

With the addition of 11:28-30 (an M saying) the identification of Jesus with Wisdom is made explicit. The invitation «Come to me» (v. 28), the image of the yoke, the promise of rest, the paradox of an easy yoke and a light burden all recall the Wisdom passages of earlier literature. The designation of the yoke as «my yoke» is particularly appropriate, for in Sirach 6:25 and 51:26, the yoke is that of Lady Wisdom. The invitation «Come to me [...] learn from me» recalls Lady Wisdom's invitation (Prov 8:1-6; 9:5; 11:24; Sir 24:19-22; 51:23). In the verses following Matthew 12:1-8, 9-14 we see Jesus interpreting *halachah* in order to justify an otherwise unacceptable action on the Sabbath. Moreover, in the context of the broader unit, Jesus' Wisdom is «greater than Solomon» (12:42), and he is acclaimed for his teaching by the astonished people in the synagogue (13:54).[73]

In describing Jesus as Wisdom in 11:25-30, Matthew portrays him as hidden, revealed and transcendent. We learn that he mediates knowledge

---

[71] Matthew 11:25-27 follows immediately the woes on the Galilean cities. We have seen that these verses are a Q saying which are found with the woes in a section on discipleship in Luke. Matthew, however, has placed both in a longer unit dominated by themes of acceptance-rejection, revelation-concealment. Cf. H.D. BETZ, «The Logion of the Easy Yoke», 10-24, 19.

[72] Cf. H. D. BETZ, «The Logion of the Easy Yoke», 19-21.

[73] In the immediate context of Matthew 11:25-29, «hidden things» refers to the Son himself and to the Father. In the context of the broader unit, «hidden things» refers to the Son's identity and the messianic significance of his teaching and deeds. Specifically, it refers to the «secrets of the kingdom of heaven» which must be hidden in parables from the crowds, and which can be understood only by the disciples to whom the secrets are given (13:10-11, 35). «Yoke», that which Jesus teaches, is Torah, as is clear from Sirach 6:37; 15:1 and 24:1-34. This is confirmed by other texts in which «yoke» refers to Torah (2 Enoch 34:1-2; 2 Baruch 41:3-5). That Jesus' yoke is a reference to Torah, specifically Jesus' interpretation of Torah, is borne out in the halachic discussions regarding Sabbath observance which follow immediately (Mt 12:1-8, 9-14).

of God and of the hidden things of the apocalyptic reign. Jesus as Wisdom proffers the proper interpretation of Torah. Mediation, revelation and Torah instruction occur precisely in the relationship of discipleship. The identification of Jesus with Wisdom in 11:25-30, moreover, authenticates Jesus' teaching, both apocalyptic and halachic. He can reveal the hidden things and give authoritative halachic decisions because he *is* Wisdom. Thus, his teaching is legitimated over against that of opposing teachers, Matthew's «scribes and pharisees». As J. P. Meier says of this text: «In Jesus the Wisdom of God, the teacher and the subject taught are one and the same.»[74] The identification also authenticates the community of disciples, Matthew's own community, in their claims to truth. After all, the disciples possess revelation or tradition unknown to outsiders and originating ultimately in a teacher who is Wisdom.[75]

(c) «Therefore, I send you prophets and wise men and scribes, some of whom you will kill and crucify, and some you will scourge in your synagogues and persecute from town to town [...]» (Mt 23:34-36);

(d) «O Jerusalem, Jerusalem, killing the prophets and stoning those who are sent to you! How often would I have gathered your children together as a hen gathers her brood under her wings, and you would not [...]» (Mt 23:37-39). The final material for our consideration is Matthew 23:34-36, 37-39. Usually vv. 34-36 and vv. 37-39 are treated separately, since they are indeed separate logia in Q.[76] However, Matthew has placed them together as a single unit.[77]

The Wisdom sayings of Matthew 23:34-36, 37-39, follow the woes addressed to the scribes and Pharisees who are called «hypocrites» (23:13-33). The woes are preceded in 23:1-12 by a passage in which Jesus is portrayed as contrasting the manner of leadership exercised by scribes and

---

[74] Cf. J.P. MEIER, *Matthew,* 128. J.P. Meier is cautious about the danger of exaggerating the place of Wisdom Christology in Matthew (*Vision of Matthew,* 78). He nevertheless writes that in Matthew we find «the meshing of the apocalyptic Son (of Man) and the figure of Wisdom», and that in Matthew's work, «the fusion of apocalyptic and sapiential themes in the service of high Christology could not be clearer.» (*Matthew,* 127 and *Vision of Matthew,* 80).

[75] Cf. S. COHEN, «The Significance of Yahweh», 30-32.

[76] Matthew 23:34-36 / Luke 11:49-51; Matthew 23:37-39 / Luke 13:34-35.

[77] This is a significant point for discovering the evangelist's redactional purpose. F.W. Burnett suggests that Matthew 23:34-36 is the departure point for anyone wishing to explore the possibility of a Wisdom Christology in the Gospel of Matthew. Cf. F.W. BURNETT, *Testament of Jesus-Sophia,* 51.

Pharisees with that required by the leaders of Matthew's community.[78] The Wisdom sayings are followed by Jesus' departure from the Temple in 24:1 and the apocalyptic discourse in 24:3–25:46, which describes the events to occur at the «close of the age» (24:3).

In 23:34-36 Matthew has replaced the Q «Wisdom of God» with «I», thus placing Wisdom's words on Jesus' lips. Consequently, in 23:34 Matthew has once again ascribed to Jesus a function possessed by Wisdom: the sending of envoys. The substitution of «I» for «Wisdom of God» makes explicit the presentation of Jesus as personified Wisdom.[79]

Matthew has introduced other changes into the oracle. The fact that he altered Q's future tense (I will send) to a present sense (I am sending) strongly suggests that he was thinking of his own present situation.[80] The «prophets, wise men and scribes» (13:52) probably denoted those commissioned by the exalted Christ for ministry in the face of an increasingly hostile rabbinic Judaism. Hence, we can understand the setting of the Q saying within the context of Matthew 23.[81] The use of the present tense and the second person (rather than the third) actualize the saying and relate it to the Matthean community. The envoys sent by Wisdom are not only, or even primarily, the prophets of old, whose sending is described in vv. 29-32. Rather, they are the disciples of Jesus and «messengers» of Matthew's community. At the conclusion of the woes, Matthew thus presents Wisdom's envoys as exercising prophetic and teaching functions in both Jesus' time and that of the Matthean community. As he does in 23:1-12, the introduction to the woes, so at the conclusion (23:31-36), Matthew places Jesus and the teachers of his own

---

[78] For a reconstruction of the woes in Q cf. J.S. KLOPPENBORG, «The Formation of Q», 443-462, 450.

[79] Moreover, it smooths the awkwardness of the Q oracle where, in the midst of woes attributed to Jesus, it is unexpected to find a saying of Wisdom. Whether Matthew's readers would have recognized here an equation of Jesus with Wisdom is uncertain; it would depend on whether the Q saying was already well known as a saying of Wisdom. Cf. E. SCHWEIZER, *Good News According to Matthew*, 284; M.J. SUGGS, *Wisdom, Christology*, 59; U. WILCKENS, *Weisheit und Torheit*, 197.

[80] Cf. S. SCHULZ, *Q*, 336; D.W. SMITH, *Wisdom Christology*, 100.

[81] That Matthew was written in the period following 70 A.D., when rabbinic Judaism and Jewish Christianity became more hostile, is implied by Matthew 23 in particular, and widely agreed among commentators. Cf. S. SCHULZ, *Q: Die Spruchquelle der Evangelisten*, 336; D.W. SMITH, *Wisdom Christology in the Synoptic Gospels*, 100.

community over against the «scribes and Pharisees», the teachers of the broader Jewish community.

Matthew's version of the saying about Wisdom's envoys expands the prediction of persecution. Whereas Luke (Q) has «[...] some of whom they will kill and persecute [...]» (11:49), Matthew has «[...] some of whom you will kill and crucify and some you will scourge in your synagogues and persecute from town to town» (23:34). The addition of the verbs «crucify» and «scourge» recalls the passion predictions, the third of which occurs at 20:19.

In 23:35-36 Matthew takes over a tradition regarding the rejection and killing of the prophets and applies it to the fate of the prophets, wise men, and scribes sent by Jesus as personified Wisdom. The fate of Jesus' envoys and of those of Matthew's day enters into the long history in Israel of prophets and Wisdom's envoys. Moreover, Matthew creates a continuity between the past history of Israel, the rejection of repentance in Jesus' day and the opposition experienced by the Matthean community and its leaders. In referring to the teachers of his community as Wisdom's envoys and placing them in the context of prophetic activity and history, Matthew legitimates their teaching and leadership, and he explains the opposition which they encounter. They are the proper teachers and interpreters of the tradition because they are Wisdom's envoys, and they experience opposition because that is the fate of prophets.[82] So whatever the precise character of Matthew's Wisdom Christology, we can say that Matthew has transformed a Q saying, in which Jesus was presented simply as the spokesman of Wisdom, into a vehicle of Wisdom Christology, in which Jesus is identified as Wisdom. In Matthew 23:34-36, as elsewhere, Jesus speaks not merely as the spokesman of Wisdom but as divine Wisdom in person.

In summary, the pre-Matthean meaning of the oracle in 23:34-36, namely, the persecution and rejection of Wisdom's envoys, has been enhanced by Matthean redaction. The evangelist links verses 32 and 34 and thereby emphasizes that the persecution and rejection of Christian prophets is still the story of the rejection of Wisdom's envoys. Matthew's redaction has made two modifications in this view of history: Jesus himself is identified with Sophia, and Wisdom's «prophets» now include

---

[82] Opposition here legitimates the perceived truth of the Matthean position. Cf. D.A. HAGNER, *Matthew*. II, 102-104.

Jesus' disciples.[83] This becomes even clearer when the other Wisdom logia (23:37-39) is investigated. This lament centres on the poignant image of Jesus as a mother hen who wishes to gather her brood under her wings.[84] In the context of the Gospel, these verses are a lament of Jesus as Wisdom over Jerusalem.[85] Matthew's redaction of the previous Q saying has the effect of transforming this present logion into a further statement of Wisdom Christology. As in Matthew 23:34, where Jesus himself is the one who sends prophets and wise men and scribes, so in Matthew 23:37 Jesus is again the sender of the prophets rather than the one sent.

3.3 Concluding Remarks

The Synoptic Gospels give us a unique opportunity to see into the developing thought of the early Christians. Because we can compare Matthew and Luke with their sources (Mark and Q), we can frequently detect where Matthew and Luke modified or expanded the traditions about Jesus which they received; and where a consistent redaction becomes evident we are wholly justified in speaking of Matthew's or Luke's theology at that point. In the context of our study we can say with some confidence that we have detected a particular christological emphasis in Matthew which emerges specifically in his redaction of Q. Furthermore, the difference between Q and Matthew is such that we can speak of a development in Christology as we move from Q to Matthew.[86]

---

[83] Cf. E. SCHWEIZER, *Good News According to Matthew*, 443- 444; M.J. SUGGS, *Wisdom, Christology*, 60.

[84] E. Klostermann points out that the Hebrew Bible uses the metaphor of a bird to indicate God himself. The word «wings» in the Old Testament is used quite often to depict the wings of Yahweh under which Israel can hide for his sustaining care and protection: Exodus 19:4; Deuteronomy 32:11; Ruth 2:12; Psalms 17:8; 36:7; 57:1; 61:4; 63:7. For a discussion of this subject cf. J.A. WHARTON, «Wings», 196. Cf. also E. KLOSTERMANN, *Das Matthäusevangelium*, 124-128.

[85] We have seen that Luke has the lament in another context (Lk 13:34-35). Whether the Matthean or Lucan version represents the original Q setting or whether both have displaced the saying is debatable. Nevertheless, oracle (vv. 34-36) and lament (vv. 37-39) do stand together in the Matthean context, whether so placed in the source or not. Moreover, the lament stands with Wisdom's oracle in the Matthean context, whether or not it was originally understood to be a Wisdom saying or not. The fact that the lament follows the oracle immediately, without so much as a transitional phrase, indicates that Matthew considers the speaker of the lament to be Jesus as personified Wisdom.

[86] Cf. R.A. EDWARDS, *A Theology of Q*, 58-79; J.M. ROBINSON, «Logoi Sophōn», 84-130; C.M. TUCKETT, *Q*, 325-354.

The Wisdom references in Q do not reflect any kind of identification or explication of Jesus as transcendent Sophia.[87] As a minimum we can say that Q (i) became the depository for what is now classified as the Wisdom thread in the Synoptic sayings, and (ii) thinks of Jesus as the last, perhaps the most authoritative, envoy of Wisdom rather than incarnate Wisdom. In Q Jesus brings Wisdom's truth to humanity while Matthew «historicizes» the Wisdom tendency in Q by identifying heavenly Wisdom with the earthly Jesus.[88] In terms of a Wisdom Christology, the development from Q to Matthew opens up new possibilities for assessing the significance and status of Christ- Jesus as messenger of Wisdom is one thing, Jesus as Wisdom incarnate is quite another. Such a development opens up prospects of moving from a Christology which thinks of Jesus as different in degree from earlier prophets to one which understands that difference in terms of kind. It is a development from a Christology which speaks of Jesus' divinely given function to one which speaks of Jesus' metaphysical status. In this regard, Matthew identifies Jesus with Wisdom in terms of function and of being. Matthew stands alone within the Synoptic tradition in maintaining an enhanced Wisdom Christology in identifying Jesus as Wisdom.

4. Summary and Conclusions

We have examined the place of Wisdom in the Synoptic Gospels. We have been especially concerned with the place these evangelists may have given in their respective Christologies to Jesus as teacher of Wisdom and also possibly to Jesus as Divine Wisdom in person.

In drawing attention to suggestions that our understanding of Mark's structure for his Gospel and of his theology may benefit by being addressed within the context of some sapiential themes, we focussed on Jesus' authoritative knowledge of the Law presented by Mark in 6:30–8:21 and his calling on the people to understand (7:14). The parallel with the *bread* motif in Sirach 15:3 and Proverbs 9:5 were considered, though this view implicitly challenges other analyses of this material.

---

[87] The Q collector was conscious of the Wisdom overtones of his material. The form of the sayings mark them out as belonging to what J.M. Robinson has called *Logoi Sophōn*, (sayings of the sages). Cf. J.M. ROBINSON, «Logoi Sophōn», 84-130; M.J. SUGGS, *Wisdom, Christology*, 58.

[88] F.W. Burnett argues that Q is moving in the direction of a Wisdom Christology. Cf. F.W. BURNETT, *Testament of Jesus-Sophia*, 52.

Furthermore, as Proverbs' Wisdom invites the unwise to her banquet, so the Markan Jesus calls not the righteous but sinners. However, such tentative associations with Wisdom hardly present a compelling reason for detecting in Mark's mind a connection with personified Wisdom. A discernible Wisdom theology does not appear in his Gospel.

Of the passages studied in Luke's Gospel, the two which illustrate most clearly Luke's use of Wisdom are 7:31-35 (on Wisdom justified by her children) and 11:49-51 (on Wisdom sending prophets). In the first, Wisdom sends John the Baptist and Jesus in particular; in the second, Wisdom sends «prophets and apostles» in general. Luke presents Jesus not as Wisdom but as the messenger of Wisdom, as the eschatological envoy of (God in his) Wisdom. The implication is that Jesus thought of himself in these terms. We speculated, given his interest in the Holy Spirit, that Luke adopted and developed a theology first stated in the Book of Wisdom where Wisdom is practically identified with the Spirit of God.

In our study of Matthew we detected a particular christological emphasis which emerges specifically in his redaction of Q. Furthermore, the difference between Q and Matthew is such that we spoke of a development in Christology as we move from Q to Matthew. The Wisdom references in Q do not reflect any kind of identification or explication of Jesus as divine Wisdom. Rather, Q, thinking of Jesus as the last and possibly most authoritative envoy of Wisdom (rather than Wisdom incarnate), became the depository for what is now classed as the Wisdom thread in the Synoptic sayings. The implication is that the same was true also of Jesus' own teaching: there is no evidence in the earliest traditions of Jesus' ministry that he understood himself as Wisdom, or as the incarnation of divine Wisdom. Throughout the earliest stages of the Synoptic tradition prior to Matthew, but including Luke, Jesus is presented not as Wisdom, but as the messenger of Wisdom. Matthew «historicizes» the Wisdom tendency in Q by identifying heavenly Wisdom with the earthly Jesus. In terms of a Wisdom Christology, the development from Q to Matthew opens up possibilities for presenting the significance and status of Jesus Christ. Matthew identifies Jesus with Wisdom in terms of function and being and consequently stands alone within the Synoptic tradition in maintaining an enhanced Wisdom Christology in identifying Jesus as Wisdom.

CHAPTER V

Wisdom in the Gospel of John

Our purpose here is to appraise the conclusions contemporary scholarship has drawn regarding the Wisdom influences on the formation of the Fourth Gospel. We shall see that Wisdom's influence upon the Christology of the Fourth Evangelist is not merely significant, but fundamental, even though no word of the *sophia / sophos* family appears in the text.

1. The Gospel of John

1.1 *Authorship, Date, and Place of Composition*

A comparison of the Fourth Gospel to the first three Gospels shows obvious differences.[1] The Johannine Gospel differs from the Synoptics in the style and content of Jesus' words, which no longer focus on the kingdom of God (only in 3:3, 5), or use proverbs and parables.[2] Instead,

---

[1] Amidst the abundant literature concerning a comparison of John to the Synoptics cf. B. LINDARS, «John and the Synoptic Gospels», 287-294; D.M. SMITH, *John among the Gospels*.

[2] John is a Gospel where style and theology are intimately wedded. (i) *Poetic format*: There is a uniquely solemn pattern in the Johannine discourses that some would call semipoetic. One explanation draws on the Old Testament: there divine speech (God through the prophets or personified divine Wisdom) is poetic, signalling a difference from more prosaic human communication. The Johannine Jesus comes from God, and therefore it is appropriate that his words be more solemn and sacral. (ii) *Misunderstanding*: Jesus frequently employs figurative language or metaphors to describe himself or to present his message. In an ensuing dialogue the questioner will misunderstand the figure or metaphor, and take only a material meaning. This allows Jesus to explain his thought more thoroughly and thereby to unfold his doctrine (2:19-21; 3:3-4; 4:10-11; 6:26-27; 8:33-35; 11:11-13). (iii) *Twofold meanings*: Sometimes playing into misunderstanding, sometimes simply showing the multifaceted aspect of revelation,

Jesus speaks in symbolic discourses and dialogues, which often refer to his relationship with the Father (conscious of having pre-existed with God before he came into the world, 17:5).[3] Chronologically, John differs in presenting the ministry of Jesus over a period of three years and having Jesus' death on the day of preparation before Passover. Geographically, John presents the ministry of Jesus as largely set in Jerusalem rather than in Galilee. This pattern departs from the Synoptic picture of a relatively extensive ministry in Galilee followed by a brief period in Jerusalem before Jesus' arrest at Passover.

Yet, there are also important similarities to the Synoptics, especially in the beginning narrative of the ministry featuring John the Baptist and in the concluding narratives of the passion and empty tomb.[4] John agrees

---

a double meaning often can be found in what Jesus says: «lifted up» in 3:14; 8:28; 12:34; «living water» in 4:10. (iv) *Irony:* By way of irony some of the statements made by the opponents of Jesus are often true or more meaningful in a sense that the speakers do not realize (3:2; 4:12; 6:42; 7:35; 9:40-41; 11:50). (v) *Inclusions and transitions*: The care structure of the Gospel is indicated by certain techniques. By inclusion is meant that John mentions a detail (or makes an allusion) at the end of a section that matches a similar detail at the beginning of the section (large inclusions are 1:1 with 20:28; 1:28 with 10:40). By way of transition from one subdivision of the Gospel to the next, John uses a «hinge» motif or section to conclude what has gone before and introduce what follows (the Cana miracle terminates the call of the disciples in chapter one, fulfilling the promise in 1:50, but also opens the next subdivision of 2:1–4:54 that runs from the first Cana miracle to the second. The second Cana miracle concludes that subdivision but by stressing Jesus' power to give life (4:50) prepares for the next subdivision (5:1–10:42) where Jesus' authority over life will be challenged. (vi) *Parantheses or footnotes*: Frequently John supplies parenthetical notes, explaining the meaning of Semitic terms or names (1:41-42; 9:7; 11:16), offering background for developments in the narrative and for geographical features (2:9; 3:24; 4:8; 6:71) and even supplying theological perspectives (2:21-22; 7:39; 11:51-52; 12:16, 33). Cf. R.E. BROWN, *An Introduction*, 333-337.

[3] For commentaries and studies on the Fourth Gospel cf. C.K. BARRETT, *Gospel according to John*; R.E. BROWN, *Gospel according to John*, I-II; R. BULTMANN, *Gospel of John*; C.H. DODD, *Interpretation of the Fourth Gospel*; J. GNILKA, *Johannesevangelium*; I. DE LA POTTERIE, *La verité*; R. SCHNACKENBURG, *Gospel according to John*, I-III. For surveys of research cf. W.F. HOWARD, *The Fourth Gospel in Recent Criticism*; R. KYSAR, *The Fourth Evangelist and His Gospel* (covering 1955-75); ID., «The Fourth Gospel», 2391-2480 (covering to 1977); ID., «Gospel of John», 314-323 (covering to 1983); G.S. SLOYAN, *What are they saying about John?* (covering 1970-90).

[4] In particular, the closest similarities are with Mark, eg., in the sequence of events shared by John 6 and Mark 6:30-54; 8:11-33; and in such verbal details as «costly ointment of pure nard» (Jn 12:3), three hundred denarii (12:5), and two hundred denarii

with the Synoptics that Jesus healed people, multiplied the loaves, and rescued the disciples from a storm at sea, but he never includes exorcisms among the healings of Jesus. Many of the miracles in the Johannine Gospel provide the occasion for symbolic insight into Jesus' identity. The Synoptics make the perception that Jesus is Messiah the climax of Jesus' Galilean ministry (Mk 8:31), whereas the disciples in John have confessed this truth from the beginning (1:41-49).[5]

The relationship of John to the Synoptics has significance for the dating of the Fourth Gospel. If it is supposed that the fourth evangelist employed the Synoptics in the composition of the Gospel, it then becomes necessary to date the Gospel of John after the writing of all three Synoptics (after 85 A.D.). Unfortunately, the issue of the fourth evangelist's knowledge and use of the Synoptics is unsettled at the present.[6] Those who think that the

---

(6:7). There are parallels with Luke, but more of motif than of wording, eg., figures like Martha and Mary. There are fewer similarities with Matthew; yet compare John 13:16 with Matthew 10:24; and John 15:18-27 with Matthew 10:18-25. Cf. A. BAILEY, *The Traditions*; R.E. BROWN, *An Introduction*, 365.

[5] A variety of solutions to the differences and similarities between the Fourth Gospel and the Synoptics has been suggested. At one end of the spectrum, some would posit John's knowledge of Mark or even of all three Synoptics. Such proposals may disagree as to whether John *also* had an independent tradition. At the other end of the spectrum, the fourth evangelist is thought not to have known any Synoptic Gospel and occasional similarities between John and the others are explained in terms of the Synoptic and Johannine traditions independently reproducing with variations the same deeds or sayings. In between the extremes a median position maintains that Mark and John shared common pre-Gospel traditions, oral or written; and that although the fourth evangelist had not seen the final form of Luke, he was familiar with traditions incorporated later into Luke. Some who make a distinction in John between an evangelist and a final redactor would posit that only the latter knew one or more of the Synoptic Gospels. Cf. R.E. BROWN, *An Introduction*, 365.

[6] The Fourth Gospel has been dated as early as 40 A.D. and as late as 110 A.D. The latest possible date has been fixed by the discovery in Egypt of the Rylands Papyrus 457, an Egyptian codex fragment of John 18:31-33, 37-38. This manuscript is usually dated between 125 A.D. and 150 A.D. Other textual finds make it undeniable that the Gospel circulated in Egypt in numerous copies in the middle and last half of the second century. Hence, no one is inclined to propose a date later than 100-110 A.D. The earliest date for the Gospel hinges upon the question of whether or not it presupposes the destruction of the temple in 70 A.D. Most scholars agree that it does, although there have been persistent attempts to argue otherwise. The reasons for positing a post 70 A.D. date include the view of the Temple implicit in John 2:13-22. Most scholars agree that the passage attempts to present Jesus as the replacement of the Temple that has been destroyed. Cf. R.E. BROWN, *Gospel According to John*. I, lxxx-lxxxiii; R. KYSAR,

Gospel was redacted by another hand after the main writer composed it may place the body of the Gospel in the 90s and the additions of the redactor around 100-110 A.D.[7] Given all the considerations, the Gospel is usually assigned a date of 90-95 A.D., which agrees with previous decades of scholarship by concluding that John is the last of the four Gospels to be written.

The authorship of the Gospel is no less easy to determine. As with the other Gospels, it is doubted by most scholars that this Gospel was written by an eyewitness of the public ministry of Jesus.[8] Intertwined with the question of authorship is the mysterious disciple «whom Jesus loved». This anonymous beloved disciple raises two related questions: Who was he and is it possible that this is the author's way of referring to himself? The beloved disciple appears five times in the narrative of the Gospel (13:23; 19:26-27; 20:1-8; 21:7; 21:20-24) and is sometimes linked with two references to «another disciple» who remains nameless (18:15-16; 19:35).[9]

While the evidence is not sufficient to identify the beloved disciple with any of the popular candidates, there is nothing preventing him from being

---

«Gospel of John», 918; P. PERKINS, «Gospel According to John», 942-946.

[7] Of importance to the dating of the Gospel is the speculation as to what date is suggested by the setting proposed for the document. We take it for granted that the Fourth Gospel was written to address a mixed community of Christian believers whose particular needs, attitudes, and situation will to some extent be reflected and addressed within the boundaries of the text. As noted in the previous chapter, because the Jesus material was shaped by each evangelist for an intended audience, indirectly the Gospels may give us theological and sociological information about the Christians who preserved, shaped, and / or received the memories of him. Cf. R.E. BROWN, *Gospel According to John*, ciii-civ; ID., *Community of the Beloved Disciple*, 13-24, also the chart on pp. 166-67. Brown's views are similar to those of J.L. MARTYN, *Gospel of John*; ID., *History and Theology*.

[8] An important exception is Martin Hengel who would identify the author as John the Elder (not John the apostle), who was head of a school in Asia Minor where he had moved from Palestine. As a young man he had known Jesus, and then he modeled himself after the beloved disciple. Cf. M. HENGEL, *The Johannine Question*.

[9] Two interesting facts are worthy of note. First, the beloved disciple does not appear in the narrative until 13:23. Second, Peter appears in all but one (19:26) of the narratives in which the beloved disciple is mentioned. The first fact has been used to argue against the effort to identify the beloved disciple with John, son of Zebedee. The second fact has been employed to argue that some kind of contrast between the beloved disciple and Peter is suggested by the author.

a real person who passed on the Jesus tradition to his community, interpreting it for them, so that the Fourth Gospel may be in some large measure, as John 21:24 suggests, his testimony.[10] Furthermore, it might be that this figure is intended to represent the Johannine community's founder, well known to the evangelist's first readers. It does seem likely that the beloved disciple is appealed to as the source of the tradition upon which the community and the Gospel were founded.[11]

Was the beloved disciple the fourth evangelist? That would be the impression given by John 21:24: «This is the disciple who is bearing witness to these things, and who has written these things; and we know that his testimony is true». Could this, however, be a simplification by the redactor who added John 21, paraphrasing the more accurate 19:35: «He who saw it has borne witness, his testimony is true, and he knows that he tells the truth, that you also may believe»? The passage in John 19 could mean that the beloved disciple was not the evangelist but a witness to Jesus and thus the *source* of the tradition that has gone into the Fourth Gospel. The evangelist who wrote that passage could have been a follower or disciple of the beloved disciple (whom he describes in the third person) and not himself an eyewitness of the ministry.[12] The beloved disciple may

---

[10] There have been, generally, three approaches to the question of the identity of the beloved disciple. First, some propose a New Testament figure. In addition to the traditional candidate (John, son of Zebedee), other proposals have included Lazarus, John Mark, and Thomas. Although there may be a passage to support each identification, if the long tradition behind John is rejected, one is reduced to guessing. Second, some scholars have evaluated the beloved disciple as a pure symbol, created to model the perfect disciple. That he is never given a name and that he appears alongside Peter in scenes known to us from the Synoptic Gospels where no such figure is mentioned have been invoked as a proof of non-historicity. However, another unnamed Johannine figure who has a symbolic role and appears when she is absent in the Synoptics, namely, the mother of Jesus (2:3-12; 19:25-27), was certainly a historical figure. Third, still other scholars theorize that the beloved disciple was a minor figure during the ministry of Jesus, too unimportant to be remembered in the more official tradition of the Synoptics. But since this figure became important in Johannine community history (perhaps the founder of the community), he became the ideal in its Gospel picture, capable of being contrasted with Peter as closer to Jesus. Cf. R.E. BROWN, *An Introduction*, 369.

[11] For a summary of the debate cf. R.E. BROWN, *Gospel According to John*. I, xciii-xcviii.

[12] Indeed, if we posit both a different writer for the Johannine epistles and a redactor for the Gospel, we could agree with those who postulate a «Johannine school», ie., various disciples employing both a style and material that were traditional in this

have lived through the historical development of the community, and so there may have been a certain symbiosis between him and the Gospel that was committed to writing a tradition that not only had its roots in his experience of Jesus but also embodied decades of his ongoing reflection on that experience. The evangelist, who wove the theologically reflected tradition into a work of unique literary skill, would presumably have been a disciple of the beloved disciple, about whom he writes in the third person. The redactor, if there was one, may have been another disciple.[13]

2. The Theology of John

The theological nature of the Fourth Gospel has long been recognised. It is clear that the fourth evangelist was concerned to nurture the readers through the explication of a number of theological themes important to the Johannine community.[14] It is clear, too, that the evangelist possessed a certain theological acumen. Hence, the analysis of the Gospel in terms of its theological themes has persistently been one of the major tasks of theologians and biblical scholars. While the language is generally uncomplicated and the vocabulary and syntax are simple, the Gospel of John presents one of the most profound and moving portraits of Jesus of Nazareth and his message found in the New Testament.

2.1 *Johannine Christology: Shaping the Fundamental Structures*

A distinctive feature of John's Gospel is the way in which, more than any other New Testament writing, John has served as a bridge between the beginnings of Christianity in Jesus and the orthodox faith which achieved definition at the various Ecumenical Councils and which has provided the dogmatic basis of Christianity ever since. John's Gospel is written about Jesus, about his ministry of word and sign in Judea and Galilee, and its traditions are certainly rooted, in greater or less degree, in the earliest

---

community, traditional because in whole or in part they were shaped by the beloved disciple. The thesis would explain how some factors in the Fourth Gospel plausibly reflect origin in the ministry of Jesus, while other factors seem distant from that ministry. Cf. R.A. CULPEPPER, *The Johannine School*.

[13] For various theories thereon, cf. R.E. BROWN, *Gospel according to John*. I, xxiv-xl; R. FORTNA, *Gospel of Signs*; ID., *The Fourth Gospel*; R.A. CULPEPPER, *The Johannine School*.

[14] Cf. the review of the debate in M. DE JONGE, *L'Évangile de Jean*; R. KYSAR, *The Fourth Evangelist*.

memories of that ministry. At the same time, John's Gospel brought together key categories which dominated the subsequent developing debates on Christology (Logos and Son of God), and the Gospel has provided a portrayal of Jesus which has served as a chief inspiration and textbook for centuries of Christ-centred apologetic and piety.

The christological claim is at the heart of the Fourth Gospel. Indeed, a primary objective of the Fourth Evangelist is christological – so to present Jesus in his Gospel that his readers may believe the Christian claim expressed in the formulation: Jesus is the Christ, the Son of God. Furthermore, it is clear that most of the Johannine *distinctives* come to clearest expression in John's Christology. Certainly we can find some Synoptic-like traditions in the Johannine discourses; but it is the thorough-going portrayal of the Son sent from the Father, conscious of his pre-existence, the descending - ascending Son of Man, making the profoundest claims in his «I am» assertions, which both dominates John's Christology and distances it most strikingly from the Synoptic tradition.

Fundamental to the whole of the Gospel is the origin of Jesus: the fact that the pre-existent Logos (1:1-2) has become flesh and dwelt among us in the person of Jesus (1:14-18). Throughout the Gospel the question of *origin* is raised: at Cana (2:9), with the Samaritan woman (4:11), by the crowd at the feast of Tabernacles (7:27; 8:14), by «the Jews» (9:29) and even by Pilate (19:9). If the origin of Jesus is turned toward God as the Logos (1:1), then his presence in history will be the result of his being the «sent one» of the Father. The fourth evangelist believes that no one has ever seen God, but that there is one person who is able to reveal him to us: the one who comes from the Father (1:18; 6:46).

Central to the revealing task of Jesus is his being the *Son of God*.[15] The Son of God sayings almost always express a relationship between God and Jesus (1:18, 34; 3:16; 5:19-26; 6:40; 14:13). This title is not only about Jesus, but also about God and God's relationship to the world and those

---

[15] The fourth evangelist is not the first to use the «Son of God» term to speak of Jesus. It can be found in one of the earliest christological confessions in the New Testament (Rom 1:3-4) and in the earliest of the Gospels (Mk 1:1,11; 9:7; 15:39). There is every indication that the concept, so important to the New Testament as a whole, had its origins in the relationship which existed between Jesus of Nazareth and the God of Israel, a relationship which Jesus summed up by his use of the term *Abba*. Yet the Johannine use of «the Son» is bolder than its earlier uses to interpret the person and significance of Jesus (3:16,17,18; 5:18 [twice] 20, 21, 22, 23 [twice] 25, 26; 6:40; 8:35-36; 10:36; 11:4; 14:13; 17:1 [twice]). Cf. *NJBC*, 1422.

who dwell in the world but are not of the world (3:16-17; 17:14-16).[16] The close link that exists between the glorification of the Son and the event of the cross is expressed in 11:4, 40 and 14:13. The glory spoken of in 11:4 is the glory that the Son will have when he returns to the presence of his Father (14:13; 17:1, 5), but this glory will be his as a result of the cross. Although the glory of God shines through all the words and deeds of Jesus, it is on the cross where he reveals love (13:1; 15:13). There is the place where God's saving revelation in his Son shines forth. Jesus claims that he is the Son of God and that because of his Sonship he has authority to reveal what he has seen with his Father and thus bring eternal life to those who believe in him. The pre-existent Word of God has become flesh, dwelling among us as God's Son, revealing the truth and making visible the «glory as of the only Son of the Father» (1:14).[17]

The fourth evangelist has his own view of the cross, not as a moment of humiliation (see Phil 2:5-11; Mk 15:33-39) but as Jesus' consummation of his life's journey and purpose, the place where he returns to the glory that was his and where he glorifies his Father by bringing to perfection the task given to him (4:34; 11:4; 13:31-32; 17:4; 19:30). The title *Son of Man* is consistently used in association with the «lifting up» on the cross, reflecting the Marcan use of this title in the passion predictions (Mk 8:31; 9:31; 10:33-34). However, while the Synoptic tradition used the title to speak of Jesus as a human figure who has a unique authority and who will eventually return as universal judge (Mk 2:10, 27-28;.8:38; 13:26; 14:21, 40; Mt 13:37, 16:13, 28; Lk 6:22, 9:58; 11:30; 21:36), in the Fourth Gospel the presence of Jesus reveals God among humanity and brings judgment (3:16-21, 31-36; 5:24-25; 12:44-50). Thus it has been said that John fuses the two Synoptic uses, drawing the judgment theme back into

---

[16] Schnackenburg affirms that the Johannine Son Christology is also the doctrine of salvation for believers and not only a doctrine about Jesus Christ in isolation but taking in the human race, with Jesus as God's emissary revealing and mediating salvation. This is made clear in 3:16-21,34-36, passages that argue fundamental Johannine themes. Jesus' mission is explained in terms of God's having so loved the world that he sent his only Son (v. 16) in order that the world may have the opportunity to accept or refuse the light and truth (vv. 19-21, 35-36) found in him (vv. 18,36). Salvation or condemnation is already made possible through the acceptance or refusal of that life available in the revelation of God in the Son (vv. 17, 36; also 5:24-25). Cf. R. SCHNACKENBURG, *Gospel according to John*. II, 185.

[17] Cf. C.H. DODD, *Interpretation of the Fourth Gospel*, 250-262; F.J. MOLONEY, «Johannine Son of God», 71-86; E. SCHILLEBEECKX, *Christ*, 427-432.

the historical encounter with Jesus (5:27; 9:35-39; 12:24-36). It appears that John uses a traditional term to present the earthly ministry of Jesus, and especially the «lifting up» on the cross, as the place where the man Jesus, the Son of Man, reveals God and thus brings life and judgment. However, in keeping with the rest of Johannine Christology, such an understanding of Jesus, the Son of Man, is possible only because he comes from the Father and will return to the Father (3:13; 6:62).[18]

In presenting Jesus as the Son of God who is also the Son of Man, the fourth evangelist wants to persuade his readers of *a heavenly origin* for Jesus the Messiah which goes back to the beginning of time, and of *a closeness of continuity* between Father and Son which is more than simply identity of will or function. From where does the fourth evangelist derive these emphases? A decisive clue is given in the prologue which provides a category in terms of which we can understand the Christology as a whole: that of Wisdom or Logos.[19]

3. Wisdom Influences on the Gospel of John

It has long been recognized that the Gospel of John contains elements of a Wisdom Christology, even though no word of the *sophia / sophos* family appears in the text.[20] Some have seen the Wisdom motifs as confined to the *logos* concept in the prologue.[21] However, if the prologue is to be seen as an integral part of the Gospel and not merely as a kind of preface attached to the beginning, then we would expect the motifs contained in it to be worked out, to some extent at least, within the Gospel as a whole. This has indeed been shown to be the case.[22]

---

[18] Cf. J. COPPENS, «Le Fils de l'homme», 28-81; S.S. SMALLEY, «Johannine Son of Man Sayings», 278-301.

[19] We have noted that, in the literature of pre-Christian Judaism, Wisdom, Word, and Spirit were near alternatives as ways of describing the active, immanent power of God. Cf. J.D.G. DUNN, *Christology in the Making*, 196.

[20] For an examination of Wisdom influences on the Gospel of John cf. R.E. BROWN, *Gospel according to John*, I-II, passim.; J.D.G. DUNN, *Christology in the Making*, 163-212; ID., «Let John be John», 309-339; M. SCOTT, *Sophia and the Johannine Jesus*; M.E. WILLETT, *Wisdom Christology* {quoted by M. SCOTT, *Sophia and the Johannine Jesus*, 28, n. 7}.

[21] Cf. R. BULTMANN, *Gospel of John*, 22.

[22] Cf. R.E. BROWN, *Gospel according to John*, I, lix-lxiv, cxxii-cxxv, 521-523; J.D.G. DUNN, «Let John be John», 330-332. Why no *explicit* connection is made by the fourth evangelist between Jesus and Wisdom will be addressed later in the

In any attempt to trace the influence of the Wisdom motif on the Gospel of John as a whole, we must immediately observe that *nowhere* in the Gospel is Jesus referred to as either Logos or Sophia outside of the prologue.[23] However, we will argue that, in drawing his portrait of Jesus, the evangelist has capitalized on an identification of Jesus with personified divine Wisdom as described in the Old Testament.[24] Just as the New Testament writers found in Jesus the fulfilment of the words of the prophets, so the fourth evangelist saw in Jesus the culmination of a tradition that runs through the Wisdom literature of the Old Testament.

3.1 *Logos and Sophia in John 1:1-18*

Without question John 1:1-18 has had more impact on Christian thinking about the Son of God as pre-existent and a divine being than any other New Testament passage. Here is where the early church derived its Logos Christology and its basic understanding of the Incarnation.[25] It is not necessary to repeat what we have already on the Wisdom character of the Logos hymn, but it may prove useful to add the voice of C.H. Dodd to reaffirm the main point:

> «The evangelist does not, like some Gnostics, set out to communicate an account of the origin of the universe, as a way to that knowledge of God which is eternal life, and then fit Christ into the scheme. He says, in effect, 'let us assume that the cosmos exhibits a divine meaning which constitutes its reality. I will tell you what that meaning is: it was embedded in the life of Jesus, which I will now describe [...]' The Prologue is an account of the life of Jesus under the form of a description of the eternal Logos in its relations with the world and with man, and the rest of the gospel an account of the Logos under the form of the record of the life of Jesus; and the proposition *ho logos sarx egeneto* binds the two together [...]»[26]

In our study of the prologue we have shown that much of what is contained therein would not have been strange to anyone familiar with the

---

[23] M. Scott argues that this need not be a problem but may in the end be a supportive argument for it. Having clarified who the Logos/Sophia actually is in the prologue, the author then works out the theme through the Gospel, but does so by allowing Sophia to present herself in the claims and person of Jesus. Cf. M. SCOTT, *Sophia and the Johannine Jesus*, 115-116.

[24] Obviously this is not the only factor that has contributed to the portrait, but here we wish to draw attention to the strength and number of the Wisdom motifs.

[25] Cf. C.H. DODD, *Interpretation of the Fourth Gospel*, 292-296.

[26] Cf. C.H. DODD, *Interpretation of the Fourth Gospel*, 285.

Wisdom tradition.[27] It is only the central and crucial affirmation that «the Word became flesh» which has no real parallel in pre-Christian Jewish thought. Yet, it is the intermingling of Wisdom themes which prepares the way for this climactic utterance. The author's central insight is summed up here, namely, the identification of Jesus Christ, revered and worshipped by Christians, with the figure of Wisdom. This stems from the realisation, expressed throughout the prologue, that the history of Wisdom has been re-enacted by Christ: the divine plan seen at work throughout the history of Israel has actually taken flesh in him.

We have already noted evidence of a developing parallelism between the concepts of *Logos* and *Sophia* in the Book of Wisdom.[28] Having introduced Wisdom as the intervener on behalf of the godly in Israel's history in Wisdom 10–11, we find that in Wisdom 18:15 it is rather the Logos who comes to the rescue of God's righteous children in their imprisonment: «Thy all-powerful Word leaped from heaven, from the royal throne, into the midst of the land [...]». What is important to note here is that the two concepts were beginning to be seen as potentially interchangeable ways of speaking about the same thing. The Book of Wisdom represents a stage on the road towards a mutual identity, a process which we saw Philo developed much further.[29]

Since, as we have seen, the writings of Philo have long been recognised as a peculiar blend of Greek philosophical tradition and the thought world of Judaism, it is hardly surprising that Philo uses the terms *Logos* and *Sophia* with a large degree of interchangeability. Both are virtually synonymous in meaning and function, while at the same time retaining some individual characteristics.

Hence, we can say that, from the opening statement in John's Gospel of the presence of the Logos at creation, through the themes of proximity to God, life and light, grace and truth, to the announcement of the refusal of some to believe, we can trace the Logos' steps in the traditional material related to Wisdom. The term *Logos* offered itself as an appropriate vehicle for expressing the fact that Jesus is the embodiment of Wisdom. The hymn to Wisdom is thus transformed into a hymn to the incarnate Logos, a term otherwise untried as a christological category in the writings of the church.

The discussion of the Wisdom influences on the Fourth Gospel normally begins, but quite often ends, with the discussion of the prologue

---

[27] Cf. pages 79-83.

[28] Cf. pages 81-83.

[29] Cf. pages 36-40.

in John 1. This is a mistake because most scholars agree that the prologue to the Gospel of John in some way anticipates the Gospel as a whole. M.D. Hooker has argued that the whole of John's Gospel must be read in the light of the prologue.[30] She maintains that the «messianic secret» in the Fourth Gospel, if we should call it that, is that Jesus is the Logos, the one who has come from above and returns to the Father. However, this is hidden to all but the reader who starts with John 1, just as in Mark 1 the story is incomprehensible without knowing the content of the very first verse. Thus the prologue is used as a christological basis for the rest of the Fourth Gospel.[31] There is a sense in which the whole of the Fourth Gospel is dependent on the prologue, with its Wisdom motifs, to set the stage for the story about the one who comes from and returns to the Father.

3.2 The «I am» sayings

One of the most unique christological presentations of the Fourth Gospel is found in the discourses in which Jesus introduces himself with the distinctive affirmation, *I am*. The background to this distinctive introduction has long been a matter of divergent scholarly opinion. Some have seen its origins in Rabbinic material,[32] others in a wider Semitic setting,[33] and yet others in the Gnostic Mandaean tradition.[34] More recently, however, the Old Testament background has been reaffirmed as the most likely point of origin for the Johannine usage, not least in the use of *I am* as a form of the Divine name in both Deutero-Isaiah and later Jewish writings.[35] R.E. Brown has also observed that here, as in other areas of the Gospel, the author of John may well have been influenced by the Wisdom tradition, in particular that of Proverbs 8 and Sirach 24.[36] In the seven key *I am* sayings Jesus is characterized variously as living bread, light of the world, the gate, model shepherd, the way, the truth and the life, and the authentic vine. All of these are said at one point or another to come from or characterize personified Wisdom. Thus:

---

[30] Cf. M.D. HOOKER, «The Johannine Prologue», 40-58.

[31] In support of Hooker's position, cf. P.S. MINEAR, «We don't know where», 125-139.

[32] Cf. A. SCHLATTER, *Der Evangelist Johannes*.

[33] Cf. E. NORDEN, *Agnostos Theos*.

[34] Cf. R. BULTMANN, *Gospel of John*; E. Schweizer, *Ego Eimi*.

[35] Cf. R.E. BROWN, *Gospel according to John*, I-II, under the individual *I am* sayings, and particularly I, 535-538; C.H.DODD, *Interpretation of the Fourth Gospel*, 93-96.

[36] Cf. R.E. BROWN, *Gospel according to John*. I, 537-538.

(i) «I am the Bread of Life» (Jn 6:35, 51)
   «Come eat of my bread and drink of the wine I have mixed» (Prov 9:5)

(ii) «I am the Light of the World» (Jn 8:12)
   «For she is a reflection of eternal light..» (Wis 7:26)

(iii) «I am the door of the sheep» (Jn 10:7, 9)
   «This is the gate of the Lord, the righteous shall enter through it»
(Ps 118:20)

(iv) «I am the Good Shepherd» (Jn 10:11, 14)
   «The Lord is my Shepherd [...]» (Ps 23)

(v) «I am the resurrection and the life» (Jn 11:25)
   «For he who finds me finds life [...]» (Prov 8:35)

(vi) «I am the Way, the Truth and the Life» (Jn 14:6)
   «[...] Happy are those who keep my ways» (Prov 8:32)
   «For my mouth will utter truth [...]» (Prov 8:7)

(vii) «I am the True Vine» (Jn 15:1, 5)
   «Like the vine I caused loveliness to bud, [...]» (Sir 24:17)

A brief examination of each individual saying will help to clarify this point further.

3.2.1 *I am the Bread of Life (Jn 6:35)*

We have already noted that the first-person style of address by Wisdom in Proverbs 8 and Sirach 24 offers an interesting parallel to the *I am* statements in the Gospel of John. However, the parallels are not confined to these two chapters. While the *I am* formula is not used, it is nevertheless evident that Wisdom makes claims for herself using the first person in a manner similar to that employed by Jesus in the Fourth Gospel. The first declarative statement using the *I am* formula in John is that in which Jesus describes himself as the «Bread of Life» (Jn 6:35, 48, 51). The specific connection here becomes more obvious when we observe that Wisdom lays claim to the idea of being the provider of sustenance, that is, of bread and wine: «Come, eat of my bread and drink of the wine I have mixed» (Prov 9:5).

The juxtaposition of bread and wine here may also be significant in respect of the eucharistic overtones in John 6:35-39 and, in particular, of the assertion in 6:53-56 regarding the eating and drinking of the Son of

Man's flesh and blood. Just as Wisdom can call upon people to eat and drink of her, so too the Johannine Jesus presents himself as the true and living bread for the nourishment of the believer. A direct parallel to this is found in the claims which Sirach makes for Wisdom: «Those who eat me will hunger for more, and those who drink me will thirst for more» (Sir 24:21).

This particular verse may, at first sight, appear to contradict Jesus' claim in John 6:35 («[...] he who comes to me shall not hunger, and he who believes in me shall never thirst»). However, R.E. Brown has highlighted that the meaning of the Sirach text is that those who taste of Wisdom «will never have too much Wisdom and will always desire more.»[37] This is surely also the import of Jesus' words. Although John 6:35 only mentions bread specifically, the latter half of the verse («[...] he who believes in me shall never thirst») implies that Jesus supplies nourishment not only through food, but also through drink. Indeed, this connection becomes explicit in the speech which Jesus makes during the Feast of Tabernacles: «[...] If anyone thirsts, let him come to me and drink [...] out of his heart shall flow rivers of living water» (Jn 7:37-38).

Since there is no Old Testament text which is directly quoted here, a number of suggestions have been made as to its origin:[38]

«Come eat of my bread and drink of the wine I have mixed» (Prov 9:5)

«She will feed him with the bread of understanding, and give him the water of wisdom to drink» (Sir 15:3)

«Those who eat me will hunger for more, and those who drink me will thirst for more» (Sir 24:21)
«The essentials for life are water and bread [...]» (Sir 29:21)

«When they thirsted they called upon thee, and water was given them out of flinty rock, and slaking of thirst from hard stone.» (Wis 11:4)

Hence, we can see the substantive connections between the claim of the Johannine Jesus to be the «Bread of Life» (Jn 6:35, 48, 51) and the claims of a similar nature made by Wisdom.

---

[37] Cf. R.E. BROWN, *Gospel according to John*, I, 269.

[38] Cf. R.E. BROWN, *Gospel according to John*, I, 327-328; B. LINDARS, *Gospel of John*, 298.

3.2.2 *I am the Light of the World (Jn 8:12)*

Allowing for the story of Jesus and the woman caught in adultery as a later insertion into the Gospel (Jn 8:2-11), Jesus' statement in John 8:12 is seen to continue his speech at the Feast of Tabernacles (Jn 7:14-39), an appropriate setting for taking up the theme of light.[39] The story of the Exodus wanderings provided the imagery of a flaming pillar that guided the Israelites through the darkness of the night (Ex 13:21). That this image could have entered into the background of Jesus' claim to be the light of the world is suggested when we remember that Wisdom 18:3-4 witnesses to the tradition that identified this pillar with «the imperishable light of the law»(v. 4). Just as with the metaphor of bread, the Wisdom literature offers some valuable background for Jesus' use of light as a symbol of his revelation.

Our starting point is Proverbs where Wisdom makes her claim to being the first of God's creations (Prov 8:22). When we look back to the Genesis creation account, we find that God's first command is: «Let there be light» (Gen 1:3). We would therefore be justified in saying that Wisdom's claim in Proverbs 8:22, «The Lord created me at the beginning of his work, the first of his acts of old», already contains within it the potential for understanding Wisdom as light. This affinity becomes explicit in Ecclesiastes: «Then I saw that Wisdom excels folly as light excels darkness» (Eccles 2:13). This is further developed in the Book of Wisdom, where Wisdom is equated with everlasting light. When compared with the light of day she is seen to be greater: «For she is a reflection of eternal light» (Wis 7:26), for neither darkness nor evil can prevail against her: «Compared with the light she is found to be superior, for it is succeeded by the night, but against Wisdom evil does not prevail» (Wis 7:29-30). R.E. Brown reminds us of the association between law and the light of life in the Qumran literature,[40] which is further evidence of the connection between the concepts of Law-Wisdom-Light at the time of the New Testament writings.

There is, then, sufficient evidence within the Wisdom tradition to underline the connection between Wisdom and light. The Johannine

---

[39] For the theme of light in the feast of Tabernacles, cf. C.K. BARRETT, *Gospel according to John*, 335; R.E. BROWN, *Gospel according to John,* I, 344-345; B. LINDARS, *Gospel of John,* 315.

[40] Cf. R.E. BROWN, *Gospel according to John,* I, 344.

assertion is once again that Jesus is the true light (1:9),[41] and this is graphically illustrated in the healing of the blind man in John 9:1-41. If Wisdom was true light, that function is now accorded to Jesus, the embodiment of the same tradition.

3.2.3 *I am the door of the Sheep (Jn 10:7)*
3.2.4 *I am the Good Shepherd (Jn 10:11, 14)*

The two statements regarding the «door of the Sheep» and the «Good Shepherd» are virtually inseparable from each other, not only because they appear in such close proximity, but also because they are both explanatory comments on the parable about entering the sheepfold which opens the chapter (Jn 10:1-5). This parable deals with false shepherds and the relationship of the true shepherd to the sheep.[42] The central point of the whole section is a christological one: «Jesus draws to himself every epithet which the picture of sheep and shepherd suggests.»[43]

Because the patriarchal civilization, and that of Israel until well after the conquest of Palestine, was largely pastoral, the imagery of shepherding is frequent in the Bible. Even when agriculture became dominant in Israel, there remained a nostalgia for the pastoral. Yahweh might be pictured as the tender of the vine and the planter of the seed, but He remained more familarly the shepherd of the flock. The Patriarchs, Moses, and David were all shepherds, and so *shepherd* became a figurative term for the rulers of God's people, a usage common throughout the ancient Near East. Impious kings were scathingly denounced as wicked shepherds (I Kgs 22:17; Jer 10:21; 23:1-2). In this regard Ezekiel 34 is important background for John 10.

However, it seems difficult to try and posit a direct dependence of John 10 on any statement comparing Wisdom with *door / gate* or *shepherd*. M. Scott recognizes that Proverbs does encourage the wise person to sit at

---

[41] That Jesus can be thought of as *light* is not only a Johannine theme. The Synoptic tradition also makes this association: Mt 5:15; Mk 4:21; Lk 2:32, 8:16-17, 11:33. Cf. C.K. BARRETT, *Gospel according to John*, 337; R.E. BROWN, *Gospel according to John*. I, 344; B. LINDARS, *Gospel of John*, 314-315.

[42] At first sight the two images of these *I am* statements seem incompatible, since one could hardly be the door and the one who leads through it at the same time. The interesting parallel cited by E.F. BISHOP, «The Door of the Sheep», 307-309, where the shepherd lies down across the entrance to the fold in order to be the door, may go some way towards a resolution of the tension between these two images.

[43] Cf. C.K. BARRETT, *Gospel according to John*, 372.

Wisdom's door rather than at that of the harlot: «Happy is the man who listens to me, watching daily at my gates, waiting beside my doors» (Prov 8:34-35).[44] However, this overlap in meaning does not strictly correspond to the idea of Jesus as the door. The background to John's use of *door* is complex,[45] the most notable parallels being the apocalyptic notion of the doors or gates of heaven,[46] and the Synoptic traditions related to entering the Kingdom.[47]

However, an aspect of the shepherd which should be noted in relation to the possible influence of the Wisdom tradition is the intimate relationship the shepherd has with the sheep, to the extent that he knows each one by name (Jn 10:3). Wisdom encourages the wise to have a similar kind of intimate relationship with her which she also shares with God. Wisdom 7:25-26 describes that relationship: «For she is a breath of the power of God, and a pure emanation of the glory of the Almighty, [...] for she is a reflection of eternal light, [...] and an image of his goodness». This in turn is followed by a description of the way in which Wisdom relates to those who come to her, and to whom she comes: «[...] makes them friends of God and prophets» (Wis 7:27). Those who are wise listen to Wisdom's voice as she cries out to them (Prov 8; Sir 24), and she provides and cares for those who know her (Sir 24:19-22).

3.2.5 *I am the Resurrection (Jn 11:25)*

It is hardly a surprise to discover that the word *resurrection* is nowhere used in the Wisdom literature. The almost total lack of any concept of resurrection outside of the Apocalyptic tradition makes a search for linguistic parallels in biblical, or even post-biblical sapiential writings, futile. However, both the Gospel of John and the Book of Wisdom have a theology of eternal life and its negative counterpart. This theology, in the way it is expressed, reflects the use of sapiential language to cope with an idea that very likely does not appear in the Wisdom corpus before the Book of Wisdom - the idea of a positive afterlife.

---

[44] Cf. M. SCOTT, *Sophia and the Johannine Jesus*, 121-123. Scott argues that although there is no evidence of Wisdom being called the *door*, she nevertheless fulfils the same function as the one who now claims that title. She is effectively the door to God and salvation for those who seek and find her.

[45] For a discussion of the background, cf. C.K. BARRETT, *Gospel according to John*, 372-373.

[46] For example, I Enoch 33–36; 72–76; 2 Enoch 13–16; 3 Baruch 3:1; 6:13.

[47] Cf. Matthew 7:13, 14; Luke 13:24, 25.

Thus, for the author of Wisdom, as for the Fourth Evangelist, physical death is not the end of the story. In Wisdom 3:1-2 the author stresses «But the souls of the righteous are in the hand of God, and no torment will ever touch them. In the eyes of the foolish they seemed to have died [...] but they are at peace [...] their hope is full of immortality». This statement about only appearing to have died is similar to the discussion in John 11 when Jesus insists that Lazarus is sleeping. This is because death in the hands of the God of life is not necessarily the end. The author of Wisdom is in fact willing to say that God did not make death (Wis 1:13); it entered the world through the devil's envy and only the devil's followers truly experience it (Wis 2:24). It was God's intention that human beings were created for «incorruption», being made in the «image of his own eternity» (Wis 2:23). By contrast with the wicked «the righteous live forever» (Wis 5:15).

With Jesus in the Fourth Gospel, as with Wisdom in the Wisdom corpus but especially in the Book of Wisdom, our destiny, whether life or death, hangs on whether we accept or reject Jesus / Wisdom. The coming of Wisdom causes a division amongst human beings, some seek and find (Prov 8:17; Sir 6:27; Wis 6:12); others, to their cost, do not seek and regret it when it is too late (Prov 1:28). The same language in the Fourth Gospel describes the effect of Jesus upon human beings (7:34; 8:21; 13:33).[48]

Furthermore, in an attempt to develop the link between Wisdom and the Johannine Jesus, M. Scott argues that we should approach this *I am* saying from the viewpoint of the main thrust of its claim rather than merely searching for linguistic parallels.[49] The point of Jesus' claim to be the resurrection, he argues, is not so much one of having the ability to resuscitate dead bodies, but rather that he is the giver of *life*, in this case specifically *eternal life*. Furthermore, R.E. Brown, agreeing with C.H. Dodd, recognizes «[...] that Jesus is the resurrection in the sense that whoever believes in him, though he may go to the grave, shall come to eternal life».[50]

In dealing with this *I am* saying, Scott concentrates his attention upon the theme of life.[51] The Old Testament consistently describes God as the

---

[48] Cf. R.E. BROWN, *Gospel according to John*, I, cxxiv.

[49] Cf. M. SCOTT, *Sophia and the Johannine Jesus*, 124-125.

[50] Cf. R.E. BROWN, *Gospel According to John*, 434.

[51] Cf. M. SCOTT, *Sophia and the Johannine Jesus*, 124-125.

giver of life and the Lord of life (Deut 32:29). This is evident from the first pages of Genesis, where Yahweh breathes life into creation, in particular animating the body of Adam (Gen 2:7). The theme of Yahweh as the life-giving force is found in every sphere of Israel's religion and life, so it is not surprising to find it celebrated in the life of worship reflected in the Book of Psalms (Ps 15:11; 20:5; 29:4; 35:10). Yahweh both gives life and takes it away (Job 1:21). In the Wisdom literature it is Wisdom who brings life (Prov 3:16; 8:35; 9:11) and who offers blessing, in contrast to the way of folly, which leads to destruction and death (Prov 9:13-18). Later Wisdom writers speak of the gift of immortality being received through the ministrations of Wisdom (Wis 8:13).

The Fourth Gospel speaks of salvation in a way (usually as life or eternal life) and to a degree that is not characteristic of the Synoptics, but it is reminiscent of Wisdom. Here, not only is immortality the reward for seeking and finding or receiving Wisdom, it is also said: «who has learned thy counsel, unless thou hast given Wisdom and sent thy Holy Spirit from on high? And thus the paths of those on earth were set right, and men were taught what pleases thee, and were saved by Wisdom» (Wis 9:17-18). It is striking too that John's theology of the penetration of believers by Christ, so that he will dwell in them (Jn 14:23), seems to echo the idea found in Wisdom 7:24, 27 that salvation amounts to Wisdom penetrating and indwelling human beings.

3.2.6 *I am the Way, and the Truth and the Life (Jn 14:6)*

In an attempt to determine the relationship between the three substantives, R.E. Brown presents two basic options: {1} «Explanations wherein the way is directed toward a goal that is the truth and/or life»; {2} «Explanations wherein the way is the primary predicate and the truth and the life are just explanations of the way».[52] The first choice includes most of the Greek and Latin Fathers as well as modern approaches such as those of Bultmann[53] and Dodd.[54] The way is already in their midst and he is at the same time their goal of truth and life. However, this does not appear to take account of the context in which John 14:6 stands. In John 14:4, Jesus has stated that, despite his departure, the disciples know the way he will take. This provokes the question from Thomas: «How can we know

---

[52] Cf. R.E. BROWN, *Gospel according to John,* II, 620-621.

[53] Cf. R. BULTMANN, *Gospel of John,* 603-612.

[54] Cf. C.H. DODD, *Interpretation of the Fourth Gospel,* 153.

the way?» (Jn 14:5). It is in response to this question that the *I am* statement of John 14:6 comes. When we add to this the evidence of the second half of 14:6, «[...] no one comes to the Father but by me», we see that the emphasis is indeed on *way*. Therefore, Brown[55], Scott[56] and I. de la Potterie,[57] all agree that the second of the above options is the preferable one. Because Jesus is the life and the truth, he is the way to the Father, the way of salvation.

In turning to the Wisdom literature to seek possible parallels, we note that *way* is not used in the same absolute Johannine manner in the Wisdom corpus. However, the need to follow in the way of Wisdom is a constantly recurring theme of both biblical and post-biblical literature:

> «Her ways are ways of pleasantness, and all her paths are peace» (Prov 3:17)
> «And now, my sons, listen to me: happy are those who keep my ways» (Prov 8:32)
> «Come to her with all your soul, and keep her ways with all your might» (Sir 6:26).

Many more similar phrases can be found expressing the understanding that following in the way of Wisdom leads to salvation. Because Wisdom is the giver of life and the true Wisdom over against the false woman in Proverbs, the disciple is encouraged to walk in her ways.

R.E. Brown points to the fact that later medieval scribes at least interpreted the reference to Jesus as the *way* against a Wisdom background:

> There is a very perceptive Christian interpolation into the words of Lady Wisdom in the Latin of Sirach 24:25. Wisdom says «In me is the gift of every way and truth; in me is every hope of life and virtue.» It is almost as if the interpolator has associated the Johannine description of Jesus in 14:6 with the claims of Wisdom.[58]

Despite the absence of the claim «I am the Way» in the mouth of Wisdom, we can nevertheless see that there is sufficient background within the Wisdom tradition on which the author of John could have based this claim.

---

[55] Cf. R.E. BROWN, *Gospel according to John,* 621.

[56] Cf. M. SCOTT, *Sophia and the Johannine Jesus,* 126.

[57] Cf. I. DE LA POTTERIE, «Je suis la Voie», 907-942, 929. He concludes that the phrase means, «I am the way because I am the truth and thus also the life». Cf. also C.K. BARRETT, *The Gospel according to John,* 458.

[58] Cf. R.E. BROWN, *Gospel according to John.* II, 630.

Regarding the theme of truth, we see that, in the Gospel of John, Jesus is the true bread from heaven (6:32); as light of the world, Jesus' witness is true (8:14); he is the good shepherd as distinct from the false hireling (10:11,14); he is the true vine (15:1). Truth is an important concept in John, as we have seen in the prologue's assertion that «[...] the Word became flesh and dwelt among us, full of grace and truth [...]» (Jn 1:14).

Truth can be related to the claims of Wisdom:

«[...] from my lips will come what is right, for my mouth will utter truth [...]» (Prov 8:6-7)

«A truthful witness saves lives, but one who utters lies is a betrayer» (Prov 14:25)
«Buy truth, and do not sell it, buy Wisdom, instruction, and understanding» (Prov 23:23)

«Never speak against the truth [...] strive even to death for the truth» (Sir 4:25, 28)

«I will tell you what Wisdom is [...] and I will not pass by the truth» (Wis 6:22)

In John 14:6 Jesus is seen to be the way on account of his being the truth, which in turn is a consequence of his relationship with God (Jn 8:40, 45-46). Wisdom, who claims to speak the truth, does so on the basis of her closeness to God. She was with God from the beginning (Prov 8:22-31), enjoys intimate communion with God (Prov 8:30-31; Wis 7:22-26), and has come down from heaven (Sir 24:3-12). She can thus stand in the street and appeal to the passers-by to hear the truth from her (Prov 8:6-7), rather than heeding the smooth words of the false woman (Prov 7:10-20; 9:16-18). In the same way, Jesus stands over against the false or inadequate representation of bread, light, life, shepherd, and vine, and is himself *the* truth.[59]

We have previously explored the background to Jesus as life.[60] This Johannine claim is seen as a development of the theme of Wisdom as the giver of life (Prov 3:16; 8:35; 9:11), with later Wisdom writers speaking

---

[59] Cf. R.E. BROWN, *Gospel according to John.* I, 500-501. He notes the contrast between the Old Testament «type» and the New Testament reality, Jesus the Bread, conveyed through the use of *true*.

[60] Cf. pages 168-169.

of the gift of eternal life being received through the ministrations of Wisdom (Wis 8:13).

3.2.7 I am the True Vine (Jn 15:1,5)

This final *I am* saying which we will consider here is steeped in Old Testament tradition. Israel is frequently compared with a vine (Is 5:1-7; Jer 6:9; Ez 15:1-6, 17:5-10, 19:10-14). Like the parallels to the good shepherd, some of the significant material is located in Ezekiel. However, even Ezekiel does not really match the imagery employed in John 15, where the main thrust is the description of the *relationship* between the vine and the branches. Here again the theme of life is prominent, the life which flows from the true vine to the disciples. Recognizing this emphasis, we turn to some passages from Sirach which may be seen to lead us closer to the Johannine concept. The most prominent Wisdom reference to Wisdom as a vine occurs in Sirach 24:17: «Like a vine I caused loveliness to bud, and my blossoms became glorious and abundant fruit».

She provides sustenance and abundance of life through the fruit of her branches and invites those who desire her to come and receive what she has to offer. In the epilogue to the book of Sirach, the author likens the process of Wisdom's influence in his life to the ripening of grapes: «From blossom to ripening grape my heart delighted in her» (51:15).

A fundamental part of the vine imagery in John 15 is the relationship of the vine to the branches. Here again we can find some traces of Sophia's influence. In Sirach 1:20 her branches offer long life, while Sirach 14:26 makes reference to the shelter which they provide. Perhaps most telling of all is the reference in Sirach 24:16 to the spreading out of her branches which are glorious and graceful. In Sirach this fruitful picture of Wisdom's branches stands in stark contrast to the warning against the woman who is unfaithful in her marriage relationship. Here «her branches will not bear fruit» (Sir 23:25). The implication behind this thinking is that those who are faithful will bear fruit, which is very similar to the image of the branches which will bear fruit through their relationship with the true vine in John 15:1-4.[61]

Ultimately, as with the other *I am* statements, we must allow for more than one influence to have been effective in the formation of the Johannine

---

[61] The meaning for the different terms for *branches* in Sirach and the Fourth Gospel (cf. Sir 1:20 and Jn 15:2) is identical.

image of the vine. It may be, as Barrett says, that «[...] fragments of meaning obscurely hinted at by other vines, are gathered up and made explicit» in the Gospel.[62] What is important in all of this is the recognition that many of the *I am* sayings of the Gospel of John do reflect the influence of the Wisdom tradition and in particular the claims of personified Wisdom. In addition to this, the *I am* statements echo the principal themes of the prologue: light, life and truth, all of which we have been able to identify as qualities applied to Jesus.

3.3 *Jesus' Relationship with the Father*

A uniquely Johannine christological emphasis is the presentation of Jesus' relationship with the Father. While the Synoptics portray Jesus as the Son of God from their own post-resurrection perspective, there is little material within those traditions to suggest that Jesus himself had any full consciousness of *divine* Sonship.[63] By contrast, John expounds the Father-Son relationship from the beginning to the end of the Gospel. He pre-existed with the Father (1:1-2, 15; 6:62; 8:58; 17:5), and descended from heaven at his Father's command (3:31-32; 6:33, 38-39, 57; 8:42; 13:3; 16:27-28; 17:8). Those who see or hear Jesus see or hear the Father (5:19, 23; 7:16-17; 8:19, 26; 10:15, 38; 12:45; 14:7, 9; 15:24; 17:21). In addition to the *I am* statements, Jesus, at times, uses the absolute form as a claim of divinity after the manner, for example, of Isaiah 43 (Jn 8:28, 58). The glory of the Father comes through the works and suffering of the Son (1:14; 2:11; 11:40; 12:23, 28; 17:4-5). Each of these themes is, in its own way, a working out of the themes of the prologue.

3.3.1 *Pre-existence of Jesus*

The Gospel of John offers lucid examples of a pre-existence Christology. The opening verses of the prologue (1:1-2) make clear not only that through the Word (who is the Son, Jn 1:18) were all things created but also that the Word existed in God's presence before creation. If in Genesis 1:1 *in the beginning* means in the beginning of creation, in John 1:1 *in the beginning* means before creation. However, the theme of pre-existence

---

[62] Cf. C.K. BARRETT, *The Gospel according to John*, 473.

[63] Cf. J.D.G. DUNN, *Jesus and the Spirit*, 21-40; ID., *Christology in the Making*, 26-29. The suggestion here is, not that the historical Jesus had no sense of unique intimacy with God, merely that this was not a full-blown notion of divinity.

extends beyond the prologue to the body of the Gospel and is a sign both of Jesus' superiority and his authority. That in John's mind the pre-existence of Jesus as God's Son is not merely hymnic figurative language or poetic license is clear from Jn 17:5, where Jesus speaks literally and consciously of having had a glorified existence with the Father before the world began (see 3:13; 5:19; 8:26, 58; 16:28). In John 1:30 John the Baptist bases the superior ranking of Jesus on Jesus' pre-existence. Jesus may come after John in terms of his earthly ministry, but he existed before John came into being. Furthermore, the authority of Jesus' words rests upon his being the incarnation of the Son of God.

In this motif of pre-existence we see one of the strongest connections between prologue and Gospel. The opening statement of the prologue, that the Logos was God, rests on the assertion of pre-existence. Throughout the Gospel as a whole, there is a very definite progression towards the recognition of Jesus Christ for who he truly is, culminating in the climactic confession of Thomas: «My Lord and my God» (Jn 20:28). As the moment of pre-existence is pushed further and further back, we are finally led to the point at which the prologue already began. In the same way that both Wisdom in the Wisdom tradition and the Logos in the Johannine prologue are seen to function as God, or to be God, so too Jesus is finally confessed as such without any hint of compromise for monotheism.[64]

The pre-existence of Wisdom functions in a similar way within the Wisdom tradition. The call to listen to the words of life (Prov 8:32-36) is based on the authority which comes from Wisdom's existence with God from the beginning, before the foundation of the world (Prov 8:22-31). Her gifts are seen to be worthwhile, over against those of the false woman on this account. She was both before creation (Prov 8:23-25) and at God's side (Prov 8:30), thus affording an authority which no one else may claim.

In the Book of Wisdom we find that Wisdom, who is the fulness of God in every possible way (Wis 7:22-26) and who, as the maker of all things, clearly pre-existed them (Wis 9:1-2), is now said to be able both to exercise power in every place (Wis 8:1) and to enable the king to rule (Wis 8:14). In all of this we see a parallel to the relationship between pre-existence and the authority of Jesus in the Fourth Gospel. Consequently, it appears to be the case that the Fourth Gospel's assertion of Jesus' pre-

---

[64] Regarding the possibility of speaking of the Logos as God without infringing monotheism, cf. J.D.G. DUNN, *Christology in the Making*, 241, 243-245, 249.

existence, announced in the prologue and developed in the body of the Gospel, is grounded on the parallel tradition concerning Wisdom, both in terms of agency (creation / life) and function within the Gospel (authority / preeminence).[65]

3.3.2 *Motif of Descent and Ascent*

A second prominent feature of Jesus' relationship with God in the Fourth Gospel is the motif of descent and ascent. Such language is found already in the testimony of the Baptist, especially in John 1:30, where it is said that Jesus in some sense comes before John and is thus above John in rank. Such an idea is not found in the Synoptic parallels at this point. John then elaborates on this in John 3:31 by saying that the one who comes from above is above all.

There is a reference to angels «ascending and descending» on the Son of Man (Jn 1:51). Jesus is the juncture between earth and heaven, the one through whom the two realms are linked. In John 3:2, Nicodemus admits that Jesus is a teacher who comes from God. However, Jesus is not merely a teacher but that which must be taught – the Word that comes from God. The birth that comes through Jesus is a birth from above (Jn 3:3, 7); he is the only one who has both descended from heaven and ascended into it as Son of Man (Jn 3:13).

M. Scott affirms Wisdom 9:10 as the most significant text relating to the descent of Wisdom.[66] That Wisdom was with God in the beginning of creation (Prov 8:22-31) and then subsequently appeared crying aloud in public places (Prov 1:20-33) implies that she must first have descended from the place where she was, even if this is not explicitly stated. Sirach 24:3-17 describes the movement of Wisdom from her heavenly home down to earth, where she established her home in Israel. Here too we find the idea expressed that it is at God's command that Wisdom descends to live with human beings (Sir 24:8), an understanding which comes to fuller expression in the sending motif of Wisdom 9:10: «Send her forth from the holy heavens, and from the throne of thy glory send her, that she may be with me and toil, and that I may learn what is pleasing to thee». As in the

---

[65] On the relationship between pre-existence Christology and Wisdom, cf. J.D.G. DUNN, *Christology in the Making*, 163-250.

[66] Cf. M. SCOTT, *Sophia and the Johannine Jesus*, 135-136.

case of the Johannine Jesus, so also Wisdom is sent out from above to make known what is pleasing to God.[67]

Not only the manner of Wisdom's sending prefigures the coming of the Johannine Jesus, but also the purpose. Both descend in order that God's true will may be known (Sir 24:3-17; Wis 9:10; Jn 4:34; 5:30; 6:38-40; 7:17), which is ultimately going to lead to eternal life and salvation (Prov 3:16; 8:35; Wis 8:13; 9:18; Jn 3:15-16; 5:24; 6:35). In both cases the combination of pre-existence and being sent by God gives authority to the claims and offers each makes.

3.3.3 *Intimacy with the Father*

The Fourth Gospel presents a more intense relationship between Jesus and the Father than do the Synoptics. The whole Gospel is woven through with the theme of the unity of the Father and the Son.[68] This is perhaps most clearly expressed through the idea of their mutual love (3:35; 5:20; 10:17; 14:31; 15:9; 17:24-26), but is also seen in their oneness of knowledge (1:18; 7:29; 8:55; 10:15; 17:25) and unity of will (5:19-30).

The focal point of Jesus' relationship with the Father is the love which passes between them. This is at the kernel of what the Son does and reveals (3:35; 5:20), and it is founded on the Son's eternal pre-existence (17:24-26). The Father's love for the Son can also be expressed as a response to the Son's work (10:17), but this should not be construed as a conditional response; rather, an expression of the bond of love that exists between the Father and the Son, a bond involving the mission and obedient death of the Son.[69] The unity of love is expressed in a unity of will and purpose.

We discover a similar picture when we consider the figure of Wisdom and her relationship with God. She shares an intimacy with God which

---

[67] The ascent of Jesus seems somewhat more difficult to explain with reference to Wisdom. There is no real idea of an ascent of Wisdom in the Wisdom corpus. It has been argued that if we move the focus from the motif of ascent and look instead at the idea of withdrawal, or going away, we find that there are indeed similarities between Jesus and Wisdom. Just as Jesus' going away means judgment on those who reject him, so too Wisdom abandons to their fate those who reject her call and counsel. Compare, for example, John 8:21 with Proverbs 1:28. Cf. M. SCOTT, *Sophia and the Johannine Jesus*, 136-140.

[68] Cf. M.L. APPOLD, *Oneness Motif.*

[69] Cf. C.K. BARRETT, *Gospel according to John*, 377; R.E. BROWN, *Gospel according to John.* I, 399.

corresponds to Jesus' relationship in terms of love, will and knowledge. Just as the Father's love for the Johannine Jesus is rooted in pre-existence, so too we see that the intimacy which existed between Wisdom and God began before the creation of the world (Prov 8:30-31). In later Wisdom tradition this understanding of Proverbs 8:30-31 is confirmed, as God is specifically reported to love Wisdom: «She glorifies her noble birth by living with God, and the Lord of all loves her. For she is an initiate in the knowledge of God, and an associate in his works» (Wis 8:3-4). This text is particularly significant for our comparison with the Johannine Jesus because it not only mentions God's love for Wisdom, but also connects the theme of love with that of knowledge and will. Wisdom is privy to the knowledge that is God's, and she participates in his works. Moreover, Wisdom is frequently placed in parallel with knowledge (Prov 2:6, 10; 3:19, 20), and even offers it as one of her gifts (Prov 8:12). More important still, in terms of the intimate relationship between God and Wisdom, is the knowledge which they have of each other. Wisdom knows God because of her presence at creation (Wis 9:9) and God knows Wisdom's origin and extent (Job 28:23, 27).

Like the Johannine Jesus, Wisdom knows «all things» (Wis 9:11), a point which is underlined in Wisdom 7:17-22; 8:8. Because of this knowledge of the intimate things of God, Wisdom, like Jesus, is in tune with God's will. While the author of John attributes authority over life and judgment to Jesus (5:19-25), the author of Proverbs assigns this task to Wisdom (1:20-33). This theme is dramatically developed in Wisdom 10 where Wisdom becomes the force by which God works out salvation history in Israel.

3.4 *The Teacher's Disciples*

The matter of discipleship in the Fourth Gospel is a complex one. Unlike the Synoptic tradition, John's Gospel does not present us with individually named disciples who follow Jesus and interact with him in the various stages and individual acts of his ministry.

R.E. Brown has noted a number of parallels between the call to discipleship in the Fourth Gospel and that of Wisdom's practice of seeking out her followers.[70] First, we may note the way in which the Johannine Jesus calls disciples: he seeks them out in public places, be it the men of John 1 or the Samaritan woman of John 4. In the course of the final

---

[70] Cf. R.E. BROWN, *Gospel according to John*. I, cxxiii, 79, 106-107.

farewell speech to those who have been chosen, Jesus makes it clear that it is on his initiative that they have been brought to the place where they are: «You did not choose me, but I chose you and appointed you that you should go and bear fruit and that your fruit should abide [...]» (Jn 15:16). So it is with Wisdom who appears in the public places to call out to people to respond and follow her ways (Prov 1:20-21; 8:1-4, Wis 6:16). Moreover, there may be a direct parallel between Wisdom 6:16 and John 1:47; Wisdom seeking out those worthy of her and Jesus seeking out Nathan'ael. Certainly, Wisdom and the Johannine Jesus are open in their search and focused in their call of disciples.

A second aspect of Jesus' call is that it is directed towards the enlightenment of those who respond. As his friends, they are called so that they may know what Jesus is about (Jn 15:15) and they are purified by the working of his word in them (Jn 13:10; 15:3). In the same way, Wisdom selects her followers by testing them and then revealing her secrets to them (Sir 4:11; Wis 7:12). In the end this means that her disciples can also be called her friends (Wis 7:14; 8:18).

The relationship of teacher and disciple goes much deeper than mere superficial friendship. Jesus loves those who love him and this leads to their being loved by the Father (Jn 14:21; 16:27). The promise given to them is that he will come and dwell in them (Jn 14:23). This again reflects what was known of Wisdom's relationship with her followers:

> «Those who serve her will minister to the Holy One; the Lord loves those who love her» (Sir 4:14)

> «He who has my commandments and keeps them, he it is who loves me; and he who loves me will be loved by my Father, and I will love him and manifest myself to him» (Jn 14:21).

The indwelling of Wisdom in those who love her is also a feature of the Book of Wisdom's understanding of the relationship between Wisdom and those who follow her teaching: «because Wisdom will not enter a deceitful soul, nor dwell in a body enslaved to sin» (Wis 1:4).

In these aspects we see a close parallel between the call of Wisdom and the resulting relationship between her and her disciples, and the picture given by the Fourth Evangelist concerning the affiliation of Jesus to his disciples.

3.5 *Logos and not Sophia*

We have noted that nowhere in the Fourth Gospel is the word *Sophia* used. Dunn has shown that, in the literature of pre-Christian Judaism, Wisdom, Word, and Spirit were «near alternatives as ways of describing the active, immanent power of God».[71]

In chapter two we affirmed that, in any consideration of why John chose Word and not Wisdom a number of key points should be kept in mind.[72] In summary, it would have been difficult for John to speak of Wisdom becoming flesh given that, in the Old Testament, Wisdom is personified as Lady Wisdom and Jesus was male. Second, in Sirach 24:23 Wisdom was identified with the Torah. Hence, had John said that Wisdom was made flesh, it could have implied that the Torah was God and had been made flesh. Third, Paul and Luke prepared the way for John's prologue by their use of *Logos* for God's revelation through Christ. Fourth, it has been shown that, both in New Testament times and later, the Johannine Word offered rich christological possibilities.[73] «Word» allows for the possibility of identification and distinction. On the one hand, words proceed from a speaker and hence are something of an extension of the speaker. In a certain sense, words can be identified with the speaker: «the Word was God» (Jn 1:1). On the other hand, there is a distinction between a word and the one who utters it: «the Word was with God» (Jn 1:1). Thus Christ is identified with, yet distinct from, the Father. Fifth, the Father has been uttering the divine Word always: «In the beginning» (Jn 1:1); the Word «was» (not «came to be») God. In this context, Word opens up reflection on the personal, eternal pre-existence of the Logos-Son.

Sixth, words reveal what is in the hearts and minds of the speakers. In the Old Testament, the Word of God designates the revelation of God and the divine will. Consequently, John's Gospel can move from the language of the Word to «[...] God; the only Son, he has made him known» (Jn 1:18). Seventh, John's Logos Christology insured that Christians not only

---

[71] Cf. J.D.G. DUNN, *Christology in the Making*, 196, 219. In pre-Christian Judaism «basically all three phrases (Spirit, Wisdom and Word) are simply variant ways of speaking of the creative, revelatory or redemptive act of God [...] all three expressions are simply alternate ways of speaking about the effective power of God in his active relationship with his world and his inhabitants» (p. 219). Cf. also T.E. FRETHEIM, «Word of God», 961-968; T.H. TOBIN, «Logos», 348-356.

[72] Cf. pages 82-83.

[73] Cf. G. O'COLLINS, *Christology*, 41-44.

recognized the influence of the Logos outside Christianity, but also initiated a dialogue with non-Christian thinkers. For those influenced by a Jewish, Platonic, and Stoic understanding the concept of the Logos allowed them to find a measure of common ground with Christians who, nevertheless, remained distinctive with their claim that «[...] the Word became flesh». Consequently, the notion of Logos offered a more effective bridge to contemporary culture than Wisdom.

4. Summary and Conclusions

We have now considered a wide range of themes which may be seen as reflecting the influence of Wisdom thought and, in particular, the figure of Wisdom on the Fourth Evangelist's understanding of Jesus. We have pointed to a number of areas where Wisdom's influence may be identified.

The *I am* sayings were shown to have roots in Wisdom speculation. These included those without a predicate (Jn 6:20; 18:5) and those where Jesus claims to be the bread of life (Jn 6:51), the light of the world (Jn 8:12; 9:5), the door (Jn 10:7, 9), the good shepherd (Jn 10:11,14), the resurrection and the life (Jn 11:25), the way, the truth and the life (Jn 14:6) and the true vine (Jn 15:1).

In drawing this portrait of Jesus, the evangelist built upon the identification of Jesus with the Old Testament's figure of Wisdom:

(i) As Wisdom speaks in the first person in long discourses (Prov 8:3-36; Sir 24) so Jesus addresses his hearers in long discourses, often beginning with *I am* ; (Jn 6:35-59; 8:12-59; 10:1-18; 14:1–16:28; 17:1-26.

(ii) As Wisdom descends to dwell among us (Prov 8:31; Sir 24:8; Bar 3:37; Wis 9:10) so Jesus descends from heaven to live among us (Jn 1:14; 3:31; 4:38; 16:28);

(iii) As Wisdom roams the streets, crying out and inviting all to hear her message (Prov 1:20-21; 8:1-4; Wis 6:16), so Jesus walks the streets, searching out women and men and crying out his invitation in public places (Jn 1:36-38, 43; 5:14; 7:28, 37; 9:35; 12:44);

(iv) As Wisdom instructs disciples who are her children (Wis 6:17-19; Prov 8:32-33; Sir 4:11; Sir 6:18), so Jesus gives instruction to disciples who are called his children (Jn 13:33);

(v) As Wisdom forms her disciples (Sir 6:20-26) and they come to love her (Prov 8:17; Sir 4:12; Wis 6:17-18), so Jesus forms his disciples (Jn 15:3; 17:17) and calls them his beloved friends (Jn 15:15; 16:27);

(vi) As some accept and others reject Wisdom (Prov 1:24-25; 8:17; Sir 6:27; Wis 6:12), so some receive the message of Jesus while others reject him (Jn 7:34; 8:21; 13:33);

(vii) As Wisdom prepares a feast and calls out, «Come, eat of my bread and drink of the wine I have mixed» (Prov 9:5; Sir 24:19-21), so Jesus cries out, «[...] I am the bread of life; he who comes to me shall not hunger, and he who believes in me shall never thirst» (Jn 6:35; 6:51); and so Jesus tells the Samaritan woman «but whoever drinks of the water that I shall give him will never thirst; the water that I shall give him will become in him a spring of water welling up to eternal life» (Jn 4:14);

(viii) As Wisdom was active in creation and was present when God made the world (Prov 8:27-30; Wis 7:22, 9:9), so in John's prologue we read that through the Word «all things were made through him, and without him was not anything made that was made» (Jn 1:3).

Wisdom language appears in the Synoptic tradition on a number of occasions. However, there is nothing to match the number of echoes of Wisdom we find in the Fourth Gospel. There can be little doubt that this background is a major element in the vocabulary and imagery for the Johannine presentation of Jesus as pre-existent who came into this world from a heavenly realm where He had been with the Father.

The Wisdom literature offers better parallels for the Johannine picture of Jesus than do the later Gnostic, Mandean, or Hermetic passages sometimes suggested. However, John has noticeably modified details of the presentation of Wisdom by introducing a much sharper historical perspective than is found in the Old Testament literature. If Jesus is incarnate Wisdom, this Incarnation has taken place at a particular time and place, once and for all. But even this adaption of the Wisdom concept, by incorporating it into salvation history, is not totally new; for we encounter the same tendency in the very late Wisdom literature. Sirach 24:23 and Baruch 4:1 identify Wisdom with the Law given on Sinai, and Wisdom 10 illustrates the activity of Wisdom in the lives of the patriarchs from Adam to Moses. The Fourth Evangelist sees in Jesus the supreme example of divine Wisdom active in history, and indeed divine Wisdom herself.

While it would be wrong to deny that other influences have been at work in the process of the formation of Johannine Christology, as we know it through the Gospel, the Fourth Evangelist has found in the Wisdom tradition much significant material to help clarify our understanding of Jesus Christ.

The survey of the biblical Wisdom tradition has presented two complementary processes at work in Wisdom Christology. In the first process, the sages of Israel, and Jesus as presented in the Gospels, offer proverbs and Wisdom sayings which articulate the religious dimension of human experience. The process employs a variety of literary forms ranging from the proverbs and poems of Lady Wisdom to the Wisdom sayings and discourses of Jesus. The second process relates the universal presence of Lady Wisdom to specific historical events of revelation thus highlighting a particularization of the tradition. Sirach and Wisdom interpreted the religious heritage of Israel as the work of Lady Wisdom linking her with the Torah (Sirach) and the Spirit of God (Wisdom). The Wisdom Christology of the New Testament, continuing the correlation between Lady Wisdom and salvation history and particularizing that tradition further in a dramatic way, interprets Jesus, the Logos through whom all things were made, as the Wisdom of God. For early Christians the religious dimension implicit in all human experience had now been uniquely and decisively revealed in the person of Jesus, the Wisdom of God.

CHAPTER VI

Wisdom in the Tradition of the Church

We focus here primarily on how the Wisdom theme was received in the early church and influenced the development of Christology in patristic and medieval theology. We consider the writings of several authors who were influenced by the Wisdom theme including Justin Martyr, Origen, Athanasius, Pope Leo I, Augustine, Hildegard of Bingen and Thomas Aquinas. While Wisdom Christology was not a major theme in post-biblical development, the early Christian centuries saw continuing use of Wisdom categories in christological reflection both alone and in combination with thought about the Logos.

1. Wisdom in Patristic Theology

The teaching of the church about Jesus Christ was forged in the centuries immediately following completion of the New Testament. In the second and third centuries, christological reflection struggled to express Jesus' relationship to the Father and counter denials of Jesus' true humanity and genuine divinity. In the fourth and fifth centuries the development of classical christological doctrine reached its climax. The fourth-century controversy centred on Arius' denial of Jesus' divinity and was addressed by the Council of Nicaea, the first Ecumenical Council, in 325. The issues of Nestorianism and monophysitism were weighed by the Councils of Ephesus (431) and Chalcedon (451). Ephesus professed that Christ's two natures (divine and human) are not separated. Chalcedon confessed that, while belonging to one person, the two natures are not merged or confused.[1]

In tracing the influence of the concept of Wisdom on the formation of classical Christology, we have selected authors who have made a contribution to this endeavour and whose works on the subject still constitute valuable points of reference.[2]

1.1 *Clement of Rome*

The anonymous letter from the Church in Rome to the Church of the Corinthians is traditionally ascribed to Clement. Written around 96-98 A.D., it is generally regarded as the most ancient patristic document. The official list of popes gives the succession: Peter, Linus, Cletus (or Anacletus), Clement. We may suppose Clement to have been a bishop; and the traditional dates of Pope Clement, 90-100 A.D., would cohere with the internal evidence of the letter.[3]

The letter was occasioned by news reaching Rome of factions within the Church at Corinth, leading to the deposition of certain blameless presbyters; evidently the Corinthian Christians had not changed much since the time when Paul had been moved by reports of schisms to write I Corinthians. In the person of Clement, the Church in Rome now intervened because of Christian concern over this difficult situation.[4]

J. Wolinski has noted that, in the letter, Clement uses the word *Sophia* eight times, principally in citations from the Old Testament: Jeremiah 9:22-23, Psalm 51: 3-19; Job 4:16-5:5 and Proverbs 1:23-33.[5] Twice the verses cited show that man does not have Wisdom by himself. Two other verses speak of the Wisdom of God. Further on, for the first time in the letter, Wisdom appears personified following the citation of Proverbs 1:23-33.[6]

---

[1] On the early history of Christology cf. A. GRILLMEIER, *Christ in Christian Tradition*, I-II; R.P.C. HANSON, *Search for the Christian Doctrine*; J.N.D. KELLY, *Early Christian Doctrines*; N.P. TANNER, ed., *Decrees of the Councils*, I-II.

[2] Cf. H. JAEGER, «Patristic Conception of Wisdom», 90-106; J. WOLINSKI, «La Sagesse», 424-426.

[3] Cf. H. BETTENSON, *Early Christian Fathers*, 1; T. BOKENKOTTER, *Concise History*, 31.

[4] Cf. H. BETTENSON, *Early Christian Fathers*, 2-3.

[5] Cf. J. WOLINSKI, «La Sagesse», 424-426.

[6] Cf. J.A. KLEIST, ed., *Epistles of St. Clement*, ACW. I, 16.

1.2 *Ignatius of Antioch*

Ignatius, Bishop of Antioch, was condemned to death in his own city and taken to Rome expecting to be thrown to the wild beasts in the amphitheatre. Apart from what we can discover from his letters, we know nothing of him. We infer from the fate which he anticipated that he was not a Roman citizen, for citizens were exempt from such a death. We gather from his letters that he was converted in adult life. The date of his death is unknown; Eusebius gives 108, while John Malalas (c.600) assigns it to 115, on the occasion of Trajan's visit to Antioch. It is not a fact beyond all doubt that Ignatius actually suffered martyrdom; for by the fourth century his bones were assumed to have been buried in his episcopal city; and if this tradition is true he could scarcely have been torn to pieces by the beasts in Rome. On the way to Rome, Ignatius wrote seven letters to the Christians of Ephesus, Magnesia, Tralles, Rome, Philadelphia, Smyrna, and to Polycarp, Bishop of Smyrna.[7]

The chief themes of the letters include warnings against the Docetic heresy, which denied the reality of Christ's human nature, and the exhortation to unity with the emphasis on the authority of the bishop. However, the theme of Wisdom also features in some of these letters. In the *Letter to the Smyrnaeans* Ignatius invokes the Christ who has made them wise while he opposes those who claim superior intelligence because all knowledge of God which comes through Christ has been given by grace (cf. I Cor 1:20).[8]

1.3 *Justin Martyr*

Justin Martyr was the most significant of the second- century apologists for Christianity. He was born of Gentile parents towards the end of the first century in Flavia Neapolis (the ancient Sichem, now called Nablus) in Samaria. He spent a large part of his life in a long and restless search for the truth. He passed through numerous philosophical schools, all of which left him unhappy. Dissatisfied with his tutors, Justin studied under a Platonist and found his doctrines more congenial. Then, in mature life, he was converted to Christianity, apparently at Ephesus, and rejoiced at finding the goal of his long search. Tradition holds that in the reign of

---

[7] For an introduction to the life of Ignatius of Antioch cf. H. BETTENSON, *Early Christian Fathers*, 3-5.

[8] Cf. J. WOLINSKI, «La Sagesse», 425.

Marcus Aurelius, about 165 A.D., Justin met the death which earned him the title afterwards affixed as a kind of surname.[9]

At Rome, the imperial capital where ideas and cultural currents flowed in from every corner of the Mediterranean world, Justin, now a Christian, founded a school of philosophy where he accepted persons wishing to deepen their understanding of Christianity. It was during these years that he wrote his *First Apology* (c.155). For Justin, while the Incarnation of Christ revealed all of truth in a definitive and comprehensive manner, it nevertheless remained true that the greatest minds of ancient paganism, such as Socrates and Plato, had gained some insight, the «seeds» of the Word. Therefore, between ancient philosophy and Christianity, there existed for Justin the relationship of the part to the whole in the substantial continuity of the revelation of the truth by one and the same divine Word.[10]

In the other of his great works, the *Dialogue with Trypho*, Justin discusses in detail the interpretation of the messianic texts of the Old Testament. While the speculations on the Logos are still modest they show clearly the significance which is given to this word and its relationship to Wisdom.[11] Justin is confronted by the fundamental objection of Jewish monotheism, championed by the Rabbi Trypho, which is scandalized by what is said of Christ. Among the «paradoxes» that Trypho cannot admit is the pre-existence of Christ.[12]

Justin's argument remains the principle of many of the Fathers up to Nicaea.[13] He argues that, while it is clear that God manifested himself in the Old Testament, it could not have been a manifestation of the Father. For Justin, it is inconceivable to say the Father would have left heaven to live in a corner of the world.[14] He concludes from this that neither

---

[9] Cf. H. BETTENSON, *Early Christian Fathers*, 9-10; H. CHADWICK, *Early Church*, 74-79.

[10] Cf. H. BETTENSON, *Early Christian Fathers*, 9-10; R.P. GRANT, *Greek Apologists*, 24-28.

[11] Cf. J. WOLINSKI, «La Sagesse», 428-431.

[12] Cf. Justin, *Dialogue*, 38, 1-2; 48, 1; 50, 1; 55, 1; 56; 128, 4, in T.B. FALLS, *Fathers of the Church*. IV, 26, 32, 34, 35, 61. References to the works of Justin are taken from T.B. FALLS, *Fathers of the Church*. I-VI.

[13] Cf. G. AEBY, *Les missions divines*, 120-124.

[14] Cf. JUSTIN, *Dialogue*, 60, 2; 127, 1-5.

Abraham, nor Isaac, nor Jacob have ever seen the Father but only He who, by God's will, is also God – his Son.[15]

In Justin's writings the title of Wisdom (like that of Logos) does not feature too prominently. He remarks once that the title is attributed to the Word by Solomon.[16] However, one passage is of significant importance.[17] Firstly, it outlines the generation of the Word in God, beginning with the image of the human word. But, above all, it attaches this reflection to the theme of the created Wisdom of Proverbs. A key verse which will be quoted down to the end of the fourth century is Proverbs 8:22: «The Lord created me at the beginning of his work, the first of his acts of long ago».

The Apologists used the concepts of Logos and Wisdom in order to find points of contact between their faith and what they had acquired from philosophy. They admit, as do many of their contemporaries influenced by Plato's *Timaeus*, Middle-Platonism, and Stoicism[18], that there is a God-creative intelligence which enables the expression of rational power and efficacious activity.[19] These expressions and other similar ones concern God. But they apply them equally to Christ. The step taken by the apologists is a double one: first, starting from faith, it poses the existence of Christ perceived as a personal being distinct from the Father and then transfers to him all the cosmological potentialities of the God of the Old Testament, all the powers of creation recognized in the Father of the universe by philosophy and in a general way all his intervention in the world. This is justified by citing the Logos of the Johannine prologue and the Wisdom of Proverbs 8:22.

1.4 *Tertullian*

Tertullian was born at Carthage about the middle of the second century, a son of a pagan centurion. He was educated for the law, and was a well-established defender at court when, in 193, he was converted to Christianity by witnessing the courage of Christians facing torture and death for the faith. Tertullian was the first great Latin Christian writer of the West. He

---

[15] Cf. JUSTIN, *Dialogue, 33.*

[16] Cf. JUSTIN, *Dialogue,* 39.

[17] Cf. JUSTIN, *Dialogue, 61,* 1.

[18] Cf. PLATO, *Timaeus,* 36, in D. LEE, *Plato and Critias,* 48-49. Cf. also JUSTIN, *Apology,* 60,1.

[19] Cf. THEOPHILUS OF ANTIOCH, *Three Books.* I, 63.

was the most learned Christian scholar of his day, having read most of the second century Christian writings as well as the works of pagan authors.[20]

The impulsive and impetuous character and the intransigent rigorism which always led Tertullian to assume extreme positions finally led him, around 206-7, to abandon Christianity in order to adhere to Montanism. This charismatic-prophetic movement, which was started by Montanus in Phrygia (a region of Asia Minor), spread rapidly in all the Christian communities of the time and soon reached Carthage. Tertullian displayed this radical turn in his life in many works. Here he expressed judgments and opinions which were often in complete opposition to his position regarding the same questions in the earlier period of his adherence to the orthodox community of Carthage.

In spite of the extreme positions expressed in various treatises of his Montanist period, Tertullian ended up breaking with Montanism and establishing an even more rigorist sect of the «Tertullianists» who survived until the time of Augustine. He left behind many works rich in doctrine and faith, such as the oldest Latin commentary on the «Our Father», a work on baptism and one on penance.[21]

Tertullian laid the foundations for the Church's doctrine of the Trinity, and this represents an important aspect of his doctrinal activity. The concepts and technical terminology which he expounded in his doctrinal treatises exercised a great influence on subsequent authors. The formula which defined the Trinity as «one substance in three persons» represented a decisive move forward. Tertullian developed the questions regarding the Godhead in a polemic against a certain Praxeas, who maintained that in God there was only the «monarchia», unity without the distinction of the single persons. This heresy took the name of «Monarchianism» but was known also as «Modalism» inasmuch as it maintained that the Father, Son and Spirit were in reality only «modes» of the one divinity. As a result, it was also called «Patripassianism» to the extent that it upheld that the Father, identical with the Son, suffered on the cross. Searching for a way to distinguish the Father and the Son, Tertullian evoked the creative Wisdom and Proverbs 8:22 affirming that God is one but adding that God has in him his Logos and Wisdom.[22]

---

[20] Cf. T.D. BARNES, *Tertullian*; H. BETTENSON, *Christian Fathers*, 14-16. Cf. also *ABD*, VI, 389-391.

[21] Cf. H. BETTENSON, *Early Christian Fathers*, 14.

[22] Cf. J. WOLINSKI, «La Sagesse», 439-444.

1.5 *Origen*

One of the earliest and substantial presentations of a Wisdom Christology in the early church was that of Origen (c.185-c.254). The structure of Origen's thought is that divine Wisdom, having had a cosmic role in creation, is now made manifest in Jesus.[23] For Origen, Jesus Christ is the divine Wisdom who is the «emanation» of the glory of God (Wis 7:25). Here Origen expresses the constant theme of all Wisdom Christology: what is revealed in creation is made manifest in Jesus.

Origen's great work of systematic theology, *On First Principles*, was written before he left Alexandria for Caesarea in 231. The first three chapters are on the Persons of the Trinity and, in his second chapter, Origen's christological vision is outlined in Wisdom categories. There he writes of the eternity of the Second Person of the Trinity:

> Wisdom, therefore, must be believed to have been begotten beyond the limits of any beginning that we can speak of or understand. And because in this very subsistence of Wisdom there was implicit every capacity and form of the creation that was to be, both of those things that exist in a primary sense and of those which happen in consequence of them, the whole being fashioned and arranged beforehand by the power of foreknowledge, Wisdom, speaking through Solomon in regard to these very created things that had been as it were outlined and prefigured in herself says that she was created as a «beginning of the ways» of God, which means that she contains within herself both the beginnings and causes and species of the whole creation.[24]

Origen sees every creature as contained in some way in Eternal Wisdom. In Sophia, as the eternal self-expression of God, every possible form of creation is already implicitly prefigured and outlined. Origen argued that the title of Divine Wisdom encapsulated all other titles for Jesus: «Whatever then we have said of the Wisdom of God will also fitly apply to and be understood of him in his other titles as the Son of God, the Life, the Word, the Truth, the Way and the Resurrection».[25] The role of the Son as mediator of meaning is delineated by Origen under two aspects: in relation to the Father and in relation to the world. In relation to the Father,

---

[23] Cf. K. ANATOLIOS, «Christian Story of Meaning in Origen», 55-77; J.A. LYONS, *Cosmic Christ in Origen,* 121.

[24] Cf. ORIGEN, De *Principiis*, in G.W. BUTTERWORTH, *Origen*, 16. References to Origen's *De Principiis* are taken from G.W. Butterworth's translation.

[25] Cf. ORIGEN, *De Principiis, 17.*

the Son is a likeness, an «image». Origen seems to conceive of the Son's imaging of the Father in terms of co-operation, insofar as «[...] there is one and the same movement, so to speak, in all they do».[26] By virtue of this co-operation, the Son's works show forth the likeness of the Father: «[...] in this very fact that the Son does all things just as the Father does, the Father's image is reproduced in the Son».[27] However, the Son's manifestation of the Father is not conceived by Origen in exclusively functional terms. He uses the term *Wisdom* to emphasize what is for him the crucial point that the Son's revelation or manifestation of the Father is constitutive of the Son's hypostatic existence: «[...] the only-begotten Son is God's Wisdom hypostatically existing».[28] This means that the Son's reference to the Father is not at any point extraneous to his own hypostatic existence; rather the Son «reveals the Father by being himself understood».[29] As Wisdom, the revelation of the knowledge of God is an activity that takes place in the Son's own person, as constitutive of his person, in a way that is at least ontologically prior to the Son's activity *ad extra*:

> See, then, whether the Son of God, who is called God's Word and Wisdom, and who alone knows the Father and reveals him to whom he will [...] may not perhaps be said to express the image of God's substance or subsistence for this reason, that he makes God understood and known; that is, when Wisdom outlines first in herself the things which she wishes to reveal to others, by means of which they are to know and understand God, then she herself may be called the express image of God's substance.[30]

Thus, in relation to the Father, the Son is conceived as being revelatory of God's substance in his own hypostasis as well as in his activity. If the Father as «Light» is ultimate meaning and intelligibility, it follows that the Son is a mediator of this meaning by virtue of his own full appropriation of it, an appropriation that constitutes his hypostatic existence as Wisdom.

When we come to consider Wisdom from the point of view of creation, we have only to expressly consider the original and intelligible principles of created realities as among those things that «[...] Wisdom outlines in herself [...] which she wishes to reveal to others, by means of which they

---

[26] Cf. ORIGEN, *De Principiis*, 26.

[27] Cf. ORIGEN, *De Principiis*, 19.

[28] Cf. ORIGEN, *De Principiis*, 15.

[29] Cf. ORIGEN, *De Principiis*, 20.

[30] Cf. ORIGEN, *De Principiis*, 21.

are to know and understand God».[31] Thus, the ultimate meaning and reality of all created things are found in the very substance and hypostatic existence of Wisdom.[32] The principle that Wisdom contains within herself the ultimate meaning and intelligible structure of all created realities has, as its correlative, the affirmation that created realities refer to ultimate reality and ultimate meaning. Thus, if the truth is essentially, comprehensively, and hypostatically contained only in Wisdom, this does not mean that created realities are devoid of truth and intelligibility. Quite the contrary, it is the participation of creation in hypostatic Wisdom that guarantees creation's true existence and intelligibility:

> But if someone is able to comprehend an incorporeal existence comprised of the various ideas which embrace the principles of the universe, an existence which is living and animate, as it were, he will understand the Wisdom of God which precedes all creation, which appropriately says of herself, 'God created me at the beginning of his ways for his works'. It is because of this creation (of Wisdom) that the whole creation has also been able to subsist, since it has a share in the divine Wisdom according to which it has been created, for according to the prophet David, God made «all things in Wisdom».[33]

Because it participates in Wisdom, creation itself is not discontinuous with ultimate truth, but contains a resemblance to it. Created truth, considered exclusively in its immanent aspect, is not truth itself but neither is it false or illusory. It contains a resemblance, and represents a certain analogue to ultimate truth.

Origen thus affirms the ultimate meaningfulness of creation. Undergirding this affirmation is his insistence on the priority of Wisdom in both the divine and human spheres. With regard to the Son, Origen will consider all the different names applied to his person, and emphasize that it is Wisdom which is the primary name; it is as Wisdom that the Son is the beginning.[34] Similarly, God's rule over creation and creation's subjection to God is not so much a matter of divine control through force but of rational governance.

According to Origen, the Son is ultimate meaning (or Wisdom) both as image of the Father and as the archetype of creation. Moreover, Origen

---

[31] Cf. ORIGEN, *De Principiis,* 21.

[32] Cf. ORIGEN, *De Principiis,* 16.

[33] Cf. ORIGEN, *Commentary on John,* Book 1, 244, in R.E. HEINE, *Origen,* 83. References to Origen's *Commentary on John* are taken from Heine's translation.

[34] Cf. ORIGEN, *Commentary on John,* 118.

makes another significant distinction within his conception of the Son as the ultimate meaning of creation. This distinction is made to correspond with the different titles of Wisdom and Word, and the distinction seems to be between the structure of meaning and its communication:

> It is Wisdom which is understood, on the one hand, taken in relation to the structure of the contemplation and thoughts of all things, but it is the Word which is received, taken in relation to the communication of the things which have been contemplated to spiritual beings.[35]

The importance of this distinction is that it reinforces the double character of the Son as both the content of meaning as Wisdom, and the conveyor of meaning as Word. The Son is not only «objectively» truth, meaning, intelligibility, but is also the first agent of the process of accessibility of the mysteries which he himself contains as Wisdom:

> Now just as we have learned in what sense Wisdom is the «beginning of the ways» of God and is said to have been created, in the sense, namely, that she fashions beforehand and contains within herself the species and causes of the entire creation, in the same manner also must Wisdom be understood to be the Word of God. For Wisdom opens to all other beings, that is, to the whole creation, the meaning of the mysteries and secrets which are contained within the Wisdom of God, and so she is called the Word, because she is as it were an interpreter of the mind's secrets.[36]

The Son is thus the principle of rationality both as the objective substance of intelligibility and as the primary agent of the subjective process whereby intelligibility is discovered and appropriated. As Logos, the Son is a light that shines on rational creatures[37] and he is the reason of rational beings.[38] This Logos within rational creatures is the same as the Logos who was in the beginning with God.[39] Thus we can sum up Origen's christological structure of meaning, which relies heavily on the Wisdom motif, by saying that he conceives the Son to be ultimate meaning precisely through the simultaneity of his roles as the image of the Father, the archetype of creation, the objective content of intelligibility and the subjective mediator or interpreter of truth and meaning.

---

[35] Cf. ORIGEN, *Commentary on John.,* 57.

[36] Cf. ORIGEN, *De Principiis,* 16.

[37] Cf. ORIGEN, *Commentary on John,* 53.

[38] Cf. ORIGEN, *Commentary on John,* 20.

[39] Cf. ORIGEN, *Commentary on John,* 111.

1.6 *Athanasius*

Arius (c. 260-336) taught that the Logos, the Son of God, is created by the Father and is therefore not identical, but essentially dissimilar, in nature to the Father. Athanasius (c. 296-373) opposed this point of view by stating that the Son is begotten of the Father, not created, and is therefore identical to Him in nature. In support of his position, Arius pointed to the figure of Wisdom. He identified her with the Logos as had other Church Fathers like Origen before him. But because of the indications that she is created (Prov 8:22; Sir 1:4, 9; 24:9) Arius deduced that the Logos was created.

Athanasius energetically opposed Arius, though not by arguing that Sophia had a separate individuality. He accepted the assumption that she and the Logos were identical, and took on the challenge of proving that Sophia was not created in spite of Scripture's apparent witness to the contrary. Athanasius thought of Jesus as the eternal Word and Son of God, but he also thought of him as divine Wisdom. He pictures the role of divine Wisdom at work in creation as a musician bringing all creatures together into a beautiful harmony:

> Like a musician who has attuned his lyre, and by the artistic blending of low and high and medium tones produces a single melody, so the Wisdom of God, holding the universe as a lyre, adapting things heavenly to things earthly, and earthly things to heavenly, harmonizes them all, and leading them by his will, makes one world and one world-order in beauty and harmony.[40]

Athanasius thinks of Jesus as Image, Expression, Word, and Son of the Father, and also as Wisdom and Light. There never was a time when Wisdom did not exist:

> If there be an Image of the invisible God, it is an Invisible Image; nay, I will be bold to add, that, as being the likeness of the Father, never was it not. For when was that God, who according to John, is called Light (for «God is Light»), without a radiance of his proper glory, that a man should presume to assert the Son's origin of existence, as if before he was not? But when was not that image of the Father's ineffable and nameless and unutterable subsistence, that expression and word, and He that knows the Father? For let him understand well who dares to say, «Once the Son was not», that he is saying, «once Wisdom was not», and «Life was not».[41]

---

[40] Cf. ATHANASIUS, *Contra Arianos*, 42, cited in H. BETTENSON, *Early Christian Fathers*, 279.

[41] Cf. ATHANASIUS, *Contra Arianos* 25, in H. BETTENSON, *Early Christian Fathers*, 178.

Athanasius considers Jesus Christ not only as Wisdom but also as Image and Expression of God. Wisdom, who is the Image and Expression of God, leaves an impress and likeness on all creatures:

> The Only-begotten, the absolute Wisdom of God is the creator and maker of all things. 'In Wisdom you made all things', scripture says; and again: «the earth is full of your creation». In order that what was made might not only be, but might be good, God willed that his own Wisdom should come down to the level of created thing and impress a sort of stamp and likeness of its image on all in common and on each individually, so that what was made would be seen to be wise, a work worthy of God.[42]

But, Athanasius explains, the world did not know God through the image of Wisdom that exists in all created things. So God sent Wisdom in the flesh that all might believe and be saved:

> The Wisdom of God formerly revealed itself through its own image impressed on created reality (by reason of which it is said to be created) and through itself revealed its own Father. It is the same Wisdom of God which later, being the Word, became flesh, as John says, and after destroying death and saving our race revealed himself still more fully and through himself his Father.[43]

The divine Wisdom and Word of God is the image of the invisible God. This image of Wisdom is impressed on all creatures by the very reality of divine creation.

1.7 *Pope Leo I*

One of the most important documents in the history of Christology is the letter of Pope Leo I to Flavian of Constantinople (13 June 449), sometimes called the *Tome of Leo*. This letter was crucial at the Council of Chalcedon and in subsequent developments in Christology.[44] At a central point in this letter, Leo employs the text of Proverbs 9:1 («Wisdom has built her house») alongside the text from John 1:14 («the Word became flesh») to affirm, against Eutyches, the human nature of Jesus Christ, the human flesh he took from his mother, and his human birth.

---

[42] Cf. ATHANASIUS, *Discourses* 2.78, in *The Divine Office*. I, 526-527.

[43] Cf. ATHANASIUS *Discourses against the Arians,*2. 81.

[44] Cf. LEO I, *Letter to Flavian,* 28, in H. BETTENSON, *Later Christian Fathers*, 278-280.

But that birth, singularly wonderful and wonderfully singular, must not be understood as meaning that, because of the new type of procreation, the intrinsic quality of the birth was changed. Fecundity was given to the Virgin by the Holy Spirit, but the reality of the body was taken from her body; and with Wisdom building a dwelling for herself (Prov 9:1), the Word was made flesh and lived among us (Jn 1:14); that is, in the flesh which he took from a human being and which he animated with the breath of rational life.[45]

Leo's strong grasp of the doctrine of the Incarnation is usually expressed in Word/Logos categories as «Word made flesh». But the same doctrine is expressed in Wisdom/Sophia categories as «Wisdom has built herself a house». In another letter, Leo again addresses the theology of the Incarnation. Speaking of Mary, the mother of Jesus, he writes:

Only then, with «Wisdom building herself a house» (Prov 9:1) would «the Word become flesh» (Jn 1:14) within her inviolate womb. Then, too, the Creator of ages would be born in time and the nature of God would join with the nature of a slave in the unity of one person. The one through whom the world was created would himself be brought forth in the midst of creation.[46]

Leo not only refers to the incarnation as «Wisdom building herself a house», but he shows the inner link in a Wisdom theology between God's work in creation and Incarnation. When Wisdom builds her house among us, the one through whom the world was created is brought forth in the midst of creation.

1.8 *Augustine*

Divine Wisdom plays a prominent role in two of Augustine's records of his personal experience of God.[47] Shortly after being baptised by Ambrose in 387, Augustine and his mother experience a conversion at Ostia that led to a mystical vision of divine Wisdom, the eternal principle who creates:

There, life is Wisdom by which all creatures come into being, both things which were and which will be. Furthermore, in this Wisdom there is no past

---

[45] Cf. LEO I, *Letter to Flavian*, 278-280.

[46] Cf. LEO I, *Letter to Flavian*, 31. This text is read as part of the Liturgy of the Hours during Advent. Cf. *The Divine Office*. I, 120.

[47] Cf. V.J. BOURKE, *Augustine's Love of Wisdom*.

and future, but only being, since it is eternal. For to exist in the past or in the future is no property of the eternal. And while we talked and panted after it, we touched it in some small degree by a total concentration of the heart.[48]

Augustine identifies Wisdom predominantly as qualities reflected in the Book of Wisdom (Wis 7:22-23) and the Platonic world of ideas in the inner life of God where certain truth may be found. He prays in the *Soliloquies* for immersion in Wisdom's qualities: «Make me to know thee, O eternal Wisdom, thee who are the source of all the life of my soul».[49] In chapter 28 he longs for «infinite Wisdom which has formed all the universe in accordance with thine eternal thoughts which has put into it the order, the beauty and the harmony that we admire».[50] Augustine equates Wisdom with the very nature of God; therefore in seeking Wisdom, he is seeking God. God is the eternal source of Wisdom who is unchanging truth, eternal light, fountain of life, who creates order out of chaos, beauty and harmony out of ugliness, who nourishes and renews the human spirit in manifold ways.

When Augustine refers to the Wisdom of Christ he identifies Christ with the creative role of God, indirectly echoing the sapiential literature where personified Wisdom is the communication of God active in creation (Prov 1:22-33; 8–9; Sir 24; Wis 7:22), and directly referring to the Logos from the prologue of John's gospel, where Christ is the Word who was in the beginning, was with God and was God. Everything is made through Christ's personal word as we read in *The Homilies on the Gospel of St. John:*

All things then, my brothers, all things, each and everyone, were made through him and without him was made nothing. But how can all things be made through him? That which is made in him is life. Now this can be taken as follows: That which was made in him is life. And if we express the sentence in this way, everything is life. For what was made in him? For he himself is the Wisdom of God and in the psalm it is said, You have made all

---

[48] Cf. AUGUSTINE, *Confessions*, 9.9.24, translated with an introduction by H. CHADWICK, 171. References to Augustine's *Confessions* are taken from Chadwick's translation.

[49] Cf. AUGUSTINE, *Soliloquies of St Augustine*, 1.1, in J.E. ROTELLE, ed., *Works of Augustine*, III /15. References to Augustine's *Soliloquies* are taken from this translation.

[50] Cf. AUGUSTINE, *Soliloquies*, 28.1.126.

things in Wisdom. If, then, Christ is the Wisdom, as all things were made through him, so they were made in him.[51]

Augustine uses Wisdom language to create a portrait of Christ as identical with God's creative Wisdom. He fuses the Pauline text «Christ is the Power and the Wisdom of God» (I Cor 1:24) with Psalm 103:24 and other implicit scriptural texts such as John 1:4 and Colossians 1:15-10 that generate an explicit identification of God's creative Wisdom with Christ, the Word of God. As the Wisdom of God, Christ gives life. Christ is the divine exemplar who fashions everything in the created world in his likeness. He holds together all creation, reconciling all things to God. He feeds us with his Wisdom, until he perfects divine Wisdom embodied in a limited form as a human being and unites us with divine Wisdom.

Augustine extends the notion of being created in and through Christ's Wisdom into historical time by linking Wisdom to the task of mothering. This expansion shows how the creative activity of the Word dwells among us. The *Confessions* presents this correlation; «for the Word was made flesh that your Wisdom, by which you created all things, might give nourishment to our soul's infancy».[52] In *Homily on Psalm 119*, Christ descends to earth to carry out the functions of a mother so that human beings may ascend to God:

> He who has promised us heavenly food has nourished us on milk, having recourse to a mother's tenderness. For just as a mother suckling her infant, transfers from her flesh the very same food which would otherwise be unsuited to the babe (the little one actually receives what he would have received at table, but the food conveyed through the flesh is adapted to the child), so our Lord, in order to convert his wisdom into milk for our benefit, came to us clothed in flesh. It is the body of Christ then which he says: And thou shalt nourish me.[53]

Wisdom is the eternal source of life in the text from the *Homilies of John,* while in texts from the *Confessions, Questions on the Good News,* and *On the Psalms,* when Wisdom becomes flesh, Christ carries out the work of a mother who feeds us so that we may grow in spiritual understanding and participate ever more in Wisdom until at last we come face

---

[51] Cf. AUGUSTINE, *Tractates on the Gospel of John*, 78, 1: 16,1 in J.W. RETTIG, *Fathers of the Church*, 55.

[52] Cf. AUGUSTINE, *Confessions*, 7. 18. 128.

[53] Cf. AUGUSTINE, *On the Psalms*, in S. HEBGIN – F. CORRIGAN, *On the Psalms*. I, 20.

to face with God in the beatific vision. Although Augustine has been accused of «masculinising» the Wisdom motif by giving more attention to the Logos[54], in these passages the message is clear. In his humanity Christ is a tender mother who attends to the temporal, visible, bodily aspects of the human condition. Given that Augustine had such a close relationship with his mother and they shared together the experience of a close relationship with Wisdom, it is not surprising that Augustine would relate the salvific work of Christ feeding us with divine Wisdom to the task of mothering. Yet, Augustine limits the analogy. Christ is only a mother in his humanity or in his salvific works within historical time.

The extension of the Wisdom of the godhead to the mothering role of Christ assists Augustine in distinguishing between the potential of human beings to reflect the Wisdom of God on the one hand, and our flawed nature on the other, that makes us incapable of digesting the true Wisdom of God which is beyond human comprehension. Christ our mother nurtures us as children at the breast until we grow spiritually, ready to digest the solid food of Wisdom which is true knowledge of God.

2. Wisdom in Medieval Theology

Among medieval theologians Jesus was understood as the Wisdom of God. Wisdom was regularly attributed to the Second person of the Trinity and Wisdom categories were used to speak of experiential knowledge of God. Thomas Aquinas quoted Augustine that «God's Wisdom became man to give us an example in righteousness of living».[55] On his own authority he also noted that «Christ, who is the Wisdom of God, orders all things sweetly and in a fitting manner, according to Wisdom 8:1».[56]

Two twelfth-century figures, Bernard of Clairvaux and Hildegard of Bingen, and two fourteenth-century mystics, Henry Suso and Julian of Norwich, also serve us well here.[57] All four discovered experiential ways of locating and conceptualizing the feminine divine. The «Wisdom writings» of Bonaventure will also be considered.

---

[54] Cf. G. JANTZEN, *Power, Gender and Christian Mysticism*, 59-74, for an historical development of the transformation of the female *Sophia* into the male *Logos*.

[55] Cf. THOMAS AQUINAS, *ST*, III, Q. 46, art. 4, translated by English Dominican Province, *ST*, 2268.

[56] Cf. *ST*, III, Q. 46, art. 4 and Q. 55, art. 6.

[57] Cf. B. NEWMAN, «Medieval Theologians», 111-130.

2.1 *Bernard of Clairvaux*

Bernard of Clairvaux (c.1091-1152) reflects the theological outlook of the monastic tradition.[58] Of his manifold works, none were better loved and more frequently imitated than his eighty-six sermons on the Song of Songs. Although he seldom personifies Wisdom directly in these sermons, he often presents the work of imparting Wisdom as the activity of a nursing mother.[59] Bernard's imagery of mothering is typical of Cistercian usage and may reflect a need to supplement monastic authority with affection and nurture - qualities that twelfth-century culture perceived as feminine.[60] Abbots like Bernard, who seemed uncomfortable with an authoritarian style of leadership, found in the tender-hearted «Mother Jesus» and Mother Church the models they needed to reshape the abbatial role. Conversely, the religious who looked to «Mother Jesus» or «Mother» monastic superior were adopting a role of childlike, even infantile, dependence and trust.[61]

Compared with the biblical Sophia, Bernard's figure of Mother Jesus is a less commanding presence. She is, in effect, Sophia-for-spiritual-beginners, and like many images of Christ intended for children, she may strike adults as somewhat sentimental.[62] Wisdom offers a banquet of food and wine, while Mother Jesus offers milk; Wisdom as a teacher is robust and vigorous, while Mother Jesus is tender and comforting. However, this is not the only way Bernard presents the feminine divine. When he wants a more awesome image of divinity in female form, he uses the persona of Charity or Love, in keeping with St. John's assertion that «God is Love» (I Jn 4:8). In Bernard's skilful rhetoric, the figure often becomes a mouthpiece for the abbot himself when he intends to speak with the authority of heaven. She also takes on many attributes of Sophia, particularly her role as mediatrix between God and humanity.[63]

In one of Bernard's early letters, written to a monk who had run away from the order, he uses the persona of Charity to heap reproaches on him:

---

[58] Cf. E. GILSON, *Mystical Theology*; E. KLEINEIDAM, «Wissen, Wissenschaft, Theologie», 128-167.

[59] Cf. BERNARD Of CLAIRVAUX, *Song of Songs*, translated and foreword by G.R. EVANS, *Life of St. Bernard*, CWS, 25 (sermon 9).

[60] Cf. C. BYNUM, «Jesus as Mother», 154-166.

[61] Cf. B. NEWMAN, «Medieval Theologians», 116.

[62] Cf. B. NEWMAN, «Medieval Theologians»,117.

[63] Cf. B. NEWMAN, «Medieval Theologians», 117.

«Our good mother Charity loves us all and shows herself differently to each one of us, cherishing the weak, scolding the restive, exhorting the advanced. But when she scolds she is meek, when she consoles she is sincere. She rages lovingly, her caresses are without guile. She knows how to be angry without losing patience, how to be indignant without being proud. It is she, the mother of angels and men, who brings peace not only on earth, but also in heaven [...] And it is this mother whom you have wounded [...]»[64]

Adapting a biblical text about Wisdom (Ecc 15:2), Bernard goes on to say that if he returns home Charity will receive him with open arms: «[...] she will meet you as an honoured mother [...] rejoicing that her son who was lost is found; who was dead has come to life again.»[65] This is the role of God the Father in Christ's parable of the prodigal son, which Bernard has feminized for his purpose.

In another letter, he again re-fashions Wisdom as Charity, calling her «the creator and ruler of the Universe, since through her all things were made».[66] Bernard uses the persona of Charity so often, and develops the image so extensively, that this manner of speech cannot be dismissed as mere rhetorical ornament. As an image and mouthpiece of God, Charity has taken over many of the functions of Wisdom in Bernard's writing: she is an imperious presence who can be as gentle or acerbic as the need requires. It is easy to see how Bernard, who placed progress in loving at the heart of the Christian life, should fashion from the bald statement that «God is Love» his most complex epitome of the feminine divine.

2.2 *Hildegard of Bingen*

Born in 1098 in the German town of Bermersheim bei Alzey, Hildegard was the tenth child of noble parents, who dedicated her to God as a tithe. Three of her siblings also devoted their lives to the Church: one brother was a cantor at the Mainz Cathedral, another became a canon in Tholey, and a sister joined religious life at Hildegard's convent.[67] From early childhood, long before she undertook her public mission or even her monastic vows, Hildegard's spiritual awareness was founded in what she

---

[64] Cf. M. L'ABBÉ, *Bernard of Clairvaux*, 10-11.

[65] Cf. M. L'ABBÉ, *Bernard of Clairvaux*, 10-11.

[66] Cf. M. L'ABBÉ, *Bernard of Clairvaux*, 44.

[67] For a biographiy of Hildegard's life cf. B. NEWMAN, *Sister of Wisdom*, 4-15.

called the *umbra viventis lucis*, the reflection of the living light.[68] However, only in retrospect, it appears, did Hildegard recognize these early experiences as a stage of preparation for her calling.

The devotional writing of Bernard of Clairvaux probably influenced Hildegard of Bingen, who used the figures of Charity (Caritas) and Wisdom (Sapientia) almost interchangeably in her visions.[69] Although the two saints never met, the story of their correspondence is well known.[70] Her writings reveal the pervasive influence of Bernard even though her spirituality was quite different, as a comparison of their Sophia-figures will show.

The devotion to Mother Jesus was totally foreign to Hildegard, although in her visions and letters she wrote a great deal about the Church as mother.[71] Elsewhere she refers to the divine nature as «my mother, because she created me and gives me life», just as Mother Church gives life through the Eucharist.[72]

Hildegard's images of the feminine divine, in contrast to Bernard's, do not stress the motherly love of God so much as the divine activity in creation and redemption. Her visions give a large place to the feminine personae she calls Virtues, who are not simply moral qualities but potent divine energies working for good in the cosmos and in human souls.[73] The most important of these, Wisdom and Charity, are virtually identical figures who fill the place of the biblical Sophia as creatrix, consort of God, and ruler of the world. Their symbolism is sometimes amorous, suggesting not mystical union so much as a sacred marriage within the Godhead. Thus Hildegard calls Wisdom «a most loving mistress» in the embrace of

---

[68] Hildegard used the word *umbra* to denote images reflected in the *fons vitae*, which is literally a shining pool or fountain. The *umbra viventis lucis* is a «shadow» with respect to the *lux vivens* itself, but the shadow is nonetheless brighter than the light of common day. Her letter to Guibert of Gembloux, written at the age of seventy-seven (1175), describes her experience of this light. Cf. B. NEWMAN, *Sister of Wisdom*, 6-7.

[69] For an account of Hildegard's sapiential visions cf. B. NEWMAN, *Sister of Wisdom*, 89-120.

[70] For the exchange of letters cf. M. SCHRADER – A. FÜHRKÖTTER, *Die Echtheit des Schrifttums*, 105-108.

[71] Cf. B. NEWMAN, «Medieval Theologians», 118-122.

[72] Cf. HILDEGARD OF BINGEN, *Scivias. II, 6, 35* in A. FÜHRKÖTTER – A. CARLEVARIS, *Corpus Christianorum*, 43-43a, 263.

[73] Cf. B. NEWMAN, «Medieval Theologians», 119.

God, and Charity says of herself, «I keep the royal marriage bed, and all that is God's is mine as well».[74]

Like several of her contemporaries, Hildegard believed that the Incarnation was, in fact, the purpose for which God fashioned the world in the first place: it was his desire to become flesh and share the existence of his creatures. Hildegard referred to this divine intention as the «eternal counsel» of Psalm 32:11 - the divine purpose for which the world was made - and frequently symbolized it through the feminine figures of Love and Wisdom.[75]

Hildegard's Wisdom theology is complex and many-sided, embracing the doctrines of creation, incarnation, prophetic inspiration and spiritual and moral growth, and including a colourful array of images for the feminine divine. B. Newman has argued that Hildegard uses feminine symbols when she wants to depict God's timeless or perpetually renewed interactions with the world, while for the linear events of salvation history, she prefers masculine imagery.[76] Above all, feminine Wisdom figures suggest for her the principle of God's self-revelation, whether in creating the world, taking human form in it, or manifesting the divine will through visions and inspired scriptures. Such figures also denote human collaboration with God in the Church and the life of virtue.

Significantly, however, Hildegard associates Wisdom theology primarily with the luminous and joyful side of Christian faith. It is not that she downplays the suffering of Christ or the power of sin. On the contrary, she refers quite frequently to the Passion, the fallenness of human nature and the continuing role of Satan. But these sorrowful mysteries are seldom evoked by means of feminine symbols. For Hildegard, it is always the historical, masculine Christ who suffers, not the alternative female persona of Love or Wisdom.

2.3 *Henry Suso*

By the fourteenth century, we find both Christology and the Sophia tradition radically transformed, though female imagery for the divine

---

[74] Cf. HILDEGARD OF BINGEN, *Liber Vitae Meritorum*. I, 46 and III, 8, in J.B. PITRA, *Analecta Sacra*, VIII, 23, 108.

[75] Cf. B. NEWMAN, «Medieval Theologians», 120.

[76] Cf. B. NEWMAN, *Sister of Wisdom*, 44-46.

persisted and in fact increased. One spiritual writer of the fourteenth century who continued to make use of Wisdom categories was Henry Suso (1295–1366). Suso rejected the family name of his father, a worldly knight, and adopted his mother's name to express his admiration of her piety.[77] As a Dominican friar, he devoted most of his ministry to the spiritual direction of nuns and had many female disciples with whom he corresponded. One of them, Elsbet Stagel, wrote a preliminary *Life* which Suso himself seems to have enlarged and altered for publication. This text in its present form is entitled *The Life of a Servant*.[78]

The *Life* purports to describe Suso's inner development in several phases: we learn of the exuberant «spiritual springtime» that followed his conversion at eighteen, then of an intensely ascetic and self-torturing period that lasted about twenty years, and finally of his spiritual maturity gained through the patient suffering of persecution and slander. For our purposes, the first phase may be the most interesting. During his novitiate, Suso tells us, he showed no particular fervor until the time when he suddenly «fell in love» with Eternal Wisdom. This happy event occurred as he sat in the friars' refectory, listening to the lector read from Sirach and Wisdom. In the words of the *Life*, «his young heart was drawn to her» as she «often attracted him and charmed him lovingly» by means of these books.[79]

Suso began to style himself the «Servant of Eternal Wisdom», like a courtly lover who has vowed homage to a lady, for in Eternal Wisdom he has wedded «the empress of his heart and giver of all grace».[80] Suso appears to be confused about the nature and gender of this being, for he asks himself, «Is the beloved God or human, woman or man?» Sometimes he treats her as divine and female, courting Wisdom as a knight offers protection to a lady, or again resting in her presence like a baby in its mother's lap. Once he compares her to a fair lady awarding prizes in a tournament.[81] At other times Eternal Wisdom is identified more or less clearly with Jesus.

When he went to study in Cologne, he commissioned an artist to make him an image of Eternal Wisdom who «has heaven and earth in her power,

---

[77] Cf. B. NEWMAN, «Medieval Theologians», 122-124.

[78] The problematic authorship of the *Life* is discussed by N. HELLER, *Blessed Henry Suso*, xviii-xli. References to Suso's *Life* will be taken from Tobin's translation.

[79] Cf. H. SUSO, *Life of a Servant*, 22-23.

[80] Cf. H. SUSO, *Life of a Servant*, 23.

[81] Cf. H. SUSO, *Life of a Servant*, 146.

and in her fair loveliness [...] surpasses all earthly creatures in beauty».[82] This devotional image did not survive, but the earliest manuscript of Suso's *Exemplar* (dated c. 1365–1370) contains a drawing which may be modelled on it. The illustration shows Suso, in his friar's habit and tonsure, pulling his cloak apart to display his soul in the form of a naked child embraced by the maternal figure of Wisdom.[83]

As he matured, however, Suso gradually discarded the feminine imagery of Wisdom. A turning-point came at the moment when Christ told the servant that if he wished to attain to his naked divinity, he must tread the path of his suffering humanity.[84] Reversing Hildegard's formula, Suso's spirituality had woman symbolize the divinity of Christ and man his humanity. Eternal Wisdom as feminine had been his muse, the object of an aspiring and sentimental love, Eternal Wisdom as masculine was Jesus, the object of an heroic and sacrificial love.

This change of heart could almost be described as Suso's second conversion.[85] His reversal of Wisdom's gender is correlated with his transition from a «theology of glory» to a «theology of the cross». It may be that, because the image of the risen and ascended Lord was absent from Suso's spiritual horizon, the sublime figure of Sophia had initially taken his place. With the ascetic's maturity, however, the divine Christ receded before the human, suffering Christ who, for Suso as for Hildegard, was decisively male.[86]

2.4 *Julian of Norwich*

In Julian of Norwich, the famed English mystic and anchoress, we can see Henry Suso's trajectory in reverse. We know almost nothing about Julian's life before her visionary experience: she may have been a laywoman, a nun or perhaps already a recluse.[87]

The course of her spiritual journey can be charted by noting her movement from a piety much like Suso's final phase, focused intensely on the Passion and vicarious suffering, toward a more balanced and optimis-

---

[82] Cf. H. SUSO, *Life of a Servant*, 104.

[83] For a copy of the drawing cf. J. HYNES, «Use of Images», 25. This reference is cited in F. Tobin's translation of H. Suso's *The Life of a Servant*, viii.

[84] Cf. H. SUSO, *Life of the Servant*, 42.

[85] Cf. B. NEWMAN, «Medieval Theologians», 124.

[86] Cf. B. NEWMAN, «Medieval Theologians», 124.

[87] Cf. B. NEWMAN, «Medieval Theologians»,, 124-126.

tic theology characterized by a Trinitarian sense of God. Linking Julian's earlier, passion-centred, spirituality with her later concerns is one of her most carefully developed themes, the Motherhood of God All-Wisdom.[88] In her theology we find Bernard's devotion to Mother Jesus, Hildegard's understanding of Wisdom as creator and redeemer and Suso's commitment to the Passion, all retained and integrated into a fresh Trinitarian synthesis.[89]

Julian introduces her teaching on the Motherhood of God with her mysterious parable of a lord and a servant, which is revealed in answer to her puzzlement over the insight that God does not blame humanity for sin. In the parable, the servant who comes to grief in the act of fulfilling his lord's will is shown to be at once Christ and Adam, Eternal Wisdom and suffering human nature. Julian teaches that «when Adam fell, God's Son fell»: at the moment that humanity fell from life to death, «God's Son fell with Adam, into the valley of the maiden's womb».[90] This mystical identification of the divine suffering Servant with our fallen nature is further developed in the teaching on Christ our Mother. Julian adapts the traditional doctrine of «appropriations», which associates the divine attributes of power, wisdom and love with Father, Son and Holy Spirit respectively.[91]

The motherhood of Wisdom has three aspects. First, Christ as the Word and Wisdom of God is our mother «substantially», in that all creatures exist from eternity in the divine will; this teaching is similar to Hildegard's view of Wisdom or Love as the «living fountain» in which all beings are eternally reflected. In the second place, Christ becomes our mother «sensually» through the Incarnation, taking on human flesh and blood. Thirdly, he is our «mother of mercy» in the redemption, suffering for us and tending us with loving care.[92] Like Suso, Julian sees that Eternal Wisdom and Christ crucified are one; but unlike the German mystic, she does not make the distinction between the suffering and the glorified Christ into a distinction of gender. For Julian, whether in his passion or in

---

[88] There is an extensive literature on Julian, especially on the theme of divine motherhood. Cf. K. BÖRRESEN, «Christ notre mère», 320-329; E. MCLOUGHLIN, «Christ my Mother», 228-248.

[89] Cf. B. NEWMAN, «Medieval Theologians», 125.

[90] Cf. E. COLLEDGE – J. WALSH, Showings of Divine Love. I, 274-275.

[91] Cf. E. COLLEDGE – J. WALSH, Showings of Divine Love, 294-295.

[92] Cf. B. NEWMAN, «Medieval Theologians», 125-126.

his celestial bliss, God's Son is still our Mother. The office of motherhood implies that Jesus gives us spiritual birth, feeds us with the sacrament of his body and blood, comforts and cleanses our souls, and also disciplines us when we have need. Julian compares the motherhood of Jesus favourably with earthly mothering:

> We know that all our mothers bear us for pain and for death [...] But our true mother, Jesus, he alone bears us for joy and for endless life, blessed may he be [...] The mother can give her child to suck of her milk, but our precious Mother Jesus can feed us with himself, and does, most courteously and most tenderly, with the Blessed Sacrament.[93]

Compared to Bernard's image of Mother Jesus, Julian's is more inclusive and embraces a wider affective range. For instance, she notes that, as a child grows older, a mother changes her mode of action, but not her love; she may chastize her child for its own good and allow it to stumble so that it can learn from its mistakes.[94] This is behaviour that Bernard would have connected with fathering not mothering. While Bernard evoked Mother Jesus especially for the consolation of beginners, Julian states that Jesus is our Mother from everlasting to everlasting.[95]

If we set Bernard and Suso beside Hildegard and Julian, we see that for the two *male* writers, images of the *feminine* divine are connected with the *earliest* stages of spiritual growth. Bernard speaks of Mother Jesus suckling infant souls, and Suso of the young lover and his lady. For the spiritually *mature*, *masculine* images are more suitable: Christ as bridegroom of the soul (for Bernard) or as the crucified Eternal Wisdom (for Suso). For the two *women*, in contrast, *feminine* imagery becomes more important with *maturity*. Hildegard did not begin to write until she was forty-three, and female personae are important in all her works; but the divine figures of Love and Wisdom play an ever larger role in her last book, which she began at the age of sixty-five. Julian said nothing about the motherhood of Wisdom in her short text, but developed this teaching in the longer one when she was past fifty.[96]

---

[93] Cf. E. COLLEDGE – J. WALSH, *Showings of Divine Love*, 297-298.

[94] Cf. E. COLLEDGE – J. WALSH, *Showings of Divine Love*, 300-301.

[95] Cf. E. COLLEDGE – J. WALSH, *Showings of Divine Love*, 292.

[96] Julian wrote what is called the «Short Text» of her *Showings*. But given twenty more years of illumination and insight, she revised her book, producing the «Long Text» on which her fame largely rests. Cf. B. NEWMAN, «Medieval Theologians», 126.

Taking a different approach, we might compare the two twelfth-century authors with those of the fourteenth century. Here we find the expected «darkening» of late medieval piety. The Passion is far more central to Suso and Julian than it is to Bernard and Hildegard, and both fourteenth-century mystics venerate Wisdom Crucified. But in this case Suso is typical and Julian exceptional: she is alone among the writers of her age in the extraordinary optimism of her theology, which co-exists throughout her work with an unblinking and rather gory vision of the Cross. This recovered balance may be accounted for, in large part, by her renewed interest in the traditional Wisdom themes of creation, the eternal existence of creatures in God, and the solidarity of created with uncreated being through the Incarnation. These interests again bring Julian close to Hildegard, whose work she could not, however, have known.

2.5 *Bonaventure*

As a Franciscan theologian, Bonaventure (c.1217–1274) gives expression to key insights of the early Franciscan movement which had their source in the religious experience of Francis himself, particularly the conviction of God's overflowing goodness and the experience of creation as expressive of this divine goodness.[97] He very often used the name «Wisdom» when describing the way that creatures reflect their Exemplar: «every creature is of its very nature a likeness and resemblance to eternal Wisdom».[98] He wrote that creatures are «nothing less than a kind of representation of the Wisdom of God, and a kind of sculpture».[99] For Bonaventure it is in eternal Wisdom that we find the basis of the fecundity to «conceive, carry and bring to birth» the forms of all things in the universe. All these exemplary forms «are conceived from eternity in the womb of eternal Holy Wisdom».[100] In Bonaventure's view, if it were not for the distortion of sin, we would be able to read the book of creation and come to know Wisdom: «In the state of innocence, when the image had not yet been distorted but was conformed to God through grace, the book

---

[97] Cf. Z. HAYES, *Bonaventure's Disputed Questions*, 32-33.

[98] Cf. BONAVENTURE, *Itinerarium*, 2.12, in J. de VINCK, *The Works of St. Bonaventure*. I, 97. References to the works of Bonaventure are taken from de Vinck's translation.

[99] Cf. BONAVENTURE, *Hexaemeron*, 12.

[100] Cf. BONAVENTURE, *Hexoemeron*, 20.5.

of creation sufficed to enable humanity to receive the light of divine Wisdom».[101]

3. Wisdom in the Liturgy

It is a venerable Advent custom to pray the «O antiphons» which are part of the Liturgy of the Hours. The first of these is the «O Wisdom» antiphon recited on 17 December as the Magnificat Antiphon of Evening Prayer: «O Wisdom, you come forth from the mouth of the Most High. You fill the universe and hold all things together in a strong yet gentle manner. O come to teach us the way of truth».[102] D. Edwards summarises well the theology presented in this antiphon: «In these lines we find a compendium of Christian theology in Wisdom categories: a Spirit theology in terms of the procession of Wisdom from the mouth of the Most High; a theology of Wisdom's work in creation, in which Wisdom is understood as not only being present to all of creation, but as holding all things together; the suggestion of a theology of divine power as non-dominating, as Wisdom is at work in creation in a 'strong but gentle manner'; the prayer «O come» as a plea for Wisdom's advent in Jesus of Nazareth; an understanding of Jesus as a Wisdom teacher, teaching us 'the way of truth'».[103]

In the Office of Readings for the feast of St. John of the Cross (14 December) Wisdom is presented as being revealed through the sufferings of Christ. In his *Spiritual Canticle* St. John of the Cross writes:

«Would that men might at least understand that it is impossible to attain to the thicket of manifold riches of the Wisdom of God without entering into the thicket of manifold suffering, making that its consolation and desire! And how the soul which really longs for divine Wisdom first longs for suffering, that it may enter more deeply into the thicket of the cross!»[104]

For St. John of the Cross, the cross, and what we can learn from its place in our lives, is the door to Divine Wisdom and the best model for this journey is Jesus Christ, the Wisdom of God: «Was it not ordained that the Christ should suffer and so enter into his glory?» (Lk 24:26).

---

[101] Cf. BONAVENTURE, *Breviloquium*, 2.12.

[102] Cf. *The Divine Office*. I, 124.

[103] Cf. D. EDWARDS, *Jesus the Wisdom of God*, 56.

[104] *The Divine Office*. I, 39*-40*.

A reference to Jesus as the Wisdom is God is found in the Prayer of Consecration during the ceremony of Ordination of a Deacon. With hands extended the bishop says: «Almighty God be present with us by your power. You are the source of all honour, you assign to each his rank, you give to each his ministry. You remain unchanged, but you watch over all creation and make it new through your Son, Jesus Christ, our Lord: he is your Word, your Power, and your Wisdom [...]».[105]

4. Summary and Conclusions

While we began with Clement of Rome and Ignatius of Antioch, it is with Justin Martyr that the significance of the Wisdom theme emerged in patristic theology and in its relationship to the Logos. Justin, reflecting on the generation of the Word in God, links this generation with the theme of created Wisdom in Proverbs. Proverbs 8:22 proved a key verse here and would continue to do so down to the end of the fourth century. The Apologists used the concepts of Logos and Wisdom in order to make connections between faith and philosophy. All the powers of creation recognized in the Father of the universe by philosophy and all his intervention in the world are transferred to Christ, and this is justified by appeal to the Wisdom of Proverbs 8:22 as well as the Johannine Logos. Tertullian, searching for a way to distinguish the Father and the Son, also evoked the created Wisdom of Prov 8:22. For Tertullian, while God is one He has in him his Logos and Wisdom.

The greatest Wisdom christologian of the patristic period was Origen. The structure of Origen's thought is that divine Wisdom, having had a cosmic role in creation, is now made manifest in Jesus. Origen expresses the constant theme of all Wisdom Christology – what is revealed in creation is made manifest in Jesus.

In his great work of systematic theology, *On First Principles*, Origen outlined his christological vision in Wisdom categories. He uses «Wisdom» to emphasize that the Son's revelation of the Father is constitutive of the Son's hypostatic existence: the only-begotten Son is God's Wisdom hypostatically existing. Furthermore, for Origen, the ultimate meaning and reality of all created things is found in the very substance and hypostatic existence of Wisdom. It is the participation of creation in hypostatic

---

[105] Cf. «Ordination of a Deacon», in INTERNATIONAL COMMISSION ON ENGLISH IN THE LITURGY, *The Rites of the Catholic Church*. II, 56.

Wisdom that guarantees creation's true existence and intelligibility. Origen thus affirms the ultimate meaningfulness of creation. For Origen, the Son is the principle of rationality or Wisdom both as the objective substance of intelligibility and as the primary agent of the subjective process whereby intelligibility is discovered and appropriated.

Thus, Origen's christological structure of meaning can be summed up by saying that he conceives of the Son as ultimate Wisdom precisely through the simultaneity of his roles as the image of the Father, the archetype of creation, the objective content of Wisdom, and the subjective mediator or interpreter of all Wisdom and Truth. Athanasius also thought of Jesus as divine Wisdom comparing the role of divine Wisdom at work in creation with a musician bringing all creatures together into a beautiful harmony.

Presentations of Jesus as the Wisdom of God are also found in medieval theology: Wisdom was regularly attributed to the Second Person of the Trinity and Wisdom categories were used to speak of experiential knowledge of God. We highlighted the continuity as well as the variety of sapiential thought in medieval Christianity.

While Bernard of Clairvaux seldom personified Wisdom directly, he often presented the work of imparting Wisdom as the activity of a nursing mother. Hildegard of Bingen's Wisdom theology was found to be complex and many-sided, embracing the doctrines of creation, incarnation, prophetic inspiration and spiritual and moral growth. Feminine Wisdom figures suggest for her the principle of God's self-revelation, whether in creating the world, taking human form in it, or manifesting the divine will through visions and inspired scriptures. She associates Wisdom theology primarily with the luminous and joyful side of Christian faith.

Julian of Norwich adapted the traditional doctrine of «appropriations», which associates the divine attributes of Power, Wisdom and Love with Father, Son and Spirit respectively. Three Wisdom references from the Church's liturgy were highlighted: the «O Wisdom» antiphon from the Liturgy of the Hours (17 December), an extract from the Office of Readings for the feast of St. John of the Cross (14 December), and a reference from the Prayer of Consecration from the Rite of Ordination to the Diaconate. The «O Wisdom" antiphon contains a compendium of Christian theology in Wisdom categories while St John of the Cross emphasizes the consolation of Wisdom which can come to the one who suffers. The Prayer of Consecration in the Ordination Rite for deacons speaks of Jesus Christ as the Father's «Word [...] Power [...] and Wisdom».

In later centuries, while largely replaced by considerations of Logos Christology (in itself partially shaped by Wisdom texts), the Wisdom tradition continued to make elusive appearances in christological reflection, while the major application of Wisdom texts turned in the direction of mariology. Hence, a more profound and comprehensive vision of Mary's participation in the plan of salvation was provided. Mary works together with Christ as Sophia was involved with creation. A Wisdom mariology provided a rich basis for articulating the church's devotion to Mary as more elevated than the angels and saints.[106]

Our journey began with an overview of Sophia in the Wisdom writings of the Second Temple Period. We then traced the influence of the Wisdom theme on the formation of substantial parts of the New Testament. We have seen some of Wisdom's influence on the faith reflection of the church. These many dimensions of Wisdom can be said to constitute a distinct perspective on the person of Jesus Christ and the faith of the church. We now move to consider what has been the influence of this perspective on contemporary Catholic Christology.

---

[106] An examination of the development of Wisdom mariology is beyond the scope of this thesis. For a cursory overview of this development cf. T. SCHIPFLINGER, *Sophia - Maria*, 393-396.

PART TWO

WISDOM IN CONTEMPORARY CHRISTOLOGY

CHAPTER VII

Wisdom Christology in Some Representatives of the German-Speaking world

We now propose to examine to what extent the Wisdom elements present in the Scriptures and the tradition of the Church have been incorporated into some contemporary Catholic Christology in three language areas (German, English and French). We begin by concentrating on some representative Christologies of the German-speaking world.

1. Representative Catholic Christology in the German-Speaking World

The three theologians whose Christology we propose to examine are Walter Kasper, Karl Rahner, and Edward Schillebeeckx. W. Kasper's *Jesus der Christus*[1] has found widespread use in colleges and seminaries because of its contemporaneity, fidelity to the tradition, and attention to exegetical and historical data. Rahner's writings on Christology span half a century and consider innumerable questions from a variety of perspectives. The closest approximation to a comprehensive summary of his Christology is found in chapter six of *Grundkurs des Glaubens*.[2] Though E. Schillebeeckx is Flemish and has written in Dutch we may include him here. Together with W. Kasper and H. Küng, Schillebeeckx contributed to the major christological publications in Europe in 1974. Schillebeeckx's *Jezus*[3] was hailed as a critical synthesis of New Testament scholarship and a new approach to theological reflection on the Christian experience.

---

[1] W. KASPER, *Jesus der Christus*; E.T. *Jesus the Christ*.
[2] K. RAHNER, *Grundkurs des Glaubens*; E.T. *Foundations of Christian Faith*.
[3] E. SCHILLEBEECKX, *Jezus*; E.T. *Jesus*.

Because of its rapid translation into German we can include him with the German-speaking theologians in this chapter.

2. Walter Kasper

2.1 Theologian and Bishop

Walter Kasper (b.1933) was born in Heidenheim, a town of the Swabian forest, not far from Tübingen, Germany. He began his theological studies at the University of Tübingen in 1952 and was to return as Professor of Dogmatics in the Catholic faculty of theology there. Apart from a short period in Münster, he remained at Tübingen until 1989 when he was appointed Bishop of Rottenburg-Stuttgart. Having been appointed Secretary of the Pontifical Council for the Promotion of Christian Unity in 1999, he was appointed to the College of Cardinals in February 2001. He is currently President of the Pontifical Council for the Promotion of Christian Unity[4]

Coming from the Catholic Tübingen theological school, Kasper «represents a total theological programme of a quite distinct kind».[5] Commitment to the Catholic tradition and openness to the modern philosophical questions are the hallmarks of his theology. He is critical of the various theological responses to the challenge of modernity and wants to develop a middle way between the two dominant theological approaches characterized as theology from below and theology from above by appealing to the inner dynamism of modernity, which he identifies as the idea of freedom.[6] J. Palakeel sums up Kasper's approach to this process in these words: «Kasper moves away from the Hellenistic essentialist metaphysics and from the radical rationalism of idealism to a relational metaphysics and theological rationality in order to establish a christological theocentrism and a christological anthropocentrism in mutual correspondence».[7]

---

[4] For an introduction to the thought of Walter Kasper see: W.P. LOEWE, «New Catholic Tübingen Theology», 30-49; A. NICHOLS, «Walter Kasper», 16-24.

[5] Cf. A. NICHOLS, «Walter Kasper», 16. W.P. Loewe characterizes it as «*new* Catholic Tübingen Theology»: see W.P. LOEWE, «New Catholic Tübingen Theology», 30-49. Cf. also W. KASPER, *Jesus the Christ*, 9; ID., *The God of Jesus Christ*, ix.

[6] Cf. J. PALAKEEL, *Use of Analogy,* 263-298. Palakeel shows how Kasper sets out to transform the doctrine of analogy from early Greek cosmological concerns and classical Greek and scholastic metaphysical terms to modern philosophical understanding by taking the historical consciousness and freedom of man as the point of departure.

[7] Cf. J. PALAKEEL, *Use of Analogy*, 263.

Jesus der Christus [8] was Kasper's formidable contribution to European christological publications in 1974.[9] Its publication confirmed his reputation as a theologian who is conceptually rigorous and historically well-informed. At the heart of Kasper's Christology are the twin ideals of the Catholic Tübingen school: commitment to a study of the origins of Christianity in Jesus Christ accessible only through biblical and ecclesiastical tradition; and a conviction that tradition has to be handed on as something living, that is, in conjunction and confrontation with the comments and questions of a particular time.[10]

2.2 *The Development of Kasper's Theology*

While inheriting the major concerns of the Tübingen theology, Kasper creatively renewed it through his encounter with Idealist thought, especially through his study of the philosopher F.W.J. von Schelling (1775-1854). Kasper's doctoral dissertation[11] is an inquiry into the doctrine of tradition of the nineteenth century Roman theologians, Perrone, Franzelin and others, who are considered architects of the First Vatican Council. He shows that the Tübingen theologians of the nineteenth century too were motivated by such an ecclesiology. The finding of the thesis is that tradition is the chief principle of authority in Christian theology and this tradition cannot be reduced to the magisterium of the Church. He addresses also the question of the nature and function of dogma. In his later writings Kasper subjected these doctrines of tradition and dogma to further analysis in the light of the modern philosophical insights into the historicity of man.[12]

Kasper attempted next to look for a philosophy capable of conceptualising the faith expressed in and through tradition. He found in the later

---

[8] W. KASPER, *Jesus der Christus*; E.T. *Jesus the Christ*.

[9] H. Küng and E. Schillebeeckx were the authors of the other two major works on Christology to be published in Europe in that year. H. KÜNG, *Christ Sein*,; E.T. *On Being a Christian*; E. SCHILLEBEECKX, *Jezus*.

[10] Cf. W. KASPER, *Jesus the Christ*, 9-10.

[11] W. KASPER, *Die Lehre von der Tradition*.

[12] Cf. W. KASPER, *Methods of Dogmatic Theology* 29, 36-37, 39. According to Kasper, exaggerated emphasis on magisterium and dogma is the result of an apologetic and defensive attitude to modernity which manifested itself in the First Vatican Council and was overcome by the Second Vatican Council. Cf. W. KASPER, *Christian Understanding of Freedom*, 20-22 [quoted by J. PALAKEEL, *Use of Analogy*, 265].

philosophy of Schelling a partner with whom to dialogue.[13] Although Kasper was not the first theologian to be interested in the theological possibilities offered by the philosophy of Schelling[14], he arrives at an independent position, arguing that a unitary intention is discernible throughout Schelling's various stages of development.[15]

Kasper showed how the key to the unity of Schelling's development, to his philosophical originality and his contemporary relevance, lies in his concept of *die Freiheit, freedom.*[16] Schelling critically limited Idealism by showing that reason does not have power over itself, and hence only the God of positive philosophy, who manifests himself in history by a free act, is the solution to the crisis of Idealism and the resultant nihilism.

The positive philosophy of Schelling is also the point of departure for Kasper's critique of the various theological traditions dealing with the challenge of Idealism and for the development of his own theological system. Thus Kasper found himself able to argue that he was not departing from strict philosophical rationality in posing the question, how does the Absolute come out of itself (in the free act of creating)? How do we (as finite spirits) come forth from the Absolute and (as free spirits) posit ourselves as other than and opposed to God?

Kasper finds the illumination he needs to answer these questions in the Church's faith in God as Trinity. He locates the means to overcome the schism between God's infinite freedom and our finite freedom in the

---

[13] Kasper's *Habilitationsschrift* presented at Tübingen was a study of the later philosophy of Schelling: *Das Absolute in der Geschichte, Philosophie und Theologie der Geschichte in der Spätphilosophie Schellings.* [Hereafter *Das Absolute*]

[14] Nichols situates Kasper's book on Schelling within the context of the various Schelling studies in Continental Europe. He has suggested that J. Habermas' dissertation *Das Absolute und die Geschichte: von der Zweispaltigkeit in Schellings Denken*, must have provided Kasper's model. He points out also that Kasper is trying to resume and to take further the project of F.A. Staudenmaier, the nineteenth-century Tübingen theologian, who had already drawn on Schelling's philosophy theologically. Cf. A. NICHOLS, «Walter Kasper», 19.

[15] For Kasper, Schelling is «[...] not just the culminating point and consummation of the philosophy from Descartes to Kant (Idealism), but at the same time the point of its radical change and inversion (*Das Absolute*, 145). Schelling represents «the last encounter in grand scale between Idealist thought and Christianity» (*Das Absolute, 6*) and secondly, even the present theological scene is characterized by the post-Hegelian crisis, in which Schelling effected this encounter (*Das Absolute, 26-28*).

[16] On the theological relevance of Schelling see W.P. LOEWE, «New Catholic Tübingen Theology», 32-35.

redemptive work of Jesus Christ. The working out of these themes was to contribute in time to Kasper's two great works: *Der Gott Jesu Christi*[17] and *Jesus der Christus*. The latter will serve here as the central text in our study of Kasper's Christology.

2.3 *The Christology of Walter Kasper*

It is not the purpose of our study to treat Kasper's Christology in detail.[18] Rather, our central focus is concerned with examining to what extent, in formulating his systematic Christology, Kasper uses the Wisdom elements in the Scriptures. However, some explication of Kasper's Christology, by way of summary and overview, will help to situate our specific study. In this regard we will draw on Kasper's presentation in *Jesus the Christ*.

2.3.1 *Summary*

Kasper formulates the primary criterion which guides a Catholic systematic Christology in terms of the earthly and exalted Jesus Christ, who is a living, personal identity in difference: thoroughly one, of God and of us.[19] He stipulates the secondary criterion in terms of the living faith of the Church, both in its foundations as testified to in the New Testament and its ongoing life of worship and witness through the ages. The subordination of the Church and its faith to the primary criterion, the reality of Christ, is evident in Kasper's formulation.[20] The starting point of Christology, which Kasper distinguishes from the criterion, is the phenomenology of the Church's faith in Christ. The reason for this is twofold: the living Christ of today is encountered only in the living faith of Christians in the twenty-first century, and the Jesus of yesterday is met only through the faith-witness of the New Testament, the book of the early Church.[21]

Kasper's Christology of reciprocity, which holds the earthly and resurrected Jesus together while, at the same time, recognising the

---

[17] W. KASPER, *Der Gott Jesu Christi*; E.T.: *The God of Jesus Christ*.

[18] For a study of the Christology of Walter Kasper see: N. MADONIA, *Walter Kasper*.

[19] Cf. W. KASPER, *Jesus the Christ*, 19.

[20] Kasper argues that «[...] only a renewed Christology can enable the Church to regain its universality and catholicity without denying the foolishness of the cross and surrendering the unique impetus of Christianity». Cf. W. KASPER, *Jesus the Christ*, 16.

[21] Cf. W. KASPER, *Jesus the Christ*, 26-28.

difference, guarantees that Kasper will make the historical aspect of Jesus of Nazareth an essential element. Thus Jesus' activity, message, and death receive close attention, with the result that he finds an implicit Christology in Jesus' preaching of the kingdom, his table fellowship, his call to discipleship, and his offering the cup of eschatological blessing in the face of his impending death.[22]

The eschatological and soteriological character of Jesus' person is grounded in the meaning of his cause, that is, his activity and message concerning the kingdom, and the inseparability of person and cause in Jesus. The kingdom of God preached, whose blessing people partook of in welcoming him, was the very content of salvation.[23] This central fact receives more weight in Kasper's Christology than any particular finding with regard to the titles such as Christ, Son of Man, Son of God, and so forth (even though he is open to Jesus' employment of some of these titles in his public life).[24] Jesus' life and ministry was service of his fellows in the name of God, a service which essentially consisted in making it possible for men and women to share in salvation, ie., in God's reign and its blessing in the form of new life and forgiveness. Later Christian confessions of Jesus as Christ and Saviour thus do no violence to the earthly Jesus but rather make explicit what is given in historical form in Jesus of Nazareth.

Clearly the pre-resurrection Jesus has a significant role to play in Kasper's Christology, but he does not allow this to be the sole content or criterion of Christology. In order to see the theological function of the pre-Easter Jesus, as understood by Kasper, it is necessary to appreciate the place which the resurrection assumes in his reflections.

---

[22] Kasper devotes five chapters in *Jesus the Christ* to a study of the historical Jesus under the headings of: (i) Jesus' Activity (65-71); (ii) Jesus' Message (72-88); (iii) Jesus' Miracles (89-99); (iv) Jesus' Claim (100-112); (v) Jesus' Death (113-123).

[23] «The centre and framework of Jesus' preaching and mission was the approaching Kingdom of God.» (*Jesus the Christ*, 72). For Kasper, the message of the imminent Kingdom of God is a fundamental concept of Christology and he devotes a chapter to explaining this view in detail. Cf. W. KASPER, *Jesus the Christ*, 72-88.

[24] Though Jesus did not see himself as Messiah, the title in a transmuted sense was, Kasper argues, rightly applied to him. He called himself Son of Man, Kasper believes, both as the eschatological representative of God and as our representative. While ontically he lived the life which the later Church determined ontologically as that of Son of God. Cf. W. KASPER, *Jesus the Christ*, 104-112. Part Three of Kasper's Christology addresses the mystery of Jesus Christ under the headings of «Son of God», «Son of Man», and «Mediator» (*Jesus the Christ*, 163-274).

Kasper acknowledges that the resurrection was the confirmation and legitimation by the Father of the earthly Jesus' message and activity.[25] But that is only one dimension of the resurrection's significance. Beyond such confirmation, it was a new, creative event which exalted Jesus, bringing him into the Father's dimension and filling him with the eschatological Spirit so that he in turn could fully share the Spirit with others. Revelationally, the resurrection is God's definitive self-disclosure which gathers up the earthly Jesus and establishes him in a radically new mode of being and activity. Soteriologically, the kingdom Jesus preached he has now become in person, thanks to God's self-disclosure and Jesus' personal consummation and public empowerment that occur indivisibly in Jesus' being raised from the dead. It is not enough to say that the resurrection makes the Christology implicit in Jesus' earthly ministry explicit; rather Jesus is now the beginning of a new creation, and the exalted one is continuous with the earthly Jesus precisely through his becoming more, through his becoming fully in person God's victorious reign in the world.

Within these perspectives on the earthly and exalted Jesus Christ, Kasper opts very clearly for a pneumatological approach to Christology.[26] The Incarnation, according to Kasper, is effected by the personal activity of the Holy Spirit, whose sanctifying presence is constitutive of the human person of Jesus. The risen Jesus, in turn, sends forth the Holy Spirit as his very own, and in this way continually inaugurates the eschatological era of salvation.[27]

The main thrust of Kasper's argument in favour of a pneumatological-oriented Christology is that the New Testament writers themselves

---

[25] Kasper devotes two chapters to his treatment of the resurrection entitled: «The Basis of Belief in Jesus' Resurrection» (124-143) and «The Content of Faith in Jesus' Resurrection» (144-162).

[26] Kasper arrives at this position by considering the weaknesses of those Christologies which explicitly adopt either the perspective of philosophy, anthropology, and cosmology or the perspective of world history. For Kasper, such Christologies are represented by, among others, P. Teilhard de Chardin, K. Rahner, and W. Pannenberg. The central weakness, as identified by Kasper, is that the universal character of Jesus Christ is preserved and enhanced at the expense of his uniqueness. As important and necessary as a universal context is for a genuine Christology, the absolute uniqueness of Jesus Christ is equally necessary and important. Kasper argues, therefore, that the danger in the above-mentioned Christologies is that they begin with a particular universal framework, into which at a later point the person Jesus Christ must somehow be inserted. Cf. W. KASPER, *Jesus the Christ*, 17-19.

[27] Cf. W. KASPER, *Jesus the Christ*, 249-268.

inevitably conceive of Jesus in terms of the central Old Testament concept of the Spirit of Yahweh.[28] It is Jesus' Spirit-filled existence which chiefly accounts for his unparalleled uniqueness in the eyes of the Evangelists. Jesus, the Messiah, is the one who is totally the bearer of the Spirit (Is 11:12), the one who is anointed with the Spirit (Lk 4:21).

But this important stress on Jesus' Spirit-filled person, work, and message would not in itself be a sufficient argument for his uniqueness over the prophets, were another aspect of Jesus' spiritual nature left out. This other aspect is the clearly unique significance of Jesus' resurrection, which completely transformed him as no prophet ever was transformed, into a «spiritual body», a «life-giving spirit» (I Cor 15:44-45), a creature fully in the dimension of God.[29] This uniqueness in turn grounds the universal significance of Jesus, in that he is the first person capable of opening the way for all other human beings to such a new form of being with God. Jesus is not only unique as the prophetic bearer of the Spirit and the royal one anointed with the Spirit; he is also divinely vindicated as the one who sends the Spirit to all, because he has become the Head and Lord of all creation through the power of God's Spirit, who effected his resurrection and glorification (Rom 8:11 and I Pet 3:18) as well as his Incarnation and human existence (Lk 1:35).

Therefore, according to Kasper, the absolute uniqueness of Jesus' ontic human life can only be understood in terms of the unquestionable universality of his resurrected and glorified existence. Jesus' real identity can be understood in terms of an unprecedented relationship to the Spirit of God. This Spirit is, in the Old Testament, the life-giving power of the Creator, who is explicitly responsible for the break-through of the totally new and unforeseen into the history of the cosmos. The Spirit continually

---

[28] Cf. W. KASPER, *Jesus the Christ*, 251, 253-256.

[29] The most significant way in which Kasper uncovers the «more» in the resurrection is by developing the outline of a Spirit Christology. The life, light, and creative power released in the world by the resurrection, ascension, and outpouring of the Spirit are the extension of being and life of the Risen One shared with the universe which longs for redemption. The historical life of the believing community and indeed of all humankind is the proper place in which to discern the content of the life and activity of the risen Christ. Tradition in this context is the transmission of the life and light of Christ through the Church to all the world. The age of the Spirit is the age of the resurrected Christ, and the pre-Easter Jesus is a partial dimension of that age but not its full measure or source. In sum, the resurrection legitimates the earthly Servant of God but, even more, fills him with the overflowing Spirit of God. Cf. W. KASPER, *Jesus the Christ*, 250-268.

inaugurates the eschatological age of healing and of hope as He leads the composite course of natural and human history towards its completion. Thus, Kasper can say that the Bible itself contains a unique and universal setting into which Christ can be placed without doing violence to his ontological singularity. The Spirit can effect in the person of Jesus what the Spirit is in Himself: God's own openness to history. The Spirit, as the divine self-mediating principle, is the «theological-transcendental condition of the very possibility of a free self-communicating of God in history».[30] To understand Jesus fully, we must appreciate his unique union with God's own principle of communicating Himself to humanity in history, that is, to the Spirit.

This fact opens up a trinitarian and an ontological ground of Jesus' uniqueness and universality without destroying the personal and historical nature of his human experience. The Spirit, who mediates between the Father and the Son in God's own inner life, is the same Spirit who mediates between the freedom of God and the freedom of the man Jesus at the centre of human history. Kasper thus asserts that the universal mediating function of the Spirit in the Scriptures in general becomes most transparent in the concrete person, work, message, and fate of Jesus of Nazareth; for in Jesus the Spirit of Yahweh was at work to create an ontologically different form of human existence. This activity of the Spirit accounts for the uniqueness of Jesus' being and mission.[31] But the Spirit also inaugurates in Jesus' resurrection a totally new form of human participation in the trinitarian life of God. Thus the universal love of God now has its locus in the person of the risen Christ, the centre and head of the new creation. God's triune being is now objectively open to all who must subjectively respond to God's openness to them through the power of the Spirit of the risen Jesus; this activity of the same Spirit who brought about Jesus' uniqueness also accounts for the universality of the being and the mission of Jesus.

2.3.2 *Awareness of Wisdom Christology in Kasper*

Having summarised Kasper's pneumatological approach to Christology, we now turn to the central focus of our discussion, namely the presence of the Wisdom theme in Kasper's Christology. We have already noted that Kasper makes the historical aspect of Jesus of Nazareth an essential

---

[30] Cf. W. KASPER, *Jesus the Christ*, 250.
[31] Cf. W. KASPER, *Jesus the Christ*, 251-256.

element in the formulation of his Christology. In this regard, while not using much of the Wisdom tradition, Kasper does make reference to some of the central Wisdom texts of the New Testament as set out in our earlier chapters. Kasper's is not a Wisdom Christology but there is to be found there an awareness of the Wisdom influences in the formulation of the doctrine of the Incarnation and, furthermore, as we shall see, a consciousness of the role that Wisdom can play in grappling with at least one question which Kasper deems important for Christology today.

While acknowledging that New Testament Christology is not simply reducible to Jewish ideas but is in fact original and innovative and can be looked for only in the preaching and ministry of the earthly Jesus himself as well as in the experience of Easter, Kasper does acknowledge the influences from the world of the Old Testament and Judaism.[32] Most important of these influences, for Kasper, is the idea of Wisdom as pre-existent at the time of creation (Prov 8:22-31).[33] In the development of New Testament Christology, he understands the categories of the Wisdom tradition as a necessary supplement to the messianic and prophetic categories and as a stage leading to the Logos Christology of John.

However, Kasper keeps all this very general. Specific references to links in the New Testament corpus with the Wisdom literature are sparse.[34]

---

[32] Kasper argues that the title «Son of God» has a firm basis in the royal messianism of the Old Testament. For this reason the two royal psalms, Psalm 2 and Psalm 110, became the mȯst important supports for the early church's christological proof from scripture. In the New Testament, too, the Davidic sonship of the Messiah and the divine sonship of Jesus are seen as closely connected (Rom 1:3-4; Lk 1:32-35). Cf. W. KASPER, *The God of Jesus Christ*, 173.

[33] Kasper goes on to conclude that the parallels to the idea of the Logos in the prologue of John's Gospel are obvious here. Furthermore, Kasper notes that «[...] the writings of Philo of Alexandria show how easy it was to connect these Jewish speculations on Wisdom with Greek philosophical ideas.» As a result, Kasper concludes, all the essential components of New Testament Christology were prepared in the Judaism of the inter-testamental period. Cf. W. KASPER, *The God of Jesus Christ*, 174.

[34] With reference to the greeting «Blessed are you [...]» which is characteristic of Jesus' preaching (Mt 5:3-11; Lk 6:20-22; Mt 11:6; Lk 7:23; Mt 13:16; Lk 10:23), Kasper notes that «[...] these beatitudes are a fixed form in Greek and Jewish Wisdom literature (Sir 25:7-10) but that Jesus uses this same form in a very different way. In the preaching of Jesus, and in contrast to these beatitudes, all worldly blessings and values recede before the good fortune of sharing in the Kingdom of God.» Furthermore, in discussing the implicit Christology included in Jesus' preaching, Kasper notes that «[...] at first sight, Jesus comes on the scene like a rabbi, a prophet, or a teacher of Wisdom but that closer inspection reveals characteristic differences between Jesus and all three such

Kasper's central point here is that the implied Christology of the earthly Jesus contains an unprecedented claim which breaks down all previous schemes. Jesus was reluctant to accept titles because He claimed to be more than they could express.

In his analysis of «Jesus Christ–Son of God» Kasper deals with two questions in which he draws upon the themes of the Wisdom tradition: the pre-existence of Christ and his mediatorship of creation.[35] He appeals to some components of New Testament Christology which have a biblical basis in the Wisdom literature of the Old Testament.[36] Firstly, with regard to pre-existence,[37] Kasper shows how this theme emerged at a very early stage, in practice at the same time as the formulation of the Christology of exaltation. The «living situation» of these ideas in the New Testament which had emerged was the eschatological character of the Christ-event.[38]

Kasper shows how the idea of pre-existence proved necessary. Only this idea could guarantee that in the earthly life and in the cross and resurrection of Jesus, God himself was involved and that in Jesus Christ God was revealing himself definitively and eschatologically.[39] Kasper highlights that what the pre-existence statements of the New Testament do is to express in a new and more profound way the eschatological character of

---

groups. The difference was noticed by Jesus' own contemporaries, who asked in amazement: 'What is this? A new teaching, and one proclaimed with authority' (Mk 1:27).» Cf. W. KASPER, *Jesus the Christ*, 84 and 102. In a similar discussion in *The God of Jesus Christ*, Kasper also notes the table-fellowship of Jesus during his public ministry as highlighting a defining theme in any Christology. However, Kasper does not recall here the table-fellowship of the great banquet as set out in the Wisdom literature. Cf. W. KASPER, *The God of Jesus Christ*, 169.

[35] Kasper appeals to some components of New Testament Christology which have a biblical basis in the Wisdom literature of the Old Testament. Here we are thinking primarily of the Johannine prologue along with other Johannine «Wisdom» texts and the Pauline hymn of Colossians 1:15-17. Kasper also makes use of Philippians 2:6-11. However, we have seen that the Wisdom basis of this hymn is more suspect. Cf. W. KASPER, *Jesus the Christ*, 163-196.

[36] Cf. W. KASPER, *The God of Jesus Christ*, 174.

[37] Kasper rightly points out that «[...] what is at issue here is not a question of extending time into eternity, but of founding salvation history in God's eternity and that the pre-existence theme does not arise from a speculative interest, but serves as a basis for the soteriological concern.» Cf. W. KASPER, *Jesus the Christ*, 172.

[38] Cf. W. KASPER, *Jesus the Christ*, 172.

[39] Cf. W. KASPER, *Jesus the Christ*, 172-185.

the person and work of Jesus of Nazareth.[40] Since in Jesus Christ God himself has definitively, unreservedly, and unsurpassably revealed and communicated himself, Jesus is part of the definition of God's eternal nature. The eschatological character of the person and work of Jesus belongs to the eternal being of God. Otherwise Jesus could not have «defined» God in an eschatological and definitive way. «It follows from the eschatological character of the Christ-event that Jesus is Son of God from eternity, and God from eternity is the Father of our Lord Jesus Christ.»[41] The history and fate of Jesus are thus rooted in the relationality of God: God's relationality proves to be an event. Thus, the New Testament pre-existence statements lead to a new and comprehensive interpretation of the term «God». Furthermore, only thus could the universal significance of Jesus Christ as the fulfilment of all meaning have been adequately expressed.

Kasper is aware that the immediate source of the New Testament pre-existence statements is found mainly in the field of Old Testament Judaism, with the parallels clearest in Old Testament speculation on Wisdom. Wisdom personified is understood as emanation, reflection, and image of God (Wis 7:25); she is present, giving counsel, at the creation of the world (Wis 8:4; 9:9) and can be called «author of all things» (7:12); God sends her (9:10, 17); he has her dwelling in Israel (Ecc 24:8-12). Kasper concludes that the ideas of the pre-existence of Jesus were conveyed to the New Testament through Judaism's speculation on Wisdom.[42]

Turning to the statements about Jesus' mediatorship of creation, Kasper notes that these statements have the same roots in the history of religion as the pre-existence statements, namely, in the Old Testament speculation on Wisdom.[43] Kasper argues that, with the aid of the sapiential tradition

---

[40] Kasper remarks that «[...] the pre-existence theme combined with the mission theme is meant to express the fact that Jesus' person and fate do not have their source within the context of events in this world, but that God himself acts in a way that is beyond any mundane explanation.» Drawing on his use of the concept of freedom, Kasper argues «[...] that this freedom, inexplicable in terms of the present world, breaks through the interconnections of fate and liberates us for the freedom of the children of God. The statement of the pre-existence of the one Son of God provides the reason for our redemption and salvation.» Cf. W. KASPER, *Jesus the Christ*, 173-175, here 173.

[41] Cf. W. KASPER, *Jesus the Christ*, 175.

[42] Cf. W. KASPER, *Jesus the Christ*, 174.

[43] Cf. W. KASPER, *Jesus the Christ*, 186.

which they had largely in common with other peoples (especially the Egyptians), the Old Testament writers already attempted to explain the universality of Yahweh's action in salvation history in and with Israel and so to link together creation and salvation history.[44] Kasper acknowledges that the New Testament developed a Wisdom Christology at a very early stage in the logia source known as Q.[45] In this regard, he notes the threats against «this generation» which does not know the Wisdom of God (Mt 23:34-36, 37-39; Lk 11:49-51; 13:34-36; cf. Mt 11:16-19; 12:41; Lk 7:31-35; 11:31).

Kasper shows how the soteriological and universal cosmic significance of the assertion of Jesus as Son of God is again taken up and developed in the hymn to Christ in Colossians 1:15-17.[46] Here the idea of creation is used to serve and justify the soteriological interest. The aim is to prove the universality of the salvation given through Christ and at the same time to assert that all other «principalities and powers» have been disposed of and that we are bound to no other Lord except Jesus Christ and are to live in the world with a Christian freedom. The statements about the mediatorship of Jesus Christ in creation are therefore intended to bring out the eschatological-definitive and universal character of the person and work of Jesus Christ in the fullness of time and to underline Christian freedom and responsibility in the world. We have already noted the numerous parallels between this hymn and the Wisdom literature, especially Wisdom and Sirach, and this debt to Old Testament Wisdom material is acknowledged by Kasper.[47]

Kasper recognises that the theme of the Wisdom of God as the folly of the cross, resisted and contradicted by the Wisdom of this world, is found in I Corinthians 1 and 2. For Kasper, «the theology of the cross cannot be played off against a sapiential Christology within a universal horizon; but it is an important corrective, so that God's Wisdom in Jesus Christ and the Wisdom of the world are not confused and the cross of Christ is not made void (I Cor 1:17).»[48] Kasper notes the extensive development of Wisdom Christology in the deuteropauline letters.[49] Ephesians 3:10 speaks of the

---

[44] In support of this view Kasper cites G. VON RAD, *Wisdom in Israel.*

[45] Cf. W. KASPER, *Jesus the Christ*, 187.

[46] Cf. W. KASPER, *The God of Jesus Christ*, 185-186.

[47] Cf. W. KASPER, *Jesus the Christ*, 187.

[48] Cf. W. KASPER, *Jesus the Christ*, 187.

[49] Cf. W. KASPER, *Jesus the Christ*, 187.

manifold Wisdom of God, which is active everywhere and assumes a variety of forms. According to God's eternal plan, it appeared in Christ, in whom all treasures of Wisdom and knowledge are hidden (Col 2:3), and is proclaimed by the Church (Col 1:26-28). For Kasper, this Wisdom Christology forms a parallel to the Logos Christology of John's prologue.

Kasper is aware of the contribution of the Church Fathers of the second and third centuries, specifically Tertullian and Origen, regarding a correct understanding of the divine sonship of Jesus Christ. We have already seen how they both drew on Wisdom imagery from the Old Testament. However, Kasper makes no explicit connections in *Jesus the Christ* between the Wisdom literature and the writings of the Fathers.[50]

We have already noted that Kasper acknowledges the presence of the pre-existence theme in the Johannine prologue. Kasper notes that the decisive step in Christology was the interpretation of the biblical image of Jesus Christ as the Son of God by means of the concept *Word of God*.[51] For Kasper, this step from image to concept had already been prepared for in Old Testament Wisdom literature and was expressly taken in the prologue of John.[52] Kasper notes the emphasis by contemporary scholarship on the Old Testament and primitive Christian roots of the Johannine concept of Logos, while also acknowledging the contribution of Philo who linked Old Testament speculation on Wisdom with Greek philosophical speculation on the Logos. Philo had no personal conception of the Logos and even less of the idea of an Incarnation. Hence, Kasper argues that the synthesis offered in the prologue of John must be regarded as an independent achievement which operated in the framework of biblical and early Christian thinking but served to disclose to Hellenistic Jews the being and meaning of Jesus.[53]

However, in his assessment of classical Logos Christology, Kasper concludes that the element of self-emptying is neglected. Logos Christol-

---

[50] However, Kasper notes elsewhere the efforts of the Fathers to formulate a Wisdom Christology, though he does not affirm this explicitly in *Jesus the Christ*. In an article, Kasper refers to the work of Origen, Augustine, Maximus the Confessor, and Bonaventure and their attempts at formulating a Wisdom Christology. Cf. W. Kasper, «Gottes Gegenwart [...]».

[51] Cf. W. KASPER, *The God of Jesus Christ*, 185.

[52] Cf. W. KASPER, *The God of Jesus Christ*, 185.

[53] Kasper acknowledges that the most important statements of a Son Christology and the ones most momentous for subsequent development are in the writings of John. Cf. W. KASPER, *The God of Jesus Christ*, 177.

ogy needs to be taken a step further and deeper in light of the idea of self-emptying. For Kasper, the cross is not simply the consequence of the earthly ministry of Jesus but the very goal of the Incarnation, the meaning and purpose of the Christ-event, so that everything else is ordered to it as to a goal. An important point for Kasper's christological reflection is the giving of the Son by the Father and the self-giving of the Son to the Father for all.[54]

Kasper believes that theology must grapple today with the questions of evil and suffering. Theodicy remains a great challenge for contemporary theology.[55] In this regard, Kasper argues that one of the most important tasks for theology today is to articulate a theology of the cross. This kenosis theology, for Kasper, will be at the same time a theology of the *Wisdom of the cross* and thus will, in accordance with the writings of Paul, *understand the cross of Christ anew as the manifestation of the Wisdom of God*.[56] Here we see Kasper, in an attempt to answer what he sees as a key question for contemporary theology, advocating a kenosis Christology which is *also* a Wisdom Christology. Kasper employs Schelling's attempts at a universal-historical interpretation of the cross. Within a freedom-orientated, historically conscious, and secular world, the cross emerges as the true Wisdom of God. However, Kasper notes there can be no «truth-verification» criteria for the cross. The crucified Wisdom cannot be forced into a scheme of worldly Wisdom which would limit, and thus empty it of meaning.[57]

Furthermore, a Wisdom Christology, understood as a Wisdom of the cross, allows the believer to understand more profoundly the implicit

---

[54] Basic to such a christological approach, for Kasper, is the hymn to Christ in Philippians 2:6-11 which speaks of the kenosis or emptying of him who was in the form of God and accepting the form of a slave. Cf. W. KASPER, *Jesus the Christ*, 168, 172-173; W. KASPER, *The God of Jesus Christ*, 189-197.

[55] «War der Gesprächspartner der neuzeitlichen Theologie der aufgeklärte gebildete Ungläubige, so ist der Gesprächspartner der heutigen Theologie der leidende Mensch». Cf. W. KASPER, «Gottes Gegenwart», 324.

[56] In setting out Kasper's understanding of a kenosis Christology as a theology of the Wisdom of the cross, I am drawing on Kasper's article where he sets out preliminary considerations for a Wisdom Christology. The article is helpful as it expands considerably the Wisdom reference in *Jesus the Christ* and *The God of Jesus Christ* linking kenosis and Wisdom Christologies. Cf. W. KASPER, «Gottes Gegenwart», 311-328.

[57] Cf. W. KASPER, «Gottes Gegenwart»., 325-326.

Wisdom of the created world. A Wisdom Christology will defend and protect the rational structure of reality and its properly understood autonomy leading to a dialogue between Church and world. The world asks, in accordance with its own innate Wisdom, questions beyond itself to which the complete and final answer is solely the Wisdom of God.

2.4 *Concluding Remarks*

We have been concerned with examining to what extent, in formulating his Christology, Kasper makes use of the Wisdom elements in the Scriptures. Kasper opts very clearly for a pneumatological approach to Christology. In this regard, he highlights the emphasis by New Testament writers on the central Old Testament concept of the Spirit of Yahweh.

However, while not using extensively the Wisdom tradition, Kasper does make passing reference to some of the central Wisdom texts of the New Testament. Kasper's is not a Wisdom Christology but there is to be found there a general awareness of the Wisdom influences in the development of Christology.

Specifically, there are four areas where Kasper draws on the Wisdom theme in the Scriptures. Firstly, in dealing with the question of the pre-existence of Christ, Kasper is aware that the immediate source of the New Testament pre-existence statements is found mainly in the field of Old Testament Judaism, with the parallels clearest in Old Testament speculation on Wisdom (Ecc 24:8-12; Wis 7:12; 7:25; 8:4; 9:9-10,17).

Secondly, regarding the statements about Jesus' mediatorship of creation, Kasper notes that these statements have the same roots in the history of religion as the pre-existence statements, namely, the Old Testament speculation on Wisdom. He shows how the soteriological and universal cosmic significance of the assertion of Jesus as Son of God is developed in Colossians 1:15-17. Thirdly, in presenting the decisive step in Christology as the interpretation of the biblical image of Jesus Christ as the Son of God by means of the concept «Word of God», Kasper argues that this step had already been prepared for in Old Testament Wisdom literature and was expressly taken up in the prologue of John.

Finally, in presenting theodicy as a great challenge to contemporary theology, Kasper argues for a kenosis theology which will understand the cross of Christ anew as the manifestation of the Wisdom of God. Thus Kasper advocates a kenosis Christology which is *also* a Wisdom Christology.

While acknowledging those positive points about Kasper's use of the Wisdom theme, it must be said also that, in his extensive treatment of the historical Jesus, Kasper does not present Jesus as a Sage or as Divine Wisdom in person. Kasper's emphasis on the Kingdom of God preached and lived as the very content of salvation receives more attention than any particular finding with regard to the titles.

Neither does Kasper advert to the feminine element in Wisdom thought. No specific references in *Jesus the Christ* are made to the development of the Wisdom theme among the Church Fathers. In conclusion, we cannot speak of Kasper's Christology as a Wisdom Christology. Rather, a general acknowledgment and passing reference to the Wisdom influence on the development of Christology is what is found there.

3. Karl Rahner

3.1 *Jesuit and Theologian*

Karl Rahner (1904-1984) is, arguably, the most influential Catholic theologian of the twentieth century.[58] Born in the town of Freiburg in Breisgau, Germany, he followed in the footsteps of his older brother, Hugo, entering the Jesuit novitiate in Feldkirch, Austria, in 1922 and was ordained a priest ten years later. The autumn of 1937 was for Rahner the beginning of a career as Professor of Theology which was to last for thirty-four years. He spent most of his priestly life teaching at Innsbruck (1937-38, 1948-64), Munich (1964-67), and Münster (1967-71). These years were also an incredibly prolific period of writing and publishing.[59] He

---

[58] Cf. G.A. McCool, «Rahner's philosophical Theology», xiii-xxviii; L.A. Roberts, *Achievement of Karl Rahner*; G. Vass, *Understanding Karl Rahner:* ix-xii; K.H. Weger, *Karl Rahner*.

[59] During the course of this section we will refer to some of Rahner's major writings. However, another side to Rahner's publishing which deserves mention is his work as an editor. In the 1950s he was the editor of the 28th to 31st editions of Denzinger's *Enchiridion Symbolorum*, the compendium of texts of the Church's official teaching. He was co-editor with Josef Hofer of a new edition of Herder's ten-volume *Lexikon für Theologie und Kirche* which appeared between 1957 and 1965. He edited with Adolf Darlap between 1967 and 1969 the six-volume *Sacramentum Mundi*, which also appeared in English, French, Spanish, Italian, and Dutch, each entrusted to its own editor. In 1961 Rahner produced along with Herbert Vorgrimler his *Concise Theological Dictionary*. He was also a co-editor of the *Handbook of Pastoral Theology* (five part-volumes, 1964-69) and an accompanying lexicon (1972), and of the thirty volume encyclopedia *Christian Faith in Modern Society* (1980-83). In addition to editing, he also

retired from teaching in 1971 but continued to write and lecture around the world. Shortly after his eightieth birthday he died on 30 May 1984.[60]

German and Roman Catholic traditions constitute the «context» of Rahner's theology. Rahner breaks away from scholastic and neoscholastic Thomism and seeks to establish a theology based on the double foundation of God's self-communication in Jesus and modern man's experience of God. While his early major works engage in a metaphysics of knowledge[61] and an ontology of man[62], the later Rahner is more explicitly concerned about theological themes such as mystery, symbol, doctrine of God, Christology, and theological anthropology. The articles, collected and published in the *Theological Investigations*[63], reveal a preoccupation with more practical theological questions, while *Foundations of Christian Faith*[64] synthesises his total theological accomplishment.[65]

---

contributed many articles to these various volumes.

[60] For Rahner's life and works see: W.V. DYCH, *Karl Rahner*, 4-17; K.H. NEUFELD, *Die Brüder Rahner*; H. VORGRIMLER, *Karl Rahner*; ID., *Understanding Karl Rahner*.

[61] Cf. K. RAHNER, *Geist in Welt*, 296 pp. Rahner entrusted the preparation of a 2nd edition to J.B. Metz, who extended the text considerably. It is this edition that was translated into English as *Spirit in the World* [Hereafter *Spirit*]. Rahner's task in this work is to establish the possibility of metaphysics and rational theology by applying the critical and transcendental method to the Thomistic epistemology. Using this method, Rahner affirms a primordial unity and convertibility of knowing and being. In every act of human knowledge there is an objective, categorical knowledge through universal concepts and a non-objective, implicit, yet conscious pre-grasp of infinite Being. The absolute openness for infinite Being is part of the essential constitution of humankind. Cf. W.V. DYCH, *Karl Rahner*, 42-46.

[62] Cf. K. RAHNER, *Hörer des Wortes*. J.B. Metz also prepared a 2nd and revised edition of this work. It is this edition which was translated into English as *Hearers of the Word* [Hereafter *Hearers*]. In this work Rahner articulates three propositions of metaphysical anthropology: (i) for man to hear the word of God he must possess an openness (*Offenheit*) for Being; (ii) authentic knowledge of God can be found only in a man's fundamental act of freedom, which determines a basic attitude towards oneself, one's world, and one's infinite horizon; (iii) the place where man must listen for a possible revelation of God is human history.

[63] Most of his theological writings are in the form of articles, which are collected and published in *Theological Investigations*, I-XXIII, (translated from *Schriften zur Theologie*, I-XVI).

[64] A synthesis of his theological programme is found in *Foundations of Christian Faith* (E.T. by W.V. Dych from *Grundkurs des Glaubens*). Although the book is not a summary of Rahner's theology, it comes closer than any of his other publications to giving a unified and systematic view of his thought. Originally given as a course at Münster and Munich under the title «An Introduction to the Idea of Christianity», it took

3.2 *The Development of Rahner's Theology*

Rahner's programme is to do theology as *mystagogy*, the process of learning what faith and theology mean from within our own existence and experience, and not merely by indoctrination from without, and theologizing is an act of translating the experience of mystery into modern man's categories of existential ontology.[66] In this perspective, human subjectivity (modern philosophy) is interpreted by Rahner as man's unlimited dynamic openness to the Absolute (transcendental metaphysics), identified with God (traditional Thomism). The openness and receptivity are human capacities but they are complemented by the *supernatural existential*, i.e., the longing for union with God.[67] In this view the term *supernatural existential*, which is an existential ontological expression of man's experience of God, is the key to interpret Rahner's theology.[68]

Rahner arrived at an understanding of human existence and human knowledge which allowed him to say that the presence of God's grace is

---

Rahner several years to get it ready for publication. Cf. K. RAHNER, *Foundations*, xiii.

[65] Looking at the chronology of his publications we could have the impression that Rahner first worked out a philosophical basis, and then built his theology upon it. Rahner himself rejected such an understanding for both theological and philosophical reasons, as falsely portraying the relationship between faith and theology on the one hand, and knowledge in the sense of reason or philosophy on the other. For Rahner, faith and theology do not begin with philosophy but with an encounter with Jesus of Nazareth. Nevertheless he acknowledges that philosophy can and should play an important role in the elaboration of theology. Cf. K. RAHNER, «Human Question of Meaning», 89-104. Cf. also W.V. DYCH, *Karl Rahner*, 18-19, 32.

[66] Cf. K. RAHNER, *Foundations*, 16-17.

[67] Rahner uses the Heideggerian notion of an existential to explain his faith conviction that God's gracious presence is an intrinsic and universal dimension of all human existence while maintaining the absolute gratuity of this presence. He uses the understanding of knowledge and being elaborated in transcendental Thomism to explain his faith conviction that, though all human knowledge is rooted in the senses, human beings can know God; and though all human existence is existence in relationship to the world and to history, human beings through grace can be personally related to God in knowledge and love. Cf. K. RAHNER, « Nature and Grace», 297-317.

[68] Rahner considers the transcendental and the historical experience of both mystery (God) and history (man) as existing together in a dynamic tension, which characterizes all philosophical and theological thinking. God's revelation starting in creation and culminating in the Incarnation is considered as adding a new dimension to human experience. Rahner has, consequently, developed a transcendental-anthropological method based on both philosophical and theological-christological foundations and has proposed it as the most legitimate one in both theology and philosophy. On theological method in Rahner see A. CARR, *Theological Method of Karl Rahner*.

also the presence of God's revelation, that a universal history of grace is also and necessarily a universal history of revelation and a universal possibility of faith. For Rahner the supernatural elevation of man's being in grace was also the elevation of his knowledge to a new horizon unattainable by any merely natural act. In theological terms, Rahner calls the horizon of human transcendence *mystery* and still later *holy mystery*.[69]

In an article entitled «The Theology of the Symbol» Rahner developed his metaphysics of being into an ontology of symbol.[70] Here Rahner states that knowledge of being is possible because being expresses itself and expresses itself in and through another. That in which the being expresses itself is called *Realsymbol*.[71] This understanding of symbol, which flows directly from the metaphysics outlined in *Spirit* and *Hearers*, leads Rahner to his interpretation of the Trinity and the Incarnation.

According to Rahner, the eternal Logos is the *Realsymbol* of the Father, the expression through which the Father knows and is known. Rahner applies to God the principle that a *Realsymbol* is the only means through which a reality can be known by others. The fact that man is spirit-in-the-world and all human knowledge is sense knowledge means that God can be known only if God becomes appearance. Thus the historical human word is the place of God's revelation and man is the symbol of God in

---

[69] Rahner distances himself from the conventional notion of mystery as «[...] something mysterious to *reason* [...]» or «[...] a provisional limit of thought». Instead he defines the holy mystery, which is accessible in the experience of limitless openness (transcendence) of the subject, as «[...] the nameless, the undeniable, the unattainable [...]» and hence «[...] essentially determinative of the necessary relationship intervening between the created spirit and God [...]» because man is a «[...] recipient of the mysteries in his natural and supernatural elevated transcendence [...]», he is «[...] always confronted by the holy mystery [...]» and «[...] lives by the holy mystery». Cf. K. RAHNER, « Mystery», 36-73; ID., *Foundations*, 1-2, 21-22, 60-61.

[70] Cf. K. RAHNER, «Theology of the Symbol», 221-252. Cf. also J.J. BUCKLEY, «On Being a Symbol», 453-473; M.E. MOTZKO, *Karl Rahner's Theology*, (referred to by J.H.P. WONG, *Logos-Symbol*, 22).

[71] The basic principle of Rahner's ontology of symbol is the fact that all beings are by their very nature symbolic, because they necessarily «express» themselves in order to attain their own nature. Every being expresses itself in something other than itself, returns to itself, and thereby fulfills itself. This expression which enables the being to constitute itself and know itself is what Rahner calls a *Realsymbol*. Cf. K. RAHNER, «Theology of the Symbol», 221-252.

matter.[72] This brings us specifically to Rahner's Christology which is our chief concern here.

3.3 *The Christology of Karl Rahner*

Rahner's writings on Christology span a half-century and pursue innumerable questions from a variety of perspectives. The closest approximation to a comprehensive summary of his Christology is found in chapter six of *Foundations*,[73] but even this presentation differs in intent and scope from an integrated christological synthesis.[74] Of the nine chapters in this work the sixth on Jesus Christ accounts for nearly one third of the whole, further emphasizing the central position occupied by Christology in Rahner's theological system.[75] It is not the purpose of our study here to treat Rahner's Christology in detail.[76] Rather, as with Kasper, our central concern is with examining to what extent, to formulate his systematic Christology, Rahner uses the Wisdom elements in the

---

[72] Obviously, Rahner accepts the doctrine of creation, and so man is not necessary to God. But he does say that if God wants to express himself outwardly, what comes to be is Jesus of Nazareth. Jesus as man is the perfect self-expression of God.

[73] Cf. K. RAHNER, *Foundations*, 176-321.

[74] The subtitle of *Foundations* is a more accurate rendering of the nature of the book for the German theologian's desire is to introduce his readers to the idea of Christianity. The term *foundations* in the title leads us to expect that Rahner is offering a philosophical or fundamental-theological exploration, whereas he is actually presenting a work which includes both fundamental and systematic theology and which operates on what he calls a «first level of reflection». This level consists in giving an account of one's faith in an intellectually responsible way by exposing the intrinsic connections between who human beings are and the message of Christianity. In other words, Rahner wants to introduce his readers to the intelligibility of Christianity, an enterprise which involves him in exploration of the human person (philosophical and theological anthropology) of the reality of faith (systematic theology) and the grounds of faith (fundamental theology). Cf. K. RAHNER, *Foundations*, xi-xv.

[75] This becomes even more evident when we look at the internal structure of the work. In his theological endeavour there, Rahner is above all concerned with man in his openness to the self-communication of God in history. The mystery of Christ is presented precisely as the climax of this two-way movement, for the Christ event is conceived as the fullness of God's self-communication and the absolute realization of human transcendence. Hence, chapters one to five can be considered as a preparation for the message of Christ. The remaining three chapters dealing with the Church, Christian living, and eschatology are only the continuation and the final fulfilment of the Christ event.

[76] For a study of Rahner's Christology cf. J.H.P. WONG, *Logos-Symbol*.

Scriptures. However, some explication of Rahner's Christology, by way of summary and overview, will help to situate our specific study. In this regard, we will use chapter six of Rahner's *Foundations* as a basic text for our examination of Rahner's Christology. We will appeal to other writings of his on Christology insofar as they help to clarify or elucidate our argument further.

3.3.1 *Summary*

When speaking of Christology a decisive point of departure for Rahner is the necessity for an encounter with the historical Jesus of Nazareth.[77] Rahner argues that the «[...] genuine Christianity of the New Testament» knew that its faith «[...] was related to a definite historical event» and that «[...] it did not simply posit this event or create it in faith» but rather «[...] receives its justification and foundation from this event».[78] In maintaining the intrinsic connection between faith and history, Rahner does not ignore or minimize the difficulties posed by modern historical research. Nevertheless faith and theology are related to a definite historical event and Christian faith today must continue to maintain the «substantial historicity» of the gospel narratives.[79]

Culling his material from what he considers reliable exegetical sources, Rahner summarizes this «substantial historicity» in broad strokes and in the question of the claim of the historical Jesus limits himself to six minimal statements.[80]

---

[77] «In giving a justification for our faith in Christ, the basic and decisive point of departure, of course, lies in an encounter with the historical Jesus of Nazareth, and hence in an "ascending Christology".» Cf. K. RAHNER, *Foundations*, 177. Rahner calls this dimension of our relationship to Jesus of Nazareth an «existentiell Christology». It is the actual process of living in a relationship of faith, hope, and love with Jesus of Nazareth wherein he is recognized and acknowledged as the true way to salvation. Cf. K. RAHNER, *Foundations*, 305-311.

[78] Cf. K. RAHNER, *Foundations*, 238.

[79] Cf. K. RAHNER, *Foundations*, 246. Rahner's treatment of the historical Jesus can be found in *Foundations* chapter 6, sections 2,5,6,8,9. Rahner is aware that scriptural exegesis, in the case of Christology, has highlighted that it is seldom possible to say with any certainty which statements can be attributed to the historical Jesus and which can «only» be ascribed to the theology of faith of the early church.

[80] (i) Jesus lived in the religious environment of his own people, that is, within the already existing historical situation in which he found himself. (ii) As a radical reformer, Jesus broke through the monopoly of the Jewish law which had set itself up in place of God. (iii) Although he hoped for success in his religious mission, Jesus became more and

Given the complexity and historical ambiguity of questions about the historical Jesus, Rahner sets out two theses which constitute for him the minimum knowledge of Jesus that is both historically credible and also keeps faith rooted in and justified by the historical Jesus of Nazareth. Firstly, Rahner points out that Jesus did not regard himself simply as one of the many prophets in a line that was always open. On the contrary, he saw himself as the *eschatological prophet* and *absolute saviour*.[81] Secondly, we are, according to Rahner, able to believe in Jesus' claim if we look in faith at the event mediated by the bringer of salvation in the whole of his existence, the resurrection of Jesus.[82] For Rahner, resurrection means the salvation of Jesus' concrete existence by God and in the presence of God, and the abiding and permanent validity of his history.[83] For Rahner, it is at least implicit in the claim of resurrection that Jesus is the *eschatological prophet* (the last of the prophets) of God's final word.[84]

---

more convinced that his mission was leading him into fatal conflict with the religious and political establishment. (iv) Jesus faced death with resolution, accepting it as the inevitable consequence of his faithfulness to his mission. (v) He preached with reforming zeal to rouse people and call them back to God because of his consciousness of the nearness of the kingdom of God. He also gathered disciples around him. (vi) From the historical point of view, a great many questions about Jesus' life and attitudes before the Easter event must inevitably remain open. Cf. K. RAHNER, *Foundations*, 247-249.

[81] What is striking about Rahner's Christology is not only that it is in accordance with his anthropological approach, but also that he prefers the term *absolute bringer of salvation* to the concept of *Incarnation*. He has even gone so far as to say that a transcendental Christology points essentially to an absolute bringer of salvation, which means that the «idea of Christ» is not primarily described in ontic categories, but is also the basis of the function that Jesus has for me personally and for humanity in general, a function of which Jesus himself was aware. According to whatever function he wishes to emphasize, Rahner varies the name, calling Jesus, in addition to the absolute bringer of salvation, the mediator of salvation, the eschatological prophet, or the last of the prophets.

[82] Rahner sees the resurrection narratives as the pre-eminent New Testament material for grounding our faith today. The resurrection of Jesus, however, must be understood as intrinsically related to the whole life and death of Jesus which preceded it, and his life and death must be understood as intrinsically related to the resurrection. Cf. K. RAHNER, *Foundations*, 266.

[83] Cf. K. RAHNER, *Foundations*, 266.

[84] For Rahner, the life, death, and resurrection of Jesus is the sign or symbol in which God's saving will reaches its full and irrevocable realization and manifestation, and this event in the life and history of Jesus is a unique event in the common history of which we are all a part. The single history which we all share has already entered into eschatological salvation in the person and history of Jesus, who is thus the first moment

This ascending Christology of the resurrection experience is the basis for the development of all the later Christologies of the New Testament and the subsequent Councils of the Church. Hence, for Rahner, there can be no opposition between the earlier, ascending, functional Christology and its later transposition into metaphysical and essential terms.

Rahner moves from the *a posteriori* experience of the Logos in history to the *a priori* elements in the christological dogma. Applying his characteristic method of transcendental Thomism to christological questions, Rahner develops what he calls a *transcendental Christology*.[85] In this regard, Rahner asks how the classical «descending» Christology of God becoming incarnate in the world and in humanity could be supplemented by an «ascending» Christology which begins with the world and humanity, and sees them as moving towards this point of unity with God. His answer is an understanding of the Christian doctrine of Incarnation within the context of an evolutionary view of the world.[86] We can trace three main steps in Rahner's attempt to show this affinity and thereby work out an ascending Christology of the world's movement towards unity with God.[87] Firstly, there is the intrinsic unity of matter and spirit in the

---

and the inauguration of the final, eschatological stage of history for all of us. Cf. K. RAHNER, *Foundations*, 264-285.

[85] The task of transcendental Christology is to develop an ontology and an anthropology within which the affirmation of Christian faith that Jesus is both God and man makes sense and is intelligible in our contemporary cultural situation. In developing a transcendental Christology, Rahner sees the dogmatic statements about Jesus in Christian tradition as the beginning and not the end of christological reflection. Rahner speaks both of the «permanent validity» and of the «limits» of the traditional dogmatic statements about Jesus formulated at the great Councils of Nicaea (325), Constantinople I (381), Ephesus (431) and Chalcedon (451). See the reflection on the Council of Chalcedon as both end and beginning in « Problems in Christology», 149-200. The classical doctrine based on the notion of Incarnation is an exclusively *descending* Christology in the sense that it speaks from the outset of the incarnate Word of God who has «come down» to us. The humanity of Jesus can be misunderstood as merely the livery which God donned in order to appear among us. The notion of Incarnation, for Rahner, should be the end and not the beginning of christological reflection. Cf. K. RAHNER, *Foundations*, 177, 289-290.

[86] Cf. K. RAHNER, «Evolutionary View», 157-192; ID., *Foundations*, 178-203.

[87] Rahner seeks to articulate an «inner affinity», «a sort of similarity of style» between Christology and an evolutionary view of the world. He stresses that «[...] the world is something in which everything is related to everything else.» The Incarnation is not a way for God to make «[...] corrections as a kind of afterthought [...]» but rather «[...] appears as the ontologically unambiguous goal of the movement of creation as a

sense of the evolutionary movement of the material world towards spiritual existence.[88] Secondly, there is the intrinsic unity between human spiritual existence and the life of grace freely bestowed by God.[89] Thirdly, there is the intrinsic link between the union of human beings with God in grace and the hypostatic union of the man Jesus with God.[90]

---

whole..». In light of this relationship, Rahner calls for a mutual interplay between ontology and Christology. On the one hand, christological statements require «[...] a general doctrine of creation (and the ontology contained in it) [...]»; but on the other hand, Rahner calls for a «[...] retrospective use [...]» of Christology in ontology. Our understanding of creation shapes our interpretation of Christ, but our experience of Christ re-shapes our understanding of the universe. Rahner's perspective stresses the uniqueness of the Christ-event, but it also establishes the ground of continuity between the Christ-event and God's universal activity. Cf. K. RAHNER, «Problems in Christology», here 164-166. Cf. also W.V. DYCH, *Karl Rahner*, 69-79.

[88] In his first step Rahner argues that it can be taken for granted in Christian theology and philosophy «that spirit and matter have more in common than they have differentiating them» (Cf. K. RAHNER, *Foundations*, 192). He recalls the anthropological starting point and the metaphysical analysis of spirit and matter developed in *Spirit and Hearers*. Matter and spirit are two correlated elements to be found individually in isolation from each other (Cf. K. RAHNER, «Evolutionary View», 162). Moreover, the intrinsic relationship is not static, but has a history. It is the history of material being in its process of becoming, not just in the sense of becoming different, but becoming more, a leap to something essentially higher (Cf. K. RAHNER, *Foundations*, 184-185; Rahner, «Evolutionary View», 164). This is possible so long as the intrinsic dynamism empowering this evolutionary process of becoming is understood as God's creative and co-operative presence as the ground of his creation. Cf. also K. RAHNER, «Unity of spirit and matter», 153-177.

[89] It is against the background of this unity between matter and spirit that we must understand the second step of Rahner's synthesis, the intrinsic unity of nature and grace. He affirms this unity by conceiving of God's gracious presence in the world through his Spirit as a *supernatural existential*. This means that in God's creative intention, from the very beginning the intrinsic dynamism and goal of the evolutionary process has been not just the transcendence of matter beyond its own power into the human life of knowledge, freedom, and love, but also the transcendence of human life beyond its own power and participation in God's own life through knowledge, freedom and love. Cf. K. RAHNER, «Nature and Grace», 297-317; ID., «Nature and Grace», 165-188.

[90] When the evolutionary process reaches the stage of human consciousness and freedom, history in the proper sense begins. That is, human freedom becomes a decisive factor in its course and direction. It is in the context of human freedom that Rahner in his third step sees the unique role of Jesus in this history, and the place of Christology in an evolutionary view of the world. For Rahner, while the offer of God's self-communication is an existential which pervades all of history, its free acceptance is an historical event that takes place at definite points of space and time. Cf. K. RAHNER,

Christian faith sees Jesus of Nazareth as the person in whose total openness to God the offer of God's self-communication met with a free and perfect response, so that in his life and death the history of grace reaches its irreversible and unsurpassable triumph over sin. Since the history of sin is the history of separation and alienation from God, the perfect union with God that Jesus achieved in his free response is the undoing of sin and the entrance into history of its opposite, that is, salvation. He is salvation and saviour in his very being, and not just in his actions. Moreover, since his union with God is irrevocable and cannot be surpassed by a still greater union, he is the «absolute saviour».[91]

In a series of further reflections Rahner tries to show that an ascending Christology, in which the self-transcending movement of all creation towards life in God reaches its culmination in Jesus' union with the Father, is perfectly compatible with the traditional descending Christology which speaks of the movement of God towards the world or God becoming flesh. Indeed, they are but two sides of the same coin, or the two poles of the single union between God and the world that is the substance and heart of Christology.[92]

Foundations, 193; ID., «Evolutionary View», 173-192.

[91] This does not mean that salvation begins or ends with Jesus in a temporal sense, but that in him the process that began before him and continues after him has reached its climax, not its end or conclusion. Christ has been at work in human history from the very beginning as the final cause, «the moving power of the movement toward the goal». What happens in Christ is that the goal of the entire cosmic process, God's self-communication «can be clearly recognized as something irrevocable, and in him it reaches its climax» (Cf. K. RAHNER, «Evolutionary View», 175). As absolute saviour Jesus must be «both the absolute promise of God to spiritual creatures as a whole», and at the same time «the acceptance of this self-communication» and thereby the fulfilment of the promise. In the unity of these two aspects Rahner sees the meaning of the traditional christological term «hypostatic union», the union of the divine and the human in a single person. Jesus is the presence of God's saving activity in the world in such a way that he is part of the world. Otherwise, the world would not have been truly united to God in him. At the same time, what he accepted in the fullest and most radical way was God's self-communication, the very life and being of God's Son, so that in him God's own Son became flesh. In this immediacy to and union with God implied in the notion of an absolute saviour Rahner sees the same content that is expressed in the doctrines of Incarnation and hypostatic union. Cf. K. RAHNER, *Foundations*, 193-202. For a treatment of Rahner's notion of «absolute saviour» see J.H.P. WONG, *Logos-Symbol*, 135-138.

[92] Cf. K. RAHNER, «Theology of the Incarnation», 105-120; ID., *Foundations*, 212-228.

In the light of Rahner's evolutionary view of Christology this process wherein the Word becomes flesh is identical with the process wherein flesh becomes the Word of God. Descending and ascending Christology, God's self-communication and man's acceptance, the Incarnation of God and the divinization of man are two sides of the same coin. Hence the Incarnation is not an abrupt interruption or aberration in the «normal» course of history, but the «fullness of time», the culmination of a movement which began with creation itself. For Rahner, this «idea» of the God-Man is a more universal and more intrinsic way of understanding and expressing for our age what Christian faith affirms of Jesus of Nazareth. It is an attempt to avoid other «ideas»: mythological ones which see God in human disguise, or monophysite ones that find Christ by suppressing the humanity of Jesus, or gnostic ones whose route to God lies outside the world and human history altogether. It is not the case, says Rahner, that God is in heaven and we are on earth. Rather, «we have to say of the God whom we profess in Christ that he is exactly where we are, and only there is he to be found».[93] For Rahner, theology is also and always anthropology, and Christology is the beginning and end of anthropology.

3.3.2 *Traces of Wisdom Christology in Rahner*

We have seen that Rahner presents, in thesis form, aspects of our historical knowledge of Jesus.[94] In setting about this task Rahner does not explicitly draw upon the Scriptures and so we cannot expect to find many references to the Wisdom literature in his writings. In thesis six Rahner acknowledges «over fifty names given to Jesus in the New Testament».[95] However, the term used most frequently by Rahner is that of «incarnate Logos/Word».[96] Rahner's Christology is based on the concept of the Word. He has developed a contemporary Logos Christology which seeks a coherent understanding of the revelation of God in Jesus Christ and the universal presence of God in all human experience and in the cosmos. In this regard, Rahner was going back to the affirmation of the Incarnation

---

[93] Cf. K. RAHNER, *Foundations*, 226.

[94] Cf. K. RAHNER, *Foundations*, 247-249.

[95] Cf. K. RAHNER, *Foundations*, 248. In his *Concise Theological Dictionary*, edited with H. Vorgrimler, Rahner acknowledges «over one hundred and thirty names given to Jesus in the New Testament». Cf. K. RAHNER – H. VORGRIMLER, *Kleines Theologisches Wörterbuch*; E.T.: *Concise Theological Dictionary*,102.

[96] Cf. J.H.P. WONG, *Logos-Symbol*, 113-148.

of the Logos, and the identification of Jesus as the incarnate Logos which dominated the Christology of the second and third centuries.

The concept *Logos* is indispensable to Rahner's Christology of the symbol. Indeed, the Johannine prologue offers Rahner the primary inspiration for his Christology «from above». Moreover, even his Christology «from below» is chiefly a reflection on man's constitution as the *potentia oboedientialis* for the Logos. Rahner considers the Logos concept an appropriate expression for the idea of revelation. He conceives of the Logos precisely as the Father's «perfect image» and his «revelatory symbol» for the world, rather than as simply his spoken word.[97] Rahner has not only revived the classical Logos concept by reaffirming its original connection to revelation; he has also enriched it with a contemporary notion *Realsymbol* which shows revelation essentially to mean *self-revelation*. We have already noted that the Logos prologue of the Gospel of John is considerably indebted to pre-Christian Wisdom speculation. To this extent we may speak of Logos Christology having some of its roots in Wisdom Christology. While acknowledging this connection we must note that Logos Christology stands independent of Wisdom Christology. However, Rahner makes no explicit reference to Wisdom Christology or to Wisdom literature in the christological chapter in *Foundations*.

It is in this context that we must refer to the work of Leo Lefebure.[98] While treating Rahner's Christology, Lefebure acknowledges from the beginning that an interchange between the concepts of *Wisdom* and *Word* is possible and, hence, he proceeds to understand Rahner's Christology as Wisdom Christology. At no point does Lefebure advert to any distinctions between Wisdom and Word Christologies. Neither does he acknowledge Rahner's emphasis on Jesus as the *eschatological prophet* or *absolute saviour*.

Lefebure draws parallels between Rahner's Christology and the biblical theme of Wisdom Christology under three headings: (i) the religious dimension of experience; (ii) Christ and creation; (iii) the play of language.[99] Regarding the religious dimension of experience, Lefebure argues that the Old Testament Wisdom image of a call coming in and through the everyday experience of the created order of the world bears a clear similarity to Rahner's more abstract and theoretical theme of a call

---

[97] Cf. K. RAHNER, *Foundations*, 248.

[98] Cf. L.D. LEFEBURE, *Wisdom Christology*.

[99] Cf. L.D. LEFEBURE, *Wisdom Christology*, 164-280.

implicit in human life, a call which we experience in and through our everyday decisions, a call in response to which we are ultimately deciding our own destiny. Furthermore, Lefebure affirms that the later stages of the Wisdom tradition correlated the experience of Wisdom with the historical revelations to the people of Israel. Rahner's interpretation of special historical revelations of God as concrete manifestations of God's universal salvific will which has already embedded itself in the entire creative process is presented by Lefebure as a parallel to this process of correlation in the later stages of the Wisdom tradition.

Secondly, Lefebure compares the disclosure/concealment dialectic evident in the Wisdom literature and in the revelation of Jesus as the Wisdom of God with a similar dialectic he claims can be observed in Rahner's Christology. Lefebure argues that while Christ is the Wisdom of God he is not recognised as such either by the «masters of our age» (I Cor 2:8) or by the Jews and Greeks (I Cor 1:22-25). Even though Jesus appears as the epiphany of the Logos in the Gospel of John, he is not recognised by the world or even by «his own» (Jn 1:10-11). For Lefebure, Rahner's Christology also involves a dialectic of disclosure and concealment. The human nature of Jesus, as the *Realsymbol* of the Logos, reveals God to mankind; and yet God remains hidden even in this revelation. The ontology of *Realsymbol* implies that there is no direct path to knowledge of any reality, including God. Even God must communicate with human thought through the medium of a symbol, a symbol in which God is both hidden and revealed. The incomprehensibility of God and the dialectic of disclosure and concealment force religious language to a paradoxical intersection of affirmation and negation. Such a paradoxical intersection, according to Lefebure, appears in the Wisdom tradition and the Christology of Rahner, and so Rahner's relating of the Christ-event to universal human experience finds precedent in the Wisdom Christology of the New Testament.

Regarding these two parallels drawn by Lefebure between Rahner's Christology and the theme of biblical Wisdom, we do not know whether Rahner himself was aware of these proposed associations. Certainly Rahner does not draw on the Wisdom literature or the notion of Jesus as the Wisdom of God. Hence, the parallels do not indicate an attempt by Rahner to present his understanding of Jesus explicitly in terms of Wisdom Christology.

Lefebure's third link between Rahner's Christology and the biblical Wisdom theme concerns an apparent relationship between the Wisdom notion of Christ as the universal ordering principle of creation and Rahner's cosmic Christology. We have seen that some central Wisdom texts of the New Testament (I Cor 8:6; Col 1:14-20; Jn 1:1-18) establish a very close relationship between the ordering power of creation and the experience of revelation and redemption in Christ. In these texts Christ or the Logos is at work throughout the cosmos from the very beginning of creation, long before the birth of the historical figure, Jesus of Nazareth. The life, death, and resurrection of Jesus reveal, illumine, and make present this universal activity. Lefebure has argued that this link between creation and Christ offers precedent for Rahner's vision of «creation and Incarnation as two moments and two phases of the *one* process of God's self-giving and self-expression».[100] Rahner's integration of Christology into an evolutionary world-view clearly moves beyond anything envisioned by the ancient sages or the New Testament writers. Yet Lefebure argues that there is within the Wisdom tradition an interest in the order of the physical universe and an openness to using forms of thought which come from diverse sources.[101] By integrating his Christology into an evolutionary view of the world, Lefebure argues that Rahner gives a contemporary and dynamic interpretation of the New Testament's presentation of Jesus as Wisdom.

As with the previous two parallels drawn by Lefebure between Rahner's Christology and the biblical Wisdom theme, this third parallel between Rahner's integration of Christology into an evolutionary world-view and the Wisdom notion of Christ as the universal ordering principle of creation can only be said to be implicitly present. As with the previous two parallels, while it may be argued that there are precedents in the Wisdom literature and early Wisdom Christology for elements in Rahner's own Christology, there is no way of knowing that Rahner himself was aware of these precedents or that they were important to him in his overall christological project. In this specific parallel, for example, Rahner makes no reference to Colossians 1:14-20; I Corinthians 8:6; or John 1:1-18, the central Wisdom texts of the New Testament which establish a close

---

[100] Cf. K. RAHNER, *Foundations*, 197.

[101] We have already seen that the Book of Wisdom made use of Hellenistic philosophy to develop the presentation of Wisdom. Moreover, it was a fundamental principle of the Wisdom tradition that there is a close link between understanding the order of the world and the activity of God. Moreover, the New Testament's identification of Christ as the power through whom all things are created and remain in being offers an invitation to relate the experience of Jesus Christ to the ordering power of creation.

relationship between the ordering power of creation and the experience of revelation and redemption in Christ. These precedents are implicit in Rahner's Christology but no explicit connections are made.

Furthermore, given Rahner's emphasis on the concept of the Word and his development of a contemporary Logos Christology, together with his presentation of Jesus as the *eschatological prophet* and *absolute prophet*, it would seem reasonable to argue that an explicit understanding of Jesus in terms of Wisdom Christology was not intended by Rahner. Hence, while these precedents point to traces of Wisdom Christology in his writings, we cannot speak of Rahner's Christology as a Wisdom Christology.

3.4 *Concluding Remarks*

We have been examining to what extent, in formulating his Christology, Rahner uses Wisdom elements in the Scriptures. Rahner's decisive point of departure for Christology is an encounter with the historical Jesus of Nazareth. In this regard, Rahner's Christology draws on the concept of *Word* to develop a contemporary Logos Christology. Explicit references to the Wisdom literature in Rahner's christological writings are not to be found. Rahner acknowledges the complexity and historical ambiguity of questions about the historical Jesus. In this context, in order to remain historically credible and to keep faith rooted in and justified by the historical Jesus of Nazareth, Rahner speaks of Jesus as the *eschatological prophet* and the *absolute saviour*.

Lefebure's failure to distinguish between Wisdom and Word Christologies, or to explicitly acknowledge Rahner's use of *absolute saviour* and *eschatological prophet* as titles for the historical Jesus, together with a failure to acknowledge Rahner's lack of use of the Wisdom theme, undermines his attempt to present Rahner's Christology as a Wisdom Christology. Rather, Lefebure is developing Rahner's christological thought in a Wisdom direction rather than expounding his Christology. Lefebure's contribution is to show that Rahner's Christology is open to development in this way though Rahner himself did not do so. The facts are that, in his treatment of the historical Jesus, Rahner does not present Jesus as a Sage or as Divine Wisdom in person. Neither does Rahner advert to the feminine element in Wisdom thought. He does not refer to the development of the Wisdom theme among the Church Fathers. In conclusion, we cannot speak of Rahner's Christology as a Wisdom

Christology. Some implicit traces of a Wisdom Christology can be identified but such traces do not warrant the position that we find in Rahner a Wisdom Christology.

4. Edward Schillebeeckx

4.1 *Dominican and Theologian*

Edward Schillebeeckx (b.1914) has proved to be one of the most widely read, influential, and controversial theologians of the twentieth century.[102] Born in the Belgian city of Antwerp, he joined the Belgian province of the Order of Preachers (Dominicans) just before his twentieth birthday. Schillebeeckx's career spans most of the twentieth century. Apart from relatively short stays elsewhere, he has spent his entire life in the Low Countries of Europe. As an adult he has worked professionally in Catholic universities publishing a vast amount of material during his career: over five hundred books and articles.[103] Because his theology has been enunciated primarily in a *European* cultural context, it is not surprising that his thought has been particularly influenced by two major European philosophical currents, both of which are connected. In broad terms, the first is a dialogue with critical philosophy inherited from the Enlightenment. The second is a twentieth-century philosophical *quest for meaning* that seeks to overcome a positivism characterizing certain currents of nineteenth-century philosophy in Europe.[104]

4.2 *The Development of Schillebeeckx's Theology*

Schillebeeckx's early years of formal studies were spent in Ghent (*Studium Philosophicum*)[105] and Louvain (*Studium Theologicum*).[106] If

---

[102] For an account of Schillebeeckx's life see: J. BOWDEN, *Edward Schillebeeckx*. Cf. also D.F. FORD, «Edward Schillebeeckx», 152-163; P. KENNEDY, *Schillebeeckx*, 13-30; R.J. SCHREITER – M.C. HILKERT, ed., *Praxis of Christian Experience*.

[103] There is no complete bibliography of Schillebeeckx's writings, but for a listing of works published up to 1983 see R.J. SCHREITER, «Bibliography», 297-321.

[104] Cf. P. KENNEDY, *Schillebeeckx*, 31-53. Cf. also R. KEARNEY, *Modern Movements*, 1-9.

[105] As a student in Ghent, Schillebeeckx's philosophical studies were especially beneficial to him because they were directed by Dominic De Petter (1905-71). De Petter stands as the pre-eminent intellectual guide in Schillebeeckx's early life. It was thanks to him that Schillebeeckx began to read philosophers such as Kant, Hegel, Husserl and Merleau-Ponty. As a professor of philosophy in Ghent, De Petter was concerned with

these years may be regarded as the first significant intellectual develop-ment of his adult life, then the second most significant stage began in 1946 when Schillebeeckx moved to France to undertake doctoral studies in theology. Even though his stay there was a brief academic *intermezzo*, ending in 1947, it was a period of intense intellectual fermentation resulting in his «conversion» to theology. While living in France, Schillebeeckx became familiar with the theological programmes of Marie-Dominique Chenu and Yves Congar. Both Chenu and Congar advocated a historical approach to theology and a creative re-interpretation of Aquinas.[107]

---

the problem of how to surmount conceptualism which he held characterized all philosophy before Kant. De Petter set Schillebeeckx this academic task. Towards that end Schillebeeckx made an analysis of the interplay between question and answer and speculated about the possibility of a non-conceptual component in reason. The all-important consequence of Schillebeeckx's attempt to obviate conceptualism in theology was that he became interested in the concept of experience. Cf. J. BOWDEN, *Edward Schillebeeckx*, 25-27.

[106] *The Code of Canon Law* (1917) brought into law Pope Leo XIII's instruction that Catholic theological studies should be undertaken with Aquinas as a model. During the period of Schillebeeckx's first sojourn in Louvain, theology was taught according to Aquinas' *Summa Theologiae*. Schillebeeckx became extremely dissatisfied with his theological studies at Louvain, largely because of the method used in the *Studium*. The problem was the identification of theology with the exposition of concepts that are not related to their historical context and to contemporary experiences. On witnessing Schillebeeckx's dissatisfaction with theology, De Petter encouraged him to read Karl Adam's works since they covered theological topics such as the church, sacraments, and Jesus Christ, but without using scholastic terminology. Adam was unlike other Catholic theologians of his day in that his theological method extended beyond medieval thinkers to the Fathers of the Church, while simultaneously incorporating the findings of modern biblical research. Through reading Adam, Schillebeeckx found a way of linking theology and philosophy and was propelled to study the work of Pierre Rousselot (1878-1915) who, by examining the medieval doctrine of the *lumen fidei,* was better able to highlight a human experiential aspect to faith. Cf. P. KENNEDY, *Schillebeeckx*, 17-21.

[107] The most significant teacher Schillebeeckx encountered in Paris was the Dominican, Marie-Dominique Chenu (1895-1990). It was largely because of Chenu's approach to theology that Schillebeeckx became more inclined to develop his interests in the subject. In his book, *Une École de Théologie: Le Saulchoir*, Chenu underscored the importance of history for theology. He argued that speculative theories occupy a place in theology secondary to the realities referred to in formulas of faith. This reflects the same starting point as De Petter. Through Chenu and De Petter, therefore, Schillebeeckx was stimulated to relativize theology conceived as a conceptual system, and to place theological reflection in a historical (Chenu) and human-experiential context (De Petter). Cf. P. KENNEDY, *Schillebeeckx*, 21-23.

After a decade teaching dogmatics at Louvain,[108] Schillebeeckx was appointed Professor of Dogmatic Theology and the History of Theology in the Catholic University of Nijmegen in the Netherlands in 1957. His move to the Netherlands triggered another major turn in his intellectual life.[109] In Louvain his method of teaching had always begun by explaining a specific dogma and its history. In a second step, the method moved on to explore what the dogma might mean for contemporary believers. In the Netherlands, however, Schillebeeckx began more resolutely to reflect theologically by taking human experiences as a methodological point of departure.

1966 is a milestone in Schillebeeckx's life mainly because during that year he first visited North America and he began to teach hermeneutics. In his publications after this time there are clear signs that he had begun to believe that classical theology was becoming increasingly ineffective in the interpretation of Christian faith for the modern world. He spoke unreservedly of his search for a solution to what he perceived as a crisis for contemporary Christians. This period of his career up to 1974

---

[108] During a decade of teaching dogmatics in Louvain, Schillebeeckx focused his attention on five main subjects: (a) sacramentology; (b) theological propaedeutics; (c) the theology of creation; (d) Christology; (e) eschatology. With all of these subjects Schillebeeckx's overriding interest was *to interpret ecclesiastical dogmas historically*, which is to say, to study dogmatic texts in their historical settings. In his teaching he applied the method of historical *ressourcement* to his subjects. While teaching in Louvain, Schillebeeckx's method was essentially dogmatic: it took as its point of departure (Catholic) dogmatic formulas, and then sought to elaborate these with the resources of Patristic texts and a historical-critical reading of Aquinas. Conspicuously absent from his work at this time was a developed historical-critical and literary-analytical methodological exegesis of *biblical* texts. His works frequently refer to biblical texts; but the texts are methodologically secondary to dogmatic pronouncements and serve to support ecclesiastical dogmas. Cf. P. KENNEDY, *Schillebeeckx*, 23-24.

[109] In the Netherlands, Schillebeeckx found himself in quite a different cultural and religious climate. Having left the largely Catholic Belgium he began to live in a region where Protestant churches were more conspicuous. Quite apart from the general socio-cultural change, the faculty of theology in Nijmegen advocated a more inter-disciplinary approach to theological study than was the tendency in Louvain. Subsequently, having moved to Nijmegen, Schillebeeckx began more emphatically to take contemporary human experiences as the starting point for his theological reflections. This meant that he broadened his field of academic enquiries to include the behavioural sciences, and that instead of viewing theology primarily as the explicitation of dogmatic prescriptions, he attended more to human history as a source for theological reflection. This closer attention to contemporary human experiences is the crucial factor which initiated a new phase in Schillebeeckx's intellectual biography. Cf. P. KENNEDY, *Schillebeeckx*, 24-28.

witnessed the development of three master-themes in his work: eschatology, orthopraxis, and hermeneutics.[110] Furthermore, it seems clear that 1966 and the years immediately following marked the time when Schillebeeckx began extensively and radically to alter his former theological opinions and method.

The hermeneutical research which Schillebeeckx began in the 1960s was brought to fruition in 1974 with his publication of *Jezus, het verhaal van een levende*.[111] This book was the first of three tomes to be published in a christological trilogy. The second volume was issued in 1977 with the title *Gerechtigheid en liefde: Genade en bevrijding*.[112] The third tome, *Mensen als verhaal van God*, was published in 1989, and re-issued in the following year in a corrected edition.[113] It is sufficient here to note that Schillebeeckx's christological trilogy was written with three pivotal hermeneutical principles in mind. The first is that revelation can be known from within experience. The second principle asserts that experience can never be divorced from interpretations of experiences. In other words, whatever may be objectively given in experience, can only be grasped as «objective», by virtue of a subjective interpretative process. The third hermeneutical hinge of the three volumes is that theology should proceed by way of establishing a correlation between contemporary experiences and the experiences of more ancient traditions.[114]

4.3 *The Christology of Edward Schillebeeckx*

As was the case with Kasper and Rahner, it is not our purpose to treat Schillebeeckx's Christology in detail. Rather, we are concerned to examine to what extent, in formulating his systematic Christology, Schillebeeckx uses the Wisdom elements in the Scriptures. Some explication of Schillebeeckx's Christology, by way of summary and

---

[110] Cf. C. DUMONT, «De trois dimensions retrouvées en théologie», 561-591 (here 571, n. 25 and n. 26). Cf. also P. KENNEDY, *Schillebeeckx*, 27.

[111] E. SCHILLEBEECKX, *Jezus;* E.T.: *Jesus. An Experiment in Christology.*

[112] E. SCHILLEBEECKX, *Gerechtigheid en liefde*; E.T.: *Christ.*

[113] E. SCHILLEBEECKX, *Mensen als verhaal van God*; E.T.: *Church.*

[114] These three hermeneutical hinges are elaborated in E. SCHILLEBEECKX, *Tussentijds verhaal*, 18-24, 60-61. Even though this text was written before the publication of *Mensen als verhaal van God*, the third part of the trilogy, it is clearly developed according to the same hermeneutical principles as the first two volumes. Cf. P. KENNEDY, *Schillebeeckx*, 104-112.

overview, will help to situate and clarify our specific study. In this regard
we will concentrate on Schillebeeckx's *Jesus: An Experiment in Christology.*[115] It is the first of Schillebeeckx's works to involve comprehensively
the findings of contemporary exegetical studies. His previous publications
frequently referred to scriptural passages and to the work of exegetes, but
on nothing like the enormous scale we find in *Jesus*.

4.3.1 *Summary*

Schillebeeckx finds the starting point and permanent context of his
Christology in the universal human experience of evil.[116] He argues that
what is needed in response to the presence of evil is not an explanation or
a theory about its origin or purpose. Wherefore, Schillebeeckx argues that
narrative with practical intent holds out more promise than theory.[117]
Schillebeeckx believes that, in the judgment of Christians, the story to be
told in the face of evil is christological. It is this understanding of the
problem that theology must confront which both necessitates for
Schillebeeckx a pursuit of christological issues and dictates his choice of
christological method. As a result his Christology does not concentrate on
a christological formula nor does it develop a soteriological theory.

---

[115] Schillebeeckx's *Jesus. An Experiment in Christology* has a fourfold structure: the
first part discusses matters of method and hermeneutics pertaining to contemporary
christological investigations. The second part undertakes a detailed reading of New
Testament texts with a view to extracting historical data concerning Jesus. The third
moves on to an analysis of early Christian interpretations of Jesus, while the fourth
responds to the question of who Jesus might be for present-day Christians. The third part
is motivated by the conviction that, in order to ascertain more of the identity of Jesus
with the aid of historical-critical methods, it is necessary to attend to the «horizon of
experience», or cultural context, in which the first Jews and Gentiles interpreted Jesus.
It should be noted that, even though the English translation is offered as a version of the
original Dutch text of 1974, in fact it also includes modifications found in later (Dutch)
editions of this work.

[116] Without disparaging the significance of other concerns, Schillebeeckx remains
convinced that the problem of evil, concretized most disturbingly in the suffering of the
innocent, is both the primary issue that has preoccupied religions and philosophies of the
past and present and the most urgent challenge faced by Christianity today. Cf. E.
SCHILLEBEECKX, *Jesus*, 19-26; 172-178; 612-625. Schillebeeckx returns to the problem
of suffering in «Mysterie van ongerechtigheid (Mystery of Iniquity)», 3-25.

[117] «People do not *argue* against suffering, but tell a *story* [...] Christianity does not
give any explanation for suffering, but demonstrates a way of life». Cf. E.
SCHILLEBEECKX, *Christ*, 698.

Instead, firmly oriented towards the narrative form of the gospels, Schillebeeckx attempts to retell «the life story of the man Jesus as a [...] (liberating) [...] story of God.»[118]

Schillebeeckx emphasizes strongly that our historical access to Jesus remains mediated through the responses he evoked from others. The constant factor in Christology is the Christian movement itself, in the sense of a community experience which refers to Jesus.[119] To reach the Jesus of history, it is necessary to retrace our way through the Gospels, which are composed from the perspectives of their early Christian authors yet enshrine earlier historical material.[120] This, for Schillebeeckx, demands careful consideration of the issues raised by modern historical-critical scrutiny of the New Testament.[121]

---

[118] Cf. E. SCHILLEBEECKX, *Jesus*, 80.

[119] «[...] the constant factor is the changing life of the "assembly of God" or "assembly (congregation) of Christ", the community-fashioning experience evoked by the impression Jesus makes and, in the Spirit, goes on making upon his followers, people who have experienced final salvation in Jesus of Nazareth.» Cf. E. SCHILLEBEECKX *Jesus*, 57. Cf. also E. SCHILLEBEECKX, *Christ*, 66.

[120] For Schillebeeckx, the starting point of christological exploration is the movement begun by Jesus, the movement which is the medium through which we encounter him. A modern christological interpretation of Jesus cannot start from the kerygma about Jesus, or indeed from a so-called purely historical Jesus of Nazareth; a historical and critical approach, set within the dynamic of faith, remains the only proper starting point. With this methodology, Schillebeeckx is developing a Christology from below, in the sense that the starting point is the encounter with and recollection of Jesus of Nazareth, as they are mediated to us through the Christian movement. But such an approach does not mean some kind of deliverance from history for faith but rather an appreciation of historical data as divine disclosure from within a faith context. Cf. E. SCHILLEBEECKX, *Jesus*, 55.

[121] The introductory section of *Jesus* ends with a survey of five different criteria helpful for distinguishing what may actually be ascribed to the historical Jesus from subsequent amplifications by the early church: (i) the presence of material that diverges from the theological tendencies of the work in which it appears; (ii) the existence of material that cannot plausibly be attributed to sources other than Jesus; (iii) the presence of the same material in diverse traditions; (iv) consistency in content between a given detail and the overall picture of Jesus; and, finally, (v) the standard of Jesus' execution - Jesus' life must be such that it accounts for his rejection and death. Application of these criteria, in wide-ranging dialogue with modern biblical scholarship, allows Schillebeeckx to provide a detailed account of Jesus' public life. However, reading the reviews of *Jesus* by some exegetes we see that many were dissatisfied with Schillebeeckx's attempt. For an overview of these reviews see G. O'COLLINS – D. KENDALL, *The Bible for Theology*, 173, n. 25.

Aware that our access to Jesus is mediated through the church's response to his person and life, Schillebeeckx, centring on the Synoptic Gospels, engages in a detailed study of Jesus' preaching and conduct and evaluates them as an offer of definitive salvation from God in a context marked by suffering.[122] The inseparability of Jesus' message from his person is a central factor in Schillebeeckx's Christology.[123] Schillebeeckx locates the foundation of Jesus' activity in his consciousness of deep intimacy with the Father, who benevolently opposes evil and refuses to allow it to have the last word.[124]

Schillebeeckx, in trying to reconstruct how Jesus interpreted his own death, rejects the assumption that Jesus' message took its meaning only from his death. For Schillebeeckx, death is an entirely negative event.[125] At the same time Schillebeeckx is at pains to make clear that Jesus did not believe that he would die for an illusion and that his mission had been a failure. A detailed analysis of what happened at the Last Supper leads to the conclusion that Jesus «has come to proper terms with his death, which

---

[122] This section deals with the parables, Jesus' attitude towards the law, his dealings with the outcasts of society and his role as the eschatological prophet. Schillebeeckx demonstrates the shock effect of the parables. He shows how Jesus radicalized the Law. He is convinced that Jesus performed at least the miracles involving the driving out of demons and the centurion's servant, while accepting that others may be additions representing the elaboration of Old Testament prophecies which were applied to Jesus. Jesus' identification with the outcast and the way in which he joined in meals with sinners leads into a demonstration of the way in which Jesus brings freedom from the Law. We are also reminded that Jesus' whole mission was based on a great intimacy with the Father. However, any attempt to establish from the Synoptic or pre-Synoptic material an uninterpreted, «first articulation» Jesus is dismissed by Schillebeeckx as an illusion. Cf. E. SCHILLEBEECKX, *Jesus*, 52.

[123] Cf. E. SCHILLEBEECKX, *Jesus,* 258.

[124] Alluding to Mark 14:36, Romans 8:15, and Galatians 4:6, though not relying on these texts in isolation, Schillebeeckx designates this reality as Jesus' *Abba-experience*. Yet Schillebeeckx's insistence that a conviction of intimacy with God lies at the source of Jesus' public activity rests on an overall consideration of Jesus' life and message, not mainly on an exegesis of the passages in which the word «Father» appears. Cf. E. SCHILLEBEECKX, *Jesus*, 260.

[125] Schillebeeckx stresses the passive character of death and its negative dimension. Such negativity is all the more evident in an unjust and violent execution like that of Jesus. The immediate agents of the crucifixion were Jesus' enemies and no theology can legitimately permit the memory of this evil to be blunted in subsequent glorification. Cf. E. SCHILLEBEECKX, *Jesus*, 272-274, 648.

he evidently does not feel to be an absurd miscarriage of his mission.»[126] For Schillebeeckx, Jesus was long aware of the possibility of a violent end and gradually became certain of death's approach. Schillebeeckx's narrative treatment of the crucifixion includes an examination of Jesus' approach to death and an analysis of early Christian interpretations of the crucifixion. In addition, he offers his own reflections on the theological meaning of the cross.[127] Confident of personal vindication and somehow integrating his approaching fate into his understanding of his mission, he left his death as a final prophetic act.

Schillebeeckx's Christology offers reflections on both the nature of the resurrection and the revelation of the risen Christ to his followers.[128] His treatment of the resurrection is marked strongly by his insistence on the negative character of death, while his analysis of the revelation of the resurrection, one of the most controversial aspects of his theology, concentrates on New Testament traditions about the empty tomb and the appearances.[129] Schillebeeckx's initial writing on the appearance tradition,

---

[126] Cf. E. SCHILLEBEECKX, *Jesus*, 309.

[127] Schillebeeckx is more favourable to portrayals of the crucifixion as the death of a prophet-martyr (*Jesus*, 274-282) and of the righteous sufferer (*Jesus*, 282-291) than he is to interpretations of Jesus' death in the categories of atonement and redemption (*Jesus*, 291-294). The first two approaches, while largely bypassed in the history of theology, tend far more than the third to link Jesus' death to his public life, thus lending themselves to use in narrative presentations.

[128] Cf. E. SCHILLEBEECKX, *Jesus*, 320-402, 516-544, 644-650.

[129] In studying the empty grave stories, Schillebeeckx notes the discrepancies in the various accounts and concentrates on their function in the different gospels as articulations of the church's faith in Jesus' resurrection. He concentrates chiefly on the New Testament tradition about appearances of the risen Jesus. His analysis of the appearance tradition rests on his conviction that, since the disciples let Jesus down at the time of his arrest, some sort of conversion must lie between this failure and their later faith. In an unusual methodical procedure, he attempts to understand the gospel accounts of Jesus' appearances by examining the three New Testament narratives of Paul's experience on the road to Damascus (Acts 9; 22; 26). From a study of these texts, he concludes that the story of this event underwent gradual transformation from an account of Paul's conversion (Acts 9) through a transitional version (Acts 22) to a report of Paul's mission (Acts 26). The gospel narratives of Jesus' appearances to the disciples parallel the final form of the tradition about Paul, inasmuch as they too accent the theme of mission. In view of all these considerations, Schillebeeckx hypothesizes that the appearance narratives found in the gospels may be the end product of a tradition that in its early stages reflected the idea of conversion. He proposes that intimate personal religious experiences of a renewed divine offer of forgiveness of sin through Jesus led

like his study of the empty tomb, has been subjected to considerable criticism, and he has modified his position in response to some objections.[130] His later treatments of the issue refrain from stressing the theme of the resurrection appearances as conversion experiences for the disciples and see Jesus' resurrection as a divine victory over the negativity of his crucifixion, a new and different event after death that confers upon Jesus' death a new meaning.

In examining the history of Christian thought about Jesus, Schillebeeckx is especially attentive to the seminal period between Jesus' death and the writing of Paul's Epistles. While acknowledging the inevitably tentative nature of such research, Schillebeeckx adapts some analyses of Helmut Koester to offer a plausible summary of the diverse assessments Jesus evoked from the earliest Christians. Following Koester, Schillebeeckx distinguishes four distinct creedal tendencies present in early Christianity: a *parousia Christology* concentrated on Jesus' future role as Son of Man and coming judge;[131] a second type, sometimes termed a *divine-man Christology*, presented Jesus chiefly as a worker of miracles;[132] a *Wisdom Christology* emphasized Jesus as the bringer and teacher of Wisdom and as the pre-existent, incarnate, humbled-yet-exalted Wisdom;[133] while, lastly, an *Easter Christology*, reflected strongly in the Pauline writings, directed attention toward Jesus' death and resurrection.[134] Each of these themes of early Christian thought, Schillebeeckx argues, captured a real facet of Jesus' life and for that reason should be recognised as fundamentally legitimate.

However, in both historical analysis and systematic reflection, Schillebeeckx favours the category of eschatological prophet, the long-awaited prophet-like-Moses with whom God speaks face to face, as a

---

to the disciples reassembling at the initiative of Peter. This conversion experience is at the root of the ancient listing of appearances in I Corinthians 15:3-8. The latter gospel appearance narratives are not historical reports, but theological elaborations of specific aspects of the church's faith in Jesus' resurrection.

[130] Cf. E. SCHILLEBEECKX, *Tussentijds verhaal*; ET: *Interim Report*. Cf. also P. CARNLEY, *Structure of Resurrection Belief*, 119-222; G. O'COLLINS, *Interpreting Jesus*, 120-124; B.L. RAMM, *Evangelical Christology*, 186-187; W.M. THOMPSON, *The Jesus Debate*, 220-223.

[131] Cf. E. SCHILLEBEECKX, *Jesus*, 405-423.

[132] Cf. E. SCHILLEBEECKX, *Jesus*, 424-429.

[133] Cf. E. SCHILLEBEECKX, *Jesus*, 429-432.

[134] Cf. E. SCHILLEBEECKX, *Jesus*, 432-438.

vehicle for articulating Jesus' status and significance.[135] Rich in theological implications, this initial identification of Jesus captured well the facts of his life; in due course, it also gave rise to the other titles and the later christological themes. For Schillebeeckx, the baptism in the Jordan marks an important breakthrough of the prophetic awareness of Jesus.[136] It provides the foundation for his radical praxis of the values of the kingdom and it finds its climax in the drama of the cross. According to Schillebeeckx, the eschatological prophet is himself a sign of the proclamation of the in-breaking kingdom which emerges from his extraordinary *Abba* experience. As a protest against the injustice and oppression which dehumanizes men and women, and as a promise of a better world to come, this solitary life takes on universal significance when the self-giving death on the cross is vindicated by the resurrection.

4.3.2 *Awareness of a Wisdom Christology in Schillebeeckx*

Having given an overview of Schillebeeckx's Christology, we now move to the central focus of our discussion, namely the presence of the Wisdom theme in his Christology. We have already noted that Schillebeeckx, in an attempt to offer a plausible summary of the diverse assessments Jesus evoked from the earliest Christians, distinguishes four distinct creedal tendencies present in early Christianity. One of these is entitled Wisdom Christology. Schillebeeckx argues that there was no single creed or *kerygma* in early Christianity that did not take a particular historical aspect of Jesus' earthly life as the starting-point and criterion for its interpretation of the faith. Underlying each of these creeds, including that of Wisdom, is an historical facet of the life of Jesus.[137] The bringing together in the canonical gospels of these diverse creedal strands, each with its own appropriate historical concern with Jesus of Nazareth, is not just a merging of various interpretations of Jesus; it also brings together information about Jesus' life on earth culled from various local church traditions. Different Christian congregations, each in its own way and

---

[135] «Whereas God is bent on showing himself in human form, we on our side slip past this human aspect as quickly as we can in order to admire a 'divine Icon' from which every trait of the critical prophet has been smoothed away.» Cf. E. SCHILLEBEECKX, *Jesus*, 671. Despite variations and qualifications, all three parts of the trilogy interpret the life, message, death, and resurrection along similar lines.

[136] Cf. E. SCHILLEBEECKX, *Jesus*, 138.

[137] Cf. E. SCHILLEBEECKX, *Jesus*, 437.

basing itself on its own creed, cultivated a particular *memoria Jesu*, and became a channel of authentic Jesus tradition.

At the outset of his discussion of Wisdom Christology, Schillebeeckx acknowledges that set formulae and hymns, adopted into the New Testament, as well as various passages in the gospels taken over from the Q tradition, reveal a close connection between Jesus and Wisdom. He treats, albeit briefly, the personification of Wisdom (and Folly) in the Old Testament, referring specifically to Proverbs 8.[138] He also is aware of the dialectic of disclosure and concealment regarding the Wisdom of God evident in parts of the Old Testament Wisdom literature. Schillebeeckx cites Job 28 where this Wisdom is hidden with God and inaccessible to human beings, except to the one to whom God reveals her.[139]

Schillebeeckx treats two aspects of Wisdom which he deems important and sets out the historical emergence of both. In the first case Wisdom comes down to earth, where she is a stranger unacknowledged and rejected, and then returns to heaven. Yet at the same time she is the teacher of humanity (Prov 9:1*)* as the mediator of divine revelation. In this period there emerged the speculation about heavenly «intermediaries» between God and the world who initiated a relationship with God.[140] Alongside that, from the Maccabean period onwards, Schillebeeckx notes the emergence of another concept of Wisdom specifically in the pietistic circles of the «Chasidim», a Jewish coterie of pious religionists. This group formed a penitential movement with a very definite apocalyptic view of human history. Schillebeeckx presents the Chasidic idea of Wisdom in terms of three layers: (a) only the righteous person is wise (Dan 12:10); the wise man is one who acquires true knowledge of the Law and practices it; (b) to these wise keepers of the Law are imparted, in the testing circumstances of the «last days», divine disclosures which enable them to understand the eschatological event; (c) complete Wisdom is an eschatological gift of the time of salvation.[141]

Schillebeeckx notes that «in the later phase of the Q community» Jesus was associated with pre-existent Wisdom; the latter sends her messengers, the prophets, and also the eschatological prophet. But Jesus is never

---

[138] Cf. E. SCHILLEBEECKX, *Jesus*, 429.

[139] Cf. E. SCHILLEBEECKX, *Jesus*, 429.

[140] Cf. E. SCHILLEBEECKX, *Jesus,*, 429-430.

[141] This Chasidic notion of Wisdom conflicted quite sharply with the hypostatizing speculations of Hellenistic Wisdom. Cf. E. SCHILLEBEECKX, *Jesus*, 430.

precisely identified with pre-existent Wisdom.[142] This understanding of Jesus presented Him as the Son known only by the Father because the Father has given him all authority and power, so that in him the heavenly Wisdom has come to dwell; he appears and acts as the eschatological emissary of a pre-existent Wisdom.[143] Schillebeeckx goes on to acknowledge that the Matthean gospel goes further and identifies Jesus with Wisdom, while, in the apocryphal Gospel of Thomas, Jesus identifies himself with Wisdom.[144]

Schillebeeckx notes that the sapiential myth of a pre-existent Wisdom is applied to Jesus most particularly in the ancient hymns in the New Testament, in the poetic form of a cosmic drama in different acts: pre-existence, coming down to earth, return and exaltation of Wisdom. In this regard Schillebeeckx refers to Philippians 2:6-11, John 1:1-14, Hebrews 1:3-4, and Colossians 1:15-20.[145]

Schillebeeckx argues that Wisdom Christology was subsequently caught up in gnostic speculations, while noting that it inspired the Logos Christology of the Church Fathers. He makes the general point that Wisdom Christology seems to have been widely diffused in diverse early Christian traditions and even to have appeared in diverse forms, with the most prevalent form to be found in the christological hymns.[146]

Schillebeeckx asks whether the historical Jesus event correlates with this Wisdom creed. Jesus quite clearly made use of Wisdom sayings and proverbs. In that sense it is historically legitimate to see Jesus as a teacher of Wisdom. In this regard, continuity is shown in the way the disciples emulate Jesus; just as Jesus is a mystagogue initiating people into God's secrets, so too the apostles are mystagogues. However, while acknowledging a clear connection between Jesus of Nazareth and Wisdom Christology, Schillebeeckx argues that the canonical Scriptures are not explicit in regard to their position on Wisdom Christology.[147] On the one

---

[142] Schillebeeckx cites Matthew 11:25-27=Luke 10:21-22 (Wis 6-10); Matthew 23:34-36=Luke 11:49-51; Matthew 9:37-38; 10:7-16=Luke 10:2-12. Cf. *Jesus*, 430. We should note here that many scholars are sceptical about an expression like the «later phase of the Q community». Cf. J.P. MEIER, *A Marginal Jew*. I, 43-45.

[143] Schillebeeckx notes that formulae suggesting a «sending forth» are a typical feature of Wisdom Christology. Cf. E. SCHILLEBEECKX, *Jesus*, 430-431.

[144] Cf. E. SCHILLEBEECKX, *Jesus*, 430-431.

[145] Cf. E. SCHILLEBEECKX, *Jesus*, 430-431

[146] Cf. E. SCHILLEBEECKX, *Jesus*, 431.

[147] Cf. E. SCHILLEBEECKX, *Jesus*, 432.

hand, the New Testament cites the christological hymns, but then they are worked over and set within the gospel tradition. Schillebeeckx also argues that we see especially in Paul a degree of hostility towards the practical consequences of this presentation: it threatens to degenerate into a «scholastic» kind of mystery doctrine meant only for initiates who «care nothing for the common herd» (see I Cor 1–4, where Paul decries «the Wisdom of the Greeks»).

However, Schillebeeckx acknowledges that what emerges from his sketch of early Wisdom Christology, as with the other three distinct creedal themes of early Christian thought, is that it testified to the immediate, permanent, and definitive significance of Jesus.[148] It also underscores the fact that, although Jesus' historical message about the coming kingdom of God is of abiding value, there is no single instance of an attempt to carry forward this Good News, either pre-canonical or in the New Testament, without linking it intrinsically with the person of Jesus.

4.4 *Concluding Remarks*

We have been concerned here with examining to what extent, in formulating his Christology, Schillebeeckx uses Wisdom elements in the Scriptures. *Jesus* was the first of Schillebeeckx's works to involve comprehensively the findings of contemporary exegetical studies. His previous publications frequently referred to scriptural passages and to the work of exegetes, but on nothing like the enormous scale which is encountered in *Jesus*. In this regard, Schillebeeckx's Christology is not a treatise that seeks to interpret Jesus in metaphysical categories. Rather, he attentions Jesus' *story*.

Schillebeeckx's Christology is fired by the desire to explain the ultimate identity of the man, Jesus, as the universal and unique disclosure of divine salvation in human history. A primary conclusion of Schillebeeckx's Christology is that access to Jesus, and interpretations of Jesus, are grounded in the life of the Christian community. In other words, Jesus can only be known by way of the praxis of a particular community. Jesus cannot be grasped and interpreted in a purely theoretical and abstract way. Schillebeeckx has shown how different generations of Christians, in diverse cultural settings, have interpreted Jesus in divergent ways and gave him various titles: «Son of Man», «Messiah», «Christ», «Son of God», «Lord». Schillebeeckx acknowledges that «Wisdom» was also a title

---

[148] Cf. E. SCHILLEBEECKX, *Jesus,* 437-438.

given to Jesus while expressing his own preference for the title «eschato-logical prophet» for interpreting Jesus. However, for Schillebeeckx, titles applied to Jesus are entirely secondary in any contemporary attempt to interpret who Jesus was. Jesus himself, as reached by way of the original Christian communities, is the primary factor.

Therefore, despite his extensive treatment of the historical Jesus, Schillebeeckx does not present Jesus as a Sage or as Divine Wisdom in person. Schillebeeckx's emphasis on the Good News of the kingdom of God preached and lived as the very content of salvation receives more attention than any particular finding with regard to the titles.

Neither does Schillebeeckx advert to the feminine element in Wisdom thought. No specific references in *Jesus* are made to the development of the Wisdom theme among the Church Fathers. In conclusion, while acknowledging its contribution as a distinct creedal understanding of Jesus present in early Christianity, Schillebeeckx's Christology cannot be deemed a Wisdom Christology.

5. Summary and Conclusions

We have concerned ourselves with examining to what extent the Wisdom elements present in the Scriptures and the tradition of the early Church have been incorporated into some representative Catholic Christologies of the German- (and Dutch-) speaking world. We have concentrated on Walter Kasper's *Jesus the Christ*, Karl Rahner's *Foundations of Christian Faith* (chapter six), and Edward Schillebeeckx's *Jesus: An Experiment in Christology*. None of these works are an explicit *Wisdom* Christology. Kasper opts very clearly for a pneumatological approach to Christology. The Incarnation, according to Kasper, is effected by the personal activity of the Holy Spirit, whose sanctifying presence is constitutive of the human person of Jesus. Rahner's Christology is based on the concept of the Word. He has developed a contemporary Logos Christology which seeks a coherent understanding of the revelation of God in Jesus Christ and the universal presence of God in all human experience and in the cosmos. Schillebeeckx, in both historical analysis and system-atic reflection, favours the category of eschatological prophet, the long-awaited prophet-like-Moses with whom God speaks face to face, as his vehicle for articulating Jesus' status and significance. However, all of them, to a lesser or greater extent, acknowledge the contribution of the Wisdom theme to the development of early Christology. This is explicitly the case with Kasper and Schillebeeckx. Rahner does not refer to Wisdom

Christology but his articulation of a contemporary Word Christology, based on the Word prologue of the Gospel of John, involves a link with Wisdom Christology.

In this regard, we criticised the work of Leo Lefebure who argues that Rahner's is a Wisdom Christology. At no point does Lefebure distinguish between a Wisdom and Word Christology. Neither does he acknowledge Rahner's emphasis on Jesus as the *eschatological prophet* and *absolute saviour*. Rahner himself makes no explicit christological connections with Wisdom Christology. While there are precedents in the Wisdom literature and early Wisdom Christology for elements in Rahner's own Christology, there is no way of knowing that these precedents were important to Rahner himself in his overall christological project. Lefebure's work develops Rahner's Christology in a Wisdom direction and has helped to show that Rahner's christological thought is the most open of the three under discussion in this chapter to be taken in a Wisdom direction. Earlier we concluded that the Gospel of John contains fundamental elements of Wisdom Christology, even though no word of the *sophia / sophos* family appears in the text. Similarily, Rahner's Christology contains elements of Wisdom Christology without specific references to the Wisdom literature.

However, given Rahner's emphasis on the concept of Word and his development of a contemporary Logos Christology, together with his presentation of Jesus as the *eschatological prophet* and *absolute saviour*, it seems reasonable to argue that an explicit understanding of Jesus in terms of Wisdom Christology was not intended by Rahner.

With regard to Kasper's Christology and a possible Wisdom emphasis, he highlights New Testament statements regarding the pre-existence of Christ and Jesus' mediatorship of creation as having their immediate source in Old Testament Judaism - with the parallels clearest in Old Testament speculation on Wisdom. Similarly, in a brief discussion on the Wisdom background of some christological hymns, Schillebeeckx, with Philippians 2:6-11, John 1:1-14, Hebrews 1:3-4 and Colossians 1:15-20 in mind, also notes that the sapiential myth of a pre-existent Wisdom is applied to Jesus in the poetic form of a cosmic drama: pre-existence, coming down to earth, return and exaltation of Wisdom. Furthermore, Kasper notes the contribution of a Wisdom Christology to the development of the Logos Christology of the Church Fathers.

Moving beyond Kasper's *Jesus the Christ,*, in an article published in 1987, «Gottes Gegenwart in Jesus Christus», Kasper presents theodicy as one of the great challenges to contemporary theology. The need for a kenosis theology, Kasper argues, also calls for a theology of *the Wisdom of the cross* and thus will, in accordance with the writings of Paul, *understand the cross of Christ anew as the manifestation of the Wisdom of God*. Here Kasper acknowledges the need for Wisdom Christology in the context of kenosis theology grappling with the questions of evil and suffering in the world.

However, Kasper's own presentation in *Jesus the Christ* does not present Jesus as a Sage or as Divine Wisdom in person. Like Schillebeeckx, Kasper's emphasis on the kingdom of God preached and lived as the very content of salvation receives more attention than any particular finding with regard to the titles. Hence, in *Jesus the Christ*, apart from a general acknowledgment and passing reference to the Wisdom influence on the development of Christology, we cannot speak of Kasper's Christology as a Wisdom Christology.

Schillebeeckx, in distinguishing four distinct creedal tendencies present in early Christianity, identifies a particular *memoria Jesu* in terms of Wisdom. He argues that underlying this creedal presentation is an historical facet of the life of Jesus. In this regard, he notes the Wisdom influence on the beliefs of the Q community, as well as Jesus' identity with Wisdom in the Gospel of Matthew and the claim of the apocryphal Gospel of Thomas that Jesus identified himself with Wisdom.

While acknowledging its influence on the emergence of Logos Christology, Schillebeeckx claims that the canonical Scriptures have reserved their judgment on Wisdom Christology. He notes that the christological hymns were set within the gospels' canonical creed and that Paul in 1 Corinthians 1–4 questioned the practical consequences of a Wisdom model which threatens to support the emergence of an elite. However, Schillebeeckx does acknowledge that what emerged from the Wisdom creedal theme was a response in faith to the immediate, permanent, and definitive significance of Jesus.

CHAPTER VIII

Wisdom Christology in Some Representatives
of the English-Speaking world

Our examination here will focus on the extent to which the Wisdom elements present in the Scriptures and the tradition of the church have been incorporated into some contemporary representative Catholic Christologies of the English-speaking world.

1. Representative Catholic Christology in the English-Speaking World

The three theologians whose Christology we propose to examine are Jacques Dupuis, Denis Edwards, and Elisabeth Schüssler Fiorenza. Though born in Belgium, J. Dupuis taught for many years in India and has written extensively in English. His *Who do you say I am?*[1] has found widespread use in colleges and seminaries because of its clarity on the central theological concern of the identity and meaning of Jesus Christ. In his book *Jesus the Wisdom of God*[2] D. Edwards, one of Australia's leading theologians, attempts to retrieve the notion that Wisdom became incarnate in Jesus of Nazareth and seeks to show how a Wisdom Christology can clarify our understanding of the trinitarian God at work in creation. Though E. Schüssler Fiorenza was born in Romania of German background, she has spent much of her academic life in the United States and has published extensively in English. While feminist scholarship in North America has not yet produced a book-length study of the historical Jesus,

---

[1] J. DUPUIS, *Who do you say I am? Introduction to Christology*.
[2] D. EDWARDS, *Jesus the Wisdom of God: An Ecological Theology*.

Fiorenza's *In Memory of Her*[3] has been acclaimed as a sophisticated attempt to reconstruct Christian origins from a feminist theological perspective.

2. Jacques Dupuis

2.1 *Jesuit and Theologian*

Jacques Dupuis (b.1923) was Professor of Systematic Theology at the Gregorian University in Rome from 1984 to 1998. Prior to coming to Rome, Dupuis lived and taught for over twenty years in an international theological college near Darjeeling in India. Born in Huppaye in French-speaking Belgium, he entered the Jesuit order in 1941 and thirteen years later was ordained to the priesthood. Dupuis' academic studies led to a Licentiate in Philosophy from the University of Louvain, a Licentiate in Theology from the University of Kurseong in India, and a Doctorate in Theology from the Gregorian University in Rome.[4] During his years in India Dupuis was founding editor of the Indian theological review, *Vidyajyoti*. Together with J. Neuner and later by himself, he edited *The Christian Faith in the Doctrinal Documents of the Catholic Church*[5] and has contributed extensively to many theological periodicals and journals.[6] Currently he is Professor Emeritus and serves as editor of the periodical *Gregorianum*.

2.2 *The Development of Dupuis' Theology*

Dupuis' theological writings have largely centred around questions in Christology.[7] He has been heavily influenced by his years in India and his contact with many of the great religious traditions of the world: Buddhism, Christianity, Confucianism, and Hinduism. His interest in and commitment to inter-religious dialogue, together with christological concerns, has ensured that his writings are dominated by the themes of a Christian understanding of other religions and an attempt to develop a «trinitarian,

---

[3] E. SCHÜSSLER FIORENZA, *In Memory of Her: A Feminist Theological Reconstruction of Christian Origins*.

[4] J. DUPUIS, *L'Esprit de l'homme*.

[5] Cf. J. NEUNER – J. DUPUIS, ed., *The Christian Faith*.

[6] Cf., for example, «Apostolic Exhortation», 218-230; «Conscience du Christ», 448-460. Cf. also the two articles both entitled «Authority in the Church», 98-111 and 151-168.

[7] Cf. J. DUPUIS, *Jesus Christ and his Spirit*; ID., *Who do you say I am?*.

christological model capable of holding in creative tension the depth of God's commitment to humankind in Jesus and the authenticity of other paths in accord with divine providence».[8]

Who do you say I am? is Dupuis' thorough and thoughtful contribution to contemporary christological discussion. In this work he uncovers the core doctrines of Christology in the context of liberationist, feminist, and inter-religious questions. It will serve here as the central text in our study of Dupuis' Christology.

2.3 *The Christology of Jacques Dupuis*

It is not the purpose of our study to treat Dupuis' Christology in detail. Rather, our central focus is examining to what extent Dupuis uses the Wisdom elements in the Scriptures to formulate his systematic Christology. However, some explication of Dupuis' Christology, by way of summary and overview, will help to situate our specific study. In this regard, we will draw on Dupuis' presentation in *Who do you say I am?*

2.3.1 *Summary*

In this work Jacques Dupuis presents a classical Roman Catholic Christology, one heavily influenced by the writings of Karl Rahner and Walter Kasper. From the outset, Dupuis advocates what he calls «an integral approach» or a comprehensive perspective to Christology.[9] What such an approach to Christology implies has been summed up by Dupuis under five hermeneutical principles[10]: dialectic tension[11], totality[12],

---

[8] Cf. J. DUPUIS, *Encounter of World Religions*; ID., *Christian Theology of Religious Pluralism*, 7.

[9] Dupuis borrows the expression *integral Christology* from the Pontifical Biblical Commission but claims to give it a more ample meaning here, where it refers to a «comprehensive perspective». Integral Christology is understood by the Biblical Commission to be one that takes into account the entire biblical witness. However, Dupuis' integral approach to Christology will also benefit from the insights that distinct theological approaches have brought to the fore. Cf. J.A. FITZMYER, *Scripture and Christology: A Statement of the Biblical Commission*. Cf. also J. DUPUIS, *Who do you say I am?* 31-32.

[10] The survey of christological approaches which Dupuis presents from two perspectives, biblical (historico-critical, existential, christological titles) and theological (critico-dogmatic, salvation history, anthropological, liberation, feminist liberation), in the opening pages of *Who do you say I am?* allows him to draw preliminary conclusions as to what an integral approach to Christology would necessarily involve. This Dupuis

plurality[13], historical continuity[14] and integration.[15] He is aware of the serious limitations of the dogmatic and genetic (historical-evaluative) methods for the christological project and proposes a new inductive method for theological speculation.[16] This proposed turn from the

does by enunciating five principles. Cf. J. DUPUIS, *Who do you say I am?* 20-32.

[11] Dupuis understands the principle of dialectical tension to be operative in the continuity-in-discontinuity between the searching Christology of man's supernatural existential (K. Rahner) and the historical event of Jesus Christ; or again between the searching Christology of the world's religious traditions and God's finding of religious humanity in Jesus Christ. In all these and other instances of the principle of dialectical tension, Dupuis argues that the rapport between continuous and discontinuous elements will have to be ascertained. Cf. J. DUPUIS, *Who do you say I am? 32.*

[12] By the principle of totality is meant that a well-poised Christology must avoid all danger of reductionism or of unilateralism, in whatever direction. Dupuis notes that the christological mystery is made up of complementary aspects, often at first sight mutually opposed, yet which must be held together, even if often in tension. Cf. J. DUPUIS, *Who do you say I am?* 32-33.

[13] Dupuis notes that the principle of plurality applies most especially where the post-biblical christological tradition and recent christological developments are concerned. Wherever it has arisen, such plurality has throughout the Christian tradition been guided by the concern to inculturate and to contextualise the christological faith. He highlights that the problem it raises is how to maintain and express the traditional faith in Jesus Christ in the context of a changing culture where, due to an evolution in the meaning of concepts, the traditional formulations run the risk of betraying the sense they were meant to convey. He notes that the same preoccupation governs the anthropological and liberation approaches to Christology. Cf. J. DUPUIS, *Who do you say I am?* 33-34.

[14] Dupuis presents this principle in terms of the large degree of christological continuity that exists between the various christological approaches at different stages of the tradition. Cf. J. DUPUIS, *Who do you say I am?* 34-35.

[15] For Dupuis an integral Christology must hold together complementary, though apparently contradictory, component elements of the mystery of Jesus Christ. It must likewise recover and reintegrate into a comprehensive presentation some aspects of the mystery which, in the course of tradition or even in recent times, have fallen by the wayside or been to a considerable extent neglected. A key question of concern for Dupuis in this regard is the universal significance of the Christ-event and the cosmic dimension of the mystery of Christ, the historical particularity of the man Jesus notwithstanding. Cf. J. DUPUIS, *Who do you say I am?* 35-36.

[16] Dupuis notes that both the dogmatic and genetic methods are deductive: both seek to draw ever more precise conclusions from previous christological data. Both are primarily speculative, proceeding from doctrine to its application to reality. However, a lack of success in establishing contact with the reality of life characteristic of much traditional theological speculation suggests for Dupuis that a new method be devised which may be called inductive and which finds its point of departure in the lived reality of a concrete situation and its challenges for faith reflection - confronting reality with

deductive to the inductive method raises the issue of the dialectical process that obtains in hermeneutical theology between a concrete context and the revealed data. Dupuis notes that the revealed data is always a faith interpretation of the Christ-event initiated by the apostolic Church.[17] Every generation of Christianity is bound to enter into the hermeneutical process which means that no single theology can claim to be valid for all times and places.[18]

Dupuis addresses the question of the earthly Jesus as the source of the church's Christology. For Dupuis, the decisive core of the christological faith offered by the resurrection of Jesus and the Easter experience of the disciples must be fully recognized.[19] These events gave rise to an explicit Christology and, in that sense, mark its point of departure. What Dupuis is concerned with here is showing that Jesus' works and words, his self-consciousness and self-revelation, his choices and options, his attitude to life and death, in sum his entire mission and human existence, are at the origin of an explicit Christology.[20]

Dupuis traces the development of Christology from the apostolic kerygma to the present. Here Dupuis draws attention to some aspects of the mystery of Jesus Christ, inadequately stressed in the past, which a renewed Christology should highlight[21]: the historical aspect[22], the

---

Jesus and his Gospel. Cf. J. DUPUIS, *Who do you say I am?* 7.

[17] Cf. J. DUPUIS, *Who do you say I am?* 8-9.

[18] Dupuis notes that the vast contextual divergences call for many diversified theologies and Christologies. What Dupuis is proposing here he hopes will be applicable to distinct situations. What is thereby unavoidably lost by way of immediate relevance to a concrete situation will, Dupuis hopes, be made good inasmuch as the primary concerns of the vastly different contexts which he describes will be kept in mind. Cf. J. DUPUIS, *Who do you say I am?* 10-11.

[19] Dupuis shows that the resurrection of Jesus and the Easter experience of the disciples completes the journey from implicit to explicit Christology. Here is where discipleship becomes faith. Cf. J. DUPUIS, *Who do you say I am?* 39-42.

[20] Though Dupuis' treatment is necessarily brief, it accounts for the «whole» Jesus of history, in his «vertical» as well as his «horizontal» dimension, his personal relation to the Father as well as his way of relating to people. His presentation is divided into four sections: the mission of Jesus; the personal identity of Jesus; Jesus facing his imminent death; Jesus' resurrection and the Easter experience. Cf. J. DUPUIS, *Who do you say I am?* 42-55.

[21] Dupuis shows that much traditional Christology has been marked by a double tendency: toward a one-sided ontology of Christ divorced from soteriology, and toward a unilateral descending approach severed from the necessary complement of an ascending perspective. Dupuis highlights the shortcomings of the christological model

personal or trinitarian aspect[23], and the soteriological aspect.[24] The process of development in New Testament Christology is followed by Dupuis through two main stages: the proclamation of the Risen Christ in the early kerygma[25], and from the proclamation of the Risen Christ to the confession of the Son of God.[26]

Dupuis summarises the distinct characteristics of the Christology of the early kerygma as an Easter Christology centred on the resurrection and glorification of Jesus by the Father.[27] His exaltation is an action of God[28],

---

of Chalcedon and continues to indicate the corresponding aspects of the mystery that need to be recovered in view of a renewed and integrated Christology. Cf. J. DUPUIS, *Who do you say I am?* 101-106.

[22] First to be recovered for Dupuis is the historical aspect, which ought to be combined with the ontological. Central to the Christian message is not a doctrine but an event, that of God's personal entry into, and decisive commitment to, history in Jesus Christ. This event takes place in the concrete history of humankind and is subject to a historical process of becoming. Dupuis emphasizes that the concrete *story* of Jesus must be rediscovered as the epitome of the personal commitment and self-communication of God to humankind. Cf. J. DUPUIS, *Who do you say I am?* 106.

[23] Dupuis argues that the trinitarian dimension of the mystery of Jesus Christ must once more be recognised. Christology cannot be severed from the mystery of the Trinity. Dupuis notes that the implications of Jesus' Sonship of the Father, for him and for us, have been brought out. He proposes that those of his relation to the Spirit ought to be equally developed. Cf. J. DUPUIS, *Who do you say I am?* 106-107; 168-170.

[24] Dupuis emphasizes that Christology cannot be severed from soteriology. The soteriological aspect of the mystery also needs to be rediscovered and reintegrated into Christology as the marvelous exchange by which the Son of God shared our concrete human existence in order to make us share in his own Sonship of the Father. Cf. J. DUPUIS, *Who do you say I am?* 107.

[25] Cf. J. DUPUIS, *Who do you say I am?* 58-65.

[26] Cf. J. DUPUIS, *Who do you say I am?* 65-78.

[27] That the Christology of the early kerygma is an Easter Christology means that the point of departure of its discourse about Jesus is the Easter event. Dupuis argues that it implies a projection into the eschatological future, by which Jesus' significance is explained in relation to the end-time of salvation. The personal origin of Jesus himself has not been touched. Dupuis notes that further developments will lead to the consideration of his pre-existence and consequently to a Christology of the Incarnation. In this sense, the earliest Christology may be termed a Christology from below, for it starts from the human reality of Jesus transformed through the resurrection, not from the pre-existence of the Son of God become man. The Christology of the early kerygma is essentially soteriological. Cf. J. DUPUIS, *Who do you say I am?* 61-65, here 63.

[28] The divine action referred to consists essentially in raising Jesus from the dead. This action is presented as God's decisive intervention in the history of salvation. Cf. J. DUPUIS, *Who do you say I am?* 61.

upon Jesus[29], for our sake.[30] He notes that functional Christology naturally ends with questions concerning the ontological person of Jesus Christ, and the answers to these necessarily marks the advent of a Christology which rises from the functional to the ontological level.[31] The New Testament testifies to a progressive and significant advance toward such a Christology.[32] In this regard, Dupuis insists that the question of pre-existence introduced the decisive step in the inquiry about Jesus' true identity and led to the deepest insights into the mystery of his person.

In moving from pre-existence to Sonship, Dupuis shows how the elaborate New Testament Christology of Jesus' ontological Sonship of God gives objective expression to the filial consciousness that had been at the centre of Jesus' subjective experience of God during his earthly life. Furthermore, the depth of Jesus' divine Sonship having been discovered, a new approach lay open for the discourse of faith which would no longer start, as the early kerygma had done, from the Lordship of the Risen One but, inverting the perspective, would resolutely take as its point of

---

[29] Dupuis notes that, in this early stage of Christology, it is not said that through his resurrection Jesus *returns* to the glory that he had with God before his earthly life. No thought had yet been given to the pre-existence of Jesus and to the Incarnation of the eternal Son of God. What is said is that between the earthly existence of Jesus and his risen condition as Christ and Lord, there is a true discontinuity: Jesus has been really transformed, and his transformation measures the distance between the Jesus of history and the Christ of faith. Cf. J. DUPUIS, *Who do you say that I am?* 62-63.

[30] Dupuis notes that what God has done to Jesus is *for us*. All the titles by which the newly acquired dignity of the risen Jesus is expressed view him in relation to us. Cf. J. DUPUIS, *Who do you say I am?* 62.

[31] Dupuis highlights the witness given by the christological hymns to the direction in which Pauline Christology, and the Christology of the apostolic Church, gradually evolved from functional to ontological: Philippians 2:6-11; Ephesians 2:14-16; Colossians 1:15-20; I Timothy 3:16; Hebrews 1:3; I Peter 3:18-22. Cf. J. DUPUIS, *Who do you say I am?* 65-67.

[32] For Dupuis, the divine condition of Jesus, first perceived by the early Kerygma in Jesus' glorified state through the resurrection, is progressively thrown back toward the past by a process of retroprojection. This happens through various stages. The virginal birth of the infancy narratives is presented as a God-given sign that Jesus is from God from the very beginning of his earthly existence. The question of the pre-existence of Jesus is not yet raised. Where and when considered, it will lead in Paul and his environment to new christological insights (Phil 2:6-11; Col 1:15-20; Eph 1:3-13) and, above all, in John's Gospel, to the heights of the prologue (1:1-18) in which, from that issue, can rightly be found the summit of New Testament Christology. Cf. J. DUPUIS, *Who do you say I am?* 65-66.

departure the togetherness of Father and Son in an ineffable communion of life prior to and independently of the Son's mission from the Father.[33]

Dupuis follows the development of post-biblical Christology or christo-logical dogma through the Councils of the patristic age.[34] He notes that the christological dogmatic formulations are never absolute points of departure and also never represent final words in the church's faith reflection on the mystery of Jesus Christ. They are additional interpreta-tions rendered necessary by the concrete circumstances of historical contexts. These are always particular by definition, that is, determined and limited in space and time, and thus dependent upon a surrounding culture. The dogmatic value of the christological definitions is, therefore, not absolute but relative and relational. Relational, in content, to the New Testament Christology; relative in expression, insofar as it does not represent the only possible way of expressing the mystery, one that would be valid for all times and places.[35] They continue to function in the living tradition of the Church as regulative within the parameters of the cultural context in which they were historically coined and within which they need to be understood. It is in this context that Dupuis highlights aspects of the christological mystery that need to be recovered in view of a renewed and integrated Christology.[36]

Dupuis gives special attention to the human psychology of Jesus and the christological problems contained therein.[37] He shows that both the

---

[33] Dupuis traces the christological development to show how the pre-existence and divine identity of Jesus came to be progressively enunciated and how it precisely came to be understood in terms of divine Sonship. Cf. J. DUPUIS, *Who do you say I am?* 69-75.

[34] Dupuis records that the christological dogma developed in the early centuries in the context of the encounter between the Christian mystery and the surrounding Hellenistic philosophy. Such an encounter, Dupuis argues, offered both an opportunity and a danger. The opportunity consisted in the way that lay open to express the mystery of Jesus Christ in terms of the prevalent culture of the Hellenistic world. The challenge was to preserve intact the meaning, and to convey the integrity, of the revealed mystery, while transposing it from the linguistic register of the New Testament to that of Hellenistic philosophy. Cf. J. DUPUIS, *Who do you say I am?* 77-101.

[35] Cf. J. DUPUIS, *Who do you say I am?* 78-83.

[36] We have noted that Dupuis highlights three aspects of the mystery of the Incarnation that need to be recovered in view of a renewed and integrated Christology: the historical aspect, the personal or trinitarian aspect and the soteriological aspect. Cf. J. DUPUIS, *Who do you say I am?* 106-107.

[37] Dupuis remarks that the Council of Constantinople III directly oriented the Church's christological reflection toward problems of the human psychology of Jesus that were already latent in its doctrine of Jesus' human will and action. Cf. J. DUPUIS,

upward and downward perspectives must be combined in a theology of the human psychology of Jesus that would do justice both to the reality of his historical human condition and his personal identity as Son of God. It must recover the historical dimension of Jesus' human life in his state of kenosis; the personal aspect of his dealings with God his Father in obedience and free submission; and the soteriological motive that underlies his messianic mission.[38]

Dupuis also addresses himself to questions regarding the uniqueness and universality of Jesus Christ. One dimension of this issue consists in asking what God's intention is in devising an order of things in which God's self-communication to human beings depends on the historical Incarnation and death on the cross of God's Son. Another is to seek how the divine plan unfolds itself through the history of mankind and the world.[39] Dupuis devotes the final chapter of *Who do you say I am?* to the two questions of the uniqueness and universality of Jesus Christ.

Dupuis observes, with K. Rahner, that the most urgent christological task today consists in demonstrating the universal significance and cosmic dimension of the Jesus Christ event, with Christ as the pinnacle of salvation history and Christology as that history's sharpest formulation.[40] He notes the need for a cosmic Christology which will show the cosmic dimension of the Incarnation, highlighting the significance of Jesus Christ not only for the salvation of human beings and their history but for the whole universe.[41]

Who do you say I am? 111.

[38] Cf. J. DUPUIS, *Who do you say I am?* 112-113.

[39] Dupuis wishes to know whether the traditional christocentric perspective of Christian faith is still defensible in the new context created by the discoveries of modern science and religious pluralism as we know and live it today. He notes that at stake is the traditional Christocentrism of Christian theology, whose profound, seemingly irreducible, demands are now judged by some to be passé and no longer defensible. Cf. J. DUPUIS, *Who do you say I am?* 141.

[40] Cf. K. RAHNER, «Current Problems», 167.

[41] Dupuis recognizes that the underlying unity between creation and «re-creation» in Jesus Christ is highlighted when seen in the context of an evolutionary view of the world. He highlights this intention of P. Teilhard de Chardin when he conceived the world evolutionary process as «Christogenesis». In this view, Jesus Christ is seen at once as the driving force and the goal that draws to itself, the beginning and the end, the Alpha and the Omega. The cosmic Christ acts as the final cause that directs the entire cosmos to its last end. Cf. J. DUPUIS, *Who do you say I am?* 149-150; 163, n. 16.

Dupuis considers some perspectives on the theology of religions and the challenge posed by the context of religious pluralism to the traditional christocentric perspective of theology.[42] A key conclusion emphasized by Dupuis here is that the christological problem constitutes the nub of this debate. The decisive question is whether a Christian theology of religions has a choice between a christocentric perspective, which acknowledges the Jesus Christ event as constitutive of universal salvation, and a theocentric perspective which somehow places in doubt or explicitly rejects this central datum of traditional faith.[43]

2.3.2 *Awareness of Wisdom Christology in Dupuis*

We have noted that Dupuis makes the historical aspect of Jesus of Nazareth an important element in formulating his Christology. In this regard, while not using much of the Wisdom tradition, Dupuis does refer to some of the central Wisdom texts of the New Testament as set out in our earlier chapters. Dupuis' is not a Wisdom Christology, but he seems aware of the Wisdom influences on the formulation of the doctrine of the Incarnation.

Dupuis begins his Christology by emphasizing that the entire New Testament Christology, including the apostolic kerygma, interprets the story of Jesus from the vantage point of the disciples' paschal experience. He notes that it does not witness to a single apostolic hermeneutics of the Jesus story, but to several. The diverse Christologies of the New Testament represent distinct interpretations of the event in the light of Easter, each conditioned by the particular context of a church to which it is addressed and by the singular personality of the author or editor of the material.[44]

---

[42] Cf. J. DUPUIS, *Who do you say I am?* 157-162.

[43] Dupuis emphasizes that christocentrism and theocentrism cannot be mutually opposed as different perspectives between which a choice can be made. Christian theology is *theocentric qua christocentric, and vice versa.* Cf. J. DUPUIS, *Who do you say I am?* 161-162.

[44] For Dupuis, theology understood as contextual interpretation must be local and diversified, since the Christian experience is always conditioned by the context in which it is lived, with its socio-political, cultural, and religious dimensions. No contextual theology can therefore claim universal relevance. Furthermore, he argues, no single expression of theological concepts can claim to be valid for all times and places. Cf. J. DUPUIS, *Who do you say I am?* 8-10.

Dupuis emphasizes that we must not choose between the distinct Christologies of the various New Testament writers. They remain distinct, fragmentary, and mutually complementary approaches to the mystery of Jesus Christ, which in itself stands beyond them all and will forever defy full comprehension. He argues that today, as in the early church, the distinct New Testament Christologies need to be kept in fruitful tension and dialogue, lest, choosing one at the expense of another, we fail to embrace in our vision the fullness of the mystery and perhaps lose sight of either the authentic manhood of Jesus or of his true divine Sonship.[45] For Dupuis, to avoid becoming unilateral in one direction or the other, christological reflection will always need to follow a twofold path, from below and from above, and to integrate both.[46]

Given Dupuis' acknowledgment of diverse Christologies in the New Testament and the positive advantage of distinct Christologies presenting mutually complementary approaches to the mystery of Jesus Christ, the titles of *Christ, Lord,* and *Son of God* are highlighted by Dupuis. He quotes Peter's answer given at Caesarea Philippi to the question posed by the title of Dupuis' book as the content of the first kerygmatic preaching of the apostolic church. When Peter stood up with the eleven to address the Jews in the first-ever Christian preaching, the decisive point in his message ran: «Let all the house of Israel [...] know assuredly that God has made him both Lord and Christ, this Jesus whom you crucified» (Acts 2:36). For Dupuis, the three titles of *Christ, Lord* and *Son of God* form the core of the early christological faith showing unmistakably the central place these confessions occupied in the faith of the christian church from the outset.[47]

---

[45] For Dupuis this is why, though in a certain sense the Christology of the Gospel of John, and particularly in the prologue, represents the climax of New Testament Christology, it can never be made into an absolute and exclusive model, leaving no room for the more ancient Christology of the early kerygma. Cf. J. DUPUIS, *Who do you say I am?* 74-75.

[46] This, we have pointed out, is what Dupuis understands by an «integral Christology». The tension in unity of the distinct Christologies of the New Testament guarantees the legitimacy and necessity of plural Christologies today. Cf. J. DUPUIS, *Who do you say I am?* 75.

[47] Throughout this work Dupuis emphasizes that there has never been, not even in the New Testament, a single Christology. He acknowledges that our own time has witnessed a variety of christological approaches. Part of the aim of such christological reflection is to evaluate the merits and limitations of various christological postures, in order to benefit by the gains they have made and remedy their shortcomings in devising a more comprehensive christological perspective. Cf. J. DUPUIS, *Who do you say I am?* 1, 15.

In chapter one of *Who do you say I am?* Dupuis discusses an approach to Christology through the titles.[48] He lists three categories for a study of New Testament «title» Christologies: messianic titles (Dupuis lists *Christ, Servant of Yahweh, Son of David*); functional titles, referring to the salvific role of Jesus toward humankind (*Prophet, Saviour, Lord*); ontological titles, referring to the personal identity of Jesus (*Word of God, Son of God*).[49] Dupuis does not refer to the title of Wisdom here. He highlights the importance of christological titles in New Testament Christology but stresses that this importance should not be exaggerated.[50] Dupuis' central point is that the implied Christology of the earthly Jesus contains an unprecedented claim which breaks down all previous schemes. Jesus was reluctant to accept titles because he claimed to be more than they could express. When dealing with the question of the personal identity of Jesus, Dupuis highlights that Jesus did not legitimise his mission by reference to the titles that had nourished the Jewish expectations of the last era and would later be applied to him by New Testament Christology. In spite of differences of opinion about different titles, Dupuis concludes that exegetes today are largely in agreement that the messianic titles occupy a secondary place in Jesus' testimony about himself.[51]

In his analysis of the development of New Testament Christology we have already noted that Dupuis deals with the question of pre-existence. Dupuis shows how only this idea could guarantee that, in the earthly life and in the cross and resurrection of Jesus, God the Father himself was involved and that in Jesus Christ the Father was revealing himself definitively and eschatologically.[52] Only thus could the universal

---

[48] Dupuis observes that some New Testament Christologies present themselves as title Christologies. He refers to O. CULLMANN, *Christology of the New Testament*; F. HAHN, *Titles of Jesus*; L. SABOURIN, *Names and Titles of Jesus*; V. TAYLOR, *Names of Jesus*.

[49] Dupuis stresses that the ontological meaning of titles may not be presumed. The overall perspective of New Testament Christology is primarily functional, not ontological. Cf. J. DUPUIS, *Who do you say I am?* 19.

[50] Dupuis notes that a Christology of titles can never constitute by itself a complete Christology. Cf. J. DUPUIS, *Who do you say I am?* 19-20.

[51] Dupuis recordes that, beyond all titles and in spite of Jesus' apparent reluctance to declare himself, an astonishing self-awareness emerges from his words and actions. Mark 14:36 testifies beyond doubt to Jesus' consciousness being essentially filial: Jesus was aware of being *the Son*. Cf. J. DUPUIS, *Who do you say I am?* 48-50.

[52] Cf. J. DUPUIS, *Who do you say I am?* 65-69.

significance of Jesus Christ as the fulfillment not only of the Old Testament but of all reality have been adequately expressed. However, unlike Kasper, Dupuis does not cite the immediate source of the New Testament pre-existence statements as found mainly in Old Testament Judaism, with the parallels clearest in Old Testament speculation on Wisdom.

Dupuis acknowledges the presence of the pre-existence theme in the Johannine prologue. Dupuis notes that the writer of the prologue applies the concept of the *Word* of God to the pre-existent Son. He recognizes that this was borrowed from the sapiential literature of the Old Testament. «He dwelt among us» recalls the Old Testament theology of the *shekinah* in virtue of which Wisdom «pitched her tent» to dwell among people.[53]

When presenting a number of theological approaches to Christology, Dupuis highlights the feminist liberation approach.[54] He notes the use by feminist theologians of the Wisdom theme in articulating a feminist liberation approach to Christology: far from laying a foundation for partriarchal attitudes in the community of his disciples, Jesus instituted a rapport of equality, mutuality, and reciprocity among its female and male members. Dupuis focuses on that function of feminist biblical interpretation concerned with retrieving aspects of the tradition which have been lost or neglected and confirms the worth of this initiative.[55] He does not engage in any critique of the more debatable presuppositions of the feminist approach to Christology.[56]

---

[53] Cf. J. DUPUIS, *Who do you say I am?* 72.

[54] Dupuis distinguishes two distinct forms of feminist theology: the post-Christian feminism which chooses to opt out of Christianity and the church, which it considers irremediably aligned to a sexist view of society and church based on patriarchy and androcentrism; reformist, which stigmatises all manifestations of sexism as militating against God's will in creation and provides the equality and mutuality in partnership that characterised the disciples in the Jesus movement. Cf. J. DUPUIS, *Who do you say I am?* 28.

[55] Cf. J. DUPUIS, *Who do you say I am?* 27-29.

[56] Dupuis highlights that the Reign of God breaking in through Jesus marks the end of sexist discrimination, as of every other discrimination; Jesus' partiality in favour of the marginalized includes women. He called them to discipleship, they were present under the cross, and became the first recipients of resurrection appearances. Dupuis acknowledges that androcentricism did return to church structures, even as they endured and continued to prevail to a great extent in society. Cf. J. DUPUIS, *Who do you say I am?* 29.

We have already noted that Dupuis identified the demonstration of the universal significance and cosmic dimension of the Jesus Christ event, with Christ as the pinnacle of salvation history and Christology as that history's sharpest formulation, as the most urgent christological task today.[57] While Dupuis remarks that a cosmic Christology is not wanting in the New Testament, least of all in Pauline theology, highlighting Colossians 1:15-20; Ephesians 1:15-23; 2:10 and John 1:1-18, he does not show how the soteriological and universal significance of the assertion of Jesus as Son of God is taken up and developed in any of these christological hymns. The numerous parallels between these hymns and the Wisdom literature, especially Wisdom and Sirach, have been highlighted. This debt to Old Testament Wisdom material is not acknowledged here by Dupuis.

Dupuis is aware of the contribution of the Church Fathers of the second and third centuries, especially Tertullian and Origen, regarding a correct understanding of the divine Sonship of Jesus Christ. We have already seen, in chapter six, how they both drew on Wisdom imagery from the Old Testament. However, Dupuis makes no explicit connections in *Who do you say I am?* between the Wisdom literature and the writings of the Fathers.

In dealing with the question of the plurality of religions and the challenge posed by religious pluralism to the traditional christocentric perspective of theology, Dupuis appeals to the active presence of the Word of God and of the Divine Spirit but not to the Wisdom of God.[58] Given that we have shown how the Wisdom books of the Old Testament offered something of a bridge to the non-Jewish world, it would have been worth considering whether Wisdom Christology might serve as a useful interpretative key here also.

---

[57] Dupuis stresses that a cosmic Christology would have to show the cosmic dimension of the Incarnation, that is, the significance of Jesus Christ not only for the salvation of human beings and their history, but for the whole universe. It would also have to illustrate the relationship between the theology of the Incarnation and the scientific understanding of the universe, and integrate into a holistic vision of reality creation, Incarnation, salvation, and consummation. Cf. J. DUPUIS, *Who do you say I am?* 149.

[58] This is also the case with Dupuis' two major works in the area of religious pluralism: *Encounter of World Religions* and *Christian Theology of Religious Pluralism*.

2.4 *Concluding Remarks*

We have been concerned here with examining to what extent, in formulating his Christology, Dupuis makes use of the Wisdom elements in the Scriptures. While not using extensively the Wisdom tradition, Dupuis does make passing reference to some of the central Wisdom texts of the New Testament. Dupuis does not offer a Wisdom Christology but reveals a general awareness of the Wisdom influences in the development of Christology.

While Dupuis addresses the christological issues which draw on the Wisdom trajectory, questions of the pre-existence of Christ and Jesus' mediatorship of creation, he does not explicitly highlight their roots in Wisdom. The one exception is Dupuis' acknowledgment that the concept of the *Word* of God, applied to the pre-existent Son in the Johannine prologue, was borrowed from the sapiential literature of the Old Testament. Like Kasper, Dupuis draws on Philippians 2:6-11 as an example of New Testament pre-existence statements though there is uncertainty regarding the roots of this hymn in Wisdom speculation.

Dupuis acknowledges not only the existence of diverse Christologies in the New Testament but also highlights the positive advantage of distinct Christologies presenting mutually complementary approaches to the mystery of Jesus Christ. Hence, while not specifically referring in any significant way to Wisdom Christology, Dupuis would support any initiative to recover a lost or forgotten «metaphor» for Jesus which helps in our understanding of the mystery.

While acknowledging those positive points about Dupuis' references to the Wisdom theme, it must be said that, in his quite substantial treatment of the historical Jesus, Dupuis does not present Jesus as a Sage or as Divine Wisdom in person. No specific references in *Who do you say I am?* are made to the development of the Wisdom theme among the Church Fathers. In conclusion, we cannot speak of Dupuis' Christology as a Wisdom Christology. Rather, a general acknowledgment and passing reference to the Wisdom influence on the development of Christology is what is to be found there.

3. **Denis Edwards**

3.1 *Priest and Theologian*

Denis Edwards is a priest of the Archdiocese of Adelaide, Australia, and one of Australia's leading theologians. Much of his time as a priest has been spent in his native country as a theology teacher, adult educator and retreat director. Currently, he is senior lecturer in systematic theology at the School of Theology of the Flinders University of South Australia and at Catholic Theological College within the Adelaide College of Divinity. Edwards engaged in post-graduate theological studies in the United States leading to an M.A. from Fordham University in 1974 and a doctorate in theology from the Catholic University of America in 1980. His doctoral thesis, under the direction of Avery Dulles, was entitled: *Experience of God and Explicit Faith: A Comparison of John of the Cross and Karl Rahner*. Edwards is the author of a number of books including *Human Experience of God, Jesus and the Cosmos, The God of Evolution: A Trinitarian Theology* and *Jesus the Wisdom of God* which will be of direct concern to us in this chapter.[59] Edwards' books are written in a down-to-earth and practical fashion and are filled with application to the life situations of believers. He writes as a priest who clearly has consider-able experience in religious education and pastoral ministry.

3.2 *The Development of Edwards' Theology*

As an Australian theologian, Edwards' context for his theological writings is his own country of Australia with its diversity of landscapes from rain forests to deserts and a unique flowering of evolution in its flora and fauna. He highlights the need for Australians to address the fact that this land was occupied for thousands of years by Aboriginal people who saw the land as revelatory of the sacred.[60] Edwards' context, therefore, is the relationship between the land and a view of God. Much of his writing centres on the relationship between ecology and theology.[61] Edwards is aware of the terrifying contribution made by Western civilization to the ecological destruction of the planet. In this regard he articulates a foundational principle: love and respect for God involves love and respect for God's creation. Much of Edwards' writing can be understood as an

---

[59] D. Edwards has published the following books: *Human Experience of God; Called to be Church; Jesus and the Cosmos; Creation, Humanity, Community; Jesus the Wisdom of God; God of Evolution*. His most recent publication is «Ecological Significance of God-language», 708-722.

[60] Cf. D. EDWARDS, *Jesus the Wisdom of God*, 1-10.

[61] *Jesus and the Cosmos, Creation, Humanity, Community* and *Jesus the Wisdom of God* all feature the challenge of contemporary ecological concerns to theology as a major theme.

attempt to reflect upon and to ground this intuition by making manifest the ecological and cosmological significance of the central insights of Christian doctrine.

As well as his writings on Christology, Edwards has attempted to build a theological approach to human experience of God. He has explored the connection between the human experience of mystery and transcendence and the Christian God. In *Human Experience of God* he probes the relationship between the development of Christian faith and the mystery lying at the heart of all human experience.[62] While acknowledging the elusive nature of God's presence, Edwards firmly holds that we do experience God.[63] Furthermore, he goes on to show how, on the one hand, such experience of God relates to society and history (the social structure), and on the other hand, how experience of God opens out into contemplative prayer (the mystical dimension).[64] He argues that the church provides the interpretative context in which religious signs and sacraments are experienced as manifestations of God's real presence to us and to our world.

Edwards notes that, in the person and example of Jesus, we have the ultimate access to God. Hence, Edwards highlights the need for a profound Christology to address contemporary theological concerns, be they explorations regarding the human experience of mystery and transcendence and belief in the God of Jesus Christ or our current cosmic and ecological concerns. In *Jesus and the Cosmos* Edwards works towards a theological response to both the ecological crisis and the new cosmology. The evolutionary and cosmic Christology developed here is used to ground what, for Edwards, is a fundamental ethical principle for our time: respect for the whole biosphere, and respect for the integrity of all creation.[65] The basic thesis of *Jesus the Wisdom of God* concerns the retrieval and

---

[62] K. Rahner, more than any other writer, has helped Catholic theology to move in this direction. Edwards relies on the thought of Rahner at several stages in his work. Cf. D. EDWARDS, *Human Experience of God*, vii.

[63] Edwards builds his argument principally on the writings of St. John of the Cross and Karl Rahner. He also relies on the «reconstructed» theory of experience that has been worked out by contemporary philosophers such as John E. Smith. Cf. D. EDWARDS, *Human Experience of God*, 90-101, 112-126.

[64] Cf. D. EDWARDS, *Human Experience of God*, 67-101.

[65] In *Jesus and the Cosmos*, 110-116, Edwards brings together, in summary form, the theological principles outlined in the book and discusses some of the consequences of this theological system for contemporary life.

exploitation of Wisdom Christology as an alternative christological starting point in addressing some contemporary theological concerns.

3.3 *The Christology of Denis Edwards*

It is not the purpose of our study to treat Edwards' Christology in detail.[66] Rather, as with Dupuis, our central concern is with examining to what extent in formulating his systematic Christology, Edwards uses the Wisdom elements in the Scriptures. However, some explication of Edwards' Christology, by way of summary and overview, will help to situate our specific study. In this regard, we will use Edwards' *Jesus and the Cosmos* to summarize his christological thought and *Jesus the Wisdom of God* to examine Edwards' attempt to retrieve Wisdom Christology and hence to use the Wisdom motif to address contemporary questions in theology.

3.3.1 *Summary*

In *Jesus and the Cosmos* Edwards sets about reflecting upon the new story of the cosmos[67], in the light of the story of Jesus that emerges from historical studies. He does this by way of some insights from the work of K. Rahner. Edwards begins by presenting the whole cosmos as having a fundamental unity in the one God, who creates, sustains, and empowers it, and brings the whole to completion.[68] Matter, life, and consciousness form one single history of evolution. Each development, however, is new and essentially different from the preceding stage. Edwards understands

---

[66] We have already noted the strong emphasis Edwards places, in his christological writings, on ecological concerns. The traditional Logos or Word Christology that has dominated the tradition since the early Councils of the church is found wanting by Edwards in his desire to address contemporary ecological concerns. Hence, his argument for the retrieval and exploitation of a Wisdom Christology. Cf. D. EDWARDS, *Jesus the Wisdom of God*, 14-15.

[67] Edwards notes that the advances made by science during this last century have led to a radically new understanding of the universe, which has left the general public, and most theologians, well behind. Edwards highlights the work of scientists who have made serious attempts to communicate the new understanding of the universe to a wider public: P. DAVIES, *God and the New Physics*; ID., *Superforce*; ID., *The Cosmic Blueprint*; S. HAWKING, *A Brief History of Time*. Cf. D. EDWARDS, *Jesus and the Cosmos*, 11-21.

[68] Cf. K. RAHNER, *Foundations*, 181-183; «Evolutionary», 161-163.

the human person to be the cosmos itself come to self-consciousness.[69] Given that it is the human alone who can conceptualize the cosmos as an entity, it could be argued in some sense that a human person is the cosmos come into consciousness. The history of the universe continues in the human community, in culture, and in human interaction with the Earth.[70] For Edwards this evolutionary history of the cosmos reaches its goal in God's self-communication by grace to conscious beings, and through them to the whole cosmos.

Edwards draws upon Rahner's notion of «active self-transcendence» which implies, first, that evolutionary shifts occur through a power that is genuinely intrinsic to the creature and, second, that this power belongs not to the nature of the creature but to God.[71] In Jesus of Nazareth, in his life, death, and resurrection, the universe reaches its goal which it could never attain of itself. Jesus is part of the history of the cosmos, truly of the earth, truly a moment in the biological evolution of the universe.[72]

Edwards affirms the intrinsic and necessary connection between God's self-communication in Jesus and God's universal self-communication through grace.[73] Jesus of Nazareth is God's absolute self-communication to the cosmos. Creation and redemption are understood as two moments in the one process of God's self-communication with the world.[74] Within the history of the cosmos, Jesus can be understood as the absolute Saviour: in him God's self-communication reaches its climax in our history, and is given irreversibly and unambiguously.[75]

---

[69] Here Edwards cites D. LAMBERT, *Cambridge Guide to Prehistoric Man*; S. and T. MCKERN, *Tracking Fossil Man*; E. STOCKTON, «Blackened Stump», 19-25. Cf. D. EDWARDS, *Jesus and the Cosmos*, 21.

[70] Cf. K. RAHNER, «Evolutionary», 172; ID., *Foundations*, 189.

[71] Cf. K. RAHNER, *Hominisation*; ID., «Evolution: II Theological», 478-488; ID., «Evolutionary», 165; ID., *Foundations*, 185.

[72] Cf. D. EDWARDS, *Jesus and the Cosmos*, 42-63.

[73] Cf. D. EDWARDS, *Jesus and the Cosmos*, 64-77.

[74] Cf. K. RAHNER, *Foundations*, 197.

[75] Edwards takes the term «absolute saviour» from Rahner. There are three dimensions to this notion of the absolute saviour: first, in this person we find God's self-communication given *irrevocably*; second, in this person it is possible to *recognize unambiguously* this self-communication; third, in this person God's self-communication reaches its *climax* in our history. Such an absolute saviour would be the irreversible and unambiguous culmination of God's self-giving to the world. Cf. K. RAHNER, «Evolutionary», 193-196.

Edwards refers to one of Rahner's later writings where he calls for an expansion of the theology of redemption in terms of the redemption of the body and the redemption of the cosmos.[76] Influenced by Rahner, Edwards argues that the body can be understood as the self-expression of the spirit in space and time. Through our bodies we are necessarily related to others, and to the whole cosmos, in a common sphere. The glorified resurrected body involves a bodily relationship with the whole cosmos. Edwards defines eternal life as time subsumed into its definitive state. It is the achievement of something definitive and final and is filled with the incomprehensible mystery of God and God's love.[77]

Edwards highlights that the whole of creation, the whole cosmos, will share in the consummation of all things in Christ. The material universe will itself be transformed. The coming kingdom will be God's deed, but it will also be the self-transcending of our cosmic history. The human task of caring for and completing creation has final salvific significance. Through his death and resurrection, Jesus of Nazareth has become an «intrinsic principle» and a «determining feature» of the whole cosmos. In his death and resurrection Christ has been poured out over the cosmos and «become actually, in his very humanity, what he has always been in his dignity, the very centre of creation».[78] He is the beginning and the pledge of the future of the material universe. The risen Christ is the power and the victory hidden in all cosmic reality drawing it toward its consummation in the new earth.[79]

Edwards concludes that this theology of the cosmic Christ attempts to capture the decisive meaning of Jesus for a new time and a new cosmology. It strives to remain faithful to Colossians 1:15-20 which did the same

---

[76] Cf. K. RAHNER, « Redemption», 252-253. What Rahner hoped for was a theology of redemption consistent with his Christology within an evolutionary view of the world.

[77] Cf. D. EDWARDS, *Jesus and the Cosmos*, 84-98.

[78] Here Edwards is quoting K. RAHNER, *Theology of Death*, 66. Cf. D. EDWARDS, *Jesus and the Cosmos*, 92.

[79] Here again Edwards is heavily influenced by the thought of K. Rahner. He had argued that there is an intrinsic and ontological connection between the resurrection of Jesus and the renewal of the world, so that Jesus can be understood as «the pledge and beginning of the perfect fulfillment of the world» and as «representative of the new cosmos». Furthermore, Rahner wrote: «[T]he resurrection is the beginning of the transformation of the world [...]» and «[...] in this beginning the destiny of the world is already in principle decided and has already begun.» Cf. K. RAHNER, «Resurrection», 332-333; ID., « Easter», 124-126, 132-133.

thing for a different time and for a different cosmology. In his later work, *Jesus the Wisdom of God*, Edwards develops further his christological reflections in the context of contemporary ecological and cosmological concerns.

3.3.2 *Outline of a Wisdom Christology in Edwards*

Edwards traces the development of the personification of Wisdom in parts of the Jewish sapiential tradition and then considers key passages of the Christian scriptures where Jesus is identified with divine Wisdom.[80] He notes the ongoing development in the relationship between Sophia and Yahweh: from the time of her earliest appearances in Proverbs[81] to that in Wisdom at the beginning of the Christian era. Edwards keeps in mind the nature of Israel's religion as being monotheistic: Sophia was seen as a symbolic figure in female guise, who took on some of the roles traditionally associated with Yahweh, while remaining within his control.

In moving to the New Testament, Edwards sets out to show that the identification of Jesus with Sophia was the bridge whereby the community who believed that God had raised up Jesus of Nazareth came to see Jesus as the pre-existent one.[82] Edwards discusses Colossians 1:15-20, Hebrews 1:2-4, and the Johannine prologue when considering the christological hymns. He notes that these hymns express the community's faith in Jesus Christ risen from the dead and attribute to him a cosmic role in both creation and redemption. For Edwards this is an important basis for a contemporary ecological approach to Christology. Jesus is celebrated as the exalted and universal Saviour, but as a Saviour whose triumph comes by way of the cross.[83]

When the hymns are considered together, there emerges a pattern for Edwards of One who was with God in the beginning, was an agent in creation, became truly human, died on the cross, rose from the dead, is exalted above all powers, and is the source of universal reconciliation. While not every hymnic text includes all these elements, some of these

---

[80] Cf. D. EDWARDS, *Jesus the Wisdom of God*, 19-43.

[81] Edwards appears to agree with R.E. MURPHY, *The Tree of Life*, 135 that Wisdom is already personified in Job. Cf. D. EDWARDS, *Jesus the Wisdom of God*, 20-21.

[82] Edwards cites J.D.G. DUNN, *Christology in the Making*. Edwards' approach to Wisdom Christology owes much to Dunn's work and to E.A. JOHNSON «Jesus the Wisdom of God», 261-294.

[83] Cf. D. EDWARDS, *Jesus the Wisdom of God*, 33-37.

elements appear in each hymn, the larger pattern appears in Colossians 1:15-20, and most elements are found in the prologue to John's Gospel.[84] Edwards concludes that, in the liturgical celebrations of the earliest Christian communities, we find a highly developed Christology, a theological connection between God's action in creation and in Jesus, a cosmic role for the risen Christ and, at least in John 1:1-18, an explicit theology of pre-existence and Incarnation.[85]

Edwards concludes that it was only through identifying Jesus as divine Wisdom that the theological insight could be reached that the Wisdom who is God's agent in creation is made flesh in Jesus of Nazareth. Not just the theology of pre-existence, but the emergence of the theology of Incarnation and the theology of the Trinity, are historically and structurally dependent upon the theology of Sophia and the identification between Jesus and Sophia.[86]

Edwards also cites I Corinthians 1–4 in the identification of Jesus and divine Wisdom as an important basis for Wisdom Christology.[87] Edwards notes that there is at least an implicit identification here between the Wisdom who was active in the creation of the world (Prov 8) and Jesus crucified. This becomes more obvious when, in I Corinthians 8:6, Paul writes of Christ's role in creation in a way which depends upon understanding Jesus as divine Wisdom. For Edwards there are clear parallels with Wisdom texts (Prov 3:19), and scholars conclude that Paul is here implicitly identifying Jesus with personified Wisdom.[88] Edwards quotes J.D.G. Dunn[89] who says that at this point we cannot say that Wisdom was,

---

[84] Cf. D. EDWARDS, *Jesus the Wisdom of God*, 33-37.

[85] Cf. D. EDWARDS, *Jesus the Wisdom of God,*, 38.

[86] Cf. D. EDWARDS, *Jesus the Wisdom of God,* 37.

[87] Edwards is aware that scholars differ in their interpretation of what Paul means by Wisdom here. What Edwards understands to be clear is that Paul is identifying Jesus with Wisdom, and, that Paul is deliberately using language that has a rich context in the Wisdom literature. Cf. D. EDWARDS, *Jesus the Wisdom of God*, 38-39.

[88] Edwards cites E.A. JOHNSON, «Jesus the Wisdom of God», 278. Johnson mentions as supporting this view, P. Bonnard, H. Conzelmann, W.D. Davies, J.D.G. Dunn, A. Feuillet, W. Knox, E. Schweizer, and U. Wilckens. Cf. D. EDWARDS, *Jesus the Wisdom of God,* 179.

[89] Cf. J.D.G. DUNN, *Christology in the Making*, 212. Cf. also I Corinthians 10:1-4 where Paul identifies the rock from which the Jewish people drank in the desert as Christ. Dunn sees this as a parallel between the rock then and Christ now, rather than a clear reference to pre-existence (pp.183-184).

for Paul, a divine being, or that Christ was explicitly understood as pre-existent with God. What we can say is that Christ is the manifestation of divine Wisdom, the «[...] climactic and definitive embodiment of God's own creative power and saving concern».[90]

Edwards notes that in Luke's Gospel the texts linking Jesus and Wisdom are found principally in four places (7:35; 10:21, 22; 11:49; 13:34). Edwards notes that twice in these texts we find the Lukan Jesus speaking of God as Sophia (7:35; 11:49). For Edwards it is clear that in Luke 11:49 Jesus is being understood as one in the line of the prophets of Sophia. He concludes that, for at least some parts of the early Christian community, Jesus was understood as Wisdom's envoy (Lk 7:35 / Mt 11:19) and Wisdom's prophet (Lk 11:49 / Mt 23:34).[91] Edwards presents Matthew as portraying Jesus as the great teacher of Wisdom and having him implicitly claim to speak as Wisdom himself (11:19; 11:25-30; 23:34; 23:37). In discussing John's Gospel, Edwards relies heavily on the work of Raymond Brown.[92] For Edwards, Jesus in the Gospel of John is personified and incarnate Wisdom, Wisdom come among us in individual and historical terms.[93]

From his study of the Wisdom influence on the Christian scriptures Edwards draws two conclusions. First, Wisdom categories can provide the

---

[90] Cf. J.D.G. DUNN, *Christology in the Making, 212*. Dunn suggests that in this text we see Paul's thought moving in a trinitarian direction, and he comments that «[...] herein we see the origin of the doctrine of the Incarnation». From this Edwards will argue that Wisdom Christology was the bridge to the theology of Incarnation.

[91] Edwards' view here will concur with that of E. Schüssler Fiorenza that at least some parts of the early Christian community understood Jesus as Wisdom's child and Wisdom's prophet. Edwards, like Fiorenza, traces the beginnings of this tradition to the elusive Q community. Cf. D. EDWARDS, *Jesus the Wisdom of God*, 50. He also cites, in support of this view, M.J. SUGGS, *Wisdom, Christology and Law*. Suggs has argued that Matthew takes this theology and transforms it by identifying Jesus and Sophia in 11:2-19 and 3:24. Matthew 11:28-30 echoes the invitation to come to lodge in Wisdom's house of instruction (Sir 51:53), to take up Wisdom's yoke (Sir 51:26), and find with her light labour and rest (Sir 51:27). While Edwards notes that J.P.Meier has urged caution regarding the exaggeration of the place of Wisdom Christology in Matthew, he highlights Meier's comments that «the fusion of apocalyptic and sapiential themes in the service of high Christology could not be clearer». Cf. J.P. MEIER, *Matthew*, 127.

[92] Cf. R.E. BROWN, *Gospel According to John, I-XIII*, cxxii-cxxxviii. Here Brown argues that, in drawing this portrait of Jesus, the fourth evangelist has capitalized on the identification of Jesus with personified Wisdom described in the Old Testament.

[93] Cf. D. EDWARDS, *Jesus the Wisdom of God*, 42-43.

basis for an authentic interpretation of the life and ministry of Jesus. Salvation in Jesus Christ (functional Christology, Christ *pro nobis*) can be understood in Wisdom categories. During his lifetime Jesus was understood as a Wisdom teacher and in the early Christian community He was understood as Wisdom's teacher and emissary and as Wisdom Incarnate. Wisdom categories, alongside others, can help Christian theology gain authentic insight into the life and ministry of the historical Jesus. Christian faith can be expressed in the language «Jesus the Wisdom of God» (I Cor 1:24).[94]

Second, this ancient Wisdom Christology is the essential structural link in the development of the doctrine of the Incarnation in the early church. It is in and through the identification of Jesus (ontological Christology, Christ *in se*) with pre-existent divine Wisdom that we find in the early Christian hymns the beginnings of a theology of Incarnation, a theology which reaches a clear and unambiguous articulation in John's gospel. Here Jesus is the eternal Word made flesh. It is through the identification of Jesus with personified Wisdom that the insight has been reached that what is divine in Jesus (Wisdom) pre-existed his life and ministry and has become incarnate in him. Even in the prologue of John's Gospel, Edwards concurs with Brown that the concept of pre-existent Wisdom lies behind the theology of the pre-existent Word.[95] It is the existence of the biblical tradition of divine Wisdom, with its understanding of Wisdom's pre-existence and presence with God in creation, that provides the conceptual framework which allows the theology of Incarnation and pre-existence to emerge in the New Testament period.[96]

Edwards is aware of the presence of Wisdom Christology in patristic and medieval theology. He specifically traces the emergence of a Wisdom Christology in Origen (c.185-c.254), Athanasius (c.296-377)[97] and Pope Leo I.[98] Edwards notes how Origen held that divine Wisdom, having had

---

[94] Cf. D. EDWARDS, *Jesus the Wisdom of God,* 50-51.

[95] Cf. D. EDWARDS, *Jesus the Wisdom of God,* 50-51.

[96] For Edwards, it is the biblical Wisdom tradition which is ultimately behind Christian thinking about the Trinity. The historical dominance of the theologies of Jesus as divine Word of God and as Son of God has obscured the Wisdom Christology which was their origin. Cf. D. EDWARDS, *Jesus the Wisdom of God,* 51.

[97] Cf. D. EDWARDS, *Jesus the Wisdom of God,* 54-55.

[98] Cf. D. EDWARDS, *Jesus the Wisdom of God,* 55-56. Edwards cites the famous letter of Pope Leo I to Flavian of Constantinople, the *Tome of Leo,* which was crucial at the Council of Chalcedon and in subsequent christological reflection, where Leo employs

a cosmic role in creation, is now made manifest in Jesus.[99] Edwards also refers to the «O Wisdom» antiphon from the Liturgy of the Hours for the Advent season.[100] He highlights that here we find a compendium of Christian theology in Wisdom categories: a trinitarian theology in terms of the procession of Wisdom from the mouth of the Most High; a theology of Wisdom's work in creation, in which Wisdom is understood as not only being present to all of creation, but also as holding all things together; the suggestion of a theology of divine power as non-dominating, as Wisdom works in creation in a «strong but gentle manner»; the prayer «O come» as a plea for Wisdom's advent in Jesus of Nazareth; an understanding of Jesus as a Wisdom teacher, teaching us «the way of truth».[101]

For Edwards, Wisdom Christology, by continually making manifest the interrelationship between creation and Incarnation, can form the basis for a contemporary ecological theology. He goes on to argue that the retrieval of Wisdom Christology can throw fresh light on seven complex areas of contemporary theology. These are issues which not only create difficulties for many Christian believers today, but also, in many cases, are difficult to deal with in traditional «Son of God» Christologies. Edwards identifies these questions as: pre-existence of Jesus[102], the issue of the «person» of

---

the text of Proverbs 9:1 («Wisdom builds her house») alongside the text from John 1:14 («the Word is made flesh») to affirm, against Eutyches, the enduring human nature of Jesus Christ. This is not an isolated instance. In another letter Leo again addresses the theology of the Incarnation in terms of Wisdom [*Epistola,* 31. 2-3]. Leo here not only refers to the Incarnation as «Wisdom building herself a home», but he also shows the inner link in a Wisdom theology between God's work in creation and Incarnation. When Wisdom builds her home among us, the one through whom the world was created is brought forth in the midst of creation.

[99] Cf. D. EDWARDS, *Jesus the Wisdom of God*, 52-54. Edwards notes that chapter two of Origen's great work of systematic Christology, *On First Principles*, sets out his christological vision in terms of Wisdom categories.

[100] «O Wisdom, you come forth from the mouth of the Most High. You fill the universe and hold all things together in a strong yet gentle manner. O come to teach us the way of truth». Cf. *The Divine Office.* I, 549.

[101] Cf. D. EDWARDS, *Jesus the Wisdom of God*, 56.

[102] Regarding pre-existence, Edwards argues that a Wisdom Christology is not only faithful to the biblical origins of a theology of pre-existence, but emphasizes the incomprehensibility of the pre-existing One. This great tradition of divine incomprehensibility must be applied to the pre-existence of Christ, and Edwards argues that Wisdom Christology can help to preserve the «unknowing» in our approach to the second person of the Trinity better than Son Christology. Cf. D. EDWARDS, *Jesus the Wisdom of God*, 57-59.

Jesus Christ[103], the maleness of Jesus in relationship to women[104], the doing of justice[105], Christology in relationship to other religious traditions[106], a theological approach to the possibility of extraterrestrial life[107], and, the principal concern of Edwards, the relationship between God's self-revelation in Jesus and the created universe.[108]

---

[103] Regarding the issue of the «person» of Jesus Christ, Edwards argues that the use of Wisdom categories can help a contemporary approach to the teaching of the Council of Chalcedon and show that the divine and human natures of Jesus Christ are united in one Person. Cf. D. EDWARDS, *Jesus the Wisdom of God*, 59-61.

[104] Edwards concurs with feminist theologians that the early Christian identification of Jesus with Wisdom can be the base for «a contemporary non-androcentric and inclusive Christology». For Edwards a paradigm shift is created when the female figure of Sophia is identified with the limited, male, Galilean Jew, Jesus of Nazareth. For Edwards this opens new possibilities «in an inclusive Christian vision of God's action in Jesus of Nazareth». Cf. D. EDWARDS, *Jesus the Wisdom of God*, 61-62.

[105] Regarding a theology of praxis, Edwards notes that there is a link between traditional Wisdom theology and practice. Wisdom is meant to be lived. Social justice is at the heart of Wisdom literature. A Wisdom Christology supports a theology of praxis. Cf. D. EDWARDS, *Jesus the Wisdom of God*, 62-64.

[106] Regarding other religious traditions, Edwards' central point here is that the Christian conviction that Jesus can be seen as the Incarnation of God's saving and universal love, the human face of divine Wisdom, can be put forward in inter-religious dialogue, without attempting to include other religions within Christianity. Cf. D. EDWARDS, *Jesus the Wisdom of God*, 64-66.

[107] Regarding the possibility of extraterrestrial life , Edwards argues that Wisdom Christology, with its understanding of the inner link between Wisdom's work in creation and Incarnation, opens up the probability that divine Wisdom would be revealed to such creatures not only through Wisdom's presence in creation, not only through the gracious presence of the Spirit of God, but also by some kind of free act of God by which divine Wisdom became present in their history. Cf. D. EDWARDS, *Jesus the Wisdom of God*, 66-68.

[108] In chapter three of his book, Edwards argues that the theology of Jesus as divine Wisdom can undergird a Christian approach to ecology and form the basis for a cosmic Christology. He argues that a Wisdom Christology can begin to show the interrelation between the inter-connected and self-organizing universe and all its creatures, and the saving work of Jesus Christ. Wisdom is dynamically present in all creation, in the great cluster of galaxies, and in every sub-atomic interaction, enabling them to be and to become. This same divine Wisdom became incarnate in Jesus of Nazareth. The crucified and risen One has a new transforming and redeeming bodily relationship with the whole universe. Edwards develops this argument by first showing the inter-relationship between creation and Incarnation in Wisdom Christology and then discussing what the cross tells us about the love that moves the universe and what the resurrection means for the creatures of the universe. Cf. D. EDWARDS, *Jesus the Wisdom of God*, 69-87.

In attempting to show that a retrieval of Wisdom Christology can throw fresh light upon this relationship, Edwards sets out two understandings of the Incarnation.[109] The Thomistic position views the Incarnation as coming about primarily to restore and redeem what was broken by human sin and, hence, presents an extrinsic relationship between God's work in creation and the Incarnation. An alternative theological approach, which Edwards associates with Irenaeus, Duns Scotus, Teilhard de Chardin, and Rahner, sees the Incarnation, while not dependent on the Fall as it was always part of God's plan, as flowing directly from God's free love for creatures.[110] Here the motive of the Incarnation is simply the free self-communicating love of the divine will. While these theologians recognize the fact of sin and the need for redemption, they see the Incarnation of the Word of God as always intended by God.

Edwards argues that Wisdom Christology lends support to this latter interpretation and can help hold together a theology of creation and Incarnation. A Wisdom Christology sees creation and Incarnation as intrinsically connected in the one divine plan, while still insisting that the Incarnation was a totally free act of God. In this view, there can be no separation of creation and redemption, no theology of creation independent of a theology of Incarnation, and no theology of Incarnation and redeeming grace not related to the created world.[111]

Edwards' argument proceeds by highlighting that in I Corinthians 1–4 the identification of divine Wisdom with the incomprehensible mystery of the cross has profound meaning for an ecological theology. The Wisdom of God revealed in creation is now revealed in a staggering way in the cross of Jesus. This suggests, for Edwards, that the love revealed on

---

[109] Cf. D. EDWARDS, *Jesus the Wisdom of God*, 70-72.

[110] Cf. D. EDWARDS, *Jesus the Wisdom of God*, 71-72.

[111] Edwards cites K. Rahner who said «we can understand creation and Incarnation as two moments and two phases of the one process of God's self-giving and self-expression, although it is an intrinsically differentiated process». Cf. K. Rahner, *Foundations of Christian Faith*, 197. Edwards notes that while Rahner is not developing an explicitly Wisdom Christology, Rahner's theology of Incarnation is compatible with Wisdom theology. This intrinsic connection, for Edwards, is fundamental to the structure of Wisdom thought. Divine Wisdom is, by definition, God's presence and self-expression. God communicates God's self through divine Wisdom; Wisdom is present in all of creation and has built herself a home among us in Jesus Christ. Wisdom, God's companion and helper in creation, becomes incarnate in this one human being. God's self-communication in creation and grace reaches its irrevocable climax in Jesus. Cf. D. EDWARDS, *Jesus the Wisdom of God*, 71.

the cross is the focal point of the Wisdom that is at work and manifest in an eco-system, a rain forest, and the Milky Way Galaxy.[112] For believers, the great size and beauty of the universe reveal the wonder and artistry and the greatness of God. We see God at work in our expanding universe sustaining all things, enabling creatures to break through to new levels of complexity and organization, and enfolding the whole curvature of space-time within divine creative love. Edwards' thesis is that Paul's theology of Wisdom confronts us with the fact that *this* Wisdom at work in the universe is now revealed in the vulnerable love expressed in the crucified One. The foolish excess of the cross reveals what is at the heart of the processes of the universe.

Edwards argues that if the Wisdom Christology of I Corinthians contributes to an ecological theology by giving insight into the love that is at the heart of evolutionary and cosmic history, the Wisdom Christology of the Colossians hymn (1:15-20) can be seen as contributing to an ecological theology by offering insight into the relationship between the resurrection of Jesus and the material universe.[113]

Edwards notes that the context for this hymn is the widespread New Testament celebration of Christ as the Wisdom of God. Part of this wider context is formed by the Pauline theology of *mystery*, where Christ is understood as the revelation of God's purpose of salvation, which had hitherto been hidden in God.[114]

---

[112] In support of his argument, Edwards refers to the commentary by H. Conzelmann on I Corinthians, where, in his treatment of I Corinthians 1–4, Conzelmann argues that Paul, as well as speaking of the historic relationship which God establishes through the cross, also says something about the nature of God and about God's relationship with creation. Cf. H. CONZELMANN, *I Corinthians*, 48.

[113] Edwards notes that the cosmic scope of the Colossians Christology is brought out sharply by the use of three different strategies to describe the universal meaning of Christ. First, there is the often-repeated expression «all things». All things were created in Christ according to the first stanza (1:16) and redeemed in him according to the second (1:20). Second, the hymn uses the standard expression for the whole of creation: everything in «heaven and earth» is both created in Christ and reconciled in him. Third, the hymn specifies that the cosmic powers are created in him: thrones, dominions, rulers and powers. Cf. D. EDWARDS, *Jesus the Wisdom of God*, 83.

[114] Edwards highlights that both in I Corinthians 1–4 and Colossians 1:15-20 the mystery of God's plan and God's Wisdom are closely related. Paul writes to the Corinthians: «But we speak God's Wisdom, secret and hidden [literally, the Wisdom of God in mystery], which God decreed before the ages for our glory» (I Cor 2:7). This idea is taken up in Colossians 1:26-27; 2:2 and developed further in Ephesians 2:1–3:13.

For Edwards Colossians 1:15-20 displays a clear movement of thought. The first stanza (Col 1:15-18a) is concerned with the *creation* of all things in Christ, while the second stanza (Col 1:18b-20) celebrates the *reconciliation* of the universe in Christ.[115] Edwards cites the work of J. Sittler regarding the meaning of the second stanza of the hymn in relation to the first with his summary proposition: «A doctrine of redemption is meaningful only when it swings within the larger orbit of a doctrine of creation».[116] Edwards concludes that Colossians 1:15-20 will not allow us to contain our theology of redemption «within the narrower (although profoundly important) orbit of human sin and forgiveness». The rest of creation cannot be seen merely as the stage on which the drama of human redemption is played out. The Colossians hymn insists that the whole universe is caught up in the Christ event.[117]

Edwards notes that the world-view of Colossians and Ephesians[118] differs markedly from contemporary views of evolutionary history and from contemporary cosmology. There is a big shift from the «powers» of Colossians and Ephesians to ecosystems, global climate change, black holes, quasars, and the choice between an open and a closed universe. Yet Edwards points out that the theological principle at work in Colossians and Ephesians applies to both ancient and modern views of creation.[119] He suggests that we need to understand the «principalities and powers» as time-conditioned language for what today we might call «the structures, laws, institutions, and constants of nature, evolution, history, society, the

---

These texts make it clear that God's saving plan includes the gathering up of all things in Christ (Eph 1:10). Cf. D. EDWARDS, *Jesus the Wisdom of God*, 78-79.

[115] Edwards cites C.F.D. Moule who has drawn attention to the fact that the «stupendous» words of this hymn apply to One who had been crucified just a few years before. The explanation can only be found in the experience of the resurrection of the crucified, and the powerful light this event throws on all things. The resurrection sheds its light in both directions - forward to God's future transformation of all things, and back to God's creation of the universe. Cf. C.F.D. MOULE, *Epistles of Paul*, 58-59.

[116] Cf. J. SITTLER, «Called to Unity», 177-78. In support of Sittler's interpretation of Colossians 1:15-20 see J. MOLTMANN, *Way of Jesus Christ*, 276-78.

[117] Cf. D. EDWARDS, *Jesus the Wisdom of God*, 81-83.

[118] Edwards notes that in Ephesians we find a cosmic Christology like that of Colossians 1:15-20 expressed in a succinct and summary form: «A plan for the fulness of time, to gather all things in him, things in heaven and things on earth» (1:10). Cf. D. EDWARDS, *Jesus the Wisdom of God*, 83.

[119] Cf. M. BARTH, «Principalities», 170-183, here 175.

psyche, the mind».[120] When Colossians and Ephesians refer to Christ and the «powers», they are testifying to the relevance of Christ's work for everything in the created world. Edwards argues that in taking up the thought of Colossians in today's world it is both possible and necessary to reflect upon the relationship between the crucified and risen Christ and the expanding universe and the evolutionary biotic community of the planet Earth. What the Wisdom Christology of Colossians is saying to our ecological and cosmological concerns Edwards highlights in seven points: (1) Christ is the mediator of creation, not only because divine Wisdom, which becomes incarnate in him, is God's creative power and presence, but because all things are created «for» Christ (1:16). (2) The Wisdom at work in creation finds ultimate expression as compassionate love in the radical vulnerability of the cross. *This* is the Wisdom of God, the art of God at work in creation and salvation. (3) Because of the resurrection of the crucified Jesus, it is no longer simply divine Wisdom at work in continuous creation, but the risen Jesus, Wisdom incarnate, and the transforming power of his death and resurrection that are at work in the universe. (4) Jesus Christ, in the power of the resurrection, has become what the Wisdom of God always was, engaged with the whole universe as a power at work shaping and transforming all things. (5) While the work of cosmic reconciliation has begun in Christ's resurrection, we live in a universe and a biotic community in which this work is not yet complete. (6) The material universe will be transformed in the power of the risen Christ. The bodily resurrection of Jesus is the promise and the beginning of the reconciliation of «all things», whether «on earth or in heaven» through the blood of the cross (Col 1:20), of the bringing together of all things in Christ, «things in heaven and things on earth» (Eph 1:10). (7) The resurrection can transform, not only individual bodies, but the universe itself through an eschatological action of God in Jesus Christ (I Cor 15:24-28).[121]

3.4 *Concluding Remarks*

We have been concerned here with examining to what extent, in formulating his Christology, Edwards uses the Wisdom elements in the Scriptures. Edwards traces the development of the personification of

---

[120] Cf. D. EDWARDS, *Jesus the Wisdom of God*, 84.

[121] Cf. D. EDWARDS, *Jesus the Wisdom of God*, 84-87.

Wisdom in the Jewish sapiential tradition, from the time of her earliest appearances in Proverbs to that in Wisdom at the beginning of the Christian era, and considers key passages of the New Testament where Jesus is identified with divine Wisdom.

Edwards sets out to show that, first, Wisdom categories can provide the basis for an authentic interpretation of the life and ministry of Jesus and, second, the identification of Jesus with Wisdom was the bridge whereby the community which believed that the Father had raised up Jesus of Nazareth came to see Jesus as the pre-existent one. Edwards, influenced by the writings of J.D.G. Dunn, concludes that it was only through identifying Jesus as divine Wisdom that the theological insight could be reached that Wisdom, who is God's agent in creation, is made flesh in Jesus of Nazareth. The theologies of pre-existence and Incarnation are historically and structurally dependent upon a Wisdom theology and the identification of Jesus and Wisdom.

Edwards is also aware of the presence of Wisdom Christology in patristic and medieval theology, specifically tracing the emergence of Wisdom Christology in Origen (c.185-c.254), Athanasius (c.296-377), and Pope Leo I, together with the «O Wisdom» Antiphon of the Advent Liturgy.

For Edwards, a Wisdom Christology, by continually making manifest the inter-relationship between creation and Incarnation, can form the basis for a contemporary ecological theology. He has isolated seven complex areas of contemporary theology which, he believes, can benefit from a retrieval of Wisdom Christology: pre-existence of Jesus, the issue of «person» of Jesus Christ, the maleness of Jesus in relationship to women, the doing of justice, Christology in relationship to other religious traditions, a theological approach to the possibility of extraterrestrial life, and, the principal concern of Edwards, the relationship between God's self-revelation in Jesus and the created universe.

Edwards favours a theological understanding of the Incarnation which highlights this great mystery as flowing directly from God's love for humanity and all creation. In this theological tradition, Edwards argues, there is the possibility for seeing a much more intrinsic link between God's action in creation and Incarnation. For Edwards, a Wisdom Christology lends support to this interpretation. In this view, Edwards argues, there can be no separation of creation and redemption, no theology of creation independent of a theology of Incarnation and no theology of Incarnation and redeeming grace not related to the created world.

In interpreting Paul's theology of Wisdom, Edwards holds that Pauline Wisdom Christology confronts us with the fact that the Wisdom at work in the universe is now revealed in the vulnerable divine foolishness of the cross. He goes on to argue that if the Wisdom Christology of I Corinthians contributes to an ecological theology by giving insight into the love that is at the heart of evolutionary and cosmic history, the Wisdom Christology of Colossians 1:15-20 can be seen as contributing to an ecological theology by offering insight into the relationship between the resurrection of Jesus and the material universe. Edwards highlights here the link between the creation and the reconciliation of all things «in Christ». Here the whole universe is caught up in the Christ event.

In taking up the thought of Colossians for today's world, Edwards stresses the necessity of reflecting upon the relationship between the crucified and risen Christ and the expanding universe, and the evolutionary biotic community of the planet Earth. The Wisdom of Colossians, for Edwards, is saying to our ecological and cosmological concerns that the resurrection promise embraces the whole creation. The whole universe will share in the consummation of all things «in Christ». In conclusion, Edwards brings together insights from the Wisdom literature and contemporary creation thought in a work that illuminates an integrated ecological theology.

4. Elisabeth Schüssler Fiorenza

4.1 Christian Feminist and New Testament Scholar

Elisabeth Schüssler Fiorenza was born in the town of Tâşnad in the Banat region of the north-west of Romania. She still vividly remembers her family's flight from Romania through Hungary and Austria to southern Germany in the closing months of 1944, as World War II swept once again through her home town where she had been born six years previously. Fiorenza's academic studies began at the University of Würzburg (1957-63) where she studied philosophy, theology, and German literature. In 1962 she was awarded the equivalent of a M.Div. Degree from the Studium Theologicum of the University of Würzburg[122] followed, in 1963, with a Licentiate in Pastoral Theology. Fiorenza's doctoral dissertation[123],

---

[122] E. SCHÜSSLER FIORENZA, Zum Herrschaft und Priestermotiv in der Apokalypse.

[123] E. SCHÜSSLER FIORENZA, Der vergessene Partner. This thesis was completed under the direction of Prof. Dr. R. Schnackenburg of the University of Würzburg and Prof. Dr. J. Gnilka of the University of Münster. Fiorenza received the Award of the

from the University of Münster, concerned the role of women historically in various church ministries and was published in Germany in 1964. She came to the United States in 1970 and subsequently taught for almost fifteen years in the department of theology at the University of Notre Dame, Indiana. In the autumn of 1988 she joined the faculty at Harvard Divinity School as Krister Stendahl Professor of Scripture and Interpretation (the first occupant of a chair named after the renowned biblical scholar who was for a decade also the Divinity School's Dean).[124] Fiorenza is a co-founder and co-editor, with Judith Plaskow, of the *Journal of Feminist Studies in Religion*, the first and arguably the most important of several academic journals in the field. The list of Fiorenza's publications, both in English and German, is extensive. Her books *In Memory of Her*[125] and *Bread not Stone*[126] have been translated into several languages and have been acclaimed for their scholarly approach.[127] Fiorenza is a significant contemporary feminist NewTestament scholar.[128]

Theological Faculty of the University of Münster for the best dissertation in the academic year 1969-70.

[124] Fiorenza has also been Talbot Professor of New Testament Studies at the Episcopal Divinity School in Cambridge, Massachusetts, Harry Fosdick Visiting Professor at Union Theological Seminary in New York and *Gastprofessorin* at (the Catholic Theological Faculty of) the Universities of Tübingen, Luzern and Berlin.

[125] E. SCHÜSSLER FIORENZA, *In Memory of Her*.

[126] E. SCHÜSSLER FIORENZA, *Bread not Stone*.

[127] Fiorenza's most recent books include: *Revelation*; *But She Said*; *Discipleship of Equals*; *Jesus*; *The Power of Naming*. She is also editor of a two volume feminist commentary work *Searching the Scriptures*. Her latest book is *Sharing Her Word*. She has served on the boards of the major biblical societies and on the editorial boards of the *Catholic Biblical Quarterly*, *Cross Currents*, *Horizons*, *Journal of Biblical Literature*, *Journal of Religion and Law*, *Kirche und Israel*, *Religious Studies Review*, *Semeia*. She is the co-editor of the feminist theology issues of the international journal *Concilium*.

[128] At the outset it should be noted that there is a fundamental confidence in tradition evident in the work of Fiorenza which does not exist among all feminist theologians. As a Christian feminist she has elected by definition to dialogue with tradition in the belief that there is a liberating core masked by centuries of misogyny. Since she articulates her egalitarian vision out of the same foundational experiences, texts, and traditions as classical theology, she represents perhaps a more profound challenge than the work of, for example, post-Christian feminists. Fiorenza contends that the stance of post-Christian feminism too easily concedes that women have no biblical history and so relinquishes their claim to a biblical heritage. As an example of post-Christian feminism see M. DALY, *Beyond God the Father*. Daly firmly rejects any priority or privilege of the Christian tradition.

Both in terms of methodology as well as in terms of historical-critical research and exegesis, her work has received acclaim.[129]

4.2 *The Development of Schüssler Fiorenza's Theology*

The work of Elisabeth Schüssler Fiorenza is seen by many as a significant attempt to reconstruct Christian origins from a feminist theological perspective. Her book *In Memory of Her* sets the theoretical agenda for feminist interpretation of the New Testament.[130] In a more recent monograph, *Jesus, Miriam's Child, Sophia's Prophet*, she is primarily concerned to set out further the implications of her views that were already stated in her earlier work.[131] In this book she does not offer any significantly new exegesis but rather concentrates on methodological and theological issues.

In *Bread not Stone*, Fiorenza articulates in a general way her aim «[...] to develop a feminist biblical hermeneutics [...] a theory, method, or perspective for understanding and interpretation [...] In doing so [...] (to) contribute to the feminist articulation of a new scholarly paradigm of

---

[129] The 1980s witnessed the publication of many studies in the area of feminist reconstructions of early Christianity and feminist hermeneutical theory. Apart from the work of Fiorenza the primary works include: A.L. LAFFEY, *Wives, Harlots and Concubines*; A. LOADES, *Feminist Theology*; L.M. RUSSELL, ed., *Feminist Interpretation*; A. YARBRO COLLINS, ed., *Feminist Perspectives*.

[130] There are of course other female New Testament scholars whose work has reached similar conclusions, such as E.A. Johnson and L. Schottroff, but to date their work has not been quite as influential as Fiorenza's. Cf. E.A. JOHNSON, «Jesus the Wisdom of God», 261-294; ID., *She Who Is*; L. SCHOTTROFF, «Women as Followers», 453-461.

[131] Cf. E. SCHÜSSLER FIORENZA, *Jesus*. Though the book is two hundred pages long, it deals as much with methodological issues as with Jesus, with the result that we still do not have an adequate study of the historical Jesus by a feminist scholar. Chapter five of this work is given over to reiterating her arguments that Jesus saw God as Sophia with himself as Sophia's prophet. As we shall see, it is crucial to Fiorenza's whole programme that she assume that the Gospel material underwent a lengthy process of transmission and substantive change (*Jesus*, 133). This assumption underpins a repeated and radical reconstruction of the Jesus tradition that rejects much material and gives a particular construal to a few passages. While we agree that historical reconstruction is necessary to sort out what goes back to the historical Jesus, we would argue that there is not a willful misconstrual or patriarchal reconstructing of most of the arguably authentic Jesus material in the Synoptic Gospels. If this argument is true, much of Fiorenza's case for her exegetical and theological programme falters.

biblical interpretation and theology».[132] In discussing the foundation for such a «new scholarly paradigm» she enunciates a basic principle of feminist theory: that «[...] the locus or place of divine revelation and grace is not the Bible [...] but the *ekklesia* of women and the lives of women who live the option of our women selves».[133] With the experiences of, who Fiorenza calls, *women-church* as the principle for evaluating scriptural texts, we are led to see whether patriarchal texts, which according to Fiorenza have been experienced as utterly oppressive and exploitative, have any place in the *ekklesia gynaikon*. For Fiorenza it is the task of a feminist biblical hermeneutics to challenge the assumption that such patriarchal texts are authoritative.[134]

The hermeneutical function of biblical interpretation within the feminist movement is, firstly, concerned with retrieving those aspects of the tradition which narrate a more positive and less steretoyped view of women than tradition might otherwise seem to suggest and also to make those aspects available as a contributory force for criticism of the present and for

---

[132] Cf. E. SCHÜSSLER FIORENZA, *Bread not Stone*, x. Feminist hermeneutics rests on the principle that biblical texts have been interpreted in such a way as to promote and legitimate secondary or oppressive social roles for women. Certain biblical texts, as mediated through many Christian traditions, are perceived in most strands of feminism to have been transposed into instruments of power, domination, and social control. A critical hermeneutical principle is sought which will unmask this «legitimating» social function to produce women's emancipation from these supposed norms and patterns. In this sense, as Fiorenza argues, feminist hermeneutics is also liberation hermeneutics. Cf. also E. SCHÜSSLER FIORENZA, *In Memory of Her*, 6 and 16.

[133] Cf. E. SCHÜSSLER FIORENZA, «The Will to Choose», 125-146, here 128. Fiorenza defines the *ekklesia gynaikon* as «[...] the movement of self-identified women and women-identified men in biblical religion [...] (whose) [...] goal is women's self-affirmation, power, and liberation from all patriarchal alienation, marginalisation and oppression» (p.126). This notion of *ekklesia gynaikon* as the critical centre of interpretation of Scripture is much disputed. Cf. F. MARTIN, *The Feminist Question*, 172-182.

[134] Feminist interpretations of the Bible, Fiorenza urges, cannot do other than operate with what amount to internal norms within feminist life-worlds or systems, because the Bible itself is already selective. It is «[...] authored by men, written in androcentric language, reflective of male experience, selected and transmitted by male religious leadership. Without question the Bible is a male book.» Therefore, Fiorenza argues, the biblical writings cannot provide a trans-contextual critical principle; the needed critical dimension emerges from the experience of women. What guides the interest of interpretation tends to be that which retrieves women's experience and corporately affirms women readers. Cf. E. SCHÜSSLER FIORENZA, «The Will to Choose», 130.

transformative action.[135] Feminist hermeneutics also embodies a deep «hermeneutic of suspicion» that conventional biblical interpretation does not represent value-neutral descriptions of biblical history, traditions and texts. All interpretation, it is argued, at least until very recently, has been mediated through male-dominated reading-communities.[136] The conclusion is urged that, because of patriarchal bias, the dominant interpreters and transmitters of early tradition transmitted only a fraction of the rich traditions about significant women and their contributions in early Christianity. Hence, most egalitarian traditions of primitive Christianity are probably lost.[137]

However, unease has been expressed regarding the extent to which Fiorenza allows her own social and hermeneutical interest to determine not simply the weighting of probability that a given historical hypothesis receives, but even the very selection of hypotheses which are presented for serious consideration and evaluation.[138] What is being referred to here is the clearly selective discussions of different explanatory hypotheses which might account for the same textual and historical data.[139] Such criticism

---

[135] Given that the women-church has the authority «to choose and reject» texts, Fiorenza sees the thrust of such a discipline to be critical evaluation rather than correlation. As such, it is obliged to articulate criteria for evaluating particular texts and traditions. Such criteria or principles must be derived from a systematic exploration of women's experiences of oppression and liberation. Fiorenza has not yet dealt with the question of the further articulation of such criteria, nor has she specified what these principles, based on the experience of *women-church*, might be. Undoubtedly, a basic difficulty with further specification of such principles may be the realization that the experience of *women-church* is not uniform. Fiorenza is rightly aware of this difficulty: what is constitutive of women's experience? what is universal? what is particular? Although she does not discuss the extent to which the term «women's experience» can be used independently of the context from which it originates, she is acutely aware of the difficulties involved in using the category of women's experience. Once she chooses to stress that the evaluative norm for hermeneutics cannot be universal, but rather is derived from specific instances of oppression and liberation, she admits that there is a certain relativism implied in her primary resources. Cf. A.C. THISELTON, *New Horizons in Hermeneutics*, 442-444.

[136] Cf. E. SCHÜSSLER FIORENZA, *In Memory of Her*, 5-6. Cf. also T.D. SETEL, «Feminist Insights», 35-42.

[137] Cf. E. SCHÜSSLER FIORENZA, «Word, Spirit and Power», 30-70, here 57; see also E. SCHÜSSLER FIORENZA, *In Memory of Her*, 55, 80.

[138] Cf. A.C. THISELTON, *New Horizons in Hermeneutics*, 442-450.

[139] Cf. A.C. THISELTON, *New Horizons in Hermeneutics,* 443-452. One of the most striking examples noted by Thiselton arises from Fiorenza's handling of the different biblical narrative-traditions of the resurrection appearances of Jesus to the women. In *In*

calls into question, at least at some decisive points, the genuinely socio-critical, rather than pragmatic, status of her work. Thiselton acknowledges that the task of holding together a hermeneutic which is explicitly aggressive, namely a hermeneutic of conflict, with genuine hermeneutical openness, imposes an exceedingly demanding and perhaps impossible task on the author.[140]

Memory of Her, Fiorenza attempts to develop the thesis that Luke attempts to play down the role of women as proclaimers of the Easter kerygma by stressing «[...] that the words of the women seemed to the eleven an idle tale, and they did not believe them (Lk 24:11)». Fiorenza drives a wedge between the positive affirmation of women found in Matthew and especially in John and an allegedly negative and suppressive anti-feminist stance in the pre-Pauline tradition, in Paul, in Mark 16:1-8, and in Luke 24:1-11. Fiorenza pursues only one set of questions: what gender-related evaluations of the status of women serve to address this problem? She does not seriously ask whether some other question might equally well, or perhaps more convincingly, invite an alternative explanation for the same data, because such questions are not a major part of her agenda. But this surely weakens the credibility of her hypotheses as genuinely critical constructions. Fiorenza, it seems, is committed to find explanations which depend wholly on gender-differences. But the crucial question is: Is this the issue in those traditions which stress the role and experience of Peter, the twelve and Paul? Further, the Lukan verse on which Fiorenza places so much weight for an allegedly anti-feminist perspective (Lk 24:11), is read by most specialists (and probably by most ordinary readers) as a rebuke to the unbelief of the *male* disciples! Does the selection of a small segment of gender-related explanatory hypotheses for historical or textual data erode claims to offer a genuinely critical, rather than pragmatic-orientated, inquiry in which social interest takes precedence over hermeneutical openness and forecloses certain possibilities before they are examined?

[140] Thiselton refers to the work of Walter Künneth in his specialist treatise on the resurrection. For Künneth, the central issue in the accounts of the resurrection appearances is that of continuity of identity in the context of transformation and change. The role of the resurrection appearances functions first of all to establish continuity of identity between the crucified Jesus and the transformed, exalted, Lord Jesus. Further, Peter denied Jesus, and in his failure shared in the apparent «failure» of the cross; in and through the resurrection he was re-commissioned to the apostolic task as one who shared in fellowship with the Risen One after coming to the end of himself and his own strength. Fiorenza has the raw material explicitly to hand to consider this hypothesis. For, ironically, she stresses again and again that while all of the texts point up the repeated failures of the men, the women remain models of unfailing discipleship. Yet, she does not even consider the possibility that, for the evangelists and for Paul, to be a witness of the resurrection has something to do with the birth of hope out of despair (Moltmann) rather than just the gender issues. Fiorenza, it seems, is committed to find explanations which depend wholly on gender-differences. Cf. W. KÜNNETH, *Resurrection*, 89.

4.3 *The Christology of Elisabeth Schüssler Fiorenza*

As was the case with Dupuis and Edwards, we will not treat Fiorenza's Christology in detail. Rather, we are concerned to examine to what extent, in formulating her Christology, Fiorenza uses the Wisdom elements in the Scriptures. Some explication of Fiorenza's Christology, by way of summary and overview, will help to situate and clarify our specific study. In this regard we will concentrate on Fiorenza's *In Memory of Her*, together with chapter five of *Jesus: Miriam's Child, Sophia's Prophet*[141], as our basic texts for our examination of Fiorenza's Christology. We will appeal to other writings of hers on Christology insofar as they help to clarify or elucidate our argument further.

4.3.1 *Summary*

Fiorenza is primarily concerned with the *politics* of christological discourses, the hidden frameworks of meaning that determine, and often distort, both malestream and apologetic feminist christological formulations. For Fiorenza, Christologies can either encourage critical thought and engagement or entrench kyriarchal processes of domination and subordination. She does not accept kyriarchal Christology as normative and insists that the best response to it is a praxis of liberation. Fiorenza argues that Jesus was a prophet of God, whom he viewed as Sophia or Wisdom, rather than Father.[142] Jesus, Fiorenza argues, led a renewal movement that stood in continuity with an egalitarian tradition within Judaism that was critical of the dominant tradition of Jewish patriarchalism.[143] Jesus preached and

---

[141] *Jesus* expands the section on the Jesus movement found in Fiorenza's earlier book *In Memory of Her*. Here Fiorenza maintains her basic thesis that Jesus was a Sophia-inspired prophet who challenged the patriarchal family and established a movement that can be characterised as «a discipleship of equals», while expanding her analysis to include a feminist critique of the theology of the cross as well as feminist reflections on the development of various Wisdom Christologies in early Christian tradition. The book has three parts which deal roughly with methodological concerns, questions of historical reconstruction, and the development of Wisdom Christology in early Christian tradition.

[142] Fiorenza is an exponent of the view that Jesus saw himself as a prophet of Wisdom/Sophia and addressed God as such; Marcus Borg, Burton Mack and others also support this interpretation of Jesus. While we have evidence for showing that the early church, even as early as Paul's earlier letters, viewed Jesus as God's Wisdom, we have little evidence that they viewed Jesus' God as Wisdom/Sophia. Cf. B. WITHERINGTON, *The Jesus Quest*, 167-168.

[143] Fiorenza wishes to avoid pitting Jesus against Israelite patriarchal religion, for that would mean alleging that Jesus was anti-semitic and had a non-Jewish point of view. Instead she argues that Jesus continues one stream of Jewish tradition that was critical

practiced a kingdom of equals and opposed patriarchy in any form, and his death is attributed to his resistance to Roman domination.[144]

Using sociological models as a way of ordering data from the earliest traditions, Fiorenza presents the group around Jesus as «an inner-Jewish renewal movement». For Fiorenza, the sociological characteristics of this movement are most clearly seen in a dialectic with the dominant ethos of the Jewish social world.[145] That ethos was expressed in the image of Israel as a «kingdom of priests and a holy nation», and its central symbols were temple and Torah. In the social system purity and holiness became correlated with the hierarchical structure of a patriarchal society.[146] Jesus and his movement challenged the purity system, offered an alternative interpretation of Torah and temple, and practiced inclusive wholeness in «a discipleship of equals», one of her most frequent epithets for the movement.[147] Its praxis was marked by festive table-sharing. As a social

---

of the dominant patriarchal system that existed in Judaism. Cf. E. SCHÜSSLER FIORENZA, *In Memory of Her*, 107. In *Jesus* Fiorenza reiterates her reconstruction of the Jesus movement as one of several renewal movements within Judaism; the Jesus movement was a particular Jewish emancipatory movement of wo/men (Fiorenza writes in such a fashion both in order to indicate the problematic character of the signifier «woman» and to use the term as inclusive of men) which grew out of a emancipatory Jewish framework. For evidence she appeals to the understanding of Jesus as a prophet of Sophia who challenged the oppressive Roman imperial system in his proclamation of the kingdom of God, sought to abolish the patriarchal family, and welcomed disenfranchised groups to his inclusive table community. Cf. E. SCHÜSSLER FIORENZA, *Jesus*, 92-94.

[144] There are various key texts from which Fiorenza argues that Jesus believed in the eschatological abolition of patriarchy: Mark 10:2-9; Mark 12:18-27; Luke 14:26; the Q material in Matthew 10:34-36 / Luke 12:51-53; Luke 11:27-28; Matthew 23:1-12. Cf. E. SCHÜSSLER FIORENZA, *In Memory of Her*, 143-148. B. Witherington comments on Fiorenza's use of these texts in *The Jesus Quest*, 169-174. Fiorenza says nothing about the *Abba* sayings or the Lord's Prayer, presumably because she wishes to argue that Jesus called and saw God as Sophia. The difficulty is that the Sophia idea is less well attested than the Father / Abba one in the Gospels. Furthermore, what little evidence we have from the teachings of Jesus suggests he was not a Zealot and did not preach resistance against the Roman authorities.

[145] Fiorenza has offered little evidence for the «emancipatory Jewish framework» which she has proposed other than an appeal to the Book of Judith (*Jesus*, 89). The Book of Judith, which is a fictional work featuring Judith as a representative of Israel who is domesticated at the end of the story, proves little about the actual role of women in ancient Judaism. Cf. A.J. LEVINE, «Sacrifice and Salvation», 17-30.

[146] Cf. E. SCHÜSSLER FIORENZA, *In Memory of Her*, 110-116.

[147] Cf. E. SCHÜSSLER FIORENZA, *In Memory of Her*, 140-151.

movement, it specifically included the impoverished and destitute, the sick and crippled, tax collectors, outcasts, and prostitutes. This egalitarian praxis was intended as an alternative ethos for Israel, subverting and intruding upon the dominant ethos. It was an alternative life-style not simply for individuals, but for a community.[148]

In reaching these conclusions Fiorenza brings certain presuppositions to her reading of the Jesus material. It is her view that women had large roles to play in both the Jesus movement in Palestine and in early Christianity throughout the Mediterranean world.[149] In addition, she assumes that the Gospel material must have gone through a lengthy process of transmission and substantive change.[150] This assumption undergirds a repeated and radical reconstruction of the Jesus tradition that

---

[148] Cf. E. SCHÜSSLER FIORENZA, *In Memory of Her*, 118-130. For Fiorenza, this political agenda was subverted by the Evangelists who depoliticized the teaching of Jesus. Cf. E. SCHÜSSLER FIORENZA, *Jesus*, 96.

[149] Cf. E. SCHÜSSLER FIORENZA, *In Memory of Her*, 101-102. Principally, Fiorenza sees Jesus as pursuing the sort of enlightened view of women to be found in the Book of Judith, which she dates to the first century B.C., and in material about the life of Jewish women in places like Egypt. Two points should be made here. First, the texts that come from Egypt must be used with care because Egypt was a place where women, including Jewish women, had considerably broader amd more valued roles than in Palestinian Jewish culture. We cannot simply extrapolate from the roles Jews took at Elephantine and elsewhere in Egypt, including Alexandria, and apply those conclusions to the role of women in Israel. Cf. B. WITHERINGTON, *Women in the Earliest Churches*. Witherington also argues that it is saying too much that «[...] the Book of Judith mediates the atmosphere in which Jesus preached and in which the discipleship of equals originated» (*In Memory of Her*, 118).While the story in the Book of Judith shows that women were, from time to time, raised up by God to perform mighty deeds and that the Jewish culture did not suppress these events but rather seems, at least on occasion, to have celebrated them, this does not mean that the story of Judith provides evidence for an early egalitarian movement in Judaism. Cf. B. WITHERINGTON, *The Jesus Quest*, 167-168.

[150] Cf. E. SCHÜSSLER FIORENZA, *In Memory of Her*, 101-102. Cf. also E. SCHÜSSLER FIORENZA, *Jesus*, 79, where Fiorenza reiterates her view that there was considerable distortion of the Jesus tradition as it was passed on. Almost all her more radical proposals about Jesus presuppose that there was a long and convoluted process in the transmission of the Jesus tradition, with considerable distortion along the way. This leads to the conclusion that much of the tradition must simply be rejected as later theologizing about Jesus which does not represent how the historical Jesus really spoke and acted, and that only in a distinct minority of passages do we see the real Jesus shining through, though no two scholars would agree on exactly which passages these are.

rejects much material and gives a particular construal to a selection of salient passages.[151]

In *Jesus*, Fiorenza seems more prepared than in her earlier work to take seriously the suggestion that the material in the Gospel of Thomas provides us with an early and authentic window on the kind of Wisdom Jesus proclaimed.[152] Furthermore, Fiorenza appears to accept and build on the theological reconstruction of the ever elusive Q community as it allows her to argue that there were a variety of alternate Christian communities from the beginning.[153] A further methodological problem with Fiorenza's approach is her assumption that all God language is simply symbolic, metaphorical and analogical, since «[...] human language can never speak adequately about divine reality».[154] This theory of language that Fiorenza espouses allows her to suggest that there are no definitive images of God, for «divine reality cannot be comprehended in human language».[155]

---

[151] While mainstream scholars would agree that historical reconstruction is necessary to establish the historical Jesus, unlike Fiorenza many would argue that there is not a willful misconstrual or patriarchal reconstructing of much of the arguably authentic Jesus material in the Synoptic Gospels. If this is true, Fiorenza's argument and justification for her exegetical and theological programme is considerably weakened. Cf. J.P. MEIER, *A Marginal Jew*. I, 167-184.

[152] Cf. E. SCHÜSSLER FIORENZA, *Jesus*, 158-159. However, the Gospel of Thomas has been shown to be a later gnosticizing re-appropriation of the Jesus tradition found in the Synoptics. Cf. J.P. MEIER, *A Marginal Jew*. I, 199-202.

[153] In *Jesus* Fiorenza traces the theme of women's proclamation of the «words of Sophia» into the earliest Christian mission, by noting the continued participation of women with men as prophets and emissaries of Sophia in the Q community. She speculates that the open-ended empty tomb traditions themselves may have come out of the matrix of traditions which understood Jesus as the prophet of Sophia as is found in Lk 7:35: «Sophia is justified by all her children». Fiorenza also claims that the theologically exclusive language of Jesus' relationship to the «Father» as «Son» in Q (Mt 11:25-27) is a later theological shift which replaced the earlier inclusive sophiology of the earliest Jesus traditions found in Q. Cf. Fiorenza, *Jesus*, 139-144. The difficulty here is that we have no solid historical evidence for the existence of such a Q community and Fiorenza is mounting one tentative hypothesis upon another. Cf. J.P. MEIER, *A Marginal Jew*. II, 177-181; B. WITHERINGTON, *The Jesus Quest*, 171-172, 176, 184.

[154] Cf. E. SCHÜSSLER FIORENZA, *Jesus*, 161.

[155] Cf. E. SCHÜSSLER FIORENZA, *Jesus*, If this is so, there is no reason to advocate alternate images or names for God, since they too must fail in the light of the impossibility of properly imaging God. Fiorenza appears not to be entirely consistent here, for clearly she believes there are more or less true images of God, or else she would not be so eloquently and passionately arguing for these alternative images. But if this is so, then we must ask: by what standard do we determine which images are more or less

Finally, it is hard to doubt that the driving engine behind such statements is Fiorenza's liberationist aims. As she says, «Nothing stops feminist theologians from critically assessing the kyriocentric framework of the Wisdom traditions (and all other biblical traditions) in order to re-articulate some of its discourses in such a way that wo/men can theologically claim it», or to «[...] open up possibilities of liberation and well-being».[156]

4.3.2 *Wisdom Christology in Schüssler Fiorenza*

As an alternative to a religion that worships God as Father, Fiorenza argues that Jesus offered a vision of God as Sophia.[157] Fiorenza's conclusion that Jesus used the Sophia image of God to speak of God's gracious presence among the chosen people is based to a large extent on Luke 7:35 / Matthew 11:19, and in particular on the conclusion that Luke preserves the earlier form of this saying, which speaks of Wisdom being

---

true or revealing of God's character? Fiorenza's answer presumably would be one from experience: those images that liberate the oppressed are «true» images of God (Cf. Fiorenza, *Jesus*, 162). The danger here is that we re-create God in our own image and especially in the image of our cultural and political agendas. While human experience should not be ignored, it should not be the starting point for deciding the issue about God language. Cf. F. MARTIN, *The Feminist Question*, 172-182.

[156] Cf. E. SCHÜSSLER FIORENZA, *Jesus*, 157, 162. F. Martin argues that if this is so, it becomes clear that theology is dictating how the historical research is going to be conducted and what the outcome must be. It is one thing to assert that no historical research is value-free and to be aware and cautious about one's own presuppositions. It is quite another to deliberately use the historical data to support or buttress one's own agenda. Unfortunately, Fiorenza's own rhetoric encourages the reader to see her reading of the Jesus material as deliberately tendentious, and this will mean that many of those who most need to hear some of her very helpful historical insights into Jesus will not do so. Cf. F. MARTIN, *The Feminist Question*, 172-182.

[157] Fiorenza insists that in order to understand the submerged early Christian traditions of Divine Wisdom, it is first necessary to trace their roots in Jewish Scriptures and theology. Consequently her argument that Jesus was a prophet of God, whom he viewed as Sophia, is based on the assumption that Israel in, for example, its Lady Wisdom material in Proverbs 1-9, had integrated language about the Egyptian goddess Isis or Ma'at into its own material as «reflective mythology», which was then used to express something about the gracious goodness of God. Cf. E.SCHÜSSLER FIORENZA, «Jesus», 231-252. Fiorenza's further conclusion is that, from the third century B.C., Jewish Wisdom theology celebrated God's goodness in allowing his gracious presence to dwell «in the female *Gestalt* of divine Sophia» in the midst of the chosen people. Cf. E. SCHÜSSLER FIORENZA, *In Memory of Her*, 132.

vindicated by her children, while the Matthean form speaks of Wisdom being vindicated by her deeds. The Matthean form suggests that Jesus saw himself as Wisdom, the Lukan form that Jesus saw God in this light.[158]

Fiorenza notes that, when we move from Jewish Wisdom literature to early Christian writings, the figure of Divine Wisdom seems to disappear. Yet, a sympathetic reading, which attends to traces and tensions inscribed in the text, can show that a submerged sophiology permeates all Christian Scriptures.[159] Early Jewish discourses on Divine Wisdom provided a theological linguistic matrix that was activated by early Christian communities. Hence, the traditions of Divine Wisdom together with other early Jewish traditions could be used to elaborate the theological significance of Jesus.[160]

In discussing the christological hymns, Fiorenza notes that the Sophia-Jesus identification appears here in a milieu quite different from that of Palestine. These hymns emerge not only in a different cultural-religious

---

[158] B. Witherington points out that there is evidence in the Gospel tradition that suggests Jesus may have seen himself in this light, but little evidence apart from this saying (and possibly Luke 11:49) that he spoke of God in this way. In texts such as Matthew 11:28-30 and Luke 13:34 Jesus does not speak as Wisdom's messenger, but simply as Wisdom. Witherington's point is that even if Fiorenza's interpretation of Luke's two sayings is correct, it is too slender a basis to support the argument that Jesus' dominant image for God was Sophia or Wisdom, rather than Father or Abba. Cf. B. WITHERINGTON, *The Jesus Quest*, 184-186.

[159] Fiorenza argues that, just as in the work of Philo, two levels of reflection can be distinguished in early Christian theological discourses on Sophia. The first level, which may go back to the historical Jesus himself but is barely traceable any longer, understands Jesus as messenger and prophet of Sophia. The second level of theological reflection identifies Jesus with Divine Wisdom. Jesus, however, is not called *Sophia* but receives «male» christological titles such as *kyrios* and *soter*, which also were titles of Isis-Sophia. Fiorenza refers to the work of Martin Hengel who has argued that the diversity of christological discourses that developed in a time span as short as twenty years after Jesus' death can be plausibly explained if we assume Jewish Wisdom theology as the generative matrix. The tradition of Jesus, the Galilean preacher and representative of Divine Wisdom, Hengel has suggested, can bridge the chasm between the actual person Jesus of Nazareth who was executed as the «King of the Jews» and Jesus Christ who was proclaimed powerful Lord, pre-existent Son of God, and mediator of creation. Jewish Sophia theology provides the language world and mythological frame of reference that can explain the earliest attempts to make meaning out of the ministry and execution of Jesus as well as the meaning-making of the later christological developments in the early church. Cf. M. HENGEL, «Jesus als messianischer Lehrer der Weisheit», 147-190. Cf. also E. SCHÜSSLER FIORENZA, *Jesus*, 139-141.

[160] Cf. E. SCHÜSSLER FIORENZA, *Jesus*, 135-137.

context but also in a different form, articulated not as sayings of Jesus but as hymnic praise.[161] She observes the cosmological understanding expressed in the christological hymns of Philippians 2:6-11, Hebrews 1:3, and Colossians 1:15-20 and argues that these hymns exemplify an early Christian «reflective mythology» which used mythological elements to speak of Jesus Christ as the Divine Sophia and cosmic Kyrios.[162] This «reflective mythology» came to function in the Christian community as a foundational myth that created its own cult. Christ's exaltation and enthronement in cosmic reconciliation and sovereignty were the central symbols of this myth.

The understanding of Christ in terms of Sophia as the mediator of the first creation and as the power of the new, qualitatively different, creation underlined the cosmic significance of Christian faith. It also retained the knowledge that their cosmic kyrios is the same Jew, Jesus, who sought a resting place in Israel. This knowledge is expressed in the categories of humiliation, Incarnation, and death.[163] Consequently, Jesus was now proclaimed in masculine mythological terms as a divine being, and the Galilean prophet and emissary of Sophia was now envisioned in kyriarchal terms as a cosmic lord / master and sovereign in universal power and world dominion.[164]

In her treatment of the Pauline corpus, Fiorenza argues that, although the polemical rhetoric of Paul in I Corinthians misconstrues the arguments and beliefs of the Corinthian wo/men, it nevertheless indicates that the early Christian missionary movements in urban centres of the Greco-Roman world understood Jesus in terms of Sophia-Spirit.[165] For Fiorenza,

---

[161] Cf. E. SCHÜSSLER FIORENZA, *Jesus*, 147-149.

[162] Cf. E. SCHÜSSLER FIORENZA, «Wisdom Mythology», 17-42.

[163] Fiorenza argues that the mythological features of these early Christians are so strong, however, that their cosmic imagination threatens to absorb the knowledge about the human life of Jesus, the prophet of Galilee.

[164] Fiorenza concludes that, while such a mythologization and kyriarchalization may or may not have served to hold together and strengthen the identity of the Christian community consisting of Jews and Gentiles, such Christology lends itself in the long run to legitimize Christian domination in christological terms.

[165] Fiorenza claims that it is evident from I Corinthians 1–4 that women were actively involved in the articulation of sophiological discourses about Jesus and that the sophiological traces embedded in I Corinthians recognize the Resurrected One as identical not only with the Spirit of God but also with Divine Sophia. Cf. E. SCHÜSSLER FIORENZA, *Jesus*, 149-150.

the meaning of the «Wisdom» against which Paul polemicizes is expressed in the traditional christological formula of I Corinthians 1:24, which confesses Christ as God's power and Sophia. The resurrected One is seen in I Corinthians as Divine Sophia who led Israel on the Exodus out of Egypt (I Cor 10).[166]

Fiorenza questions the view that the Corinthians, under the leadership of Apollos, cultivated a rarefied (Gnostic) spirituality of eloquence and wisdom, as Paul claims. In this view it is Paul who, against such an «otherworldly» enthusiasm, insists on the proclamation of Christ crucified in the everyday realities of life. Fiorenza highlights the opposite view, underscored by other recent feminist writing.[167] It holds that the Corinthian wo/men prophets understood themselves and other apostles as standing in a long line of Sophia's emissaries. Moreover, they interpreted baptism as the inauguration into a «new creation» in which status differences and divisions were abolished (Gal 3:28). They believed that the crucifixion was a violent act of the kyriarchal powers of this world and that they had direct access to the Resurrected One's life in the Spirit of Sophia, whose life-giving power was with them in their struggles. In this latter view, Paul insists on Christ's death as a model whose downward path unto death and subordination to God must be imitated.[168]

We have already noted that Fiorenza stakes a lot on certain key texts which she sees as revealing the earliest stages of the tradition.[169] In using Luke 7:35[170], we note that Fiorenza does not refer to the parallel in Matthew 11:19.[171] She seems to assume that Luke preserves the earliest version of this saying. This is not certain, and the Matthean reference is to

---

[166] Fiorenza argues that such an early sophiological theology might also be expressed in the characterization of Jesus Christ in I Corinthians 1:30 which, for Fiorenza, may refer to baptism. Christ is the divine Sophia, secret and hidden (1 Cor 2:7) but revealed to the initiates of Sophia.

[167] Cf. L.M. RUSSELL, ed., *Feminist Interpretation*, 25-31; A. YARBRO COLLINS, ed., *Feminist perspectives in Biblical Scholarship*, 32-36.

[168] Cf. E. SCHÜSSLER FIORENZA, *Jesus*, 150.

[169] Luke 7:35; Luke 11:49; Luke 13:34; Matthew 11:28-30. Fiorenza favours Lukan texts or texts in their Lukan version. She nowhere faces the possibility that Luke's version of things may be a later adoption of more Jewish texts for a Gentile audience. Cf. E. SCHÜSSLER FIORENZA, *Jesus*, 140-143.

[170] «Yet Wisdom is justified by all her children» (Lk 7:35).

[171] «Yet Wisdom is justified by her deeds» (Mt 11:19).

Jesus.[172] In Luke 11:49[173] it is possible that the Father is spoken of as Wisdom, but this is not certain.[174] Luke 13:34[175] is indeed a lament using female imagery, but it does not suggest that Jesus is acting as the agent of God / Sophia in speaking this way. Rather, it suggests that Jesus is speaking about himself and the personal rejection he experienced during his own ministry. The same may be said about Matthew 11:28-30[176], which appears to be a modification of material found in Sirach 51:26-28, where Wisdom is the one who offers a yoke.

Fiorenza argues that the Matthean identification of Jesus with Divine Sophia is rooted in the conflict between the Matthean community and the rival Jewish schools of the Scribes and Pharisees. Matthew portrays Jesus as Divine Wisdom in order to authorize the disciples as Sophia's envoys.[177] Fiorenza's fundamental point here is that we cannot simply take Matthew's conventional androcentric language at face value and assume that Matthew's Sophia envoys were all male.[178]

Fiorenza notes that, unfortunately, the Wisdom matrix of John's Gospel remains almost completely hidden in a cursory reading of the text because

---

[172] Scholars have argued that the reading «children» in Luke may not be original in view of Luke 7:32, where children are the subject of the discussion at the beginning of these sayings (Lk 7:31-35). Cf. B. WITHERINGTON, *The Christology of Jesus*, 49-50. «Deeds» is the more difficult reading here and thus more likely to be original.

[173] «Therefore also the Wisdom of God said 'I will send them prophets and apostles, some of whom they will kill and persecute'» (Lk 11:49).

[174] Two other conclusions have been drawn: (1) the text refers to Jesus' own agents and emissaries, whom Luke has styled in later Christian terms (ie. Apostles). If so, this text calls Jesus the Father's Wisdom; (2) «the Wisdom of God» may not refer to a person, whether the Father or Jesus, but to a source from which this saying comes, or to an attribute of the Father (God's Wisdom). Cf. B. WITHERINGTON, *The Jesus Quest*, 183.

[175] «O Jerusalem, Jerusalem, killing the prophets and stoning those who are sent to you! How often would I have gathered your children together as a hen gathers her brood under her wings, and you would not!» (Lk 13:34).

[176] «Come to me, all who labour and are heavy laden, and I will give you rest. Take my yoke upon me, and learn from me; for I am gentle and lowly in heart, and you will find rest for your souls. For my yoke is easy, and my burden is light» (Mt 11:28-30). Nothing in this text suggests anything other than the conclusion that Jesus saw himself as Wisdom or Wisdom's manifestation in the flesh and offered his yoke as Wisdom's yoke.

[177] Fiorenza cites the work of Celia Deutsch who has suggested that the identification of the Matthean Jesus with Sophia reflects competition among the schools and legitimates a male teaching class. Cf. C. DEUTSCH, *Hidden Wisdom*.

[178] Cf. E. SCHÜSSLER FIORENZA, *Jesus*, 152.

the narrative does not introduce Jesus as the Son of Divine Sophia but as the only begotten Son of the Father.[179] She argues that the Christology of John's Gospel appears to integrate the hymnic and narrative traditions that see Jesus as a paradigmatic representative of Divine Wisdom, developing this tradition further by taking over the cosmic-journey aspects of the pre-Pauline hymns, and by combining them with the kind of Sophia reflection found in Matthew's Gospel.[180] The narrative characterization of Jesus, for Fiorenza, highlights Jesus as Wisdom incarnate.[181] By introducing the «father-son» language in the very beginning and using it throughout the Gospel, Fiorenza argues that John's Gospel «[...] reinscribes the metaphorical grammatical masculinity of the expressions "logos" and "son" as congruent with the biological masculine sex of the historic person of Jesus of Nazareth».[182] For Fiorenza, both the christological discourses of the Gospels of Matthew and John that identify the mission and life of Jesus with Divine Sophia seem to have their «setting in life» in a rhetorical situation in which the Christian community no longer understands itself in continuity with Israel but rather defines its identity in opposition to its Jewish roots.[183]

The shift from the linguistic chain of Sophia-prophets to that of Father-Son-Logos suggests to Fiorenza either a shift in the self-understanding of the believing community or a different understanding within the community. The «Father-Son» language indicates that now the «Father-Son» relationship, both of the patriarchal household and of the Wisdom school, is operative. Yet, this shift in social location is not only linguistic; it also constitutes a theological shift in the Jesus traditions. The Q people who have articulated this saying have replaced the inclusive sophiology of the earliest Jesus traditions with an exclusive understanding of revelation. In any case, Fiorenza argues, this introduction of the Father-Son language

---

[179] Fiorenza notes that in John 1:14-18 the glory of the Logos that became flesh was the «[...] glory of the only Son of the Father». The prologue ends with the assertion that «[...] no one has ever seen God; the only Son, who is in the bosom of the Father, he has made him known» (Jn 1:18).

[180] Cf. E. SCHÜSSLER FIORENZA, *Jesus*, 154.

[181] Fiorenza notes that, like Sophia-Isis, Jesus speaks in the revelatory *I am* style. With the symbolism of bread, wine, and living water he invites people to eat and drink. Like Sophia, Jesus proclaims his message aloud in public places. Like Sophia, Jesus is the light and life of the world.

[182] Cf. E. SCHÜSSLER FIORENZA, *Jesus*, 153.

[183] Cf. E. SCHÜSSLER FIORENZA, *Jesus*, 153-154.

into early Christian sophiology is intrinsically bound up with a theological exclusivity that reserves revelation for the elect few and challenges the boundaries of communal identity between insiders and outsiders.

From her study of the canonical scriptures Fiorenza concludes that the canonical processes and kyriarchal «strategies» that have marginalized or eliminated sophiology have had far-reaching consequences for christological articulations. In this process, early Christian sophiological reflection not only has become intertwined with anti-Judaism but also has been erased from Christian «orthodox» consciousness. However, the kyriocentric framework of masculine-feminine gender dualism, which has shaped the Wisdom traditions, has not been eliminated but rather strengthened by this process.[184]

4.4 *Concluding Remarks*

The influential work of Elisabeth Schüssler Fiorenza argues that Jesus was a prophet of God, whom he viewed as Sophia, or Wisdom, rather than Father. Fiorenza adopts a hermeneutic of suspicion toward the Gospels. Specifically, since in her view the Jesus tradition underwent a long process of transmission and change including christological transformation, the historical and egalitarian Jesus can be only critically discerned behind the veil of androcentric, patriarchal, and christological overlays.

Fiorenza argues that in her own work she has elaborated the Sophia traditions as one but not the sole early Christian discourse that might open up unfulfilled possibilities for feminist liberationist theological reflection. She finds the early Jesus as prophet of Sophia traditions theologically significant because they assert the unique particularity of Jesus without having to resort to assertions of exclusivity and superiority. Building on feminist discussions, Fiorenza has suggested a way in which feminist theological reflection can approach the remnant discourse on Divine Wisdom in Christian Scriptures. Such an approach shifts the discussion of

---

[184] Here Fiorenza is returning to her point regarding God language, namely, that conventional masculine gender language is as metaphoric as the grammatical feminine gender language is for Sophia. She concludes that this overt masculinization and covert genderization of Christian theology has determined the theological articulations of pneumatology, mariology, and spiritual experience that understood Woman, Wisdom, or Mary as the representative of humanity or the soul. Feminine discourses have tended to follow this logic of the canonical exclusion of Divine Sophia and to reinstitute Sophia rather than to challenge the overall masculine / feminine kyriocentric framework of the malestream orthodox tradition. Cf. E. SCHÜSSLER FIORENZA, *Jesus*, 154.

the female figure of Wisdom from the ontological-christological level to a linguistic-symbolic level of reflection. Fiorenza argues that such a shift is justified insofar as Wisdom theology is best understood not as producing a unified discourse but as a reflective methodology.

In short, for Fiorenza, the rediscovery of Wisdom theology and Wisdom Christology inscribed in biblical writings requires that feminist theologians reflect on the inadequacy of andro-kyriocentric language and critically assess its function in Christian theological discourse. A rediscovery of Wisdom traditions does not invite us to repeat the language of early Jewish-Christian Wisdom theology. Rather it compels us to continue the struggle with what Fiorenza understands as conventional masculine language for God and the exclusivist authoritarian functions and implications of such language. Feminist theology, Fiorenza argues, must re-articulate the symbols, images, and names of Divine Sophia in the context of our own experiences and theological struggles in such a way that the absolutist masculine language about God and Christ is radically questioned and undermined and the Western cultural sex / gender system is radically deconstructed. A feminist exegetical attempt to reconstruct the traces of Sophia as emancipatory Christology invites us to develop a critical praxis of reflective sophialogy. Such a critical feminist practice has to sort out and evaluate those traces of emancipatory Christology in general and biblical Wisdom theology in particular that open up possibilities of liberation and well-being but have not yet been fully realized in history.

Fiorenza's work is an important contribution to feminist christological conversation in that she remains committed to the eradication of anti-Judaism from feminist historical reconstructions and christological formulations as well as being deeply engaged with both feminist theory and African-American and liberationist theology. However, many of Fiorenza's assumptions are problematic, not least of which are her reliance on problematic interpretations of a small number of isolated Gospel texts and some unsupported conclusions about Judaism, the Q community, and the development of the earliest christological affirmations. All of Fiorenza's major proposals are interconnected and in many cases depend on each other for viability. Also her use of Wisdom texts in the Jesus tradition is both selective and idiosyncratic. Many would certainly be contested by the majority of mainstream New Testament scholars. Though Fiorenza is surely right to place Jesus within the context of sapiential traditions and concepts, her argument that these Jesus traditions reveal a purely theocentric focus even in their earliest stages is difficult to maintain.

5. Summary and Conclusions

We have concerned ourselves with examining to what extent the Wisdom elements present in the Scriptures and the tradition of the early Church have been incorporated into some representative Catholic Christologies of the English-speaking world. We have concentrated on Jacques Dupuis' *Who do you say I am?*, Denis Edwards' *Jesus the Wisdom of God*, and Elisabeth Schüssler Fiorenza's *In Memory of Her* and *Jesus: Miriam's Child, Sophia's Prophet* (chapter five). Both Edwards' and Fiorenza's work are explicit Wisdom Christologies. Dupuis' is not a Wisdom Christology but there is to be found there an awareness of the contribution of the Wisdom material to the development of early Christology.

Both D. Edwards and E. Schüssler Fiorenza make extensive use of the Wisdom themes in order to articulate their respective contemporary Christologies. Edwards' interest lies in the development of a cosmic Christology. In this context he sets out explicitly to retrieve Wisdom Christology and hence to use the Wisdom motif to address contemporary questions in theology. Edwards argued in favour of Wisdom categories providing the basis for an authentic interpretation of the life and ministry of Jesus. The identification of Jesus with Wisdom as the bridge whereby the community which believed that God had raised up Jesus of Nazareth came to see Jesus as the pre-existent one was also highlighted by Edwards. Furthermore, Edwards concluded that it was only through identifying Jesus as divine Wisdom that the theological insight could be reached that the Wisdom of God who is God's agent in creation is made flesh in Jesus of Nazareth. Edwards concludes that the theologies of pre-existence and Incarnation are historically and structurally dependent upon Wisdom theology and the identification of Jesus with Wisdom.

Fiorenza's objective, through the re-discovery of Wisdom theology and Christology, is to highlight the inadequacy of andro-kyriocentric language and critically assess its function in Christian theological discourse. A re-discovery of the Wisdom tradition compels us to continue the struggle with what Fiorenza understands as conventional masculine language for God and the exclusivist authoritarian functions and implications of such language. As an alternative to a religion that worships God as Father, Fiorenza argues that Jesus offered a vision of God as Sophia. Fiorenza adopts a hermeneutic of suspicion toward the Gospels. Specifically, since in her view the Jesus tradition underwent a long process of transmission and change, including christological transformation, the historical and egalitarian Jesus can be only critically discerned behind the veil of androcentric, patriarchal, and christological overlays.

At the socio-pragmatic level, Fiorenza's work comes into its own as a way of calling attention to elements of tradition and memory that need to be retrieved and re-affirmed. Some of Fiorenza's work remains invaluable in setting the record straight; other aspects are more speculative and less firmly grounded in critical inquiry than she seems to concede; a third category performs a useful pragmatic function of affirming values which serve the needs of a particular hermeneutical situation and community, and in this way also serve the wider community.

Dupuis highlights the titles of *Christ, Lord,* and *Son of God* as forming the core of the early christological faith. However, Dupuis acknowledges the presence of many diverse Christologies in the New Testament and highlights the positive advantage of the existence of distinct Christologies presenting mutually complementary approaches to the mystery of Jesus Christ. Dupuis advocates what he calls an «integral approach» or a comprehensive perspective to Christology. Every generation of Christianity, he argues, is bound to enter into the hermeneutical process which means that no single theology can claim to be valid for all times and places. In this regard, while not appealing explicitly himself to a Wisdom Christology, Dupuis would support the retrieval of the language of Wisdom as a «root metaphor» which can generate new perspectives on issues which face contemporary Christology.

While Dupuis addresses the christological issues which draw on the Wisdom material, questions of the pre-existence of Christ and Jesus' mediatorship of creation, he does not explicitly highlight their roots there, with the one exception of the Johannine prologue where Dupuis notes that here the concept of *Word* of God, borrowed from the sapiential literature of the Old Testament, is applied to the pre-existent Son. Dupuis highlights the use by feminist theologians of the Wisdom material in the articulation of a feminist liberation approach to Christology articulating an understanding that, far from laying a foundation for patriarchal attitudes in the community of his disciples, Jesus instituted a rapport of equality, mutuality, and reciprocity among its female and male members. Dupuis focuses on that function of feminist biblical interpretation concerned with retrieving aspects of the tradition which have been lost or neglected.

Dupuis calls for a cosmic Christology which will show the cosmic dimension of the Incarnation, highlighting the significance of Jesus Christ not only for the salvation of human beings and their history but for the whole universe. Dupuis does not show how the soteriological and universal significance of the assertion of Jesus as Son of God is taken up and developed in any of the christological hymns of the New Testament. Neither does Dupuis present Jesus as a Sage or as Divine Wisdom in person or refer to the connections between the Wisdom literature and the writings of some of the Church Fathers.

In his understanding of Paul's theology of Wisdom, Edwards' thesis is that Pauline Wisdom Christology confronts us with the fact that the Wisdom at work in the universe is now revealed in the vulnerable divine foolishness of the cross. He argues that, if the Wisdom Christology of I Corinthians contributes to an ecological theology by giving insight into the love that is at the heart of evolutionary and cosmic history, the Wisdom Christology of Colossians 1:15-20 can be seen as contributing to an ecological theology by offering insight into the relationship between the resurrection of Jesus and the material universe.

Edwards highlighted the presence of Wisdom Christology in significant parts of the New Testament and in patristic and medieval theology, specifically tracing its emergence in Origen, Athanasius, and Pope Leo I. Edwards believes the retrieval of Wisdom Christology will throw fresh light on a number of complex areas of contemporary theology: pre-existence, the *person* of Jesus Christ, the maleness of Jesus in relationship to women, justice issues, Christology and other religious traditions, and the principle concern of Edwards, the relationship between Christology and cosmology. Edwards' theological approach here is to understand the motive of the Incarnation as the free self-communicating love of the divine will and thus articulating a more intrinsic link between God's action in creation and Incarnation. For Edwards, a Wisdom Christology lends support to this interpretation and can help hold together a theology of creation and Incarnation as intrinsically connected in the one divine plan, while still insisting that the Incarnation was a totally free act of God.[185]

Dupuis devotes some consideration in his Christology to the debate among the various perspectives of the theology of religions and the challenge posed by the context of religious pluralism to the traditional christocentric perspective of theology. In this context Dupuis appeals to the active presence of the Word of God and of the Divine Spirit but not to the Wisdom of God. While not challenging the validity of these titles, the Wisdom of God would also serve as another very helpful interpretative key.

---

[185] In our final chapter we will address the apparent lack of emphasis on soteriology and the necessity of redemption in some contemporary Christologies.

CHAPTER IX

Wisdom Christology in Some Representatives
of the French-Speaking world

We focus here on the extent to which the Wisdom elements present in the Scriptures and the tradition of the church have been incorporated into some contemporary representative Catholic Christologies of the French-speaking world.

1. Representative Catholic Christology in the French-Speaking World

The three theologians whose Christology we will examine here are Louis Bouyer, Christian Duquoc, and Joseph Moingt. L. Bouyer's *Le Fils éternel*[1] has been hailed as an exceptional work in its scope and competence. C. Duquoc is one of the best known theologians to have written in French and has addressed all the major questions in systematic theology including Christology. His *Christologie. Essai Dogmatique*[2] will be our chief concern here. J. Moingt's *L'homme qui venait de Dieu*[3] has found widespread use in universities because of its contemporaneity and fidelity to the tradition.

2. Louis Bouyer

2.1 *Priest and Theologian*

Louis Bouyer was born into a Lutheran family in Paris in 1913. Educated at the universities of Paris and Strasbourg where his teachers

---

[1] L. BOUYER, *Le Fils éternel*. E.T.: *The Eternal Son*.
[2] C. DUQUOC, *Christologie* I-II.
[3] J. MOINGT, *L'homme qui venait de Dieu*.

included Auguste Lecerf and Oscar Cullman, he renewed his profession of Christian faith in the Catholic church and was ordained a priest of the Oratorians. Bouyer has been professor in the faculty of theology at the Institut Catholique in Paris for many years and is author of numerous books and articles in ecclesiology, ecumenism, liturgy, and spirituality.[4]

2.2 *The Development of Bouyer's Theology*

Bouyer's thesis to obtain his licence in theology was entitled *The Incarnation and the Church as Body of Christ in the Theology of St Athanasius*. His hypothesis was that only the existence of the church as Body of Christ in the world constitutes the principle which accounts for the communication of the life of God to man through the Incarnation of the Word.[5] A cursory examination of Bouyer's publications point to three main periods in the development of his theological writings. In the first stage (1936-44) Bouyer published works on Scripture, ecumenism, together with other questions associated with his university studies.[6] Indeed, ecumenism was to remain one of his principal themes and an important backdrop to all of Bouyer's theological writings.

The second period of Bouyer's theological writing coincides with his participation in the work of the *Centre de Pastorale Liturgique* in Paris together with his teaching at the *Institut Catholique* (1945-61). During this time Bouyer also lectured at various universities throughout the United States. These years saw Bouyer publish a number of books on spirituality and liturgy.[7] This second stage in the development of Bouyer's

---

[4] For an introduction to the thought of L. Bouyer cf. E. LEIVA-MERIKAKIS, «Louis Bouyer», 257-282.

[5] Cf. L. BOUYER, *L'Incarnation et l'Église*.

[6] Cf. L. BOUYER, *Le quatrième évangile*, E.T.: *The Fourth Gospel*. Later in his theological career, Bouyer dedicated two important works to ecumenism. Cf. L. BOUYER, *Du protestantisme à l'Église*, E.T.: *The Spirit and Forms and Protestantism*; ID., *Parole, Église et Sacrement*, E.T.: *The Word, Church and Sacraments*. Another important publication by Bouyer during the first period was *La vie de saint Antoine*.

[7] Cf. L. BOUYER, *Le Mystère Pascal*, E.T.: *The Paschal Mystery* which is a meditation on the liturgy of the last three days of Holy Week. It contributed significantly to the beginnings of liturgical renewal before Vatican II. While teaching in the United States Bouyer published *Liturgical Piety*, which was later translated into French: *La vie de la liturgie*. In this work Bouyer, reacting against an understanding of liturgy in terms of rubrics, addresses the nature of liturgical spirituality. His teaching in the United States found its clearest expression in *Le rite et l'homme*, E.T.: *Rite and Man*.

theological writing underlines an important theme in his work: the close link between liturgy, theology, and spirituality. This theme is most explicitly underlined by Bouyer in *Le Mystère Pascal*.

The final period in the unfolding of Bouyer's thought is characterized by his attempt at a theological synthesis (1962-82). With this task Bouyer wished to emphasize the intrinsic relationship between the life God has in himself from all eternity and the life which God communicates to creation and invites creation to share. Volume one of a trilogy of writings develops a theology of creation and the whole economy of grace which God has ordered for creation. *Le trône de la Sagesse* is dedicated to the Virgin Mary and presents her as representing creation in its highest form of union with God and as the type and model for Christians.[8]

The second volume, *L'Église de Dieu, corps du Christ et temple de l'Esprit,* is hailed as Bouyer's finest work.[9] He presents the history of the Church as *mystery*, highlighting the active, continuous, and purposive presence of God in the world through the Christian community. God calls and moves the world towards the kingdom of God. The Church is the sign and instrument of that call and movement. In the final volume, *Cosmos: le monde et la gloire de Dieu,* Bouyer attempts a Christian interpretation of the scientific vision of the world.[10]

Bouyer's first trilogy of writings served to introduce a second trilogy. Here Bouyer dedicated a volume to each of the persons of the Trinity. Volume one, *Le fils éternel: théologie de la Parole de Dieu et christologie,* is our chief concern in this chapter. The second volume, *Le Père invisible. Approches du mystère de la divinité,* is concerned with the God question and addresses the uniquely Christian experience of God.[11] The final volume, *Le Consolateur: Esprit-Saint et vie de Grâce,* presents the Holy Spirit as a divine person who constitutes the seal of unity within the Trinity and through whom we are able to accept the self-communication of the Father.[12]

2.3 *The Christology of Louis Bouyer*

It is not our purpose to treat Bouyer's Christology in detail. Rather, our central focus involves examining to what extent, to formulate his

---

[8] Cf. L. BOUYER, *Le trône de la Sagesse,* E.T.: *The Seat of Wisdom.*

[9] Cf. L. BOUYER, *L'Église de Dieu,* E.T.: *The Church of God.*

[10] Cf. L. BOUYER, *Cosmos.*

[11] Cf. L. BOUYER, *Le Père invisible.*

[12] Cf. L. BOUYER, *Le Consolateur.*

systematic Christology, Bouyer uses those Wisdom elements in the Scriptures. However, some explication of Bouyer's Christology, by way of summary and overview, will help situate our specific study. In this regard, we will draw on Bouyer's presentation in *The Eternal Son.*

2.3.1 *Summary*

When speaking of Christology, Bouyer begins by situating Christ clearly and precisely into our total human history, which is primarily the history of our search for God, and into that particular history of the people of Israel into which he is born and which can best be described as the history of God's search for us. Consequently, the first task of a truly authentic Christology is to scrutinize Christ's historical roots and their meaning.[13]

Bouyer presents a unified view of the mystery of Christ within the context of a theology of the Word of God.[14] Bouyer's main argument in favour of a Logos-oriented Christology is that the New Testament writers themselves conceive of Jesus in terms of the central Old Testament concept of the Word of Yahweh. More than half of *The Eternal Son* is devoted to the theme of the expectation of the Saviour in the Old Testament and the fulfillment of that expectation in the New. This is due not simply to Bouyer's determination to set his Christology on a firmly biblical foundation, but also to his conviction of the need to rescue Christology from a growing and excessive individualism which he sees to have characterized it in the West from the Middle Ages onwards.[15] Bouyer also affirms a biblical Christology for developing a theology of the psychology of Jesus that does justice both to the reality of his historical

---

[13] Bouyer concludes that any attempt to develop a theology of the divine Word must endeavor to discover, within the reality of a particular history, a tradition that has a creative power to reveal the destiny of our humanity, the divine meaning of all of life and existence, whose ultimate mystery will be found in Jesus Christ. Cf. L. BOUYER, *The Eternal Son*, 18-19.

[14] Bouyer notes that a study of Christ, both in terms of what he has done for us and of his person as the unique foundation of all his saving actions, must be presented in such a way that Christ is seen as the centre of the various divisions of the whole of theology. He highlights the dubious consequences of reducing all theology to a single Christology: there is no place for a natural theology and the Old Testament itself no longer has enduring meaning except when considered in relation to the direct knowledge of Christ. Any Christology, therefore, that attempts to reduce or radically absorb all theology to Christology destroys itself. Cf. L. BOUYER, *The Eternal Son*, 13-16.

[15] Cf. L. BOUYER, *The Eternal Son,* 22.

human condition and his personal identity as Son of God.[16] Furthermore, a biblical Christology, as Bouyer understands it, is essentially ecclesial. The living faith of the church, both in its foundations as testified to in the New Testament and its ongoing life of worship and witness through the ages, is a key norm guiding Catholic systematic Christology.[17]

Bouyer affirms that the Word of God in the Old Testament must be studied as the primary and most basic introduction to any and all Christology. For the major theme of Christology in the New Testament is the Logos, the Word of Johannine writings.[18] Bouyer notes that, from the beginning of biblical history, the Word as revelation and communication expressed through words is intimately linked to events that presuppose a special presence and unique manifestation of the «Spirit and power» of God in our history. This unity of word and event becomes the powerfully active presence of God among his people awakening a renewed consciousness of God.[19]

---

[16] Bouyer is convinced of the need to rescue Christology from a psychologism whose roots he traces to Thomas Aquinas but which later resulted in «a virtual expulsion of metaphysics». He argues that even for a scholastic as traditional, spiritual, and sensible as Thomas, it is dangerously easy, when using an *a priori* deductive metaphysics, to congeal nearly whole parts of his Christology, no matter how traditional, with claims that try to justify the formulations. When using words like nature and hypostasis, Bouyer argues that remembrance of the analogical character of our affirmations about God seems to disappear even among the greatest scholastics. Cf. L. BOUYER, *The Eternal Son,* 368-369.

[17] Cf. L. BOUYER, *The Eternal Son,* 14.

[18] Bouyer's objective here is to situate the whole activity of Jesus within the context of the traditional religion of Israel. He notes, by way of example, that the prophets never conceived the word addressed to them as an isolated word. Every illumination and message is for them an organic part of the one Word of God of which they know themselves to be the bearers. The prophets themselves unanimously admit that, regardless of the individuality of each of their messages, their personal message is never seen apart from a tradition that is much broader. Cf. L. BOUYER, *The Eternal Son,* 41-63.

[19] Bouyer notes that this does not mean that revelation is reduced to mere history, but rather that the Word of God is so inextricably linked to the history within which it is recognized and given expression, that history and revelation are inseparable. On the one hand, the Bible is a narrative of facts that are pregnant with meaning, facts through which God, their primary author, reveals himself by the process of a gradual unfolding of his design. On the other hand, the Bible at the same time interprets these facts without which the revelation they contain would never be known to us. We might say that, at the heart of this organic development, facts and ideas are constantly caught up in a process of reciprocal revelation and interpretation. Cf. L. BOUYER, *The Eternal Son,* 53.

Bouyer's Christology grounds the eschatological and soteriological character of Jesus' person in the meaning of his cause, that is, his activity and message concerning the kingdom, and the inseparability of person and cause in Jesus. The kingdom of God preached, whose blessing people partook of in welcoming him, was the very content of salvation.[20] Jesus' life and ministry served his fellows in the name of God, a service which essentially consisted in making it possible for men and women to share in salvation, ie., in God's reign and its blessing in the form of new life and forgiveness.[21] Rooted in the historical institution of kingship in Israel and eventually transposed to that of an eschatological king in whom the kingdom of God will ultimately be realized, the figure of the Suffering Servant embodied the eschatological future of Israel.[22]

Bouyer's stress on the Bible makes a discussion of New Testament criticism inevitable, and Bouyer's account of its evolution and his «critique of the critics» is of value in itself, apart from its relevance to the main theme of the book. He attacks vigorously the Bultmannian postulates of a discontinuity between Jesus and the church and of a location of the

---

[20] For Bouyer, the message of the imminent kingdom of God is a fundamental concept of Christology. Cf. L. BOUYER, *The Eternal Son*, 185-188.

[21] Bouyer notes that it is the historical institution of kingship in Israel and in myths related to it that we have our point of departure for the divine concepts of kingship and the kingdom which permeate the biblical Word. He affirms that Psalm 101, a sapiential psalm, mirrors the ideal king of Israel to be revealed. He must be a «son of David» in spirit as well as in lineage, who faithfully and humbly strives to fulfill the divine will revealed to him through the Word. Only then will the prophet's anointing make him truly God's king and anointed one, his Messiah. The thought of a future king who would re-establish the kingdom of David is eventually transposed to that of an eschatological king in whom the kingdom of God will ultimately be realized. The first decisive element in this change is the eschatological character of Israel's destiny. This is something unique to Hebrew thought from which their messianic hope will come. The Messiah will project the prophetic hope of an ideal king «according to God's heart» into the eschatological future of the kingdom conquered by God. Cf. L. BOUYER, *The Eternal Son,* 86-94.

[22] Bouyer notes that the messianic hope, inasmuch as it is hope for the eschatological kingdom of God, has to go beyond the image of Messiah into another figure besides that of the Servant. While not shown to us as God himself entering into his own kingdom, this new figure, who will be presented as God's champion and final mediator, is the apocalyptic figure of the «Son of Man». This vision will be the unique contribution made by the apocalypse to the eschatological vision of the coming of the kingdom of God. Bouyer observes that the references made in the Gospels presuppose an understanding of the role and character of the Son of Man similar to that presented in Daniel 7 and the Book of Enoch. Cf. L. BOUYER, *The Eternal Son,* 117-121.

Gospels in the literary category of myth and folklore.[23] He expresses great respect for the school of Riesenfeld and Gerhardsson, and he pointedly remarks that «the Bultmannians or post-Bultmannians, by their education, have become incapable of profiting by a whole world of data, which they are even less capable of rebutting and which show the falsity of the presuppositions from which they start».[24] Bouyer concludes this section with six conclusions which will be the basis of all that will follow.[25]

In addressing the resurrection and the kerygma of the early church, Bouyer confronts three interpretations opposed to the traditional interpretation of the resurrection.[26] He affirms that the resurrection was the

---

[23] Cf. L. BOUYER, *The Eternal Son*, 148-149.

[24] Cf. L. BOUYER, *The Eternal Son,* 185.

[25] The six conclusions are as follows: (1) the critical-historical approach to the person of Christ must be even more truly critical and historical than ever before; (2) this means that one cannot impose demands on the Gospel documents other than those imposed on any documents serving history, while the historian must bring to them the same «objective sympathy» that is required of him in all of his research; (3) it will be particularly important that we approach the documents with which we are concerned in the light of their cultural context; (4) one fundamental mistake to be avoided absolutely regarding the primitive Christian texts is the insistence that a choice be made in identifying the text as either historical or dogmatic; (5) it would likewise be a mistake to presuppose that tradition, since it is ecclesiastical tradition, so radically modified the *Sitz im Leben* of Jesus that it distorted of whatever he said or did and all that was related to him in any way; (6) to achieve his purpose of bringing the people of God to fulfillment, Christ used at least some of the rabbinical methods of teaching in order that the Twelve might be able to transmit his message and ultimately his own interpretation of himself. Cf. L. BOUYER, *The Eternal Son,* 164-166.

[26] A summary of these interpretations are: (i) a personal but not a bodily immortality, in which Christ simply represents a future that has been promised to all of us because of our basic nature; (ii) the same kind of immortality, but one which is unique to Christ and which he could communicate to us; (iii) the possession by Christ of a simple metamorphic immortality, which would only be an incomplete demythologized name given to the survival of an exceptional personal influence. For Bouyer, the first, in spite of the pains to hide the fact beneath eloquent vocabulary, is simply a return to a philosophy of natural immortality which is substantially Platonic. Such a view is as foreign to the modern mentality, whatever meaning might be given under this name, as it is to the biblical mentality. Regarding the second position, if it intends to retain the essentials of Christian affirmation while discarding whatever might be judged unacceptable to contemporaries, it seems doomed to failure on both counts. It does not diminish the possible scandal to the strictly scientific mentality, since it presupposes in Christ a change in the nature of things, a kind of radical transfiguration of human evolution. On the other hand, by presupposing that such a transfiguration evades the field

confirmation and legitimation by God of the earthly Jesus' message and activity. Furthermore, the resurrection is God's definitive self-disclosure which gathers up the earthly Jesus and establishes him in a radically new mode of being and activity.[27] For Bouyer, the decisive core of the christological faith offered by the resurrection of Jesus and the Easter experience of the disciples must be fully recognised. Soteriologically, the kingdom Jesus preached he has now become in person, thanks to God's self-disclosure and Jesus' personal consummation and public empowerment that occur indivisibly in Jesus' being raised from the dead. Jesus is now the beginning of a new creation, and the exalted one is continuous with the earthly Jesus precisely through his becoming more, through his becoming fully in person God's victorious reign in the world.

Bouyer affirms the originality of Paul's preaching. He highlights that it is in Galatians and Romans that Paul develops his fundamental Christology of filial relationship which is our call to share in Jesus' own filial relationship because of his death and resurrection. Paul tells us that we are given the unique privilege that the Gospels imply belonged only to Jesus: to call God «Abba, Father!» Such a privilege presupposes a dynamic identification with Jesus, which Paul develops in a way that is rooted in the teachings of Jesus. It is a kind of second Christology for Paul, which he calls the Christology of the second Adam, and enhances his Christology of Jesus as the Son of God. This Christology of the second Adam, Bouyer sees as outlined in Romans 5 and I Corinthians 15.[28]

Bouyer follows the development of the christological dogma through the Councils of the patristic age emphasising the importance of theological developments after the Council of Chalcedon.[29] He is unable to see

---

of physics and experimentation, either we make it a reality simply dreamed or purely imaginary and thus fall back into the third solution, or we surreptitiously reintroduce the possibility of a reality that is not only out of the realm of our phenomenological world but totally independent of it, bringing us back to the first solution. Cf. L. BOUYER, *The Eternal Son,* 201-206.

[27] Bouyer sees the resurrection narratives as the pre-eminent New Testament material for grounding our faith today. The resurrection of Jesus, however, must be understood as intrinsically related to the whole life and death of Jesus which preceded it, and his life and death must be understood as intrinsically related to the resurrection. Cf. L. BOUYER, *The Eternal Son,* 201-213.

[28] Cf. L. BOUYER, *The Eternal Son,* 221-232.

[29] Bouyer makes the point that some theologians, in their presentation of the historical development of dogma, implicitly maintain that nothing of theological importance happened after the Council of Chalcedon and so neglect some important figures

Chalcedon as an entire success, and the separation of the so-called monophysite and Nestorian churches is for him proof of this. He does not see the separation as simply due to politics, either secular or ecclesiastical, but to the failure of Chalcedon, perhaps unavoidably, to recognise genuine theological insights.[30] Passing to the Latin Middle Ages, of which he is in general highly critical, he discusses in detail the Christology of St. Thomas Aquinas.[31]

When he turns to the modern epoch, he faults contemporary Christologies for their excessively psychological orientation where a more ontological direction is necessary.[32]

2.3.2 Awareness of Wisdom Christology in Bouyer

In the early chapters of The Eternal Son Bouyer summarises the Hebrew Wisdom literature and highlights its roots in Canaanite and Mesopotamian Wisdom.[33] We have already noted that Bouyer makes the historical aspect

---

including Leontius of Jerusalem and Maximus the Confessor. Cf. L. BOUYER, The Eternal Son, 332-342.

[30] Bouyer writes: «It seems clear that a work of healing and of liquidation of the problems in question was sketched out at Chalcedon but was not brought to a satisfactory conclusion [...]Consequently, even the Christologies which can be called orthodox, in the degree in which they do not bring into debate the conciliar definitions, betray an uneasiness, a duality that has not been overcome, in their elaborations. This is so undeniable that we must recognise [...] that the problem needs to be reopened on a wider basis, even if we do not agree with those [...] who [...] declare the Chalcedonian solution so unsatisfactory that they propose to set it aside altogether. Nevertheless, I do not believe that it is a matter of rejecting the vision, or the successive and relatively complementary visions, of Ephesus and Chalcedon, but to recognise that the christological problem cannot move towards a solution with the sole data that they provide». Cf. L. BOUYER, The Eternal Son, 400.

[31] Bouyer sees Aquinas' Christology as hitherto equalled «neither in the richness and understanding of its delving into the traditional sources, nor in the correctness and rational coherence of its structure and its exposition, nor in the visible and almost palpable profundity with which it is rooted in a contemplative life of faith». Nevertheless, he sees it as having serious weaknesses, in particular the rigorous deductive rationality which arises from the scholastic notion of theology as a «science»; thus «the chain of meditation upon mystery is periodically distorted by a web of univocal conceptualism». However, he stands firmly with St. Thomas against Duns Scotus. Cf. L. BOUYER, The Eternal Son, 418-419.

[32] Cf. L. BOUYER, The Eternal Son, 368-386.

[33] Bouyer notes that we have at least three thousand years of documentation regarding the development of Egyptian Wisdom, from Hardedef, in the first half of the three thousand years before Christ, up to the time of the Ptolemies. These texts reveal a

of Jesus of Nazareth a significant element in the formulation of his Christology.[34] In this regard we can observe that, while not using much of the Wisdom tradition, Bouyer does refer to some central Wisdom texts of the New Testament. Bouyer's is not a Wisdom Christology but it shows an awareness of some of the Wisdom influences in the formulation of the doctrine of the Incarnation. Furthermore, we will see that Bouyer is aware of one Russian theologian's attempt to link Kenosis Christology and Wisdom Christology.

From the beginning Bouyer emphasizes that the entire New Testament Christology does not witness to a single apostolic hermeneutics of the Jesus story, but to several. The diverse Christologies of the New Testament represent distinct interpretations of the event in the light of Easter. Following his acknowledgment of diverse Christologies of the New Testament, Bouyer highlights the titles of *Word, Son of Man* and *Lord*. He argues that these titles form the core of the early christological faith.[35] In this context, Bouyer highlights references in the Gospels of Matthew and Luke which, he argues, confirms the use of the Wisdom motif by these evangelists. Furthermore, Bouyer believes that this approach to an understanding of Jesus influenced the author of the Fourth Gospel.[36] However, while highlighting the importance of some of the christological titles in New Testament Christology, Bouyer stresses that this importance

---

Wisdom intimately related to the institution of royalty. He notes that, before the link with royalty, there existed a Wisdom that was simply transmitted within the family structure. Bouyer also emphasizes the experiential nature of Wisdom: the transmission from father to son, from master to disciple, of a treasure of accumulated experience which, from beginning to end, is constantly tested and considered. Cf. L. BOUYER, *The Eternal Son*, 75.

[34] Bouyer notes that «Christology must [...] situate Christ clearly and precisely into our total human history [...] If today we want to develop a truly authentic Christology, our first task will be to scrutinize Christ's historical roots and their meaning». Cf. L. BOUYER, *The Eternal Son*, 18.

[35] Bouyer notes that during his earthly life Jesus never claimed the title of Messiah and allowed no one to call him by this title. In the synoptic gospels Jesus constantly speaks of the Son of Man, sometimes in the third person and without identification with himself, and at other times in a way that identifies the Son of Man with himself, as in relatively numerous texts where he says the Son of Man must suffer and die before being glorified. Bouyer concludes that Jesus very definitely and consistently identified himself with the title of Son of Man. Cf. L. BOUYER, *The Eternal Son*, 28.

[36] Bouyer refers to Matthew 11:19 («Yet time will prove where Wisdom lies») and Luke 7:35 («God's Wisdom is vindicated by all who accept it»). Cf. L. BOUYER, *The Eternal Son*, 182.

should not be exaggerated. His central point is that the implied Christology of the earthly Jesus contains an unprecedented claim which breaks down all previous schemes. Jesus was reluctant to accept titles because he claimed to be more than they could express. For Bouyer, Jesus did not legitimise his mission by reference to the titles that had nourished Jewish expectation of the last era. Rather the titles occupy a secondary place in Jesus' testimony about himself.

Bouyer cites I Corinthians 1–4 and its identification of Jesus with divine Wisdom as a basis for Wisdom Christology.[37] He notes that there is at least an implicit identification here between the Wisdom who was active in the creation of the world (Prov 8) and Jesus crucified. Bouyer affirms that the theme of the Wisdom of God as the folly of the cross, resisted and contradicted by the Wisdom of this world, is found in I Corinthians 1 and 2. Paul's theology of Wisdom confronts us with the fact that this Wisdom at work in the universe is now revealed in the vulnerable love expressed in the crucified one.[38]

In his treatment of the Christologies of the Synoptics, Bouyer presents Matthew's Christology in terms of a radically allegorized Messianism.[39] In treating Luke's Christology he speaks of a pneumatological Christology: Luke's Christology is a pneumatic extension and clarification of Pauline Christology. Beginning with Paul's presentation of Jesus as the second Adam who shares his filial relationship with all of humanity, and linking it with our sharing of his Spirit, Luke reverses this presentation by showing how Jesus manifested himself as the second Adam, the Son of God, by revealing himself to us as the one through whom and with whom the Spirit will be given to all of humanity.[40] Bouyer underlines what he sees as a strong affinity between the gospels of Mark and John claiming that both rest on the same basic Christology, with only John developing it to the full. Both see Christ as essentially the Son of God. Both clarify the meaning of this title by identifying Jesus with his message, with the *Gospel* considered as the fullness of God's Word.[41]

---

[37] Cf. L. BOUYER, *The Eternal Son*, 232.

[38] Cf. L. BOUYER, *The Eternal Son*, 232-237.

[39] Cf. L. BOUYER, *The Eternal Son*, 243-248.

[40] Cf. L. BOUYER, *The Eternal Son*, 253-260.

[41] Bouyer believes that a study of their parallel structure makes this observation very evident. Both link Jesus to the «beginning», Mark with a prophecy and John with creation. The prologue of each considers Christ as the divine Word, and both prologues are followed by narratives revealing Jesus' unique filial relationship throughout

In his treatment of Johannine Christology Bouyer is conscious of the Old Testament background, most especially in the Old Testament Wisdom literature.[42] He acknowledges that the fourth evangelist saw in Jesus the culmination of a tradition that runs through the Wisdom literature of the Old Testament. Bouyer notes that it is in Proverbs 8 that we have the first identification of the Word of Genesis 1 with Wisdom, and in Sirach 24 the final identification of Word / Wisdom with the *Shekinah*, the localized presence in history of the simultaneously transcendent and immanent God. For Bouyer it is clear that every verse of the prologue has its root in some phase of the progressive development found in the Old Testament: first of the Word and then through Wisdom to the *Shekinah* culminating in the definitive presence of God with us.

Bouyer is aware of the contribution of the Church Fathers of the second and third centuries regarding a correct understanding of the divine Sonship of Jesus Christ.[43] We have seen already how some of the Fathers drew on Wisdom imagery from the Old Testament. Bouyer makes one connection in *The Eternal Son* between the Wisdom literature and the writings of the Fathers. He notes that, to the Arians who objected to the eternity of the Logos and to its uncreated character described in the Old Testament, (especially in Proverbs 8, which speaks of God's Wisdom «created as the principle of all his works»), Athanasius, in the second book of *Contra Arianos*, responds by saying that the divine Wisdom, who in God was uncreated and identical with his eternal Son, became created through the creation and redemption of which he is the principle.[44]

In his study of modern Christology Bouyer assesses the contribution of Russian kenotic Christologies with specific reference to the work of Serge

---

persistent conflict with the powers of this world. This conflict affirms the all-powerful presence of God in him. The cross will be his victory, ie., the victory of God which is also ours. Cf. L. BOUYER, *The Eternal Son*, 262-267.

[42] Cf. L. BOUYER, *The Eternal Son*, 273-282.

[43] Bouyer follows the evolution of the christological problem through the centuries, tracing the origins of the main questions. He divides his summary of its historical development into five periods: (i) Christian beginnings to the end of the fourth century; (ii) focus on integrity and fullness of Christ's humanity; (iii) Latin Middle Ages: Anselm, Duns Scotus and Aquinas; (iv) reaching to our time, difficulties of the Christology based on the Thomistic approach; (v) existentialist Christology versus essentialist Christology. Cf. L. BOUYER, *The Eternal Son*, 299-302.

[44] Cf. L. BOUYER, *The Eternal Son*, 321.

Bulgakov (1871–1944).[45] Bulgakov's literary output was prodigious.[46] The *leitmotif* present in all his works is Sophia and his work *Sophia the Wisdom of God* presents his understanding of Sophia.[47] Bouyer notes that Bulgakov wanted to demonstrate the relationship between the Wisdom inherent in creation and the Wisdom in God. His intention was to oppose Manichaeism by emphasizing creation's unity and value, and also to oppose the prevalent atheism of the time by emphasizing creation's origin and significance in God. He wanted to develop a new «theology of creation» which for him was synonymous with sophiology.[48] Through sophiology he wanted to penetrate to the world's hidden meaning, which he believed he had attained by coming to understand Sophia as the universal and living element at the basis of all existence both created and divine.

For Bouyer the first anticipation of modern kenotic Christologies was preoccupied with defining the content of this kenosis or self-emptying of Christ about which Paul speaks in Philippians 2:6-11. Bouyer outlines some basic propositions underlying Bulgakov's kenotic theory: Wisdom, in God, is the essence of the divine life, the object of God's eternal

---

[45] Sergej Bulgakov was born in Livny, the son of an orthodox priest. Cf. «Sergej N. Bulgakov» in H.J. RUPPERT, *Klassiker der Theologie*. II, 263-276. Cf. Cf. also L. BOUYER, *The Eternal Son*, 381-383. In the 1930s Eastern Orthodoxy was abundantly represented in Paris as a result of post-revolutionary Russian emigration. During this time Bouyer met Bulgakov who was to leave a profound mark on Bouyer's outlook and theological work. Bulgakov was then developing a deeply sapiential form of the Christian vision viewing the world as continually assumed and transformed by the creative Wisdom of God. For an introduction to the writings of S. Bulgakov cf. M.R. LANGELLA, *Salvezza come illuminazione*. Chapter three of this book is entitled «Salvezza come illuminazione nella teologia di Sergej Bulgakov», 73-129.

[46] Bulgakov wrote a dogmatic trilogy concerning the divineness of humanity: *The Lamb of God* (addressing the study of Christology), *The Comforter* (Pneumatology), and *The Bride of the Lamb* (Ecclesiology). Cf. T. SCHIPFLINGER, *Sophia - Maria*, 273.

[47] Bulgakov began to express his sophiological ideas in his *Economic Philosophy* (published 1912) and honed them further in his trilogy about the divineness of humanity. He summarized his thinking about Sophia in *The Wisdom of God*. A French edition also exists which the translator claims is based on the original and unpublished Russian text: S. BULGAKOV, *La Sagesse de Dieu,* (translated by C. Andronikov). The French edition appears to be different from the English translation mentioned above.

[48] Bulgakov says that sophiology is a Christian vision of the world, a particular interpretation of the entirety of Christian teaching, from the teachings about the Trinity and the origin of humanity, to the practical questions of Christianity today. Cf. S. BULGAKOV, *The Wisdom of God*, 13, 15.

knowledge and love. However, Wisdom is also one with God's creative project, his design to create a world and especially a humanity that will participate in his own divine life. This presupposes a kenosis in creation by which God limits himself because he brings into existence a freedom other than his own, together with a decision never to abolish it. This kenosis of creation is, nevertheless, only a reflection of the eternal kenosis within the Trinity, by which the Father exists only in projecting himself in the Son, with the Spirit attesting to the reciprocity of their love. In the Incarnation, finally, we have a third kenosis, through which the Word, by assuming an individual humanity, will lead all of humanity back again through this same identification with its eternal reality. The resurrection and ascension of Christ are brought to gradual fulfillment through the suffering but ultimately victorious life of Christ's members, the fulfillment of the glorious divine kenosis. [49]

In his conclusion to this section Bouyer notes that we are speaking about the fulfillment of divine Wisdom in history when we speak of the divine Word, the eternal Logos, where the Father speaks himself in the Son, taking on his own flesh and earthly humanity at birth. Bouyer affirms that in God there is no distinction between the Wisdom through whom he disposed all things, and especially foresaw and preordained our human history, and the Logos in whom he reveals himself. This is why in history, where the divine Word reveals himself, there is an intimate correlation and concordance between the revelation of God and God's design for us.

We have already observed that the christological title used most frequently by Bouyer is that of *Word*.[50] Bouyer's Christology is based on the concept of the Word. In this regard, Bouyer was going back to the affirmation of the Incarnation of the Logos, and the identification of Jesus as the incarnate Logos which dominated the Christology of the second and third centuries. In the development of New Testament Christology Bouyer understands the categories of the Wisdom tradition as a necessary supplement to the messianic and prophetic categories and as a stage leading to the Logos Christology of John. We have already noted that the Logos prologue of the Gospel of John is considerably indebted to pre-Christian Wisdom speculation. This is acknowledged by Bouyer.[51] To this extent we have spoken of Logos Christology having some of its roots in

---

[49] Cf. L. BOUYER, *The Eternal Son*, 382-383.

[50] Cf. L. BOUYER, *The Eternal Son*, 41.

[51] Cf. L. BOUYER, *The Eternal Son*, 182, 269-270.

Wisdom Christology. While acknowledging this connection we also noted that Logos Christology stands independent of Wisdom Christology.

Given Bouyer's emphasis on the concept of the Word it is reasonable to argue that an explicit understanding of Jesus in terms of Wisdom Christology was not intended by Bouyer.

2.4 *Concluding Remarks*

We have been concerned here with examining to what extent, in formulating his Christology, Bouyer uses the Wisdom elements from the Scriptures. Bouyer focuses on a Christology of the Word. In this regard, he highlights the emphasis by New Testament writers on their understanding of Jesus in terms of the central Old Testament concept of the Word of Yahweh. This forms the basis for Bouyer's argument in favour of a Logos oriented Christology.

However, while not using extensively the Wisdom tradition, Bouyer does make passing reference to some of the central Wisdom texts of the New Testament. Bouyer's is not a Wisdom Christology but there is to be found there a general awareness of some of the Wisdom influences in the development of Christology.

Specifically, in the early chapters of *The Eternal Son*, Bouyer offers an overview of Wisdom in the Hebrew Wisdom literature and highlights its roots in Canaanite and Mesopotamian Wisdom. He refers to I Corinthians 1–4 and its identification of Jesus with divine Wisdom as a basis for Wisdom Christology. Bouyer notes that there is at least an implicit identification here between the Wisdom who was active in the creation of the world (Prov 8) and Jesus crucified. He affirms that the theme of the Wisdom of God as the folly of the cross, resisted and contradicted by the Wisdom of this world, is found in I Corinthians.

Bouyer highlights references in the Gospels of Matthew and Luke which, he argues, confirm the use of the Wisdom motif by these evangelists: Matthew 11:19 («Yet time will prove where Wisdom lies») and Luke 7:35 («God's Wisdom is vindicated by all who accept it»). However, while highlighting the importance of some of the christological titles in New Testament Christology, including Wisdom, Bouyer maintains that this importance should not be exaggerated. His central point, like that of W. Kasper, is that the implied Christology of the earthly Jesus contains an unprecedented claim which breaks down all previous schemes. Jesus was reluctant to accept titles because he claimed to be more than they could express. For Bouyer, Jesus did not legitimise his mission by reference to the titles that had nourished Jewish expectation of the last era. Rather the titles occupy a secondary place in Jesus' testimony about himself.

In his treatment of Johannine Christology Bouyer is conscious of the Old Testament background, most especially from the Old Testament Wisdom literature. He acknowledges that the fourth evangelist saw in Jesus the culmination of a tradition that runs through the Wisdom literature of the Old Testament.

In his study of modern Christology Bouyer assesses the contribution of the Russian theologian Serge Bulgakov. In Bulgakov's works Sophia is the key *leitmotif*. Bouyer notes that, for Bulgakov, sophiology presents a Christian vision of the world, a particular interpretation of the entirety of Christian thinking, from teachings about the Trinity and the origin of humanity right through to the particular questions of Christianity today.

Bouyer does not advert to the feminine element in Wisdom thought, and makes only one reference to the development of the Wisdom theme among the Church Fathers. While acknowledging positive points in Bouyer's use of the Wisdom theme, in his treatment of the historical Jesus Bouyer does not present Jesus as Sage or as divine Wisdom in person. Indeed, like Walter Kasper, Bouyer's emphasis on the kingdom of God preached and lived as the content of salvation is, for him, more important than any particular finding with regard to the titles. A general acknowledgment and passing reference to the Wisdom influence on the development of Christology is what is to be found in Bouyer's *The Eternal Son*.

3. Christian Duquoc

3.1 *Dominican and Theologian*

Christian Duquoc was born in Nantes in 1926. In 1948, at the age of twenty-two, he joined the Order of Preachers (Dominicans). After studies in Lyons, Freiburg, and the École Biblique in Jerusalem, he obtained a doctorate in theology from the University of Lyons in 1967. He was a member of the faculty of theology at the University of Lyons from 1957 to 1992. Presently he is Professor Emeritus at the University of Lyons and is editor of the periodical *Lumière et vie*.

3.2 *The Development of Duquoc's Theology*

Throughout his theological career Duquoc has addressed many of the central questions in systematic theology. The titles of some of his publications indicate the breath of his theological interests.[52] He has also concerned himself with developments in contemporary theology and spirituality, displaying particular interest in theology's dialogue with secularism and liberation theology[53] as well as in other prevailing theological questions.[54]

3.3 *The Christology of Christian Duquoc*

It is not the purpose of our study to treat Duquoc's Christology in detail.[55] Rather, our central focus is concerned with examining to what extent, to formulate his systematic Christology, Duquoc uses Wisdom elements found in the Scriptures. However, as with the other theologians under review, some explication of Duquoc's Christology, by way of summary and overview, will help to situate our specific study. In this regard, we will draw on Duquoc's *Christologie. Essai Dogmatique.*

3.3.1 *Summary*

In volume one of *Christologie. Essai Dogmatique* entitled *L'homme Jésus*[56] Duquoc introduces his Christology by highlighting that renewal within theology represents a return to the origins of Christianity bringing

---

[52] C. Duquoc has addressed the major questions in systematic theology. Cf. *Christoloie.* I-II; *Jésus, homme libre*; *Dieu différent*; *Messianisme de Jésus*; *Des Églises provisoires.* For a complete bibliography of Duquoc's works to 1995 see: M. DEMASION, ed., *La liberté du théologien* , 171-181.

[53] Cf. C. DUQUOC, «Le Christ», 43-59; ID., *Ambiguitiés des théologiens.*

[54] Cf. C. DUQUOC, «Le christianisme», 75-85; *La femme, le clerc et le laïc*; «Une coexistence conflictuelle», 165-171.

[55] For studies on the Christology of C. Duquoc see: M. SERENTHÀ, «Cristologie», 61-113; B. SESBOÜÉ, «Bulletin Christologie I», 628-671, esp. 656-663; ID., «Bulletin Christologie II», 423-465, esp. 427-433.

[56] C. DUQUOC, *Christologie,*I. In this first volume Duquoc wishes to affirm the historical basis of the life of Jesus and to underline the humanity of Jesus, undiminished by his divinity. From this Duquoc derives the title for the volume: *L'homme Jésus* - the man Jesus. Clear and significant differences between the two volumes concerning Christology have been highlighted with the claim that two different images of Jesus emerge. Volume one addresses the difficulties arising from the «God is dead» theology (T. Altizer, P. van Buren, J.A.T. Robinson); the second considers the place of the Christian in society and in history in the context of issues raised by German Protestant post-Bultmannian theology (J. Moltmann, W. Pannenberg). These difficulties aside, Duquoc's principal pre-occupation in these two volumes was to set forth a discourse of faith in Jesus Christ, beginning from the humanity of Jesus.

us into contact with the person of Jesus Christ. Theology is once again rediscovering its christological base. Our acceptance and appropriation of the mystery of Jesus Christ determine our attitude towards everything else within Christianity, most especially our response to the ultimate mystery in life which is God.

Following the chronological events in the life of Jesus, Duquoc's opening chapter seeks to uncover the message that Matthew and Luke sought to transmit in the accounts of the birth of Jesus.[57] Reflecting on the christological development in the «infancy» narratives,[58] Duquoc affirms a sophisticated theology hidden behind the candid simplicity and lyricism of these scenes.[59] Rather than narrating facts concerning the birth of Jesus, the evangelists employ graphic and theological narratives to announce Jesus of Nazareth (who and what he is) to the believing communities.

Duquoc makes the historical aspect of Jesus of Nazareth an essential element in his Christology, with special emphasis on the place of the kingdom. Thus Jesus' baptism, activity, and message receive close attention. The eschatological and soteriological character of Jesus' person is grounded in his activity and message concerning the kingdom. The kingdom of God preached was the very content of salvation. For Duquoc, to reach the Jesus of history, it is necessary to retrace our way through the Gospels, which are composed from the perspectives of their early Christian authors yet enshrine earlier historical material. Duquoc studies

---

[57] Duquoc affirms the use in the infancy narratives of the *haggadah midrash*. This literary form takes a scriptural fact or saying and embellishes it with the intention of underlining some truth of faith and proclaiming it in an unequivocal way. Cf. C. DUQUOC, *Christologie*, I, 24-28.

[58] Duquoc notes the word «infancy» here is a misnomer: These narratives are, in fact, accounts of the birth of Jesus. Cf. C. DUQUOC, *Christologie*, I, 24.

[59] Duquoc highlights a central question for the believing community: At what point did God institute Jesus as Saviour, Messiah, and Son of God? I Corinthians 15:3-8 and Acts 10:34-43 had pointed to the death and resurrection of Jesus. Mark, with no infancy account, inferred that this event took place with Jesus' baptism by John in the Jordan. Matthew and Luke emphasize the birth of Jesus in this regard. Finally, John, inheriting the long and profound meditation on the matter, concluded that Jesus was Son of God before he was born, in his pre-existence at the side of God, before the creation of the world, because «in the beginning was the Word [...]». Given the understanding gained in the brightness of the resurrection, the apostles began to reread the whole life of Christ, to re-interpret his words, to retell his miracles; and they began to discover in the facts of his birth the latent presence of the Messiah and Saviour patently revealed only after the resurrection. Cf. C. DUQUOC, *Christologie*, I, 39-42.

Jesus' preaching and conduct, and evaluates these actions as an offer of definitive salvation from God. The inseparability of Jesus' message from his person is a central factor in Duquoc's Christology. He locates the foundation of Jesus' activity in his consciousness of deep intimacy with God.[60]

The emerging point, for Duquoc, is that the historical Jesus stands out as an integral part of Christian faith. This is not to suggest that the historical Jesus is the object of Christian faith. Rather, the historical Jesus is the foundation stone for the development of Christian faith.[61] In the end the legitimation of our confession of Jesus as Lord must go back to the historical Jesus and, once legitimated, this Christian faith must remain in close contact with the historical Jesus if it is to remain integral. Otherwise the kerygma without Jesus becomes a verbal vacuum and Jesus without the kerygma appears as a meaningless surd. It is in this sense that the historical Jesus assumes a position of permanent significance within Christology.

Within this position of permanent significance that obtains between the historical Jesus and Christology, Duquoc addresses the question as to what kind of relationship exists between the Jesus of history and the Christ of faith. Within the unified development of the words and deeds of the historical Jesus giving rise to his death, and his death being the horizon against which the mystery of the resurrection unfolded itself, the gradual transition from the Jesus of history to the Christ of faith took place. Within this gradual transition there is a fundamental relationship of underlying personal continuity between the Jesus of history and the Christ of faith.[62] Three distinct levels of continuity between the Jesus of history and the Christ of faith can be detected from Duquoc's presentation. First, Duquoc speaks of a progressive unfolding of eschatological meaning through the

---

[60] Cf. C. DUQUOC, *Christologie,* I, 52-90.

[61] Duquoc notes that it is not enough to suggest, as Bultmann does, that it is merely the existence of Jesus in his givenness without historical details that lies behind Christian faith. To affirm such a Christ of faith without historical details would be to accept a content-less, characterless and impersonal reality as the object of faith. Rather, if as the early Post-Bultmannians pointed out the person to whom the Christ of faith refers is in no way concretely definable in his historicity, then he becomes pure myth. Cf. C. DUQUOC, *Christologie*, I, 43.

[62] Duquoc notes that the impact of biblical research in the nineteenth century drove a wedge between the Jesus of history and the Christ of faith. This barrier has now been removed thanks to the advances of biblical research and understanding. C. DUQUOC, *Christologie.* I, 97-102.

experience of the life, death, and resurrection of Jesus as a unified whole. Duquoc classifies this level as one of eschatological continuity.[63] Second, Duquoc underlines that, on the level of Christology implicit and explicit, there is a continuity between the Jesus of history and the Christ of faith.[64] A third continuity on the level of faith itself is identified by Duquoc.[65] Yet, in spite of this heavy emphasis on the continuity between the Jesus of history and the Christ of faith, Duquoc highlights a dimension of discontinuity within the line of continuity. The mode of existence belonging to the risen Christ of faith is radically different from and therefore discontinuous with the mode of historical existence in the earthly life of Jesus. In this sense there is a distinct dimension of discontinuity, a discontinuity which is specifically historical. The reality of the risen Christ of faith is trans-historical and is therefore, to that extent, discontinuous with the Jesus of history.[66] In the light of his analysis of continuity and

---

[63] For Duquoc the words and deeds of Jesus gave rise to his death and resurrection and the death and resurrection explain the meaning of his words and deeds. The eschatological suggestiveness of the words and deeds of Jesus is the background against which the resurrection experience unfolds itself meaningfully upon the consciousness of the apostles in terms of the dawning of a new era. Cf. C. DUQUOC, *Christologie*, I, 100-103.

[64] Duquoc notes that evidence for the presence of an implicit Christology in the life of Jesus can be found in the prefacing of his sayings with the expression *Amen*, the addressing of God as Father, the existence of a filial relationship towards God, the teaching contained in his parables, and the forgiving of sins. It was on the basis of these historical phenomena in the life of Jesus that the apostles could attribute in the light of the resurrection different biblical titles to Jesus: *Christ, Lord, Son of God,* and *Word,* which in fact make up the content of explicit Christology. Because of this continuity between the Jesus of history and the Christ of faith the evangelists had no difficulties in projecting back the post-paschal titles into the earthly life of Jesus. Thus Duquoc underlines a basic continuity on the level of Christology between the Jesus of history and the Christ of faith. Cf. C. DUQUOC, *Christologie*. I, 105-107.

[65] By this Duquoc means that the faith of the Jesus of history as the founder of Christianity is continued in the Christian faith of his followers. Jesus believed in faith that the kingdom of God was being made manifest through his missionary activity. It is this faith of Jesus which inspires the faith of the apostles in his own person. As such this faith of Jesus is continued after the resurrection in Christian faith, which now recognises Jesus as *the* one in whom the power and presence of God have been fully realised and through whom the kingdom of God is made manifest as present reality and future promise. Cf. C. DUQUOC, *Christologie*. I, 107-109.

[66] Duquoc highlights that such qualities of discontinuity are derived from the theological fact that, in and through the resurrection, the Jesus of history is transformed into a new mode of existence, an eschatological mode of existence which lies outside

discontinuity the relationship between the Jesus of history and the Christ of faith is one of personal sameness within historical differentiation. The person referred to is one and the same reality, whereas the mode of being belonging to this person has been changed historically.

Duquoc summarises the distinct characteristics of the Christology of the early kerygma as an Easter Christology centred on the resurrection and glorification of Jesus by the Father. He notes that functional Christology naturally ends with questions concerning the person of Jesus Christ, and the answers to these necessarily mark the advent of a Christology which rises from the functional to the ontological level. The New Testament testifies to a progressive and significant advance toward such a Christology.[67]

In moving from pre-existence to Sonship, Duquoc shows how the elaborate New Testament Christology of Jesus' ontological Sonship of God gives objective expression to the filial consciousness that had been at the centre of Jesus' experience of God during his earthly life. Furthermore, the depth of Jesus' divine Sonship having been discovered, a new approach lay open for the discourse of faith which would no longer start, as the early kerygma had done, from the lordship of the Risen One but, inverting the perspective, would resolutely take as its point of departure the togetherness of Father and Son in an effable communion of life prior to the Son's earthly mission from the Father.[68]

Duquoc follows the development of christological dogma through the Councils of the patristic age and highlights Chalcedon as a normative christological landmark in saving the human dimension of the mystery of Jesus Christ and providing us with a balanced formulation of the universal significance of the Christ-event, a formulation that needs to be interpreted

---

space and time. As in the case of personal continuity, we can also detect different levels of discontinuity between the Jesus of history and the Christ of faith. On the eschatological level there is discontinuity in that the end of time has already occurred in the resurrection of Jesus and the new era has begun in Jesus as the risen Christ. On the level of Christology there is also a discontinuity between the Jesus of history and the Christ of faith, in that the risen Christ reigns as universal Lord in a way that was impossible to the particularity of the Jesus of history. Thirdly, on the level of faith, there is a discontinuity insofar as the risen Christ has become the new object of faith which is now specifically called Christian faith. As the object of faith Jesus Christ defines, personalises, and concretises the content of basic faith in a new way. Cf. C. DUQUOC, *Christologie.* I, 109-112.

[67] Cf. C. DUQUOC, *Christologie.* I, 111-117.

[68] Cf. C. DUQUOC, *Christologie.* I, 189-194.

according to the experience of the Christian community under the influence of the Spirit.[69]

Duquoc also addresses himself to questions regarding the uniqueness and universality of Jesus Christ. For Duquoc, the decisive core of the christological faith offered by the resurrection of Jesus and the Easter experience of the disciples must be recognised.[70]

3.3.2 *Awareness of Wisdom Christology in Duquoc*

Duquoc makes the historical aspect of Jesus of Nazareth an important element in the formulation of his Christology. Duquoc's is not a Wisdom Christology, but he seems aware of some of the Wisdom influences on the formulation of the doctrine of the Incarnation. Duquoc treats, albeit briefly, the personification of Wisdom in the Old Testament, referring specifically to Proverbs 8. Furthermore, in the development of New Testament Christology, Duquoc understands the categories of the Wisdom tradition as a necessary supplement to the messianic and prophetic categories and as a stage leading to the Logos Christology of John.[71]

However, specific references to links in the New Testament corpus with the Wisdom literature are scant. Duquoc's central point is that the implied Christology of the earthly Jesus contains an unprecedented claim which breaks down all previous schemes. The bringing together of diverse creedal strands in the canonical gospels, each with its own appropriate historical concern with Jesus of Nazareth, is not just a merging of various interpretations of Jesus; it also brings together information about Jesus' life on earth culled from various local church traditions. Different Christian congregations, each in its own way and basing itself on its own creed, cultivated a particular *memoria Jesu*, and became a channel of authentic Jesus tradition. The diverse Christologies of the New Testament represent distinct interpretations of the event in the light of Easter, each conditioned by the particular context of a Church to which it is addressed and by the singular personality of the author or editor of the material. For Duquoc, all aspects of titular Christology remain distinct, fragmentary, and mutually complementary approaches to the mystery of Jesus Christ, which in itself stands beyond them all and will forever defy full comprehension.[72]

---

[69] Cf. C. DUQUOC, *Christologie*. I, 282-298.

[70] Cf. C. DUQUOC, *Christologie*. I, 299-321.

[71] Cf. C. DUQUOC, *Christologie*. I, 272.

[72] Cf. C. DUQUOC, *Christologie*. I, 130-132.

Duquoc is aware of the contribution of the Church Fathers of the second and third centuries, specifically Tertullian and Origen, regarding a correct understanding of the divine Sonship of Jesus Christ. We have already seen how the Fathers drew on Wisdom imagery from the Old Testament. However, Duquoc makes no explicit connections between the Wisdom literature and the writings of the Fathers.[73]

Duquoc acknowledges the presence of the pre-existence theme in the Johannine prologue, noting that the writer of the prologue applies the concept of the «Word of God» to the pre-existent Son. The decisive step in Christology was the interpretation of the biblical image of Jesus Christ as the Son of God by means of the concept *Word of God*. For Duquoc, this step from image to concept has already been prepared for in Old Testament Wisdom literature and was expressly taken in the prologue of John.[74] Duquoc notes the emphasis by contemporary scholarship on the Old Testament and primitive Christian roots of the Johannine concept of Logos. Duquoc makes no reference to the theme of the Wisdom of God as the folly of the cross as found in I Corinthians.[75]

Given Duquoc's acknowledgment of diverse Christologies in the New Testament and the positive advantage of distinct Christologies presenting mutually complementary approaches to the mystery of Jesus Christ, he goes on to highlight a number of key titles in Christology: prophet[76], servant[77], mediator[78], son of man, son of God[79] and word of God. For

---

[73] Cf. C. DUQUOC, *Christologie*. I, 282-293.

[74] Duquoc cites Proverbs 8:22-26, Wisdom 7:25– 8:10, Sirach 1:1-20, Sirach 24:3-21.

[75] Cf. C. DUQUOC, *Christologie*. I, 263-276.

[76] Duquoc notes that there are prophetic forms of speech attributed to Jesus which link him to the classical prophets of Israel and their concern with justice, oppression, and the historical direction of their nation's life. Jesus also performed actions which recalled the symbolic acts of the prophets (Mark 11:1-10; 15-17). Moreover, the tradition refers to Jesus as a prophet, as he reportedly did himself (Mark 6:4; Luke 13:33). Duquoc focuses on the notion of Jesus as the eschatological prophet highlighting Jesus' attack on the temple system as a prophetic symbolic gesture. Jesus is presented as a prophet of restoration theology, a prophet of the coming judgment but also of the coming new age, who predicted that God would destroy the temple in order to raise up a new one in its place. Cf. C. DUQUOC, *Christologie*. I, 131-170.

[77] Here Duquoc cites Philippians 2:6-11 as the biblical basis for the title of servant, and articulates a kenosis Christology grounding the Old Testament background in the Suffering Servant Songs of Isaiah. Cf. C. DUQUOC, *Christologie*. I, 171-186.

[78] In his treatment of statements concerning Jesus' mediatorship of creation Duquoc does not refer to the roots of these statements in the Old Testament speculation on Wisdom. We have already noted that, with the aid of the sapiential tradition, which they

Duquoc these have proven to be classic titles for Christian creeds and christological teaching. He notes that all titles help to define the role and identity of Jesus. All are indispensable in articulating a definition of who Jesus is. Thus the titles orient us toward the radical identity of Jesus by signifying the mission humanely accomplished by Jesus.[80]

In his chapter on Jesus as the Word of God Duquoc develops a contemporary Word Christology which seeks a coherent understanding of the revelation of God in Jesus Christ. He stresses the identification of Jesus as the incarnate Logos which dominated the Christology of the second and third centuries.[81]

3.4 *Concluding Remarks*

We have been examining to what extent, in formulating his Christology, Duquoc uses Wisdom elements from the Scriptures. An important point of departure for Duquoc's Christology is an encounter with the historical Jesus of Nazareth. In this regard, Duquoc's Christology draws on a number of the titles, particularly that of Word. Significant references to the Wisdom literature in Duquoc's Christology are not to be found.

In his treatment of a Word Christology Duquoc understands the Wisdom categories as a necessary supplement to the messianic and prophetic categories and as a stage leading to the Logos Christology of the Fourth Gospel. However, specific references by Duquoc to links between the New Testament corpus and the Wisdom literature are scant. For Duquoc, all aspects of titular Christology remain distinct, fragmentary, and

---

had largely in common with other peoples (especially the Egyptians), the Old Testament writers already attempted to explain the universality of Yahweh's actions in salvation history in and with Israel and so to link together creation and salvation history. Neither does Duquoc show how the soteriological and universal cosmic significance of the assertion of Jesus as Son of God is taken up and developed in the hymn to Christ in Colossians 1:15-17. Cf. C. DUQUOC, *Christologie*. I, 187-188.

[79] Duquoc notes that the decisive step in Christology was the interpretation of the biblical image of Jesus Christ as the Son of God by means of the concept «Word of God». No link here with the Old Testament Wisdom literature is spoken of by Duquoc. Cf. C. DUQUOC, *Christologie*. I, 277-281.

[80] Each chapter identifies the Old Testament background of the title under discussionand then addresses the contribution that the title opens up towards an understanding of the mission and person of Jesus Christ. Cf. C. DUQUOC, *Christologie*. I, 130-131.

[81] Cf. C. DUQUOC, *Christologie*. I, 265-270.

mutually complementary approaches to the mystery of Jesus Christ, which in itself stands beyond them all and will forever defy full comprehension.

Duquoc does not advert to Wisdom influences on some of the christological hymns, on Paul's writing in I Corinthians 1–4, or on the Gospel of Matthew. Neither does he address the feminine element in Wisdom or the development of the Wisdom theme among the Church Fathers. Moreover, in his treatment of the historical Jesus, Duquoc does not present Jesus as Sage or as divine Wisdom in person. Only a brief acknowledgment of the Wisdom influence on the development of Christology is to be found in Duquoc's christological writings.

4. Joseph Moingt

4.1 Jesuit and Theologian

Joseph Moingt was born in Britanny in 1915. He entered the Jesuit order in 1938 and was ordained a priest in 1949. He studied philosophy and theology at the universities of Lyons and Paris. His doctoral dissertation, from the university of Paris, is a study of the trinitarian theology of Tertullian.[82] Moingt's early teaching career was spent at the Jesuit House of Studies at Lyons. He moved to Paris in 1968 to begin teaching at the *Institut Catholique* and the *Centre Sèvres*. He continues to teach at the *Centre Sèvres* and is editor of the periodical *Recherches de science religieuse*.

4.2 The Development of Moingt's Theology

A cursory look at Moingt's publications highlights the breath of his theological interests.[83] Clearly, Christology was a subject to which he has devoted considerable study.[84] His work, *L'homme qui venait de Dieu,*

---

[82] J. MOINGT, *Théologie trinitaire*, I-IV.

[83] Cf. J. MOINGT, *Le devenir chrétien*; La *transmission de la foi*. Notable articles by Moingt include the following: «Caractère et ministère sacerdotal», 563-589; «Nature du sacerdoce ministériel», 237-272; «Certitude historique et foi», 561-574; «L'initiation des jeunes», 437-454, 599-613, 744-762; «Le mariage des chrétiens», 631-654; «Le Dieu de la morale chrétienne», 631-654; «Montre nous le Père», 305-338; «L'echo du silence», 329-356; «Morale et catéchèse», 147-180; «Moralité de la morale», 195-212; «L'avenir du Magistère», 299-308; Le récit fondateur du rite», 337-353; «Un avenir pour la théologie», 601-628; «L'ailleurs de la théologie», 365-380; «Un corps pour l'Eglise», 391-400; «Transmettre un avenir de de foi», 11-27.

[84] For a complete bibliography of Moingt's works up to 1992 see J. DORÉ – C. THEOBALD, ed., *Penser la foi.* 1077-1084.

received lavish praise following publication in 1994. In a very favourable review, his fellow countryman, B. Sesboüé, underlined the originality of Moingt's work as well as its speculative significance.[85]

4.3 *The Christology of Joseph Moingt*

As was the case with Bouyer and Duquoc, we will not treat Moingt's Christology in detail. Rather, we are concerned to examine to what extent, in formulating his Christology, Moingt uses those Wisdom elements from the Scriptures. Some explication of Moingt's Christology, by way of summary and overview, will help to situate and clarify our specific study. In this regard we will concentrate on Moingt's *L'homme qui venait de Dieu* as the basic text for our examination of his Christology.

4.3.1 *Summary*

Moingt finds the starting point and permanent context of his Christology in the contemporary existential situation of doubt and unbelief. He argues that a new language to talk about Christology is needed so as to speak of Jesus Christ against the background of atheism.[86] For Moingt, Vatican II marked a breakthrough in Church attitudes in its opening up to the realities of unbelief.[87] Moingt argues that what is needed in response to the challenge of atheism is not an explanation of or a theory about its origin or purpose. He believes that, in the judgment of Christians, the story to be told amidst the encounter with atheism is christological.[88]

---

[85] Cf. B. Sesboüé, «De la rumeur de Jésus», 87-102, here 87. Sesboüé writes: «Le tout récent livre de J. Moingt, *L'homme qui venait de Dieu*, est une oeuvre personnelle et forte qui, si elle s'enrichit naturellement du travail de ses devanciers, apporte du neuf, tant par l'originalité de son point de vue principal que par l'ampleur de l'effort spéculatif entrepris. Elle est un travail qui restera à l'égal des grandes christologies de ce siècle» (p. 87).

[86] Cf. J. Moingt, *L'home qui venait de Dieu*, 9-10.

[87] Vatican II's realism towards the challenge of atheism is seen in three principal achievements of the Council: (i) a new sense of the complexity of unbelief; (ii) a new level of sympathetic understanding of unbelievers; (iii) a desire for mutual dialogue between believers and atheists. The text of *Gaudium et Spes* was to mirror the variety of forms of atheism found around the globe and the final document lists some fourteen different types of unbelief. Cf. Second Vatican Council, *Gaudium et spes*.

[88] Moingt's emphasis will be on what scripture authorizes us to say in response to the questions of faith posed by critical reason. Cf. J. Moingt, *L'homme qui venait de Dieu*, 9-10.

Moingt divides his work on Christology into two parts: the first studies the history of the dogmas on Christology, while part two treats the person and message of Jesus constructed systematically on the basis of the Gospel accounts.[89] In these latter chapters, which encompass the largest part of the book, Moingt makes the historical aspect of Jesus of Nazareth an essential element in his Christology emphasizing the return to Scripture in the facilitation of our meeting with and understanding of Jesus of Nazareth.[90] Furthermore, Moingt stipulates a second element in terms of the living faith of the Church, both in its foundations as testified to in the New Testament and its ongoing life of worship and witness through the ages. Like Kasper, Moingt affirms that the living Christ of today is encountered only in the living faith of Christians in the twenty-first century; the Jesus of yesterday is met only through the faith-witness of the New Testament, the book of the early Church.[91]

Moingt begins his study of the historical Jesus with the events of Jesus' death and resurrection. For Moingt the resurrection was the confirmation and legitimation by God of the earthly Jesus' message and activity. Beyond such confirmation, it was a new, creative, event which exalted Jesus, bringing him into God's dimension and filling him with the eschatological Spirit so that he in turn could fully share the Spirit with others. For Moingt, resurrection means the salvation of Jesus' concrete existence by God and in the presence of God, and the abiding, permanent validity of his history.[92] The resurrection is God's definitive self-disclosure which gathers up the earthly Jesus and establishes him in a radically new mode of being and activity. Moreover, the kingdom Jesus preached he has now become in person, thanks to God's self-disclosure and Jesus' personal consummation and public empowerment that occur indivisibly in Jesus' being raised from the dead.[93]

The ascending Christology of the resurrection experience is the basis for the development of all the later Christologies of the New Testament and

---

[89] Part one recounts the history of the dogma of the Incarnation in three parts: (i) the origins of the dogma; (ii) its definitions; (iii) contemporary challenges to the dogma. He begins his study in the first half of the second century with Justin of Rome and leaves the New Testament corpus to be treated in part two. Part two is oriented towards the narrative form of the gospels.

[90] Cf. J. MOINGT, *L'homme qui venait de Dieu*, 285-295.

[91] Cf. J. MOINGT, *L'homme qui venait de Dieu*, 291-294.

[92] Cf. J. MOINGT, *L'homme qui venait de Dieu*, 339-394.

[93] Cf. J. MOINGT, *L'homme qui venait de Dieu*, 370-390.

the subsequent Councils of the church. Hence, for Moingt, there can be no opposition between the earlier, ascending, functional Christology and its later transposition into metaphysical and essential terms. In the early chapters of his work Moingt follows the development of christological dogma through the Councils of the church.[94] Moingt summarises the various quests for the historical Jesus from the middle and late nineteenth century in Europe when, as one of the final effects of the Enlightenment, historical-critical scholarship began to be applied in earnest to the Gospel narratives.[95]

Moingt emphasizes that our historical access to Jesus remains mediated through the responses he evoked from others. The constant factor in Christology is the Christian movement itself, in the sense of a community experience which refers to Jesus. To reach the Jesus of history, it is necessary to retrace our way through the Gospels, which are composed from the perspectives of their early Christian authors yet enshrine earlier historical material.[96] The inseparability of Jesus' message from his person

---

[94] Cf. J. MOINGT, *L'homme qui venait de Dieu*, 141-220.

[95] Moingt highlights some of the various scholars who began writing new summaries of the life of Jesus. One of the most influential was David Strauss's *Das Leben Jesu* (1835-1836). This work was a clarion call for «unbiased» historical research to be done on the life of Jesus, a call based on the assumption that the Gospels could no longer be read straightforwardly as unvarnished historical records of what Jesus actually said and did. Yet by the end of the century various scholars, especially Albert Schweitzer (*The Quest of the Historical Jesus*, 1906), had come to the conclusion that most of these fresh attempts to say what we could *really* know about the historical Jesus actually told us more about their authors than about the person they sought to describe. The result was that for much of the first half of the twentieth century the scholarly quest for the historical Jesus was assumed to be dead. However, in 1953 Ernst Käsemann argued against his mentor, Bultmann that, while the Gospel traditions were certainly interpreted by believing followers of Jesus, this did not mean they could preserve authentic historical memories. Bultmann's scepticism about what could be known about the historical Jesus had been too extreme. Consequently, various scholars produced significant works reflecting the newfound confidence that we can know something about the historical Jesus by fully implementing the tools of critical inquiry. As the towering influence of Bultmann and the enthusiasm for existentialism waned, so did the enthusiasm for the Second Quest leaving the movement *passé* by the early 1970s. In a final section, Moingt draws attention to the work of a number of contemporary christologians: Rahner, Schillebeeckx, Kasper, Pannenberg, Moltmann. Cf. J. MOINGT, *L'homme qui venait de Dieu*, 224-280.

[96] Cf. J. MOINGT, *L'homme qui venait de Dieu*, 285-294.

is central to Moingt's Christology and he locates the foundation of Jesus' activity in his consciousness of deep intimacy with God.

Moingt returns to the significance of Jesus' resurrection, which completely transformed him, as no prophet ever was transformed, into a «spiritual body», a «life-giving spirit» (I Cor 15:44-45), a creature fully in the dimension of God. This uniqueness in turn grounds the universal significance of Jesus, in that he is the first person capable of opening the way for all other human beings to such a new form of being with God. For Moingt, the absolute uniqueness of Jesus' ontic human life can only be understood in terms of the unquestionable universality of his resurrected and glorified existence.[97]

Moingt addresses the question of the earthly Jesus as the source of the church's Christology. For Moingt, the decisive core of the christological faith offered by the resurrection of Jesus and the Easter experience of the disciples must be fully recognized. These events gave rise to Christology and, in that sense, mark its point of departure. What Moingt is concerned with here is showing that Jesus' works and words, his entire mission and human existence, are at the origin of Christology.[98] He traces, in broad strokes, the development of Christology from the apostolic kerygma to the present summarising the distinct characteristics of the Christology of the early kerygma as an Easter Christology centred on the resurrection and glorification of Jesus by the Father.[99]

4.3.2 *Awareness of Wisdom Christology in Moingt*

Of the three theologians under review in this chapter Moingt makes the least use of the Wisdom tradition in the formulation of his Christology. Not only is Moingt's not a Wisdom Christology, there is no explicit reference by him to the Wisdom influences on the formulation of the doctrine of the Incarnation.

In his analysis, Moingt addresses two questions which we have already seen other theologians raise in the context of the Wisdom theme: the pre-existence of Christ and his mediatorship of creation. However, in his discussion Moingt does not draw upon the trajectory of the Wisdom tradition. Addressing the pre-existence of Christ, Moingt shows how the notion of pre-existence proved necessary. Only this concept could

---

[97] Cf. J. MOINGT, *L'homme qui venait de Dieu*, 395-448.

[98] Cf. J. MOINGT, *L'homme qui venait de Dieu*, 340-390.

[99] Cf. J. MOINGT, *L'homme qui venait de Dieu*, 683-706.

guarantee that in the earthly life, death, and resurrection of Jesus, God himself was involved and that in Jesus Christ, God was revealing himself definitively and eschatologically. Moingt argues that what the pre-existence statements of the New Testament really do is express in a new and more profound way the eschatological character of the person and work of Jesus of Nazareth. Only thus could the universal significance of Jesus Christ as the fulfillment not only of the Old Testament but of all reality have been adequately expressed.[100]

We have noted already that the immediate source of the New Testament pre-existence statements is found mainly in Old Testament Judaism, with the parallels clearest in Old Testament speculation on Wisdom. Wisdom personified is understood as emanation, reflection and image of God (Wis 7:25); she is present giving counsel at the creation of the world (Wis 8:4; 9:9) and can be called «author of all things» (7:12); God sends her (9:10, 17); he has her dwelling in Israel (Ecc 24:8-10). However, Moingt does not highlight that the ideas of the pre-existence of Jesus were conveyed to the New Testament through Judaism's speculation on Wisdom.

Moingt acknowledges the presence of the pre-existence theme in the Johannine prologue. He notes that the decisive step in Christology was the interpretation of the biblical image of Jesus Christ as the Son of God by means of the concept *Word of God*. He argues that the synthesis offered in the prologue of John must be regarded as an independent achievement which operated in the framework of biblical and early Christian thinking but served to disclose to Hellenistic Jews the being and meaning of Jesus. In chapter ten of his Christology Moingt develops a Logos Christology which seeks a coherent understanding of the revelation of God in Jesus Christ. We have already noted that the Logos prologue of John's Gospel is considerably indebted to pre-Christian Wisdom speculation. To this extent we have spoken of Logos Christology having some of its roots in Wisdom Christology. Moreover, while acknowledging this connection we noted that Logos Christology stands independent of Wisdom Christology. Moingt makes no explicit reference to Wisdom Christology or to the influence of the Wisdom literature in articulating his Logos Christology.[101]

4.4 *Concluding Remarks*

We have been concerned here with examining to what extent, in formulating his Christology, Moingt makes use of the Wisdom elements

---

[100] Cf. J. MOINGT, *L'homme qui venait de Dieu*, 133-140.

[101] Cf. J. MOINGT, *L'homme qui venait de Dieu*, 623-682.

in the Scriptures. Moingt does not use the Wisdom tradition or refer to the central Wisdom texts of the New Testament. Moreover, he shows no explicit awareness of the Wisdom influences in the development of Christology.

In his treatment of the historical Jesus Moingt does not present Jesus as Sage or as Divine Wisdom in person. Neither does Moingt advert to the feminine element in Wisdom thought. He does not refer to the development of the Wisdom theme among the Church Fathers.

5. Summary and Conclusions

We have been concerned with examining to what extent the Wisdom elements present in the Scriptures and the tradition of the church have been incorporated into some representative Catholic Christologies of the French-speaking world.[102] We have concentrated on Louis Bouyer's *Le Fils éternel*, Christian Duquoc's *Christologie. Essai Dogmatique*, and Joseph Moingt's *L'homme qui venait de Dieu*. We have concluded that none of these works are an explicit *Wisdom* Christology.

In the early chapters of *The Eternal Son* Bouyer sets out the development of Wisdom in Israel taking us through an overview of the Hebrew Wisdom literature and affirms its roots in Canaanite and Mesopotamian Wisdom. He highlights references in the Gospels of Matthew and Luke which, he argues, confirms the use of the Wisdom motif by these evangelists. He also notes that a Wisdom approach to an understanding of Jesus influenced the author of the Fourth Gospel.

Bouyer cites I Corinthians 1–4 and its identification of Jesus with divine Wisdom as a basis for Wisdom Christology. He notes that there is at least an implicit identification here between the Wisdom who was active in the creation of the world (Prov 8) and Jesus crucified. Bouyer affirms that the theme of the Wisdom of God as the folly of the cross, resisted and contradicted by the Wisdom of this world, is found in I Corinthians 1 and 2. As Bouyer observes, Paul's theology of Wisdom confronts us with the

---

[102] While coming to this conclusion we should note some of the major exegetical works and commentators in French that have studied Wisdom literature: ASSOCIATION CATHOLIQUE FRANCAISE POUR L'ÉTUDE DE LA BIBLE, *La Sagesse biblique*; A. BARUCQ, *Le Livre des Proverbes*; A.M. DUBARLE, *Les sages d'Israël*; C. LARCHER, *Le Livre de Job*; ID., *Job et son Dieu*; ID., *Le Livre de la Sagesse*, I-III; J. LÉVÈQUE, *Études sur le Livre de la Sagesse*; D. LYS, *L'Ecclésiaste ou que vaut la vie?*; C. SPICQ, *L'Ecclésiastique*; J. VERMEYLEN, *Job*.

fact that this Wisdom at work in the universe is now revealed in the vulnerable love expressed in the crucified one.

In his treatment of Johannine Christology Bouyer is conscious of the Old Testament background, most especially from the Old Testament Wisdom literature. He acknowledges that the fourth evangelist saw in Jesus the culmination of a tradition that runs through the Wisdom literature of the Old Testament. Bouyer notes that it is in Proverbs 8 that we have the first identification of the Word of Genesis 1 with Wisdom, and in Sirach 24 the final identification of Word / Wisdom with the *Shekinah*, the localized presence in history of the simultaneously transcendent and immanent God. For Bouyer it is clear that every verse of the prologue has its root in some phase of the progressive development found in the Old Testament: first of the Word and then through Wisdom to the *Shekinah* culminating in the definitive presence of God with us.

In his study of modern Christology, Bouyer assesses the contribution of Russian Christologies with specific reference to the work of S. Bulgakov (1871-1944). Bouyer notes that, for Bulgakov, sophiology presents a Christian vision of the world, a particular interpretation of the entirety of Christian thinking, beginning with the teachings about the Trinity and the origin of humanity and moving to the particular questions of Christianity today.

A general acknowledgment and passing reference to the Wisdom influence on the development of Christology is found in Bouyer's *The Eternal Son*.

Turning to C. Duquoc's *Christologie*, he is aware of some of the Wisdom influences on the formulation of the doctrine of the Incarnation. In the development of New Testament Christology, Duquoc understands the categories of the Wisdom tradition as a necessary supplement to the messianic and prophetic categories and as a stage leading to the Logos Christology of John. However, there are few links drawn by Duquoc between the New Testament corpus and Wisdom literature. For Duquoc, all aspects of titular Christology remain distinct, fragmentary, and mutually complementary approaches to the mystery of Jesus Christ, which in itself stands beyond them all and will forever defy full comprehension. As with Bouyer, only a brief acknowledgment of the Wisdom influence on the development of Christology is found in Duquoc's *Christologie*.

Of the three theologians under review, J. Moingt makes the least use of the Wisdom tradition in the formulation of his Christology. He makes no references to the Wisdom influences on the formulation of the doctrine of the Incarnation.

None of our three authors refer to the feminine element in Wisdom thought and no significant reference to the development of the Wisdom theme among the Church Fathers is identified. Neither is Jesus presented as Sage or as Divine Wisdom in person. There is no significant influence of the Wisdom elements present in the Scriptures and the tradition of the church on the three chosen representative Catholic Christologies of the French-speaking world.

CHAPTER X

Towards a Contemporary Wisdom Christology
Critical Implications and Prospects

We are concerned here with opening up new avenues for Wisdom Christology. We will show that the language of Wisdom can be retrieved as a «root metaphor» which can generate new perspectives on issues which face contemporary theology. In the contemporary life of the church, at least five important areas are amenable to being led along the path of Wisdom: the call to justice, outlining the significance of Wisdom for feminist concerns in Christology, the dialogue with other religions, grounding ecological and environmental responsibility, and presenting a face of God for the modern world.

The metaphor of the path, the way, appears regularly throughout the Wisdom literature as Wisdom calls people to walk her way (Prov 3:17; 8:32; Sir 6:26).[1] In ordinary life, a path is created by many feet over a period of time. As each individual chooses to walk the path, that act cuts the path more deeply. Ultimately, the path orders the world in a particular way, establishing relations between places and offering a common and recommended way of getting there. In just this way, Wisdom lays down a path which, if followed by many, increasingly leads the believing community to right relations with God, the world, and each other.

1. Critical Implications of and Prospects
   for Wisdom Christology

We now turn to the challenge that the five areas highlighted pose for contemporary theology and to the resources for addressing them to be

---

[1] For a presentation of the metaphor of *the way* see; E.A. JOHNSON, *Jesus - Sophia: Ramifications for Contemporary Theology*, 5.

found in Wisdom Christology. Our discussion will illustrate the contribution to be made by the Wisdom tradition, and specifically Wisdom Christology, to contemporary theological reflection.

1.1 The Call to Justice

Contemporary Catholic theology continues to reflect on the relationship of Christian faith to the quest for justice in the world. This reflection is rooted in the biblical tradition. G. von Rad has said that «[...] there is absolutely no concept in the Old Testament with so central a significance for the relationships of human life as that of *ṣedāqāh*, justice / righteousness».[2] The ministry of Jesus was guided by his image of God as the Compassionate One concerned with justice (Mk 2:17; Mt 6:33; 23:23). The biblical idea of justice can best be described as *fidelity to the demands of a relationship* which extend in four directions: to God, to oneself, to one's neighbour both as individual and society, and to creation as a whole.[3] The biblical world is one where the person lives united with others in a social context either by bonds of family or by covenant relationships.

In this time when a theology of justice remains important to contemporary theology, we must recognize that social justice is a central concern both of the Wisdom tradition of ancient Israel and the New Testament. Indeed it is scarcely possible to separate justice from Wisdom, for unjust conditions are perceived to be a violation of the right order of creation, which is established and cherished by Wisdom herself.[4] Lady Wisdom betrays a strong identification with the concerns of justice. «I walk», she proclaims, «in the way of righteousness, in the paths of justice» (Prov 8:20). Elsewhere, Lady Wisdom demands justice and threatens sudden disaster on those who refuse her call (Prov 1:10-33). It is noteworthy that the punishment of the wicked is not the result of a special supernatural intervention by God but the natural result of unjust action in a justice-loving world order.[5]

In Job and Proverbs the just man preserves the peace and wholeness of the community. He cares for the poor, the fatherless, and the widow (Job 29:12-15; 31:16-19; Prov 29:7) and defends their cause in court (Job 29:16; Prov 31:9). Such a person «strengthens the weak hands and him

---

[2] Cf. G. VON RAD, *Old Testament Theology*. I, 370.

[3] Cf. J. FUELLENBACH, *Kingdom of God*, 157.

[4] Cf. B. MALCHOW, «Social Justice», 120-124.

[5] Cf. G. VON RAD, *Wisdom in Israel*, 124-137.

who was stumbling» (Job 4:3-4). According to Proverbs, «He who oppresses the poor insults his Maker» while those who reach out to the poor honour God (14:31). Accordingly, the Wisdom literature is replete with calls to care for the widow, the orphan, and the poor; with warnings that those who are greedy for gain will be caught in their own snare: «A righteous man knows the rights of the poor; a wicked man does not understand such knowledge» (Prov 29:7). The marginal groups in society, the poor, the widows, the orphans, the strangers, become the scale by which the justice of society is measured.[6] J. Donahue highlights that, in a biblical perspective, concern for the poor is rooted not simply in compassion for the plight of others but in claims of justice. The goods of the earth have been given for the benefit of all.[7]

Furthermore, the just are good stewards of the land and their relations with their workers create peace and harmony (Job 31:13). They live at peace with their neighbours and are a joy to their families (Job 31:1-12; Prov 23:24). From justice flows peace and prosperity to the land and to all in the community.[8] Yahweh rewards according to justice (Ps 18:20) and vindication comes from the justice of God (Ps 35:24). The statements on justice in Job and Proverbs reveal that living in the ways of justice creates a harmony within the community which comes from a right relationship to the covenant Lord and to one's neighbour to whom a person is related by covenant bond.[9]

During the period from the exile to the time of Jesus, the Hebrew terms for justice and their Greek translations retained the same connotations which we find in the early period.[10] Justice is associated with mercy (Sir 44:10), goodness of heart (Wis 1:1), and truth (Wis 5:6). During the inter-

---

[6] The development of this view lived on in both Judaism and Christianity. In Judaism it produced a large system of care for the poor in the community. In the New Testament it is mirrored in the view of the relation of faith and works in the Letter of James where true faith demands acts of charity (Jas 2:16-17).

[7] Cf. J.R. DONAHUE, «Biblical Perspectives», 68-112, here 84-85.

[8] Realism characterizes Israel's view of justice. Injustice is not simply a bad moral attitude but a social cancer which destroys society and a physical force which can bring chaos to the goods of the earth. At the same time biblical thought has a dialectical counter to the naive view of Proverbs 11 that the unjust suffer and the just prosper. Job lived a just life and yet he suffers. He is restored when he discards his claim on God's justice and accepts it as gift (Job 42:10-17). To live justly is to recognize that life is a gift even in the face of loss and destructiveness.

[9] Cf. J.R. DONAHUE, «Biblical Perspectives», 70-78.

[10] Cf. A. CRONBACH, «Righteousness», 85-91.

testamental period, reflection on the call to be just before the Lord, coupled with a growing awareness of the transcendence of God, led to a theology where God alone is just (Sir 18:2) and that man alone is devoid of justice (Sir 5:8).

Allied to the individualization of justice is the rise of the motif of suffering as a sign of justice. In the Old Testament the command was to remain faithful to the covenant God amid suffering and see God's saving power as the vindication of his justice. In the inter-testamental period suffering itself became a sign of a just person. This emphasis culminates in the Book of Wisdom. Here the unjust «lie in wait for the righteous man» who reproaches them for sins against the law. The just man reproves their thoughts because he «opposes our actions» (2:12). The unjust plan to test the just one with torture and put him to death (2:18-20). However, the death of the just one will vindicate God's justice, since «the righteous man who has died will condemn the ungodly who are living» (4:16). At the final judgment the vindication of the suffering just man will take place (5:1).[11]

In the Wisdom writings of the Second Temple period, Sirach knows the demand for justice, the threat of judgment upon economic injustice, and God's special preference for the poor (4:9; 21:4-5, 8). Furthermore, Sirach has an acute sense of the dilemma of business ethics: the desire for wealth leads to sinful business practices, which in turn brings inevitable destruction (26:29 - 27:3; 31:5-6).

When speaking of the Exodus event, Sirach describes Moses and Aaron as «illustrious men» who merit praise and imitation. They stand as models who show clearly to all nations the benefits of Wisdom (45:1-22). For Sirach, the revelatory experience of the Exodus is neither individualistic nor subjective but rather cosmological.[12] As we have seen, Sirach

---

[11] It is in the inter-testamental period that we see the emergence of the motif of the true justice of God being manifest only at the end time by a final judgment of God. The just will be vindicated and the deeds of evil persons will come to light (Sir 16:11-14). This conjunction of justice and suffering may have provided a background for the Pauline idea of the cross as a stumbling block (I Cor 1:23) as well as a manifestation of the saving justice of God (Rom 4:25). Cf. J.C. BEKER, *Paul*, 16-18.

[12] J.L. Segundo sees the post-exilic Wisdom tradition as becoming «[...] more individualistic, inner-directed, and apolitical [...]», and he questions the Wisdom tradition's «[...] more spiritualistic and subjective interpretation of the Exodus event». Segundo has directly questioned the usefulness of the Wisdom tradition for liberation theology. His charge of becoming individualistic and apolitical, which may apply to

understands the revelation of the Torah as the dwelling of Wisdom in Israel (24:13). The commandments of Moses reveal the ordering principle of creation and allow the wise to live in harmony with the order of the universe. As the dwelling of Wisdom in Israel, the Torah articulates the demand for justice which is built into creation itself. This correlation of Wisdom and Torah allows for a genuine knowledge of God throughout the earth, for Wisdom is everywhere (24:6). It also gives a cosmological grounding to «the Law which Moses enjoined on us» (24:23).

What is significant about the Book of Wisdom is its development of the potential we discovered in the earlier tradition for a political critique of injustice. Lady Wisdom is closely associated with «avenging justice» who spares no one who «gives voice to injustice» (Wis 1:8). The Book of Wisdom presents itself as an explicitly political document, a message from King Solomon to the other rulers on earth (1:1; 6:1, 4-6). The opening line proclaims its central call: «Love righteousness, you rulers of the earth» (1:1). Lest there be any lingering doubt about the intended audience, the author reiterates: «[...] you monarchs, my words are directed, that you may learn Wisdom and not transgress» (6:9).[13] As with Sirach, Wisdom's interpretation of the Exodus is cosmological and a basis for just government. The disaster which befell Pharaoh and the Egyptians is a harsh warning of the avenging justice which threatens the rulers of every society. Wisdom broke the yoke of slavery by leading her people out from a nation of oppressors, bringing them through the deep waters of the Red Sea, and becoming to them a flame of guidance until they find a safe home (Wis 10:15-19). Whenever corruption creeps into the social sphere, Wisdom reproves and corrects, shouting in the streets and at the city gates, judging wrongdoing in robust and stinging terms (Prov 1:20-33). At the same time, she keeps on making all things new. Ultimately, we are assured in our

---

Qoheleth, does not offer an interpretation of the Exodus event. The two works of the later Wisdom tradition that do introduce the Exodus event are Sirach and the Book of Wisdom. Cf. J.L. SEGUNDO, *Liberation of Theology*, 111, 115.

[13] It is noteworthy that, in the Book of Wisdom, the problem of injustice in this world is resolved by means of an apocalyptic vision of judgment after death. The confidence of the older Wisdom tradition in Proverbs that justice would be done in this world appears to be under some strain, for the Book of Wisdom must look beyond the grave for a vindication of the just and wise. Nevertheless, the account of the history of Israel in Wisdom 10-19 does look to historical events as confirmation of the power of justice to avenge oppression in this world.

struggles. She will triumph over even the worst evil: «against Wisdom evil does not prevail» (Wis 7:30).

This perspective clearly possesses the potential for developing a political criticism of unjust practices and powers in society. While the ancient sages themselves had no sense of changing the social and political structures of Israelite society, they did reiterate the basic principle of justice upon which such change could be based. Injustice is inherently unstable and leads to its own destruction. Justice brings fulfilment and lasting prosperity because it is demanded by the very structure of the world in which we live. Although the Wisdom tradition could function among the upper classes as a guide to success, it could also offer a sharp criticism of the wealthy classes from within their own ranks.[14] Moreover, the Wisdom tradition was never limited to the upper classes; its origins and its appeal were rooted in the folk Wisdom of the people and the tradition is essentially universal in scope.[15] While Wisdom literature did find a home in the royal court and the upper classes of Israel, these circles were drawing upon a tradition that had existed on every level of society from the earliest times in Israel.[16]

---

[14] The association of the Wisdom teachers with the royal court in Jerusalem and with the upper classes in general has led some scholars to interpret the Wisdom tradition as fundamentally conservative. Cf. J. CRENSHAW, *Old Testament Wisdom*; R. GORDIS, «The Social Background», 81-92. Gordis argues that the Wisdom literature was fundamentally the product of the upper classes in society, who lived principally in the capital, Jerusalem, and that the upper classes were conservative in their outlook, satisfied with the status quo, and opposed to change. In a similar vein, Crenshaw stresses the «emphasis upon moderation» by the professional class of sages (p. 20). However, we have observed that Wisdom was the fruit of a tradition originally rooted in the mores of the family, tribe, and local community and hence, arguably, as old as society itself.

[15] While Wisdom literature did function in the royal court and the upper classes of Israel as counsel to the powerful and formation to the young, recent scholarship has stressed the broader and less affluent origins of the Wisdom tradition in families, clans, and local communities. R.N. Whybray in particular has argued against the assumption that Wisdom literature was produced by a professional class of sages paid by the wealthy. For Whybray, Wisdom was not the product or prerogative of any one class but formed part of the common cultural stock of Israel. Wisdom referred to simply a natural endowment which some persons possess in greater measure than others. As such it was not a static possession or set content to be learned but rather a natural shrewdness and ability to cope with life. Cf. R.N. WHYBRAY, *The Intellectual Tradition*.

[16] Recent studies have found substantial parallels between Wisdom and prophetic literature. Cf. J. FICHTNER, «Isaiah», 429-438; S. TERRIEN, «Amos», 448-455; J. WHEDBEE, *Isaiah and Wisdom*; H. WOLFF, *Amos the Prophet*. If the prophet and the sage

We have seen that the Wisdom focus in the New Testament continues many themes of the Hebrew and Jewish Wisdom tradition. Interpreting the ministry, death, and resurrection of Jesus in the context of the Wisdom tradition, seeing him as Wisdom's prophet and indeed as the human being Wisdom became, shows that the desire of God is clearly directed toward lifting injustice and social oppression and establishing right relations and harmony among people. As with Wisdom herself, it is scarcely possible to divorce Jesus from the path of justice. In Matthew Jesus says «seek first his [the Father's] kingdom and his righteousness» (6:33), and Jesus criticizes the scribes because they have neglected the weightier matters of the Law, «justice and mercy and faith» (23:23). Jesus' alliance with the marginalised of society, his compassion for those who suffer, his acts of healing and words of enlightenment, his rebuke of oppressive leadership, his seeking and finding the lost, and his encouragement of others to do likewise carve a footpath in history for those who would follow his way (Mt 5:1-11; 18:1-14; 26:6-15; Mk 1:32-45; 4:1-32; 10:13-16; Lk 5:40-44; 6:20-49; 10:29-37; 15:1-32).

In the teaching and practice of Jesus traditional Wisdom insight was made radical by the theology of the kingdom of God.[17] Jesus called for a radical change of heart, a *metanoia*, in the light of the imminent Reign of God. The kingdom of God finds expression in Jesus' own life and ministry, in his concern for the poor (Mt 5:3), the ill, the outcasts (Mt 5:4) and sinners (Mk 2:17). In associating with these groups Jesus is a parable of God's justice where mercy (*hesed*) and justice (*ṣedāqāh*) are not in opposition, but in paradoxical agreement. As the proclaimer of God's Kingdom, Jesus is the sacrament of God's justice in the world.

The attitude Jesus is calling for here is to go beyond abstract norms in our conduct to a way of relating because of our experience of God's own

---

share a common concern for justice and a common conviction that injustice will be punished, they do differ nonetheless in basing their appeals on different kinds of experience. Where the prophet appeals to the extraordinary experience of being specially called by God (Is 6, Jer 1, Ez 1, Hos 1, Amos 1; 7:14-16; Joel 1), the sage makes no claim of special experience but appeals to experience accessible to all and to the listener's own understanding and desire for well-being (see the repeated appeals in Proverbs 1-7 that Wisdom and virtue bring a full and happy life).

[17] As a symbol *kingdom* carries with it all the overtones of meanings it has in the Old Testament. Yahweh's rule and the establishment of justice are closely joined (Ps 97:1-2; 96:10). By identifying the advent of God's kingdom with his ministry and teaching, Jesus proclaims the advent of God's justice.

goodness. Jesus experiences his heavenly Father as acting in the same manner that he is exhorting his followers to act. Just as his Father acts benevolently toward his children rather than on the basis of a pre-judgment about their relative merits, so Jesus' listeners are urged to act toward one another.

In the Wisdom of Jesus, relationship to his Father is intimately linked to the practice of mercy (Lk 6:36). A Wisdom Christology springs from, and leads to, discipleship in the light of Jesus' life and message, his death and resurrection: «We proclaim Christ crucified [...] Christ the Power and the Wisdom of God» (I Cor 1:23-25). Like the figure of Wisdom in Proverbs 9, Jesus invites all to come and eat of his bread and drink of his wine. Like the wise person of Sirach 14, 20 who encamps near Wisdom's house and pitches a tent by her side, those who hear the message of Jesus are invited to choose lifelong companionship with him.

From this perspective, the conflict of Jesus with the Jewish and Roman authorities of his time reveals the relation of Wisdom to the ruling powers of every human society. The fate of Jesus, like that of the wise man in the Book of Wisdom, is a critical judgment upon the powerful of every age who ignore the call of Lady Wisdom to practise justice.

What is needed is for us, under the influence of Wisdom Christology, to collaborate as a Wisdom community with God's struggle to resist evil and establish right order, the harmony of justice, in the world. The biblical Wisdom tradition is concerned with justice and with practical action in society, but realizes the impossibility of prescribing specific courses of action for all times. The Wisdom sayings of Israelite sages and of Jesus, the Wisdom of God, do not claim to make our concrete political decisions for us but offer us resources, the expression of others' insights and experiences, which help form our judgment and shape the perspective in which we decide our actions. Living Wisdom Christology the believing community walks the compassionate path of justice.

1.2 *The Significance of Wisdom for Feminist Concerns in Christology*

In our study of the work of Elizabeth Schüssler Fiorenza, we noted the essential characteristics of a feminist liberationist Christology.[18] It is

---

[18] Feminist Christology follows a liberationist hermeneutical method that has an analogue in the method described by J.L. Segundo in *The Liberation of Theology*. There, Segundo describes theology as progressing on the basis of the following logic: an experience of something wrong, an analysis and critique of Christian symbols insofar as

women's understanding of their situation in the world today that drives feminist theology generally and feminist Christology in particular. We shall not dwell on this since the issues involved have already been highlighted.[19] However, it is helpful to underscore aspects of its logical significance. First, feminist Christology is a Christology from below in several respects, and one is that it begins with experience. That experience is not merely Christian experience narrowly conceived, but the general experience of people in society: secular experience. For some that experience is a negative one. As well as reacting against this negativity, there is also a drive by some feminist theologians to redress the situation taking the form of a positive reconstruction of what Jesus Christ means.

Second, feminist Christology undertakes a critical analysis and appraisal of how traditional Christology is implicated in the negative situation of «patriarchy and sexism».[20] The conclusion drawn is that the negative experience of women and more generally those who suffer from

---

they contribute to the negativity, a search for biblical sources for a renewed interpretation, and with their help a theological reconstruction. Cf. J.L. SEGUNDO, *Liberation of Theology*, 7-9. Applying this logic to a feminist approach to Christology, a first stage, for feminist theologians, consists in a recognition of the negative situation that requires a feminist Christology, a second is an analysis of how traditional Christology is perceived to be implicated in sexism and patriarchy, while a third stage is a constructive Christology in response to the situation.

[19] Cf. pages 296-299.

[20] The argument regarding Christology's connection with sexism can be reduced to two points. Both have to do with Jesus being male. First, it is argued, Jesus' maleness has been allowed by both theologians and general consciousness to define the nature of God as male, which is detrimental of women because it reinforces patriarchy. It is argued that it indicates, if not an identification, then more of an affinity between maleness and divinity than is the case with femaleness. However, neither Scripture nor the theological tradition support the exclusive application of male images and names for God. The Eleventh Council of Toledo in 675, for example, speaks of the Son being begotten «from the womb of the Father». Furthermore, the Fourth Lateran Council in 1215 definitively expressed the necessary but limited nature of our language about God in terms of there being a greater dissimilarity than similarity between Creator and creature. Cf. J. NEUNER – J. DUPUIS, ed., *The Christian Faith*, 142-150, here 143 and 150. The second point is that the other side of Jesus' function as revealer of God involves Jesus' maleness coming to be regarded as the definition of what it means to be human. An androcentric anthropology, it is argued, is given religious sanction because a particular honour, dignity, and normativity accrues to the male sex because it was chosen by the Son of God for the enfleshment of Incarnation. Consequently, it is claimed, women are subordinated or excluded from what may be called a full human existence.

human oppression, together with the traditional christological construals, calls out for retrieval and re-appropriation.

Addressing this analysis involves a certain number of basic tasks that are intrinsic to the discipline of theology generally and have a particular bearing on Christology. First, a Christology listening to feminist concerns must plot its course between two false anthropological alternatives. One involves a theory of complementarity in which the two sexes complement each other. At the other extreme, we find a stress on the singularity of human nature that neglects the differences between the sexes and other differences among human beings generally. A balanced position must lie in a conception of human nature as one yet differentiated: «one human nature celebrated in an interdependence of multiple differences».[21] There is a complementarity between male and female which does not play down the differences between the sexes. The complementarity of the sexes is part of human nature.[22] This elementary conviction about the coincidence of unity and difference marking the human will allow such a Christology to integrate Jesus' maleness into a larger pattern of understanding. This might be considered a first step in a Christology listening to feminist concerns with the possibility of providing a framework for other issues of concern in feminist theology.

The second step is more concrete; it consists in a turn to the historical Jesus. Two dimensions will mark the treatment of the historical Jesus. The first is the telling of the story of Jesus of Nazareth; the second is the theoretical justification of why this consideration is essential to an understanding of the person of Jesus Christ and his message. Historical research provides the basis for a narrative Christology. Its method is to uncover the story of Jesus in history and then to correlate this story with the situation of the believing community today. It contains three moments: (i) telling the story in a vivid contemporary way; (ii) living the story, allowing the story to shape the community and individuals in it; (iii) theorizing about the story, and responding to the question of how God and the risen Jesus are present and alive in the faith community today.

The New Testament itself is vitally interested in the historical Jesus because he is the referent of christological faith. Generally, a failure to recognize the place of the historical Jesus in christological faith is due to a reaction against efforts to «ground», in the sense of «prove», Christian

---

[21] Cf. E.A. JOHNSON, *She Who Is*, 155.
[22] Cf. K. WOJTYLA (Pope John Paul II), *Love and Responsibility*, 21-44.

faith historically. However, a view that exalts an existential appreciation of Jesus over against the historical figure rests implicitly not on a distinction but on an illicit division between existential faith and its historical object who is a person of history. Epistemologically, the faith of the community is always accompanied by an historical memory image of Jesus that is the medium for the content of its faith.

The third major step in a Christology responding to feminist concerns may be called a theological reflection on the symbol of Christ. This is an extensive process which includes a consideration of the development of New Testament interpretations of Jesus. Constructing such a Christology consists in examining the development of the New Testament communities and their Christologies. Here we will underline a distinctive element of a feminist Christology, namely, a drawing out of the significance of the biblical symbol, Wisdom.[23]

The re-discovery of Wisdom Sophia can serve as a key by which a Christology responding to feminist concerns interprets Jesus. We have seen that, in addressing the theological significance of Lady Wisdom, it is the interpretation of Wisdom as the personification of God's own self in creative and saving involvement with the world which best describes Wisdom as divine and thus provides a female image for God without distorting the structure of Israel's faith and falling into the error of ditheism. We have seen the personification of Wisdom used extensively in the New Testament to interpret Jesus as the Christ, so much so that one of the New Testament Christologies proposes Jesus as the Incarnation of Wisdom. This interpretation gave Jesus cosmic significance and related him to the governance of the world; it linked God's saving action in Jesus with God's action in the past in Israel and in the whole world; it served as a vehicle for the development of an understanding of Jesus' divinity.

---

[23] The Wisdom tradition appears, initially, to be ambiguous for feminist reflection. The tradition shared and supported the patriarchal bias of its culture and tended to view women as either dangerous temptresses to male virtue or as helpful assistants to their husbands. Students of Wisdom are repeatedly warned against the seductive snares of alluring and adulterous women (Prov 5:2-6; 23:27-28). Women are viewed as a source of temptation and destruction (Prov 2:16-19; 5:20-23; 6:23-35; 22:14; Sir 9:1-9; 23:16-27; 25:21). When the sages praise women, it is usually because of their relationships to their husbands and children (Sir 25:2-3). The perfect wife of Proverbs 31:10-31 is exceedingly industrious and capable at home, but her diligence and competence allow her husband to participate in civic affairs at the city gates. Regarding the Gospel tradition, a presentation of Wisdom Christology as found in the Synoptics and the Gospel of John is presented in chapters four and five of this dissertation.

More specifically, Wisdom opens Christology to the use of female images to interpret Jesus Christ, thus enhancing our understanding of his already inclusive framework of relationships with human beings and with his Father.[24] Moreover, the feminine dimension of the symbol of Sophia deepens our appreciation of Jesus' gracious goodness, life-giving creativity, and passion for justice, as key hermeneutical elements in understanding the breath and depth of his mission to humanity. Wisdom enables retelling the story of Jesus and transforming the symbol of Christ to practical and critical effect.

Wisdom language evokes Sophia's characteristics from the Jewish Scriptures for Christian speech about the nature and mission of Jesus. This in turn allows us to retell the story of Jesus and here is where the gender of Wisdom becomes important. For symbols function to shape the believing community that uses them. Sophia, God's Wisdom as portrayed in a feminine way in the tradition, becomes a lens for interpreting the story of Jesus. Jesus' message of the reign of God proclaims the equality of all. Though the God of Israel was presented as a male Deity, aggressive in his anger and severe in his chastisements, yet he was also boundless in his love and was Mother as well as Father to his people. Like the psalmist, the Chosen People discovered the depth of his maternal peace: «But I have calmed and quieted my soul, like a child quieted at its mother's breast» (Ps 131). Jesus preached on behalf of all on the margins and was attentive to the negative position of women. In his ministry feminine metaphors are brought together to accommodate the mystery which the Incarnation enfolds.

---

[24] The idea of many names for God has not been absent from recent official Catholic teaching about God. In 1988, Pope John Paul II pointed to the anthropomorphism of biblical language for God, and to the importance of recognizing the limits of our analogies when we speak of God in male or female terms. Taking account of the Old Testament passages on God's motherly love, he finds in biblical anthropomorphic language a way of pointing indirectly to 'the mystery of the eternal «generating» which belongs to the inner life of God'. Generating however, he explains, is neither exclusively masculine nor feminine; it is both. Hebrew literature may have attributed male parenthood to the Godhead but since God is not man or woman, motherhood is as equally valid a category to describe the divine begetting as fatherhood is. John Paul then went on to direct attention to the ways in which the Scriptures speak of God in motherly images (Is 49:14-15; 66:13; Ps 131: 2-3) and to texts that describe God as carrying us within the womb, giving birth to us, and nourishing and comforting us (Is 42:14; 46:3-4). See the apostolic letter of John Paul II, Apostolic Letter *Mulieris Dignitatem*, n. 8. The text is found in *AAS* 80 (1988), 1653-1729.

Hence, a feminist Christology proceeds to describe Jesus in terms of Sophia incarnate, the Wisdom of God. Throughout his ministry, his compassionate and liberating words and deeds are the works of Wisdom re-establishing the right order of creation: «Wisdom is justified by her deeds» (Mt 11:19). In summary, Jesus was «named» Wisdom, and this opens up feminine imagery for understanding God and Jesus Christ. The move to retrieve and appropriate the symbol of Wisdom, and then to centre christological interpretation through this lens, contains a key which has the potential to provide a Christology responding to some feminist concerns.[25]

We have already affirmed that the Wisdom tradition is interested not only in God's mighty deeds in history but in everyday life with the give and take of its relationships. People connect with the holy mystery that surrounds their lives as they actually live in the world, in the non-heroic moments, in the effort to be decent and just, in anguish over suffering, in appreciating nature, in trying to work out relationships harmoniously, in the gift and struggle of the everyday - in this, as in the peak experiences of personal and community life. More specifically, the figure of personified Wisdom offers an augmented field of female metaphors with which to interpret the saving significance of Jesus the Christ.

Along with other forms of political and liberation theology, some feminist theologies criticize an interpretation of the death of Jesus as required by God in repayment for sin. They argue, rather, that Jesus' death was an act of violence brought about by threatened human beings, that it occurred historically in consequence of Jesus' fidelity to the deepest truth and love he knew, expressed in his message and behaviour. What becomes clear in the event, they suggest, is not Jesus' passive victimization divinely decreed as a penalty for sin, but rather a dialectic of disaster and powerful human love through which the gracious God of Jesus enters into solidarity with all those who suffer and are lost. From this point of view, the cross

---

[25] The christological doctrines, principally those of the Councils of Nicaea and Chalcedon, formulated in the philosophical and theological language of the time define the true divinity and the true humanity of Jesus. Consideration of the formation of these doctrines would normally be part of any Christology. In a Christology responding to feminist concerns they also provide the occasion to correct the error of assigning theological or soteriological significance to the maleness of Jesus. The issue that became prominent after the definition of the Nicene Creed concerned Christ's full and integral humanity, or so it came to be called, the human nature of Jesus, and not his maleness. Cf. J. NEUNER – J. DUPUIS, ed., *The Christian Faith*, 194-222.

in all its dimensions, violence, suffering, and love is the parable that enacts God's participation in the suffering of the world.

We have already focused on the place of the Wisdom theme in the writings of Paul.[26] We affirmed that the most explicit linguistic identification of Jesus with divine Wisdom in the writings of Paul occurs in the First Letter to the Corinthians. In the context of pre-Christian Jewish talk of divine Wisdom, we noted that what Paul is saying here is that the same divine Wisdom which was active in creation, Christians believe to have been active in Jesus. The creator God was himself acting in and through Christ. The distinctive character of divine Wisdom, we noted, is to be read off not from creation or in terms of speculative knowledge but from the cross (I Cor 1:18-25). What we see in Christ's life, death and resurrection is the very Wisdom and Power by which God created and sustains the world (I Cor 8:6). That divine Wisdom which shaped the world and established the covenant with Israel, and which had hitherto been seen as expressed most clearly in the Torah, is now to be recognized as most fully and finally manifested in Jesus the crucified and risen one. The cross is the icon of God's Wisdom. The «word of the cross» (I Cor 1:18) puts Christ himself at the centre of soteriology and everything else in Paul's teaching is oriented to this christocentric soteriology.

Moreover, in our treatment of John's Gospel, we affirmed that the focal point of Jesus' relationship with the Father is the love which passes between them. This is at the kernel of what the Son does and reveals (3:35; 5:20), and it is founded on the Son's eternal pre-existence (17:24-26). The Father's love for the Son can also be expressed as a response to the Son's work (10:17), an expression of the bond of love that exists between the Father and the Son, a bond involving the mission and obedient death of the Son.

Feminist theology, for the most part, has neglected to reflect on the paradox of the cross, folly to Wisdom humanly conceived but also God's folly that is at the same time God's Wisdom and Power. Much of feminist theology is more favourable to portrayals of the crucifixion as the death of a prophet-martyr than to interpretations of Jesus' death in the categories of atonement and redemption. Christ is the Wisdom of God precisely because he is the Power of God for the salvation of everyone who believes (I Cor 1:18-25).[27] We have already referred to Walter Kasper's argument

---

[26] See pages 100-109, 111-112.

[27] In chapter three we noted the argument of G.D. Fee that I Cor 1:24 is not a christological statement but a soteriological one. Cf. G.D. FEE, *First Epistle to the Corinthians*, 77.

that, within a freedom-orientated, historically conscious, and secular world, the cross emerges as the true Wisdom of God.[28] Wisdom Christology, as found in the Pauline corpus, can assist feminist theology to articulate a soteriology of the Wisdom / foolishness of the cross and to reclaim the doctrines of atonement and redemption.[29]

Christ crucified and risen, the Wisdom of God, manifests the truth that divine justice and renewing power leavens the world in a way different from the techniques of dominating violence. The victory of *shalom* is won not by the sword of the warrior god but by the awesome power of compassionate love, in and through solidarity with those who suffer. Guided by Wisdom categories, the story of the cross, rejected as passive and penal victimization, is reappointed as the life-giving power that radiates the self-sacrificing love that liberates others to a new and deeper understanding of life. The suffering accompanying such a life as Jesus led is neither passive nor useless but is linked to the ways of God forging justice and peace in a selfish and antagonistic world. As such, the cross is part of the larger mystery of pain-to-life, of that struggle for the new creation evocative of the rhythm of pregnancy, delivery, and birth (Rom 8:22-23). It is interesting to note that at the moment of final crisis Mary Magdalene, Mary the mother of James and Joseph, Salome, and «many other women» disciples (Mk 15:41) appear strongly in the story and in fact are the moving point of continuity between the ministry, death, burial, and resurrection of Jesus. Near or afar off they keep vigil at the cross, standing in a solidarity with this vilified victim that gives powerful witness to women's courage throughout the ages. Their presence is a sign of the Father's fidelity to the dying Jesus, their faithful friendship a witness to the fact that he is not abandoned. Having assisted at the burial, they know the path to the tomb. They are the first to encounter the risen Christ, to recognize what has happened, to receive the call to tell the good news to those of their circle in hiding. This they do: «Now it was Mary Magdalene, Joanna, Mary the mother of James, and the women with them who told this to the apostles» (Lk 24:10), persisting despite the ridicule and disbelief that was associated with the testimony of women as witnesses at that time.

---

[28] See pages 227-230.

[29] Cf. F.W. DILLISTONE, *Christian Understanding of Atonement*; C.J. DEN HEYER, *Doctrine of the Atonement*; D. WIEDERKEHR, *Belief in Redemption*; S.K. WILLIAMS, *Jesus' Death as Saving Event*.

Feminist hermeneutics has shown how the gospel story of Jesus resists being used to justify domination in any form. His preaching about the reign of God and his inclusive lifestyle lived and breathed the opposite, creating a challenge that brought upon him the wrath of religious and civil authority. When the story of Jesus is told in this way, a certain appropriateness accrues to the historical fact that he was male. If, in a culture of this kind, a woman had preached compassionate love and enacted a style of authority that serves, it is reasonable to presume that opposition would have been even more intense from the beginning.

When considered in this way, the cross is raised as a challenge to the view that domination is a source of authentic power in human relations. The crucified Jesus embodies the exact opposite and shows how steep the price is to be paid in the struggle for authentic liberation. The cross thus stands as a poignant symbol of the self-emptying of any dominating power in favour of a new humanity of compassionate service. On this reading, Jesus' maleness is prophecy announcing the end of domination, at least as divinely ordained.

In the light of the gospel theme of Jesus as the Wisdom of God, it becomes clear that the heart of the problem is not that Jesus was a man but that too many men have not followed his footsteps, insofar as domination may have defined their self-identity and relationships. Jesus' story of ministry, suffering, final victory, and new community signify love, grace, and *shalom* for everyone equally and for the outcast, including the women of his time.

Christology speaks not only of the story of the historical Jesus but of his saving significance and rootedness in God, typically summing up its insight in the confession that Jesus is the Christ. Using the female figure of personified Wisdom so influential in biblical Christology to speak about Jesus as the Christ affirms an inclusive interpretation of this symbol. In summary, a Wisdom Christology opens up feminine images for understanding God and Jesus Christ. The move to retrieve and appropriate the symbol of Wisdom, and then to centre christological interpretation through this lens, contain a key which has the potential to provide a Christology responding to some feminist concerns.

In conclusion, I suggest that the feminist implications of the Wisdom theme might be elaborated further by an exploration of the co-incidence and connections implicit in the notion of the Church as the Seat of Wisdom and the Bride of Christ as well as the Marian ecclesiology elaborated in *Lumen Gentium*, chapter eight. One of the obvious limitations of much of feminist theology has been its failure to consider the positive implications of the theology of the Church as the Bride of Christ (Jn 19:34) and other ecclesiological considerations and concepts including Mary as the type of the Church (*LG*, VIII, 63). The Wisdom theme in christological discourse disappeared, by and large, during the course of the Middle Ages. However, it re-emerged with Mary, captured by her title as the Seat of Wisdom.

Such an approach by feminist theology, together with a soteriology of the foolishness of the cross, would be faithful to the depth of Wisdom and Truth that is contained in the church's tradition and would thus avoid any risk of mere anthropology as the basis for a feminist Christology. Living Wisdom Christology, the community highlights the significance of Wisdom for some feminist concerns in Christology.

1.3 *Dialogue with Other Religions*

The challenge of religious pluralism is an important theological issue of our time. The encounter with other world religions has radically challenged Christianity's self-understanding and has raised questions about traditional Christian claims of revelation.[30] If the reality of God for

---

[30] *Nostra Aetate,* the Declaration on the Relationship of the Church to Non-Christian Religions (1965), was one of the last and shortest decrees to be issued by the Second Vatican Council. Its shortness, however, belies its significance. In many respects it gathers up theological principles from other documents and applies them to non-Christian religions. These principles include statements about the universality of God's grace in the world (*GS*, 22), the possibility of salvation outside the church (*LG*, 16), the existence of universal revelation (*DV*, 6), and knowledge of God through human experience (*DV*, 8, 14). These principles and others are woven together synthetically to give a positive evaluation of the other religions of the world. *Nostra Aetate* situates all religions in the context of the shared search for answers to ultimate questions about the meaning of existence, with particular reference to the origins and destiny of life. Many religions, and here the Declaration mentions explicitly Judaism, Islam, and Buddhism «often reflect a ray of that truth which enlightens all» and consequently a spirit of «dialogue and collaboration» should take place between Christians and the followers of other religions (art. 2). The document also talks about the special relationship that exists between the church and Muslims as well as the spiritual bond that obtains between Christians and Jews. Furthermore, the Decree *Ad Gentes* (1965) talks about «elements of grace and truth» as well as «seeds of the word in other religions» (arts. 9, 11, 15). While these statements may today appear rather general, they did at the time mark a watershed in the history of the church's approach to other religions. In particular, they paved the way for the acceptance of inter-religious dialogue as an integral part of Catholic life and mission (*DI*, 22). Hence, the positive appreciation of other religions

Christians is actively present throughout human experience in a wide variety of religious traditions, how then are Christians to understand the revelation of God experienced in Jesus Christ? This question is answered by working out a specifically Christian theology of religions affirming: (i) the full and complete revelation of the salvific mystery of God in Jesus Christ; (ii) the unicity of the salvific economy of the one incarnate Word, Jesus Christ, the only-begotten Son of the Father, highlighting a single trinitarian economy, willed by the Father and realized in the mystery of Christ by the working of the Holy Spirit; (iii) the source, centre, and fullness of salvation history in Jesus Christ; (iv) the continuing presence and salvific work of Jesus in the church and by means of the church, which is his body; (v) the intimate connection between Christ, the kingdom and the church; (vi) the real possibility of salvation in Christ for all mankind and the necessity of the church for this salvation (*RM*, 9).[31]

The biblical Wisdom tradition offers not a resolution of the questions raised by the encounter with other religions but rather suggests perspectives for approaching the encounter. In this era of the encounter with world religions and the inculturation of the gospel, it is encouraging to note that affirming the religious value of all God-seekers is characteristic of the Wisdom tradition. The Wisdom trajectory offers solid precedent for acknowledging a general activity of God throughout human experience and for correlating the universal activity of God with specific historical events of revelation. The sages of Israel recognised a genuine knowledge of God and a real grasp of Wisdom in non-Israelite traditions, and they were open to learning and borrowing from other Near Eastern traditions.[32]

given by the Second Vatican Council created a new context for Christology inviting it to enter into a respectful dialogue with other religions without losing contact with the substance of classical Christology.

[31] Cf. CONGREGATION FOR THE DOCTRINE OF THE FAITH, Declaration *Dominus Iesus: On the Unicity and Salvific Universality of Jesus Christ and the Church*; INTERNATIONAL THEOLOGICAL COMMISSION, *Christianity and the World Religions*. For those who are not formally members of the church, «salvation in Christ is accessible by virtue of a grace which, while having a mysterious relationship to the church, does not make them formally part of the church, but enlightens them in a way which is accommodated to their spiritual and material situation. This grace comes from Christ; it is the result of his sacrifice and is communicated by the Holy Spirit» (*RM*, 9).

[32] On the relation of Wisdom in Israel to the Wisdom traditions of Egypt and Mesopotamia, see H. DUESBERG – I. FRANSEN, *Les Scribes Inspirés*, 15-95; O.S. RANKIN, *Israel's Wisdom Literature*, 35-39; R.N. WHYBRAY, *Wisdom in Proverbs*, 53-71; A. WURTHWEIN, «Egyptian Wisdom», 113-131.

The Wisdom tradition focuses not so much on once-for-all deeds in history, although it remembers these, as on everyday, mundane life, being interested in personal and social relationships, in nature and its workings, in the meaning of human life, and in the anguishing problem of suffering. Here is where God is manifested; arguably for many it is the primary way. Wisdom is given to anyone who searches out the divine order of creation in order to live in harmony with it. An example here is the Logos theme of Greek philosophy as the principle of order in the universe, an appreciation of which could be achieved through the wisdom of natural reason alone. This, of course, became the basis, in its own right, of the Logos Christology tradition typified by the prologue of John's Gospel. Perhaps significantly, Wisdom is not exclusive to Israel but has an affinity with the insights of the sages of Egypt and other advanced cultures of the ancient Near East. As a result, the sages tend to talk not so much about the «God of Israel» or the «God of our fathers» as about the Creator of the whole world whose Spirit is present and active everywhere.

The sapiential themes of trust in the rhythms and natural order of life and the awareness of the limits of all human understanding combine to encourage dialogue and mutual exchange between different traditions. Since the sages base their claims on experience that is open to all humans, it is possible for representatives of different sapiential traditions to find a common ground for discussion.[33] Since Lady Wisdom's activity is universal, it is possible for non-Israelites to respond to her invitation and receive her gift of insight and understanding (Prov 8:3-36; 9:1-6; Sir 24:19-21; Wis 6:14, 16). Thus, representatives of various sapiential traditions can acknowledge one another's genuine insights into the meaning of experience.

On the other hand, the sages' insistence on the limits of all human claims of Wisdom undercuts any claim to have understood totally the meaning of experience or the patterns of God. For example, the necessity of discerning the time for the application of a particular proverb implies an awareness that every human perspective is limited and every insight is partial and time-bound. Thus in approaching dialogue with other traditions, representatives of the biblical Wisdom tradition do not claim either to have definitively understood the mystery of God, notwithstanding

---

[33] For an introduction to the use of Wisdom in the Byzantine tradition see A. LOUTH, «Sophiology of Fr. Sergei Bulgakov», 169-181; T. SCHIPFLINGER, «Sophia According to the Russian Sophiologists», 247-280.

the claim to possess the definitive revelation of God in Jesus Christ. The trust in experience and the recognition of human limits did not eliminate the sages' acknowledgment of the revelation offered by Lady Wisdom. It was in ordinary human experience that Lady Wisdom made her call, and it was in the limits of human understanding and control that the sages gained a sense of the power and incomprehensibility of the Absolute Transcendent.

Moreover, as we have seen, the Wisdom tradition itself includes a variety of competing perspectives. Not only does the Wisdom tradition represent a distinct form within the religion of Israel, it includes a pluralism within its own development. Job and Qoheleth challenge the basic presuppositions of the accessibility of Wisdom, the intelligibility of the patterns of experience, and the graciousness of God. The Wisdom tradition of Israel reaches for descriptions of universal human experience, but it repeatedly avoids the claim to have completely understood the mystery of God or to have articulated universal human experience. By juxtaposing alternate perspectives, the sages challenged their students to recognise in their discernment the complexity of human experience and the perpetual call to understand what has been revealed.

The Wisdom tradition in general and the figure of Lady Wisdom in particular offer intriguing possibilities for discussion in the encounter with other religions. Many cultures have a tradition analogous to the biblical Wisdom tradition.[34] As part of the Bible, this universalizing Wisdom tradition reflects a genuine and primary element of biblical faith in all its integrity. Lady Wisdom symbolizes God's presence moving throughout the whole world, not just in Israel. This renders the Wisdom tradition particularly helpful to contemporary theological efforts seeking to find ways of respecting other world religious traditions, of entering into dialogue with them, and even learning from them and also drawing the discriminating line that separates them, allowing room for positive distinction, so necessary for progress. For while these religious traditions

---

[34] Similarities have been noted between various geographical and biblical proverbs. The image of Lady Wisdom as the ordering power of the universe bears analogies to such widely separated concepts as the Logos in Greek, *rta* in India (Cf. M. ELIADE, *A History of Religious Ideas*. I, 201), *dharma* in Hinduism and Buddhism (Cf. J.Y. FENTON, ed., *Religions of Asia*, 29), and the *Tao* in China (Cf. T. MERTON, *Mystics and Zen Masters*, 72). These concepts clearly are not to be identified, but they do offer analogous ranges of meaning that can provide an entry-point into inter-religious dialogue.

do not share in the particularity of Israel's salvation history, their own paths of holiness and «rays of truth» (*NA*, 2) nonetheless reflect the truth and holiness of God to be found in natural wisdom rather than in privileged sources of revelation.

The Wisdom tradition thus posits a real continuity as well as a discontinuity of divine action between Christian and Jewish religions and the multitude of world religions.[35] Interpreting the meaning of Jesus in this context, allowing it to fertilize and guide our understanding, highlights the universal and missionary intent inherent in his ministry, death, and resurrection. Jesus, the Wisdom of God, personally incarnates Wisdom's gracious care in one particular history for the benefit of all, while Wisdom provides a multiplicity of paths in diverse cultures along which all people may find resonances of her presence.

The interpretation of Jesus as the Incarnation of Lady Wisdom in the New Testament served to universalize the claims of Christianity. By presenting Jesus Christ as the Wisdom of God, the Logos through whom all things were made, the New Testament writers were claiming that the religious dimension implicit in all human experience has been revealed in a definitive and unsurpassable way in the life, death, and resurrection of Jesus Christ. This interpretation makes possible a limited knowledge of God in other religious traditions through the presence of natural wisdom, while at the same time holding to a definitive and normative preeminence for the revelation of God experienced in Jesus Christ. The claim that there is Wisdom or Logos at the heart of creation holding all things together implies a fundamental intelligibility in reality and human experience. The claim that Lady Wisdom or the Logos has been revealed in Jesus Christ implies that the ordering power of creation can only be fully interpreted and understood in light of the revelation of Jesus Christ.[36]

The paradoxical intertwining of the themes of intelligibility and incomprehensibility in Wisdom Christology offers principles for a possible approach to inter-religious dialogue. The reality of God for Christians is a universal reality who cannot be confined to the limits of any area or period of the history of humankind or the cosmos. Indeed if Jesus

---

[35] Cf. J. RATZINGER, *Called to Communion*, 32.

[36] This facilitates an answer to the difficulty raised by *Dominus Iesus* concerning those who «[...] put great stress on the mystery of creation, which is reflected in the diversity of cultures and beliefs, but [...] keep silent about the mystery of redemption». Cf. *DI*, 19.

Christ is the revelation of God, then this revelation possesses significance for all human history, indeed for the entire cosmos. However, even the rhythm and natural order of the cosmos possess an inevitable incomprehensibility which, of itself, has the potential, at least, to open the question of God to human reason.

In this spirit, Wisdom Christology directs the community of disciples toward global perspectives and ecumenical actions deeply respectful of other religious faiths.[37] At the same time it affirms our understanding regarding the full and complete revelation of the salvific mystery of God in Jesus Christ who through the event of his Incarnation, death, and resurrection has brought the history of salvation to fulfilment for the benefit of all.[38] It is a central dimension of Christian faith that God's self-communication and universal will to save are decisively, uniquely, gratuitously, and irrevocably expressed in Jesus of Nazareth, in his life, death, and resurrection. However, we ourselves because we are limited and finite human beings, historically conditioned and subject to error, cannot always grasp the totality of the Divine. Our reception of what is revealed can be inconsistent in terms of understanding. Augustine reminds us that if we have fully understood, then it is no longer God. It is within this framework that Christians can recognize that divine Wisdom may well be present, though not in any new way, in other religious traditions.[39] Certainly, other religious traditions «contain and offer religious elements which come from God» (*AG*, 11; *NA*, 2; *DI*, 21) and are part of what «the Spirit brings about in human hearts and in the history of peoples, in cultures, and religions» (*RM*, 29; *DI*, 21). Living Wisdom Christology, the community walks the appreciative path of respect for and dialogue with other religious traditions in the world.

1.4 *Ecological and Environmental Responsibility*

A Wisdom Christology invites reflection on the significance of the Incarnation for an ecological vision of the world. We begin with the faith

---

[37] Cf. R.S. SUGIRTHARAJAH, «Wisdom», 42-46.

[38] Cf. *DI*, 5-8, 13-15.

[39] Cf. *AG*, 7, *RM*, 29, *DI*, 21.The Australian theologian, Denis Edwards, has highlighted the invitation to Australian Christians to listen to the teaching of Aboriginal religious traditions concerning the sacredness of the land. He argues that here an Australian Christian has to be in apprenticeship to the Aboriginal religious view of the land, listening to hear a word of divine Wisdom. He has developed this argument in chapter one of his book *Called to be Church in Australia*.

understanding that Jesus Christ, God's Word made flesh, is «[...] our Wisdom, our righteousness, our sanctification, and redemption» (I Cor 1:30). This means that ultimately we shall find our salvation, including our ecological salvation, in God's grace. It is appropriate to approach the ecological question from a christological centre and on a biblical basis. If we believe we have a decisive divine disclosure in the flesh of Jesus Christ, and in his life, death, and resurrection, the decisive appearance of God's reign, then all our theological thought, including our ecological theology, needs to be governed in him.

We aim to show that a theology of Jesus as divine Wisdom can undergird a Christian approach to ecology and form the basis for a cosmic Christology.[40] Interpreting the ministry, death, and resurrection of Jesus by means of the Wisdom tradition orients Christology beyond the human world to the ecology of the earth and indeed the whole universe, a vital move in this era of planetary plundering.[41] As the model of Sophia who is the fashioner of all that exists, Jesus Christ's redeeming care extends to the flourishing of all creatures and the living planet itself. The cosmic Christology of the New Testament, evocatively expressed in Wisdom

---

[40] The quest of the cosmic Christ has been brought to the fore by the emergence of a new cosmic consciousness concerning the immensity and antiquity of the universe we live in. The last number of decades has seen a series of significant developments which raise questions either explicitly or implicitly about the relationship of Christ to the cosmos. These developments include the emergence of creation-centred theologies, the promotion of a new dialogue between science and religion, the re-discovery of the importance of cosmology, as well as the recognition of an ecological crisis. What is the relationship of the Incarnation to creation? Can Christian faith engage in a meaningful dialogue with the new stirrings in science? Is the care of the earth a purely practical expedient or a Christian responsibility rooted in the Incarnation? How can we move towards some appreciation of the cosmic significance of the Incarnation? Cf. I. BRADLEY, *God is Green*; G. DALY, *Creation and Redemption*; D. EDWARDS, *Jesus and the Cosmos*; S. MCDONAGH, *To Care for the Earth*; ID., *The Greening of the Church*; ID., *Greening the Christian Millennium*; J. Moltmann, *The Way of Jesus Christ*.

[41] This is a main theme of ecological theology: the criticism of «anthropocentrism», the de-centring of the human, and so the insistence that humanity as such is not the goal of all things, or the crown of creation. A certain credibility gap exists about a human-centred universe, given what the geologists and astronomers are telling us about the age of the planet and the cosmos. After all, it was only 600 million years ago that mammals became prominent on the earth, and thirty-five million years since our ancestors the higher primates appeared. Humanity has existed for perhaps just two or three hundred thousand years, a mere blink of God's eye in the fifteen billion years or so since the so-called «big bang».

categories, makes this quite evident.[42] A Wisdom Christology can begin to show the interrelation between the expanding, interconnected, and self-organizing universe and all its creatures, and the saving work of Jesus Christ. The concern with justice, which we have examined, is also connected with Wisdom's role in creation. Hers is the power to arrange the whole universe into a harmony: she reaches from end to end of the world, and orders all things prudently and well (Wis 8:1). When disorder breaks out Wisdom works to deliver and preserve life and to restore the right order of things.

Anyone reading the newspapers today will become alarmed by what we are hearing from various scientific communities regarding possible global climate change, the rapid disappearance of thousands of biological species, the vast destruction of forests, the creation and expansion of deserts, the depletion of the ozone layer of the atmosphere.[43] We have been affected in recent years by droughts, famines, mass starvation, great floods and forest fires, unheard-of ice storms, and increasing numbers of hurricanes and tornados; many of these may be linked to global warming. A grave crisis of the earth's environment exists and we urgently need an ecological vision of the world which will empower us to reverse our political and economic priorities.[44]

----

[42] One of the major points of reference for understanding and interpreting Jesus is creation. The New Testament abounds with references to principalities and powers, heaven and earth, angels and spirits, stars and clouds, above and below, all of which are symbols of one kind or another referring to the cosmic context of the Christ-event. One of the principal horizons of New Testament Christology is creational and such exists in stark contrast to the horizon of christological thinking from the seventeenth century to the present. The missing link in modern Christology has been the absence of a living cosmology. The emergence of a new cosmic story today is a challenge and an opportunity to redress this imbalance, not at the expense of a necessary anthropological and ecclesiological emphasis but to their mutual benefit.

[43] Cf. S. MCDONAGH, *To care for the Earth*, 17-103; ID., *The Greening of the Church*, 9-106; ID., *Greening the Christian Millennium*, 62-118.

[44] A consideration here is the historical claim implicit in much ecological thought that the Bible, and especially Western Christianity, is fundamentally responsible for the environmental crisis. A famous critique came from Lynn White in a much quoted essay. He suggested in 1967 that «the historical roots of our ecological crisis» are to be found in the Judaeo-Christian doctrine of creation. He argued that, more specifically, these roots lie in the belief that man was made in God's image and shares in God's transcendence of nature, and that the whole natural order was created for the sake of humanity. Cf. L. WHITE Jr., «The Historical Roots of our Ecological Crisis», 1203-1207. Needless to say, White has been challenged from many directions. We cannot enter into

In this era when scientific discoveries awaken our wonder at the intricacies of the universe and its history, while at the same time the human race wreaks devastation on ecological systems and their living inhabitants, it is challenging to note that interest in and love for the world of nature is an inherent characteristic of the biblical Wisdom tradition. Its interest lies in the right order of creation, which it finds expressed in human lives lived justly amidst the ever-beautiful natural world, both ideally forming a harmonious whole. In Proverbs we find Wisdom, who is the first-created, describing herself as a partner with God in the work of creation (8:22-31); then we are told that she has made her home among us, prepares a great feast for us, and invites the simple to come to her table (9:1-6). Here two great themes are interconnected: Wisdom's role in the vastness of cosmic creation, and Wisdom's simple and homely presence among human beings. These interconnected themes are found in a developed way in Sirach where Wisdom, who makes her home among us, is identified with Torah (24:3-23). In the Book of Wisdom we find both an exalted view of Wisdom's role in creation and a more mysterious and personal theology of Wisdom's presence to human beings (7:25-28). In this text Wisdom is understood as the divine presence working in continuous creation throughout the universe. So we find the author saying of Wisdom that «while remaining in herself, she renews all things» (7:27), and «she reaches mightily from one end of the earth to the other and orders all things well» (8:1).

Personified Wisdom is called the mother of all these good and intricate things, responsible for their existence and therefore knowing their inmost secrets (Wis 7:12). She exists before the beginning of the world and acts as the master craftswoman through whom all things were made. The great creation poem in Proverbs 8:22-31 depicts her playing with delight in the newly created world, and playing among new human creatures who are a

---

this complex debate here, but a voluminous amount of historical and theological literature exists on the topic. Certainly it is inappropriate for Christians to simply plead innocence. Christians, including theologians, share guilt in this matter. At the same time, theologians need to avoid exaggerated self-criticism which reflects an unseemly self-importance, taking on more than their share of responsibility for the evils of the world. The theory of Christian culpability has been substantially criticized by both historical and biblical scholars. The upshot of the debate seems to be that the theory bears some important insight, but in itself is too simple. Cf. R. BOOTH FOWLER, *The Greening of Protestant Thought*, 72; R. RADFORD RUETHER, *Gaia and God*, 22-31; A. SIMPKINS, *Creator and Creation*, 4, 6, 36, 156.

part of this great design. This portrait of Wisdom's creative agency «in the beginning» is completed by affirmations of her continuing presence. For Wisdom reaches mightily from one end of the world to the other, ordering all things well. Her spirit, which is characterized as holy, intelligent, more mobile than any motion, all-powerful and beneficent, pervades all things, weaving connections and holding everything together.

It is clear from the Scriptures that divine Wisdom speaks of the self-communication of God in and through creation. Wisdom is present with God at creation as a skilled co-worker (Prov 8:30; Wis 7:22; 8:6). Yet Wisdom takes delight in human beings (Prov 8:31). She «has built her house» among them and invites them all to her feast (Prov 9:1-6). Wisdom revealed in the marvels of creation now makes her home among humanity. This biblical structure was a wonderful resource for the early Christian communities as they reflected on God's action in Jesus of Nazareth. They could see Jesus as the Wisdom of God, present and active in all of creation, pitching a tent among them on earth.

We have already affirmed a clear reference to Jesus as the Wisdom of God in I Corinthians 1:22-24: «For the Jews, demand signs and the Greeks seek Wisdom, but we preach Christ crucified, a stumbling block for the Jews and folly to the Gentiles, but to those who are called, both Jew and Gentile, Christ the Power of God and the Wisdom of God». For Paul, Jesus is the Wisdom of God and this identification of Jesus with the Wisdom of God links Jesus with the cosmic role of Wisdom in the Hebrew scriptures which we have seen it to be one of creating, caring, and ordering the world and the affairs of history. Further on in I Corinthians, Paul explicitly attributes to Jesus the creative role of Wisdom: «Yet for us there is one God, the Father, from whom are all things and for whom we exist, and one Lord Jesus Christ, through whom are all things and through whom we exist» (I Cor 8:6).

A further three New Testament texts that directly link Jesus Christ with the work of creation are also part of the Wisdom tradition. In the Letter to the Hebrews we find Jesus understood as «the reflection of God's glory and the exact imprint of God's very being». As such, he is the one «through whom» the universe is created (Heb 1:2), and «he sustains all things by his powerful word» (1:3). This echoes the language of the Book of Wisdom, where Wisdom is the reflection and the image of God's goodness (7:26). The concept of Christ as the image of the invisible God is taken up in the hymn to Christ in Colossians 1:15-20 which is the supreme celebration of Christ's role in creation.[45] Here Jesus Christ is presented as the «image of God», the firstborn, the one *in* (v. 15), *through* (v. 16) and *for* (v. 16) whom all things were created, the one in whom all things hold together, and the one through whom God will reconcile all things. Again, the risen Christ is understood in Wisdom terms as the image of God, in that he is both the pattern from which all things are created and the agent through which they are created. The hymn praises Christ as the firstborn from the dead, the one through whose blood the whole universe is reconciled. By thus connecting the crucified Lord with Sophia, the agent and mediator of creation, this text attributes cosmic significance to the history of Jesus. What is instructive about this early Wisdom Christology of the New Testament is the insistent reference to creation as the primary context for understanding the universal significance of the Christ event. Creation, we are told, cannot be understood apart from Jesus Christ. In him we have the disclosure of creation's hidden source, meaning, and destiny. Moreover, in this text it is clearly not only human beings but all things (*ta panta*) which have their peace in Christ and his cross.[46]

In this Colossians text and others (I Cor 8:6, Eph 1:10) Christ is ascribed an immanent cosmic role like that of *Sophia* in the Wisdom literature. Christ's power and Wisdom permeates and fills all things (Eph 4:10). The immanent power of God that providently guides the universe is identified with Christ. What we have to note here is not only the divinity of the exalted Christ, but the constant reference to «all things» (*ta panta*).

---

[45] The cosmic scope of the Colossians Christology is brought out sharply by the use of three different strategies to describe the universal meaning of Christ. First, there is the often-repeated expression «all things». All things were created «in him» according to the first stanza (1:16) and «reconciled to himself» according to the second (1:20). Second, there is the use of the standard expression for the whole of creation: everything «in heaven and on earth» is both created in Christ and reconciled in him. Third, there is the specification of the fact that the cosmic powers are created in him: thrones, dominions, rulers, and powers. Colossians is claiming that everything is «in Christ» and there are no exceptions. Cf. J. GNILKA, *Der Kolosserbrief*; E. LOHSE, *Commentary on the Epistles to the Colossians and to Philemon*.

[46] J. Moltmann draws the startling conclusion that «[...] If Christ has died not merely for the reconciliation of human beings, but for the reconciliation of all other creatures too, then every created being enjoys infinite value in God's sight, and has its own right to live; this is not true of human beings alone [...] And it is this that provides the foundation for an all embracing reverence for life.» Cf. J. MOLTMANN, *The Way of Jesus Christ*, 256.

The saving work of Jesus Christ pertains not only to humans and certainly not only to human souls, but to all creatures.

Furthermore, in Colossians 1:15-20 there is a clear movement of thought between the two stanzas: it flows from creation to redemption. The first stanza is concerned with the creation of all things in Christ, while the second stanza celebrates the reconciliation of the universe in Christ. The rest of creation cannot be seen merely as the stage on which the drama of human redemption is played out. The Colossians hymn insists that the whole universe is caught up in the Christ event.

What does the Wisdom Christology of Colossians say to our ecological and cosmological concerns?

First, all creation is directed towards Jesus Christ and will find its fulfillment in him. Colossians tells us that all things not only have been created «in him» but also «through him»,
and «for him» (1:16). All things are created toward Christ - in this way not only the statements about the origin of creation are summarized, but also the goal of creation is indicated: creation finds its goal in Christ alone.

Second, if Jesus is the Wisdom of God, then in him, in his words and deeds, in his life, death, and resurrection, the mystery of God's purpose and work in creation is revealed. Divine, cosmic Wisdom is revealed in Jesus who was filled with a sense of the divine compassion and concerned with new familial relationships within creation and with the Creator. Furthermore, the Wisdom at work in creation finds ultimate expression as compassionate love in the radical vulnerability of the cross. *This* is the Wisdom of God at work in creation and salvation.

Third, this means that we must see the crucified and risen Jesus as achieving a radically new relationship with the universe. The power of resurrection is at work in creation, in a work which is not yet complete, not yet reached its goal of transfiguration in Christ. Fourth, the material universe, then, is not a stage on which human beings play out their relationship with God. The material universe itself will be transformed in the power of the risen Christ. The resurrection promise embraces not just human beings but the whole of creation. The bodily resurrection of Jesus is the promise and the beginning of the reconciliation of «all things». Whether «on earth or in heaven» through the blood of the cross (Col 1:20), there will be the uniting of all things in Christ, «things in heaven and things on earth» (Eph 1:10), and «a new heaven and a new earth» (Rev 21:1).

In the Letter to the Ephesians we find a cosmic Christology like that of Colossians 1:15-20 but expressed in a succinct and summary form in a one-sentence description of the mystery of God's plans: «[...] a plan for the fullness of time, to unite all things in him, things in heaven and things on earth» (1:10). In the prologue of John's Gospel we find another great hymn to Christ, again linking Christ to the whole of creation: «all things were made through him, and without him was not anything made that was made» (1:3). The structure of the prologue follows the structure of the Wisdom hymns which celebrate Wisdom as God's companion in creation who now makes her home among us. Like Wisdom, the Word was with God in creation and now pitches a tent among us. We have seen the close parallels in the Wisdom literature not only for the structure of the Logos hymn, but also for almost every detail of the prologue's description of the Word.[47] These New Testament Christologies, situated in the context of creation, are a challenge to modern Christology to deepen and extend its cosmic implications especially in this time of ecological crisis. A further aspect arising out of the conversation between cosmology and Christology is the need to widen the terms of reference in the dialogue. Christological references to creation, in both the New Testament and subsequent theology, will have to begin to include not only the earth inhabited by human beings but also the whole of the universe.

Throughout the Gospels Jesus is presented as a lover of all God's creatures. When in the desert Jesus was tempted for forty days; we are told that he was «with the wild beasts» (Mk 1:13). Is this, for example, not an allusion to his redemptive significance for the beasts? More significantly, Jesus is depicted as the preacher of the coming Reign of God, the

---

[47] John 1:14 tells us that «the Word became flesh» (sarx). John is telling us that, in Jesus, the Holy One of Israel has become truly enfleshed deep within the creaturely order. Of course Jesus, as flesh, is human. But the text affirms, significantly, the unity of the divine Word and Wisdom not only with humanity, but also with all flesh. In the Incarnation of Jesus Christ, God has shared the life and joy, vulnerability and dying, of all creatures. In the flesh of Christ, God has shared the exuberance and delight in life which all creatures enjoy, but also the pain and misery - the persecution and murder of the Jew, the humiliation of the colonized and the slave, the execution of the innocent victim, and the natural suffering, disability and death of all human beings. But more than that: in the flesh of Christ, God has participated in the life, suffering, and mortality of all living creatures. J. Moltmann has expressed this poignantly: «He died in solidarity with the whole sighing creation, human and non-human - the creation that "sighs" because it is subjected to transience. He died the death of everything that lives.» Cf. J. MOLTMANN, The Way of Jesus Christ, 69.

eschatological prophet who announces the Reign which will transform the world. It is the reign of his *Abba*, who knows when a sparrow falls (Mt 10:29), who feeds the birds of the air, who adorns the lilies and who clothes the grass of the field (Mt 6:26-30). Jesus sees these little creatures as the objects of God's tender care. The yeast and the mustard tree that shelters the birds are dignified as teachers of the nature of God's rule. Neither must we forget Jesus' healing of human bodies, these bodies of ours by which we are integrally part of the whole physical order. The apocalyptic expectation of Jesus and of his early followers was not only for their souls to go to heaven, but for the resurrection of their bodies together with the transformation of God's dearly beloved earth. Jesus loved and cherished God's good creation and expected its transformation and salvation.

Wisdom Christology is a bridge to the theology of Incarnation, but it is also a bridge to a creation Christology.[48] A Wisdom Christology holds together a theology of creation and Incarnation. A Wisdom Christology sees creation and Incarnation as intrinsically connected in the one divine plan, while still insisting that the Incarnation was a totally free act of God and that redemption was necessary. In this view, there can be no separation of creation and redemption, no theology of creation independent of a theology of Incarnation, and no theology of Incarnation and redeeming grace not related to the created world. The intrinsic connection is fundamental to the structure of Wisdom thought. Divine Wisdom is, by definition, God's presence and self-expression. God communicates God's self through divine Wisdom; Wisdom is present in all creation and has built herself a home among us in Jesus Christ. Wisdom, God's companion and helper in creation, becomes incarnate in this one human being. God's self-communication in creation and grace reaches its climax in Jesus.

The point of John 1:14 in this context («The Word became flesh»), promising the salvation of all things, is to diminish our human arrogance, commonly called «anthropocentrism». This is surely a proper goal for ecological theology. Yet, the fact remains that when God's Word became flesh, it was the flesh of a human being. According to the New Testament

---

[48] R.E. Murphy has noted that it is practically an axiom of biblical studies that «[...] Wisdom theology is creation theology». The Wisdom tradition is an approach to life and faith that is grounded in the experience of nature and of daily life. When Wisdom is personified, she is consistently presented as closely connected to the work of creation. Cf. R.E. Murphy, *The Tree of Life*, 118.

proclamation, offering salvation to all things comes through the redeeming life, death, and resurrection of this human being Jesus. Nor can we deny the *de facto* «dominion» of humanity in relation to other creatures on earth. Long before modern science and technology, it was evident to the author of Genesis 1 that human beings actually do have dominion. However we may deplore the abuse of human power, any attempt to deny its reality is surely futile.

Furthermore, the particular beauty of human beings with their consciousness and self-consciousness, their power to think, plan, and build, to create music and poetry, to reflect and to pray, is surely God's most amazing creation. Genesis 1 expresses this with the concept of the image of God. Human beings are to co-operate with the creator in the ordering of the chaos. It is unhelpful, then, to deny the specialness of the human being, or the reality of human dominion. Rather, we must allow our Christology to inform our understanding of this dominion. The full import of the Wisdom tradition insists that we are the stewards of creation with responsibility for the care of the handiwork of God. There is a fundamental unity between creation, Incarnation, redemption, and consummation.

Let us recall our christological and biblical starting point: Jesus Christ, God's Word made flesh, «is our Wisdom, our righteousness, our sanctification and redemption» (I Cor 1:30). It is through God's grace that the gospel of Christ frees us from our false lordship over the earth and empowers us to live joyfully as creatures, beside other creatures, within the good creation. The gospel does not so much burden us with a heavy duty of environmental care, as though it is we who, in lordly fashion, hold all things together. Rather, it moves us to a sense of care for the earth as an intrinsic part of the call to discipleship. We seek, then, to discern and follow the lead of Jesus, the Wisdom of God.

Once again a path is laid down for the community of disciples to follow. In fidelity to the meaning of Christ, we are challenged to break out of a self-centeredness to embrace the natural earth as a subject of religious value that demands our responsible care. The power of Jesus-Sophia's spirit is evident wherever human beings share in concern for the earth, tending its fruitfulness, respecting its limits, restoring what has been damaged, and guarding it from further destruction. No community that follows the way of Jesus, the Wisdom of God, can omit the earth from the circle of its passionate love. Living Wisdom Christology, the believing community walks the responsible path of ecological care.

1.5 *Jesus Crucified and Forsaken: Wisdom of God for the Modern World*

We have already drawn attention to W. Kasper's argument that theology today must continue to grapple with the questions of evil and suffering.[49] In this regard, we saw Kasper highlighting an articulation of a theology of the cross as one of the most important tasks for theology today. This kenosis theology, for Kasper, will be at the same time a theology of the Wisdom of the cross and thus wil, in accordance with the writings of Paul, understand the cross of Christ anew as the manifestation of the Wisdom of God.[50] Kasper, in an attempt to answer what he sees as a key question for contemporary theology, advocates a kenosis Christology which is also a Wisdom Christology.[51] Moreover, we highlighted the absence of a soteriology of the Wisdom / foolishness of the cross in much of contemporary feminist Christology. In this section, we will show how our understanding of Jesus crucified and forsaken can be presented as the Wisdom of God for the modern world.

In the history of salvation, God manifests and communicates himself by a combination of deeds and words. This pattern of deed and word is adopted as the formal teaching of the Church in *Dei Verbum*, the Second Vatican Council's Dogmatic Constitution on Divine Revelation. *Dei Verbum* 3 speaks of «the plan of salvation» being «realized by deeds and words having an inner unity».[52]

The deeds wrought by God in the history of salvation manifest and confirm the teaching and reality signified by the words.[53] This has a central hermeneutical importance showing why the single event of cross and

---

[49] Cf. pages 229-230.

[50] Cf. W. KASPER, «Gottes Gegenwart», 311-328.

[51] We highlighted Kasper's use of Schelling's attempts at a universal-historical interpretation of the cross. Within a freedom-oriented, historically conscious, and secular world, the cross emerges as the true Wisdom of God. However, Kasper notes there can be no «truth-verification» criteria for the cross. The crucified Wisdom cannot be forced into a scheme of worldly wisdom which would limit, and thus empty it of meaning. Cf. KASPER, «Gottes Gegenwart», 325-326.

[52] Commentators have noted the sequence «deeds and words». They stress «[...] that God reveals himself to mankind by deeds and words in close connection with one another; not simply by words, nor by words and deeds, but by deeds and words. There is a point in that order; the deeds come first, and the words interpreting the deeds come second. Cf. *DV*, 3. Cf. also B.C. BUTLER, «Divine Revelation», 660.

[53] The words follow upon the deeds and their function is also vital, since «[...] they proclaim the deeds and clarify the mystery contained in them». Cf. *DV*, 3.

resurrection is pivotal to the New Testament. In some way, the very core of the Word to mankind becomes *this* Deed. Hence, we understand St. Paul's statement to the Corinthians: «When I came to you, brethern, I did not come proclaiming the testimony of God in lofty words or Wisdom. For I decided to know nothing among you except Jesus Christ and him crucified» (I Cor 2:1-2). This Deed, this Non-Word, is the core of the Word.[54]

It is this specific Deed of the cross which deserves our special attention.[55] It is the moment of Jesus' dramatic experience of forsakenness by the one He had called «Abba». On the cross Jesus experienced the summit of his suffering when he cried out «with a great voice» *«E'lo-i, E'lo-i / Eli, Eli, la'ma sabach-tha'ni»* (Mk 15:34 / Mt 27:46). The content of the cry is the abandonment felt by Jesus because his Father does not intervene to take him out of the situation of abandonment in which he finds himself. He no longer experiences the beatifying light and presence of his Father. The experience of this absence constitutes the core and the summit of his suffering. Furthermore, the cry happens in the context of Jesus' fidelity to his Father and to the mission he had received from him

---

[54] Mark's Gospel brings out this truth well. In fact Mark seems to structure his highly dramatic narrative that the succession of events is meant to challenge the disciples both to dismantle dramatically their notion of the Messiah and to accept increasingly the kind of Messiah being manifested in the ministry of Jesus of Nazareth. Thus, Jesus announces three times in rapid succession his passion and death at the hands of the authorities (8:31-33; 9:30-32; 10:32-34). The net impact of these declarations on the disciples was «[...] that they were in a daze, and [...] were apprehensive» (10:32). Cf. H.U. VON BALTHASAR, «Centre of the Word», *The Glory of the Lord*. VII, 77-89.

[55] The connotation of the cross in the Old Testament and in the Hellenistic world of Paul's time was both stark and terrible. The Romans reserved this form of execution for traitors, public criminals, rebels, and those guilty of sedition against the state. In Israel the significance of death by crucifixion was even more appalling since it connoted expulsion from the Covenant and its incalculable benefits and, as a result, the notion of perdition. «Cursed be anyone who hangs on a tree» (Dt 21:23; Cf. Acts 5:30; 10:39; I Pet 2:24). This meaning is validated by Paul explaining in Galatians the purpose of Jesus' crucifixion as a reaching after those hitherto considered beyond any hope of redemption, that is, the Gentiles (Gal 3:13-14). By his crucifixion, Jesus was cursed with the accursed in order to redeem the accursed and include them in the blessings of Abraham's posterity. This is the soteriological function of the Incarnation and the cross. What is of importance here, however, is the theology that is glimpsed *through* this soteriology, the image of God that emerges from taking seriously the self-emptying of Christ for the world. Cf. M. HENGEL, *Crucifixion in the Ancient World and the Folly of the Message of the Cross.*

to «[...] give his life as a ransom for many» (Mk 10:45) and to drink the chalice of suffering to the dregs (Mk 14:36).

This immense suffering, consisting as it does in Jesus' experience of forsakenness by his Father, is still the expression of the Son's love both for the Father and for those who crucify and reject him. Through this forsakenness, which results precisely from the Son's love for the Father's redemptive will in our regard (Mk 14:35-36), he loses everything in human terms except that which binds him to the Father and to humankind, namely, his love. By doing so he places that very love precisely where it seems to be most absent, namely, in the sin-dominated history of humankind. The Son of God revealed his Father and completed his work in terms of the forsakenness of the cross and the *kenosis* of crucifixion. In this resides the wonder of the Christian faith in the redemptive power of the cross.

The governing theological perspective of the Second Vatican Council highlighted two dimensions of the mystery of faith. The first was the mystery of Christ,[56] while the second was the necessity of addressing the central issues and questions of the age, what the Council calls «the signs of the times», in order to continue the dialogue of salvation with the men and women of our times.[57] The practical import of these two dimensions is that, having reflected upon the mystery of Christ, we must also show the striking Wisdom of such a Christology to both the aspirations and the problems of the men and women of our times.

In this regard, let us note that our era emphasizes two concepts more than others. First, it emphasizes freedom. The Second Vatican Council pointed out that «many of our contemporaries seem to fear that a closer bond between human activity and religion will work against the independence of men, societies, or of the sciences.»[58] The fact of a Supreme Being whose laws govern human activity, whose Word demands «the obedience of faith» (Rom 16:26), and whose providence decides the destiny of individuals and of nations, seems to restrict human initiative and the yearning for autonomy inordinately and unacceptably.

This emphasis on freedom is sometimes so strongly made that it results in the denial, or at least the marginalization, of the idea of God. If God exists and he is everything, how can I be anything? In the name of

---

[56] Cf. *LG* 1; *DV* 1; *OT* 14.

[57] Cf. *NA* 1, 2; *GS* 4, 8, 9, 22.

[58] Cf. *GS* 36.

this freedom, such a mentality plans society and designs culture in such a way as to marginalize God. We well know how this inspires frequently a rejection of God and religious faith, or at least a practical agnosticism where people live as if God did not exist.

The second emphasis is that of the aspiration to human solidarity or community. Many movements in our time, as well as many of the world's recent ideologies, emphasize this central aspiration. We could say that a certain unitary consciousness now pervades humanity. This aspiration to community, however, often makes little or no room for the religious dimension. Sometimes, in fact, the achievements of science, technology, and commerce are proffered as a replacement for the universal bonding value of religion and faith. The ultimate achievement, in this view, is the taming of nature by these same means.

Is not the God revealed by Jesus, crucified and forsaken, the God of communion? Furthermore, is he not the God of freedom, since his whole being consists in the event of trinitarian love? He is a God who both emphasizes freedom and brings communion. The very distinction between the divine Persons, a distinction that is manifest in Jesus' dialogue with his Father («Abba») in Gethsemane, in his sense of forsakenness by him on Golgotha, and in his resurrection from the tomb by the Father's glory (I Pet 1:3; I Cor 15:15), highlights the space opened up by this trinitarian God for human freedom and its expression.

In Christianity there is the fact of the *Other* at the heart of reality: the Son is other than the Father and the Holy Spirit is other than the Father and the Son, within the indivisible unity of the divinity. Here we find the transcendent Ground for the centrality of the neigbour in Christian revelation, which teaches the way to the neighbour at the same time that it opens up the way to the Father. The Other is always «the brother for whom Christ died» (I Cor 8:11) entering forsakenness by the Father so that every neighbour's forsakenness could be accompanied and overcome. Here we find the revealed antidote to every form of individualism.

The modern world aspires to freedom and community. Ironically, this aspiration has become entangled with a false autonomy that, in the end, leads to and perpetuates man's godforsakenness. Thus, Jesus forsaken remains the Wisdom of God for humanity today because he alone can liberate from within, that is, redeem, humanity's attempts to find freedom and build community.

As well as aspirations, however, there are also great problems confronting humanity. There is the phenomenon of atheism in its various guises.[59] Atheism of whatever kind either forgets or deliberately abandons God. However, in the reality of Jesus crucified and forsaken, in that moment of Calvary, Jesus, though always being the only begotten Son, no longer *senses* the presence of the loving Father. Is not this forsaken Jesus precisely the God for the atheists?

Furthermore, there is the problem of the great divisions that mark the panorama of modern culture. There is the division between generations, divisions between the rich North and the poor South. There are the divisions within the Christian family itself and, in the wake of the Enlightenment, the division between faith and culture, perhaps the most startling phenomenon of the contemporary world. Once again, Jesus forsaken, who stretches out his limbs on the wood of the cross in order to gather together the scattered children of God (Jn 11:52) and to draw all unto himself, is the God for divided and fragmented humanity. His ideal, indeed the very purpose of his forsakenness, consists in the overcoming of the many tragic divisions: «[...] that they may all be one; even as thou, Father, art in me, and I in thee» (Jn 17:21).

Moreover, there are the phenomena of science and technology. The key characteristic of this technological civilization of our time is a turning outwards and away from the interior. It leads inexorably towards a culture devoid of human and spiritual content and unresponsive to the divine. Jesus forsaken who loves «to the end» (Jn 13:1), and in that way locates the divine where it seems most absent and turns the pain of his crucifixion and abandonment into a way of manifesting God's love for humanity. He is the perfect antidote to the spiritual and human emptiness threatening contemporary culture. He challenges believers to give a soul to our society and thus a context necessary for the proper placing and use of science and technology.

Jesus crucified, then, reveals the face of God as Trinitarian communion in love and brings this same communion into humankind. He also teaches us the art of living both communion and suffering in all its forms. First, he enables us to be architects of unity wherever we live. Jesus does not cease to love on the cross. On the contrary, he loves to the point of giving his life for those who had no love for him and who did not know his Father. Since in his crucifixion and abandonment he still continues to love, reaching those furthest away from his Father and bringing them into communion with his Father, he points the way for us to follow. Like him,

---

[59] This matter of atheism was considered in some depth in *GS* 19-21.

we must know how to build this communion. But such a communion is impossible without Christians walking «[...] in love as Christ loved us and gave himself up for us» (Eph 5:2), enduring suffering even to the extreme of experiencing forsakenness by his Father.

Second, he teaches us how to live every suffering and turn it into a springboard towards communion. In fact, he enables us to see every suffering as a reflection of his own. In each suffering, whether it is personal or social, we are invited to perceive a face, the face of Jesus forsaken and crucified, since he has entered into each and every suffering and has paid the price for the bringing of divine love where it was previously absent. It remains for us to live in tune with what he has already done and so to unite our own bodies with Christ's sufferings for the sake of his Body, the Church (Col 1:24). The achievement of such attunement is the task of the Christian life (Phil 3:10; I Cor 1:17-25) Is this not the practical Wisdom shouted out from the cross of the Word made flesh, foolishness indeed in the eyes of the worldly-wise and a stumbling-block to those who do not believe, but to those who do believe the Power and the Wisdom of God (I Cor 1:23-25)?

If this is the Wisdom of love as shown in the Incarnation and as culminating in the forsakenness of Calvary, if this is the very life of the Blessed Trinity, it is also the imperative for Christians to follow in order to walk in a manner worthy of their calling (Eph 4:1-3). It is the technique that the Apostle of the Gentiles employs. He made himself a Jew to the Jews, a Gentile to the Gentiles, «that I might by all means save some» (I Cor 9:23). Jesus crucified and forsaken, the Wisdom of God, is the model for whoever would make himself one with every brother or sister as Jesus crucified did.

2. Summary and Conclusions

We have been concerned here with opening up new avenues for Wisdom Christology. We have shown that the language of Wisdom can be retrieved as a «root metaphor» which can generate new perspectives on issues which face contemporary theology. We identified five important areas which are amenable to being led along a Wisdom path: the call to justice, outlining the significance of Wisdom for feminist concerns in Christology, the dialogue with other religions, grounding ecological and environmental thinking, and presenting a face of God for the modern world.

We noted that social justice is a central concern both of the Wisdom tradition of ancient Israel and the New Testament. There is no concept in the Old Testament with so central a significance for the relationships of human life than *ṣedāqāh,* justice. Indeed it is scarcely possible to separate justice from Wisdom, for unjust conditions are perceived to be a violation of the right order of creation, which is established and cherished by Wisdom herself. We affirmed that the biblical Wisdom perspective on justice possesses the potential for developing a political criticism of unjust practices and powers in society. While the ancient sages themselves had no sense of changing the social and political structures of Israelite society, they did reiterate the basic principle of justice upon which such change could be based. Injustice is inherently unstable and leads to its own destruction. Justice brings fulfilment and lasting prosperity because it is demanded by the very structure of the world in which we live.

Moreover, the ministry of Jesus was guided by his image of God as the Compassionate One concerned with justice. Interpreting the ministry, death, and resurrection of Jesus in the context of the Wisdom tradition, seeing him as Wisdom's prophet and indeed as the human being Wisdom became, shows that the desire of God is clearly directed toward lifting injustice and social oppression and establishing right relations and harmony among people. In the teaching and practice of Jesus traditional Wisdom insight was made radical by the theology of the kingdom of God. Jesus called for a radical change of heart, a *metanoia,* in the light of the imminent Reign of God. The kingdom of God finds expression in Jesus' own life and ministry, in his concern for the poor, the sick, the outcasts, and sinners. As the proclaimer of God's kingdom, Jesus is the sacrament of God's justice in the world.

The believing community, under the influence of Wisdom Christology, works to establish the harmony of justice in the world. Wisdom Christology offers us resources, including the expression of others' insights and experiences, which help form our judgment and shape the perspective in which we decide our actions.

Second, we emphasized that the move to retrieve and appropriate the symbol of Wisdom, and then to centre christological interpretation through this lens, contains a key which has the potential to provide a Christology responding to some feminist concerns. The figure of divine Wisdom offers an augmented field of female metaphors with which to interpret the saving significance of Jesus Christ and enhance our understanding of his already inclusive framework of relationships with human beings and with his Father. Throughout his ministry, his compassionate and liberating words and deeds are the works of Wisdom re-establishing the right order of creation: «Wisdom is justified by her deeds» (Mt 11:19). We highlighted feminist theology's neglect of the theological categories of redemption and atonement and argued that Wisdom Christology, as found in the Pauline corpus, can assist feminist theology to retrieve a soteriology of the Wisdom / foolishness of the cross. Moreover, we recommended that the feminist implications of the Wisdom theme might be elaborated further by an exploration of the connections implicit in the notion of the church as the seat of Wisdom and bride of Christ as well as the Marian ecclesiology of *LG*, 8.

Third, we noted that the biblical Wisdom tradition suggests perspectives for approaching the dialogue with other religions. The Wisdom tradition affirms the value of all God-seekers offering solid precedent for acknowledging a general activity of God throughout the human experience and for correlating the universal activity of God with specific historical events of revelation. The sapiential themes of trust in general human experience and the awareness of the limits of all human understanding combine to encourage dialogue and mutual exchange between different traditions. Moreover, the Wisdom tradition in general and the figure of Lady Wisdom in particular offer possibilities for discussion in the encounter with other religions. Many cultures has a tradition analogous to the biblical Wisdom tradition. As part of the Bible, this universalizing Wisdom tradition reflects a genuine and primary element of biblical faith in all its integrity. Lady Wisdom symbolizes God's presence moving throughout the whole world. This renders the Wisdom tradition particularly helpful to contemporary theological efforts seeking to find ways of respecting other world religious traditions. For while other religious traditions do not share in the particularity of Israel's salvation history, their own paths of holiness and «rays of truth» (*NA*, 2) nonetheless reflect the truth and holiness of God to be found in natural wisdom rather than in privileged sources of revelation. Jesus, the Wisdom of God, personally incarnates Wisdom's gracious care in one particular history for the benefit of all, while Wisdom provides a multiplicity of paths in diverse cultures along which all people may find resonances of her presence.

Fourth, we affirmed that a Wisdom Christology underlines the significance of the Incarnation for an ecological vision of the world.

Interpreting the ministry, death, and resurrection of Jesus by means of the Wisdom tradition orients Christology beyond the human world to the ecology of the earth and to the whole universe. The portrait of Wisdom's creative agency «in the beginning» is completed by affirmations of her continuing presence. It is clear from the Scriptures that divine Wisdom speaks of the self-communication of God in and through creation.

We identified five New Testament texts standing in the Wisdom tradition that directly connect Jesus Christ to the work of creation: I Corinthians 8:6, Hebrews 1:2-3, Colossians 1:15-20, Ephesians 1:10 and John 1:3. We highlighted a Wisdom Christology that sees creation and Incarnation as intrinsically connected in the one divine plan, while still insisting that the incarnation was a totally free act of God. There can be no separation of creation and redemption, no theology of creation independent of a theology of Incarnation, and no theology of Incarnation and redeeming grace not related to the created world. This intrinsic connection is fundamental to the structure of Wisdom thought. Divine Wisdom is, by definition, God's presence and self-expression. God communicates God's self through divine Wisdom; Wisdom is present in all creation and has built herself a home among us in Jesus Christ. Wisdom, God's companion and helper in creation, becomes incarnate in this one human being. God's self-communication in creation and grace reaches its irrevocable climax in Jesus. A Wisdom Christology challenges the believing community to walk the responsible path of ecological care.

Fifth, we showed how our understanding of Jesus crucified and forsaken can be presented as the Wisdom of God for the modern world. We highlighted the concepts of freedom and the human aspiration to solidarity or community as important principles for our time, and concluded that Jesus forsaken is the Wisdom of God for humanity because he alone can liberate from within and redeem humanity's attempts to find freedom and build community. Moreover, the forsaken Jesus is the God for atheists, for in the reality of Jesus crucified and forsaken we encounter the fact of God experiencing abandonment by God for the sake of all including those who are without God. In addition, Jesus forsaken is the God for divided and fragmented humanity. On the cross Jesus stretches out his limbs in order to gather together the scattered children of God (Jn 11:52). He is the antidote to the spiritual and human emptiness threatening contemporary culture. The imitation of such an example is the task of the

Christian life (Phil 3:10; I Cor 1:17-25), and this is the practical Wisdom shouted from the cross (I Cor 1:23-25).

We have highlighted *in embryo* five perspectives for Wisdom Christology. Each requires further reflection and study. Clearly, Wisdom Christology offers theological resources for the future. The Wisdom tradition as a whole with its symbol of Lady Wisdom and its sapiential Christology is a largely untapped resource for contemporary questions in Christology. But it can be a beneficial field of metaphors, concepts, and values with which to articulate the meaning of Christ, the cosmos, and ourselves as a believing community.

CONCLUSION

As we draw this dissertation to a close, certain lasting impressions and implications deserve to be stated. Our study began with the questions: Who is Wisdom, what are her ways, and how is she connected with Jesus the Christ? Until quite recently the biblical Wisdom tradition has been relegated to a position of minor importance, while the powerful female figure of Lady Wisdom has been largely ignored. In contemporary Christology the pivotal role of this symbol in articulating the meaning of Christ has been largely overlooked.

This thesis began from the premise that the Wisdom tradition, with its insights and imagery, is too valuable a resource to be forgotten. In our opening six chapters we saw how early Christians tapped deeply into the tradition of personified Wisdom to articulate the saving goodness they experienced in Jesus the Christ. Our study highlighted the scope and richness of the sapiential material, and when we focused on the New Testament, the extensive impact of Wisdom thinking and material on the Christian canon was underlined. The protest of Old Testament scholars that the Wisdom corpus, at least until recent times, has been much neglected is warranted. While Old Testament scholarship has now gone some way to make up for lost time, New Testament scholars have only begun to explore the possible benefits that come from reading the New Testament in light of the Jewish Wisdom corpus and assessing the extent and nature of its influence.

In our opening chapter we noted that in the midst of the biblical Wisdom writings arises the figure of Lady Wisdom, a female figure of power and care. The biblical picture of her is a composite one, formed of differing presentations in the Wisdom books. She is portrayed as sister, mother, bride, hostess, female beloved, woman prophet, teacher, and friend, but above all as a divine spirit. Overall, there is no other personification of such depth and magnitude in the entire Hebrew Scriptures. Scholarly debate on how to interpret this powerful female figure abounds, not least because various biblical books depict her in differing ways, so that no one interpretation can be applied to every verse where Wisdom appears. Taking the whole Wisdom tradition into account, it is the interpretation of Wisdom as the personification of God's own self-coming toward the world, dwelling in it and active for its well-being, that was to bear fruit in Christology, as early Christians grew in the realization of what God had done in Jesus Christ. For Wisdom's creative and saving actions are divine ones. The Wisdom of God in late Jewish thought is simply God, revealing and known.

In their exuberant effort to interpret their experience of salvation coming from God in Jesus and consequently his ultimate meaning, early Christians combed their Jewish religious tradition and the surrounding Hellenistic culture for interpretative elements. Consequently, they named him the Messiah / Christ, the Son of Man, Lord, Son of God, Word of God, allowing the meaning of these traditions to interact with his particular history and so shed light on his significance. In a way fraught with importance for later development they also connected him with Wisdom, allowing her symbol and myth to focus and filter his significance. As the theme of Wisdom Christology shows, Jesus was so closely associated with Wisdom that by the end of the first century he is presented not only as a Wisdom teacher, not only as a child and envoy of Wisdom, but also as an earthly appearance of Wisdom in person, the incarnation of Wisdom herself.

We observed that what Judaism said of Wisdom Christian hymn makers and epistle writers came to say of Jesus: he is the image of the invisible God (Col 1:15); the radiant light of God's glory (Heb 1:3); the firstborn of all creation (Col 1:15); the one through whom all things were made (I Cor 8:6). From Paul, who calls Jesus the Wisdom of God (I Cor 1:24), to Matthew, who puts Sophia's words in Jesus' mouth and has him do her compassionate deeds, to John, who presents Jesus as Wisdom incarnate emulating her ways, her truth, and her life, the use of Wisdom to interpret Jesus had profound consequences. It enabled the fledgling Christian communities to attribute cosmic significance to the crucified Jesus, relating time to the creation and governance of the world. It deepened their understanding of his saving deeds by placing them in continuity with Wisdom's saving work throughout history. It was also the vehicle for developing insight into Jesus' ontological relationship with his Father.

None of the other biblical symbols used, Son of Man, Messiah, Son of God, connotes divinity in its original context, nor does the Word, which is barely personified in the Jewish Scriptures. But Wisdom does. To identify the human being Jesus with Divine Wisdom, God's gracious nearness and activity in the world, was to reflect that Jesus is not simply a human being inspired by God but must be related in a more personally unique way to God. Jesus came to be seen as God's only-begotten Son only after he was identified with Wisdom. Then her relation of intimacy with God was seen to be manifest in his relation to God, her spirit seen in his, and his identity shaped by hers. "Herein we see the origin of the doctrine of the Incarnation" (J.D.G. Dunn). Without the presence and strength of New Testament sapiential Christology, insight into Jesus' identity and significance would have been very different indeed.

The reception of the Wisdom theme in the early church together with its influence on the development of Christology in patristic and medieval theology was appraised. The writings of several authors who were influenced by the Wisdom theme including Justin Martyr, Origen, Athanasius, Pope Leo I, Augustine, Hildegard of Bingen, and Thomas Aquinas were considered. While Wisdom Christology in itself was not a major theme in post-biblical development, the early Christian centuries saw continuing use of Wisdom categories in christological reflection, both alone and in combination with thought about the Logos. In the East, from the mid-second century onwards, the Apologists and others exegeted Proverbs, Sirach, and Wisdom christologically, identifying Wisdom with Jesus Christ in order to ground their argument for his eternal origin and divinity. While not as prominent in the West, traces of Wisdom Christology are found in the writings of Jerome and Augustine. Eight hundred years later the theme featured in the work of Thomas Aquinas. In later centuries in the West, while largely replaced by considerations of Logos Christology (in itself partially shaped by Wisdom texts), the Wisdom tradition continued to make elusive appearances in christological reflection, while the major application of Wisdom texts turned in the direction of mariology.

The opening six chapters of this dissertation, addressing the place of Wisdom in the Bible and the tradition of the church, provide a scholarly and scientific basis for evaluating and adjudicating to what extent these Wisdom elements present in the Scriptures and the tradition of the church have been incorporated into some representative contemporary Catholic Christologies in three language areas (German, English and French). Over the course of three chapters we examined the christological writings of nine theologians from three language groups: Walter Kasper, Karl Rahner and Edward Schillebeeckx (German / Dutch); Jacques Dupuis, Denis Edwards and Elizabeth Schüssler Fiorenza (English); Louis Bouyer, Christian Duquoc and Joseph Moingt (French). With some notable exceptions, what emerged was a story of lost opportunities. Our study established the absence of significant influence of Wisdom elements on Catholic Christology over the past thirty years.

Kasper opts very clearly for a pneumatological approach to Christology while acknowledging the need for a Wisdom Christology in the context of a kenosis theology grappling with the questions of evil and suffering. This was something we addressed in our final chapter noting that a number of theologians under review in our study (D. Edwards, E. Schillebeeckx, E. Schüssler Fiorenza) are more favourable to portrayals of Jesus' death as the death of a prophet-martyr than to an interpretation of his death in terms of the categories of atonement and redemption. Schillebeeckx, in both historical analysis and systematic reflection, favours the category of eschatological prophet as his vehicle for articulating Jesus' status and significance. Rahner's christological thought, based on the Word prologue of the Gospel of John and hence involving some link with a Wisdom Christology, is the most open of our three German / Dutch- speaking authors to be taken in a Wisdom direction though this task is not undertaken explicitly by Rahner himself.

Our study of some English-speaking authors established that both Edwards and Schüssler Fiorenza make extensive use of the Wisdom theme in order to articulate their respective contemporary christologies. Edwards sets out explicitly to retrieve Wisdom Christology and hence to use the Wisdom motif to address contemporary questions in theology. Fiorenza's objective, through the re-discovery of Wisdom theology and Christology, is to highlight the inadequacy of andro-kyriocentric language and critically assess its function in Christian theological discourse. In our concluding chapter we attempted *in embryo* to bring together some Wisdom perspectives valuable to the feminist search. We highlighted ecclesiological and soteriological issues which require the attention of feminist theologians. Wisdom Christology, we concluded, can facilitate feminist theology in this exchange and thus help the feminist quest to avoid any risk of mere anthropology as the basis for a Christology responding to feminist concerns.

We established the absence of significant influence of the Wisdom theme on some representative theologians of the French-speaking world. However, we did highlight the influence on Louis Bouyer of Sergj Bulgakov, who developed a deeply sapiential form of the Christian vision viewing the world as continually transformed by the creative Wisdom of God. Indeed, a study of the sapiential writings of Bulgakov, together with some other contemporaries of his time and place, would be of benefit to Wisdom Christology.

Our final chapter set about opening new avenues for Wisdom Christology. In the light of what had been presented, this chapter showed how the language of Wisdom can be retrieved as a *root metaphor* which can generate new perspectives on five key issues facing contemporary Christology: the call to justice, outlining the significance of Wisdom for feminist concerns in Christology, the dialogue with other religions, grounding ecological and environmental thinking, and presenting a face of God for the modern world. All five of the key issues identified require further reflection and study, thus ensuring that the theme of Wisdom Christology remains a subject for contemporary theological reflection. The Wisdom tradition accords a high value to reflection on human experience, while also acknowledging the limits of all human understanding, and the necessity of receiving Wisdom as a gift from God revealed in a definitive and unsurpassable way in the life, death, and resurrection of Jesus Christ. It also maintains an openness to philosophical and cosmological reflection which invites further dialogue with the philosophical and cosmological perspectives of our time. The interpretation of Jesus Christ as the Incarnation of Lady Wisdom claims a cosmic dimension for Christology and opens the way for reflection on the relation of Christ to the order of creation and the world-process. Lady Wisdom as a feminine figure was historically an important support for using feminine imagery to describe God and invites further reflection in dialogue with contemporary perspectives. Moreover, the universalizing character of the Wisdom tradition renders it particularly helpful to contemporary efforts to find ways of dialoging with other world religious traditions.

As one of the most evocative images of the Bible, it is clear that the figure of Wisdom was of decisive importance for the early Church's interpretation of Jesus Christ, that it continues to have an impact upon the history of Christian reflection, and that it offers an immense resource for the future development of Christology.

ABBREVIATIONS

AAS	*Acta apostolicae sedis*
AB	Anchor Bible
ABD	Anchor Bible Dictionary, ed. D.N. Freedman, I-IV, New York 1992
ACW	Ancient Christian Writers
AG	*Ad gentes* - Decree of the Second Vatican Council on the Church's Missionary Activity 1965
AnBib	Analecta Biblica
AusJBA	*Australian Journal of Biblical Archaeology*
BETL	Bibliotheca Ephemeridum Theologicarum Lovaniensium
Bib	*Biblica*
BJRL	*Bulletin of the John Rylands University Library*
BT	*The Bible Translator*
BTB	*Biblical Theology Bulletin*
BZ	*Biblische Zeitschrift*
CBQ	*Catholic Biblical Quarterly*
CivCat	*La Civiltà Cattolica*
ClerRev	*The Clergy Review*
CNT	Commentaire du Nouveau Testament
Conc(F)	*Concilium.* French edition
CTJ	*Calvin Theological Journal*
CWS	Classics of Western Spirituality Series
DI	*Dominus Iesus*
DJD	Discoveries in the Judaean Desert
DR	*The Downside Review*
DV	*Dei Verbum* - Dogmatic Constitution of the Second Vatican Council on Divine Revelation 1965

EB	Études bibliques
EKKNT	Evangelische-Katholischer Kommentar zum Neuen Testament
ER	*Ecumenical Review*
E.T.	English translation
ETL	*Ephemerides Theologicae Lovanienses*
ExpTim	*Expository Times*
EvQ	*Evangelical Quarterly*
Gr	*Gregorianum*
GS	*Gaudium et spes* - Pastoral Constitution of the Second Vatican Council on the Church in the Modern World 1965
HAT	Handbuch zum Alten Testament
HBT	*Horizons in Biblical Theology*
HeyJ	*Heythrop Journal*
HNTC	Harper's New Testament Commentaries
HTR	*Harvard Theological Review*
HUCA	*Hebrew Union College Annual*
ICC	International Critical Commentary
IDB	*Interpreter's Dictionary of the Bible*, ed. G.A. Buttrick I-IV, Nashville 1962-76
IDB Sup	Supplementary volume to *IDB*, ed. K. Crim, Nashville 1976
Int	*Interpretation*
JAAR	*Journal of the American Academy of Religion*
JBL	*Journal of Biblical Literature*
JSOT	*Journal for the Study of the Old Testament*
JSNT	*Journal for the Study of the New Testament*
JSNTSS	Journal for the Study of the New Testament Supplement Series
JTS	*Journal of Theological Studies*
KD	*Kerygma und Dogma*
LD	Lectio divina
LG	*Lumen gentium* - Dogmatic Constitution of the Second Vatican Council on the Church 1964
LS	*Louvain Studies*
LTK	*Lexikon für Theologie und Kirche*
LV(L)	*Lumière et vie.* Lyon
MFCG	Mitteilungen und Forschungsbeiträge der Cusanus Gesellschaft
MT	*Modern Theology*
NA	*Nostra aetate* - Declaration of the Second Vatican Council on the Relationship of the Church to Non-Christian Religions 1965
NBl	*New Blackfriars*

NCB	New Century Bible Series
NCTC	Nuova Collana di Teologia Cattolica
NICNT	New International Commentary on the New Testament
NIGTC	New International Greek Testament Commentary
NJBC	*New Jerome Biblical Commentary*, ed. R.Brown - J.A. Fitzmyer - R.E.Murphy, London 1990
NQR	*Nashotah Quarterly Review*
NRT	*Nouvelle revue théologique*
NT	*Novum Testamentum*
NTS	*Novum Testament Studies*
OTM	Old Testament Message
OTL	Old Testament Library
Pac	*Pacifica*
PEQ	*Palestine Exploration Quarterly*
PUG	Pontificia Università Gregoriana, Roma
RB	*Revue biblique*
RelS	*Religious Studies*
RelSRev	*Religious Studies Review*
RevExp	*Review and Expositor*
RHPR	*Revue d'histoire et de philosophie religieuses*
RQ	*Römische Quartalschrift für christliche Altertumskunde und Kirchengeschichte*
RevQ	*Revue de Qumrân*
RM	*Redemptoris missio* - Encyclical of John Paul II on the Mission of the Redeemer 1990
RSPT	*Revue des sciences philosophiques et théologiques*
RSR	*Recherches de science religeuse*
RTL	*Revue théologique de Louvain*
RTP	*Revue de théologie et de philosophie*
Sal	*Salesianum*
SBLASP	Society of Biblical Literature Abstracts and Seminar Papers
SBLDS	SBL Dissertation Series
SBT	Studies in Biblical Theology
ScC	*Scuola cattolica*
ScEs	*Science et esprit*
SJT	*Scottish Journal of Theology*
SNTSMS	Society for New Testament Studies Monograph Series
ST	St. Thomas Aquinas, *Summa Theologica*
StTh	*Studia theologica*
TD	*Theology Digest*
TI	*Theological Investigations,* ed. K. Rahner, I-XXIII, London 1961-92

TS	*Theological Studies*
TZ	*Theologische Zeitschrift*
VE	*Vox Evangelica*
VT	*Vetus Testamentum*
WBC	Word Biblical Commentary, ed. B.M. Metzger - al., Nashville 1977-
WW	*Word and World*
ZAW	*Zeitschrift für die alttestamentliche Wissenschaft*
ZNW	*Zeitschrift für die neutestamentliche Wissenschaft*

BIBLIOGRAPHY

ACHTEMEIER, P.J., «The Gospel of Mark», *ABD*, IV 541-557.

AEBY, G., *Les Missions Divines de saint Justin à Origène*, Fribourg 1958.

ALETTI, J.N., *Colossiens 1:15-20: Genre et exégèse texte: Fonction de la thématique sapientielle*, AnBib 91, Rome 1981.

ALLEGRO, J.M., «The Wiles of the Wicked Woman, a Sapiential Work from Qumran's Fourth Cave», *PEQ* 96 (1964) 53-55.

————, *Qumran Cave 4.1 (4Q158 - 4Q186)*, Oxford 1968.

ALONSO SCHÖKEL, L. – SICRE DÍAZ, J.L., *Job*, Madrid 1981.

ALONSO SCHÖKEL, L. – VÍLCHEZ LÍNDEZ J., *Sapienciales. I. Proverbios*, Madrid 1984.

ANATOLIOS, K., «Christ, Scripture, and the Christian Story of Meaning in Origen», *Gr* 78 (1997) 55-77.

APPOLD, M.L., *The Oneness Motif in the Fourth Gospel: Motif Analysis and Exegetical Probe into the Theology of John*, Tübingen 1976.

ASHTON, J., «The Transformation of Wisdom: A Study of the Prologue of John's Gospel», *NTS* 32 (1986) 161-186.

————, ed., *The Interpretation of John*, Philadelphia 1986.

————, *Understanding the Fourth Gospel*, Oxford 1991.

ASSOCIATION CATHOLIQUE FRANCAISE POUR L'ÉTUDE DE LA BIBLE, *La Sagesse biblique de l'Ancien au Nouveau Testament*, LD 160, Paris 1995.

ATTRIDGE, H.W., *Hebrews*, Philadelphia 1989.

BAASLAND, E., «Der Jakobusbrief als Neutestamentliche Weisheitsschrift», *ST* 36 (1982) 119-139.

BAER, R.A., *Philo's Use of the Categories Male and Female*, Leiden 1970.

BAILEY, A., *The Traditions Common to the Gospels of Luke and John*, Leiden 1963.

BAIRD, W., «What is the Kerygma?», *JBL* 76 (1957) 181-191.

BALCHIN, J.F., «Colossians 1:15-20: An Early Christological Hymn ? The Arguments from Style», *VE* 15 (1985) 65-94.

BARCLAY, J.M.G., «Paul among Diaspora Jews: Anomaly or Apostate?», *JSNT* 60 (1995) 89-120.

BARNES, T.D., *Tertullian: A Historical and Literary Study*, Oxford 1985.

BARRETT, C.K., *The First Epistle to the Corinthians*, HNTC, New York 1968.

———, *The Prologue of St. John's Gospel*, London 1971.

———, *The Gospel According to John*, Philadelphia 1978.

———, «Christianity at Corinth», in *Essays on Paul*, Philadelphia 1982 1-27.

———, *Paul: An Introduction to His Thought*, Louisville 1993.

BARTH, M. *Ephesians 1-3*, AB 34A, Garden City, New York 1974.

BARUCQ, A., *Le Livre des Proverbes*, Sources bibliques, Paris 1964.

BAUCKHAM, R., ed., *The Gospels for all Christians: Rethinking the Gospel Audiences*, Grand Rapids 1997.

———, *James. Wisdom of James: Disciple of Jesus the Sage*, New York 1999.

BEARDSLEE, W.A., «The Wisdom Tradition and the Synoptic Gospels», *JAAR* 35 (1967) 231-240.

BEARE, F.W., *A Commentary on the Epistle to the Philippians*, London 1959.

———, *The Gospel According to Matthew*, Oxford 1981.

BEASLEY MURRAY, P., «Colossians 1:15-20», in D.A. HAGNER – M.J. HARRIS, ed., *Pauline Studies*, Grand Rapids 1980, 169-183.

BECK, N.A., «Reclaiming a Biblical Text: The Mark 8:14-21 Discussion about Bread in the Boat», *CBQ* 43 (1981) 49-56.

BEKER, J.C., *Paul the Apostle*, Philadelphia 1982.

BENOIT, P., *L'Évangile selon Saint Matthieu*, Paris 1972.

———, «L'hymne christologique de Col 1: 15-20», in J. NEUSNER, ed., *Christianity, Judaism and other Greco-Roman Cults*, ed. J. Neusner, Leiden 1975, 226-263.

BEST, E., *Mark: The Gospel as Story*, Edinburgh 1983.

BETTENSON, H., *The Early Christian Fathers*, Oxford 1969.

————, *The Later Christian Fathers*, Oxford 1972.

BETZ, H.D., «The Logion of the Easy Yoke and of Rest (Mt 11:28-30)», *JBS* 86 (1967) 10-19.

————, *Der Apostel und die sokratische Tradition*, Tübingen 1972.

————, «Hellenism», *ABD* III 127-135.

BEYSCHLAG, K., *Clemens Romanus und der Frühkatholizismus*, Tübingen 1966.

BISHOP, E.F., «The Door of the Sheep: Jn 10:7-9», *ExpTim* 71 (1959) 307-309.

BLEEKER, C.T., «Isis as Saviour Goddess», in S.G.F. BRANDON, ed., *The Saviour God: Comparative Studies in the Concept of Salvation*, Manchester 1963.

BLENKINSOPP, J., *Wisdom and Law in the Old Testament*, Oxford 1983.

BOCCACCINI, G., *Middle Judaism: Jewish Thought 300 B.C. to 200 A.D.*, Minneapolis 1991.

BOCK, D.L., *Luke*. I-II, Grand Rapids 1996.

BOKENKOTTER, T., *A Concise History of the Catholic Church*, New York 1990.

BONNARD, P.É., *L'epître de Saint Paul aux Philippiens*, Neuchâtel 1950.

————, *La Sagesse en personne, annoncée et venue: Jésus Christ*, Paris 1966.

————, «De la sagesse personnifiée dans l'Ancien Testament à la Sagesse en personne dans le Nouveau», in M. GILBERT, ed., *La Sagesse de l'Ancien Testament*, Leuven 1979, 117-149.

BOOTH FOWLER, R., *The Greening of Protestant Thought*, North Carolina 1995.

BORNKAMM, G., «Das Bekenntnis im Hebräerbrief», in *Studien zu Antike und Urchristentum*, 2nd ed., Bonn 1963.

BÖRRESEN, K., «Christ notre mere, la theologie de Julienne de Norwich», *MFCG* XIII 320-329.

BOTTE, D.B., «La Sagesse et les origines de la Christologie», *RSPT* 21(1932) 54-67.

BOURKE, M.M., «The Epistle to the Hebrews», *NJBC* 920-941.

BOURKE, V.J., *Augustine's Love of Wisdom*, Notre Dame, IN 1992.

BOUYER, L., *L'Incarnation et l'Église: Corps du Christ dans la théologie de saint Athanase* Paris 1943.

————, *Le Mystère Pascal*, Paris 1945; E.T.: *The Paschal Mystery* London 1951.

————, *Le quatrième évangile*, Paris 1955; E.T.: *The Fourth Gospel*, Westminister 1964

————, *Le trône de la Sagesse. Essai sur la signification du culte marial* Paris 1957; E.T.: *An Essay on the place of the Virgin Mary in Christian Theology* New York 1962.

————, *Le rite et l'homme: Sacralité naturelle et liturgie*, Paris 1962; E.T.: *Rite and Man: Sacredness and Christian Liturgy*, Notre Dame, IN 1963.

————, *L'Église de Dieu corps du Christ et temple de l'Esprit*, Paris 1970; E.T.: *The Church of God, Body of Christ and temple of the Spirit*, Chicago 1982.

————, *Le Fils éternel. Théologie de la Parole de Dieu et christologie*, Paris 1974, E.T. *The Eternal Son: A Theology of the Word of God and Christology*, Huntington, ID. 1978.

————, *Le Père invisible. Approches du mystère de la divinité*, Paris 1976.

————, *Le Consolateur: Esprit-Saint et vie de Grâce*, Paris 1980.

————, *Cosmos: le monde et la gloire de Dieu*, Paris 1982.

BOUZARD, W.C., «The Theology of Wisdom in Romans 1 and 2», *WW* 7 (1987) 281-291.

BOWDEN, J., *Edward Schillebeeckx: Portrait of a Theologian*, London 1983.

BRADLEY, I., *God is Green. Christianity and the Environment*, London 1990.

BRANDENBURGER, E., «Text und Vorlagen von Hebr 5:7-10», *NT* 11 (1969), 222-238.

BRANICK, V., «Source and Redaction Analysis of I Corinthians 1-3», *JBL* 101 (1982) 251-269.

BRENNER, A. – FONTAINE, C., *Wisdom and Psalms*, Sheffield 1998.

BRING, R., «Paul and the Old Testament», *ST* 25 (1971) 21-60.

BROWN, R.E. – PHERKINS, P. – SALDARINI, A.J., «Apocrypha, Dead Sea Scrolls, Other Jewish Literature», *NJBC* 1055-1082.

BROWN, R.E., *The Gospel of St. John and the Johannine Epistles*, Collegeville, MN. 1960.

————, *The Gospel According to John*, I-II, London 1966.

————, *The Community of the Beloved Disciple*, London 1979.

BROWN, R.E., *An Introduction to the New Testament*, New York 1997.

————, «Dead Sea Scrolls», *NJBC*, 1069.

BROWN, R.E., – MEIER, J.P., *Antioch and Rome*, New York 1983.

BRUCE, F.F., «Paul and the Historical Jesus», *BJRL* 56 (1973) 317-335.

BRUCE, F.F., *The Epistles to the Colossians, to Philemon, and to the Ephesians*, Grand Rapids 1984.

BULTMANN, R., «Der religionsgeschichtliche Hintergrund des Prologs zum Johannes-evangelium», *Eucharisterion, Festschrift für H. Gunkel*, II, Göttingen 1923, 3-26.

————, *De Geschichte der Synoptishen Tradition*, Göttingen 1967

————, *The Gospel of John*, Oxford 1971.

BURNETT, F.W., *The Testament of Jesus Sophia: A Redaction - Critical Study of the Eschatological Discourse in Matthew*, Washington, D.C. 1981.

BURNEY, C.F., «Christ as the αρχH of Creation», *JTS* 27 (1976) 160-177.

BUTLER, B.C., «The Vatican Council on Divine Revelation», *ClerRev* 150 (1965) 658-661.

BUTTERWORTH, G.W., *Origen: On First Principles*, New York 1966.

BYRNE, B., «The Letter to the Philippians», *NJBC*, 791-797.

CADBURY, H.J., «The Grandson of Ben Sira», *HTR* 46 (1953) 219-225.

CAIRD, G.B., *Paul's Letters from Prison*, Oxford 1976.

CALDUCH – BENAGES, N., *En el crisol de la prueba*, Estella 1997.

————, «Jesús de Nazaret: Sophia de Dios», in I. GÓMEZ-ACEBO, ed., *Y vosotras, quién decís que soy yo?*, Bilbao 2000, 173-210.

CAMP, C.V., *Wisdom and the Feminine in the Book of Proverbs*, Sheffield 1985.

CAPIZZI, N., *L'uso di Fil 2:6-11 nella Cristologia Contemporanea 1965-'93*, Roma 1997.

CARLSTON, C.E., «Eschatology and Repentance in the Epistle to the Hebrews», *JBL* 78 (1959) 296-302.

CARNLEY, P., *The Structure of Resurrection Belief*, Oxford 1987.

CARR, A., *The Theological Method of Karl Rahner*, Missoula 1977.

CERFAUX, L., «L'hymne au Christ-Serviteur de Dieu (Phil 2:6-11=Is 52:13-53:12)», in L. CERFAUX, ed., *Miscellanea Historica in honorem A. de Meyer*, I, Louvain 1946, 117-130.

CHADWICK, H., *The Early Church*, New York 1967.

CHRIST, F., *Jesus Sophia: die Sophia - Christologie bei den Synoptikern*, Zürich 1970.

CLARK, D.K., «Signs in Wisdom and John», *CBQ*, 45 (1983) 201-209.

CLIFFORD, R.J., «Proverbs IX: A Suggested Ugaritic Parallel», *VT* 25 (1975) 298-306.

COHEN, S., «The Significance of Yahweh: Pharisees, Rabbis, and the End of Jewish Sectarianism», *HUCA* 55 (1984) 30-32.

COLLEDGE, E., – WALSH, J., *Showings of Divine Love: Introduction to Julian of Norwich*. I-II, Toronto 1978.

COLLINS, J.J., *Jewish Wisdom in the Hellenistic Age*, Edinburgh 1997.

COLLINS, R.F., *Letters that Paul did not Write*, Wilmington 1988.

COLSON, F.H. – WHITAKER, G.H., *Philo*. I-XII, cambridge, MA 1960-'68.

CONZELMANN, H., *The Theology of St. Luke*, London 1960.

———, «Paulus und die Weisheit», *NTS* 12 (1965) 231-244.

———, «The Mother of Wisdom», in J.M. ROBINSON, ed., *The Future of our Religious Past*, New York 1971, 230-243.

———, *A Commentary on the First Epistle to the Corinthians*, Philadelphia 1975.

———, «Der Brief an die Kolosser», *Das Neue Testament deutsche*, Göttingen 1976.

COOK, R.B., «Paul: Preacher or Evangelist?», *BT* 32 (1981) 441- 444.

COPPENS, J., «Le Fils de l'homme dans l'Évangile Johannique», *ETL* 52 (1976) 28-81.

CORY, C., «Wisdom's Rescue: A New Reading of the Tabernacles Discourse», *JBL* 116/1 (1997) 95-116.

COTHENET, É., «La Sagesse dans la letter de Jacques», in ASSOCIATION CATHOLIQUE FRANCAISE POUR L'ETUDE DE LA BIBLE, *La Sagesse biblique de l'Ancien au Nouveau Testament*, Paris 1995, 413-419.

COX, D., *Proverbs*, OTM 17, Wilmington, Delaware 1982.

———, *Man's Anger and God's Silence: The Book of Job*, Slough 1990.

CRANFIELD, C.E.B., *The Letter to the Romans*, I-II, Edinburgh 1979.

CRENSHAW, J.L., *Old Testament Wisdom: An Introduction*, London 1982.

———, «Qoheleth in Current Research», *HAR* 7 (1983) 41-56.

———, «The Acquisition of Knowledge in Israelite Wisdom Literature», *WW* 7 (1987) 248-262.

CRONBACH, A., «Righteousness in Jewish Literature, 2000 B.C. - 100 A.D.», *IDB.* IV 85-91.

CROSS, F.M., *The Ancient Library of Qumran*, Minneapolis 1995.

CULLMANN, O., *The Christology of the New Testament*, London 1963.

CULPEPPER, R.A., *The Johannine School*, Missoula 1975.

DAHL, N.A., «Paul and the Church at Corinth According to I Corinthians 1:10 - 4: 21», in W.R. FARMER, ed., *Christian History and Interpretation*, FS. J. Knox, Cambridge 1967, 313-335.

DALY, G., *Creation and Redemption*, Dublin 1988.

DALY, M., *Beyond God the Father: Toward a Philosophy of Women's Liberation*, Boston 1973.

D'ANGELO, M.R., «Colossians», in E. SCHÜSSLER FIORENZA, ed., *Searching the Scriptures, II*, New York 1994, 313-324.

DAVIES, J., *Wisdom and Spirit: An Investigation of I Cor 1: 18 - 3: 20 Against the Background of Jewish Sapiential Traditions in the Greco-Roman Period*, Lanham, Maryland 1984.

DAVIES, P., *God and the New Physics*, London 1983.

———, *Superforce*, London 1984.

———, *The Cosmic Blueprint*, London 1987.

DAVIES, W.D., – DAUBE, D., ed., *The Background of the New Testament and Its Eschatology*, Cambridge 1956.

DAVIES, W.D., *The Setting of the Sermon on the Mount*, Cambridge 1966.

———, *Paul and Rabbinic Judaism*, Philadelphia, 1981.

DAVIES, W.D., – ALLISON, D.C., *Matthew*. I-III, Edinburgh 1988-'98.

DE JONGE, M., *L'Évangile de Jean: Sources, Rédaction, Théologie*, Louven 1975.

DE LA POTTERIE, I., «Je suis la Voie, la Véritié, et la Vie (Jn 14:6)», *NRT* 88 (1966) 907-929.

DEICHGRÄBER, R., *Gotteshymnus und Christushymnus in der frühen Christenheit*, Göttingen 1967.

DEMARIS, R.E., *The Colossian Controversy: Wisdom in Dispute at Colossae*, Sheffield 1994.

DEMASION, M., ed., *La liberté du théologien*, Paris 1995.

DEN HEYER, C.J., *Jesus and the Doctrine of the Atonement*, London 1998.

DEUTSCH, C., *Hidden Wisdom and the Easy Yoke. Wisdom, Torah, and Discipleship in Matthew 11:25-30*, Sheffield 1987.

DEUTSCH, C., «Wisdom in Matthew: Transformation of a Symbol», *NT* 32 (1990) 13-46.

DHORME, P., *Le Livre de Job*, Paris 1967.

DI LELLA, A.A., «Sirach», *NJBC*, 496-509.

DILLISTONE, F.W., «Wisdom, Word and Spirit: Revelation in the Wisdom Literature», *Int* 2 (1948) 275-287.

———, *The Christian Understanding of Atonement*, Philadelphia, 1969.

DODD, C.H., *The Interpretation of the Fourth Gospel*, Cambridge 1953.

DONAHUE, J.R., «Biblical Perspectives on Justice», in J.C. HAUGHEY, ed., *The Faith that does Justuce*, New York 1977, 68-112.

DORÉ, J., – THEOBALD, C., ed., *Penser la foi. Recherches en théologie aujourd'hui*, Paris 1973.

DOTY, W.G., *Letters in Primitive Christianity*, Philadelphia 1973.

DUBARLE, A.M., *Les Sages d'Israël*, Paris 1946.

DUESBERG, H., – FRANSEN, I., *Les Scribes Inspirés*, Paris 1966.

DUMONT, C., «De trois dimensions retrouvees en theologie: Eschatologie – Orthopraxie – Hermeneutique», *NRT* 6 (1970) 561-591.

DUNN, J.D.G., *Jesus and the Spirit*, London 1975.

———, «Was Christianity a Monotheistic Faith from the Beginning?», *SJT* 35 (1982) 303-336.

———, «Let John be John: A Gospel for its Time», in P. Stuhlmacher, ed., *Das Evangelium und die Evangelien*, Tübingen 1983, 309-339.

———, *Christology in the Making: An Inquiry into the Origins of the Doctrine of the Incarnation*, London 1989.

———, *Unity and Diversity in the New Testament: An Inquiry into the Character of Earliest Christianity*, London 1990.

———, «Christology (N.T.)», *ABD* I 979-991.

———, *The Theology of Paul the Apostle*, Grand Rapids 1997.

———, *The Christ and the Spirit*. I, Grand Rapids, MN. 1998.

———, «Jesus Tradition in Paul», in J.D.G. DUNN, *The Christ and the Spirit*. I, 1998, 169-189.

DUPUIS, J., *L'Esprit de l'homme. Étude sur l'anthropologie religieuse d'Origine*, Rome 1967.

———, *Jesus Christ and his Spirit*, Bangalore 1977.

———, *Jesus Christ at the Encounter of World Religions*, Maryknoll 1986.

DUPUIS, J., *Who do you say I am ? Introduction to Christology*, Maryknoll 1994.

————, *Toward a Christian Theology of Religious Pluralism*, Maryknoll 1998.

DUQUOC, C., «Le Christ e la mort de Dieu», *LV* (L) 89 (1968) 43-59.

————, *Ambiguitiés des théologiens de la sécularisation. Essai critique*, Gembloux 1972.

————, *Christologie: essai dogmatique*, Paris 1972.

————, «Le christianisme et la prétention à l'universel», *Conc* (F) 155 (1980) 75-85.

————, ed., *Job and the Silence of God*, Edinburgh 1983.

————, *La femme, le clerc et le laïc. Oecuménisme et ministère*, Paris 1989.

————, «Une coexistence conflictuelle: théologie critique et magistère en catholicisme», *RTP* 121 (1989) 165-171.

————, *Figures du démoniaque, hier et aujourd'hui*, Paris 1992.

DYCH, W.V., *Karl Rahner*, London 1992.

EDWARDS, D., *The Human Experience of God*, New York 1983.

————, *Called to be Church in Australia*, New South Wales 1989.

————, *Jesus and the Cosmos*, New York 1991.

————, *Creation, Humanity, Community*, Dublin 1992.

————, *Jesus the Wisdom of God: An Ecological Theology*, Maryknoll 1995.

————, «Evolution and the God of Mutual Friendship», *Pac* 10 (1997) 187-200.

————, *The God of Evolution: A Trinitarian Theology*, NewYork 1999.

————, «The Ecological Significance of God -language», *TS* 60 (1999) 708-722.

EDWARDS, R.A., *A Theology of Q: Eschatology, Prophecy and Wisdom*, Philadelphia 1976.

EISENMAN R.H., and WISE, M.O., *The Dead Sea Scrolls Uncovered. The First Complete Translation and Interpretation of 50 Key Documents withheld over 35 Years*, Rockport, MA. 1992.

ELGVIN, T., «Admonition Texts from Qumran Cave 4», in M.O. WISE et al, ed., *Methods of Investigation of the Dead Sea Scrolls and the Khirbet Qumran Site. Present Realities and Future Prospects*, New York 1993, 137-152.

ELGVIN, T., «The Reconstruction of Sapiential Work A», *RevQ* 16 (1995) 559-580.

ELIADE, M., *A History of Religious Ideas*. I, Chicago 1978.

ELLIS, E.E., *Paul and his Recent Interpreters*, Grand Rapids 1961.

————, *Paul's Use of the Old Testament*, Tübingen 1981.

ELLIS, P.F., *Matthew*, Collegeville, 1974.

ENGELSMANN, J.C., *The Feminine Dimension of the Divine*, Philadelphia 1979.

ERNST, J., *Das Evangelium nach Lukas übersetzt und erklärt*, Regensburg 1977.

————, *Das Evangelium nach Markus*, Regensburg 1981.

EVANS, C.A., *Word and Glory*, Sheffield 1993.

EVANS, G.R., *The History of the Life of St. Bernard*, Mahwah, NY 1987.

FALLS, T.B., *The Fathers of the Church*. I-VI, Washington, DC 1971-'77.

FEE, G.D., *The First Epistle to the Corinthians*, Grand Rapids 1987.

FELDER, C.H., *Wisdom, Law and Social Concern in the Epistle of James*, Columbia 1982.

FENTON, J.Y. ed., *Religions of Asia*, New York 1983.

FEUILLET, A., *Le Christ, Sagesse Dieu d'après les épîtres paulinennes*, Paris 1966.

FICHTNER, J., «Isaiah among the Wise», in J. CRENSHAW, ed., *Studies in Ancient Israelite Wisdom*, New York 1974, 429-438.

FITZMYER, J.A., *The Gospel According to Luke*, AnBib 28, Rome 1985.

————, *Scripture and Christology: A Statement of the Biblical Commission with a Commentary*, New York 1986.

————, «The Aramaic Background of Phil 2:6-11», *CBQ* 50 (1988) 470-483.

————, *Paul and His Theology*, New Jersey 1989.

————, «The Letter to the Romans», *NJBC*, 830-835.

————, *Luke the Theologian*, New York 1989.

————, *Responses to 101 Questions on the Dead Sea Scrolls*, New York 1992.

————, *The Letter to the Romans*, New York 1993.

————, *According to Paul*, New York 1993.

FORD, D.F., «Edward Schillebeeckx», in D.F. FORD, ed., *The Modern Theologians: An Introduction to Christian Theology in the Twentieth Century.* I, Oxford 1989, 152-163.

FORTNA, R., *The Gospel of Signs*, Cambridge 1970.

———, *The Fourth Gospel and Its Predecessor*, Edinburgh 1988.

FOSSUM, J., «Colossians 1:15-18a in the light of Jewish Mysticism and Gnosticism», *NTS* 35 (1989) 183-201.

FOWL, S.E., *The Story of Christ in the Ethics of Paul: An Analysis of the Function of the Hymnic Material in the Pauline Corpus*, JSNTSS 36, Sheffield 1990.

FOWLER, R.M., *Loaves and Fishes: The Function of the Feeding Stories in the Gospel of Mark*, Chico, CA 1981.

FOX, M.V., *Qoheleth and his Contradictions*, Sheffield 1989.

———, «Ideas of Wisdom in Proverbs 1-9», *JBL* 116/4 (1997) 613-633.

FRANKLIN, E., *Luke: Interpreter of Paul, Critic of Matthew*, Sheffield 1989.

FRANKOWSKI, J., «Early Christian Hymns Recorded in the New Testament: A Reconstruction of the Question in the Light of Heb 1:3», *BZ* 27 (1983) 183-194.

FRETHEIM, T.E., «Word of God», *ABD*, IV, 961-968.

FRIEDRICH, G., «Das Lied vom Hohenpriester im Zusammenhang von Hebr 4:14-5:10», *TZ* 18 (1962) 95-115.

FUELLENBACH, J., *The Kingdom of God: The Message of Jesus Today*, New York 1995.

GAMMIE, J.G., ed., *Israelite Wisdom. Theological and Literary Essays in Honour of Samuel Terrien*, Missoula 1990.

GARCIA MARTINEZ, F., *The Dead Sea Scrolls Translated. The Qumran Texts in English*, Leiden 1994.

GARLAND, D.E., «The Composition and Unity of Philippians», *NT* 27 (1985) 141-173.

GARRETT, G., «Rule 4? Gender Difference and the Nature of Doctrine», *Pac* 10 (1997) 173-186.

GEMSER, B., *Sprüche Salomos*, HAT 16, Tübingen 1963.

GEORGI, D., «Der vorpaulinische Hymnus Phil 2:6-11», in E. DINKLER, ed., *Zeit und Geschichte: Dankesgabe an R. Bultmann zum 80 Geburtstag*, Tübingen 1964, 263-294.

———, *Weisheit Salomos*, Gütersloh 1980.

GESE, H., *Essays on Biblical Theology*, Minneapolis 1981.

GEYER, J., *The Wisdom of Solomon*, London 1963.

GIBLIN, C.H., «Two Complimentary Literary Strustures in John 1:1-18», *JBL* 104 (1985) 87-103.

GILBERT, M., ed., *La Sagesse de l'Ancien Testament*, Leuven 1979.

————, «Le Discours de la Sagesse en Proverbes 8», in M. GILBERT, ed., *La Sagesse de l'Ancien Testament*, Leuven 1979.

GILSON, E., *The Mystical Theology of Bernard of Clairvaux*, New York 1940.

GLASSON, T.F., «Col 1:15,18 and Sirach 24», *NT* 11 (1969) 154-156.

GNILKA, J., *Das Evangelium nach Markus*, Zurich 1978.

————, *Der Kolosserbrief*, Freiburg 1980.

————, *Der Philipperbrief*, Freiburg 1980.

GNILKA, J., *Johannesevangelium*, Freiburg 1983.

GOODENOUGH, E.R., *By Light, Light: The Mystic Gospel of Hellenistic Judaism*, New Haven 1935.

GORDIS, R., «The Social Background of Wisdom Literature», *BTB* 2 (1972) 81-92.

GOULDER, M.D., «Sophia in I Corinthians», *NTS* 37 (1991) 516-534.

GOWAN, D.E., «Wisdom and Endurance in James», *HBT* 15 (1993) 145-153.

GRANT, R.P., *Greek Apologists of the Second Century*, Philadelphia 1988.

GRASSER, J., *Hebräer 1:1-4*, Rome 1964.

GRILLMEIER, A., *Christ in Christian Tradition*. I-II, London 1974-'94.

GRUNDMANN, W., *Das Evangelium nach Matthäus*, Berlin 1971.

————, «Weisheit im Horizont des Reiches Gottes: Eine Studie zur Verkundigung Jesu nach der Spruchüberlieferung Q», in R. SCHNACKENBURG, ed., *Die Kirche des Anfangs*, Freiburg 1975 175-199.

GUELICH, R.A., *Mark*, Dallas 1989.

GUNDRY, R.H., *Mark*, Grand Rapids 1993.

HAGNER, D.A., *Matthew*. I-II, Dallas 1993-'95.

HAHN, F., *The Titles of Jesus in Christology. Their History in Early Christianity*, London 1969.

HAMERTON-KELLY, R.G., *Pre-existence, Wisdom and the Son of Man*, Cambridge 1973.

HANSON, R.P.C., *The Search for the Christian Doctrine of God*, Edinburgh 1988.

HARE, D.R.A., *The Theme of Jewish Persecution of Christians in the Gospel according to St. Matthew*, Cambridge 1967.

HARRINGTON, D.J. – STRUGNELL, J., «Qumran Cave 4 Texts: A New Publication», *JBL* 112 (1993) 491-499.

HARRINGTON, D.J., «The Gospel According to Mark», *NJBC*, 1989, 596-629.

―――, *Wisdom Texts from Qumran*, London 1996.

HARRINGTON, W., *Mark*, Wilmington 1979.

HARRIS, E.A., *Prologue and Gospel*, Sheffield 1994.

HARTIN, P.J., *James and the Q Sayings of Jesus*, Sheffield 1991.

HAWKING, S., *A Brief History of Time: From the Big Bang to Black Holes*, London 1988.

HAWTHORNE, G.F., *The Letter to the Philippians*, WBC, Dallas 1983.

HAYES, J., *An Introduction to the Study of the Old Testement*, Nashville 1979.

HAYES, Z., *Saint Bonevanture's Disputed Questions on the Mystery of the Trinity: An Introduction and a Translation*, New York 1979.

HEINE, R.E., *Origen. Commentary on the Gospel According to John*, Cambridge 1975.

HELLER, N., *The Exemplar: Life and Writings of Blessed Henry Suso*, Mahwah, NY 1989.

HENGEL, M., *Judaism and Hellenism: Studies in their Encounter in Palestine, during the Early Hellenistic Period*, I-II, London 1974.

―――, *The Son of God*, Philadelphia 1976.

―――, *Crucifixion in the Ancient World and the Folly of the Message of the Cross*, Philadelphia 1977.

―――, «Jesus als messianischer Lehrer der Weisheit und die Anfänge der Christologie», in E. JACOB, ed., *Sagesse et Religion*, Paris 1979, 147-190.

―――, «Hymns and Christology», *Between Jesus and Paul. Studies in the Earliest History of Christianity*, Philadelphia 1983, 78-96.

―――, «Psalm 110 und die Erhöhung des Auferstandenen zur Rechten Gottes», in C. Breytenbach – H. Paulsen, ed., *Anfänge der Christologie*, Göttingen 1984, 201-218.

―――, *Studies in the Gospel of Mark*, Philadelphia 1985.

―――, *The Cross of the Son of God*, London 1986.

―――, *The Hellenization of Judea in the First Century after Christ*, Philadelphia 1989.

―――, *The Johannine Question*, Philadelphia 1989.

HÉRING, J., «Kyrios Anthropos (Phil 2:6-11)», *RHPR* 16 (1936) 196-209.

————, *L'Epître aux Hébreux*, Paris 1954.

HOFIUS O., *Der Christushymnus Philipper 2:6-11,* Tübingen 1976.

HOLM NIELSEN, S., *Hodayot. Psalms from Qumran*, Aarhus 1960.

HOOKER, M.D., «The Johannine Prologue and the Messianic Secret», *NTS* 21 (1974) 40-58.

————, «Philippians 2:6-11», in E. Earle – E. Graesser, ed., *Jesus und Paulus,* Göttingen 1975, 151-164.

————, *From Adam to Christ: Essays on Paul*, Cambridge 1990.

————, *Mark*, London 1991.

HORGAN, M.P., «The Letter to the Colossians», *NJBC*, 877-882.

HORSLEY, R.A., «Wisdom of Word and Words of Wisdom in Corinth», *CBQ* 39 (1972) 224-239.

————, «How can some of you say that there is no Resurrection of the Dead? - Spiritual Elitism in Corinth», *NT* 20 (1978) 203-231.

————, «The Background of the Confessional Formulae in I Cor 8:6», *ZNW* 69 (1978) 130-135.

HOWARD, G.E., «Philippians 2:6-11 and the Human Christ», *CBQ* 40 (1978) 368-387.

HOWARD, W.F., *The Fourth Gospel in Recent Criticism and Interpretation*, London 1955.

HUGHES, P.E., *A Commentary on the Epistle to the Hebrews*, Grand Rapids 1977.

HUMPHREY, H.M., «Jesus as Wisdom in Mark», *BTB* 19 (1989) 48-53.

HURD, J.C., *The Origins of I Corinthians*, London 1965.

HURST, L.D., «Re-enter the Pre-existent Christ in Philippians 2:5-11?», *NTS* 32 (1986) 449-457.

HURTADO, L.W., «Jesus as Lordly Example in Phil 2:5-11», in P. Richardson – J.C. Hurd, ed., *From Jesus to Paul,* Waterloo 1984.

————, *One God, One Lord: Early Christian Devotion and Ancient Jewish Monotheism*, Philadelphia 1988.

JACOBSON, A.D., «The Literary Unit of Q», *JBL* 101 (1982) 365-389.

JAEGER, H., «The Patristic Conception of Wisdom in the Light of Biblical and Rabbinical Research», in F.L. CROSS, ed., *Studia Patristica*. XIV, 1992, 90-106.

JANTZEN, G., *Power, Gender, and Christian Mysticism*, Cambridge 1995.

JEREMIAS, J., «Zur Gedankenführung in den paulinischen Briefen», in J.N. Sevenster – W.C. van Unnik, ed., *Studia Paulina in honorem J. de Zwaan septuagenarii*, Leiden 1983, 146-154.

―――, *The Servant of God*, Philadelphia 1957.

―――, «The Key to Pauline Theology», *ExpTim* 76 (1964) 27-30.

―――, *Die Sprache des Lukasevangeliums*, Göttingen 1980.

JERVELL, J., *Imago Dei: Gen 1:26f im Spätjudentum in der Gnosis und in den paulinischen Briefen*, Göttingen 1960.

―――, *Luke and the People of God*, Minneapolis 1972.

JOHNSON, E.A., «Jesus the Wisdom of God: A Biblical Basis for Non-Androcentric Christology», *ETL* 61 (1985) 261-294.

―――, *She Who Is: The Mystery of God in Feminist Theological Discourse*, New York 1992.

―――, *Jesus - Sophia: Ramifications for Contemporary Theology*, Cambridge 1999.

JOHNSON, E.E., *The Function of Apocalyptic and Wisdom Traditions in Romans 9-11*, Atlanta, GA. 1989.

JOHNSON, L.T., *The Letter of James*, AB Commentary Series, New York 1995.

JOHNSON, M.D., «Reflections on a Wisdom Approach to Matthew's Christology», *CBQ* 36 (1974) 44-64.

KARRIS, R.J., «The Gospel According to Luke», *NJBC*, 675-721.

KÄSEMANN, E., «A Primitive Christian Baptisimal Liturgy», in *Essays on New Testament Themes*, SBT 41, London 1964, 149-168.

―――, «A Critical Analysis of Philippians 2:5-11», in R.W. Funk, ed., *God and Christ: Existence and Providence*, New York 1968, 45-88.

―――, *Commentary on Romans*, Tübingen 1980.

―――, *The Wandering People of God: An Investigation of the Letter to the Hebrews*, Minneapolis 1984.

KASPER, W., *Die Methoden der Dogmatik*, München 1967; E.T.: *Methods of Dogmatic Theology*, New York 1969.

―――, *Jesus der Christus*, Mainz 1974; E.T.: *Jesus the Christ*, London 1976, 1993.

―――, *Der Gott Jesu Christi*, Mainz 1982; E.T.: *The God of Jesus Christ*, London 1984, 1992.

KASPER, W., «Gottes Gegenwart in Jesus Christus. Vorüberlegungen zu einer weisheitlichen Christologie», in S. WIEDENHOFER, ed., *Weisheit Gottes - Weisheit der Welt*, St Ottilien, 1987, 311-328.

KEALY, S.P., *Mark's Gospel: A History of Its Interpretation*, New York 1982.

KEARNEY, R., *Modern Movements in European Philosophy*, London 1992.

KEHL, N., *Der Christushymnus in der frühen Christenheit*, Göttingen 1967.

KELLY, J.N.D., *Early Christian Doctrines*, London 1968.

KENNEDY, P., *Schillebeeckx*, London 1993.

KERTELGE, K., «Das Apostelamt des Paulus, sein Ursprung und seine Bedeutung», *BZ* 14 (1970) 161-181.

KIDNER, D.A., *Proverbs*, Downer's Grove 1967.

KIEWELER, H.V., *Ben Sira zwischen Judentum und Hellenismus*, Frankfurt 1992.

KIM, S., *The Origin of Paul's Gospel*, Tübingen 1981.

KINGSBURY, J.D., *The Christology of Mark's Gospel*, Philadelphia 1983.

KIRK, J.A., «The Meaning of Wisdom in James: Examination of a Hypothesis», *NTS* 16 (1969) 24-38.

KITTEL, B., *The Hymns of Qumran: Translation and Commentary*, Chico, CA.1981.

KLEINEIDAM, E., «Wissen, Wissenschaft, Theologie bei bernhard von Clairvaux», in J. LORTZ, ed., *bernhard von clairvaux; Mönch und Mystiker*, Wiesbaden 1955.

KLEIST J.A., ed., *The Epistles of St. Clement of Rome and St. Ignatius of Antioch*, Westminister, MD. 1949.

KLOPPENBORG, J.S., «Isis and Sophia in the Book of Wisdom», *HTR* 75 (1982) 57-84.

———, «The Formation of Q and Antique Instructional Genres», *JBL* 105 (1986) 450-462.

KLOSTERMANN, E., *Das Matthausevangelium*, Tübingen 1938.

———, *Das Lukasevangelium*, Tübingen 1975.

KNOX, W.L., «The Divine Wisdom», *JTS* 38 (1937) 230-237.

KOESTER, H., «Review of U. Wilckens' *Weisheit und Torheit*», *Gnomon*, 33 (1961), 590-595.

———, «Paul and Hellenism», in P.J. Hyatt, ed., *The Bible in Modern Scholarship*, New York 1965, 121-134.

KÜMMEL, W.G., *Introduction to the New Testament*, Nashville 1986.

KÜNNETH, W., *The Theology of the Resurrection*, London 1965.

KUSS, O., *Der Brief an die Hebräer*, Regensburg 1966.

KYSAR, R., «The Gospel of John», *ABD*, III, 912-931.

————, *The Fourth Evangelist and His Gospel*, Minneapolis 1975.

LAFFEY, A.L., *Wives, harlots, and Concubines: The Old Testament in Feminist Perspective*, London 1990.

LAMPE, P., «Theological Wisdom and the Word about the Cross. The Rhetorical Scheme in I Corinthians 1-4», *Int* 44 (1990) 117-131.

LANG, B., *Frau Weisheit: Deutung einer biblischer Gestalt*, Düsseldorf 1975.

LANGELLA, M.R., *Salvezza come illuminazione. Uno studio comparato di S. Bulgakov, V. Lossky, P. Evdokimov*, Roma 2000.

LAPORTE, J., «Philo in the Tradition of Biblical Wisdom Literature», in R.L. WILKEN, ed., *Aspects of Wisdom in Judaism and Early Christianity*, Notre Dame, IN 1975, 103-141.

LARCHER, C., *Études sur le Livre de la Sagesse*, Paris 1969.

————, *Le Livre de la Sagesse ou la Sagesse de Salomon*. I-III, Paris 1983-85.

LAUB, F., *Bekenntnis und Auslegung*, Regensburg 1980.

LAWS, S., *The Letter of James*, HNTC, New York 1980.

LEA MATTILA, S., «Wisdom, Sense Perception, Nature, and Philo's Gender Gradient», *HTR* 89 (1996) 103-129.

LEAHY, T.W., «The Epistle of James», *NJBC*, 909-916.

LEE, D.A., «Abiding in the Fourth Gospel: A Case-Study in Feminist Biblical Theology», *Pac* 10 (1997) 123-136.

LEFEBURE, L.D., *Toward a Contemporary Wisdom Christology: A Study of Karl Rahner and Norman Pittenger*, New York 1988.

LEHMANN, M.R., «11Q5 and Ben Sira», *RevQ* 11 (1983) 239-251.

LEIVA MERIKAKIS, E., «Louis Bouyer the theologian», *Communio* (US) 16 (1989) 257-282.

LÉVÈQUE, J., *Études sur le Livre de la Sagesse*, Paris 1969.

————, *Job et son Dieu*, Paris 1970.

LEVINE, A.J., «Sacrifice and Salvation», in J.C. VANDERKAM, ed., *One Spoke Ill of Her: Essays on Judith*, 1992, 17-30.

LINDARS, B., *The Gospel of John*, London 1972.

————, «John and the Synoptic Gospels: A Test Case», *NTS* 27 (1981) 287-294.

LINDEMANN, A., *Der Kolosserbrief*, Zürich 1983.

LIPSCOMB, W.L., – SANDERS, J.A., «Wisdom at Qumran», in J.G. GAMMIE et al, ed., *Israelite Wisdom*, Missoula 1990, 277-285.

LOADER, W.R.G., *Sohn und Hohepriester*, Bonn 1981.

LOADES, A., *Feminist Theology. A Reader*, London 1990.

LOEWE, W.P., «The New Catholic Tübingen Theology of Walter Kasper: Foundational Issues», *HeyJ* 21 (1980) 30-49.

LOHMEYER, E., *Kyrios Jesus. Eine Untersuchung zu Phil 2:6-11*, Göttingen 1928.

———, *Die Briefe an die Philipper, an die Kolosser und an Philemon*, Göttingen 1956.

LOHSE E., *A Commentary on the Epistles to the Colossians and to Philemon*, Philadelphia 1971.

LOTTZ, J., ed., *Bernhard von Clairvaux: Mönch und Mystiker*, Wiesbaden 1955.

LOUTH, A., «Wisdom and the Russians: The Sophiology of Fr. Sergei Bulgakov», in S.C. BARTON, ed., *Where shall Wisdom be Found? Wisdom in the Bible, the Church, and the Contemporary World*, Edinburgh 1999, 169-181.

LÜDEMANN, G., *Paulus, der Heidenapostel. II*, Göttingen 1983.

LUZ, U., *Das Evangelium nach Matthäus*, Zürich 1985.

LYONNET, S., *Quaestiones in epistulam ad Romanos. I-II.*, Rome 1962.

LYONS, J.A., *The Cosmic Christ in Origen and Teilhard de Chardin: A Comparative Study*, Oxford 1982.

LYS, D., *L'Ecclésiaste ou que vaut la vie?*, Paris 1977.

MACKENZIE, R.A.F. – MURPHY, R.E., «Job», *NJBC*, 466-488.

MACKENZIE, R.A.F., *Sirach*, OTM 19, Wilmington 1983.

MCCOOL, G.A., «Introduction to Rahner's Philosophical Theology», in *A Rahner Reader*, London 1975, xiii-xxviii.

MCCREESH, T.P., «Proverbs», *NJBC*, 453-461.

MCDONAGH, S., *To Care for the Earth*, London 1986.

———, *The Greening of the Church*, New York 1990.

———, *Greening the Christian Millennium*, Dublin 1999.

MCKANE, W., *Proverbs*, Philadelphia 1977.

MCKEATING, H., «Jesus Ben Sira's Attitude to Women», *ExpTim* 85 (1973) 85-87.

McLOUGHLIN, E., «Christ my Mother: Feminine Naming and Metaphor in Medieval Spirituality», *NQR* 15 (1975) 228-248.

McMULLEN, R., *Paganism in the Roman Empire*, New Haven 1981.

MACK, B.L., *Logos und Sophia: Untersuchungen zur Weisheitstheologie im hellenistischen Judentum*, Göttingen 1973.

MADONIA, N., *Ermeneutica e Cristologia in Walter Kasper*, Roma 1989.

MALCHOW, B., «Social Justice in the Wisdom Literature», *BTB* 12 (1982) 120-124.

MARBÖCK, J., *Weisheit im Wandel*, Bonn 1971.

MARSHALL, I.H., «Incarnational Cristology in the New Testament», in H.H. ROWDON, ed., *Christ the Lord*, Downer's Grove 1982.

MARTIN, F., *The Feminist Question: Feminist Theology in the Light of Christian Tradition*, Grand Rapids, MN. 1994.

MARTIN, R.P., *Commentary on Colossians and Philemon*, London 1981.

MARTIN, R.P., «Some Reflections on New Testament Hymns», in H.H. Rowdon, ed., *Christ the Lord*, Leicester 1982.

————, *Carmen Christi. Philippians 2:5-11 in Recent Interpretation and in the Setting of early Christian Worship*, Grand Rapids 1983.

MARTYN, J.L., *The Gospel of John in Christian History*, New York 1978.

————, *History and Theology in the Fourth Gospel*, Nashville 1979.

MASTON, T.B., «Ethical Dimensions of James», *SJT* 12 (1969) 23-39.

MEIER, J.P., *The Vision of Matthew: Christ, Church and Morality in the First Gospel*, New York 1979.

————, *Matthew*, Wilmington 1981.

————, «Symmetry and Theology in Heb 1:1-4», *Bib* 66 (1985) 504-533.

————, *A Marginal Jew: Rethinking the Historical Jesus*, I, New York 1991.

MENGEL, B., *Studien zum Philipperbrief*, Tübingen 1982.

MENOUD, P.H., «Revelation and Tradition: The Influence of Paul's Conversion on His Theology», *Int* 7 (1953) 131-141.

MERTON, T., *Mystics and Zen Masters*, New York 1967.

MICHEL, D., *Qohelet*, Darmstadt 1988.

MICHEL, O., *ber Brief an die Hebräer*. Göttingen 1966.

MIDDENDORP, T., *Die Stellung Jesus ben Siras zwischen Judentum und Hellenismus*, Leiden 1973.

MILIK, J.T., – BARTHELEMY, D., *Qumran Cave I*, Oxford 1955.

MILIK, J.T., *Ten Years of Discovery in the Wilderness*, London 1959.

MILLER, E.L., «The Logic of the Logos Hymn: A New View», *NTS* 29 (1983) 552-561.

MILLER, R.J., «The rejection of the Prophets in Q», *JBL* 107 (1988) 225-240.

MILLS, W., *An Index to Periodical Literature on the Apostle Paul*, Grand Rapids 1960.

MINEAR, P.S., «We Don't Know Where... Jn 20:2», *Int* 30 (1976) 125-139.

MOINGT, J., *Théologie trinitaire de Tertullien*. I-IV, Paris 1966-'69.

————, *Le devenir chrétien*, Paris 1973.

————, *La transmission de la foi*, Paris 1976.

————, *L'homme qui venait de Dieu*, Paris 1994.

MOLONEY, F.J., «The Johannine Son of God», *Sal* 38 (1976) 71-86.

MOLTMANN, J., *The Way of Jesus Christ: Christology in Messianic Dimensions*, San Francisco 1990.

MORGAN, D.F., *Wisdom in the Old Testament Traditions*, Oxford 1987.

MOULE, C.F.D., *The Epistles of Paul the Apostle to the Colossians and to Philemon*, Cambridge 1958.

MUNCK, J., *Paul and the Salvation of Mankind*, London 1959.

MURPHY, R.E., «Qohelet Interpreted: The Bearing of the Past on the Present», *VT* 32 (1982) 331-336.

————, «Wisdom's Song: Proverbs 1:20-33», *CBQ* 48 (1986) 456-460.

————, «Wisdom in the Old Testament», *ABD*, VI, New York 1992, 887-902.

————, «Introduction to Wisdom Literature», *NJBC*, 447-452.

————, *The Tree of Life: An Exploration of Biblical Wisdom Literature*, Grand Rapids 1996.

MURPHY O'CONNOR, J., «Christological Anthropology in Phil 2:6-11», *RB* 83 (1976) 25-50.

————, The First Letter to the Corinthians, *NJBC*, 798-815.

————, «Tradition and Redaction in Colossians 1:15-20», *RB* 102 (1995) 231-241.

MYERS, C.D., «Epistle to the Romans», *ABD*, V, New York 1992, 816-830.

NEBE, G.W., «Qumranica I: Zu unveröffentlichen Handschriften aus Höhle von Qumran», *ZAW* 106 (1994) 307-313.

NEIRYNCK, F., «Synoptic Problem», *NJBC* 587-595.

NEUFELD, K.H., *Die Brüder Rahner*, Freiburg 1994.

NEUNER, J. – DUPUIS, J., eds., *The Christian Faith in the Doctrinal Documents of the Catholic Church*, London 1996.

NEWMAN, B., *Sister of Wisdom: St. Hildegard's Theology of the Feminine*, Los Angeles, CA 1987.

———, «Some Medieval Theologians and the Sophia Tradition», *DR* 108 (1990) 111-130.

NICHOLS, A., «Walter Kasper and his Theological Programme», *NBl* 1 (1986) 16-24.

NICKELSBURG, G.W.E., *Jewish Literature between the Bible and the Mishnah*, London 1981.

NOMOTO, S., «Herkunft und Struktur der Hohenpriestervorstellung im Hebräerbrief», *NT* 10 (1968) 668-675.

NORDEN, E., *Agnostos Theos*, Stuttgart 1956.

OCHSHORN, J., *The Female Experience and the Nature of the Divine*, Bloomington, IN 1981.

O'BRIEN, P.T., *The Epistle to the Philippians: A Commentary on the Greek Text*, NIGTC Series, Grand Rapids 1991.

O'COLLINS, G., *Interpreting Jesus*, London 1983.

———, *Christology: A Biblical, Historical and Systematic Study of Jesus*, Oxford 1995.

———, «Images of Jesus and Modern Theology», in S.E. PORTER, ed., *Images of Christ Ancient and Modern*, Sheffield 1997, 128-143.

———, «Images of Jesus: Reappropriating Titular Christology», *TD* 44:4 (Winter 1997) 303-318.

O'COLLINS, G. – KENDALL, D., *The Bible for Theology: Ten Principles for the Theological Use of Scripture*, New York 1997.

O'CONNOR, K., *The Wisdom Literature*, Wilmington, DL 1988.

O'NEILL, J.C., «The Source of Christology in Colossians», *NTS* 30 (1984) 460-474.

O'TOOLE, R.F., *The Unity of Luke's Theology*, Wilmington, DL 1984.

PAINTER, J., «Christology and the History of the Johannine Community in the Prologue of the Fourth Gospel», *NTS* 30 (1984) 460-474.

PALAKEEL, J., *The Use of Analogy in Theological Discourse: An Investigation in Ecumenical Perspective*, Rome 1995.

PEARSON, A., *The Pneumatikos-Psychikos Terminology in I Corinthians*, Missoula, MT 1973.

PEARSON, B.A., «Hellenistic-Jewish Wisdom Speculation and Paul», in R.L. Wilken, ed., *Aspects of Wisdom in Judaism and Early Christianity*, South Bend, IN 1975, 43-66.

PERDUE, L.P., *Wisdom and Creation: The Theology of Wisdom Literature*, Nashville, TN 1994.

PERKINS, P., «The Gospel According to John», *NJBC*, 942-985.

PERRIN, N., «Wisdom and Apocalyptic in the Message of Jesus», *SBLASP* 2 (1972) 543-572.

PETERS, F.E., *The Harvest of Hellenism: A History of the Near East from Alexander the Great to the Triumph of Christianity*, New York 1970.

PFEIFER, G., *Ursprung und Wesen der Hypostasenvorstellung im Judentum*, Stuttgart 1967.

PHILO OF ALEXANDRIA, *The Complete Works*, E.T.: F.H. Colson – G.H. Whitaker, Cambridge, MA 1930, re-printed 1954, 1960, 1968.

PLÖGER, O., *Spruche Salomos (Proverbia)*, Neukirchen 1984.

POLHILL, J.B., «The Wisdom of God and Factionalism: I Cor 1-4», *RevExp* 80 (1983) 325-339.

POLLARD, T.E., «Colossians 1;12-20: A Reconsideration», *NTS* 27 (1980) 572-575.

POPE, M.H., *Job*, AB Commentary 15, New York 1973.

POTTERIE, I. DE LA, *La verité dans saint Jean*. I-II, Paris 1977.

PRATO, G.L., *Il problema della teodicea in Ben Sira*, Rome 1975.

QUESNELL, Q., *The Mind of Mark*, Rome 1969.

RADFORD RUETHER, R., *Gaia and God: An Ecofeminist Theology of Earth Healing*, San Francisco 1992.

RAHNER, K., *Hominisation: The Evolutionary Origin of Man as a Theological Problem*, New York 1965.

——, *On the Theology of Death*, New York 1967.

——, «Resurrection: [D]. Theology», in K. RAHNER, ed., *Sacramentum Mundi: An Encyclopedia of Theology*. V, New York 1970, 332-333.

——, *Grundkurs des Glaubens: Einführung in den Begriff des Christentums*, Freiburg 1976, E.T..: *Foundations of Christian Faith: An Introduction to the Idea of Christianity*, New York 1978.

——, «Concerning the Relationship between Nature and Grace», *TI* I 297-317.

——, «Current Problems in Christology», *TI* I 149-200.

RAHNER, K., «The Concept of Mystery in Catholic Theology», *TI* IV 36-73.

————. «On the Theology of the Incarnation», *TI* IV 105-120.

————, «Dogmatic Questions on Easter», *TI* IV 124-133.

————, «Christology within an evolutionary view of the world», *TI* V 157-192.

————, «Theology of the Symbol», *TI* IV 221-252.

————, «Christology within an Evolutionary View of the World», *TI* V 157-192.

————, «The Unity of Spirit and Matter in the Christian Understanding of Faith», *TI* VI 153-177.

————, «The Human Question of Meaning in face of the Absolute Mystery of God», *TI* XVIII 89-104.

————, «The Christian Understanding of the Redemption», *TI* XXI 252-253.

RAHNER, K., – VORGRIMLER, H., *Kleines Theologisches Wörterbuch*, Freiburg 1961; E.T.: *Concise Theological Dictionary*, New York 1975.

RAHTJEN, B.D., «The Three Letters of Paul to the Philippians», *NTS*, 6 (1959) 167-173.

RAMM, B.L., *An Evangelical Christology: Ecumenic and Historic*, New York 1985.

RANKIN, O.S., *Israel's Wisdom Literature. It's Bearing on Theology and the History of Religion*, Edinburgh 1936.

RATZINGER, J., *Called to Communion: Understanding the Church Today*, San Francisco 1996.

REED, W.L., «Asherah», *IDB*. I, 250-252.

REESE, J.M., «Plan and Structure in the Book of Wisdom», *CBQ* 27 (1965) 391-399.

————, *Hellenistic Influence on the Book of Wisdom and its Consequences*, AnBib 41, Rome 1970.

————, «Paul Proclaims the Wisdom of the Cross: Scandal and Foolishness», *BTB* 9 (1979) 147-153.

RETTIG, J.W., *The Fathers of the Church*, Washington, DC 1988.

RIDDERBOS, H.N., *Paul and Jesus: Origin and General Character of Paul's Preaching of Christ*, Philadelphia 1958.

RINGGREN, H., *Word and Wisdom: Studies in the Hypostatization of Divine Qualities and Functions in the Ancient Near East*, London 1947.

ROBERTS, L.A., *The Achievement of Karl Rahner*, New York 1967.

ROBINSON, D.W.B., «The Literary Sources of Hebrews 1-4», *AusJBA* 2 (1972) 178-186.

ROBINSON, J.M., «A Formal Analysis of Col 1:15-20», *JBL* 76 (1957) 278-279.

———, «Kerygma and History in the New Testament», in J.M. ROBINSON – H. KOESTER, ed., *Trajectories through Early Christianity*, Philadelphia 1971.

———, «Logoi Sophōn: on the Gattung of Q», in J.M. Robinson – H. Koester, ed., *Trajectories through Early Christianity*, Philadelphia 1971.

ROCHAIS, G., «La formation du prologue Jn 1:1-18», *ScEs* 37 (1985) 5-44.

ROMANIUK, C., «Le Livre de la Sagesse dans le Nouveau Testament», *NTS* 14 (1968) 498-514.

———, «Le thème de la Sagesse dans les Documents de Qumrân», *RevQ* 9 (1977) 429-435.

ROTELLE, J.E., ed., *The Works of St. Augustine*. I-III, New York 1994-'97.

RUDMAN, D., «Woman as Divine Agent in Ecclesiastes», *JBL* 116 (1997) 411-427.

RUPPERT, H.J., *Klassiker der Theologie*. I-II, Munich 1981-'83.

RUSSELL, L.M., ed., *Feminist Interpretation of the Bible*, Oxford 1985.

SABIN, M., «Women Transformed: The Ending of Mark is the beginning of Wisdom», *Cross Currents* 48 (1998) 149-168.

SABOURIN, L., *The Names and Titles of Jesus. Themes of Biblical Theology*, New York 1967.

SANDERS, E.P., *Paul and Palestinian Judaism*, London 1977.

SANDERS, J.A., «The Psalms Scroll of Qumran Cave 11», *DJD* 4 (1965) 91-92.

———, *The Psalms Scrolls of Qumran Cave 11 (11QPsa)*, Oxford 1965.

SANDERS, J.T., *The New Testament Christological Hymns: Their Historical Religious Background*, SNTSMS 15, Cambridge 1971.

———, *Ben Sira and Demotic Wisdom*, Chico, CA 1983.

———, «Nag Hammadi, Odes of Solomon and New Testament Christological Hymns», in J.E. Goehring, ed., *Gnosticism and the Early Christian World*, Sonoma 1990, 51-66.

SCHIFFMAN, L.H., *Reclaiming the Dead Sea Scrolls. The History of Judaism, the Background of Christianity, the Lost Library of Qumran*, Philadelphia 1994.

SCHILLE, G., *Frühchristliche Hymnen*, Berlin 1965.

SCHILLEBEECKX, E., *Jezus - het Verhaal vaneen Levende*, Bloemendaal 1974, E.T.: *Jesus: An Experiment in Christology*, New York 1979.

―――, *Gerechtigheid en Liefde: Genade en bevrijding*, Baarn: Nelissen, 1978; E.T.: *Christ: The Christian Experience in the Modern World*, London 1980.

―――, *Tussentijds verhaal over twee Jezus boeken*, Bloemendaal 1978; E.T.: *Interim Report on the Books «Jesus» and «Christ»*, London 1980.

―――, *Mensen als verhaal van God*, Baarn: Nelissen, 1989, 1990; E.T.: *Church: The Human Story of God*, London 1990.

SCHIPFLINGER, T., *Sophia - Maria: A Holistic Vision of Creation*, York Beach, MA 1998.

SCHLATTER, A., *Der Evangelist Johannes*, Stuttgart 1930.

SCHLOSSER, J., «Jésus le sage et ses vues sur l'homme d'après l'Évangile de Marc», in ASSOCIATION CATHOLIQUE FRANCAISE POUR L'ÉTUDE DE LA BIBLE, *La sagesse biblique de L'Ancien au Nouveau Testament*, Paris 1995.

SCHMITHALS W., *Gnosticism in Corinth*, New York 1972.

SCHNACKENBURG, R., «Logos-Hymun und johanneischer Prolog», *BZ* 1 (1957) 69-109.

―――, *The Gospel According to St. John*. I-III, New York 1968-1982.

SCHOTTROFF, L., «Women as Followers of Jesus in New Testament Times» in N.K. GOTTWALD – R.A. HORSLEY, ed., *The Bible and Liberation: Political and Social Hermeneutics*, New York 1993, 453-461.

SCHRADER, L., *Leiden und Gerechtigkeit. Studien zu Theologie und Textgeschichte des Sirachbuches*, Frankfurt 1994.

SCHRADER, M., – FÜHRKÖTTER, A., *Die Echtheit des Schrifttums der heiligen Hildegard von Bingen*, Köln, 1956.

SCHREITER, R.J., «A Bibliography on the Writings of Edward Schillebeeckx from 1945 to 1983», in R.J. SCHREITER, ed., *The Schillebeeckx Reader*, New York 1984.

SCHREITER R.J. – HILKERT M.C. (eds.), *The Praxis of Christian Experience: An Introduction to the Theology of Edward Schillebeeckx*, San Francisco 1989.

SCHULZ, S., *Q: Die Spruchquelle der Evangelisten*, Zurich 1972.

SCHÜSSLER FIORENZA, E., «Wisdom Mythology and the Christological Hymns of the New Testament», in R.L. WILKEN, ed., *Aspects of Wisdom in Judaism and Early Christianity*, Notre Dame, IN 1975, 17-41.

SCHÜSSLER FIORENZA, E., «Word, Spirit, and Power: Women in Early Christian Communities», in R. RUETHER – E. MCLOUGHLIN, ed., *Women of Spirit: Female Leadership in the Jewish and Christian Traditions*, New York 1979, 30-70.

―――, *In Memory of Her: A Feminist Theological Reconstruction of Christian Origins*, New York 1983.

―――, *Bread not Stone: The Challenge of Feminist Biblical Interpretation*, Boston 1984.

―――, «The Will to Choose or to Reject: Continuing our Critical Work», in L. M. RUSSELL ed., *Feminist Interpretation of the Bible*, Oxford 1989.

―――, *Revelation: Vision of a Just World*, Augsburg 1991.

―――, *But She Said: Feminist Practices of Biblical Interpretation*, Boston 1992.

―――, *Discipleship of Equals: A Feminist Ekklesialogy of Liberation*, New York 1993.

―――, *Searching the Scriptures*. I-II, New York 1993-'94.

―――, *Jesus: Miriam's Child, Sophia's Prophet: Critical Issues in Feminist Liberation Theology*, New York 1994.

―――, «Jesus - Messenger of Divine Wisdom», *ST* 49 (1995) 231-252.

―――, *The Power of Naming: A Concilium reader in Feminist Liberation Theology*, New York 1996.

―――, «Struggle is a Name for Hope: A Critical Feminist Interpretation for Liberation», *Pac* 10 (1997) 224-248.

―――, *Sharing Her Word*, Boston 1998.

SCHWEIZER, E., «The Church as the Missionary Body of Christ», *NTS* 8 (1961) 1-11.

―――, *Ego Eimi*, Göttingen 1965.

―――, *The Good News According to Matthew*, Wilmington, DL. 1981.

―――, *The Letter to the Colossians*, Minneapolis 1982.

―――, *Jesus Christ: The Man from Nazareth and the Exalted Lord*, Macon, GA 1987.

SCOTT, M., *Sophia and the Johannine Jesus*, Sheffield 1992.

SCOTT, R.B.Y., *Proverbs*, AB Commentary 18, New York 1965.

―――, *The Way of Wisdom in the Old Testament*, New York 1971.

SCROGGS, R., «Paul - Sophos and Pneumatikos», *NTS* 14 (1967) 33-55.

SEGUNDO, J.L., *The Liberation of Theology*, New York 1982.

SELLIN, G., «Das *Geheimnis* der Weisheit und das Rätsel der *Christuspartei* (zu I Kor 1-4)», *ZNW* 73 (1982) 69-96.

SERENTHÀ, M., «Cristologie nella prospettiva dell'uomo Gesù: Schoonenberg, Duquoc, Rahner, Küng, Schillebeeckx», *ScC* 105 (1977) 61-113.

SESBOÜÉ, B., «Bulletin de théologie dogmatique. Christologie», *RSR* 56 (1968) 628-671.

———, «Bulletin de théologie dogmatique. Christologie.», *RSR* 61 (1973) 423-465.

———, «De la rumeur de Jésus à la génération du Verbe. Du Nouveau en Christologie», *RSR* 82 (1994) 87-102.

SETEL, T.D., «Feminist Insights and the Question of Method», in A. YARBRO COLLINS, ed., *Feminist Perspectives on Biblical Scholarship*, Chico, CA 1985.

SHEPPARD, G.T., *Wisdom as a Hermeneutical Construct*, New York 1980.

SIMPKINS, A., *Creator and Creation: Nature in the World-View of Ancient Israel*, Peabody, MA 1994.

SISTI, A., *Il libro della Sapienza*, Assisi 1992.

SITTLER, J., «Called to Unity», *ER* 14 (1961) 177-178.

SKEHAN, P.W. «Structures in Poems on Wisdom: Prov 8 and Sir 24», *CBQ* 41 (1979) 365-379.

SKEHAN P.W., – DI LELLA, A.A., *The Wisdom of Ben Sira*, AB Commentary 39, New York 1987.

SLOYAN, G.S., *What are they saying about John?*, New York 1991.

SMALLEY, S.S., «The Johannine Son of Man Sayings», *NTS* 15 (1968) 278-301.

SMITH, D.M., *John among the Gospels: The Relationship in Twentieth-Century Research*, Minneapolis 1992.

SMITH, D.W., *Wisdom Christology in the Synoptic Gospels*, Rome 1970.

SPICQ, C., *L'Ecclésiastique*, Paris 1951.

———, *L'Epître aux Hébreux*. I-II, Paris 1952-53.

STANLEY, D.M., «The Theme of the Servant of Yahweh in Primitive Christian Soteriology and its Transposition by St. Paul», *CBQ* 16 (1954) 385-425.

———, «The Pauline Conception of Apostolic Tradition», *Bib* 40 (1959) 859-877.

STANLEY, J.L., «The Structure of John's Prologue: Its Implications for the Gospel's Narrative Structure», *CBQ* 48 (1986) 241-264.

STANTON, G.N., «On the Christology of Q», in B. Landers – S.S. Smalley, ed., *Christ and Spirit in the New Testament*, Cambridge 1973, 27-42.

STAUFFER, E., *New Testament Theology*, London 1955.

STOB, H., «The Doctrine of Revelation in Paul», *CTJ* 1 (1966) 182-204.

STRECKER, G., «Redaktion und Tradition im Christushymnus Phil 2:6-11», *ZNW* 55 (1964) 63-78.

STRUGNELL, J., «Notes on Volume V of "Discoveries in the Judaean Desert of Jordan"», *RevQ* 7 (1970) 269-273.

SUGGS, M.J., *Wisdom, Christology and Law in Matthew's Gospel*, Harvard, MA 1970.

SUGIRTHARAJAH, R.S., «Wisdom, Q, and a proposal for a Christology», *ExpTim* 102/2 (Nov 1990) 42-46.

TANNER, N.P., ed., *Decrees of the Ecumenical Councils*. I-II, London 1990.

TAYLOR GENCH, F., *Wisdom in the Christology of Matthew*, Washington, D.C. 1997.

TAYLOR, J.E. – DAVIES P.R., «The So-called Therapeutae of *De Vita Contemplativa*: Identity and Character», *HTR* 91 (1998) 3-24.

TAYLOR, V., *The Names of Jesus*, London 1954.

TAYLOR, V., *The Gospel According to St. Mark*, London 1966.

TERRIEN, S., «Amos and Wisdom», IN J. CRENSHAW, ed., *Studies in Ancient Israelite Wisdom*, New York 1974, 448-455.

THEISSEN, G., *Untersuchungen zum Hebräerbrief*, Gutersloh 1969.

THISELTON, A.C., *New Horizons in Hermeneutics: The Theory and Practice of Transforming Biblical Reading*, Grand Rapids, MN. 1992.

THOMPSON, W.M., *The Jesus Debate: A Survey and Synthesis*, New York 1985.

TOBIN, T.H., «Logos», *ABD* IV 348-356.

TUCKETT, C.M., *Q and the History of Early Christianity*, Edinburgh 1996.

TREANOR, O., *This is My Beloved Son. Aspects of the Passion*, London 1997.

ULRICH E. – VANDERKAM J., ed., *The Community of the Renewed Covenant. The Notre Dame Symposium on the Dead Sea Scrolls*, Notre Dame, IN. 1994.

VANDERKAM, J.C., *The Dead Sea Scrolls Today*, Grand Rapids 1994.

VASS, G., *Understanding Karl Rahner: A Theologian in Search of a Philosophy*, London 1985.

VAWTER, B., «The Colossians Hymn and the principle of Redaction», *CBQ* 33 (1971) 62-81.

VERMES, G., *The Dead Sea Scrolls in English*, London 1995.

VERMEYLEN, J., *Job: ses amis et son Dieu*, Leiden 1986.

VIVIANO, B.T., «The Gospel According to Matthew», *NJBC*, 630-674.

VON RAD, G., *Old Testament Theology*. I, New York 1962.

———, *Wisdom in Israel*, London 1972.

VORGRIMLER, H., *Karl Rahner: His Life, Thought and Works*, London 1965.

———, *Understanding Karl Rahner: An Introduction to His Life and Thought*, New York 1986.

WACHOLDER, B.Z., – ABEGG, M.G., *A Preliminary Edition of the Unpublished Dead Sea Scrolls: The Hebrew and Aramaic texts from Cave Four, Fascicle Two*, Washington, DC 1991.

WAINWRIGHT, E., «But Who Do you Say That I Am? An Australian Feminist Response», *Pac* 10 (1997) 156-172.

WALL, R.W., *Community of the Wise: The Letter of James*, Valley Forge 1997.

WANAMAKER, C.A., «Phil 2:6-11: Son of God or Adamic Christology ?», *NTS* 33 (1987) 179-193.

WEDDERBURN, A.J.M., «Some Recent Pauline Chronologies», *ExpTim* 92 (1980) 103-108.

WEGER, K.H., *Karl Rahner: An Introduction to his Theology*, London 1980.

WENGST, K., *Christologische Formeln und Leider des Urchristentums*, Bonn 1967.

WHARTON, J.A., «Wings», *IDB*. IV, 196.

WHEDBEE, J., *Isaiah and Wisdom*, Nashville 1971.

WHITE, L., «The Historical Roots of our Ecological Crisis», *Science* 155 (1967) 1203-1207.

WHITE CRAWFORD, S., «Lady Wisdom and Dame Folly at Qumran», in A. BRENNER – C. FONTAINE, ed., *Wisdom and Psalms. A Feminist Companion to the Bible*, Sheffield 1998, 205-217.

WHYBRAY, R.N., *Wisdom in Proverbs*, London 1965.

———, *The Intellectual tradition in the Old Testament*, Berlin 1974.

———, «Qoheleth, Preacher of Joy», *JSOT* 23 (1982) 87-98.

WIEDERKEHR, D., *Belief in Redemption: Explorations in Doctrine from the New Testament to Today*, Atlanta 1979.

WILCKENS, U., «Kreuz und Weisheit», *KD* 3 (1957) 27-108.

―――, *Weisheit und Torheit*, Tübingen 1959.

WILKEN, R.L., ed., *Aspects of Wisdom in Judaism and early Christianity*, Notre Dame, IN. 1975.

WILLETT, M.E., *Wisdom Christology in the Fourth Gospel*, San Francisco 1992.

WILLIAMS, S.K., *Jesus' Death as saving Event: The Background and Origin of a Concept*, Missoula 1975.

WILSON, J.H., «The Corinthians who say there is no resurrection of the dead», *ZNW* 59 (1968) 90-107.

WINK, W., «The Hymn of the Cosmic Christ», *The Conversation Continues. Studies in Paul and John in Honour of J.L. Martyn*, Nashville 1990, 235-244.

WINSTON, D., *The Wisdom of Solomon*, Garden City, NY. 1979.

WISCHMEYER, O., *Die Kultur des Buches Jesus Sirach*, Berlin 1995.

WITHERINGTON, B., *Women in the Earliest Churches*, Cambridge 1984.

―――, *The Christology of Jesus*, Minneapolis 1990.

―――, «Three Modern Faces of Wisdom», *ATS* 25 (1993) 96-122.

―――, *Jesus the Sage*, Philadelphia 1994.

―――, *John's Wisdom: A Commentary on the Fourth Gospel*, Cambridge 1995.

―――, *The Jesus Quest: The Third Search for the Jew of Nazareth*, Downers Grove, IL 1997.

―――, *The Many Faces of the Christ*, New York 1998.

WOJTYLA, K., (POPE JOHN PAUL II), *Love and Responsibility*, London 1981.

WOLFF, H.,*Amos the Prophet*, Philadelphia 1973.

WOLFSON, H.A., *Philo: Foundations of Religious Philosophy in Judaism, Christianity and Islam.* I-II, Cambridge, MA. 1947.

WOLINSKI, J., «La Sagesse Chez Les Pères De L'église. De Clément de Rome à Augustin», in ASSOCIATION CATHOLIQUE FRANCAISE POUR L'ETUDE DE LA BIBLE, *La Sagesse de l'Ancien au Nouveau Testament*, Paris 1995, 424-426.

WONG, J.H.P., *Logos-Symbol in the Christology of Karl Rahner*, Rome 1981.

WOOD, H.G., «The Conversion of St. Paul», *NTS* 1 (1954) 276-282.

WRIGHT, A.G., «Ecclesiastes (Qoheleth)», *NJBC*, 489-495.

―――, «Wisdom», *NJBC*, 510-522.

WRIGHT, N.T., «*Harpagmos* and the Meaning of Philippians 2:5-11», *JTS* 37 (1986) 321-352.

————, «Poetry and Theology in Colossians 1:15-20», *NTS*, 36 (1990) 444-468.

————, *The Climax of the Covenant: Christ and the Law in Pauline Theology*, Edinburgh 1991.

YARBRO COLLINS, A., ed., *Feminist Perspectives in Biblical Scholarship*, Chico, CA 1985.

YONGE, C.D., *The Works of Philo: Complete and Unabridged*, new updated ed., Peabody 1993.

ZIEGLER, J., ed., *Sapientia Salomonis*, Göttingen 1962.

AUTHOR INDEX

TABLE OF CONTENTS

TESI GREGORIANA

Since 1995, the series «Tesi Gregoriana» has made available to the general public some of the best doctoral theses done at the Pontifical Gregorian University. The typesetting is done by the authors themselves following norms established and controlled by the University.

Published Volumes [Series: Theology]

1. NELLO FIGA, Antonio, *Teorema de la opción fundamental. Bases para su adecuada utilización en teología moral*, 1995, pp. 380.

2. BENTOGLIO, Gabriele, *Apertura e disponibilità. L'accoglienza nell'epistolario paolino*, 1995, pp. 376.

3. PISO, Alfeu, *Igreja e sacramentos. Renovação da Teologia Sacramentária na América Latina*, 1995, pp. 260.

4. PALAKEEL, Joseph, *The Use of Analogy in Theological Discourse. An Investigation in Ecumenical Perspective*, 1995, pp. 392.

5. KIZHAKKEPARAMPIL, Isaac, *The Invocation of the Holy Spirit as Constitutive of the Sacraments according to Cardinal Yves Congar*, 1995, pp. 200.

6. MROSO, Agapit J., *The Church in Africa and the New Evangelisation. A Theologico-Pastoral Study of the Orientations of John Paul II*, 1995, pp. 456.

7. NANGELIMALIL, Jacob, *The Relationship between the Eucharistic Liturgy, the Interior Life and the Social Witness of the Church according to Joseph Cardinal Parecattil*, 1996, pp. 224.

8. GIBBS, Philip, *The Word in the Third World. Divine Revelation in the Theology of Jen-Marc Éla, Aloysius Pieris and Gustavo Gutiérrez*, 1996, pp. 448.

9. DELL'ORO, Roberto, *Esperienza morale e persona. Per una reinterpretazione dell'etica fenomenologica di Dietrich von Hildebrand*, 1996, pp. 240.

10. BELLANDI, Andrea, *Fede cristiana come «stare e comprendere». La giustificazione dei fondamenti della fede in Joseph Ratzinger*, 1996, pp. 416.

11. BEDRIÑAN, Claudio, *La dimensión socio-política del mensaje teológico del Apocalipsis*, 1996, pp. 364.

12. GWYNNE, Paul, *Special Divine Action. Key Issues in the Contemporary Debate (1965-1995)*, 1996, pp. 376.

13. NIÑO, Francisco, *La Iglesia en la ciudad. El fenómeno de las grandes ciudades en América Latina, como problema teológico y como desafío pastoral*, 1996, pp. 492.

14. BRODEUR, Scott, *The Holy Spirit's Agency in the Resurrection of the Dead. An Exegetico-Theological Study of 1 Corinthians 15,44b-49 and Romans 8,9-13*, 1996, pp. 300.

15. ZAMBON, Gaudenzio, *Laicato e tipologie ecclesiali. Ricerca storica sulla «Teologia del laicato» in Italia alla luce del Concilio Vaticano II (1950-1980)*, 1996, pp. 548.

16. ALVES DE MELO, Antonio, *A Evangelização no Brasil. Dimensões teológicas e desafios pastorais. O debate teológico e eclesial (1952-1995)*, 1996, pp. 428.

17. APARICIO VALLS, María del Carmen, *La plenitud del ser humano en Cristo. La Revelación en la «Gaudium et Spes»*, 1997, pp. 308.

18. MARTIN, Seán Charles, *«Pauli Testamentum». 2 Timothy and the Last Words of Moses*, 1997, pp. 312.

19. RUSH, Ormond, *The Reception of Doctrine. An Appropriation of Hans Robert Jauss' Reception Aesthetics and Literary Hermeneutics*, 1997, pp. 424.

20. MIMEAULT, Jules, *La sotériologie de François-Xavier Durrwell. Exposé et réflexions critiques*, 1997, pp. 476.

21. CAPIZZI, Nunzio, *L'uso di Fil 2,6-11 nella cristologia contemporanea (1965-1993)*, 1997, pp. 528.

22. NANDKISORE, Robert, *Hoffnung auf Erlösung. Die Eschatologie im Werk Hans Urs von Balthasars*, 1997, pp. 304.

23. PERKOVIĆ, Marinko, *«Il cammino a Dio» e «La direzione alla vita»: L'ordine morale nelle opere di Jordan Kuničić, O.P. (1908-1974)*, 1997, pp. 336.

24. DOMERGUE, Benoît, *La réincarnation et la divinisation de l'homme dans les religions. Approche phénoménologique et théologique*, 1997, pp. 300.

25. FARKAŠ, Pavol, *La «donna» di Apocalisse 12. Storia, bilancio, nuove prospettive*, 1997, pp. 276.

26. OLIVER, Robert W., *The Vocation of the Laity to Evangelization. An Ecclesiological Inquiry into the Synod on the Laity (1987), Christifideles laici (1989) and Documents of the NCCB (1987-1996)*, 1997, pp. 364.

27. SPATAFORA, Andrea, *From the «Temple of God» to God as the Temple. A Biblical Theological Study of the Temple in the Book of Revelation*, 1997, pp. 340.

28. IACOBONE, Pasquale, *Mysterium Trinitatis. Dogma e Iconografia nell'Italia medievale*, 1997, pp. 512.

29. CASTAÑO FONSECA, Adolfo M., *Δικαιοσύνη en Mateo. Una interpretación teológica a partir de 3,15 y 21,32*, 1997, pp. 344.

30. CABRIA ORTEGA, José Luis, *Relación teología-filosofía en el pensamiento de Xavier Zubiri*, 1997, pp. 580.

31. SCHERRER, Thierry, *La gloire de Dieu dans l'oeuvre de saint Irénée*, 1997, pp. 328.

32. PASCUZZI, Maria, *Ethics, Ecclesiology and Church Discipline. A Rhetorical Analysis of 1 Cor 5,1-13*, 1997, pp. 240.

33. LOPES GONÇALVES, Paulo Sérgio, *Liberationis mysterium. O projeto sistemático da teologia da libertação. Um estudo teológico na perspectiva da regula fidei*, 1997, pp. 464.

34. KOLACINSKI, Mariusz, *Dio fonte del diritto naturale*, 1997, pp. 296.

35. LIMA CORRÊA, Maria de Lourdes, *Salvação entre juízo, conversão e graça. A perspectiva escatológica de Os 14,2-9*, 1998, pp. 360.

36. MEIATTINI, Giulio, *«Sentire cum Christo». La teologia dell'esperienza cristiana nell'opera di H.U. von Balthasar*, 1998, pp. 432.

37. KESSLER, Thomas W., *Peter as the First Witness of the Risen Lord. An Historical and Theological Investigation*, 1998, pp. 240.

38. BIORD CASTILLO Raúl, *La Resurrección de Cristo como Revelación. Análisis del tema en la teología fundamental a partir de la* Dei Verbum, 1998, pp. 308.

39. LÓPEZ, Javier, *La figura de la bestia entre historia y profecía. Investigación teológico-bíblica de Apocalipsis 13,1-8*, 1998, pp. 308.

40. SCARAFONI, Paolo, *Amore salvifico. Una lettura del mistero della salvezza. Uno studio comparativo di alcune soteriologie cattoliche postconciliari*, 1998, pp. 240.

41. BARRIOS PRIETO, Manuel Enrique, *Antropologia teologica. Temi principali di antropologia teologica usando un metodo di «correlazione» a partire dalle opere di John Macquarrie*, 1998, pp. 416.

42. LEWIS, Scott M., *«So That God May Be All in All». The Apocalyptic Message of 1 Corinthians 15,12-34*, 1998, pp. 252.

43. ROSSETTI, Carlo Lorenzo, *«Sei diventato Tempio di Dio». Il mistero del Tempio e dell'abitazione divina negli scritti di Origene*, 1998, pp. 232.

44. CERVERA BARRANCO, Pablo, *La incorporación en la Iglesia mediante el bautismo y la profesión de la fe según el Concilio Vaticano II*, 1998, pp. 372.

45. NETO, Laudelino, *Fé cristã e cultura latino-americana. Uma análise a partir das Conferências de Puebla e Santo Domingo*, 1998, pp. 340.

46. BRITO GUIMARÃES, Pedro, *Os sacramentos como atos eclesiais e proféticos. Um contributo ao conceito dogmático de sacramento à luz da exegese contemporânea*, 1998, pp. 448.

47. CALABRETTA, Rose B., *Baptism and Confirmation. The Vocation and Mission of the Laity in the Writings of Virgil Michel, O.S.B.*, 1998, pp. 320.

48. OTERO LÁZARO, Tomás, *Col 1,15-20 en el contexto de la carta*, 1999, pp.312.

49. KOWALCZYK, Dariusz, *La personalità in Dio. Dal metodo trascendentale di Karl Rahner verso un orientamento dialogico in Heinrich Ott*, 1999, pp. 484.

50. PRIOR, Joseph G., *The Historical-Critical Method in Catholic Exegesis*, 1999, pp. 352.

51. CAHILL, Brendan J, *The Renewal of Revelation Theology (1960-1962). The Development and Responses to the Fourth Chapter of the Preparatory Schema* De deposito Fidei, 1999, pp. 348.

52. TIEZZI, Ida, *Il rapporto tra la pneumatologia e l'ecclesiologia nella teologia italiana post-conciliare*, 1999, pp. 364.

53. HOLC, Paweł, *Un ampio consenso sulla dottrina della giustificazione. Studio sul dialogo teologico cattolico luterano*, 1999, pp. 452.

54. GAINO, Andrea, *Esistenza cristiana. Il pensiero teologico di J. Alfaro e la sua rilevanza morale*, 1999, pp. 344.

55. NERI, Francesco, *«Cur Verbum capax hominis». Le ragioni dell'incarnazione della seconda Persona della Trinità fra teologia scolastica e teologia contemporanea*, 1999, pp. 404.

56. MUÑOZ CÁRDABA, Luis-Miguel, *Principios eclesiológicos de la «Pastor Bonus»*, 1999, pp. 344.

57. IWE, John Chijioke, *Jesus in the Synagogue of Capernaum: the Pericope and Its Programmatic Character for the Gospel of Mark. An Exegetico-Theological Study of Mk 1:21-28*, 1999, pp. 364.

58. BARRIOCANAL GÓMEZ, José Luis, *La relectura de la tradición del éxodo en 1 libro de Amós*, 2000, pp. 332.

59. DE LOS SANTOS GARCÍA, Edmundo, *La novedad de la metáfora κεφαλή – σῶμα en la carta a los Efesios*, 2000, pp. 432.

60. RESTREPO SIERRA, Argiro, *La revelación según R. Latourelle*, 2000, pp. 442.

61. DI GIOVAMBATTISTA, Fulvio, *Il giorno dell'espiazione nella Lettera agli Ebrei*, 2000, pp. 232.

62. GIUSTOZZO, Massimo, *Il nesso tra il culto e la grazia eucaristica nella recente lettura teologica del pensiero agostiniano*, 2000, pp. 456.

63. PESARCHICK, Robert A., *The Trinitarian Foundation of Human Sexuality as Revealed by Christ according to Hans Urs von Balthasar. The Revelatory Significance of the Male Christ and the Male Ministerial Priesthood*, 2000, pp. 328.

64. SIMON, László T., *Identity and Identification. An Exegetical Study of 2Sam 21–24*, 2000. pp. 386.

65. TAKAYAMA, Sadami, *Shinran's Conversion in the Light of Paul's Conversion*, 2000, pp. 256.

66. JUAN MORADO, Guillermo, *«También nosotros creemos porque amamos». Tres concepciones del acto de fe: Newman, Blondel, Garrigou-Lagrange. Estudio comparativo desde la perspectiva teológico-fundamental*, 2000, pp. 444.

67. MAREČEK, Petr, *La preghiera di Gesù nel vangelo di Matteo. Uno studio esegetico-teologico*, 2000, pp. 246.

68. WODKA, Andrzej, *Una teologia biblica del dare nel contesto della colletta paolina (2Cor 8–9)*, 2000, pp. 356.

69. LANGELLA, Maria Rigel, *Salvezza come illuminazione. Uno studio comparato di S. Bulgakov, V. Lossky, P. Evdokimov*, 2000, pp. 292.

70. RUDELLI, Paolo, *Matrimonio come scelta di vita: opzione – vocazione – sacramento*, 2000, pp. 424.

71. GAŠPAR, Veronika, *Cristologia pneumatologica in alcuni autori cattolici postconciliari. Status quaestionis e prospettive*, 2000, pp. 440.

72. GJORGJEVSKI, Gjoko, *Enigma degli enigmi. Un contributo allo studio della composizione della raccolta salomonica (Pr 10,1–22,16)*, 2001, pp. 304.

73. LINGAD, Celestino G., Jr., *The Problems of Jewish Christians in the Johannine Community*, 2001, pp. 492.

74. MASALLES, Victor, *La profecía en la asamblea cristiana. Análisis retórico-literario de 1Cor 14,1-25*, 2001, pp. 416.

75. FIGUEIREDO, Anthony J., *The Magisterium-Theology Relationship. Contemporary Theological Conceptions in the Light of Universal Church Teaching since 1835 and the Pronouncements of the Bishops of the United States*, 2001, pp. 536.

76. PARDO IZAL, José Javier, *Pasión por un futuro imposible. Estudio literario-teológico de Jeremías 32*, 2001, pp. 412.

77. HANNA, Kamal Fahim Awad, *La passione di Cristo nell'Apocalisse*, 2001, pp. 480.

78. ALBANESI, Nicola, *«Cur Deus Homo»: la logica della redenzione. Studio sulla teoria della soddisfazione di S. Anselmo arcivescovo di Canterbury*, 2001, pp. 244.

79. ADE, Edouard, *Le temps de l'Eglise. Esquisse d'une théologie de l'histoire selon Hans Urs von Balthasar*, 2002, pp. 368.

80. MENÉNDEZ MARTÍNEZ, Valentín, *La misión de la Iglesia. Un estudio sobre el debate teológico y eclesial en América Latina (1955-1992), con atención al aporte de algunos teólogos de la Compañía de Jesús*, 2002, pp. 346.

81. COSTA, Paulo Cezar, *«Salvatoris Disciplina». Dionísio de Roma e a Regula fidei no debate teológico do terceiro século*, 2002, pp. 272.

82. PUTHUSSERY, Johnson, *Days of Man and God's Day. An Exegetico-Theological Study of ἡμέρα in the Book of Revelation*, 2002, pp. 302.

83. BARROS, Paulo César, *«Commendatur vobis in isto pane quomodo unitatem amare debeatis». A eclesiologia eucarística nos Sermones ad populum de Agostinho de Hipona e o movimento ecumênico*, 2002, pp. 344.

84. PALACHUVATTIL, Joy, *«He Saw». The Significance of Jesus' Seeing Denoted by the Verb εἶδεν in the Gospel of Mark*, 2002, pp. 312.

85. PISANO, Ombretta, *La radice e la stirpe di David. Salmi davidici nel libro dell'Apocalisse*, 2002, pp. 496.

86. KARIUKI, Njiru Paul, *Charisms and the Holy Spirit's Activity in the Body of Christ. An Exegetical-Theological Study of 1Cor 12,4-11 and Rom 12,6-8*, 2002, pp. 372.

87. CORRY, Donal, *«Ministerium Rationis Reddendae». An Approximation to Hilary of Poitiers' Understanding of Theology*, 2002, pp. 328.

88. PIKOR, Wojciech, *La comunicazione profetica alla luce di Ez 2–3*, 2002, pp. 322.

89. NWACHUKWU, Mary Sylvia Chinyere, *Creation–Covenant Scheme and Justification by Faith. A Canonical Study of the God-Human Drama in the Pentateuch and the Letter to the Romans*, 2002, 378 pp.

90. GAGLIARDI, Mauro, *La cristologia adamitica. Tentativo di recupero del suo significato originario*, 2002, pp. 624.

91. CHARAMSA, Krzysztof Olaf, *L'immutabilità di Dio. L'insegnamento di San Tommaso d'Aquino nei suoi sviluppi presso i commentatori scolastici*, 2002, pp. 520.

92. GLOBOKAR, Roman, *Verantwortung für alles, was lebt. Von Albert Schweitzer und Hans Jonas zu einer theologischen Ethik des Lebens*, 2002, pp. 608.

93. AJAYI, James Olaitan, *The HIV/AIDS Epidemic in Nigeria. Some Ethical Considerations*, 2003, pp. 212.

94. PARAMBI, Baby, *The Discipleship of the Women in the Gospel according to Matthew. An Exegetical Theological Study of Matt 27:51b-56, 57-61 and 28:1-10*, 2003, pp. 276.

95. NIEMIRA, Artur, *Religiosità e moralità. Vita morale come realizzazione della fondazione cristica dell'uomo secondo B. Häring e D. Capone*, 2003, pp. 308.

96. PIZZUTO, Pietro, *La teologia della rivelazione di Jean Daniélou. Influsso su Dei Verbum e valore attuale*, 2003, pp. 630.

97. PAGLIARA, Cosimo, *La figura di Elia nel vangelo di Marco. Aspetti semantici e funzionali*, 2003, pp. 400.

98. O'BOYLE, Aidan, *Towards a Contemporary Wisdom Christology. Some Catholic Christologies in German, English and French 1965-1995*, 2003, pp. 448.

Finito di stampare
nel mese di Maggio 2003

presso la tipografia
"Giovanni Olivieri" di E. Montefoschi
00187 Roma • Via dell'Archetto, 10, 11, 12
Tel. 06 6792327 • E-mail: tip.olivieri@libero.it